GLOBAL STUDIES

Volume I

Asia, Africa, and Latin America

Second Edition

by

Erwin M. Rosenfeld

and

Harriet Geller

BARRON'S EDUCATIONAL SERIES

All inquiries should be addressed to:
Barron's Educational Series, Inc.
250 Wireless Boulevard
Hauppauge, New York 11788

Library of Congress Catalog Card No. 92-40894

Paper Edition
International Standard Book No. 0-8120-4771-0

Cloth Edition
International Standard Book No. 0-8120-6197-7

Library of Congress Cataloging-in-Publication Data

Rosenfeld, Erwin M.
    Global studies / Erwin M. Rosenfeld, Harriet Geller.
        p.   cm.
    Includes index.
    Summary: Introduces the civilizations of Asia, Africa, and Latin
America.
        ISBN 0-8120-6197-7 (hardcover).—ISBN 0-8120-4771-0 (paper)
        1. Civilization—Juvenile literature. 2. Human geography—Juve-
nile literature. [1. Civilization. 2. Human geography.]
I. Geller, Harriet. II. Title.
CB69.2.R67   1993
909—dc20   92-40894
                                                        CIP
                                                        AC

PRINTED IN THE UNITED STATES OF AMERICA
    56   100   987654

Table of Contents

UNIT
I

Introduction to Global Studies

Culture and Survival	1
Habitat and Culture	2
People of the World	6
Civilization	9
Cultural Diffusion	13
"What It Is Like to Be Underdeveloped"	14
Twentieth-Century Nationalism	16
Our Global Village	18
Our Endangered Planet	19
Destruction of the Rain Forests	20
The Greenhouse Effect and Global Warming	21
Depletion of the Ozone Layer	22
The Chernobyl Nuclear Accident	23
The Population Explosion	24
Feeding the World's Growing Population	25
Nuclear Proliferation—A Global Threat	27
Summary of Key Ideas	30
Exercises and Questions	32
Developing Answers to Regents-Type Essay Questions	38
Puzzle	39

UNIT
II

The Middle East and North Africa

Introduction	41
Land and Climate	44
The People of the Middle East and Their Way of Life	45
The Jews and Judaism	49
Islam—The Religion of the Middle East and North Africa	53
Early History of the Middle East	58
The Triumph of Islam—Muslim Civilization (622–1453)	64
The Middle East in Decline	66
The Ottoman Empire	67
European Imperialism in the Middle East	69
The Middle East After World War II—Nationalism and the Question of Arab Unity	71
Economic Development	74
Oil Is King	75
The Arab-Israeli Conflict: The Israeli Side	82
The Arab-Israeli Conflict: The Arab Side	86
The Problem of the Palestinians	88
Terrorism	94
Issues Dividing the Arabs and Israel: 1967 to the Present	99

War, Oil, Politics: The Yom Kippur War and Its Aftermath 101
Israel and Egypt: A New Relationship 104
The Peace Initiatives: Efforts to Resolve the Arab-Israeli Conflict 108
The Civil War in Lebanon 110
The Resurgence of Islam 116
A Revolution in Iran 118
The War Between Iraq and Iran 120
War in the Gulf: Iraq, Kuwait, and the U.S.-Led Coalition 125
The Middle East After the Gulf War 128
The Gulf War in Retrospect: What the Gulf War Did and Didn't Do 131
The Middle East in World Affairs 131
Summary of Key Ideas 134
Exercises and Questions 137
Developing Answers to Regents-Type Essay Questions 149
Puzzle 151

UNIT III

Africa—South of the Sahara

Geography and Isolation 153
Topography 155
The Climate 159
The People and Their Languages 160
African Families 163
African Tribalism 166
Religious Beliefs 168
African Arts 170
Agriculture 176
Famine in Africa 179
Natural Resources and Industrial Development 184
Early History 187
Kingdoms of West Africa 191
East Africa—Cities of the Coast 194
East Africa—Kingdoms of the Interior 195
Arabs, Islam, and Africa 197
The Arrival of the Europeans 198
The Slave Trade 200
Africa Is Opened to the Western World: Explorers and Missionaries 202
European Imperialism in Africa 204
Nationalism and Independence 207
Africa Today—Problems of Independence 211
South Africa and The Problem of Separate Development (Apartheid) 223
The Struggle Against Apartheid (1960–1984) 225
South Africa Since 1984 227
Movement Away From Apartheid 232
Summary of Key Ideas 243
Exercises and Questions 246

Developing Answers to Regents-Type Essay Questions 257
Puzzle 259

UNIT IV China

Topography of China 263
Climate 265
Agriculture and Natural Resources 267
The Peoples of China 272
Population Growth and Population Control 275
Life and Society in Traditional China 277
Social Classes in Traditional China: The Gentry and the Peasants 281
The Chinese Family 284
The Role of Women 286
Language and Writing System 289
Education 291
The History of China: Ancient China 292
Imperial China 293
China's Contributions to World Civilization:
    Achievements in Science and Technology 299
Manchu China—The Qing (Ch'ing) Dynasty 303
The Chinese Republic (1911–1949) 309
Mao Zedong and the People's Republic of China (1949–1976) 312
China and the World: Foreign Relations Under Mao Zedong 322
China Under Deng Xiaoping 328
The Massacre at Tiananmen Square 338
Foreign Policy Under Deng Xiaoping 342
Summary of Key Ideas 348
Exercises and Questions 350
Developing Answers to Regents-Type Essay Questions 366
Puzzle 368

UNIT V The Subcontinent of India and South Asia (Pakistan and Bangladesh)

The Land 371
Climate 374
Agriculture 376
Peoples and Languages 380
The Village in Indian Life 381
The Hindu Religion 384
The Literature of Ancient India 386
Early History 390
The Muslims in India 397
The British in India 399
Development of Indian National Feeling 402
Independence and Partition 403
India Attempts to Modernize 407

India in the 1990s 414
Pakistan 421
Bangladesh 424
Nepal, India's Neighbor to the North 430
India and World Politics 432
Summary of Key Ideas 440
Exercises and Questions 443
Developing Answers to Regents-Type Essay Questions 457
Puzzle 459

UNIT VI

Southeast Asia

Introduction and Setting 461
Topography 462
Climate 465
Peoples, Languages, and Population Distribution 466
Village Life 470
Agriculture 472
Religion 473
Early History of Southeast Asia 476
The Empires of Southeast Asia 479
The Arrival of Westerners in Southeast Asia 480
Nationalism in Southeast Asia 482
World War II and Japanese Control 485
Independence and Its Results 486
The Economy of Southeast Asia 495
Foreign Relations 504
Summary of Key Ideas 514
Exercises and Questions 517
Developing Answers to Regents-Type Essay Questions 526
Puzzle 528

UNIT VII

Japan and Korea

Japan—Land and Climate 531
The People and Their Language 536
Religion 538
Life in Japan 541
Japanese Arts 547
Early History of Japan 556
Japan Enters the Modern World 568
Japan After World War II 572
Japan's Economy 573
Japan's Place in the World Today 583
Korea—Land and Climate 589
Korea's People 590
Religion 590

History of Korea 591

The Korean War 593

Korea's Economy 594

The Two Korean Situations in the 1990s 596

Summary of Key Ideas 597

Exercises and Questions 599

Developing Answers to Regents-Type Essay Questions 612

Puzzles 614

UNIT VIII   Latin America

Introduction 617

Geography 618

Climate 625

The People and Customs of Latin America 629

Pre-Columbian Latin America 635

Arrival of Europeans in Latin America 645

Colonial Period 648

Revolution and Independence 650

After Independence: Latin America in the 19th Century 653

Economy 655

The Arts in Latin America 665

The Caribbean Islands (West Indies) 668

Latin America in the 20th Century 674

Latin America and the United States 684

Governments in Latin America 688

Summary of Key Ideas 697

Exercises and Questions 704

Developing Answers to Regents-Type Essay Questions 715

Puzzle 717

Glossary 718

Index 722

UNIT I Introduction to Global Studies

Culture and Survival

Could you survive alone in the jungle? The desert? The Arctic? Most Americans are "civilized," and they know almost nothing of the ways of life of many peoples. If you can answer more than half of the following questions correctly, you are good. Remember, however, that only one incorrect answer in a real situation might easily result in your death.

Directions: **True or False**

NOTE: An answer key appears at the end of the unit.

Jungle

1. The chances of being bitten by a poisonous snake in the jungle are about as remote as being struck by lightning.
2. While food is plentiful in the jungle, good water is difficult to obtain.
3. Tincture of iodine can be used to purify water in an emergency.
4. All jungle animals except a few travel toward water at dawn and dusk.
5. One should seldom, if ever, follow a direct compass line in the jungle.
6. Anything you see monkeys eat you can eat.
7. Humanity's worst enemy in the jungle is the mosquito.

Desert

1. In the desert, on very hot days, it is very important for one to wear a woolen band around the stomach.
2. When walking in the desert it is desirable to wear two pairs of socks.
3. If one lies down to escape the force of a sandstorm, one should move around frequently.
4. Salt tablets should only be taken if there is water available.
5. Chewing gum increases thirst.
6. Because of the dry air, food spoilage is not a serious problem in the desert.
7. As long as you stay under cover, there is little danger of heatstroke.

Arctic

1. Very little snow falls in the Arctic during the winter.
2. Wearing loose clothing usually leads to frostbite.
3. A heavy beard is good protection against frostbite.
4. In the Arctic few if any clothes should be worn inside a sleeping bag.
5. The worst Arctic pest is the mosquito, but it is not a disease carrier.
6. Generally speaking, the Arctic coastline is friendlier than the interior.
7. Snow blindness can occur during a bright, overcast day as quickly as during bright, sunny weather.

Now that you have tried to answer the questions, you can see that it would not be easy for you to survive in a jungle, a desert, or the frozen Arctic. In order to survive people learn to adapt themselves to the place in which they live. They learn to live and make use of the things around them. You can live well in a city; but people who have lived all their lives in a desert would find the city strange and frightening, just as you and I would find the jungle or desert a frightening place.

Culture refers to the methods people use to live, or the way of life of a group of people at a particular time. There are many different cultures throughout the world. On the following pages we will discuss the various ways in which cultures are formed, and the reasons they are different.

At this point, it is important to know that there are many differences and similarities among peoples of the world. In studying other cultures, our main goal should be to explore the ways other groups of human beings have developed their cultures in response to problems of survival and in order to fulfill their dreams. We must try to look at them not through American eyes, but as they see themselves. We must not study them in the light of our history and culture, which is very young, but in the light of their own histories and cultures.

Habitat and Culture

To really understand people, you must know something about the **environment** in which they live. Environment is the setting in which humans live. The environment helps to determine the way in which people live.

Habitat

From the beginning of human existence, people have adapted their way of life to the natural environment, the **habitat**. The habitat consists of physical features or **topography**, (landforms and bodies of water), resources (soil and underground rocks, minerals, and water), living things (plants and animals), and **climate** (general weather conditions). These things are different throughout the world. For this reason people have had to learn to use them differently.

FOUR PARTS OF THE NATURAL ENVIRONMENT

Physical features (landforms and bodies of water)

Soil, underground rocks, and underground water.

Climate

Living things

People in the warmer climates have ways of living that are different from those in colder climates. They build houses, wear clothing, and eat foods that are different. Where soil is fertile and climate is favorable, people earn their living by farming. In places where the land is rocky and the soil poor, people have had to make their living in other ways, such as herding or hunting.

As technological knowledge has grown, so has our ability to use the environment. Early people were primarily hunters and gatherers who depended on what nature provided for survival. As domestication of plants and animals made farming possible, humans became more capable of altering and managing their habitat. More recently, the Industrial Revolution has increased humanity's control on the environment, with both positive and negative results.

CONTINENTS AND OCEANS

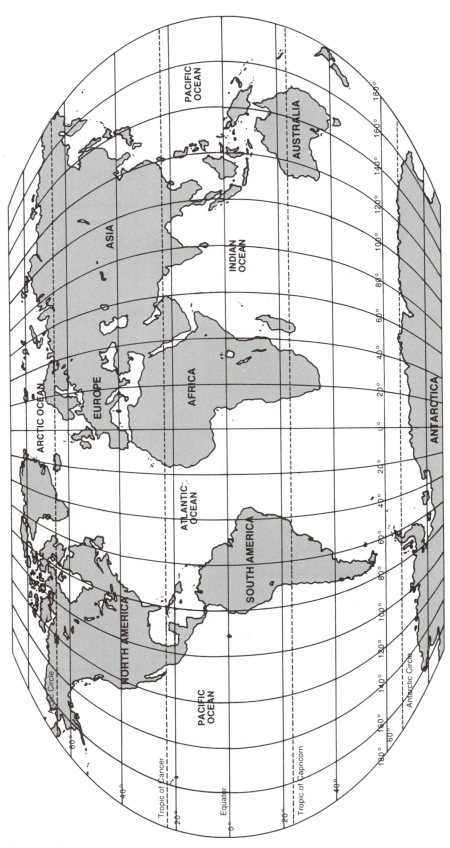

The earth is divided between large masses of land and large bodies of water. The large land masses are called **continents**. The large bodies of water are called **oceans**. The oceans lie between the continents. The line that separates the land from the water is called the **coastline**.

There are seven continents. The largest is Asia. Asia and Europe are joined and are sometimes called the Eurasian land mass. Australia is an **island** continent. Australia is also the smallest of the continents. North and South America are connected by the **Isthmus** of Panama. Africa is the second largest continent and lies directly south of Europe. Antarctica is a frozen continent. Few people live on the Antarctic continent.

There are four oceans (Arctic Ocean, Atlantic Ocean, Pacific Ocean, and Indian Ocean). The largest ocean is the Pacific.

Culture

While the habitat is important, there is another equally important part of the environment. This part is called the culture. Culture is the part of the environment that is created by human beings. The culture includes all the changes that we have made in our habitat. As people worked with the materials provided by the habitat, they developed habits and customs of living. They set up **communities**, religions, and governments. They created music, art, and language. They set up rules of conduct. These rules of conduct are called **values**.

The culture of a people develops over a long period of time. Culture is affected by materials available in the habitat, as well as by ideas and materials brought in from the outside. Culture is learned rather than inherited. Every group of people has a particular way of acting or behaving. Each individual learns the accepted ways of the group from the example of parents and from other children. He or she learns through the process of education. People learn to live according to their culture.

A culture consists of traditional ideas and purposes, ways of communication, and material objects, such as tools, buildings, and machines. The following outline suggests the variety of things that combine to make up a culture.

    a.   Material culture: Tools and skills, buildings, ways of making a living
    b.   Social institutions: Family, community, education, government, political parties
    c.   Attitudes toward the unknown: Religion, magic, superstition
    d.   Art: Graphic and plastic arts, folklore, music, drama, the dance
    e.   Language and writing: The means of communication

Clearly, the different parts of a culture can be separated only for the purposes of study. Any attempt to understand the way a people lives must take into account how these different parts of a culture relate to each other. To take one example, religious beliefs sometimes have an important effect on the way people make a living, and on the things they eat and drink.

Culture, Habitat, and People

The material things that people have developed are things that can be touched. We can find them and study them. We can see how they differ from place to place (farms, factories, tools, food, clothing, shelter). The ideas that people have developed cannot be touched, but how these ideas affect their lives can be examined.

People have used their intelligence to create religion, government, and education. The ideas behind them differ from one culture to another. However, the purpose for all cultures is the same, to set up an orderly way of life and to control how people act.

We must realize that to fully understand different ways of life, all aspects of the habitat and culture must be considered and studied.

People of the World

The world's population is approaching 6 billion. Because most of the land on earth is north of the equator, we should not be surprised to find that more than nine-tenths of the world's population lives north of the equator. This fact has been true throughout history.

ESTIMATES OF WORLD POPULATION BY REGIONS (1650–1990)
(Population in Millions)

Date	World	North America	Latin America	Africa	Europe	Asia	Oceania
1650	545	1	12	100	103	327	2
1750	728	1	11	95	144	475	2
1800	906	6	19	90	192	597	2
1850	1,171	26	33	95	274	741	2
1900	1,608	81	63	120	423	915	6
1950	2,406	166	162	199	594	1,272	13
1970	3,678	226	283	354	460	2,091	19
1980	4,478	252	365	472	484	2,618	23
1990	5,321	277	450	625	499	2,994	26

The Population Explosion

As you can see from the chart, more than half the world's people live in Asia, about one-eighth live in Africa, and about one-tenth live in Europe. The rest are scattered over the other four regions. Note that there has been a steady increase in the growth rate of population throughout the world. It has been especially rapid during the past 70 years. This growth in the number of people is called the population explosion. The world population doubled from 2 billion in 1930 to 4 billion in 1976, and will probably double to over 8 billion by the year 2025.

Population Distribution

Within the area where people live they are not evenly distributed. There are areas of dense population, where many people live close together, and other areas of sparse population, where few people live. The areas of densest population are in Southeast Asia, India, Western Europe, Eastern China, and the eastern part of the United States.

An accurate way of measuring the **population density** of a region is to divide the number of people in the region by the number of square miles. Thus, if an area has one million square miles and ten million people, the population density would be ten people per square mile.

SIZE, POPULATION, AND DENSITY OF THE WORLD'S LARGEST NATIONS AND REGIONS

Country	Size	Population (U.N. Estimate) 1968	1990	People Per Sq. Mi. 1968	1990
USSR	8,600,000 Sq. Mi.	238,000,000	290,122,000	28	33.5
Canada	3,850,000 Sq. Mi.	21,000,000	26,620,000	5	7.5
China	3,700,000 Sq. Mi.	730,000,000	1,133,000,000	197	306.7
USA	3,600,000 Sq. Mi.	200,000,000	251,394,000	57	68.3
Brazil	3,300,000 Sq. Mi.	88,000,000	150,368,000	27	45.8
India	1,200,000 Sq. Mi.	534,000,000	853,373,000	437	698.0
Other Areas					
Japan	143,000 Sq. Mi.	101,000,000	123,692,000	706	848.0
Southeast Asia	1,692,000 Sq. Mi.	270,000,000	447,000,000	159	262.9
Middle East	3,784,000 Sq. Mi.	261,000,000	306,400,000	69	81.0
Africa— south of the Sahara	8,600,000 Sq. Mi.	254,000,000	500,000,000	30	62.2

(Note the great increase of population in the 22 years that separate the two sets of figures. Scientists estimate that the earth's present population will double in the next 50 years or sooner.)

Some Parts of the World Are More Desirable Than Others

If you look around any large city, you will notice that people try to live in certain sections and avoid others. Just as people move to desirable areas of the city or a town, so do the peoples of the whole world tend to move to more desirable places and away from less desirable places.

What makes one part of the earth a desirable place to live and other parts less desirable? We can best answer this by taking actual examples. Few people live in Greenland because of the year-round cold climate. Few people live in the Sahara region of Africa because of the lack of rainfall. Thus, we see there are certain parts of the earth that are thinly populated because of extremes of temperature and rainfall. The world areas with the largest populations, such as eastern China, Japan, India, Europe, and the eastern United States, have a generally temperate climate, enough rainfall, level land, and fertile soil for raising food crops.

Climate is not the only reason people move from place to place. Many people came to the United States because land was cheap and they could own a farm of their own. Others came to escape the poverty of their land of birth, hoping to find new opportunities and a decent livelihood here. Land hunger has always been a strong reason for people to move from place to place.

Water is another attraction for people. People always move near rivers because most large rivers are bordered by level plains suitable for farming. In addition, rivers are sources of water for irrigation and drinking and a means of easy transportation.

In modern times, industries and factories need tremendous amounts of raw materials. They need coal, iron, aluminum, copper, tin, and oil. They also need cheap electric power obtained from moving water. Because of these needs, many people are attracted to towns and cities near important natural resources.

Thus, we see that for a variety of reasons people move from place to place. The places of their choice influence their customs and institutions and their occupations.

WORLD CLIMATE REGIONS

Climate Region	Location (Examples)	Climate	Description	Human Use
Low latitudes Tropical rain forest	Near the Equator: Amazon River Basin; Congo River Basin; west coast of Colombia and Ecuador; Indonesia, the Philippines; west coasts of India, Burma and Malaysia	Rainy, hot all year: "Night is the winter of the Tropics"	Jungle—tall trees, dense foliage; rivers	Rivers—most important highways; hardwood forests—rubber, bananas; shifting cultivation—"slash and burn"
Wet and dry tropical (tropical savanna)	North and south of tropical rain forests: Sahel—West Africa; Ilanos in South America; India, Southeast Asia	Winters, dry; summers, rainy; hot all year	Tall grasslands, some trees; East African plateau, low grass savanna	Cattle raising, sugarcane, paddy rice; thinly populated except in India
Tropical desert	North and south of savannas: Sahara—North Africa; west coasts of continents—southwest Africa, southwest South America, southwest United States; southwest Asia—Arabian Desert	Hot, with little or no rain	Vast sandy areas (Erg Desert); vast rocky dry areas (Hamada Desert); desert shrubs, some low grasses	Nomad cattle herders move from watering place (oasis) to watering place; irrigation needed for agriculture
Middle latitudes Maritime	West coast of continents: Great Britain, northwest Europe; U.S. Pacific Northwest; southern half of Chile	Rainy, moderate temperatures	Mixed forest, good farmland, low grasses	Farming, manufacturing: northwest Europe, one of most densely populated areas in the world; wheat, fruits, sugar beets, grazing
Humid continental	Two-thirds of United States—northern United States, East Coast United States; western former Soviet Union	Hot summers, cold winters, dependable, moderate rainfall	Plains—mixed forest, low grasses	"bread baskets" of United States and former Soviet Union—wheat, corn, grazing; also industrial center of United States and former Soviet Union
Continental steppe	Far inland, often on plateaus: Great Plains—central North America; southern former Soviet Union	Very hot summers, very cold winters, light and undependable rainfall	Low grasses, shrubs; trees along streams	Grazing, herding; grains grown with irrigation
Continental desert	North and south of continental steppe (Asian Gobi Desert)	Dry—extreme temperatures	Very little vegetation	Grazing, herding, mining

Climate Region	Location (Examples)	Climate	Description	Human Use
Mediterranean (subtropical)	West side of continents near the sea: southern Europe, central Chile; southern California	Mild wet winters; very hot summers	Grasses, evergreen trees	Fruit—olives, wheat, grapes; need for irrigation
Humid subtropical	East coasts of North America, Asia, (China, Japan); pampas of South America	Long humid summers, short mild winters	Mixed forest, low grassland	Rice, cotton, citrus fruits, vegetables, tobacco, grazing
High latitudes Taiga (forest)	North of humid continental areas in North America, Europe, Asia, former Soviet Union, Canada, Alaska	Low rainfall, snow and ice, long cold winters, short cool summers	Evergreen forests, snow and ice covers land most of year	Thinly settled; mining lumbering, fishing, hunting, herding
Tundra	North of taigas	Little rainfall, long cold winters, short cool summers	"Arctic prairie": few trees, permafrost—land frozen	Thinly settled; hunting, fishing, herding; permafrost prevents farming
Polar ice cap	Coasts of Arctic region, Greenland, north Canada, Siberia in former Soviet Union	Very cold, very short frost-free summer	Permafrost; moss, lichens, shrubs	Fishing, trapping, hunting, oil

Civilization

Most **anthropologists** (social scientists who study the origin, development, customs, and beliefs of human beings) use the term **civilization** to describe a complex level of human development (political, economic, and technological).

CHARACTERISTICS OF CIVILIZATION

Ways of making a living	Food produced by a majority of people; different goods and services provided by others
Government	Full-time leaders, laws, some kind of taxes
Settlement	Generally in cities with buildings built with tax money, but dependent upon large areas populated by farmers
Ways of life (customs)	Certain ways of doing things that are followed by all the people; importance placed on religion, art, science
Language	Spoken and written language, often but not always

Other factors may be added but are not necessary. They include the development of the arts (painting, music) and of advanced methods of communication and manufacturing.

The words *civilization* and *city* come from the same Latin word, *civis*, which means a citizen, someone who lives in the city. The word *city* can be traced even further back in history to the Greek word meaning "to settle down in." Where people settle down, towns develop. Civilization begins with **permanent** (lasting) settlements.

The Agricultural Revolution

A key event in the growth and spread of civilization was the human discovery of how to grow food. This allowed people to switch from being **nomadic** hunters and gatherers, constantly moving from place to place, to farmers settled in permanent homes.

Agriculture seems to have developed in several areas of the world where natural conditions were favorable. Humans developed a variety of crops from wild plants already in use as food sources. With the discovery of farming, people also learned to **domesticate** (tame) animals and use them as a source of food or to do heavy work. Agriculture as a way of life soon spread in all directions. New plants were raised, and new uses for animals were developed.

CENTERS OF PLANT AND ANIMAL DOMESTICATION

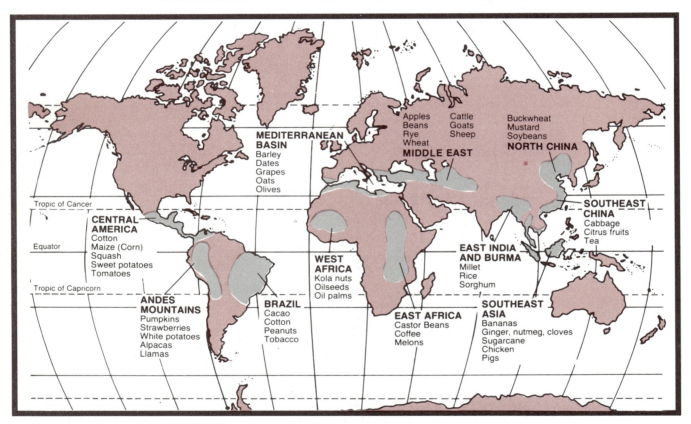

MEDITERRANEAN BASIN
Barley
Dates
Grapes
Oats
Olives

MIDDLE EAST
Apples
Beans
Rye
Wheat
Cattle
Goats
Sheep

NORTH CHINA
Buckwheat
Mustard
Soybeans

CENTRAL AMERICA
Cotton
Maize (Corn)
Squash
Sweet potatoes
Tomatoes

SOUTHEAST CHINA
Cabbage
Citrus fruits
Tea

EAST INDIA AND BURMA
Millet
Rice
Sorghum

WEST AFRICA
Kola nuts
Oilseeds
Oil palms

ANDES MOUNTAINS
Pumpkins
Strawberries
White potatoes
Alpacas
Llamas

BRAZIL
Cacao
Cotton
Peanuts
Tobacco

EAST AFRICA
Castor Beans
Coffee
Melons

SOUTHEAST ASIA
Bananas
Ginger, nutmeg, cloves
Sugarcane
Chicken
Pigs

Tropic of Cancer
Equator
Tropic of Capricorn

Communication

Communication is the keystone of human culture. Language and writing are the main methods we use to communicate.

Language

Of all human cultural developments, perhaps the most important is the development of language. A **language** is a set of signs and symbols used in communicating thought and ideas. It may be written or spoken or both. The sounds, symbols, and signs must be understood by the people who use them.

Time Period	Development
10,000 B.C. to 9,000 B.C.	First permanent communities
	Stone-based architecture
	Use of flint for fire
	Composite tools
9,000 B.C. to 8,000 B.C.	Long-distance trade
	Herding animals
8,000 B.C. to 7,000 B.C.	Agriculture
	Household crafts
	First building with communal purpose
7,000 B.C. to 6,000 B.C.	Pottery
	Earliest metal work
	Full-time craft specialists (artisans)
6,000 B.C. to 5,000 B.C.	Irrigation
5,000 B.C. to 4,000 B.C.	Ranked society
4,000 B.C. to 3,000 B.C.	Writing
	Plow
	Wheel
	Bronze metallurgy
3,0000 B.C. to 2,000 B.C.	Cities
	Class society
	Full-time armies
	State bureaucracy
2,000 B.C. to 1,000 B.C.	Written legal codes
	Iron metallurgy
	Chariots
	Alphabet

Every group of people in the world has a language. Some languages are spoken by millions of people; others may be spoken by only a few hundred.

No one knows how long ago people developed language. Anthropologists can tell that language has been part of human life for a very long time, because people have worked together and cooperated with each other in ways that required communication. For example, **archaeologists** (scientists who study pottery, tools, and weapons of people from the past) have found the remains of large pens or corrals where early hunters trapped the animals they needed for food. Those hunters must have had language. Without it they could not have planned ahead for the hunt or cooperated to build the pens or traps.

Wherever there is evidence that **prehistoric** people worked and planned together, researchers know those people had language. No one today knows what their languages were, because they left no written records.

The languages people use today are thousands of years old. Each language contains clues that help trace that language's roots. Some of these clues show that the languages of one culture may be related to other languages. Like people, languages can come in families. English is part of the Indo-European language family.

The exact nature of the relationship between language and culture is not easy to determine. Is language simply a reflection of culture, a mirror on our ways of thinking and behavior? Or does language instead somehow serve to set up the ways we look at the world around us?

George Orwell, in his novel *1984*, writes about "Newspeak," a language that makes it impossible to think certain thoughts. By constructing a new vocabulary and grammar, leaders of nations are able to mold citizens' thoughts in "acceptable" ways. Language here becomes a tool for creating a new culture. (*1984* was written by Orwell in 1949 and therefore was a novel of the future.)

Describing Newspeak, Orwell says:

Its vocabulary was so constructed as to give exact meanings to all words and excluded all other meanings . . . . To give a single example. The word "free" still existed in "Newspeak," but it could only be used in such statements as "This dog is free of lice" or "This field is free from weeds." It could not be used in its old meaning of "politically free" or "intellectually free" since political freedom and intellectual freedom no longer existed in fact or in ideas . . . . Many other words such as honor, justice, morality, internationalism, democracy, science and religion had simply ceased to exist. A few blanket words covered them, and in covering them, abolished them. All words grouping themselves around the ideas of liberty and equality for instance, were contained in the single word "crimethink." All words grouping themselves around the concepts (ideas) of objectivity and rationalism were contained in a single word "oldthink" (Orwell, 1984, pp. 246–251.)

Written Communication

Writing is language or speech written down. Writing is a much newer way of communicating than speaking. Writing is only about 5,000 years old. Language is recorded by many kinds of symbols. The symbols we use today in writing developed slowly throughout human history. Through the ages people have invented many kinds of writing systems.

Some of the earliest writing systems were **pictography** (picture writing). Picture messages were simple pictures drawn in a series. The pictures told a story or expressed an idea. Native Americans used picture writing. Many people in Europe, Asia, and Africa once used pictography. Pictography took time and many picture symbols to communicate an idea or a series of ideas.

Since there was a need to communicate, some societies developed writing systems. The Egyptians, for example, used pictures and other symbols to represent words or syllables. Languages that contained thousands of words needed more symbols. As such languages grew, so did the number of word symbols that had to be memorized. In China, picture-writing developed into a complex system of symbols called characters, which requires great discipline and study to master.

Most languages today have alphabets. In an alphabet, letters stand for sounds. These letters can be arranged to stand for any word. Fewer symbols than pictures are needed for all the words in the language. With an alphabet it is easier to write a spoken language.

English and most other Western European-based languages are written with letters developed by the Romans about 3,000 years ago. The Romans had borrowed many of these letters from the Greek alphabet. In fact, the word *alphabet* comes from the first two Greek letters, *alpha* and *beta*. The Greeks developed their alphabet from one used earlier by the Phoenicians. The Phoenicians sailed the Mediterranean Sea and traded with the Greeks. The Phoenician alphabet used symbols for consonants. The Greeks added letters for vowel sounds. All the speech sounds could then be written. In Eastern Europe, Russian and other Slavic languages are written in the **cyrillic** alphabet. In India, Hindi is one of a number of alphabetic scripts.

Writing made it possible for people to communicate without meeting. Through writing, knowledge of historical events could be passed along. Knowledge therefore could be spread more easily. Discoveries by explorers, scientists, and doctors could be communicated through writing. This in turn led to new discoveries. People became aware more easily about what was going on around them in places far away. People became linked to events away from them.

People with common interests, such as business, trade, and government, are able to share information and establish contact more easily. Understanding through written communication is a valuable tool in bringing people together to share not only information, but goods and services as well.

Cultural Diffusion

Our solid American citizen awakens in a bed built on a pattern which originated in the Near East, but which was modified in Northern Europe before it was transmitted to America. He throws back covers made from cotton first grown in India, or linen first made in the Near East, or silk, the use of which was discovered in China. All of these materials have been spun or woven by processes invented in the Near East. He slips into moccasins invented by the Indians of the eastern United States, and goes to the bathroom, whose fixtures are a mixture of European and American inventions, both of recent date. He takes off his pajamas, a garment invented in India, and washes with soap invented by the ancient Gauls. He then shaves, a custom which seems to have been developed in ancient Egypt.

Returning to the bedroom, he removes his clothes from a chair of Southern European type, and proceeds to dress. He puts on clothes whose form originally developed from the skin clothing of the nomads of the Asiatic steppes, puts on shoes made from skins tanned by a process invented in ancient Egypt, and cut to a pattern developed in ancient Greece, and ties around his neck a bright-colored cloth which is a survival of the shoulder shawls worn by 17th-century Croatians of Southern Europe. Before going out to breakfast he glances through the window, made of glass invented in Egypt, and if it is raining, puts on overshoes made of rubber first used by Central American Indians, and takes an umbrella invented in Southeast Asia. Upon his head he puts a hat made of felt, a material first used on the Asiatic steppes.

On his way to breakfast he buys a newspaper, and pays for it with coins of ancient Lydian invention. At the restaurant a new series of borrowed things face him. His plate is made of a form of pottery invented in China. His knife is of steel, an alloy first used in southern India, his fork is a medieval Italian invention, and his spoon comes from a Roman original. He begins breakfast with an orange from the eastern Mediterranean, a cantaloupe from Persia, or perhaps a piece of African watermelon. With this he has coffee, an African plant. After his fruit and first coffee he goes on to waffles, cakes made by a Scandinavian technique from wheat first raised in the Near East. As a side dish he may have eggs, first eaten in eastern Asia, or then strips of the flesh of an animal first tamed in eastern Asia, which has been salted and smoked by a process developed in Northern Europe.

When our friend has finished eating, he settles back to smoke, an American Indian habit, consuming a plant first developed in Brazil, in either a pipe developed by the Indians of Virginia, or a cigarette, derived from Mexico. If he is hardy enough, he might even smoke a cigar, brought to us from the Antilles by way of Spain. While smoking, he reads the news of the day, imprinted in characters invented in Germany. As he absorbs the information in the newspapers of the problems that exist in other countries he will, if he is a good conservative citizen, thank a Hebrew deity in an Indo-European language that he is 100 percent American.

This article by Ralph Linton clearly shows the origins of certain objects and activities with which Americans are familiar. He shows the origins to be outside of America. When cultural traits or cultural patterns are spread from one group of people to another and from one culture to another, this action is called **cultural diffusion**.

Most of the cultural background and heritage of America was brought here from England, Spain, and other European countries. Some items of America's culture, such as the potato, maize, types of cooking and methods of warfare were contributed by Native Americans. African traditions have influenced music and religion, and more recently, immigrants from Asia and Latin America have added new aspects to the mix of American culture.

England and France diffused much of their culture from Italy. Italy, in turn, borrowed from the Greeks. It was once believed that Greece created its own culture. However, we now know that the Greeks borrowed much from Crete, and that Crete borrowed from Egypt. Egypt exchanged cultural traits with the cultures of the Tigris-Euphrates Valley. The Tigris-Euphrates cultures exchanged traits with the Indus River civilizations. India, in turn, had interchanges with China. As you can see, there has been a vast amount of borrowing by one people from another.

If a new cultural pattern or object appeals to a groups of people because it is useful and meets the needs of the group, cultural diffusion takes place. The new pattern or object is made part of the group's culture in a way that best serves the group.

Diffusion is not automatic when two groups come together. It is selective. If a particular trait fits in easily with a culture, it is quickly diffused. If it can be used or is needed, it will be **adapted** or changed slightly to fit the needs of a society. The Russians borrowed the Greek religion, but made it fit the existing culture of Russia.

"I approach my older brother with respect, my father and mother with veneration (honor), my grandfather with awe (fear)."—an old Chinese saying—expresses how the Chinese placed great importance on the past. They borrowed little from the outside, and what they did borrow, they made Chinese. Custom and tradition ruled in China. Cultural diffusion was resisted. Few new ideas entered. The Chinese civilization fell behind and began to crumble under the force of 20th century progress.

It is important to note that societies and nations borrow from each other to better themselves. There is no single culture that has developed without diffusion. We will note many examples of cultural diffusion in our study of the world.

"What It Is Like to Be Underdeveloped"

Most Americans look at the developing areas of the world without having the slightest idea of the difficulties with which they are faced. We must try to understand what life is like for the almost 4 billion human beings who live in developing nations.

It is not easy to make the mental jump. Let us try, however, by imagining how an American family, living in a housing development on a very low yearly income could be changed into a family of the underdeveloped world.

Our first step is to strip our American home of its furniture. Everything from the living quarters goes: beds, chairs, tables, television set, lamps. Leave a few old blankets, a kitchen table, a wooden chair. For clothing, each member of the family may keep his oldest suit or dress, plus a shirt or blouse. Permit a pair of shoes to the head of the family, but none for the wife.

In the kitchen the appliances have already been taken out, the water and electric power shut off. The box of matches may stay, as well as a small bag of flour and some sugar and salt. A few moldy potatoes, already in the garbage can, must be hastily rescued, for they will be much of tonight's meal. We will leave a handful of onions and a dish of dried beans. All the rest must go: the meat, fresh vegetables, canned goods, crackers.

The house itself, as well as the other houses of the development, must go. The family can move into a small shack. It may be crowded. Still, they are fortunate to have any shelter at all; an estimated 250,000 people in the Indian city of Calcutta live in the streets.

Communication must go next. No more newspapers, magazines, books. However, they will not be missed, since we are not able to read. Instead, in our community we will allow one radio—and that is generous.

Government services must go also. No more mail delivery or fire protection. There is a school, but it is three miles away and consists of two classrooms. It is not overcrowded, since only half of the children in the neighborhood go to school. There are, of course, no hospitals or doctors nearby. The nearest clinic is ten miles away. It can be reached by bicycle, if the family has one, which is unlikely. Or you can go by bus—not always inside, but there is usually room on the top.

Money? We will allow our family a cash treasure of ten dollars. This will help cover some of the costs of unexpected medical and family problems. Meanwhile, the head of the family must earn a living. As a peasant with three acres to farm, he may raise the equivalent of 100 to 300 dollars worth of crops a year. If he is a tenant farmer, which is more than likely, a third of his crop will go to his landlord, and another 10 percent to the local money lender. But there will be enough to eat—or almost enough. The human body requires a daily input of at least 2,300 calories to make up for the energy used by the body. If we do no better than the Latin American peasant, we will average no more than 2,000 to 2,100 calories per day. Our bodies, like a machine that is not oiled enough, will run down.

And so we have brought our American family down to the very bottom of the human scale. When we are told that more than half the world's population "enjoys" a standard of living of "less than 100 dollars a year," this is what that figure means.

The Road to Development

The description you have just read was adapted from Robert Heilbroner's book *The Great Ascent.* It gives you a vivid picture of what poverty means to individual people. What does it mean to a country?

When we refer to a nation as "developing," we are comparing it to the United States, Canada, Australia, Japan, or most of the nations of Western Europe. The term suggests that there is a potential for improved living standards, though now the majority of that nation's people live in poverty. The term *developing* has replaced *underdeveloped.*

The Role of Human Resources

A large supply of natural resources, such as water power and minerals (oil, coal, iron ore), alone does not guarantee development. A country's human resources are even more important than its natural resources. To turn rivers into electric power, there must be trained and educated people. They must build the dams and generators to produce and move the electricity. Crude oil lying under the ground is not valuable unless there are people who know how to get it out, refine it, and use it. The education of an engineer, a scientist, or a teacher cannot be accomplished overnight.

The Role of Capital

Development means not only improving the standard of living and education of the people. It also means the development of a sense of pride and satisfaction in oneself and one's country. The leaders of the "developing" nations are asking their people to work harder. The people are asked to raise more food than they themselves can use. The extra, or surplus, food can be exported for money. This money, or capital, can be used to build schools, factories, and roads. The term **capital** can be used to describe goods, such as machinery and buildings, that are used directly in the production of other goods. Some forms of capital, such as a textile mill or a hydroelectric plant, immediately produce new goods, which create more capital. Other forms of capital, such as schools, hospitals, and roads, are often called "social capital" because they, too, have a role to play in producing wealth, although not as immediate a role as capital goods (machinery, factories).

Outside Aid

Capital, then, can be raised from within a country only if the people do not use all that is produced. If the birth rate is high, and production of food does not keep up with the growth in population, there will be no surplus. No surplus means no capital for development. A "developing" nation must, therefore, get help from the outside.

Over a century ago, Abraham Lincoln said that the United States could not exist half slave and half free. Today the world cannot exist one-quarter rich and three-quarters poor. The developed nations must be aware of the potential and the challenge this situation presents, and they must help change the situation by supplying aid and assistance.

The Third World of Developing Nations

You may have heard people speak of the "Third World." We have learned that there are political and economic differences among nations and peoples. These differences give us a basis for the term the *Third World*.

The world can be divided into three parts: The industrialized and developed nations of Western Europe, Australia, the United States, and Canada make up the "First World." The former Communist nations of Eastern Europe and Asia make up the "Second World." The developing nations of Africa, Latin America, and Asia make up what is known as the **Third World**. Many of these countries are former colonies of "First World" nations, and became independent between 1945 and 1970.

As some of these nations become more prosperous, and as great changes take place in the former Communist nations, such divisions no longer are very descriptive or accurate. We must look at individual nations or related groups of nations and examine information that depicts their specific possibilities and problems.

Twentieth-Century Nationalism

Every morning the American flag is raised over the school. Soldiers and sailors salute the flag as it passes by in a parade. When we go to baseball, basketball, or football games we sing our national anthem, "The Star-Spangled Banner." We do these things to show we are proud of our nation. We are also showing our respect and loyalty for the ideals upon which our nation is built. This feeling of pride, loyalty, and respect to our nation is called **nationalism**.

What is a nation? A nation may be defined as a group of people united by common history, common customs, and a common language. Such a group of people is called a **nationality**. What makes a nation? A nation must have (1) a definite area of land; (2) a government obeyed by all of the people; (3) a people who have a feeling of nationality and nationalism; and (4) a government that is fully independent and not forced to obey any outside group or nation.

The spirit of nationalism is found all over the world today. It is found in many places where a "nation" itself does not exist. In recent years the spirit of nationalism has shown itself in Northern Ireland, where the Irish Republican Army (IRA) wishes to dispose of the British. In Canada the French-speaking Canadians of Quebec are discussing the establishment of a separate Quebec nation. In Africa the Somali nationalists in Kenya and Ethiopia wish to become independent. The Palestinian nationalists want a homeland in the Middle East. These are only a few examples of existing nationalist movements.

Nationalism and Terrorism

In an effort to achieve their goals, some nationalists have used the tactics (methods) of terrorism. Terrorism is an old method, based on the fact that people can be influenced by fear. Terrorism is not new, but only recently have new means become available for a different type of international terrorism.

Today terrorists obtain weapons that can be used to threaten those in power. The terrorists aim to frighten and impress those in power so that they may grant the terrorists demands.

Today's terrorists are well aware of the power of the media. They play to and for an audience. Their actions are carefully planned to gain maximum attention, thereby winning the sympathy of the world. Claims of ill-treatment, a seeming "desire for justice," and a variety of sophisticated propaganda methods combine to create a performance. In the interests of their "sacred (holy) nationalist cause," they use all possible means to create fear, thus forcing their opponents to yield to the threats.

The reaction of the world to the terrorist acts is often varied. In the eyes of some countries, such actions are viewed as necessary to achieve freedom from oppression. At times, terrorists have traveled freely from country to country, with diplomatic immunity (freedom from punishment). They have sometimes been welcomed to the United Nations. The media have made the terrorists famous by publicizing their actions on radio, on television, and in newspapers.

As mentioned before, terrorism is not new. In 1914, a Bosnian nationalist hurled a bomb and killed the Archduke Ferdinand, the heir to the throne of Austria. This terrorist wanted Bosnian independence from Austria, but his action caused the beginning of World War I. Joseph Stalin robbed banks to help raise money to finance the Communist terrorism in Russia before the Revolution of 1917. Jomo Kenyatta of the Mau Mau terrorist campaign in Kenya in 1952, fought against both blacks and whites and later became president of that country. Menachem Begin was the leader of the Irgun, which was a terrorist organization that fought the British and Arabs in Palestine before 1948. Begin became prime minister of Israel. Algeria's Bouteflike was a member of the FLS (Front de Libération Nationale), which fought for Algeria's independence from France.

Terrorist acts have escalated. Whereas Kenyatta and Begin, as well as the Algerian nationalists, created terrorist acts only in their countries, the Palestine Liberation Organization (PLO) hijacked planes traveling all throughout the world. The Japanese Red Army terrorists attacked Christian pilgrims in the Israeli Lod Airport. German terrorists hijacked a plane full of people in Athens, Greece, and took it to Entebbe, Uganda, in Central Africa.

Our Global Village

Our world has become a "**global village**." What happens in one country not only affects the people in that nation, but also the people in neighboring nations and possibly in nations on the other side of the planet.

With the coming of electricity, the telephone and telegraph, radio and television, as well as air travel, the planet has become smaller and its nations more interdependent. **Interdependence** means that nations of the world depend on one another for goods and services. All nations benefit from this exchange of trade. Nations often need something other countries have in abundance. Interdependence based on trade is called economic interdependence. Cultural interdependence is the exchange of ideas and knowledge.

Still another example of interdependence is the role played by international and regional organizations (United Nations, Organization of American States, European Economic Community). Each provides help and support to member nations.

The events of the Cold War and Soviet Russia's control of Eastern Europe in the postwar period (1945–1990) forced the countries of Western Europe, the United States, and Canada to form the North Atlantic Treaty Organization (NATO). NATO has become history's most lasting and successful attempt at collective security.

During this period the European community pioneered the establishment of a regional economic union—European Economic Community (EEC). The EEC has become the model for regional economic groups throughout the world.

The internal affairs of a nation used to be off-limits to the world community. Now the principle of "humanitarian intervention" is gaining acceptance. A turning point came in April, 1991, shortly after Saddam Hussein's withdrawal from Kuwait. At that time, the Security Council of the United Nations authorized allied troops to assist starving Kurds in Northern Iraq. This policy continues with U.N. intervention in Somalia and Bosnia (Yugoslavia).

The "global village" has also contributed to the spread of terrorism, the growth of worldwide drug traffic, the spread of AIDS, and the continued destruction of the environment. The reappearance of nationalism in its most violent and destructive form is also a result of this phenomenon—the "global village."

However, because these threats are more than any one nation can cope with on its own, they may create the necessary incentive for interdependent and international cooperation.

Issues of global concern:
1. Maintaining international peace and security.
2. Controlling the international drug trade.
3. The effects of a rising population which is outgrowing food production.
4. The problems related to food scarcity and the unequal distribution of resources that create hunger and poverty.
5. The issues of human rights and civil liberties throughout the world.

6. The destruction of the environment due to unwise and many times selfish practices.
7. The problems related to international trade, international debt, and world finance.
8. The unequal distribution of energy resources throughout the world.
9. The international problem of terrorism and its affect on the terrorists and those who are terrorized.
10. The growth of nationalism in its most negative and most destructive forms.

Our Endangered Planet

For most of the 2 million years of human existence, people lived in harmony with the environment. This situation began to change after 1800 with the Industrial Revolution. Technological advances provided the means for destroying nature's balance. Smokestacks began to discharge poisonous gases into the air while factories dumped toxic wastes into rivers and streams. More serious deterioration came in the 1900s. Automobiles, trucks, and other vehicles seriously added to air pollution. Rivers, lakes, and even oceans became dumping sites for all kinds of wastes. Toxic garbage in landfills contaminated the soil in many places and made drinking water unsafe.

For decades scientists warned of the possible consequences, but no one paid much attention. Now there is increasing evidence that our planet is in serious trouble and that reckless treatment of the environment is affecting our lives and endangering our health.

Examples of environmental damage can be found in every part of the globe. The serious effects of pollution on the Atlantic coast of the United States were evident during the last few summers. Many beaches had to be closed because medical waste and other solid wastes dumped into the ocean washed up on the beaches. The deaths of large numbers of dolphins off the coasts of the Middle Atlantic states is further evidence of the pollution in our coastal waters. Fish caught in many parts of the Hudson River cannot be sold because they are considered to be contaminated. For years, chemical, mineral, and organic waste was dumped into the Great Lakes. Much of this has now stopped, but the dangerous contamination in the Great Lakes will be around for decades, threatening the health of fish, wild life, and humans. This is because contamination levels can remain high years after direct discharges cease.

In Europe, the situation is even worse. For years, Europeans disposed of their industrial and radioactive waste by dumping it at sea. The deaths of large numbers of seals in the North Sea drew attention to its terrible pollution. In many parts of Western Europe, excessive levels of nitrates and pesticides are found in ground water that is used for drinking. The countries of Eastern and Central Europe are in worse condition. For four decades, the Communist governments of these nations promoted rapid industrialization; however, little attention was paid to environmental impact. In recent years, many forests in Central Europe have died from acid rain. The major rivers in Poland are so polluted they are useless for drinking, fishing, or swimming. Air pollution is destroying buildings and with them the cultural heritage of many of these nations. In the mining districts people suffer from many different diseases and there is a shortened life expectancy.

In 1970, a strong citizens' movement for environmental protection began. This is celebrated every year as Earth Day. All over the world citizens' groups and organizations are pressuring governments to clean up and protect the environment. Many of the industrialized countries are now investing billions of dollars to reduce air and water pollution. Some of these efforts have been successful. In many cities air quality has been improved and many rivers are being rescued from pollution. However, much still remains to be done.

Moreover, there are several environmental issues that require international cooperation. These issues include the destruction of the rain forests, the greenhouse effect and global warming, and the depletion of the ozone layer.

Destruction of the Rain Forests

All around the globe habitats are being destroyed and with them entire **ecosystems**. An ecosystem is a community of plants, animals, birds and insects, and the environment where they exist.

The ecosystem in which this destruction is most serious is that of the tropical rain forests. Trees and vegetation are being slashed and burned and large areas of forest land are disappearing. In Central America, forests have been destroyed to create cattle ranches that produce beef for export. In Malaysia, trees are cut down for timber and to create rubber plantations. In Brazil, forest land is cleared to provide fields for agriculture and economic opportunities for corporations. The reasons for this destruction include poverty, population growth, poor planning, and greed. The consequences are enormous.

The rain forests of the world are the home of thousands of species of insects, birds, animals, and plants. In the rain forests there is a diversity of life (biodiversity) that is not found anywhere else in the world. While the tropical rain forests cover only 7 percent of the earth's surface, they house between 50 and 80 percent of its species.

As the rain forests are destroyed, many species of plants and animals are being wiped out. It is believed that hundreds of thousands of species may be extinct by the year 2000. We will never even know what some of those species were. Of the estimated 5 million to 30 million different life forms on earth, only 1.7 million have been identified and cataloged. The disappearance of these species will be a great, irreversible loss to humanity.

Humans benefit greatly from the earth's biodiversity. Approximately 25 percent of the pharmaceuticals (drugs and medicines) in use in the United States today contain ingredients derived from wild plants. Hidden in the plants and vegetation about to be destroyed might be cures for still unconquered diseases. The diversity in nature also offers many opportunities for agriculture. Scientists are using **biotechnology** to improve crops by transferring desirable genes from the wild strains of some plants. The possibilities for improvement are endless: drought- and frost-resistant crops may be developed as well as natural fertilizers and pesticides. But these possibilities will be limited as more species of plants disappear.

The question of saving the rain forests from destruction is very complicated. Almost all the rain forests are found in developing countries of Africa, Asia, and Latin America. These nations are struggling to feed their people, to raise cash to modernize, and to pay their huge international debts. Many countries are chopping down their forests to earn capital from timber exports. They are also doing it to create living and farming space for their growing populations. How can countries worry about biodiversity when their people need to feed themselves?

The developed nations can take some steps to help preserve the world's rain forests. For example, the rich nations can reduce the debt burden of the developing nations. They can send conservation information and experts to the developing nations and train local people in conservation techniques. Most important, they must convince people in the developing countries that it is in their own interest to preserve their environment. There is increasing evidence for these countries that the destruction of forests has disastrous consequences. In recent years, deforestation has contributed to the terrible droughts in Africa and to devastating mud slides in Brazil.

Development must go hand in hand with preservation. For example, if trees are cut selectively it is possible for forests to provide profit and to survive.

The Greenhouse Effect and Global Warming

For more than a decade, scientists have warned that gases coming from cars, factories, and even agriculture are heating up the earth causing a **greenhouse effect** that could eventually produce disastrous climate changes. The gases causing this are called "greenhouse gases." The threat of global warming and severe climatic changes resulting from the greenhouse effect has become the number one environmental issue of the 1990s.

One of the main greenhouse gases is carbon dioxide (CO_2) which is released into the air in large quantities when wood and fossil fuels such as coal, oil, and natural gas are burned. An important function of trees is to absorb carbon dioxide which exists in nature. However, increasing population has led to widespread cutting down of trees throughout the world. Now with more carbon dioxide coming from cars and factories, there are fewer trees to absorb it.

Carbon dioxide causes only part of the problem. Other gases such as chlorofluorocarbons that are used in spray cans and as coolants in refrigerators and air conditioners are also responsible. So are nitrogen oxides, which are released from automobiles and power plant smokestacks. Another greenhouse gas is methane which comes from natural gas and from rotting garbage in landfills.

Many scientists say if more greenhouse gases are released into the atmosphere, the earth's average temperature may rise by 3°F to 8°F by the middle of the 21st century. This warming could produce disastrous changes in climate. For example, shifting rainfall patterns could result in increased rainfall and flooding in some areas and droughts in other areas. This could have a serious impact on agriculture around the world. It has even been suggested that the main wheat growing area in the United States could turn into a dustbowl. Another possible result of climate change is rising sea levels caused by the melting polar ice caps. Some scientists predict that if the Mediterranean Sea rises, Venice, Alexandria, and other cities would be flooded. The same could be true for coastal villages and cities in many parts of the world.

Scientists disagree over the question of global warming. Some scientists claim that global warming is already occurring. They point to data showing that the thickness of sea ice north of Greenland has decreased. Some say that the sea level might already be rising and that the rising sea level is destroying large areas of low lying tropical forests in parts of Queensland in Australia and causing coastal erosion in Britain. These scientists claim that the heat waves, droughts, floods, and hurricanes of the 1980s are indications that global warming is taking place.

However, some scientists say that these changes have nothing to do with the greenhouse effect. These events in the 1980s could simply have been part of the natural year to year variations in weather.

Although scientists do not agree about global warming and its consequences, no one disputes that the amount of greenhouse gases in the atmosphere has increased and continues to increase rapidly. Everyone also agrees that preventive measures are necessary to avoid possible disaster. Several steps must be taken to slow or even prevent global warming. Car and industrial emissions must be drastically reduced by encouraging energy conservation and developing alternatives to fossil fuels.

Conservation

When oil prices sky-rocketed in the 1970s, industries became more energy-efficient. Individuals also changed their habits and conserved energy. But when oil prices declined in the 1980s, people became less interested in conservation. Governments must encourage industries to use the most advanced energy-saving technology. Minimum efficiency standards must be set for cars, appliances, and machinery. Some suggest that raising the cost of oil and gas or putting a tax on carbon dioxide emissions will encourage conservation. Individuals must also conserve energy.

Develop Alternatives to Fossil Fuels

Conserving energy is not enough. Even if carbon dioxide emissions are reduced, carbon dioxide is still being released into the atmosphere and atmospheric concentrations will continue to rise. The world must move away from its dependence on oil and gas and find other sources of energy.

The two main alternatives are nuclear energy and solar energy, neither of which produces greenhouse gases. However, the building of nuclear power plants to provide energy is controversial. Many Americans are opposed to nuclear power plants because of the accidents at Three Mile Island and Chernobyl, the problem of radioactive waste, and the effects of radiation on people. Those who favor nuclear energy claim that it is possible to build safe nuclear power plants. They point out that France gets more than 70 percent of its electricity from nuclear plants and has a good safety record. Solar energy produces no waste and is inexhaustible. More research is needed to find ways to lower the cost of solar energy and help it become more widely used.

Global warming can also be reduced by stopping or slowing down **deforestation** (cutting down large numbers of trees). This is often difficult because thousands of jobs in the timber industry are at stake. **Reforestation**, planting trees, is extremely important. This can be done by individuals planting trees in their backyards, local communities and private organizations planting a few acres, and state and national governments creating wilderness areas and reforesting on a much larger scale.

Depletion of the Ozone Layer

The ozone layer is a natural layer of gas located between six and 30 miles above the earth's surface. It protects humans and other living things from the damaging effects of the sun by absorbing most of the sun's ultraviolet radiation. Ultraviolet rays are very dangerous. Besides causing sunburn, they have been linked to cataracts and weakened immune systems in humans and animals. Ultraviolet light disrupts the workings of cells and is thought to be a primary cause of some skin cancers.

In 1985, scientists found a "hole" or a thinning in the ozone layer over Antarctica. Since the 1970s, scientists had warned that chemicals known as chlorofluorocarbons (CFCs) were destroying ozone molecules and depleting the ozone layer. (CFCs are also blamed for adding to the greenhouse effect.) Chlorofluorocarbons are used as propellants in spray cans and as coolants in refrigerators and air conditioners. They are also ingredients in plastic-foam materials such as styrofoam that is used to make drinking cups, hamburger containers, and packaging materials. Although the United States banned the use of chlorofluorocarbons in spray cans after scientists warned against them, CFCs were used in other products. Moreover, the rest of the world continued to use CFCs for many purposes and their production kept growing. The former Soviet Union was an especially heavy user of CFCs.

As the danger became more evident, 24 nations, including the United States and the Soviet Union, met in Montreal in 1987 and accepted an agreement known as the Montreal Protocol. It called for a step-by-step reduction in the production of chlorofluorocarbons during the 1990s. Three years later, as evidence of ozone loss increased, representatives of many nations met in London and agreed to a total ban on CFCs by the year 2000.

In 1992, there was alarming new information. The National Aeronautics and Space Administration (NASA), together with a number of prominent scientists, announced findings from several atmospheric studies. These indicated that the ozone layer over the northern United States, Canada, Europe, and Russia could be depleted by as much as 40 percent before 1995. Scientists fear that a huge ozone hole could open over these heavily populated regions. If this occurs, the long-term effects on animal and plant life could be disastrous.

The Chernobyl Nuclear Accident

In 1986, the nuclear power plant at Chernobyl in the former Soviet Union exploded. A number of people died immediately following the accident and several hundred people were treated for radiation sickness and burns. The Soviet government evacuated 135,000 people from the area, slaughtered contaminated livestock, and discontinued farming over a 37-mile radius around Chernobyl. The difficult process of decontaminating the soil was undertaken.

The radioactive particles released into the air were carried by winds to much of Scandinavia and the Baltic region. Higher levels of radiation were also found in Eastern and Western Europe and large quantities of food and livestock had to be destroyed. In some places, drinking water was considered unsafe. Above-average radioactivity was detected as far away as North America, Israel, and Japan.

The 1986 disaster at the Chernobyl nuclear power plant is used by people opposed to nuclear power to show its dangers and to push for a ban on all new nuclear plants and to abandon existing ones. This was the most serious accident in the history of the nuclear power industry and was the first time that such an accident resulted in immediate deaths and a large release of radioactivity. Its effects on humans and on the environment will be felt for years to come. However, those who favor nuclear power point out that other nations use nuclear power safely.

The Population Explosion

July 11, 1987 was designated by the United Nations as the "Day of Five Billion" to mark this milestone in world population growth. World population is now growing by 93 million people per year and is expected to pass the 6 billion mark before the year 2000. This increase is larger than expected and is due to a rise in China's birthrate since 1985 as well as larger increases in population in India.

China's population in 1990 was estimated at 1,133,000,000. India's population was estimated to be 853,373,000. Together, these two countries make up 37 percent of the world's total population.

United Nations population projections (predictions) are as follows:

Year	World Population
1997	6,000,000,000
2000	6,260,800,000
2025	8,504,223,000

These estimates are based on the assumption that birth rates will drop significantly during the next 30 years in Asia (except Japan), Africa, and Latin America. If this does not happen, world population in 2025 could be as high as 9,423,000,000.

It is estimated that 90 percent of future growth in population will take place in the developing nations of Asia (except Japan), Africa, and Latin America. These countries are growing at a rate of 2 to 4 percent a year, a rate that will double their population every 29 years. For example, the population of Kenya, with an annual growth rate of 4 percent, is expected to jump from 23 million to 79 million in 30 years. The growth rate is smaller in Brazil, Indonesia, China, and India, but the sheer size of their already existing populations means a huge increase in people in the future. In 1990, 77 percent of the world's population lived in the developing countries of the Third World. This percentage will increase as the populations increase in these countries.

Explosive growth in world population is the greatest environmental threat to the earth. In the poorer countries, population is growing at a much faster rate than agricultural production. These nations are increasingly unable to provide the bare necessities of life—food, housing, and fuel. As a result, trees are being cut down for fuel and building materials, grasslands are overgrazed by livestock, and farmland is overused by desperate farmers.

Total food production will have to increase by at least 33 percent just to maintain present per capita consumption levels. However, present levels of consumption are quite inadequate in many places. The greatest food shortages due to explosive population growth are expected in Africa and Latin America. In addition, the former Soviet Union and the countries of Eastern Europe are expected to have serious shortages.

Many countries will depend on large amounts of imported food to feed their people for some years to come. The countries that presently export food—the United States, Australia, and Argentina—will continue to play a vital role in the future.

Environmentalists claim that limiting population growth is the only way to prevent possible calamity in the future. They urge the adoption of family planning programs in countries with high population growth rates. Some call for a goal of two children per family for the world as a whole. In some countries it may be necessary to set a goal of one child per family, as China did in 1979. Although many developing countries opposed the idea of family planning in the past, almost all these countries now are committed to limiting population growth. The most difficult obstacle is changing the cultural attitudes that encourage high birth rates. Many families in poor countries see children as a source of labor and a protection against poverty in old age. People need to be taught that with lower infant mortality, fewer children can provide the same security.

Feeding the World's Growing Population

There is a cruel paradox with regard to food. While people in some countries have never experienced hunger in their lives, people in other countries face starvation almost every day. In the United States, storage facilities overflow with surplus agricultural products and farmers receive government payments to cultivate fewer acres. In drought stricken Africa, famine takes the lives of millions of people and millions more suffer the debilitating effects of malnutrition.

Why are some countries able to produce enough to feed their people with more left over for export, while others can barely feed their people? Many factors are involved; soil quality; amount of rainfall; methods of cultivation; transportation; government policies; agricultural research; and population growth.

Success in agricultural production in the 20th century is largely the result of science-based agriculture. With a growing knowledge of soil chemistry, plant physiology, genetics, and other related sciences, agricultural scientists have increased food production throughout the world.

Science-Based Agriculture

Methods for high-yielding agricultural production were first widely applied in the United States during World War II. The new practices included: the use of newly developed high-yielding crop varieties; increased irrigation; a large increase in the use of chemical fertilizers to restore soil fertility; more effective weed control; improved control of diseases and insects; and economic incentive to farmers to adopt the new practices.

As a result of the new technology, American farmers achieved dramatic increases in corn, wheat, and other crop yields. Today, American farmers, who represent less than 2 percent of the nation's work force, feed the nation, and produce a huge surplus for export. During the past several decades this new technology has also reached the farmers of Western Europe, Canada, Australia and New Zealand, Japan, and parts of Eastern Europe and the former Soviet Union.

The Third World—Agriculture a Low Priority

Until recently, agricultural development, especially of food crops, was given a low priority in much of the Third World. In many cases, the colonial powers (England, France, and other European nations) who had ruled these countries had emphasized the production of cash crops such as cocoa, tea, coffee, and rubber for export. Following independence, the governments of these new nations believed that economic development rested on industrialization. Although 70 to 90 percent of the work force in these countries was engaged in agriculture, government investment went into industrial projects.

By the early 1960s, rapid population growth together with low agricultural output resulted in severe food shortages in parts of Asia and Africa. Most of the countries were too poor to import large amounts of food. Without food aid from the developed nations, millions in these regions faced continual famine. Consequently, many Third World leaders began to focus on their nations' agricultural problems and discovered that improvement in agriculture was essential to economic growth.

The Third World's Green Revolution

By the middle of the 1960s, agronomists (specialists in crop production and soil management) had developed high-yielding wheat and rice plants that were highly disease resistant and were able to withstand strong winds. Even when farmers used traditional methods of cultivation, the new wheat and rice varieties yielded substantially more grain than the traditional local varieties.

Leaders in India and Pakistan, facing desperate food shortages, decided to introduce these new wheat and rice varieties as well as new farming technologies. Demonstration programs were set up for farmers to try the new technologies. Money was diverted from industry to invest in agriculture. Increased use of irrigation and large quantities of fertilizer were emphasized. As a result, wheat and rice output in both countries increased enormously and more food became available to consumers at lower prices. The successes in India and Pakistan during the 1960s and 1970s were repeated in the Philippines and later in other countries.

This breakthrough in wheat and rice production came to be known as the Green Revolution. It involved using the principles of modern science and technology to increase agricultural production.

The greatest success story of the 1980s was China which moved ahead of the United States and the former Soviet Union to become the world's largest food producer. Several factors were responsible. In 1979, the Chinese government reformed its agriculture policy and abandoned the old system of centralized planning and government control over agriculture. A new "responsibility system" gave individual peasants a great deal more control and encouraged initiative, innovation, and hard work because the peasants were allowed to keep most of the profits. Also the rapid increase in agricultural research after 1977 led to the development of high-yielding crop varieties, greater use of fertilizers; more effective weed, disease, and insect control; and improved water use. After 1978, agricultural production in China rose by 8 percent a year, the highest rate in the world. Average income in rural areas grew by 70 percent.

But the Green Revolution has not had the same successes everywhere. Crop yields in many parts of the Third World remain very low. During the 1980s, many parts of sub-Saharan Africa experienced prolonged periods of famine. For almost 20 years, food production in most of sub-Saharan Africa has not kept up with demand. Poor soils, low and uncertain rainfall, a shortage of capital, and prolonged periods of drought all played a part in holding back progress. Another reason was explosive population growth. Africa's population is growing faster than that of any other continent. Government policies also contributed to food shortages. Although 70–85 percent of the people in most African countries are engaged in agriculture, agricultural development was not a high priority. Investment in research, education, and other agricultural programs was very low.

Despite the problems, the programs that worked in Asia can also work in Africa. To increase food production these nations must: invest in agricultural research; educate farmers in the new technologies; increase the use of high-yielding crop varieties, increase the use of fertilizers; expand irrigation; and create government policies that promote agricultural development.

Nuclear Proliferation—a Global Threat

Until recently, only a few nations in the world possessed nuclear weapons—the United States, the former Soviet Union, Britain, France, and China. In addition, it was believed that India, Pakistan, and Israel also had atomic weapons. Today, the world is faced with the very real danger that many more nations will soon have nuclear weapons. This is known as **nuclear proliferation**. As more nations come to possess nuclear weapons, there is an increased possibility that they will be used. Local or regional conflicts could turn into a nuclear war affecting the entire planet.

The Former Soviet Union and Its Nuclear Arsenal

For over 40 years, the Soviet Union manufactured and stockpiled nuclear weapons. Despite the danger, the world gradually came to trust Soviet rulers to use caution, since a nuclear war would destroy the Soviet Union along with the rest of the planet.

Since the break up of the Soviet Union in late 1991, the danger of nuclear proliferation has greatly increased. The Soviet arsenal is believed to contain almost 30,000 atomic weapons located in four of the former Soviet republics—Russia, the Ukraine, Byelorussia, and Kazakhstan. Since these are now independent nations, the question is, who will have control over the atomic weapons? Will they be placed under one centralized control or will each of the four nations have control over the weapons on its territory? Boris Yeltsin, as President of Russia, proposed that all the nuclear weapons be placed under Russian authority. The leaders of the other three republics agreed but the matter is not resolved. Each republic knows that control of the atomic weapons gives it considerable power.

Because the situation in the former Soviet Union is so unstable, the danger exists that some of these weapons "will fall into the wrong hands." Some Soviet military commanders might get hold of nuclear arms that they could sell to foreign governments or even terrorist groups. If current efforts to create democratic institutions fail, it is possible that a dangerous dictatorship could take over and control the atomic weapons.

Difficult economic conditions including serious shortages of food, fuel, and consumer goods and high unemployment are also a threat. Thousands of former atomic scientists and weapons designers are out of work. The danger exists that some unemployed scientists might sell their skills and knowledge to foreign countries.

Consequently, the United States and many European countries would like the Soviet atomic weapons and the missiles that carry them to be destroyed. Various proposals to provide financial aid to the former Soviet republics to help them dismantle their nuclear weapons have been suggested.

Third World Nations and "The Bomb"

A number of Third World nations including Iraq, Iran, North Korea, Algeria, and possibly Libya, are actively engaged in developing nuclear weapons. Many experts believe that these countries will be able to produce atomic weapons in ten years or less.

Iraq

In 1990, experts believed that Iraq would need five to ten years to develop nuclear weapons. However, secret Iraqi documents and other information obtained by U.N. inspectors indicate that Iraq was only 18 to 24 months away from building an atomic bomb when the Gulf War began in January 1991. During the 1980s, Saddam Hussein obtained the materials for his nuclear program from Western nations. Many important purchases came from the United States. The Commerce Department approved sales of machinery, equipment, and computers to Iraq that could be used in a nuclear weapons program. The Iraqis claimed that these items were intended for peaceful purposes.

Iraq received the greatest assistance for its nuclear program from Germany. Many German companies provided equipment and blueprints and sent experts and technicians to Iraq. Other European firms also sold important equipment to Iraq, among them French, Swedish, and Swiss companies. Iraq purchased a computer, cameras, and other sensitive instruments from Japan.

Before the Gulf War, Iraq began relocating much of its vital nuclear equipment to secret sites all over the country. During the war, an important allied goal was to destroy Iraq's nuclear capability. However, it is not known how much of Iraq's nuclear equipment and material was actually destroyed. The cease-fire at the end of the war gave U.N. inspectors responsibility for the "destruction, removal, or rendering harmless" of Iraq's nuclear weapons. However, Iraqi officials have refused to cooperate with the inspectors and hid reactor fuel and nuclear equipment from them.

Iraq has become a test case for nuclear proliferation. If a war, pressure by the United Nations, and U.N. inspection cannot stop Iraq from making the bomb, what will it take to stop Iran, North Korea, and Libya?

Iran

Since 1987, Iran has been engaged in a full scale nuclear weapons program. It has received help from China in the form of nuclear technology and equipment. Iran has bought a plutonium-producing reactor from China and is currently negotiating with India to buy another one. China has confirmed that it has a nuclear cooperation program with Iran, but says the program is intended for "peaceful purposes." Experts believe that with continued Chinese assistance, Iran will have an atomic bomb in ten years or less.

North Korea

Experts believe that North Korea is closest to developing an atomic bomb. Some believe that North Korea may have an atomic bomb by the end of 1993. It has the reactors that produce plutonium for use in weapons and it is believed that North Korea has built an underground research facility to construct atomic bombs. Recently, North Korea refused to allow U.N. inspectors to visit its facilities. Moreover, North Korea produces missiles that can carry nuclear weapons. It sells these missiles to countries ruled by dangerous dictators. In 1991, North Korea sold Syria SCUD missiles that can carry larger warheads and travel twice as far as the missiles Iraq launched in the Gulf War. In early 1992, North Korea delivered a large shipment of SCUD-C ballistic missiles to Iran and Syria.

Algeria   Algeria also may have an atomic bomb within ten years. China provided the technology by building a nuclear reactor in Algeria in the late 1980s. The Algerians claim that the reactor is for research purposes, but experts say that a reactor of that size is intended to produce plutonium for bomb fuel. Experts fear that Algeria may not just be developing a bomb for itself, but may be helping other nations to build nuclear weapons. There are indications that some Iraqi nuclear scientists are working in Algeria and that Iraq has provided Algeria with important nuclear technology.

The Chinese Role

Since the 1980s, China has become the world's greatest proliferator of nuclear technology. (Before that France sold its nuclear technology to many nations, including the first nuclear reactor to Iraq.) The United States has repeatedly asked China to stop selling this technology but China has refused to do so.

Summary
of
Key Ideas

Introduction to Global Studies

A. Culture is an important aspect of human life.

1. Different groups of human beings have developed different cultures to meet their needs and desires to survive.

2. Culture should be studied in the light of the environment in which individual groups of people live.

3. Habitat has a great effect on the development of culture.

4. Cultural diffusion (outside influences) also greatly affect the development of culture.

B. People select a place to live because it meets their needs.

1. Climate and topography affect the selection of a place to live.

2. World population has shown a tremendous growth in the past 100 years.

3. A study of the "density of population" of an area gives us a clearer picture of population in that area than just a study of "total population."

4. Civilization began to spread following the agricultural revolution and the revolution in communication and transportation.

C. Cultural diffusion has an important effect on the lives of people.

1. People carry ideas with them when they move from place to place.

2. Diffusion is not an automatic process. It is a selective process based on the needs of the group.

3. New ideas and customs are usually adapted to traditional customs and actions.

4. Cultures and societies borrow from each other to better themselves.

5. Nationalism is a very powerful feeling that affects people all over the world.

D. Many areas of the world can be said to be developing.

1. Development is an economic idea that suggests that appropriate use of natural, human, and capital resources can create improvements in standards of living.

2. A nation can be considered "developing" when the material standards of living of its people are relatively low when compared with those of the industrialized nations of North America and Western Europe.

E.   **International cooperation can benefit developing nations.**

   1. In the 20th century, the nations of the world have become interdependent, thus creating a global village.

   2. International cooperation between industrial nations and developing nations can help to expand trade, stop inflation, and raise living standards for all.

   3. Economic and political cooperation can lead to a peaceful and secure world.

   4. Many problems of global concern can only be solved by international cooperation and action.

F.   **A major global concern at the end of the 20th century is saving our endangered planet earth.**

   1. Many of the problems are global in scope and require international cooperation.

   2. Water, air, and soil pollution are major problems.

   3. Destruction of large areas of rain forest around the globe will have serious consequences for human beings.

   4. Many scientists are concerned that greenhouse gases will produce global warming. This could result in serious climate changes.

   5. The "hole" or thinning in the ozone layer can have dangerous, long-term effects on animal and plant life.

   6. The nuclear accident at Chernobyl in the former Soviet Union is an example of the dangers involved in nuclear power. It is also an example of how an event that occurs in one country can affect people in many other countries.

   7. The use of modern science and technology to increase agricultural production in the Third World is known as the Green Revolution.

   8. The explosive growth in the world's population is the greatest threat to our planet earth.

   9. Many countries in Asia have increased their food production substantially, while other countries in Africa and Latin America face serious food shortages.

   10. The proliferation of nuclear weapons threatens the safety and well-being of people all over the world.

Answers: **Culture and Survival Questions**

JUNGLE	**DESERT**	**ARCTIC**
1. True	1. True	1. True
2. True	2. True	2. True
3. True	3. True	3. True
4. True	4. True	4. True
5. True	5. True	5. True
6. False	6. False	6. True
7. True	7. False	7. True

UNIT I

Exercises and Questions

Vocabulary

Directions: Match the words in Column A with the correct meaning in Column B.

Column A

1. culture
2. habitat
3. environment
4. values
5. climate
6. cultural diffusion
7. civilization
8. communication
9. anthropologists
10. domesticate

Column B

(a) The weather of an area over a period of time
(b) The setting in which people live, our total surroundings
(c) The spreading of ideas, inventions, and products from one nation to another
(d) Social scientists who study the origins, customs, and beliefs of human beings
(e) The rules of conduct of a group
(f) The natural part of the environment
(g) The part of the environment that people create
(h) The act of talking; the exchange of ideas or opinions
(i) To tame
(j) A complex level of development

Completion

Directions: Select from the following terms the one that best completes each sentence.

ecosystem	conservation	chlorofluorocarbons	biodiversity
greenhouse gases	environmentalists	ozone	reforestation
biotechnology	nuclear proliferation		

1. The gases used in spray cans, refrigerators, and air conditioners are known as _____ .

2. A natural layer of gas that protects humans and animals from the damaging rays of the sun is _____ .

3. Emissions from cars and factories that can ultimately cause severe climatic changes are known as _____ .

4. The great variety of plant and animal life is known as _____ .

5. Ways of saving energy and protecting life is known as _____ .

6. A community of plants, animals, insects, and the environment in which they live is known as an _____ .

7. Planting trees is known as _____ .

8. People who are concerned with protecting our environment are _____ .

9. Using science to create improved crops is called _____ .

10. The development of atomic weapons in many countries is known as _____ .

Multiple Choice

Directions: Select the letter of the correct answer.

1. The way of life of a group of people is called
   (a) diffusion.   (b) density.   (c) culture.   (d) attitudes.

2. All of the following are part of the habitat *except*
   (a) soil.   (b) topography.   (c) climate.   (d) religion.

3. An example of topography is
   (a) rain.   (b) mountains.   (c) government.   (d) factories.

4. Which of the following statements is true about survival?
   (a) The ability to survive is born with a person.
   (b) People must learn to adapt themselves to a place to survive.
   (c) Survival has little or no relation to the culture of a group.
   (d) Civilized people learn to survive in all areas more quickly than "primitive" people.

5. In studying other cultures our main objective should be to
   (a) look at the riches gathered by those societies.
   (b) learn how they have answered the question of survival.
   (c) compare them to our culture.
   (d) learn how to survive in other cultures.

6. People are affected by their habitat in
   (a) the type of house they live in.
   (b) the type of clothing they wear.
   (c) the kinds of foods they eat.
   (d) all of these

7. The formation of a group's culture is affected by
   (a) the environment.   (b) cultural diffusion.   (c) both a and b.
   (d) neither a nor b.

8. Most of the world's people live
   (a) north of the equator.   (b) near the equator.   (c) south of the equator.
   (d) in Southeast Asia.

9. Density of population gives us an idea of
   (a) how many people live in a country.
   (b) why people live in certain places.
   (c) where large numbers of people live closely together.
   (d) why population has grown larger in the last hundred years.

10. Which of the following would *not* be an example of cultural diffusion?
    (a) the use of certain French words in English
    (b) the use of the Arabic (Hindu) number system in the United States
    (c) the belief in ancestor worship in China
    (d) the playing of baseball in Japan

11. Which of the following statements is *true* about cultural diffusion?
    (a) Diffusion occurs automatically when two cultures come together.
    (b) Adaptation is an important part of cultural diffusion.
    (c) Diffusion has had a great effect on the development of China.
    (d) Diffusion had almost no effect on the development of Greek culture.

12. All of the following are characteristics of civilization *except*
    (a) a system of laws.
    (b) permanent settlements.
    (c) hunting and gathering.
    (d) customs followed by a majority of people.

13. A good example of a developing area is a country
    (a) where many people still live in poverty for improvement in the standard of living
    (b) that is controlled by another country
    (c) without any natural resources
    (d) that has a high standard of living

14. Which of the following countries would be considered developing?
    (a) Japan   (b) United States   (c) Germany   (d) India

15. Which of the following countries might be considered part of the "Third World"?
    (a) Japan   (b) United States   (c) former Soviet Union   (d) India

16. Which of the following is true about the destruction of the rain forests?
    (a) It affects only those countries that have rain forests.
    (b) It is a minor problem in Central America.
    (c) It has positive affects in that it kills harmful insects.
    (d) It can have negative effects on human life.

17. What can be done about the destruction of the rain forests?
    (a) Nothing can be done to prevent further damage.
    (b) Since it helps progress, there is no need to do anything about it.
    (c) Third World nations must invest money to stop the destruction.
    (d) Third World nations and developed nations must begin to use conservation techniques to save the rain forests.

18. The "Greenhouse Effect" refers to:
    (a) planting crops in a greenhouse.
    (b) the possibility of severe climatic changes resulting from the release of harmful gases into the atmosphere.
    (c) solid waste pollution.
    (d) the growing of new varieties of crops.

19. Further depletion of the ozone layer:
    (a) may cause skin cancers in humans.
    (b) would have no affect on humans.
    (c) will reduce the strength of the sun's rays.
    (d) all of the above.

20. Which of the following is believed to be true about the depletion of the ozone layer?
    (a) With the help of a few nations the process can be reversed.
    (b) The recycling of bottles and cans will solve the problem.
    (c) An international ban on CFCs may slow the process.
    (d) There is little danger from the depletion of the ozone layer.

21. What resulted from the explosion at the Chernobyl nuclear power plant?
    (a) Only the area around Chernobyl was affected.
    (b) It caused damage to the land, people, and animals over a large area.
    (c) The radioactivity which was released was quickly contained by the Soviet government.
    (d) The damage that was done was only minor and very temporary.

22. The Green Revolution refers to:
    (a) the development of high yield, disease resistant crops.
    (b) the pollution of the earth's atmosphere.
    (c) the conservation methods used to preserve rain forests.
    (d) the use of machinery to produce manufactured goods.

23. Which of the following is true about crop yields in the 20th century?
    (a) Crop yields have increased all over the world.
    (b) Crop yields have remained about the same as in the 19th century.
    (c) Crop yields have decreased all over the world.
    (d) Most countries using science-based agriculture have increased crop yields.

24. Which Third World area has successfully used science-based agriculture?
    (a) India   (b) Africa   (c) Western Europe   (d) United States

25. A major problem in feeding the world's population is:
    (a) the supply of food has not kept up with the growing population.
    (b) long periods of drought in some areas of the world has kept food production low.
    (c) outdated farm methods used in some countries keep crop yields low.
    (d) all of the above.

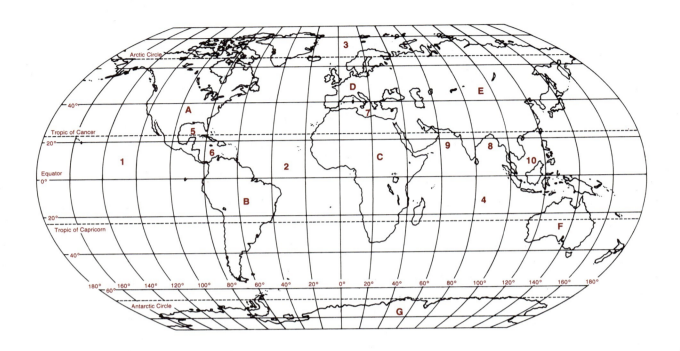

Map Exercises

Directions: Identify each of the continents by placing the correct name next to the letter that is indicated.

A _____   D _____   F _____

B _____   E _____   G _____

C _____

Directions: Select the letter of the correct answer using the map above.

1. The *Atlantic Ocean* is shown by the number
   (a) 1   (b) 2   (c) 3   (d) 4

2. A *gulf* is shown by the number
   (a) 5   (b) 6   (c) 7   (d) 10

3. The direction from 9 to 8 is
   (a) north   (b) south   (c) east   (d) west

4. The *Mediterranean Sea* is identified by the number
   (a) 6   (b) 7   (c) 8   (d) 10

5. The *ocean* which touches both Africa and Asia is the
   (a) Pacific   (b) Atlantic   (c) Arctic   (d) Indian

Thought Questions

1. How does environment affect the lives of people?

2. How have people tried to use their environment to better their lives?

3. Why is it difficult to study the ideas of a culture?

4. Why have people decided to settle in certain areas of the world instead of others?

5. Why is it important to study cultures in relation to their own environments?

6. How does the process of cultural diffusion take place?

7. "Habitat determines the culture of an area." Do you agree or disagree with this statement? Why?

8. "The different parts of a culture cannot be separated from each other." Do you agree or disagree? Why?

9. (a) If you were the leader of a newly independent nation, what problems of development would you face?
   (b) How would you try to solve these problems?

10. Describe some of the characteristics of "Third World" countries.

11. If you were the American representative in the United Nations, what steps might you recommend to help developing nations?

12. Explain why there has been a great deal of environmental damage in the 19th and 20th centuries.

13. Explain how the destruction of the rain forests can have very negative effects on our lives.

14. Why is saving the rainforest a very difficult problem for many Third World nations?

15. Why is the problem of global warming considered to be the number one environmental issue today?

16. Why is the construction of nuclear power plants a very controversial issue?

17. How can the depletion of the ozone layer harm us?

18. Why is the explosive growth in the world's population such a serious problem?

19. How has science helped many nations produce more food?

20. What has the Green Revolution accomplished in China, India, and Pakistan?

21. Why is nuclear proliferation a very serious threat today?

22. What can you do to help save our environment?

Developing Answers to Regents-Type Essay Questions

Helpful Hints

In developing your answers to the essays be sure to:

1. Include specific factual information and evidence whenever possible.

2. Answer the question being asked; do not go off on tangents.

3. Keep these general definitions in mind:
   (a) *discuss* means "to make observations about something using facts, reasoning, and argument; to present in some detail."
   (b) *describe* means "to illustrate something in words or to tell about."
   (c) *show* means "to point out, to set forth clearly an idea or position by stating it and giving data that support it."
   (d) *explain* means "to make plain or understandable; to give reasons for or causes of; to show the logical development or relationship."

Sample Essay Question

Our world has become a "global village." What happens in one country has effects throughout the world.

The following headlines illustrate the statement above:

Thousands Face Death by Starvation in Somalia
Overpopulation Continues to Increase in Developing Nations
Croatians and Serbians Attempt to "Sanitize" Bosnia
Government of South Africa Grants Equal Rights to All Residents
Terrorist Bombings Kill Innocent Civilians in London
Destruction of the Amazon Rain Forest in Brazil Damages Ecosystems

For *each* of the headlines:

- Describe its impact on the area in which it occurred.
- Discuss what impact it might have on nations around the world.

Puzzle

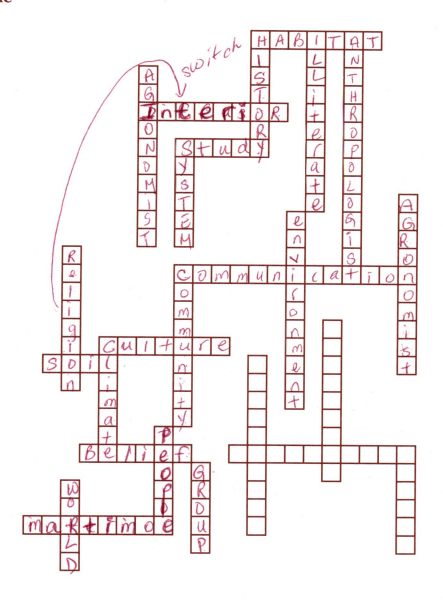

Directions: Place the words below in their proper place in the puzzle.

4 LETTERS	5 LETTERS	6 LETTERS	7 LETTERS	8 LETTERS
SOIL	STUDY	SYSTEM	CULTURE	SURVIVAL
	GROUP	PEOPLE	HABITAT	INTERIOR
	WORLD	BELIEF	CLIMATE	MARITIME
		TERROR	HISTORY	RELIGION

9 LETTERS	10 LETTERS	11 LETTERS	13 LETTERS	14 LETTERS
COMMUNITY	AGRONOMIST	ENVIRONMENT	COMMUNICATION	ANTHROPOLOGIST
DIFFUSION	ILLITERATE			
MOUNTAINS	GOVERNMENT			
	DEVELOPING			

THE MIDDLE EAST AND NORTH AFRICA

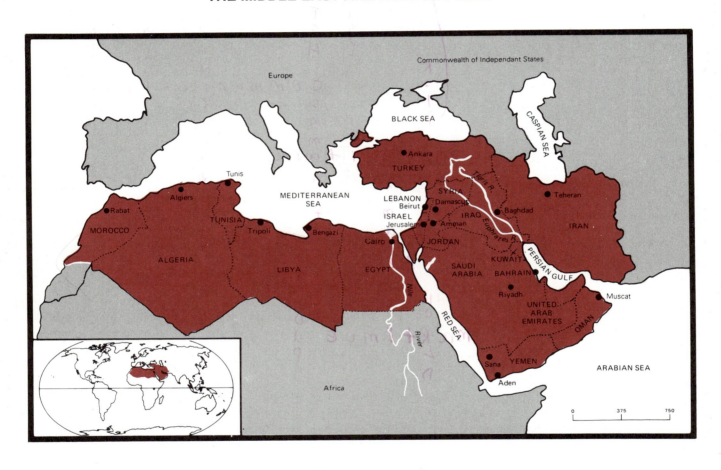

Commonwealth of Independant States

Europe

BLACK SEA

CASPIAN SEA

Ankara

TURKEY

Teheran

Tunis

MEDITERRANEAN
SEA

SYRIA

Tigris R.

LEBANON
Beirut
Damascus

IRAN

Algiers

Rabat

TUNISIA

ISRAEL
Jerusalem

IRAQ
Amman

Baghdad

Euphrates R.

MOROCCO

Tripoli

Bengazi

JORDAN

ALGERIA

LIBYA

EGYPT

Cairo

SAUDI
ARABIA

KUWAIT

BAHRAIN

PERSIAN GULF

Muscat

Nile

Riyadh

UNITED
ARAB
EMIRATES

OMAN

RED SEA

River

Sana

YEMEN

ARABIAN SEA

Aden

Africa

0   375   750

UNIT II The Middle East and North Africa

Introduction

The term *Middle East* was coined by British geographers to describe a geographic area and to distinguish this area from other lands that are referred to as the Far East. But the terms *middle* and *far* only have meaning if looked at from the point of view of Europe.

Nevertheless, the Middle East refers to the area that connects three great continents—Europe, Asia, and Africa. The Middle East includes: Turkey, Syria, Lebanon, Israel, Jordan, Iraq, Iran, and the countries of the Arabian Peninsula—Saudi Arabia, Yemen, Oman, The United Arab Emirates, Bahrain, Qatar, and Kuwait. Geographically, this area is located in southwestern Asia. In recent years, some people have referred to this area as Southwest Asia instead of the Middle East to avoid being Eurocentric (seeing the world from the point of view of Europe). The U.S. State Department uses the term *Southwest Asia*.

To the west of these lands, along the Mediterranean coast, are the nations of North Africa—Morocco, Algeria, Tunisia, Libya, and Egypt. The countries of the Middle East and North Africa are usually studied together because they have many things in common.

1. The climate is generally hot and dry—much of the land is desert.
2. Most of the people here are Arab and speak the Arabic language.
3. Over 90 percent of the people in the Middle East are Muslims—that is, they follow the religion known as Islam.
4. The people of the area share a related history and have similar problems today.

It is important to know about the Middle East for many reasons.

1. Some of the earliest civilizations in the world developed in the Middle East in Egypt, Mesopotamia, ancient Israel, and Persia.

2. Three of the world's great religions—Judaism, Christianity, and Islam—began in this part of the world. Many places in Israel, Jordan, and Saudi Arabia are thought of as holy by Christians, Muslims, and Jews.

3. The Middle East has always been of great importance because it is located at the crossroads of three continents. Trade between Asia, Africa, and Europe has passed through the Middle East, and its waterways have been used as trade routes since the beginning of civilization. The Mediterranean Sea is one of the busiest trade routes in the world. The Suez Canal, which connects the Mediterranean Sea to the Red Sea and the Indian Ocean, is also found here. The Canal shortens the distance between Western Europe and India, Southeast Asia, and China by thousands of miles. The countries of Western Europe and the United States send their products to Asia and Africa through the Canal. In turn, rubber, oil, tin, and other products from Africa and Asia are shipped through the Canal to the countries of the West.

4. The Middle East is very rich in oil. It is believed that two-thirds of the world's total oil reserves lie here. Many countries around the world import oil from the Middle East.

5. The Middle East is constantly in the news. This is because the Middle East is one of the most unstable areas in the world. Religious, ethnic, and national conflicts divide many of the people and have resulted in almost continual violence and warfare. A few examples are: the bitter conflict between Israel and its Arab neighbors; the war between Iran and Iraq (1980–1988); the civil war in Lebanon (1975–1990); and Iraq's invasion of Kuwait (1990). (Each of these will be discussed in detail later in this unit.) These conflicts affect other countries outside the Middle East. In recent years, wars in the Middle East have resulted in oil shortages and higher oil prices. Iraq's invasion of Kuwait led to the Gulf War which involved the United States and a number of other nations. In addition, many Middle Eastern organizations as well as countries have employed international terrorism to further their political goals. Americans and others have been the victims of kidnappings, hijackings, and killings by Middle Eastern terrorists.

6. Between 1945 and 1990, the United States and the Soviet Union were rivals in the Middle East. Each superpower tried to gain influence and power in the area and prevent the other from becoming too powerful. One way of winning allies was to sell armaments. The United States sold weapons to Israel, Jordan, Saudi Arabia, Turkey, and others. The Soviet Union armed Egypt, Syria, and Iraq. The sale of highly sophisticated weapons to these nations contributed to the instability of the region. The United States and the Soviet Union also became involved in the conflicts of their Middle Eastern allies. On several occasions this involvement almost led to war between the two superpowers.

7. Finally, the Jewish state of Israel stands in the middle of the Arab countries of the area. Since Israel was formed in 1948, the Arab nations have wanted to destroy it. Four wars have been fought—in 1948, 1956, 1967, and 1973. All have been won by Israel, but a lasting peace has not been achieved. The United States has always feared that continued trouble in the area might lead to a world war.

Oasis in Saudi Arabia. This moist and fertile oasis is found on one of the driest places on earth.

The famous pyramids of Giza are considered one of the seven wonders of the ancient world. They were built about 5,000 years ago as tombs for the kings of Egypt.

Land and Climate

An Area of Deserts

North Africa and the Middle East are regions of deserts. There are mountains and plateaus as well, but the desert most affects the life of the people. The largest desert on earth, the Sahara, is located in northern Africa and covers the southern portions of Morocco, Algeria, Libya, and Egypt. These desert lands extend eastward to the Red Sea. Beyond the Red Sea there is a desert again. The Arabian Peninsula contains one of the most barren deserts in the world—the Rub àl Khali (roob' al Kah'lee), which is known as the "Empty Quarter." There are no settlements in the Empty Quarter and few people have ever crossed it. This region is a continuation of the Sahara and part of a desert chain that extends through large parts of Southwest Asia some 5,000 miles from the Atlantic to the Indian Ocean.

Rainfall is Scarce

The Middle East is one of the driest places on earth. The major economic problem faced by the people living here is water. Although some areas may have a lot of rainfall, the rain is concentrated so that it falls over a short period of time, leaving the ground dry through most of the year. During the rainy period, the water flows into seasonal streams called **wadis**. This water runs off rapidly, carrying with it much of the topsoil. As a result the land is left in worse condition than if it had not rained at all. It is along the Mediterranean coast and some of the other coasts as well as in the mountains that rain falls most heavily during the rainy season. The rainy season comes in the winter and the spring. Summers are hot and dry with very little rainfall. Farther away from the coast there is even less rainfall. Where there are tall mountains along the coast, these mountains block the rain from moving into the interior regions. This is true of Arabia, where in some regions of the interior, the amount of rainfall cannot even be measured. Because of the lack of rainfall much of the Middle East is totally **uninhabitable** (people cannot live there). Only about 15 percent of all the land is suitable for agriculture.

Mountains

Parts of the Middle East and North Africa are hilly or mountainous. The highest mountains are found in northern Turkey and Iran. In northwest Africa are the Atlas Mountains of Morocco and Algeria, which lie between the desert and the Mediterranean Sea. The Atlas extend well into the interior and form a high plateau several hundred miles wide. Plateaus make up most of the land in Turkey and Iran.

The mountains are very important to the people living in the area. It is in the mountains that most of the rain falls (in addition to the rainfall along the coasts). Water trapped by the mountain peaks travels for hundreds of miles underground. In some places it comes to the surface of the earth in springs. In others it is reached by digging wells at the base of the mountains.

Rivers

Because of the water from the mountains there are two great riv
Euphrates Rivers in Iraq and the Nile in Egypt. The Tigris River
south from the mountains of Turkey. The two rivers flow almost parallel
wind through Iraq. They finally join together and empty into the Persian Gulf.
where the two rivers almost meet, the ancient city of Baghdad is located. For thousands
years the people living along these two rivers have used the rivers to irrigate their land.

The Nile is the longest river in the world. It begins south of Egypt in the highlands of
East Africa. The Nile is joined by other streams that rise in Ethiopia. The great river flows
northward through Egypt until it reaches the Mediterranean Sea over 4,000 miles from its
source (beginning). The river brings both water and rich soils to the people of the Nile
Valley. Without the Nile few people could live in Egypt. Beyond the waters of the Nile is
the desert—approximately 96 percent of the total land of Egypt.

Climate and Agriculture

The best land for farming is found in the river valleys and along the seacoasts. The land
along the Mediterranean Sea has a pleasant climate. This is known as a Mediterranean climate and is similar to that of California. The summers are long, hot, and dry; winters are
mild and moist. Olives, fruits, and grapes are grown on the hillsides along the coastal
areas. In addition, the waters and banks of the many seas of the Middle East have long provided food. Fishing and sailing are possible on the Black, Caspian, Mediterranean, Red,
and Arabian Seas and on the Persian Gulf. All the countries of the Middle East have at
least some access to the sea.

The People of the Middle East and Their Way of Life

There are three very different ways of life in the Middle East. The farmer, the nomad
herder, and the city dweller almost seem to live in separate worlds. Yet, each is dependent
on the others for the fulfillment of basic needs.

Nomads of the Desert

The nomads who inhabit the deserts of the Middle East make up about 5 percent of the
people of the area. They are known as **bedouins** and they live in **tribes**. A tribe is a group
of people who share a common language and religion and are united under one leader.
Their time is spent moving through the desert in search of water and grass for their herds
of sheep, goats, and camels.

The animals provide the nomads with most of their needs. Whatever their animals do
not supply, the nomads buy when they reach an **oasis**. An oasis is a place in the desert
where there is water from underground streams and vegetation. Part of the nomads' diet
consists of flour, dates, and fruits that come from the farms and groves. From the towns

and cities they obtain utensils, cloth, coffee, tea, and sugar. In this way the nomads are dependent on the farms and cities that lie beyond the desert. The bedouins in turn provide the farmers and city people with animals and animal products.

The bedouins are very proud individuals who believe in equality and do not like to be ruled by other people. Nevertheless, the family, **clan**, and tribe are considered to be more important than the individual. (A group of related families make up a clan and a number of clans together form a tribe.)

For the bedouin the tribe carries out the same functions that the government does in our society. The tribal leader, or **sheik**, meets together with a council of elders to make all the important decisions for the tribe. They make treaties with other tribes, fix wanderings in the desert, educate the children to be loyal members of the tribe, and punish those who have committed crimes.

Bedouin shepherd. Sheep herding is an important bedouin occupation throughout the Middle East.

In the past, the nomads of the desert did as they pleased. They crossed and recrossed borders. They were able to attack the village farmers and force them to give up a large part of their crops because the nomads could move swiftly on their horses and camels. The bedouins policed the desert and protected the caravans that crossed it.

Today, as a result of changes in transportation and communication, the bedouins have come under the control of the governments in the cities. As a result, their whole way of life has changed. Thousands have left the desert to take jobs in the oil industry—especially in Iraq and Saudi Arabia. Others have become soldiers. Large numbers have settled down on the oases and in the cities. Many of the tribal chiefs are now rich landowners. Those living on land where oil has been discovered have adopted a way of life that is totally different from that of their fellow bedouins in the desert.

The Village Farmers

In the Middle East, more than 75 percent of the people are farmers, or **fellahin** as they are known in Arabic. Wherever there is enough water to grow crops there is certain to be a farming village. Basically the farming villages of the Middle East show great similarities.

Most of the farmers own small plots of land—often too small to support their families. In some cases, however, the farmers do not own their land but rent land from the rich landlords who live in the cities (absentee landlords). These farmers are known as tenants, and the rent they pay to the landlord is very high. There are also farmers who work as sharecroppers on the land belonging to the landlord. They use the tools, seeds, animals, and water that belong to the landlord. In the past, this situation existed all over the Middle East. Today it has been almost entirely abolished in Egypt, Syria, Libya, and Iraq, but it continues to exist in many of the other countries.

While some farms are now modernized, many peasants continue to work with simple tools—the hoe, the wooden plow, the hand sickle, and the threshing board. The farmers of the Middle East live out their lives in poverty. Because the amount of land they own is small and the tools they use are primitive, their production is very low. As a result their income is low, debts pile up, and they often have to borrow from the money lenders whose interest rates are extremely high—often 100 percent. The fellahin also have many children, another factor that contributes to their poverty. Until recently the villages where the farmers live had no electricity, no running water, and no paved roads. Disease was widespread and there were few medical facilities. The village peasants were isolated from the cities and unaffected by what was happening in the rest of the world.

Now the Arab villages are undergoing changes. Newspapers and radios are making villages aware of the world outside. Village youths are going to the cities to study. Welfare centers are being built to improve the health of the villagers. Some governments have passed land reform laws taking land away from the rich landlords and distributing it to the poor peasants. Even though some progress has been made, much remains to be done to improve the lives of the fellahin.

The only country in the Middle East where farming does not follow the pattern described above is Israel. In Israel there are no rich landlords and very few private landowners. Most of the land is organized into large collective farms called **kibbutzim**. All the farmers on a kibbutz own the land, the tools, the animals, and the farm buildings. The work is divided up among the kibbutzniks (members of the collective farm), and after the crops have been sold, the profits are divided up among them as well. Israeli farmers use the most advanced methods and equipment.

Cities of the Middle East—The City Dweller

In the Middle East as elsewhere, it is the city that dominates the rest of the country. All power is concentrated in the city—political, economic, social, and cultural. This is where decisions are made and styles set that affect the entire nation. From the cities come the trained and educated people to lead the country.

In the cities of the Middle East, the old and new exist side by side—the old Arab town alongside the modern 20th-century city. The old Arab town was built with two things in mind—religion and protection. For the sake of security the town was built on a hill or near a river or a sea. Religion required that the **mosque** or temple of worship be built in the center of the city. The mosque is the main gathering place for all purposes.

Not far from the mosque, the **bazaar** or marketplace is located. Here there are booths with all kinds of wares for sale, which provide a living for skilled craftspeople and merchants. Working chiefly with their hands, Middle East craftspeople turn out products of remarkable quality and beauty. Moroccan leather and Persian rugs are world famous. Gold and silversmiths, workers in metal, and jewelers produce objects that are equally fine. Parents pass their skills on to their children. The bazaar is a fascinating place. In addition to the craftspeople, villagers from the countryside sell their goods.

Tel Aviv, a modern city that blossomed from a sand dune.

MAJOR CITIES IN THE MIDDLE EAST

Country	City	Population
Algeria	Algiers	1,507,241
Egypt	Cairo	6,052,836
	Alexandria	2,917,327
Iran	Teheran	6,042,584
	Isfahan	986,753
Iraq	Baghdad	4,648,609
	Basrah	616,700
	Mosul	570,926
Israel	Jerusalem	493,500
	Tel Aviv	317,800
	Haifa	222,600
Jordan	Amman	936,300
Lebanon	Beirut	1,500,000
Libya	Tripoli	591,062
	Benghazi	446,250
Morocco	Casablanca	2,139,204
	Rabat	518,616
Saudi Arabia	Riyadh	1,308,000
	Jidda	1,500,000
	Mecca	550,000
Syria	Damascus	1,361,000
	Aleppo	1,308,000
Tunisia	Tunis	596,654
Turkey	Istanbul	5,475,982
	Ankara	2,235,035
	Izmir	1,489,772

Source: *Encyclopedia Britannica Book of the Year 1991*

Farther away from the center of town are the residential districts. These are divided into different quarters (sections). People living in each quarter usually share the same occupation, religion, nationality, and customs.

The new sections of the city are built in the European style. Broad avenues contain modern residential and commercial buildings, fine shops, hotels, theaters, and restaurants. People wear Western clothes and motion picture theaters show American, British, and French films.

The cities of the Middle East today have the problems of modern cities anywhere—slums, housing shortage, traffic congestion. But the worst problem is poverty. Middle Eastern cities have not yet developed into major industrial centers. There are some factories, such as spinning and weaving, cement plants, flour mills, fertilizer factories, and soap factories. But there are not enough factories to provide jobs for the thousands of people who leave the countryside each year and come to the cities. Since there are far more people than there are jobs many people find themselves without work and those who do work earn very little money.

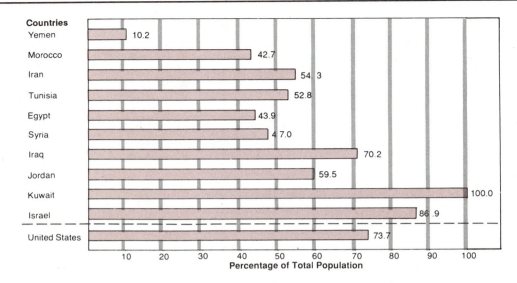

Countries

Country	Percentage
Yemen	10.2
Morocco	42.7
Iran	54.3
Tunisia	52.8
Egypt	43.9
Syria	47.0
Iraq	70.2
Jordan	59.5
Kuwait	100.0
Israel	86.9
United States	73.7

Percentage of Total Population

Source: *Encyclopedia Britannica Book of the Year 1991*

What conclusions can we reach from the information given in this graph?

The Jews and Judaism

The Ancient Hebrews

About 1400 B.C., a group of people called Hebrews moved into the land that is now called Israel. This land, which was formerly known as Canaan or Palestine, is a small fertile region located between the Arabian Desert and the Mediterranean Sea. These people were shepherds, and it is believed that they came from Mesopotamia (Iraq) in search of water and new land. After reaching Palestine they settled down, became farmers, set up a government, and began to develop as a nation. Under King David and King Solomon, ancient Israel reached its greatest glory. Trade was carried on with distant lands, wealth poured into Israel, and Solomon built a magnificent temple in Jerusalem. But the Hebrew nation lasted only a short time before it was destroyed by outside enemies. The Hebrews, or Jews as they were later called, were scattered over the entire world. However, during the few hundred years that the Hebrews lived in Palestine they developed ideas that influenced other civilizations, especially our own. The ideas about God and people, which the Hebrews put into the Bible, live on today not only in Judaism (the religion of the Jews), but in Christianity and Islam as well.

The Hebrews and God

The Hebrews were the first people to believe in one God. Other nations before and after the Hebrews continued to believe in many gods which were connected with the forces of nature—sun, moon, rain, trees. In the beginning, the Hebrew religion also involved the worship of many gods, but gradually the idea of one God developed. The Hebrews called their God Yahweh (YHWH), and believed that he created man and the entire universe. The belief in one God is known as **monotheism**.

The Western Wall of the Temple (Wailing Wall) is one of the most sacred Jewish sites in the Holy Land.

Orthodox Jew blowing the traditional ram's horn.

The Hebrews believed that their God demanded strict obedience. God made his demands known in the Ten Commandments which he gave to Moses on Mount Sinai. Yahweh was a jealous God, and his first commandment was, "Thou shalt have no other god before me."

But the Hebrew God was also a loving father who looked upon people as his children whom he protected. The Hebrews believed that God had made a covenant, or agreement, with them. God promised that if the Hebrews obeyed his commandments he would protect them. The Bible tells many stories that show how God protected his people. According to one story, God asked Abraham to sacrifice his only son, Isaac. As Abraham laid Isaac on the altar and took the knife to kill him, an angel appeared telling him not to touch his son, "for now I know that you fear God." God then promised that Abraham's descendants would multiply and be victorious over their enemies. Other stories tell how the Egyptians who pursued the escaping Hebrews were drowned in the Red Sea; David defeated Goliath; and the Hebrews were able to conquer Canaan and create a Hebrew state.

The Ideas of Justice and Righteousness

The God of the Hebrews demanded worship, but not worship alone. God was much more interested in man's ethical (moral) behavior. God was just and demanded justice for his people; he was righteous and he demanded righteousness of his people. After the Hebrews settled down and gained wealth and power, many people began to worship other gods. Then the prophets (Elijah, Jeremiah, Amos, Isiah) came on the scene to keep the faith in Yahweh alive by condemning the worship of other gods and by saying "The Lord is one." But the prophets were also concerned with man's relation with his fellow man. The prophets claimed that God was not interested in sacrifice and offerings but in justice and right living. The prophets spoke out against the oppression of the poor by the rich and the powerful. They criticized the kings for living in luxury while the people suffered. The prophets said that God would punish those people who had strayed from the path of righteousness. And when the ancient Hebrew state in Palestine was destroyed by powerful neighbors, the prophets explained this by saying that God was punishing the Hebrews for their wicked ways. Thus, for the first time in history, religion was combined with ethics and morality. The other people of the ancient world believed that by offering sacrifices they could make their gods happy. These gods could bring rain and made the sun shine, but they were not concerned with the affairs of men. It was the Hebrews who believed that man was responsible for his fellow men and that God demanded righteousness of his people. It is because of these ideas that the Hebrew (Jewish) religion has had such a powerful influence on the rest of the world.

The Dignity of Man

Not only was the Hebrew idea of God different from that of other people, but their idea of man differed as well. Other nations of the ancient world thought of man as a lowly creature, who was nothing more than a slave of the gods. The Hebrews developed the idea of the dignity of man. In the psalms they wrote,

What is man, that thou shouldst think of him,
And the son of man that thou shouldst care for him?
Yet thou hast made him but little lower than God,
And dost crown him with glory and honor!

The Bible and the Talmud

Originally the Old Testament (Bible) contained all the teachings and laws that Jews were expected to follow. As the years passed, new situations and living conditions arose for which no provision was made in the Bible. **Rabbis**, or religious teachers, interpreted the laws and made new decisions to fit the new situations. After several hundred years all these decisions were put together in volumes called the **Talmud**. The observance of these laws is what kept the Jews together for almost 2,000 years even though they were scattered all over the world.

Islam—The Religion of the Middle East and North Africa

In the Middle East and North Africa most of the people are **Muslims**, that is, people who are believers in the religion known as **Islam**. Islam is more than a religion, however. It is a way of living, affecting almost every aspect of a person's life.

Mohammed—Founder of Islam

Islam was founded by Mohammed* in the 7th century. Mohammed was an Arab merchant who lived in the city of Mecca in Arabia. The people of Mecca worshipped many different gods, but Mohammed, who had frequent contacts with Christians and Jews, came to believe in only one God, **Allah**. Mohammed tried to spread his ideas to the people of Mecca, but they would not accept them. In the year 622, Mohammed was driven from Mecca and fled to Medina. Muslims call this flight the *Hegira*, and that year is considered to be the year one of the Muslim calendar. In Medina the people accepted Mohammed as their leader. Here Mohammed built the first mosque and continued to preach his religion. From here the religion spread to the rest of Arabia and, within a century after Mohammed's death, to distant parts of the world. Mohammed was recognized as the Prophet, or messenger of God.

Mohammed called his religion Islam. *Islam* means "submission to God," that is, living according to God's will. After Mohammed's death, all his teachings were collected and put together in one book called the **Koran**. The Koran is the holy book of the Muslims. They believe that the words in it were spoken to Mohammed by God. Every aspect of life is regulated by the teachings in the Koran. The Koran is the most important book used in Muslim schools.

Mohammed's Teachings—The Ideas of Islam

Mohammed taught that there is only one God, Allah. In this Mohammed was influenced by the monotheism of the Jews and the Old Testament. He also taught that God rewards people who act according to his laws and punishes those who disobey them and that there are angels who intercede for men. Muslims are taught to believe in the prophets

---

*Also spelled Muhammad

of Allah, of whom Mohammed is considered the most important. The Koran speaks of the Day of Judgment when Allah will reward all people with either everlasting bliss or punishment.

Mohammed set up rules that all Muslims must follow. These are known as the Five Pillars of Islam.

1. Muslims must repeat every day in Arabic, "There is no God but Allah, and Mohammed is his prophet."
2. A Muslim must pray five times a day. When praying, the person must turn towards Mecca, the holy city.
3. Muslims are required to give charity to the needy.
4. Muslims are supposed to fast (go without food or drink) from sunrise to sunset during the holy month of Ramadan. Fasting is considered to be the best means of atoning for one's sins.
5. It is the duty of every Muslim to try to make a trip to Mecca at least once. This religious trip is called a pilgrimage. Every year, thousands of Muslims from different parts of the world travel to Mecca to fulfill this duty.

Throughout Muslim history, the pilgrimage has been an important unifying force, uniting Muslims from many different countries. In Mecca, as well as while traveling to and from Mecca, the pilgrims have exchanged ideas, information, agricultural and other products, and seeds. This has helped to maintain a common Islamic culture among the many diverse people who are Muslims.

Each Muslim city has at least one mosque, or temple of worship. Every morning the Muslim is awakened by a call to prayer from the mosque. Every adult male must attend the Friday noon service. There are no statues or images (pictures of people or animals) in the mosque.

Islam, like Judaism and Christianity, emphasized kindness and forgiveness, respect for parents, protection of the weak, and charity towards the poor. Mohammed taught that all men who followed Islam were brothers. "Know ye that every Muslim is a brother to every other Muslim, and that ye are now one brotherhood." All Muslims were considered equal before the law.

Muslims believe that theirs is the only true religion. However, they honor Moses and Christ and other figures in the Bible as prophets of the one God. Jews and Christians are called "People of the Book" and are given a special place in the Islamic religion. A careful study of Islam will reveal that many of its ideas and practices have their roots in Judaism and Christianity.

The religious beliefs that Muslims share have brought Muslims all over the world closer together. These beliefs have been carried over into the modern world and into present forms of government.

Jihad—Holy War

Another important idea of Islam is the duty of **jihad**, or holy war. A key belief in Islam is that the world is divided into two parts. One is "the land of Islam" (dar al- Islam) which consists of all the lands that are Muslim. The other is the "war territory" (dar al- harb), the non-Islamic lands. It is believed that every Muslim has the duty to expand the frontiers of Islam until the entire world has been won. A war that is fought against the "enemies" of Islam is considered a holy war. It is also believed that anyone who dies while fighting for

The Dome of the Rock in Jerusalem is holy to Moslems because according to tradition Mohammed ascended to heaven from this spot. It is holy to Jews as well because the Dome marks the site of Solomon's Temple and it is believed to be the site where Abraham prepared Isaac for sacrifice.

The Great Mosque of Mecca, Saudi Arabia, filled with pilgrims. The stone building in the center is the Kaaba that contains a sacred black stone. It is toward Mecca, Islam's holiest city, that Moslems throughout the world turn five times each day and pray.

Islam will go straight to heaven. Centuries ago, one of the principle duties of the **Caliph** (the leader of the Muslim world) was to expand the territory of the Islamic world. It was this duty that resulted in the spread of Islam to many different parts of the world. In recent years, especially in the 1980s, the idea of jihad was used by Arab terrorists, as well as some of the Muslim governments (especially Iran) to attack the United States and Israel as the "enemies" of Islam. During the 1990–1991 Gulf crisis, Saddam Hussein called on the Iraqi people to fight in a jihad against the United States and its allies.

Muslims: Sunnis and Shi'ites

Muslims are divided into two sects or groups—Sunni Muslims and Shi'ite Muslims. Approximately 85 percent of all Muslims are Sunnis and 15 percent are Shi'ites. Shi'ites are found mainly in Iran, where they account for 91 percent of the population. Shi'ites are also in the majority in Iraq, and are found in large numbers in Lebanon and the Persian Gulf states.

The two groups split soon after the death of Mohammed. Since then (more than 1,300 years) relations between the two groups have often been bloody. Civil wars have been fought and Shi'ites have often suffered persecution by the Sunnis.

Origins of the Split in Islam

The division between Shi'ites and Sunnis developed over the question of who should succeed Mohammed as leader of the Muslim community. When Mohammed died in 632, leaving no male heir, possible successors, or *Khalifahs* (caliphs), were named by several different groups. One group, known as the Shia, claimed that Allah and Mohammed had chosen Ali as the legitimate successor. Ali was a cousin of Mohammed and the husband of Mohammed's daughter, Fatimah.

However, Ali did not succeed in becoming caliph at first. Three others were chosen as caliph before him. Finally in 656, Ali was proclaimed the fourth caliph. Five years later he was assassinated.

In 680, Husein, the son of Ali and grandson of Mohammed, refused to recognize the new caliph. Husein was declared caliph by his Shi'ite supporters. In the war that followed, Husein and his supporters were massacred by the caliph's troops when they refused to surrender. This massacre marked the beginning of the Shi'ites as a religious sect. The great division made in Islam has never healed.

The Imam

The Shi'ites came to believe that true religious guidance could come only from Mohammad's heirs because Mohammed had transmitted a secret interpretation of the Koran to them. These people were chosen as imam, or religious leaders of the community. In time, the imams were believed to be infallible and without sin. Shi'ites believe that it is from the imam that they receive the original light of Mohammed's revelation. This is very different from the Sunni Muslims, who believe that they receive all their religious guidance from the Koran, Muslim traditions, and the holy law.

The Position of Women

Men have authority over women because God has made the one superior to the other and because they spend their wealth to support women.

—The Koran

The position of women in Islamic society is a sensitive subject that arouses much controversy among Muslims. Islamic law seems to assert openly the superiority of men over women. However, some Muslims deny this and insist that Islam merely recognizes the different roles of men and women.

Women Under Islamic Law

According to Islamic law (the Koran), a man may marry up to four wives at one time, but if a woman takes more than one husband at a time, she is subject to the severest penalties in this world and the next. In court, a man's testimony has twice the value of a woman's. When parents die, the daughters' share of the inheritance is half that of the sons'.

Under Islam, women may not reveal their person to anyone except their husband or close relatives. This is why many Muslim women veil themselves from head to foot when they leave their homes. Even at home, women live in separate quarters known as the harem.

Those who deny that Islam enforces women's inferiority claim that: wearing a veil in public protects women from unwanted advances; women are secluded because they need protection in their role as wives and mothers; women inherit only half as much as their brothers because men are charged with the care of the family. They also stress that husbands are charged with the proper care of their wives. "Be sure to treat your wives well" Mohammed ordered. Moreover, the spiritual equality of women is emphasized throughout the Koran.

Islam established practices regarding women that were quite advanced for their time. It made the education of girls a sacred duty and established a woman's right to own and inherit property. It outlawed female infanticide (the killing of girl babies), a common practice in many parts of the world centuries ago.

However, as a result of Islamic law and customs, Muslim women have not played an important role in history. Although some women exercised influence from the harem, examples of women attaining real power and importance are rare.

Marriage

In traditional Islamic marriages, young people do not choose their marriage partners. Marriages are arranged by the parents. Negotiations between the two families are carried out by kinsmen (relatives). They must agree upon the dowry, the amount of money that the groom pays to the bride's father. They must also agree upon a sum to be paid in case the husband dies or divorces his wife. The bride must provide the furniture and everything else needed to set up a home. In parts of the Islamic world the preferred marriage is between cousins on the father's side.

Divorce

According to the Koran, a husband may divorce his wife by simply making a public declaration three times. Traditionally, the principal cause for divorce has been childlessness, especially the lack of sons. However, it is very difficult for a woman to get a divorce and she must obtain her husband's consent. In case of divorce, custody of the children goes to the husband. The woman retains the property that she brought to the marriage.

The 20th Century Brought Changes

This situation began to change in the 20th century as Muslims came in contact with Europe and America. Western ideas encouraged a freer role for women outside the home. Women started attending universities and pursuing careers as doctors, engineers, teachers, social workers, and more. They became active in politics. Many governments, recognizing the talents of women, encouraged women to play a more active role in their countries.

Laws were passed in many countries giving women specific rights. Today, women hold relatively high positions in a number of Muslim nations.

**Women's Rights
Since the 1980s**

Since the 1980s, however, some of these gains have been reversed. The Muslim world as a whole is becoming more religious. In some countries, Muslim fundamentalists (religious extremists who want to return to the true teachings of Islam) have gained power. They reject Western values and have revised laws to take away the legal rights that women recently won. This is especially true in Iran, but it has also happened in Egypt, Sudan, Algeria, and other countries. In Iran, until the 1979 revolution, women in the cities wore Western clothes and had a lifestyle similar to women in Europe and America. Now, women wear veils in public and their rights have been greatly restricted. In Sudan, the military government that seized power in 1989 refused to allow women to leave the country without permission from a husband, father, or brother. In Saudi Arabia, long the most conservative Islamic country, women are forbidden to wear Western clothes or appear without a veil in public; they are forbidden to drive and may travel only if accompanied by a husband or male blood relative.

In Saudi Arabia in November 1990, a group of 47 women gathered in a parking lot. They dismissed their chauffeurs and drove through the streets of downtown Riyadh in an orderly procession. The presence of American soldiers, especially female, in Saudi Arabia had encouraged the Saudi women to press for change in the restrictions placed on them. Within minutes the police arrived to arrest the women.

A government commission found that the women had not committed a crime since there was no specific prohibition in the Koran against driving. But the women were advised not to repeat the experiment. Unfortunately the incident did not end here. Six of the women were suspended from their jobs as university professors after organized bands of students staged angry protests. Leaflets were passed out at mosques during Friday prayers accusing the women of undermining Saudi morality. Some of the women received threatening phone calls after their names, addresses, and phone numbers were printed and distributed. Finally the Saudi government issued a statement declaring that "driving by women contradicts the Islamic traditions followed by Saudi citizens."

Early History of the Middle East

River Valley Civilizations

The first great civilizations in the world developed along the banks of rivers. Historians believe that there were four cradles of civilization and that two of these were in the Middle East. (The other two developed in India and China.) One was in Egypt, in the Nile Valley. The other was in Mesopotamia (known as Iraq today) between the Tigris and Euphrates Rivers. From the Nile Valley and Mesopotamia civilization spread northward and westward, eventually reaching Europe and America.

Conditions in the Nile Valley and Mesopotamia favored agriculture. The great rivers annually overflowed their banks, depositing a rich layer of soil. This fertile, well-watered soil produced abundant harvests. These in turn made possible a large increase in population. Cities and villages arose.

In 1799, the Rosetta Stone was found by Napoleon's troops when they invaded Egypt. The Rosetta Stone (196 B.C.) is inscribed with a royal decree (law) written in Egyptian in two different scripts, hieroglyphic and demotic, and in Greek.

Tomb painting depicting the ideal life that the deceased hoped to enjoy eternally.

It was in these river valleys that people first worked out rules for living together in communities. The earliest rules dealt with irrigation. In order for a farmer to get water from the river to his fields, there had to be a system of dams and canals. The cooperation of whole villages and often whole districts was required to build and defend these canals. Leaders were needed to supervise the building, and laws were needed to ensure that every farmer repaired his own ditches and used only his fair share of water. Thus, the need for water helped create the need for government.

So fertile was the soil of the Nile Valley and Mesopotamia that farmers could produce more than enough food for themselves and their family. They could sell the surplus. As a result trade and commerce developed and with it came the exchange of ideas and inventions between people of different regions. Since there was enough food available, some people could turn their attention to developing art and other skills. Potters learned to shape clay into beautiful vases; weavers learned to make fabrics; carpenters learned to build furniture; and architects and stonemasons learned to construct elaborate buildings.

Cities and towns grew. These were places where farmers could sell their crops, where craftspeople could live and practice their skills, and where rulers could establish their centers of government. In the cities where people lived close together ideas developed and spread.

Let us examine the various nations that developed in the Middle East and see what contributions they have made.

The Ancient Egyptians

The history of ancient Egypt dates back to 5000 B.C., or even earlier. At that time the Egyptians were already using copper tools. Great advances in agriculture had been made through the introduction of the plow and the use of irrigation systems. During the next few thousand years Egyptian civilization reached a very high level.

Although most Egyptians were farmers, many industries existed. Copper mining, stone quarrying, and cabinet making, tanning, metal working, glass blowing, and weaving were some of the most important occupations. Egyptian craftsmen produced wares that were exceptionally beautiful. Since these products were in great demand, seagoing ships carried them to distant lands.

Progress was made in the art of government. The villages were united to form one nation with all power in the hands of the **pharaoh**, or god-king, who maintained order throughout the kingdom. Religion was very important to the ancient Egyptians, whose main concern was the immortality of the soul. They believed that by mummifying, or preserving the corpse, the soul would have eternal life. Later they developed the idea that everlasting life was a reward for those who were good while alive.

One of the most important Egyptian contributions to civilization was the development of the art of writing. The Egyptians did not develop a real alphabet. Their system of writing was known as **hieroglyphics**. Picture-like signs represented objects and later ideas. Still later these signs were used to represent the sounds of words and then the sounds of syllables. Ink was made, and writing was done on rolls of papyrus which were stored in earthen jars. This made it possible to accumulate knowledge and pass it on to future generations.

It is believed that the first calendar in the world was developed in Egypt, perhaps as early as 4241 B.C. This calendar consisted of 12 months with 30 days each. At the end of the year five days were added on.

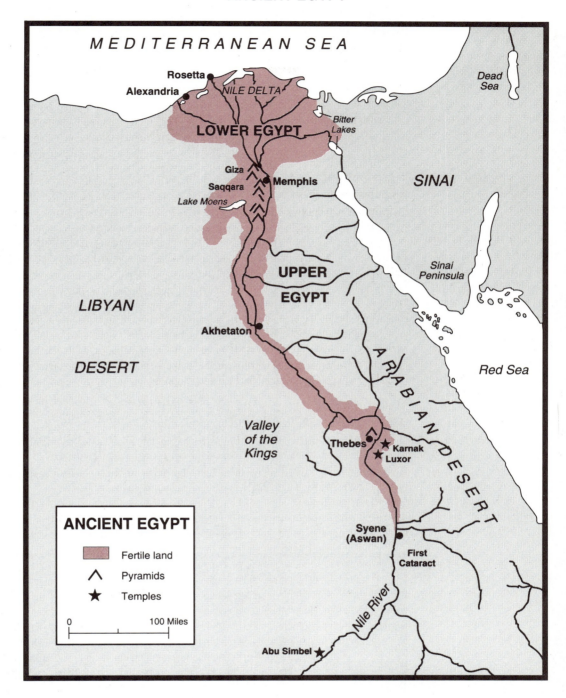

Architecture was highly advanced in ancient Egypt. Because of their concern with life after death, the pharaohs concentrated on building huge tombs to preserve their bodies and to hold all the objects they would need in the next life. These pyramids still stand today, 4,000 years after they were constructed. The pyramids, as well as the magnificent temples that were built, are proof that the Egyptians were skilled engineers who knew the principles of architecture and mathematics. Sculpture and painting were also developed and were used for decoration of the palaces and pyramids.

The Egyptians were well advanced in the science of mathematics. Exact measurements were needed to build pyramids. Since the Nile frequently overflowed its banks and erased field boundaries, precise land measurements were necessary. To meet these needs the Egyptians learned to add and subtract. They also could multiply and divide by two and three. They knew the basic principles of geometry and algebra.

The Peoples of Mesopotamia and the Fertile Crescent

During the 3,000 years that the Egyptians were developing their civilization, equally important advances were being made by other people living in Mesopotamia between the Tigris and Euphrates Rivers and along the Mediterranean Sea. However, since there were no natural barriers to protect them, this area was the scene of constant warfare and the rise and fall of numerous nations.

Sumerians

By 3500 B.C., the Sumerians already had an advanced civilization in the fertile land lying between the Tigris and Euphrates Rivers. Here, as in Egypt, the mild climate and good soil produced abundant harvests. The need for irrigation led to the growth of government. Flourishing cities arose where craftspeople produced textiles, metal products, and other goods. The Sumerians are given credit for being the first people to use wheeled vehicles. They also made important progress in mathematics. They developed a number system based on 60, which today is the basis for dividing a circle into 360° and an hour into 60 minutes. Geometric formulas were devised to compute the area of a triangle. It is believed that the Sumerians were the first people to develop a system of writing. Their writing is known as **cuneiform**. There were 350 signs representing complete words or syllables. Writing was done on soft clay tablets. Many other people of the Middle East borrowed this system of writing and used it until the introduction of the alphabet centuries later. The Sumerians were practical business people and were probably the first to use contracts in business. Sumerian literature included stories of the creation and the flood, which are similar to the later Hebrew stories found in the Bible.

THE ANCIENT MIDDLE EAST

Babylonians

The Sumerians were conquered by a group of people whose capital was Babylon, and who came to be known as Babylonians. The Babylonians are famous for the law code of Hammurabi, their greatest ruler. This law code provided that "If a man destroys the eye of another man, they shall destroy his eye. If a builder builds a house for a man and does not make its construction firm, and the house which he has built collapses and causes the death of the owner of the house, that builder shall be put to death." Although the punishments were harsh, the code was an attempt to provide some form of justice.

Hittites

The Hittites reached the height of their power around 1500 B.C. in the area that is today Turkey and Syria. They were among the earliest people to use iron, and it was through them that the metal came to be used throughout the Middle East.

Lydians

The Lydians were the first people to use coined money in the 9th century B.C.

Phoenicians

The Phoenicians lived in cities along the Mediterranean in the land that is today Lebanon. They were the greatest traders, navigators, and colonizers of their day. They were skilled manufacturers, and their purple dye, textiles, metal goods, and glassware were famous throughout the Mediterranean world. Their most important contribution was the alphabet which they developed, consisting of 22 consonant signs arranged in definite order. Their first two symbols were called aleph and beth, and it is from these that the word alphabet comes.

Hebrews

The major contribution of the Hebrews was in religion, which was discussed earlier.

Chaldeans

In the 7th century B.C., Mesopotamia came under the control of the Chaldeans. These people were important because of the progress they made in astronomy. Through systematic observation of the heavens, the Chaldeans were able to identify many stars and planets and even predict eclipses.

Persians

By 500 B.C., all the lands in the Middle East has been conquered by the Persians, the people who now live in the area we know as Iran. In fact, the Persian empire was so large that it extended up to the frontiers of India in the east and included parts of Greece in the west. In this vast empire many different people mingled together and exchanged ideas and inventions. The Persians ran their empire very efficiently. Roads were built connecting distant lands. It may be said that the Persians developed the first pony express. Every 14 miles there was a post station where fresh horses could be obtained by the king's messengers. The Persians treated the conquered peoples humanely, granting equal rights to all and respecting the gods of all. Their religion, Zoroastrianism, taught that there was a continuous struggle in the world between two great forces—righteousness and evil, and that righteousness would prevail (triumph).

Decline of the Middle East Kingdoms

As we have seen, the ancient Middle East made tremendous contributions to civilization. However, after several thousand years of advance, progress seemed to level off and come to a standstill. By the 5th century B.C., the center of civilization had shifted west along the Mediterranean Sea to Greece. For the next thousand years most of the advances in Western civilization came from the Greeks and the Romans. However, many of the ideas and discoveries of the ancient Middle East were borrowed by the Greeks and then developed still further.

The Triumph of Islam—Muslim Civilization 622–1453

The Spread of Islam

Until the 7th century A.D., the people of Arabia had never played a large part in the development of the Middle East. Living in an area that was mainly desert, most of their time was spent looking after their flocks and wandering in search of water. In the 6th century, the Arabs had not yet reached the high level of civilization that the Hebrews, Egyptians, and other people of the Middle East had reached centuries earlier. However, in the 7th century, inspired by the teachings of Mohammad, the Arabs swept over Persia, Mesopotamia, Palestine, Egypt, and North Africa in search of converts to the new religion and economic gains.

They conquered one settlement after another. In the west, Arab armies conquered Spain. They swept across south and central France until they were finally stopped at Tours, in the famous battle of 732 A.D. Although stopped in the west, the Arabs continued their successes in the east, extending their power into Central Asia and later into India and Southeast Asia. Within a century after Mohammed's death, the Arab empire extended from the Atlantic Ocean in the west to India in the east.

THE SPREAD OF ISLAM 632–750 A.D.

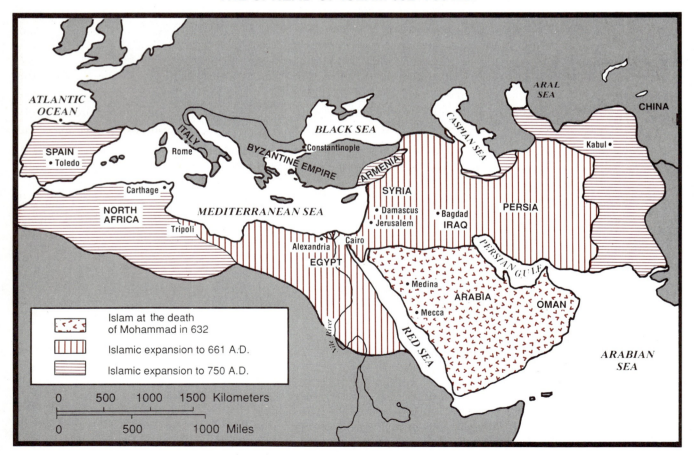

Legend:
- Islam at the death of Mohammad in 632
- Islamic expansion to 661 A.D.
- Islamic expansion to 750 A.D.

0 500 1000 1500 Kilometers
0 500 1000 Miles

The dhow has been used by Arabs for centuries to carry goods to and from Asia and Africa.

How were the Arabs able to conquer and rule so vast an empire? First the Arabs were magnificent warriors. Mohammed had taught that any Muslim dying in battle while fighting to spread Islam was assured entry into heaven. This made the Arabs fearless in battle. Their life in the desert gave the Arabs a toughness that enabled them to defeat many who stood in their way. Second, after the poverty of desert life, the possibility of gaining rich and fertile lands only encouraged the Arabs to fight harder. Third, many people found it easy to become Muslim because Islam did not discriminate against people on account of their race. Finally, the Muslims were tolerant rulers and allowed the Christians, Jews, and other non-Muslims to continue their way of life and follow their own religion.

Contributions of the Muslims

For the next 500 years Muslim civilization far surpassed that of Europe. Historians have used the words *magnificent, splendid,* and *brilliant* to describe the civilization of the Muslims during this time. No other people contributed so much to learning during this period as did the scholars and scientists of the Muslim world. The luxury and wealth that existed in the Muslim lands was unknown in Europe.

The book *Arabian Nights* gives a good description of the splendor of Baghdad, which was the capital of the Muslim world from 750 to 1258. Around the bazaars were merchants who brought fabulous carpets from Persia; silks from China; steel from Damascus; cotton from Egypt; leather from Morocco; spices and dyes from India; ivory, gold, and slaves from Africa; honey, wax, and white slaves from Russia. Industry and commerce prospered.

The cultural contributions of the Muslims were tremendous. This was partly due to the generosity of the caliphs who welcomed artists, writers, scholars, and scientists to their courts and encouraged them in their work. The Muslims had an ability to recognize what was best in other cultures, adopt it, add to it, and then pass it on to other people. The Muslims were especially influenced by the philosophy and science of ancient Greece and India. Most of the outstanding Greek writers were translated into Arabic. This learning was improved upon and later transmitted by the Muslims to Western Europe.

The Muslims made important advances in medicine. Various diseases were diagnosed and described, including measles and smallpox; all the medical knowledge of the day was collected and published in several huge encyclopedias; the first drug stores and schools of pharmacy were set up; druggists and doctors had to pass an examination; hospitals were built throughout the empire. Physics and chemistry also progressed under the Muslims. To advance the study of astronomy, they developed good astronomical instruments and built observatories. Most of their knowledge of mathematics came from the Hindus in India. This knowledge included the numbers we use today, but since it was the Arabs who introduced these numbers to Western Europe, they are commonly referred to as Arabic numbers. The Arabs made great progress in algebra, which is itself an Arabic word. Because of their trade with distant lands as well as their pilgrimages to Mecca, the Muslims became the most important geographers of the time. A great deal of geographical knowledge was collected, and maps were printed.

The Muslims made important contributions to literature as well. Arabs have always had the special gift of storytelling and poetry. The Arabic language itself is suited to colorful tales about life in the desert or palace. Hundreds of poets created poems of great beauty. The one most known in the West was the Persian poet Omar Khayyám. The *Arabian Nights* is a collection of tales that is quite popular all over the world. Many histories were written during this period. Arab historians specialized in biographies of Mohammed and other important Muslim leaders, accounts of the spread of Islam, and world histories.

In art the two fields in which the Muslims excelled were architecture and the decorative arts. Beautiful mosques were built with spacious interiors, large domes, great pillars, and arches. Besides the mosques, the Muslims built large palaces, of which the most famous is the Alhambra in Granada, Spain. Beautiful patterns of flowers and geometric figures were used to decorate the interior of mosques and palaces. Skilled craftspeople produced rugs, pottery, tiles, and metalwork of original and delicate designs.

The Middle East in Decline

Between the years 700 to 1200 A.D., the Muslims had the most advanced civilization in the world. Then Muslim civilization stopped advancing. By 1600, the civilization of Europe began to develop more rapidly and surpass that of the Muslims. There are a number of reasons that help to explain this decline.

1. Political disunity

By the middle of the 10th century there was no real unity in the Muslim lands. Although most of the countries recognized the caliph in Baghdad as their ruler, local leaders did pretty much as they wished. Different religious groups arose, each claiming to be the true followers of Islam. These groups plotted against and fought with each other. Arabs, Persians, and Turks rivaled one another for important positions and for leadership. Therefore, in the face of a common enemy, the Muslim lands could not really put up any resistance.

2. The Crusades

From 1097 to 1291 the Christians in Europe tried to reconquer the Holy Land from the Muslims. The coastal cities of Palestine, parts of Syria, and Turkey were captured by the Christians. During this period, Muslim rulers made alliances with Europeans against other Muslims. Finally the famous ruler of Egypt, Salah-al-Din (Saladin), was able to unite enough territory in 1187 to defeat the Christians and drive them from Jerusalem. During the 200 years of warfare there was considerable destruction in the Middle East.

3. Nomadic attacks

Periodically, over several hundred years various groups of nomads invaded the Middle East and North Africa and caused tremendous destruction from which the area never recovered. In the middle of the 11th century, nomadic Arabs invaded North Africa destroying the land and the irrigation systems. These were never repaired and as a result farming seriously declined.

During the 13th century, far greater destruction was caused by the Mongols. The Mongols were nomadic warriors on horseback who came from the steppes of Central Asia. Sweeping down on the Middle East, the Mongols conquered Persia, Iraq, and Syria. Baghdad, the capital of the Islamic world, fell in 1258. Hundreds of thousands of people died, cities vanished, and governments fell. Great disorder followed the invasion. Trade routes became dangerous and trade broke down. Industry declined. Iraq, which had been the center of the Muslim world, was ruined. The final blows by the Mongols came in 1380 under the leadership of Timur Leng (Tamerlane). The Mongols captured Baghdad, Damascus, Aleppo, Ankara, and other cities. Schools, mosques, libraries, and palaces were destroyed. The Mongols left pyramids of human heads behind them in each city.

4. European expansion

In general, as the Christians in Europe grew stronger, they began to expand at the expense of Islam. Areas such as Spain, which had been part of the Muslim world, were gradually taken over by the Europeans.

5. Sea route to India

The discovery in 1497 of an all-water route between Europe and India contributed to the decline of the Middle East. Formerly Middle Eastern cities profited from the overland trade between Asia and Europe. With goods moving by sea, these cities lost their main source of income.

The Ottoman Empire

The Rise of the Ottomans

During the same period that the Arab world was declining in power and importance, a new people in the Middle East were beginning to make their strength felt. They were the Turks, who had originally come from Central Asia and over the centuries settled in the country that is today known as Turkey. At the beginning of the 14th century they created a small, powerful state in Turkey. For the next few centuries the Turks fought a series of wars to capture territory and extend their empire. By the 16th century, southeastern Europe, North Africa, and most of the Middle East had been conquered by the Turks. These Turks were known as Ottoman Turks, and, therefore, the territory under their control was known as the Ottoman Empire.

During the 16th century, Ottoman civilization reached its peak. The Turks were great soldiers and good administrators and ruled their vast empire quite efficiently. Under their greatest ruler, Suleiman the Magnificent, who ruled from 1521–1566, the Ottomans built a strong navy and became the strongest naval power in the Mediterranean. The Turks of this period were also master builders and poets as well. Many beautiful mosques and palaces were built, and there were important achievements in literature, especially in the field of poetry, essay writing, and history.

Government in the Ottoman Empire

Although the Turks were Muslims, there were a number of other religious and **ethnic** (national) groups in the Ottoman Empire. The Turks allowed each group to keep its own religion, laws, language, and customs. Each group had its own courts, which tried all cases except those involving public security and crime. These groups were required to pay taxes to the Ottoman government, but in other respects they enjoyed a good deal of freedom.

The **sultan** was the ruler of the empire and the head of Islam. He had absolute authority over all matters. The second most powerful official in the empire was the grand vizier who was the sultan's chief deputy. To rule such a vast empire many qualified officials were needed. Every five years representatives of the sultan traveled through the European provinces selecting the healthiest and most intelligent Christian boys between the ages of 12 and 20. They were converted to Islam, taught Turkish, and assigned to military units. The most talented boys were brought to the royal palace and trained to govern the empire. Others were recruited for the army. Education, religious matters, and laws were exclusively in the hands of Muslim mullahs (wise men).

Decline of the Ottomans

During the 17th century, the Ottoman Empire began to decline. By the 18th century, the Ottomans were already losing territory to the more powerful Europeans. There were many reasons for this decline. In the early years the Empire was ruled by capable sultans. After Suleiman the Magnificent, however, the sultans became more interested in the luxuries and pleasures of life than in ruling the empire. In the beginning also, government officials were appointed on the basis of merit—those most qualified to do the job. Later, important positions were given to favorites who were often not suited for the job. Bribery was used to obtain many jobs, and the government became very corrupt. As the sultans grew weaker and the officials less capable, the problems of ruling a vast empire increased. At this time the Europeans were making great progress in science and industry. However, the Turks thought the Europeans were inferior to them and refused to learn new ideas from them. With the trade between Europe and Asia now controlled by the Europeans, an important source of wealth was lost. As the Ottoman Empire grew weaker, Russia and Austria tried to capture some of its territories and wars with these nations further weakened the Empire. Gradually the Turks lost control over many of their territories.

European Imperialism in the Middle East

European Interest in the Middle East

During the 19th century, the Ottoman Empire became known as "the sick man of Europe." The Empire was falling apart and the Europeans stood by waiting to take their share of it when the opportunity arose. The Europeans were expanding just when the Ottoman Empire had reached its lowest point. They wanted to rule over the less developed countries to gain markets for the goods that their factories produced and invest their money with the promise of high profits. The Europeans at first tried to avoid sending armies to conquer and rule the people directly. They found it easier to create puppet rulers to protect European interests. When the local ruler could not control the people, the Europeans sent armies in to protect their citizens and their investments.

The Europeans Gain Control

The period of European penetration into the Middle East began with Napoleon's invasion of Egypt in 1798. Napoleon defeated the Egyptians who were still part of the Ottoman Empire. A few weeks later an English fleet arrived and defeated the French forces. This incident was important for two reasons. First, it demonstrated that European military power was superior to that of the Middle East. Second, the British became the protector of the Ottoman Empire and gained a very important voice in the affairs of the Middle East.

Throughout the 19th century, Russia fought many wars against Turkey in the hope of gaining territory belonging to the Turks. It was only because of Britain's coming to the aid of Turkey that the Russians were prevented from breaking up the Empire.

Nevertheless, the British and French began to take over parts of the Empire themselves. France gained Algeria in 1830 and Tunisia in 1881. In 1882, the British took over Egypt. In 1912, France and Spain set up protectorates in Morocco. Italy held Libya from 1911 until World War II. The Arab countries of the Middle East came under the control of the British and French after World War I.

In 1856, the ruler of Egypt granted permission to Ferdinand de Lesseps, a French engineer, to dig a canal connecting the Mediterranean with the Gulf of Suez. The Suez Canal, which was opened in 1869, shortened the sea voyage between Europe and Asia by thousands of miles. Although built by the French, the Canal soon became Britain's most important waterway for trading with India. In 1875, when the ruler of Egypt was in need of cash, he sold his shares in the Canal Company to the British. In this way the British came to own a major share in the Canal, and their future policy in Egypt was determined by the need to protect this investment.

In 1881, rioting broke out in Egypt, and the Egyptian government called on the British for help. The British sent troops and promised to withdraw them from Egypt as soon as order was restored. British armed forces did not leave the country until 1956! Egypt never really became a colony, because the occupation was considered to be temporary. Until World War I, Egypt continued to be an Ottoman province, but the real power was in the hands of the British.

World War I and the Middle East

World War I brought about the collapse of the Ottoman Empire. The Empire fought on the side of Germany against England, France, and Russia. Consequently, the British encouraged the Arabs to revolt against the Ottomans. In return, the British promised independence and the establishment of an Arab state for the Arab lands east of Suez. But these promises were very vague, and no boundaries were specified. Moreover Britain and France had already secretly agreed to divide up the territory between themselves. The British had also promised that they would accept the establishment of a Jewish homeland in Palestine. The Arabs revolted against the Turks in 1916 and fought hard, expecting to be rewarded at the end of the war. Their leader, Sharif Hussein, dreamed of an Arab state that would stretch from Iraq to the Mediterranean Sea and would include the Arabian Peninsula.

At the end of the war, the League of Nations turned over Syria and Lebanon to the French as **mandates**. Iraq, Palestine, and Transjordan became British mandates. This meant that these countries were to be ruled by the British and French until they were considered ready for independence. The Arabs were very bitter over what they regarded as betrayal by the Europeans.

The Growth of Nationalism Between the Wars

During the 1920s and 1930s, nationalist feeling grew throughout the Middle East. The nationalists demanded total independence from Britain and France. They formed political organizations to achieve their goals. They organized mass rallies, strikes, and economic boycotts against the British and French. They also engaged in many acts of violence. In 1920, there was an insurrection in Iraq. In Palestine, the Arabs engaged in guerrilla warfare against the British. Syria, Lebanon, Tunisia, and Morocco were scenes of outbreaks against the French.

Saudi Arabia's independence was recognized in 1927. Iraq was declared independent in 1922, but the British mandate did not end until 1932. Even then British troops continued to occupy important places in Iraq, and major decisions continued to be made by the British. In Syria and Lebanon the French held absolute power until the end of World War II. Control over the foreign affairs, education, justice, and economy of these two countries was in French hands.

The Middle East During World War II

When Italy entered World War II on the side of Germany in June 1940, the Middle East became one of the main battlefields of the war. Mussolini, the Italian dictator, sent an Italian army of 250,000 to invade Egypt in August. Britain's Prime Minister, Winston Churchill, believed that Egypt was vital to the security of the British Empire and to the survival of Britain as a great power. Therefore, the British government decided to defend Egypt and the Middle East. A British offensive was begun in December, driving the Italian army out of Egypt. But British successes led the Germans to send General Erwin Rommel to take command of the Axis (German and Italian) troops in North Africa. Rommel's army moved into Egypt in April 1941 and once again the Suez Canal was threatened.

Between 1940 and 1943, the threat of Axis occupation hung over the entire Middle East. The Arab nationalists hoped to use this opportunity to finally rid themselves of British and

French domination. Some Arabs actively collaborated with the Germans and the Italians. In Egypt, King Farouk and many army officers were ready to welcome the Germans and the Italians and to turn against the British. In February 1942, the British forced the king to appoint a government that would cooperate with the Anglo-American war effort. But strong anti-British feeling remained. In Iraq a rebellion led by Rashid Ali overthrew the pro-British government. Rashid Ali's forces then attacked the British Air Force training base in Iraq. The Nazis provided Rashid Ali with aircraft and other forms of military aid. but with the arrival of more troops the British were able to suppress the rebellion. In Syria and Lebanon Nazi agents succeeded in arousing anti-French feeling among the Arabs.

The British launched an all-out offensive against Rommel's North African army in October 1942. The British victory at El Alamein in November marked the beginning of the end of the Axis' presence in North Africa. Britain remained firmly in control of the Middle East until the end of the war.

The Middle East After World War II—Nationalism and the Question of Arab Unity

The Europeans Leave the Middle East

In the years that followed the end of World War II the nations of the Middle East and North Africa gained their complete independence. (Even though a number of nations had been declared independent earlier, they were not really independent as long as Britain and France made important decisions for them and kept troops in their country.) During this same period, Britain and France lost their colonies in Africa and Asia as well. There are several reasons that explain why decolonization (giving up one's colonies) took place around the world.

1. In many of these colonies, revolutionary groups fought wars against the British and French and the other colonial powers that were expensive and bloody.
2. People in Britain were weary and exhausted after six years of fighting in World War II. They were unwilling to make any more sacrifices to hold onto the colonies.
3. The United States and the Soviet Union became the two superpowers after World War II and tried to take the place of Britain and France in many parts of the world. By 1949, U.S. power had replaced that of Britain in the Middle East.

British Decolonization

After 1945, Britain found it increasingly difficult to hold on to Palestine. (See "The Arab-Israeli Conflict," page 83). In May 1948, the British pulled their troops out of Palestine and left. Britain's position in the Middle East had begun to crumble.

In 1954, Egypt's new prime minister, Gamal Abdel Nasser, induced the British to remove all of their troops from the Suez Canal Zone by 1956. Although British troops left on schedule, Nasser **nationalized** (the government took over) the Suez Canal Company in July 1956. This marked the end of British control over this vital waterway that Britain had controlled since 1875. In 1958, the pro-British monarchy in Iraq was overthrown. Britain's last remaining possessions in the Middle East were the oil-rich principalities on the Persian Gulf. Britain gave these up in 1971.

French Decolonization

In the early 1950s, the Arabs in Morocco, Tunisia, and Algeria began waging guerrilla warfare against the French. In March 1956, France granted complete independence to Morocco and Tunisia. But the French fought a long and bloody war to hold onto Algeria. There were approximately 1 million European settlers living in Algeria. They considered themselves French and wanted French rule to continue. The Arab population of Algeria demanded complete independence. They received help from the rest of the Arab world, especially Egypt, to fight the French. After eight years of violence and bloodshed President de Gaulle of France realized that the cost of holding on to Algeria was too great for France. Algeria was granted independence in 1962.

The Sinai-Suez Campaign

On October 29, 1956, the Israeli army marched into the Sinai Peninsula and quickly defeated the Egyptian army. This was in retaliation for continued Arab raids across the border into Israel. (See "The Arab-Israeli Conflict," page 84.) Within 48 hours, British and French troops landed in the Sinai and were fighting the Egyptians. The British and French hoped to regain control over the Suez Canal and also to overthrow the anti-Western government of President Nasser. Before the invasion could accomplish anything, the United Nations with the support of the United States and the Soviet Union put enormous pressure on Britain and France to stop their advance and pull out. A U.N. emergency force was sent to patrol the borders. The Suez campaign was a disaster for both Britain and France. It showed that both nations had lost control over events in the Middle East. Nasser came out of the Suez War triumphant. The Canal was firmly in Egyptian hands. The outcome was seen as a great victory for the Egyptian people and for Arab nationalism.

Nationalism and Arab Unity

Common Heritage and Traditions

The Middle East is a region of great diversity. Each country has its unique history. Nevertheless, despite the many differences, most of the countries of the area (with the exception of Israel) have some very important things in common. One is Islam and the accomplishments of Islamic civilization. The other is pride in their Arab heritage and feelings of a common destiny for all Arab people. (This feeling is not shared by the people of Iran, Turkey, or Israel who are not Arabs.) The common religion, traditions, and Arabic language unite the diverse peoples of the region. This bond is the basis of Arab nationalism. Even as these nations adopt Western ideas in order to modernize, they continue to hold onto their Islamic traditions and heritage.

Pan Islamism

The goal of uniting all Muslims is known as Pan Islamism. An important idea in Islam is that there is one unified Islamic state. Those people who promote Muslim unity believe that the Muslims are one nation and one civilization and that this civilization is intrinsically (by nature) superior to that of the West.

Pan Arabism

The goal of uniting all the Arabs in a single state is known as Pan Arabism. When the Arabs revolted against the Ottoman Empire in World War I, Arab leaders hoped to create a unified Arab state in the liberated territory. Instead, the Arab lands were divided up and placed under British and French control. After 1945, the idea of Pan Arabism gained renewed importance. Gamal Abdel Nasser, Egypt's ruler from 1954 to 1970, championed the cause of Pan Arabism and tried to take over the leadership of the Arab world. In 1958, Egypt and Syria joined together to form the United Arab Republic (UAR). Nasser hoped that the UAR would some day include the entire Arab world. Syria withdrew in 1961 but Egypt continued to be known as the United Arab Republic. Even though Nasser had the support of the Arab masses in the Middle East, he failed in his ambition to create a unified Arab world. But Nasser's actions did give the Arabs a greater voice in world affairs.

The Arab League

To promote Arab unity the Arab League was formed in 1945. The original members of the League were Egypt, Syria, Lebanon, Iraq, Transjordan (now Jordan), Saudi Arabia, and Yemen. Over the years other Arab countries joined. In the beginning the Arab League concentrated mainly on improving the economic, cultural, and social programs of its members. It mediated disputes among them, or between them and third parties. Following the creation of the state of Israel in May 1948, the Arab League played an important part in organizing the fighting against Israel. Since then, whenever a major problem or confrontation has occurred between Israel and the Arabs, the Arab League has met to discuss a common strategy. In April 1950, several members of the League signed an agreement providing for joint defense and economic cooperation.

The Arabs have set up a number of other regional organizations. The Council of Arab Economic Unity was established in 1957 to achieve economic integration. The Arab Common Market was formed to facilitate the movement of capital, goods, and people. The Arab Fund for Economic and Social Development was established in 1968. It serves 21 Arab countries and the PLO (Palestine Liberation Organization). It finances development projects, promotes investment, and provides technical assistance.

Disunity and Division

Although Pan Arabism has a strong hold on people's minds in the Middle East, it remains a dream and not a reality. Despite the feelings of a common past, present, and future, which most Arabs share, there is also great disunity and division in the Arab world. The recent history of the Middle East, 1945 to the present, is full of revolutions, assassinations, **coup d'etats** (overthrowing of governments), wars, and civil war. Political differences and rivalry for leadership have created tensions and enmity between Arab nations. There are numerous examples of these divisions. Egypt and Syria are longstanding rivals for power in the Middle East. Their union did not last more than three years. Relations between Syria and Jordan have been very tense at times. In 1970, Syrian troops invaded Jordanian territory and King Hussein of Jordan ordered his troops to attack thousands of Palestinian Arabs living in Jordon. In Lebanon a bloody civil war has been waged since 1975. Iran and Iraq fought a bitter war from 1980 to 1988 that was in part caused by religious differences, although both countries are Muslim. Syria, an Arab country, helped Iran, which is not Arab, against Iraq, a fellow Arab country. Relations between Egypt and Libya have been strained for years. Several times both nations were on the brink of war.

There have been numerous assassinations for political reasons, from kings and presidents to mayors and local officials. King Abdullah of Jordan, King Faisal of Iraq, and President Anwar Sadat of Egypt are among the more famous leaders who have been assassinated. King Hussein of Jordan has survived many attempts on his life. The PLO has killed many Palestinian officials who, in any way, cooperated with Israel.

Economic Development

Problems Facing the Middle East

After World War II, many countries in the Middle East became independent and took charge of their own affairs. One of the primary goals of the new leaders was to develop and modernize their nations. But the problems they faced were enormous. The Middle East was economically underdeveloped and backward. In most of the countries there was a small group of people who lived well—mainly large landowners and merchants. A huge gap existed between this small, well-off minority and the large, poverty-stricken majority.

Approximately 80 percent of the people were peasants living on the land. Their standard of living was very low. It was necessary to improve agriculture and increase food production. However, there were many obstacles. There is a great shortage of usable land in the region since most of the Middle East is desert. There is also a shortage of water for irrigation. Other problems included: primitive agricultural methods, poor water use, crop diseases and pests, and a system of land distribution whereby most of the land was owned by a few large landowners. Soaring population growth further aggravated the situation.

It was also necessary to develop new industries. But again there were enormous obstacles. Large amounts of capital are needed to build industry. Most of the countries did not have the money and had to resort to borrowing. There was a shortage of engineers, factory managers, technicians, and skilled workers to run the new plants and mills. The Middle East was an area of widespread illiteracy. It was necessary to provide basic education and professional training to more people in order to have a skilled work force.

The biggest obstacles to economic development in the Middle East were political instability and war. So much money and energy were spent on war preparations and actual warfare that economic development was held back. For example, for years Egypt spent a large part of its budget for military purposes and very little was left for anything else.

Economic Gains

Yet, despite the many problems, most of the countries of the Middle East made great progress in the years after World War II. There was a rapid expansion of industry in many countries. In agriculture, success was more limited, and, in some places, it is still necessary to import large amounts of food.

Agriculture

To make more land available for farming, a number of river development projects were started. The most successful one was the Aswan High Dam in Egypt. This dam, completed in 1970 at a cost of $1 billion, is one of the world's great engineering works. The dam provides enormous benefits for Egypt's economy. For the first time in history, the annual flooding of the Nile can be controlled. About 1 million acres of land, which formerly were irrigated only during the summer flooding, can now be irrigated year round. Sugar cane, lentils, corn, and wheat are grown on this land. Sugar refining, a new industry, has developed in the area of the dam. Thousands of acres of former desert land are now watered as well. Lake Nasser, which was created by the dam, supports a fishing industry. The Aswan High Dam also produces most of Egypt's electricity.

In order to improve the lives of the peasants and increase agricultural production, a number of countries passed Agrarian Reform Laws. The purpose of these laws was to take away some of the land from the rich landlords and distribute it to the poor peasants. The results have been mixed. In Iran, the Land Reform Law of 1962 redistributed most of the land to small farmers. The power of the landlords was broken. In Iraq, an Agrarian Reform Law was passed in 1958. It set the maximum amount of land a person could hold; the rest had to be distributed to the peasants. However, a decade later, less than half the land had been distributed. A new Agrarian Reform Law was passed in 1970. Peasants were provided with seeds, irrigation water, fertilizer, and insecticides. Again, the results were disappointing. The quality of argicultural production did not improve. Many peasants left their farms and moved to the cities. President Nassar of Egypt broke up the large land-holdings and distributed the land to the poor. But rapid population growth wiped out the resulting benefits.

Industry

The Middle East is a major producer of **petroleum** (oil) and natural gas. Many oil-related industries have developed in the area—the refining of oil and the manufacture of fertilizer and plastics. Natural gas, a by-product of oil production, is used as a fuel in many industries in the region. These include steel making, textiles, and cement-making plants. The steel mills and manufacturing plants that have been built in recent years provide jobs and income for thousands. Saudi Arabia is a good example of how oil money has been used to develop industry. Besides oil, Saudi Arabia is now producing steel, gasoline, diesel fuel, lubricating oil, chemical fertilizer, and the petrochemicals that are used in a variety of plastics and synthetics. Much of the production is shipped to the United States, Europe, Japan, and China.

Another growing industry in the Middle East is mining. Egypt produces iron ore, phosphates, manganese ore, granite, gypsum, and salt. Morocco is the world's leading exporter of phosphates. Morocco also exports iron ore, lead maganese, and zinc ore. Turkey is a leading producer of chromite, and, to a lesser degree, iron ore and coal.

Oil Is King

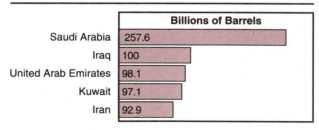

MIDDLE EAST OIL RESERVES

	Billions of Barrels
Saudi Arabia	257.6
Iraq	100
United Arab Emirates	98.1
Kuwait	97.1
Iran	92.9

Source: *National Geographic*, Feb. 1991.

The major natural resource of the Middle East is oil. The Middle East is the world's leading producer of oil. Most of this oil is found in Saudi Arabia, Kuwait, Iran, Iraq, Libya, the United Arab Emirates, and Qatar. Saudi Arabia alone is the world's largest exporter of oil. In addition, the Middle East has the largest oil reserves in the world. These oil reserves are for future use. Saudi Arabia is considered to have the largest proven oil resources, estimated at 257.6 billion barrels. This is 23.9 percent of the world's total oil reserves. Kuwait's known reserves, at the end of 1990, totalled 97.1 billion barrels and could last for more than 230 years at current rates of production.

Foreigners Develop Oil Resources

Oil was first discovered in Iran in 1908. In 1927, the Kirkuk oil fields of Iraq began to produce, and in 1935 oil fields in the Arabian Peninsula were developed.

The oil fields of the Middle East were developed by European and American companies. The countries of the Middle East did not have the money, the trained personnel, or the equipment to carry out their own oil operations. They, therefore, granted concessions (special privileges) to American and European (mainly English, French, and Dutch) companies. In Saudi Arabia, the major concession was obtained in 1932 by the Arabian American Oil Company (ARAMCO). Some of the other companies were British Petroleum, Gulf Oil, Royal Dutch Shell, Compagnie Française De Petroles, Mobil, and Exxon. These companies operated the oil wells of Kuwait, Iraq, Iran, Qatar, and the United Arab Emirates.

The companies were responsible for surveying, drilling, and finally transporting the oil by means of pipelines to seaports along the Mediterranean. From there it was shipped abroad, mainly to Europe. As a result, the foreign companies had almost complete control of the oil. The companies decided how much oil to produce, where to sell it, and how much to charge. And, of course, most of the profits went to the companies. The government of the country in which the oil was located received a fixed royalty (payment), usually 12.5 percent of the sale price and a tax.

OIL FIELDS, REFINERIES, AND PIPELINES OF THE MIDDLE EAST

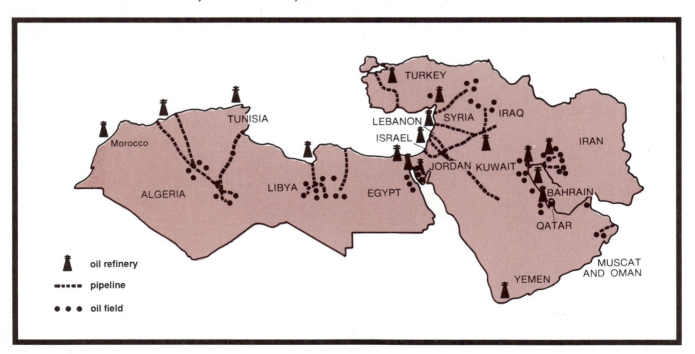

An Arabian American Oil Company (ARAMCO) drilling rig in Saudi Arabia. Note that drilling takes place in the heart of one of the world's great deserts.

Middle East Nations Gain Control of Their Oil

In the 1960s, disputes developed between the companies and the governments of the oil producing companies. These governments engaged in a major struggle with the oil companies to get a larger share of the profits and to gain greater control over the oil companies. In 1972, Iraq nationalized the big Kirkuk fields. Other countries nationalized their oil fields as well.

Since the early 1970s, the oil producing countries have had control over their oil resources. They are able to dictate prices and terms to the companies and to the countries that must import this oil.

Oil Brings Wealth

The oil producing countries have accumulated vast fortunes. Saudi Arabia's oil income in 1972 was over $2 billion. In 1981, it had grown to $100 billion. Other Arab oil-producing countries, such as Kuwait and the United Arab Emirates, have also earned billions of dollars for their oil. In addition to the oil-producing countries, other nations in the Middle East receive a substantial income from oil. Pipelines from Saudi Arabia and Iraq pass through Syria, Lebanon, and Jordan. These countries are paid a fair amount of money for the movement of oil through their territories. Oil tankers that move through the Suez Canal pay millions of dollars in tolls to Egypt annually.

In the past, much of this money was wasted on luxuries by the rulers of the oil producing nations. In recent years, oil money has been used to develop and modernize the countries of the Middle East.

Oil Companies Bring Modernization

Much of the progress and modernization in the Middle East originally centered around the oil company. When an oil company entered an area in the Middle East changes followed rapidly. Nomadic herders, drawn by attractive wages, left their flocks to work for the oil company. Complete new towns were built for workers in the oil fields. Instead of tents, workers found themselves living in concrete homes. Many received wages for the first time and bought goods they could never have afforded before. Companies like ARAMCO established schools for workers and their children. Technical training was provided for the workers as well as free medical care. The companies played a major role in building railroads and highways, clearing ports, and constructing hospitals and housing developments. Since most of the oil produced in the Middle East is also refined there, oil refineries were built that provided thousands of people with jobs.

Kuwait and Saudi Arabia

Since the 1970s, with so much oil money flowing in, the governments of the oil producing countries spent large sums on local development projects. Kuwait is a good example. This tiny country has had one of the highest per capita incomes in the world. The government provides for the health and welfare of its people almost from the moment they are born. Great sums of money are spent on education. Kuwait City, located in the middle of the desert, was converted into a modern city with broad avenues, steel and glass buildings, and thousands of automobiles. The government of Saudi Arabia has spent hundreds of billions on roads, schools, industrial plants, telecommunications networks, hospitals, and other major facilities. An example is the industrial city of Jubail, completed in 1986. It was built on 340 square miles of what was a barren desert only a decade ago. It has hotels, an airport, highways, schools, mosques, shopping centers, a hospital, and a number of industrial plants. The government of Saudi Arabia provides scholarships for study abroad. Thousands of people who have benefited from these scholarships are now working in the government and in business. At the Petroleum College young people are trained as engineers. Tuition, board, and study materials are free, and Saudi Arabian students receive a monthly stipend (payment for expenses).

Oil and International Politics

Since the 1970s, oil has become a very important factor in international politics. Western Europe depends on the Middle East for most of its oil. This dependence influences the way the nations of Europe act in their relations with the Middle Eastern nations. Japan is also very dependent on oil from the Middle East. Japan's relations with Israel and the Arabs is greatly influenced by this dependence. As for the United States, the supply of oil from the Middle East has been less important than it is for Europe, although the United States imports 50 percent of its oil. The Arab states of the Middle East therefore have been in the position to use oil as a "weapon" by limiting or halting supplies.

OPEC and the "Oil Weapon"

Since 1973, the Organization of Petroleum Exporting Countries, or OPEC, has become a powerful force in global politics and economies. OPEC is made up of the major oil producing countries in the world, including nations in the Middle East, Africa, and South America. The organization was formed in the early 1960s to give the oil producing nations a means of coordinating their policies. If these nations worked together, it was believed that they could get the best deal for their oil.

The Oil Embargo June, 1967

In June 1967, just after Egypt, Syria, and Jordan were defeated by Israel in the Six-Day War (discussed later in this unit), the Arab nations imposed an oil embargo against the United States, Israel, and its allies in Western Europe. They hoped that this would pressure Israel into withdrawing from the Arab areas it had captured in the war. However, since many nations continued to sell their oil, the embargo was a failure. The Arabs realized that oil could be an effective political weapon only if *all* the producers, including non-Arab nations, acted together.

Oil Crisis of 1973

Two days after the Arab-Israeli War of 1973 began, the Arab oil producers ordered a 25 percent cutback in production and a total embargo against the United States and Holland because of their support for Israel. This created a critical shortage of oil in the world. As the countries competed for the oil that was available, OPEC raised the price of oil from $2.50 a barrel to $10 a barrel. The cutback in production as well as the embargo lasted several months. Western Europe and Japan were badly hit and oil rationing went into effect. Many difficulties were experienced in the United States as well.

Effect on the Third World

The countries that were most seriously affected by the increase in oil prices were the nations of the Third World. Most of the countries in Asia and Africa have to import almost all of their oil. Since their cash reserves are extremely limited, many industrial development projects were cancelled and food production slowed down. The Arab oil producers had promised to set up a special fund using their surplus **petrodollars** (money received for oil) to aid the developing countries but not much was done. Until 1973 most of the African countries enjoyed a very good relationship with Israel. During the Arab-Israeli War they broke relations with Israel, hoping to win the favor of the Arabs and oil benefits as well. But they received very little in return.

Effects on Industrialized Nations

The possibility of an embargo forced the industrialized countries to search for new sources of energy. The United States turned to the Alaska pipeline as one possible answer. After the 1979 oil price crisis, President Carter promoted a comprehensive energy program to reduce oil imports. British Petroleum and other companies speeded up their development of fields under the North Sea. It was hoped that oil from the North Sea would make Britain and the Scandinavian countries almost completely independent of Arab oil.

WORLD OIL RESERVES

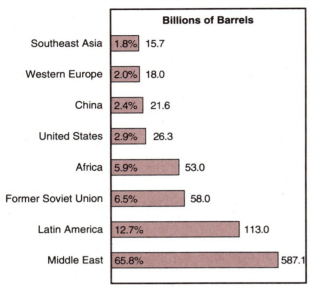

% are % of world's total reserves

Source: *Encyclopedia Britannica Book of the Year 1991*

WORLD OIL PRODUCTION

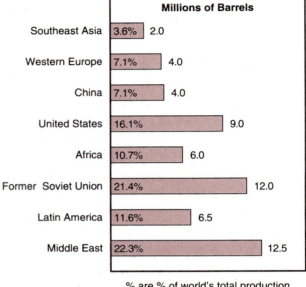

% are % of world's total production

Source: *Encyclopedia Britannica Book of the Year 1991*

OPEC's Power in the 1970s

During the 1970s, the price of oil continued to increase. The power of OPEC grew and the oil-producing Arab countries grew richer and more powerful. With their oil money, Arabs bought numerous corporations, banks, and real estate properties in Western Europe and, to a lesser degree, in the United States. The Arabs also spent billions of dollars on weapons, building up huge arsenals.

The Oil Crisis of 1979

During 1979, there was another oil price crisis as the price of oil produced by members of OPEC more than doubled. The following shows the increase in the price of oil from Saudi Arabia:

December 1978	$12.70 per barrel
June 1979	$18.00 per barrel
December 1979	$24.00 per barrel

Other OPEC members charged even more by the end of 1979. Iran's price was $28.50 per barrel and Libya's was $34.70. Part of the reason for these enormous increases was that the revolution in Iran had cut off oil exports for many months. The shortages caused panic buying and the members of OPEC took advantage of the situation to raise their prices. For the first time, prices for gasoline rose above $1.00 per gallon in the United States. During 1980, prices continued to rise. At the OPEC meeting in December 1980, a maximum price of $41 per barrel was set. The effect of these price increases was very serious. In the industrialized countries the increases resulted in high inflation, which in turn led to unemployment and lower growth in demand for imports. Third-world countries suffered also as demands for their exports fell and the prices they paid for oil rose.

By the end of 1980, the major characteristic of the Middle East was its oil wealth. It seemed that Arab banks and Arab money would play a vital role in world affairs. During the 1980s this situation changed dramatically.

OPEC's Problems in the 1980s

The price of oil, as the price of most other things, is determined largely by supply and demand. When supply is low and demand is high, prices go up. However, when the supply is greater than the demand, prices go down. The problem for OPEC throughout the 1980s was that there was a worldwide oversupply of oil—an oil glut—that was far greater than the demand. The decline in the demand for oil was caused by several factors. The high prices of the 1970s led to worldwide conservation. Several mild winters in Western Europe and the United States reduced the demand for home heating oil. The economic recessions in the United States and in many other nations during the early 1980s and again in the late 1980s caused these economies to reduce their consumption of petroleum and petroleum products.

Some oil-producing countries began to sell their oil below the official OPEC prices. As a result, OPEC lowered the official price from $34 a barrel to $29 a barrel in 1983. However, OPEC members continued to quarrel over prices and over how much oil to produce. Finally, they agreed to place a ceiling (a maximum amount) on total OPEC oil production. Each member country was assigned a **quota**—the amount that it was allowed to produce. It was hoped that the cut in production would reduce the oversupply of oil in the world and this would cause prices to stabilize and eventually to go up.

Saudi Arabia reduced its oil production substantially. But most of the other OPEC members produced more oil than their quotas and some countries sold their oil below the official OPEC price. Consequently, the oversupply of oil continued.

By following the OPEC agreement alone, Saudi Arabia suffered a serious drop in oil revenues from $100 billion in 1981 to $19 billion in 1986. The Saudis decided to increase their production. In December 1985, lead by Saudi Arabia, OPEC decided to abandon its policy of trying to maintain prices by limiting production. By March 1986, the price of oil had fallen to below $10 a barrel. As a result, OPEC member countries promised not to go above their production quotas. Since 1987, OPEC has tried to maintain the price of oil at $18 a barrel. However, with OPEC members continuing to produce above their quotas and non-OPEC countries producing at high levels, there continues to be an oversupply of oil in the world.

Iraq Invades Kuwait

Iraq's invasion of Kuwait in August 1990 and the resulting uncertainty over the supply of oil caused the price of crude oil to increase rapidly. By October 1990, prices had reached $40 a barrel, compared with about $22 at the time of the invasion. The close down of the Kuwaiti oil industry, combined with the embargo and blockage of Iraq, removed more than 4 million barrels of oil a day from the world's supply. However, no actual oil shortage developed. World supplies were high and other oil producing countries increased their production. By December 1990, the price of a barrel had dropped to the mid-$20 range.

In February 1992, OPEC oil ministers met in Geneva to discuss the problem of the oversupply of oil and low prices. Since November 1991, oil prices had fallen by 20 percent to about $16 a barrel. This sharply reduced the income of OPEC countries and hurt their economies. The OPEC ministers agreed to cut production in order to raise prices.

In the early 1980s, OPEC members believed their problems were temporary. However, in recent years there have been major oil discoveries outside the Middle East. In 1988, the Soviet Union announced that an oil field near the Caspian Sea had been evaluated as one of the world's largest. In the same year, Brazil discovered the world's largest offshore oil field. This could make Brazil an oil exporter in the 1990s. Important new oil discoveries continue to be made in the North Sea. Continued improvements in the technology for locating and producing oil at ever greater ocean depths add to the prospects of large supplies of oil in the future.

This is good news for the United States and other nations who import oil. Since the United States now imports 50 percent of its oil, oil prices are of great concern to Americans. But as more oil is produced all over the world, Middle Eastern countries will no longer be able to use oil as a "weapon."

The Arab-Israeli Conflict: The Israeli Side

The Jewish Dream: A Homeland in Israel

The roots of the Jewish people in the Middle East are very ancient. When Moses led the Hebrews out of slavery in Egypt to find the "promised land," their history as a nation began. In 70 A.D. the Jewish state came to an end when the Romans destroyed Jerusalem. Many Jews left Palestine and settled in other parts of the Middle East, North Africa, and Europe. But the Jews regarded Palestine (Israel) as their true homeland and prayed that they would one day return to their ancient land.

Those Jews who settled in Europe often found life very difficult. In some countries Jews were able to participate in commerce, banking, and the professions. But in most countries restrictions were placed upon them. They were forbidden to own land, hold political office, or enter many professions. In many countries the Jews could only live in areas that were set aside for them, known as ghettos. In addition, they were forced to pay heavy taxes and even wear special garments to identify them as Jews. The main reason for this discrimination was that the Jews wanted to preserve their religion and traditions. They resisted efforts to convert them to Christianity. Also, the Jews were a minority in the Christian countries in which they lived. As a minority they became a convenient scapegoat (target) for whatever problems existed. During bad times, feeling against them reached such a pitch that they were tortured and massacred. The situation was particularly bad in Russia, where the Jews were ordered to live in ghettos in a specific region and could not move to the large cities. Periodically, there were *pogroms* in which hundreds of homes were looted and burned and many people were killed.

Toward the end of the 19th century there was a great increase in antisemitism in Europe. Many Jews came to believe that the only solution was to have a land of their own. During the 1880s, some Jews left Russia to settle in Palestine, which was then part of the Ottoman Empire. In the 1890s, Theodore Herzl, an Austrian Jew, wrote a pamphlet called *The Jewish State*. This was the beginning of the **Zionist** movement. Zion is the name of one of the hills in Jerusalem and it became the symbol for the land of Israel. A Zionist is a person who wishes to have a Jewish homeland in Israel. Zionist organizations were set up in many countries and money was raised. Small groups of Jewish pioneers began to settle in Palestine, where they were determined to create a new way of life. Land was purchased from the Turks and as more people came, towns and cities grew.

The British and Palestine

During World War I, the British Foreign Secretary Lord Balfour issued a document that has become known as the Balfour Declaration. This document stated that Britain would "view with favor the establishment in Palestine of a national home for the Jewish people…" At the same time, however, the British made promises to Arab leaders about the future of the Arab provinces of the Ottoman Empire. At the end of the war, with the defeat of the Ottoman Empire, Palestine became a British mandate. This meant that Britain was to rule Palestine until it was ready for independence.

The Arabs Protest

As Jewish immigration increased, the Arabs living in Palestine began to fear that they would soon be outnumbered. They demanded an end to Jewish immigration and the creation of an independent Arab state in Palestine. Many times the Arabs expressed their resentment through violence, attacking Jewish settlements and killing the people.

World War II

In the 1930s, Hitler's persecution of the Jews speeded up the rate of Jewish immigration to Palestine. But just at the outbreak of World War II, in response to Arab violence, Britain severely limited this immigration. During the war, hundreds of thousands of Jews died in Nazi concentration camps. When it became known that the Nazis had killed 6 million Jews, Jewish leaders around the world began to demand the immediate establishment of a Jewish state in Palestine. The Jews felt that only by having their own country could they avoid such catastrophes in the future.

A Jewish State Is Set Up

The British realized that they could not find a solution that would be acceptable to both Jews and Arabs. Therefore, they turned the matter over to the recently created United Nations. In November 1947, the United Nations voted to divide Palestine into a Jewish state and an Arab state. The Jews accepted this solution; the Arabs did not. In May 1948, the new state of Israel declared its independence. As the British withdrew their troops, armies from six neighboring Arab states attacked Israel. Although outnumbered and fighting with inferior military equipment, the new state of Israel proved to be more than a match for the Arabs, who failed in their effort to "drive the Jews into the sea."

Israel: A Modern, Western Democracy in the Middle East

Palestine was a barren wasteland of desert and swamps when the first Jewish settlers began to arrive in the 1880s. These early Zionists brought with them the talents and skills they learned in Europe. They drained the swamps, irrigated the deserts, and planted forests. Their hard work and technology caused the deserts to bloom. Agriculture thrived and a dairy industry developed. Today, Israel is an exporter of fruits and vegetables to Europe, the United States, and other areas.

After the creation of the state of Israel in 1948, hundreds of thousands of new immigrants arrived. Many of them were trained professionals and skilled workers. They turned to manufacturing, commerce, and trade. Their skills turned Israel into a modern, industrial state. Today, many people in Israel have a high standard of living. With the exception of the oil-rich Arab lands, Israel has the highest per capita income in the Middle East.

The Jews who settled in Israel also brought with them the ideas and ideals of Western democracy and culture. They set up a system of government that is a parliamentary democracy, similar to that of Great Britain. Freedom of speech, press, and assembly, as well as many other rights, are guaranteed and protected. In fact, Israel is the only democracy in the Middle East.

Israel, like the United States, is a nation of immigrants. Soon after its independence, Israel passed the "Law of Return." This stated that any Jew who wished to settle in Israel would automatically become a citizen. Jews from almost every country in the world have immigrated to Israel. These people came with different languages, customs, and cultures. It was necessary to integrate them, to make them part of the new country. Special classes were set up to teach the new immigrants Hebrew, the language of Israel. The public schools and the Israeli Army brought people of different backgrounds together. They succeeded in creating a new nation, a new people—the Israelis.

During the 1980s, almost 20,000 Ethiopian Jews immigrated to Israel and since the late 1980s, Israel has absorbed over 300,000 Soviet Jews.

Israel Protects Its Independence

The Arabs refused to accept the existence of the state of Israel. They engaged in many border attacks against Jewish settlements and in terrorist acts inside Israel.

In 1956, Israel and Egypt fought a brief war in the Suez Canal area. The war was in part caused by continued guerrilla attacks from Egypt against Israeli settlements. Israel invaded the Sinai Peninsula and the Gaza Strip where the guerrillas were based. The United Nations stepped in to stop the fighting and then set up a U.N. Emergency Force (UNEF) to patrol the frontier between Israel and Egypt.

Between 1956 and 1967, the UNEF succeeded in preventing serious problems along the border between Israel and Egypt. However, there were occasional raids into Israel from Jordan and major attacks from Syria.

"The Six-Day War"—June 1967

In May 1967, President Nasser of Egypt began moving large numbers of Egyptian troops and tanks into the Sinai Peninsula. He demanded that the UNEF peacekeeping force leave

Egyptian territory. Egypt then closed the Strait of Tiran, preventing ships from reaching Israel through the Gulf of Aqaba. At the same time, King Hussein of Jordan gave in to mounting pressure to join the Arab cause.

Israel decided it could not allow the Arabs to strike first and risk fighting a defensive war on three fronts. Consequently, on June 5, Israel launched a "preemptive attack." This means Israel decided to attack first, before its enemies could attack. Israeli planes hit Egypt's airfields, largely destroying the Egyptian Air Force. Mastery of the air enabled the Israeli army to go after the Egyptian ground forces. At the same time, the Israeli army was engaged in fighting the Syrians in the north and the Jordanians in the west. After six days of fighting, Israel won a decisive victory. The Israeli Army occupied large amounts of Arab territory—the Sinai Peninsula and Gaza Strip belonging to Egypt, the Golan Heights of Syria and the West Bank which had been part of Jordan since Jordan annexed it in 1950. The Israelis also captured vast amounts of Soviet weapons and equipment from the Arabs.

The Six-Day War changed the map of the Middle East. It also created problems that exist to this day. Arab bitterness over Israel's victory was intense. Anti-Western feeling swept across the Arab world because of United States support for Israel. Soviet influence in the Middle East grew because the Soviet Union championed the Arab cause. After the war the Soviet Union rearmed the Egyptian, Syrian, and Iraqi armies.

After the 1967 war, there were frequent attacks along Israel's borders. Arab guerrillas entered Israeli territory, planted mines, and killed Israeli soldiers. Israeli troops retaliated.

In August 1970, a ceasefire between Israel and Egypt came into effect. For three years all was quiet along the Suez Canal, which separated the armies of the two countries.

Jerusalem

Jerusalem is a city that is sacred to people of three religions: Jews, Christians, and Muslims. For Jews, it is the holiest of all places. The Western (Wailing) Wall is all that remains of the ancient Temple of Jerusalem. It is the holiest site in Judaism. The Jewish people have a deep emotional attachment to Jerusalem. They regard it as the cradle of their culture, their religion, and their nation. King David made Jerusalem the capital of ancient Israel.

During the war of 1948, Arabs and Jews battled for control of the city. As a result of the fighting, the Israelis gained control over West Jerusalem, also known as the New City, while Arab armies occupied East Jerusalem, known as the Old City.

An armistice agreement signed by Israel and Jordan in 1949 gave each side control over the area held by its armed forces. For the next 19 years Jerusalem remained a divided city. Part of the city was Israeli and part was Jordanian—a wall and barbed wire separated the two sides. In December 1949, the Israeli government voted to make West Jerusalem the capital of Israel. For 19 years the government of Jordan did not allow Jews to enter East Jerusalem and visit the sacred sites there.

This situation was changed by the "Six-Day War," during which the Israelis captured the Old City. The Israeli government acted quickly to make East Jerusalem a permanent part of Israel. On June 27, Israel's Parliament voted to annex East Jerusalem. Soon after, a program of construction and resettlement was begun. The Israelis built new housing developments, commercial centers, and government and university buildings. Jews were resettled in and around the Old City.

Jerusalem, a city with history important to three religions: Christianity, Judaism, Islam.

At the same time, Israel promised that the religious rights of all people would be preserved. The government passed the "Protection of the Holy Places Law." This law stated that Israel would safeguard the holy places of all religions; that Christians and Muslims would have freedom of access to their Holy Places; and that each group would administer its own shrines.

Since 1967, Israel has insisted that the question of Jerusalem is different from that of the other occupied territories, that Jerusalem is not negotiable, and that it will never give up any part of Jerusalem.

The Arab-Israeli Conflict: The Arab Side

The Arabs see Israel as a foreign nation situated in the heart of the Arab world. They consider it a great injustice that people with an alien language, culture, and religion have taken over land that the Arabs regard as theirs. The area that is now Israel they call Palestine. The Arabs claim that for centuries Arabs lived in Palestine and, therefore, Palestine should be an Arab state.

As you read, during World War I, Great Britain made many conflicting promises regarding the Middle East. It promised the Arabs independence in the Arab lands that belonged to the Ottoman Empire. It issued the Balfour Declaration, saying it would view with favor a Jewish national home in Palestine. At the same time Britain and France made secret agreements to divide the Middle East into "spheres of influence"—areas that each one would dominate.

For a short time after the Balfour Declaration was issued, some important Arab leaders expressed their support for Jewish settlement in Palestine. Sherif Hussein, the chief spokesman for the Arabs at that time, called on the Arabs in Palestine to welcome the Jews as brothers and to cooperate with them for their common welfare. His son, the Amir Feisal, met with Jewish leaders in London and told them, "No true Arab can be suspicious or afraid of Jewish nationalism." In 1919, Feisal and Dr. Chaim Weizman, leader of the World Zionist Organization, signed a document assuring the Jews of their right to free immigration into Palestine and to settle on the land. Feisal came to the Paris Peace Conference in February 1919 to demand independence for the Arabs. He agreed that Palestine should be considered separately from the other Arab lands since this was the area set aside for the Jews.

Arab Opposition to a Jewish National Home

By the middle of 1919, Arab nationalism was growing throughout the Middle East. The Arabs saw their hopes for independence frustrated by Britain and France and felt betrayed. At the same time Palestinian Arab nationalism was slowly developing. The Arabs claimed that British promises for Arab independence included Palestine. Arab opposition to Zionism increased.

In 1919, Arab nationalists met and issued a statement opposing the creation of a Jewish homeland in Palestine and opposing "Zionist migration to any part of our country."

The Arabs felt that Jewish immigration had been forced on them without their consent. They were afraid that if this immigration continued, they would end up living as a minority under Jewish rule. The Arabs also feared that the Jews would dominate Palestine and that their own culture would become subordinate and eventually disappear. In addition, the Arabs regarded Zionism as another form of Western imperialism that they had to fight to protect their heritage.

The 1920s

Arab opposition to a Jewish homeland expressed itself in constant unrest in Palestine. During 1919, there were anti-Zionist demonstrations and riots. In 1920 and 1921, Arabs attacked a number of Jewish settlements, killing many Jews. Rioting in Jerusalem and in Jaffa resulted in many deaths. The Palestine Arab Congress met in 1920 and in 1921 and called on Britain to put an end to the policy of a Jewish National Home in Palestine. The Arabs demanded: (1) an end to Jewish immigration into Palestine; (2) an end to Jewish land purchases; and (3) full Arab self-government in Palestine. Arab unrest in Palestine continued throughout the 1920s.

The 1930s

In the 1930s, Palestine nationalists began a guerrilla war against the British and the Jews. In April 1936, the nationalists called a general strike. Its purpose was to force Britain to end Jewish immigration and land purchases and to grant the Palestine Arabs self-government. The strike turned into open rebellion and bands of armed guerrillas were organized. The guerrillas received active support from the neighboring Arab countries. "Committees for the Defense of Palestine" sprang up in Syria, Egypt, Iraq, and Transjordan. Syrian and Iraqi volunteers arrived in Palestine. Before 1936, the other Arab countries had not been very involved in the Palestine dispute. During the 1936 revolt, interest in the Palestine problem was awakened. Support for the nationalists in Palestine grew steadily.

After 1936, Arab nationalists also received material and moral support from Nazi Germany and Fascist Italy. The Nazis and Fascists spread anti-Jewish propaganda throughout the Middle East. They also tried to use the anti-British feeling for their own purposes.

By November 1936, Britain succeeded in putting down the rebellion. The British Government appointed a Royal Commission to study the Palestine problem. In 1937, the Commission recommended the **partition** (division) of Palestine into a Jewish State, and Arab State, and a British zone. The Arabs rejected the partition of Palestine and the establishment of a Jewish state.

The Arab revolt was resumed in the fall of 1937. Arab acts of terrorism grew in number during 1938 and 1939. At the same time Britain was facing an increasing danger of war in Europe. The British felt that their security would be endangered if the violence in the Middle East continued. Thus they gave in to Arab demands. Britain dropped the idea of partition.

White Paper

In 1939, Britain issued a "White Paper," which severely limited Jewish immigration to Palestine for the following five years. After that, Jewish immigration would depend on Arab consent. A well-known historian claims "these events taught the lesson that the use of violence as a political weapon produced results which otherwise appeared unobtainable."[1]

The Problem of the Palestinians

The Palestinian Refugees

As you read, when the state of Israel was declared in May 1948, it was attacked by armies from six Arab countries. As a result of the war, approximately 725,000 Arabs who had lived in Palestine (Israel) before the war fled to the neighboring Arab countries. These people came to be known as the Palestinian refugees. The Arabs claim that the Palestinians were forced out by the Israelis. Israel claims that the Palestinians were encouraged to leave by Arab leaders who promised them that they would soon return after Israel had been destroyed.

The Palestinians became a people without a country. Israel refused to take the refugees back, claiming their presence would endanger the survival of Israel. The Arab countries, in which the Palestinians found themselves, treated them as second-class citizens. In Egypt, Jordan, Lebanon, and Syria, the Palestinians lived in refugee camps under miserable conditions. The United Nations ran the camps and provided for the basic needs of the refugees—food, medicine, clothing, housing, and education. The Arab countries used the refugees as a political weapon against Israel. The anger and frustration felt by the Palestinians was intense. Many Palestinians became guerrillas. Encouraged by Arab leaders, they took part in bloody raids inside Israel from their bases in Egypt, Syria, and Jordan.

---

[1]J.C. Hurewitz, *The Struggle for Palestine.*

Today there are an estimated 5,500,000 Palestinians. This number includes the Arabs who live in Israel, the Arabs of the West Bank and Gaza Strip that Israel occupied in 1967, and the Palestinian Arabs who live in neighboring Arab countries.

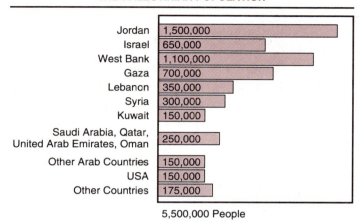

THE PALESTINIAN POPULATION

Jordan	1,500,000
Israel	650,000
West Bank	1,100,000
Gaza	700,000
Lebanon	350,000
Syria	300,000
Kuwait	150,000
Saudi Arabia, Qatar, United Arab Emirates, Oman	250,000
Other Arab Countries	150,000
USA	150,000
Other Countries	175,000

5,500,000 People

Source: *N.Y. Times Magazine* May, *1991*

Formation of the PLO

Between 1948 and 1964, the Palestinians were leaderless and unorganized. Their cause was argued for them by others. The Arab states took the lead in fighting against Israel while the Palestinians played a passive role. This situation changed after the Palestine Liberation Organization (PLO) was formed in 1964. The PLO is an "umbrella organization" with which various Palestinian groups are associated. The largest of these is al-Fatah, organized in 1959 as a secret organization by Yasir Arafat. Others are the Popular Front for the Liberation of Palestine, the Popular Democratic Front for the Liberation of Palestine, and Black September.

The goal of these organizations is the establishment of an independent Palestinian state. The PLO has tried to achieve this goal through terrorism and armed struggle. "Armed struggle is the only way to liberate Palestine." For this reason the PLO has trained and organized guerrillas to carry out terrorist acts against Israel. The PLO has also publicized the cause of the Palestinians worldwide in order to receive international support for the creation of a Palestinian state. In 1969, Yasir Arafat was named chairman of the PLO. Since 1973, Arafat has called for the acceptance of the PLO as a government-in-exile.

Jordan and the PLO

Jordan has a larger Palestinian population than any other Arab country. Approximately 70 percent of Jordan's 2,500,000 people are Palestinian. Jordan (Transjordan) was created as a country by the British in 1920 out of territory that had been Palestine. At that time most of its population was Bedouin. However, during the war of 1948 over 300,000 Arabs from Palestine fled to Jordan. In 1950, Jordan annexed the West Bank and East Jerusalem bringing hundreds of thousands more Palestinians under Jordanian rule. When Israel captured the West Bank in 1967, another 380,000 Palestinians moved to Jordan.

The PLO found it easy to recruit, train, and arm guerrillas in the refugee camps in Jordan. During the 1960s, the PLO used Jordan as a base of operations against Israel. Palestinian guerrillas crossed the border into Israel, killing civilians and soldiers and destroying property. Armed clashes along the border were frequent. By 1970, the guerrillas in Jordan had become so powerful that they were practically a state within a state. The PLO openly challenged the authority of King Hussein. This led to a brief but bloody civil war between the government and the guerrillas. Other clashes between the PLO and the Jordanian army also occurred in 1970.

In January 1971, fighting again broke out between the Palestinian guerrillas and the Jordanian Army and continued during the next few months. In July, the Jordanian Army began a major operation against the guerrilla strongholds. Within weeks the PLO strongholds were destroyed and the guerrilla movement was crushed. The struggle came to an end with the expulsion of the guerrillas from Jordan in July 1971. Although the other Arab governments protested, they failed to intervene on the side of the Palestinians. King Hussein was firmly in power.

The Palestinian guerrillas bitterly resented the actions of the Jordanian government. They referred to the events of September 1970 as "Black September." Several attempts were made to assassinate government leaders. In November 1971, the Prime Minister of Jordan was shot and killed in Cairo. An unsuccessful attempt was made on the life of the Jordanian ambassador in London. In February 1973, a group of Palestinian guerrillas was arrested after entering Jordan from Syria with a plot to overthrow the government.

The PLO in Lebanon

After the Palestinian guerrillas were crushed in Jordan in 1970–71, Lebanon became their last refuge. Beirut became the headquarters of their movement. By 1973, 10 percent of the people in Lebanon were Palestinian. The Palestinians, who were landless, poor, and exploited as a source of cheap labor, soon became more militant. They acquired armaments and used the refugee camps to train guerrillas. As the Palestinian guerrillas grew stronger, other radical groups in Lebanon sought them out as allies. During the Lebanese civil war, which began in 1975, the Palestinians became heavily involved in the fighting. (The civil war in Lebanon will be discussed later.)

The Lebanese government made repeated attempts to bring the Palestinians in Lebanon under its control but was unsuccessful. The Palestinians used southern Lebanon to shell Israeli border settlements with Soviet-made rockets and artillery fire. They also crossed the border into Israel and engaged in terrorist activities. Each attack led to Israeli retaliation. Israeli planes bombed refugee camps in southern Lebanon that Israel claimed were being used as guerrilla bases.

During the next few years the PLO and Israel continued the cycle of attacks and counterattacks.

By the early 1980s, the Palestinian guerrillas in Lebanon had become so powerful that they were practically a state within a state. It was a situation similar to that which had existed in Jordan a decade earlier. The guerrillas had accumulated an enormous arsenal of weapons supplied in large part by the Soviet Union and paid for by Saudi Arabia and some of the other Arab states. The government of Lebanon was unable to control their activities.

The Israeli Invasion—June 1982

In June 1982, Israeli troops invaded Lebanon. Israeli leaders felt it was necessary to destroy the PLO arms buildup that they regarded as a grave threat to Israel's security. Israeli troops captured town after town, while Israeli tanks and fighter planes bombed Palestinian camps in an attempt to wipe out all the guerrilla bases in southern Lebanon. Israel's stated goal was to create a 25-mile zone in southern Lebanon that would be free of Palestinian guerrillas. But it was believed that Israel hoped to completely destroy the PLO.

Israeli troops blockaded West Beirut and bombed Palestinian targets in the city. The Israelis stated that the bombardment of Beirut would not cease until the PLO removed its fighters from the city. Finding themselves trapped, the PLO had no choice but to give in. The United States helped Israel and the PLO reach an agreement providing for the evacuation of the guerrillas. In late August, approximately 6,000 PLO fighters and their leaders left Beirut to seek refuge in other Arab countries. The PLO had suffered a devastating military defeat.

The Massacre at Sabra and Shatila

In August 1982, Bashir Gemayel, leader of the Christian Phalange Party, was elected President of Lebanon. Gemayel was killed on September 14 when a bomb exploded. It was not clear who was responsible for the killing, since Gemayel had many enemies. However, the Lebanese Christians and Palestinians were long-standing enemies.

On September 16, Lebanese Christian militiamen entered the Palestinian refugee camps of Sabra and Shatila in West Beirut. They were to round up remaining Palestinian guerrillas and arms believed to have been hidden among the refugees. For the next two days the militiamen went on a rampage, brutally killing hundreds of Palestinian men, women, and children.

Israeli troops were accused of allowing the militiamen into the camps and of not intervening soon enough to stop the killings. The government of Israel appointed a commission to investigate the massacre. Its report found several Israeli generals indirectly responsible through negligence or lack of forethought. The report stated that they should have foreseen that the Christian Lebanese forces who were sent into the camps "to flush out remaining terrorists" might exact vengeance on the population after the assassination of President-elect Gemayel.

The PLO Receives Recognition

During the 1970s, the PLO made a great effort to win international support of the Palestinian cause. It also tried to win recognition for the PLO as the only representative of the Palestinian people. These efforts met with a great deal of success.

The PLO and the United Nations

In September 1974, the United Nations General Assembly for the first time included the "Palestine question" on its agenda as a subject for debate. It invited the PLO to take part in that debate. In November 1974, Yasir Arafat appeared before the General Assembly and demanded the establishment of a Palestinian state. The PLO became became the first nongovernment organization to address a session of the General Assembly.

For a number of years there was a question of who would speak for the Palestinians in any future peace talks. King Hussein and Yasir Arafat each claimed to speak in their name.

In October 1974, an Arab summit meeting was held in Rabat, Morocco. There a resolution was signed by the leaders of all the Arab states naming the PLO as the sole legitimate representative of the Palestinian people and affirming their right to an independent Palestinian state. King Hussein, under pressure from all the other Arab leaders, signed the resolution.

The PLO and Other Governments

The PLO made steady progress in gaining acceptance by other governments. In October 1974, Arafat met with the Foreign Minister of France. This was the first meeting of a Western leader with Arafat. Later that year Arafat paid official visits to several Communist countries in Eastern Europe. In 1979, Arafat held meetings with Austrian and German leaders.

He also visited Spain and Portugal. After the revolution in Iran in 1979 brought the Ayatollah Khomeini to power, Iran became an important supporter of the PLO. Israel, however, has refused to have any dealings with the PLO. Israel claims that the PLO is a terrorist organization and, therefore, refuses to negotiate with it.

The United States and the PLO

Between 1975 and 1988, the United States followed a policy of refusing to talk to or have any dealings with the PLO. This was because of the PLO's involvement in international terrorism and its refusal to recognize Israel's right to exist. But as more nations came to accept the PLO as the sole representative of the Palestinian people, there was pressure on the United State to do the same. The U.S. government insisted that it would not talk to the PLO until it officially renounced terrorism in all its forms and accepted the right of Israel to exist in peace and security with its neighbors. Although the PLO was anxious to open talks with the Americans, time and again Arafat and the PLO leadership failed to meet the American conditions.

In 1988, Arafat addressed the General Assembly of the United Nations and called for peace and a just settlement in the Middle East. He also called for a UN-sponsored peace conference. Arafat indicated that the PLO renounced terrorism and recognized Israel's right to exist.

The United States immediately announced that it would open talks with the PLO. Two days later, American and PLO officials met in Tunisia. The American decision was a victory for Arafat and the PLO. It won praise from Arab governments but was criticized by the Israeli government which called it a "dangerous blunder." However, the United States broke off its dialogue with the PLO in June 1990 after Palestinian terrorists tried unsuccessfully to land on a beach in Israel. The United States demanded that Arafat condemn the terrorists. When he refused, the United States broke off relations.

The Intifada

Causes of the Uprising

The term *intifada* refers to the Palestinian uprising in the West Bank and Gaza Strip that began in December, 1987 and continued into the 1990s. A road accident in Gaza on December 8th in which four Arabs were killed by an Israeli driver triggered the uprising. The underlying cause, however, was Palestinian frustration over the failure to achieve their goals. After 25 years their hopes for an independent Palestinian state seemed no closer.

Within hours of the accident, rioting broke out in Gaza and spread to the West Bank. Thousands of Palestinians, mainly youths, marched through the streets throwing rocks and fire bombs at Israeli soldiers, smashing windows, overturning vehicles, and setting tires on fire on the roads. In East Jerusalem, mobs of Palestinian youths also rioted in the streets.

Israel's Response

The Israeli government, army, and police were surprised by the outbreak and were unprepared for it. Young Israeli soldiers, untrained in riot-control, were sent to contain the rioting. Israeli soldiers responded with force, using tear gas, rubber bullets, and beatings to control the rioters. They shot into crowds. Suspected leaders and agitators were arrested and some were deported. Some Arab newspapers and many Arab schools were closed by the government.

Despite these measures, the Israeli army was unable to crush the revolt. Violence continued throughout 1988 and even increased in 1989. By the end of 1989 more than 600 Palestinians has been killed and thousands injured. Thousands more were in Israeli detention camps. During 1990 the rioting quieted down somewhat, but there were occasional violent eruptions.

Hamas and Other Terrorist Groups

Since the beginning of the intifada, a number of Islamic terrorist groups have emerged in the occupied territories, each claiming to represent the Palestinian people. Their violence is directed at Israelis as well as Palestinians. The most powerful and feared of these groups is the Islamic Resistance Movement, also known as *Hamas*, which means zeal in Arabic. Hamas has won over many young Palestinians who are disillusioned with the PLO's failure to achieve its goals.

Hamas is violently opposed to any compromise with Israel. It calls for an Islamic state in both Israel and the West Bank and Gaza. It insists that "there is no solution to the Palestinian problem except for Holy War." Preaching violence, Hamas incites Palestinians to attack Israelis and Israeli targets. Hamas and the other groups are also responsible for the deaths of hundreds of Arabs suspected of cooperating with the Israelis.

Effect of the Intifada

The intifada has affected Israel in a number of ways. Almost every Israeli family has a son or husband who has been called up for military service in the West Bank and Gaza. They have experienced fear and anxiety. The Israeli economy has suffered some damage. The effect of the uprising on the Palestinians has been disastrous. Normal, everyday life has come to a stop. Many schools are still closed, stores open only a few hours a day, and the curfews force people to stay indoors after dark. The Palestinian economy has suffered greatly. Businesses have lost money because of the curfews and strikes. Many Palestinians who used to work in Israel have lost their jobs because they are regarded as dangerous. This has increased unemployment in the West Bank and Gaza.

The Palestinians, Kuwait, and the Gulf War

Before Iraqi troops invaded Kuwait in August 1990, more than 300,000 Palestinians lived in Kuwait. Many of them were professionals—doctors, engineers, accountants, teachers. Many held vital jobs in oil, banking, and other industries. Others were workers who kept the economy of Kuwait running. The Palestinians in Kuwait were the wealthiest in the Middle East. Many sent money to their families in the West Bank and Gaza and this greatly helped the Palestinian economy.

The Kuwaiti people and government supported the Palestinian cause and the PLO. The Kuwaiti government provided the PLO with hundreds of millions of dollars. Many of the founders of the PLO including Yasir Arafat lived in Kuwait in the late 1950s where they planned and organized their revolutionary strategy.

All this changed with the Iraqi invasion of Kuwait. The PLO, Yasir Arafat, and most Palestinians openly sided with Iraq because Saddam Hussein promised to destroy Israel and create an independent Palestinian state. The Palestinians saw Saddam as their liberator. Many Palestinians in Kuwait collaborated with the Iraqi army. They provided the Iraqis with information that was used to arrest, torture, and kill Kuwaitis.

Iraq's defeat in the Gulf War was a terrible blow for the Palestinians. They paid dearly for backing Saddam Hussein. More than 200,000 Palestinians fled from Kuwait and they were forbidden to return. Many Palestinians still living in Kuwait are unemployed and some fear for their lives. After the war, the Kuwaiti people were very angry with the Palestinians for siding with Iraq. Some Palestinians were stopped on the streets and beaten up. Palestinians suspected of collaborating with the Iraqis were arrested and tortured. Kuwaiti courts tried accused collaborators and gave out severe penalties, including the death penalty. The government took away many of the social services the Palestinians previously had, such as free medical care and education. The Kuwaiti government replaced the Palestinians with workers from India, Pakistan, the Philippines, and other countries.

Many of the Palestinians in Kuwait would like to leave but they have no place to go. Egypt, Saudi Arabia, and the Persian Gulf states have refused to admit them. They are unwelcome in Jordan, which took in 200,000 Palestinian refugees during the Gulf crisis. The PLO lost more than $250 million a year in financial assistance that it formerly received from Kuwait, Saudi Arabia, and the other Gulf states.

Life for the Palestinians in the West Bank and Gaza worsened during the war. Fearing a real threat to Israeli security, the government clamped down on the Palestinians. The West Bank and Gaza were placed under 24-hour curfew that lasted the entire war. Palestinians could not leave their homes except to buy food and medicine. Palestinians from the territories were forbidden to travel in Israel. Because of the curfew and travel ban, most of the 120,000 Palestinians from Gaza and the West Bank who worked in Israel lost their jobs. The Palestinian economy, already crippled by the three-and-a-half year intifada, was devastated.

Palestinian support for the Iraqi occupation of Kuwait undermined their cause and lost them world support. Moreover, the war deepened the feelings of hopelessness and despair of the Palestinians.

Terrorism

In the years after World War II, many groups who were not able to win their nationalist goals began to use terrorism as a weapon. Terrorism increased dramatically during the 1970s and 1980s. Its primary targets were Israel, the United States, and several countries in Western Europe. In order to understand terrorism, it is necessary to first define it.

What is Terrorism?

Experts on the subject of terrorism have defined it in the following way, "Terrorism is the deliberate and systematic murder, maiming, and menacing of the innocent to inspire fear for political ends." The word *innocent* must be stressed. Terrorists choose innocent civilians as their victims—young children on a school bus, tourists in an airplane, or at an airport. By such actions the terrorists tell the world that they will do anything to achieve their purpose, which is to make governments give in to their demands. The word *deliberate* is also important. In every war there are civilian casualties, but in most cases these deaths are tragic accidents. Terrorists, however, deliberately choose civilians as their victims. The word *systematic* indicates that an act of terrorism is not an isolated incident, but part of a campaign of repeated attacks.

Terrorists describe themselves as freedom fighters and guerrillas to win sympathy for themselves and their cause. This is not true. There is a difference between guerrillas and terrorists. Guerrillas are irregular soldiers who wage war on regular military forces, not on civilians. Terrorists attack defenseless civilians.

Terrorists try to explain their acts as resulting from the desperation of their group. They seek worldwide publicity for their cause. The media—television, radio, newspapers—plays a very important role in their actions. The terrorists hope to get a worldwide audience to accept their point of view.

Terrorism is not something new in history. But today's terrorism differs greatly from earlier forms of terrorism. Present-day terrorism began its rapid growth in the 1960s. It was then that the PLO introduced airline hijacking as an international weapon. At the same time European terrorist groups carried out bombings, kidnappings, and assassinations throughout the continent. Terrorist groups soon spread throughout Europe, Japan, North America, South America, and the Middle East. Evidence shows that these groups are often linked to one another and to various governments that support them. There is also a strong tie between the PLO and terrorist groups in other countries.

The Central Role of the PLO

Between 1968 and 1991, the PLO carried out hundreds of terrorist attacks against civilian targets inside Israel and Israeli and Jewish targets abroad. In addition, the PLO cooperated with many terrorist groups in other nations.

During the 1970s, southern Lebanon fell under the control of the PLO. It became the center for operations against Israel and for international terrorism as well. For nearly a decade, until 1982, the PLO was the only terrorist group in existence to possess a "ministate." Terrorists from all over the world came to Lebanon where they were trained, armed, and indoctrinated.

"State-Supported Terrorism"

Terrorism could not have reached such proportions without the support of a number of governments. Terrorist groups acting alone do not have the means to carry out continued attacks or to survive for very long. Governments provide sanctuary—a place to escape capture or punishment. Governments also provide terrorists with money, weapons, training, and intelligence. Several Middle Eastern nations have actively supported terrorist organizations. They are Libya, Iran, Syria, Iraq, and South Yemen. Terrorist groups also received support directly or indirectly from the former Soviet Union, some of the former Communist countries of Eastern Europe, North Korea, and Cuba.

Libya

Since Colonel Qaddafi came to power in 1969, Libya has supported many terrorist groups around the world. Hijackers of planes and other terrorists were able to escape justice by finding a haven in Libya where they were received as heros. Moreover, the government of Colonel Qaddafi claims the right to "eliminate" Libyans living abroad who were opponents of his regime. In the 1980s, assassination attempts, some successful and others unsuccessful, took place in Italy, Greece, West Germany, Britain, Egypt, and the United States.

Libya supplied money and weapons to terrorists for their activities abroad. For some years Libya sent weapons and Libyan "volunteers" to the PLO in Lebanon. In 1985 and 1986, Libya was implicated in a number of terrorist attacks. In November 1985, an Egyptian plane was hijacked and flown to Malta. The hijacking and the Egyptian rescue operation resulted in 67 deaths. The Egyptian government claimed that Libya planned and financed the hijacking and said that two of the hijackers came from Libya. The United States blamed Libya for bombing a West Berlin discotheque frequented by American military personnel in April 1986. Two people were killed and about 200 injured.

In April 1986, United States planes bombed the Libyan cities of Tripoli and Benghazi and their surrounding areas. President Reagan claimed that the attack was in response to Libya's involvement in "international terrorism."

Syria Syria actively supported a number of Palestinian terrorist organizations. These include the Popular Front for the Liberation of Palestine, Popular Front for the Liberation of Palestine—General Command, and Democratic Front for the Liberation of Palestine. Syria also supported the Abu Nidal group, a radical terrorist organization that broke away from the PLO in 1974. From 1980 to 1985, the headquarters of the Abu Nidal organization was in Damascus. In 1985, Abu Nidal moved his headquarters to Libya, but he continued to maintain an office in Damascus, as well as training camps in various parts of Syria. In December 1985, terrorists attacked passengers at the El Al check-in counters at the Vienna and Rome airports. The Abu Nidal group claimed responsibility for the attacks. The two terrorist gangs that carried out the massacres came from Damascus. The United States claimed that Libya was also involved in the attacks.

Iran In 1979, Ayatollah Khomeini and his religious followers took power in Iran. They are followers of the Shi'ite branch of Islam. One of the beliefs of this sect is that it is the duty of Muslims to "offer themselves in sacrifice for the sake of their cause." Since then Iranian and pro-Iranian "suicide squads" have been involved in many terrorist activities. Iran provides money, weapons, and sanctuary for terrorists.

Iraq Iraq has been an active supporter of terrorist groups. Its involvement in a longstanding war with Iran, however, limited Iraq's ability to provide assistance to terrorist groups. Iraq supports the Abu Nidal group which was based there until 1980.

Except for Iran, all of these countries—Libya, Syria, Iraq, and Yemen, had close ties with the Soviet Union. They received most of their arms from the Soviet Union. The Soviet Union supported the PLO politically and militarily. PLO leaders publicly acknowledged that thousands of their people had been trained in the USSR. Most of the PLO's weapons came from the Soviet Union. The Soviet Union justified its support for terrorist groups by calling them "national liberation movements."

Islamic Jihad

In 1982, a new group emerged in the Middle East: Islamic Jihad or "Islamic Holy War." In 1983–84, it claimed responsibility for four attacks on United States diplomatic and military installations that killed more than 315 people. Islamic Jihad is made up of Shi'ite Muslims loyal to Iran. All of its targets have been Western nations or pro-Western Muslim nations. The people who carry out its missions are known as "volunteers for martyrdom."

In October 1983, a suicidal terrorist drove a truckload of explosives into the U.S. Marine Corps headquarters in Beirut. The explosion demolished the building and killed 239 U.S. servicemen. Almost simultaneously, another truck filled with explosives smashed into the building used as a barracks by French paratroopers in Lebanon, killing 58. One of the groups claiming responsibility for the attacks was Islamic Jihad. It is believed that Iran was connected with the attacks.

Terrorism: 1968–1991

Since the Six-Day War of 1967, there has been an increase in Arab terrorism against Israel. The targets have been Israeli civilians in Israel and Israeli representatives and tourists abroad. Jewish religious institutions and Jewish-owned businesses in Europe and other places have also been targets. In some cases, non-Arab terrorist groups were involved. In recent years, Americans and Europeans have become victims of terrorism as well.

The following chart is a partial list of some of these terrorist attacks. Israel has often responded to these attacks by bombing Palestinian camps in Lebanon.

TERRORIST ATTACKS

1968	Nov.	Dynamiting of a Jerusalem market results in 12 deaths.
	Dec.	Two terrorists attack El Al plane in Athens; 1 killed, 2 wounded.
1969	Feb.	Four Arab terrorists machine-gun Israeli (El Al) plane in Zurich, Switzerland; co-pilot killed, 5 passengers injured.
		Terrorist bombing of Jerusalem supermarket causes 2 deaths.
	Mar.	Cafeteria at Jerusalem's Hebrew University bombed.
	Aug.	Arab hijackers order TWA jet to Damascus, bomb the cockpit, and hold 2 Israelis hostage.
	Nov.	Arabs bomb El Al office in Athens. A child is killed.
1970	Feb.	Bomb aboard Swissair plane bound for Israel causes plane to explode in midair, killing all 38 passengers.
	May	Arab bazookas attack Israeli school bus near the Lebanese border, killing 8 children and wounding 20.
1971	May	Israeli Counsul General kidnapped and slain in Istanbul.
1972	July	Three Japanese guerrillas, supporting the Palestinian cause, open fire with their machine guns at Israel's airport, killing 28.
	Sept.	Arab terrorists kidnap and kill 11 Israeli athletes at the Olympics in Munich, Germany.
	Nov.	Letter bombs are mailed to Israeli embassies in many countries, as well as Jewish firms.
1973	Apr.	Arab terrorists bomb the residence of Israel's ambassador in Cyprus.
		Arabs murder Italian clerk at El Al office in Rome.
	July	Palestinians attack El Al office in Athens; release hostages after negotiations with police.
	Aug.	Two Palestinians machine-gun passengers in lounge of Athens airport; 4 dead, 55 wounded.
	Sept.	Three Jewish immigrants from Russia taken hostage by 2 Palestinians aboard train bound for Vienna; hostages released after Austrian government promises to close transit camp for Russian emigrants en route to Israel.
	Dec.	Five Arabs attack Pan American and Lufthansa planes at Rome airport; 32 passengers killed; Pan Am plane badly damaged and Lufthansa plane hijacked with 13 hostages.
1974	Apr.	Three Arab terrorists kill 18 men, women, and children in Israeli town of Qiryat Shemona.
	May	Three Arab terrorists kill 20 teenage students, a four-year-old boy and his parents, 2 Arab-Israeli women, and 1 Israeli soldier at the Israeli village of Ma'alot.
	June	Three Arab terrorists murder 3 women at farm settlement of Shamir; 4 Israelis killed in raid on Nahariya by Arab terrorists.
	Nov.	Three Palestinian terrorists machine-gun their way into apartment building in Israeli town of Beit She-an; 4 dead, 23 wounded.
1975	Jan.	Two Arab terrorists attempt to machine-gun El Al jet; 20 people wounded.
	Mar.	Eight Arab terrorists shoot their way into Savoy Hotel in Tel Aviv and take hostages; 3 Israeli soldiers and 8 civilians killed.
	July	Bomb explodes in Zion Square in Jerusalem, killing 13 and wounding 63.
1976	June	Arab and other terrorists hijack an Air France plane carrying a majority of Israeli and other Jewish passengers and fly it to Entebbe airport in Uganda. They threaten to blow up the plane and kill the passengers unless their demands are met. On July 4, 1976, Israeli commandos, in a daring raid, free the captives and fly them to safety.
1977	Dec.	Explosion in Netanya, Israel; 2 killed, 2 wounded.

1978	Jan.	Explosion in Jaffa, Israel; 2 killed.
	Feb.	Explosion on a Jerusalem bus; 2 killed, 46 wounded.
	Mar.	Arab terrorists hijack bus outside Tel Aviv; 34 Israelis, 1 American killed.
	May	Three terrorists attack passengers waiting at El Al terminal at Orly Airport, Paris, killing 2 people, wounding 2 others.
	June	Bomb explodes on Jerusalem bus; 6 killed, 19 injured.
		Explosion in Jerusalem market; 2 killed, 35 wounded.
	Aug.	Explosion in Jerusalem's Carmel Market; 2 killed, 50 wounded.
		Five terrorists attack bus carrying El Al crew members in Great Britain, killing 1 stewardess, wounding 3 other crew members.
1979	Mar.	Bomb explodes in Jewish-owned restaurant in Paris, injuring 26 people.
	Apr.	Bomb explodes at Israeli Embassy in Ankara, Turkey.
		Three terrorists attack El Al passengers at Brussels, Belgium, airport, wounding 12.
		Explosion at Jewish community center in Vienna, Austria and at a Vienna synagogue.
1980	Jan.	Manager of El Al office in Turkey murdered.
	Apr.	Explosion in Cairo, Egypt synagogue.
	July	Terrorist throws grenade at a group of children near Agudat Israel office in Antwerp, Belgium, killing 1 child and wounding 19 adults and children.
	Oct.	Bomb explodes in front of synagogue in Paris, killing 3 and wounding 20.
	Dec.	Bomb explodes in Jewish-owned hotel in Nairobi, Kenya, killing 20 and injuring 85.
1981	Aug.	Bomb explodes next to El Al office at Rome, Italy, airport, killing 1.
		Terrorists attack synagogue in Vienna, Austria with grenades and machine guns, killing 2 and wounding 19.
	Oct.	Bomb explodes in front of El Al office, Rome, Italy, wounding 8.
		Car bomb explodes opposite synagogue in Antwerp, Belgium, killing 2, wounding 90.
1982	Jan.	Bomb explodes at Israeli restaurant in West Germany, killing 1, injuring 24.
	Apr.	Terrorist assassinates Israeli embassy attaché outside his residence in Paris France.
	June	Israel's ambassador to Britain shot in the head and badly injured. Abu Nidal group held responsible.
	Aug.	Grenade attack on Jewish restaurant in Paris; 6 killed and 25 wounded.
	Sept.	Terrorists attack synagogue in Brussels, Belgium; 4 injured.
	Oct.	Two terrorists attack worshippers at Rome's central synagogue, killing an infant and wounding 34 people.
1983	Dec.	Two terrorists throw incendiary bombs at car of Israeli Counsul General in Alexandria, Egypt.
1984	June	Terrorists injure Israeli embassy officer in Cairo, Egypt.
1985	Feb.	Bomb explodes at Marks and Spencer department store in France, killing 1, wounding 15.
	June	Terrorists hijack TWA plane en route from Cairo to Athens, and force it to be flown to Beirut. Passengers held hostage from June 14 to June 30; 1 American soldier killed.
	Aug.	Israeli embassy employee killed, his wife and secretary injured in Cairo.
	Sept.	Two bombs explode in businesses affiliated with Israel in Copenhagen, Denmark, injuring 78.
		Three terrorists from Yasir Arafat's Fatah organization take over Israeli yacht at the Larnaca marina in Cyprus; 3 Israelis murdered.
	Oct.	Two Israeli sailors kidnapped and murdered in Madrid, Spain.
		Four Arab terrorists hijack Italian cruise ship, Achille Lauro, off the coast of Egypt. One passenger, Leon Klinghoffer, an invalid from New York, murdered and thrown into the Mediterranean.
	Nov.	Egyptian plane hijacked and forced to land at Malta; 8 killed, 7 injured. During Egyptian rescue operation, 58 killed, 23 injured.

	Dec.	Two explosions at large department stores in Paris, killing 3, injuring 39. Three terrorists attack El Al counter at Vienna Airport, killing 3, injuring 75. Four terrorists attack El Al counter at Rome Airport, killing 13 and injuring 74.
1986	Mar.	Israelis leaving Cairo International Trade Fair in their car attacked by gunmen; 1 dead, 3 wounded. Bomb explodes on Champs-Elysées in Paris, killing 2 and wounding 21.
	Apr.	Explosion on TWA plane en route to Athens; 4 killed, 9 wounded. Bomb explodes in West Berlin discotheque frequented by American military personnel, killing 2 and wounding about 200. Terrorist attack on El Al plane in London Airport averted by security personnel. Woman carrying explosives arrested before boarding.
	June	Booby-trapped suitcase explodes at El Al check-in counter in Madrid Airport, wounding 13.
	Sept.	Five bomb explosions in Paris during September were linked to demands for the release of a Lebanese terrorist, Georges Ibrahim Abdallah, who had been convicted of terrorist acts in France; 10 dead, more than 160 wounded. Iran and Syria linked with the terrorists.
	Sept.	Massacre of worshippers at Istanbul, Turkey, synagogue; 22 people killed. It is believed that Abu Nidal group carried out the massacre and that governments of Syria, Libya, and Iran cooperated.
1991	Mar.	Bombing of the Israeli Embassy in Buenos Aires, Argentina; 32 people killed, more than 250 people wounded.

Pan Am Flight 103

On December 21, 1988, Pan Am flight 103 exploded in mid-air and crashed to the ground in the small town of Lockerbie, Scotland. All 259 passengers and crew members were killed. Many of the passengers were U.S. servicemen and college students returning home for the Christmas holidays.

It soon became known that the plane was destroyed by plastic explosives. It was also revealed that American embassies in Europe and the Middle East had received warnings from Washington more than a week earlier that a bomb threat had been made against Pan Am flights.

After many months of investigation by Scotland Yard (British National Police) and the FBI, it was revealed that the bombing was a widespread operation. Evidence pointed to the involvement of Palestinian, Syrian, Iranian, and Libyan terrorists. Government investigations continued until the fall of 1991, when the United States and Britain formally accused two Libyan terrorists of responsibility. Both governments demanded that Libya turn over the terrorists to stand trial, but the Libyan government refused. In March 1992, the United Nations threatened Libya with sanctions if it did not agree to turn over the terrorists. After Libya refused, the sanctions went into effect. All international flights to and from Libya were prohibited.

Issues Dividing the Arabs and Israel: 1967 to the Present

The Occupied Territories

As you read, during the War of 1967, the Israeli army captured large amounts of Arab territory: the Sinai Peninsula and the Gaza Strip from Egypt, the Golan Heights from Syria, and the West Bank from Jordan. Immediately after the war, Israeli leaders said they were prepared to trade the land for peace. They called on the Arab leaders to meet with them to negotiate a peace settlement. But the Arabs refused to negotiate with Israel. They demanded that Israel return all the territories occupied during the war.

In November 1967, the U.N. Security Council passed Resolution 242. It called for the establishment of peace and security in the Middle East and for Israel to withdraw from the Arab territories captured in the War of 1967.

Over the years Israel repeatedly called for direct negotiations with the Arabs; however, the Arabs refused. In 1977, Egypt became the first Arab state to negotiate with Israel. (See page 104.) This resulted in Israel returning the Sinai Peninsula to Egypt several years later.

The Golan Heights

Syria demands that Israel return the Golan Heights, a mountainous area that overlooks northern Israel. Israel claims it can never return this area to Syria. Before the 1967 war, the Syrians kept artillery and missiles there that they fired at Israeli towns and villages. Israel says that to return the Golan Heights to Syria would expose its northern communities to grave danger.

The West Bank and Gaza

The problem of the West Bank is very complicated. Immediately following the 1967 war, Israel declared that it was willing to return most of the West Bank, but would hold onto small sections for security reasons. As the years passed without a peace settlement, many people in Israel became determined to hold onto much or all of the West Bank permanently. A look at a map of the Middle East shows why this is so. Israel claims that returning to the insecure boundary lines that existed before the 1967 war would leave Israel about 9 to 12 miles wide at its narrowest points and in danger of being cut in two by its enemies. Israel insists that it must have defensible borders. In addition, many people in Israel claim that the West Bank and the Gaza Strip should not be returned to the Arabs because they were historically part of the land of Israel and are part of the biblical heritage of the Jews. Many Israelis, however, disagree and believe that Israel should give up most of this territory in return for peace with the Arabs.

ISRAEL—1948–PRESENT

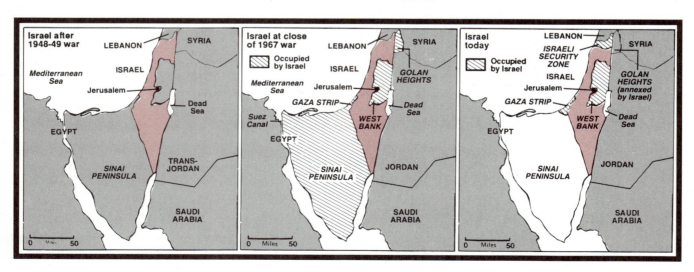

Israeli Settlements in the Occupied Territories

During the first decade of Israeli occupation, there was not much resistance on the part of the Arabs living in the West Bank. This was partly due to the fact that Israel provided the Arabs with improved housing, health care, electricity, jobs, and economic opportunities. In the late 1970s, however, when the Israeli government began to build Jewish settlements in the West Bank, the Arabs reacted with anger. They claimed this showed that Israel had no intention of returning the West Bank. Since the 1970s, the government of Israel has continued to encourage Israelis to build settlements in the occupied territories. Thousands of Israelis have moved to these areas and built houses, factories, roads, and schools. Some of the settlements are now small cities.

A Palestinian State

There are over 1 million Arabs (Palestinians) living in the West Bank and 700,000 living in Gaza. The Arabs demand that Israel give up these areas so that a Palestinian state can be established there. The Palestinian Arabs claim they have the right to independence and a country of their own. The Israeli government and most Israelis oppose the creation of an independent Palestinian state on Israel's borders fearing it would be a threat to Israel. Many Israelis claim that the Palestinians already have a country—Jordan, which is over 70 percent Palestinian in population. The Israeli government favors autonomy or self-rule for the Palestinian Arabs living in the West Bank and Gaza. This means that the Arabs would elect officials to carry out most functions of local government, except police and military control.

Jerusalem   To Muslims, the city of Jerusalem is next in holiness after Mecca and Medina. When Israel captured and annexed East Jerusalem in 1967 the Arabs were outraged that the Israelis became the guardians of the Muslim Holy Places. Soon after the annexation, a meeting of the Islamic Council in Cairo called on Muslims throughout the world to wage a jihad to liberate Jerusalem. For years the rulers of Saudi Arabia and other Arab leaders continued to call on Muslims everywhere to join in the struggle to recover Jerusalem. The Arabs insist that Muslims will never accept Israeli control over East Jerusalem.

War, Oil, Politics: The Yom Kippur War and Its Aftermath

The Yom Kippur War

On October 6, 1973, Egyptian troops crossed the Suez Canal and attacked Israeli troops stationed in the Sinai Peninsula. At the same time, Syria attacked Israeli forces in the Golan Heights. In this way the fourth Arab-Israeli war began. This war has come to be known as the Yom Kippur War because the Arab attack came on Yom Kippur, the holiest day of the Jewish year. The Israelis were caught off guard and were unprepared.

Soviet Assistance

For the Arabs, much had changed since the War of 1967. The Soviet Union had poured more than $3 billion worth of planes, tanks, missiles, and other sophisticated weapons into Egypt and Syria. Thousands of Soviet advisors and technicians had been sent to teach them how to use the equipment.

Israel used its excellent air force very effectively in 1967. However, in 1973, the Soviet-built missile systems of the Arabs largely reduced the effectiveness of Israel's air force. The Syrians also used Soviet-built missiles against Israeli towns and kibbutzim in the north, killing and injuring civilians.

Arab Strengths

The Syrian and Egyptian forces were joined by troops from other Arab countries. Iraq, Jordan, and Morocco sent troops to aid the Syrians. Kuwaiti, Tunisian, and Sudanese troops joined the Egyptians. Although Lebanon stayed out of the war, Palestinians on the Lebanese border fired at Israeli villages. North Korean pilots flew the latest Soviet jets for the Egyptians, and North Vietnamese instructors helped the Syrians with their surface-to-air missiles. For Israel, fighting in the 1973 war was the bitterest and casualties were the heaviest for all four Arab-Israeli wars.

The Syrian Front

During the first two days of fighting, the Syrians outnumbered the Israelis 10 to 1. The Israeli Air Force suffered heavy losses because of the Soviet missiles. By the sixth day of fighting, however, Syrian troops were repelled and pushed off the Golan Heights. Israeli troops then moved toward Damascus, the Syrian capital, and came within 20 miles of it. Syria lost 50 percent of its tanks and 30 percent of its jets in the first week of fighting.

The Egyptian Front

On the Egyptian front the Israelis also suffered early losses. Within days, however, the Israelis were able to stop the Egyptian offensive. By the third week the tide of war had changed. Israeli tank forces crashed through the Egyptian line in the Sinai and swept across the Suez Canal. Israeli tanks destroyed many of Egypt's missile installations, enabling the Israeli Air Force to operate freely. The Egyptians suffered heavy losses.

The Cease-fire

On October 16, Soviet Premier Alexei Kosygin arrived in Cairo. Convinced that the Egyptian forces faced disaster, he urgently requested a cease-fire. The United States immediately agreed to the Soviet demand for a cease-fire between Israel and Egypt. Israel was pressured into accepting the U.N. cease-fire even though it was close to winning the war. Egypt, then Syria, accepted the cease-fire. Iraq, Kuwait, Algeria, and the Palestinians rejected it. Libya called for a continued all-out war to destroy Israel.

Big Power Politics

Almost as soon as the fighting began, the Soviet Union started a massive round-the-clock air and sea lift to Egypt and Syria. The Soviet Union sent them hundreds of tanks, anti-tank missiles, and surface-to-air missiles. This rearming continued throughout the war and for many months afterwards. In addition, Soviet diplomats in the Middle East tried to encourage Lebanon, Algeria, and Jordan to join in the fighting. In response to the Soviet airlift, American cargo planes were soon carrying 1,000 tons of war equipment to Israel each day—roughly the same amount that the Soviets were sending to the Arabs.

Israel's Isolation

Most of the nations of the world turned away from Israel. Western Europe and Japan, depending heavily on oil from the Middle East, were afraid the Arabs would cut off their oil supplies. Some African countries broke off relations with Israel. These nations, realizing how wealthy and powerful the Arabs had become, hoped to win favor with them. Israel became much more dependent on the United States for military, economic, and political support.

As soon as the war broke out, King Faisal of Saudi Arabia threatened the United States with an oil embargo if the United States supplied Israel with war materials. The leader of Kuwait stated that "we will use oil as a means of putting pressure on countries that side with Israel." The OPEC oil embargo against the United States and Holland, as well as the cutback in oil production, lasted many months. In the United States there were gasoline shortages for months and in many parts of the country gasoline was rationed. The price of oil for heating homes increased greatly.

In Europe and Japan a real state of emergency developed. All over Europe oil was rationed. Japan faced the "worst threat to its economy and way of life since World War II." The Arabs, taking advantage of the situation, demanded that Japan break off diplomatic relations with Israel. The Japanese finally admitted that they might have to shift their foreign policy closer to the Arabs to avoid economic catastrophe.

The First Israeli-Egyptian Agreement

Following the war, since the Arabs and Israelis could not agree on prisoner exchange or any other issues, they turned to the United States for help. Secretary of State Henry Kissinger worked for almost two years to bring about several agreements between the two sides. He traveled from the United States to Israel, Egypt, and Syria many times. This came to be known as shuttle diplomacy.

In January 1974, with Kissinger's help, Israel and Egypt reached an agreement. It provided for Israel to withdraw from the area along the Suez Canal, a United Nations force to be stationed between the two armies, and limits on the number of tanks, artillery, and missiles in the area along the U.N. buffer zone.

The agreement was a set of compromises. Many important things were left out. Israel had demanded that Egypt issue a statement of nonbelligerence (a promise not to go to war), but the Egyptians refused. Egypt had demanded a timetable for total Israeli withdrawal from all Arab territory occupied in the 1967 war. Israel had refused. But the agreement was viewed by many as a first step toward future agreements.

Agreement with Syria

One of the many unsolved problems was the border between Israel and Syria. During the 1967 war, Israel occupied the Golan Heights. In the 1973 war, Israel captured more Syrian territory. Syria demanded the return of all its territory, but Israel would only discuss the return of territory captured in the 1973 war.

After many months of negotiations, Kissinger worked out an agreement that was signed by Israel and Syria in July 1974. This meeting was historic because it was the first time that these two bitter enemies met face to face other than on the battlefield. The agreement provided for Syria to recover the land it lost in the 1973 war, assigned a United Nations force to police the cease-fire, and allowed for the repatriation (return to their own country) of the prisoners of war and the return of the dead.

The Second Israeli-Egyptian Agreement

In 1975, Kissinger began another round of shuttle diplomacy between Israel and Egypt. In September 1975, after many months of negotiations, an agreement was signed between Israel and Egypt. It provided for further Israeli withdrawal from the Sinai Peninsula, including the return to Egypt of important oil fields. Egypt agreed to allow ships carrying nonmilitary cargoes for Israel to pass through the Suez Canal, provided they did not fly the Israeli flag. Both parties agreed not to resort to the threat or use of force against each other, but to settle any conflict between them by peaceful means.

The United States made secret promises to Israel and Egypt to help bring about the settlement. It promised Israel large quantities of additional U.S. weapons, compensation for the loss of the Sinai oil fields, and approximately $2.5 billion in aid. Egypt was promised $500 million in grants and increased food aid. United States prestige in the Middle East grew.

Opposition

There was much opposition to the agreement. In Israel, many people felt that Kissinger had forced them to give up positions that were vital to their security and that they received nothing in return from Egypt. The main opposition came from other Arab countries. Iraq, Libya, Algeria, Syria, and the PLO condemned the agreement and called Sadat a "traitor" to the Arab cause. Syria and the PLO opposed any separate agreement between Egypt and Israel. They wanted a general agreement that would provide for Israeli withdrawal from all occupied territory. They were afraid that if they could not count on Egypt to go to war against Israel they might never recover these territories.

After the agreement, the Arabs concentrated their efforts on having Israel expelled from the United Nations. The conference of Islamic foreign ministers, held in Saudia Arabia, unanimously adopted a resolution proposed by Syria and the PLO. It called on Islamic states to cut all ties with Israel and to press for Israel's expulsion from the United Nations. Egypt's opposition was critical in preventing Israel from being expelled from the United Nations. After they failed in this attempt, the Arabs were successful in getting the General Assembly of the United Nations to pass a resolution condemning Zionism as "a form of racism." (This resolution was repealed at the end of 1991.)

Israel and Egypt: A New Relationship

President Sadat's Visit to Israel

On November 19, 1977, President Anwar el-Sadat of Egypt arrived in Israel on what he called "a sacred mission," to speak directly to the people of Israel about peace. It was the first visit ever of an Arab leader to the Jewish state.

In the months preceding Sadat's visit, the United States had tried to get Israel and the Arabs to come together to discuss a peace settlement. Discussions continued for months but there was no real movement toward peace.

Sadat decided to take the initiative and Prime Minister Begin responded with an invitation. Sadat believed that peace was necessary to improve the Egyptian economy, which had debts of $13 billion. In a peaceful climate, Egypt could spend less money on weapons and improve the lives of its people. Investors from the industrial nations would be eager to invest money in Egypt to build up its economy.

Anwar Sadat, President of Egypt 1970–1981.

Gamal Abdel Nasser, Prime Minister of Egypt 1954–1956, President of Egypt 1956–1970.

Hosni Mubarak, President of Egypt since 1981.

Sadat was taking a big risk. Reaction to his trip by many of the Arab countries was violent. There were threats to assassinate him. But, for the most part, the Egyptian people stood behind Sadat and, most important, he had the backing of the military. Three moderate Arab states, Tunisia, Morocco, and the Sudan, approved of the trip.

Arab opposition to Sadat's trip was based on the following reasons: (1) fear that Sadat might abandon the Arab cause and make a separate peace agreement with Israel; (2) fear that Sadat, by setting foot in Israel, was granting *de facto* recognition to (recognizing the existence of) a state that Arab radicals refused to accept; (3) that Sadat, by addressing the Knesset (Israel's Parliament) in Jerusalem was acknowledging Jerusalem as Israel's capital.

When Sadat addressed the Israeli Parliament, he told the Israelis that he accepted the existence of Israel and that "we welcome you to live among us in security and safety." Sadat made a strong plea for peace, but neither he nor Begin offered any compromise on the major problems dividing the Arabs and Israelis. A lasting peace in the Middle East, Sadat said, depended on Israeli withdrawal from all the occupied Arab lands, including East Jerusalem and recognition of the rights of the Palestinians for the establishment of a Palestinian state.

Further Contacts—The Meeting in Ismailia

On December 25, 1977, the second meeting between President Sadat and Prime Minister Begin of Israel took place. It was held in the Egyptian city of Ismailia. The meeting did not produce any major breakthrough. Begin offered to return to Egypt almost all of the Sinai Peninsula that was still occupied by Israel. Sadat refused to accept a separate agreement on the Sinai. He demanded full Israeli withdrawal from all occupied Arab territories. The two leaders pledged to continue their efforts for peace.

The United States as Intermediary

Many meetings were held between Egyptian and Israeli officials between November 1977 and January 1978 to try to work out a solution to the problems that divided them. When these direct discussions broke down, the United States stepped in as an intermediary. President Carter visited the Middle East and met with Israeli and Egyptian leaders. Prime Minister Begin and President Sadat came to the United States on separate occasions for talks with President Carter. Both sides remained deadlocked, however, with no movement toward a peaceful settlement. The issues that divided them were deep and crucial.

The Camp David Accords

In 1978, President Carter invited Israeli Prime Minister Begin and Egyptian President Sadat to meet with him in the United States. The three leaders met at Camp David and there Begin and Sadat reached an historic agreement. In return for the establishment of normal relations between Israel and Egypt, Israel agreed to return all of the Sinai Desert to Egypt and to remove its settlements from the region. Both sides agreed to begin peace talks within a few weeks that would lead to an Egyptian-Israeli peace treaty.

Many questions were left open, however, such as the future of the West Bank and the Israeli settlements there as well as Palestinian rights. The agreements did not commit Israel to withdraw from all of the occupied Arab territories. There was violent opposition to the Camp David accords (agreements) in the Arab world.

President Anwar el-Sadat, President Jimmy Carter, and Prime Minister Menachem Begin join hands after signing the historic peace treaty on May 26, 1979.

Egypt and Israel Sign a Peace Treaty Ending a State of War of 30 Years

In October 1978, Israeli and Egyptian representatives came to Washington to begin negotiations for a peace treaty based on the accords reached at Camp David. Negotiations between Israeli and Egyptian officials continued for weeks and then broke down. President Carter personally intervened. He invited Prime Minister Begin to the United States and presented him with U.S. compromise proposals. Carter then flew to the Middle East and met with President Sadat in Egypt and with Prime Minister Begin in Israel.

On March 26, 1979, Prime Minister Begin and President Sadat signed the historic peace treaty on the White House lawn in Washington. The treaty formally ended the state of war that had existed between Israel and Egypt since 1948. Egypt became the first Arab nation to sign a peace treaty with Israel.

According to the treaty, Israel was to return the Sinai Peninsula to Egypt, withdrawing in stages over a period of three years. Egypt would grant Israel full diplomatic recognition. The treaty provided for Israeli and Egyptian officials to carry on negotiations for Palestinian autonomy. The treaty left out the very complicated issues of Israeli withdrawal from the other occupied Arab territories, Israeli settlements on the West Bank, and the status of Jerusalem.

President Carter tried to win "moderate" Arab support for the treaty, mainly from Saudi Arabia and Jordan. These efforts failed. The Arab League Council suspended Egypt's membership in the League and transferred headquarters from Cairo to Tunis. Most of the Arab states broke diplomatic relations with Egypt. The Arab oil-producing nations ended their substantial subsidies to Egypt, which hurt its economy. It was not until 1989 that Egypt was readmitted to the Arab League.

The Peace Initiatives: Efforts to Resolve the Arab-Israeli Conflict

Although Israel and Egypt officially made peace, peace between Israel and the rest of the Arab world has not yet been achieved. In recent years many attempts have been made to resolve the Arab-Israeli conflict. These attempts have focused on the future of the Palestinians and the "occupied territories." So far, all attempts have failed.

Arab Peace Proposals

Between 1979 and 1981, Egyptian and Israeli representatives met numerous times to negotiate an agreement on autonomy (self-government) for the Palestinians living in the West Bank and Gaza Strip, but failed to come to an agreement.

Saudi Arabia's Peace Plan

In August 1981, Crown Prince Fahd (now King Fahd) of Saudi Arabia proposed a peace plan. It called for Israel to withdraw from all the occupied territories, for the dismantling (tearing down) of Israeli settlements in these areas, and the establishment of an independent Palestinian state with East Jerusalem as its capital. The plan accepted Israel's right to exist within secure boundaries. Yasir Arafat, leader of the Palestinian Liberation Organization (PLO), said he was willing to consider the plan, but radical Palestinians rejected it as did Syria, Libya, Algeria, and Israel.

Arab League Peace Plan

In September 1982, leaders of the Arab League nations met in Fez, Morocco and adopted a peace plan very similar to the Fahd plan of the year before. A major difference was that the plan specifically recognized the PLO as "the sole legitimate representative" of the Palestinians. This meant that only the PLO could speak for or negotiate on behalf of the Palestinians.

The Reagan Peace Proposal—"The Jordanian Option"

In September 1982, President Reagan announced his own peace proposal. It called for King Hussein of Jordan, not the PLO, to negotiate about the future of the West Bank and Gaza on behalf of the Palestinians. The Reagan plan recommended the establishment of an **autonomous entity** (not an independent state) for the Palestinians linked with Jordan in a **confederation** (some kind of union).

The Role of King Hussein

Between 1982 and 1988, King Hussein worked tirelessly to promote Middle East peace talks based on the ideas in the Reagan plan. He held numerous meetings with PLO chief Arafat and also held secret meetings with Israeli leaders. In 1985, Hussein and Arafat reached an agreement on a joint peace initiative that called for Israel to give back the occupied territories in return for peace. It also called for the creation of an "autonomous Palestinian entity in confederation with Jordan." However, negotiations between Hussein and Arafat soon broke down. In 1988, Hussein announced that he was giving up his role as spokesman for the Palestinians and was cutting all ties with the West Bank.

Calls for An International Conference

After 1985, there were repeated calls for an international peace conference to resolve the Arab-Israeli dispute. Arab leaders pressed for such a conference. The Soviet Union, the European Community, and finally the United States went along with the idea. In Israel, opinion was divided. Some favored an international conference. The majority, however, were afraid that the Arab countries, the Soviet Union, and other nations would force Israel to make concessions.

The Baker Peace Initiatives

In the spring of 1991, soon after America's victory in the Gulf War against Iraq, United States prestige and influence in the Middle East were at a high point. President Bush decided to take advantage of this situation and push for a Middle East Peace Conference. He sent his Secretary of State, James Baker, to the Middle East to meet with the leaders of Egypt, Syria, Jordan, Saudi Arabia, Kuwait, and Israel. Baker also met with Palestinian representatives.

Baker traveled to the Middle East many times over a period of several months trying to resolve basic differences related to a peace conference. The most complicated question was who would represent the Palestinians at the conference. Israel refused to talk with representatives of the PLO. It would not accept any Palestinians from East Jerusalem because Jerusalem is Israel's capital and the Israelis felt it could not be represented by Palestinians. In order to get Israel to attend a peace conference, Baker accepted several Israeli conditions. It was agreed that the Palestinian representatives to the conference would not be linked to the PLO in any way. They would come as part of a Jordanian delegation. There would be no Palestinians from East Jerusalem.

The Middle East Peace Conference: Madrid, 1991

The long awaited Middle East Peace Conference opened in Madrid, Spain, on October 30, 1991. It was sponsored by the United States and the Soviet Union. The conference consisted of representatives from Syria, Lebanon, Egypt, Israel, and a joint Palestinian-Jordanian delegation. Representatives from the United States, the Soviet Union, and the European Community also attended.

The Arabs and Israelis presented their cases to the world and each denounced the other. What mattered, however, was that Israelis and Palestinians and other Arabs, bitter enemies for so long, were finally sitting around a table and talking.

It was agreed in advance that after the conference in Madrid ended the peace talks would continue between Israel and its Arab enemies. These talks would be **bilateral** (between two sides) involving Israel and Lebanon, Israel and Syria, and Israel together with a joint Palestinian-Jordanian delegation. There were many arguments as to where these talks were to be held. Finally, the first of these bilateral talks was held in Madrid. The talks then resumed in Washington in December 1991, in January 1992, then in Cairo in

July 1992. Israeli representatives met with Palestinians and Jordanians to discuss proposals for Palestinian self-rule in the occupied territories.

The Civil War in Lebanon

Another trouble spot in the Middle East for many years was Lebanon. A civil war that began there in the middle of 1975 lasted until 1990.

Lebanon: A Unique Country

In many ways, Lebanon is a unique country in the Middle East. It is made up of many different religious and ethnic groups. The main religious groupings are Christians, Muslims, and Druzes. Within the Christian group there are many different sects, the Maronite Christians being the largest. The Muslims are divided between the Sunni and Shi'ites.

For this reason, when Lebanon received its independence from France in 1943, a government structure was set up that was to maintain balance between the different religious groups. This political system was based on a census taken in 1932 when the Christians held a slight majority. Accordingly, the president of Lebanon and commander of the armed forces had to be Maronite Christians; the job of prime minister was reserved for a Sunni Muslim and the president of the legislature was a Shi'ite Muslim. The legislature had to consist of a 6–5 Christian to Muslim ratio. Many key posts in the government and administration were also reserved for Christians.

After independence, Lebanon worked toward achieving several goals: furthering democracy, developing the economy, maintaining a livable arrangement between Christians and Muslims, and maintaining good relations with the other Arab nations as well as with the West. For many years Lebanon prospered under these conditions. It became one of the most economically developed countries in the Middle East. It was an important commerical and financial center. Unlike other Arab countries, it had a large, thriving middle class and about 75 percent of its population was literate.

Lebanon, however, also had many problems. One of the most serious was the Palestinian presence. After 1948, when the state of Israel was established, about 150,000 Palestinian refugees moved to Lebanon. By 1975, there were 400,000 Palestinians in Lebanon. Many of these Palestinians became guerrillas and organized raids into Israel. The Israeli government retaliated and caused heavy destruction in Lebanon. For many years the Phalange party, the main party of the Lebanese Christians, was violently opposed to the PLO's use of Lebanese soil to attack Israel. The Christians wanted to drive the Palestinians out of the country or force the government to bring them under stricter control. There were numerous armed clashes between the Phalangist Party militia and Palestinian guerrilla groups.

Another problem was that, although Lebanon had a large and properous middle class, much of the population was poor and deprived. This was especially true of the Shi'ite Muslims living in southern Lebanon. The Shi'ites felt that the government was not doing enough to improve their lives. The Shi'ites also protested that the government failed to protect them against Israeli attacks, which resulted in much suffering and heavy damage.

The third problem was that the Muslims resented the Christian domination of the country. By 1975, approximately 60 percent of Lebanon's population was Muslim. The Muslims demanded a total restructuring of the political system to give them more power.

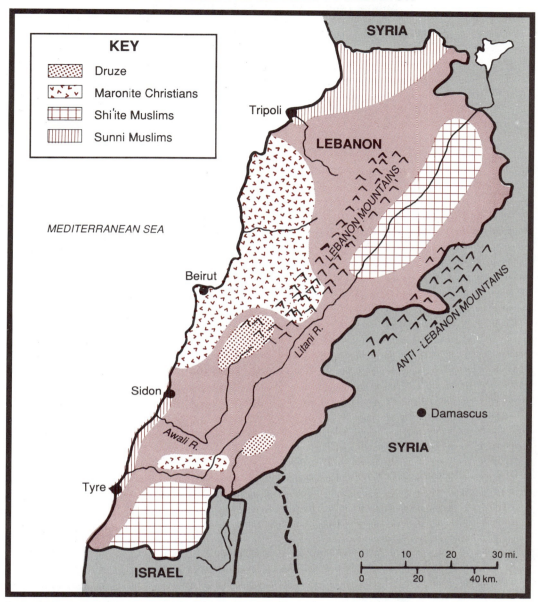

Source: *Encyclopedia Britannica Book of the Year 1984*

Civil War Breaks Out

In April 1975, fighting broke out between right-wing Christian Phalangists and left-wing Muslims aided by Palestinians. The fighting soon turned into open warfare between Christians and Muslims. The Muslims saw this as an opportunity to change the structure of the government. They decided that they would fight until they were successful in achieving a dominant position in the government. This fighting turned into a full-scale civil war which lasted 15 years.

Sectarian Violence

Between 1975 and 1990, Lebanon was torn apart by **sectarian** violence (violence between rival religious, ethinic, and political groups and even between powerful families). These rival groups armed themselves and formed their own **militias** (private armies). The rival militias engaged in street battles, car bombings, kidnappings, and political assassinations. Christian militias fought against Muslims, Palestinians, and Druzes. Rival Christian militias fought each other. Shi'ite Muslims fought Palestinians and pro-Arafat Palestinians fought anti-Arafat Palestinians. Pro-Syrian Muslims battled against anti-Syrian Muslims.

Thousands of innocent civilians lost their lives as a result of the street battles, car bomb explosions, and when their villages came under fire. The warring groups carried out assassinations of rival political leaders. Some of Lebanon's most prominent leaders lost their lives. Among them were: Druze leader Kemal Jumklatt in 1977; President Bashir Gemayel in 1982; and Prime Minister Roshid Karami in 1987.

The Lebanese government and army were too weak to control the warring militias. Business in Lebanon came to a standstill. Many of the foreign businesses and banks closed and left Lebanon. During the years of fighting, ceasefires were agreed to and temporary truces established, but each time they broke down and the fighting resumed.

Foreign Involvement: Syria

In 1976, Syria became actively involved in Lebanon's civil war, sending 200,000 troops into Lebanon. Syria always wanted to control Lebanon and even to annex it. The civil war gave Syria its opportunity. Earlier, Syria had supplied the PLO and the Muslims with Soviet made weapons. However, in April 1976, Syria changed its position and decided to help the Christians. Syrian troops and Christian forces attacked Palestinian strongholds, resulting in a heavy loss of life.

A civilian carrying a wounded child after a booby-trapped car exploded killing or wounding at least 30 people in the civil war in Lebanon.

However, in 1978, Syria turned against the Christians because some of Lebanon's Christian forces were receiving support from Israel. In July 1978, the Syrians began bombing Christian villages and Christian East Beirut. The intense bombardment continued for months. Syrian troops surrounded East Beirut and during the next few years there was bitter fighting between Syrian troops and some of the Christian militias.

By 1983, Syrian troops occupied a large part of Lebanon's territory. Christian leaders and others criticized Syria's occupation of their country and demanded that Syrian troops leave. The Syrians, however, were determined to stay. They claimed that they were in Lebanon to end the fighting and to restore order.

Foreign Involvement: Israel

As you read, during the 1970s and 1980s, the Palestinians in Lebanon turned their refugee camps into guerrilla bases. As the government of Lebanon became weaker and lost control, the Palestinians in southern Lebanon began to attack towns and villages in northern Israel with rockets and artillery. They also crossed the border into Israel and engaged in terrorist acts. Each Palestinian attack led to Israel retaliation. Israeli planes bombed refugee camps in southern Lebanon. Several times Israeli planes bombed PLO targets in and near Beirut. This cycle of attacks and counterattacks continued for years.

The Christians in Lebanon opposed the actions of the Palestinians. Many wanted the Palestinans driven out of Lebanon and some of the fiercest battles in the civil war were fought between Christians and Palestinians. Israel and the Christians became allies. Israel supplied the Christian militias with artillery, tanks, money, and training. However, most of Israel's support went to the militia of Major Saad Haddad who controlled a 350-square mile area in southern Lebanon near the Israeli border. Israel hoped that, by giving military supplies to Haddad's militia, he would be able to prevent the Palestinian raids into northern Israel.

In 1978, Israeli troops invaded southern Lebanon. They remained there for several months in an effort to destroy the PLO's guerrilla bases. In 1982, Israeli forces again invaded Lebanon, this time moving as far north as Beirut. Israel's goal was to destroy Palestinian military bases. (The details of these invasions are found on pages 90–91). Israel also hoped to push the Syrians out of central and southern Lebanon back toward the Bekaa Valley.

In 1983, approximately 40 percent of Lebanon was occupied by Israeli and Syrian troops. Lebanese and Israeli representatives met to negotiate the withdrawal of Israeli forces and signed an agreement in May 1983. The agreement ended the state of war between them and called for the withdrawal of all foreign forces from Lebanon. It also provided for a security zone in southern Lebanon that would assure Israel of adequate protection. Israel hoped that Lebanon would become the second Arab country to make peace with it. Syria, the PLO, and other groups were opposed to any normalization of relations between Israel and Lebanon. The accord, although approved by the Lebanese Parliament, never went into effect and was cancelled in 1984.

Israel insisted that it would not pull its troops out of Lebanon until Syrian troops agreed to leave. But the Lebanese civil war was becoming increasingly unpopular in Israel. Shi'ite guerrillas in southern Lebanon engaged in guerrilla attacks on the Israelis, resulting in many casualties. In January 1985, Israel announced plans for the total withdrawal of its troops from Lebanon. Israel's withdrawal was completed in June 1985. This did not end Israel's involvement in Lebanese affairs, however. Israeli military advisers remained behind to assist the South Lebanon Army, a militia composed mainly of Maronite Christians, who helped prevent raids into northern Israel.

Efforts to End the Civil War

By the early 1980s, it appeared that Lebanon would cease to exist as a country and would be broken up into a number of mini-states. The country was split into zones, each controlled by a warring group. The Lebanese government was too weak to govern the country and the army was unable to restore order.

Over the years many attempts were made to end the fighting. There were hundreds of cease-fire agreements between the warring groups, but fighting broke out almost as soon as the cease-fires had been agreed to. The Arab League held many meetings and tried to mediate among the various groups. The United Nations sent a peace-keeping force to Lebanon. Sixteen hundred U.S. Marines were part of this force. All these attempts to bring peace to Lebanon failed.

Muslim and Druze leaders insisted that the violence in Lebanon would continue until a new political structure was worked out to end the Christian domination of the government.

In 1985, Syria attempted to bring the Lebanese civil war to an end. Christian, Druze, and Muslim representatives were brought together to work out plans for political reforms. An agreement was reached providing for a gradual end to the Christian-dominated system of government. It also provided for the disbanding of the militias and called for a complete cease-fire. The agreement signed by the leaders of Lebanon's main militias fell apart a few weeks later as fighting broke out once again.

In 1989, Lebanon's warring groups accepted a peace agreement worked out by the nations of the Arab League. This "National Reconciliation Pact" established the structure for a new government for Lebanon. It established parity (equal power) between Muslims and Christians in the legislative and executive branches of government.

The fighting continued for another year, however. Christian forces under the command of General Michel Aoun refused to accept the agreement and demanded the expulsion of Syrian troops from Lebanon. In October 1990, Syrian troops crushed General Aoun's forces.

Results of the War

The civil war in Lebanon resulted in thousands of deaths. Thousands more were wounded. More than 500,000 Lebanese left the country during the war. Violence affected the daily lives of the Lebanese people. A serious refugee problem was created as thousands of people fled when their villages came under attack. The refugees added to the economic and social problems of the country. Large parts of Beirut were completely destroyed and Lebanon's economy was devastated.

The End of the Civil War

Lebanon's 15 year civil war came to an end in October 1990. By the summer of 1991, the Lebanese government and army had regained control of most of the country. The militias were disbanded and most of their weapons were handed over to the government. In July, the Lebanese Army attacked the Palestinian's last major stronghold—the camps at Sidon—an area 25 miles south of Beirut. The PLO fighters surrendered their last heavy weapons.

Thousands of Lebanese who had fled the country during the war began to return. Businesses reopened. In Beirut efforts were made to restore basic services—electricity, water, communications, garbage collection, and above all, security. Western aircraft returned to

Beirut airport after having stayed away since 1985. Attempts were made to unify Beirut which for so long had been a divided city—split into Muslim West Beirut and Christian East Beirut. To underline this unity the capital was renamed Greater Beirut. Although order has been restored, political violence is not entirely over.

The Lebanese government now controls most of the country. However, the real power in Lebanon is Syria. Syria still maintains 40,000 troops in Lebanon and controls all major decisions of the Lebanese government. In May 1991, Syria and Lebanon signed an agreement called the "Treaty of Brotherhood, Cooperation, and Coordination." This agreement established a special relationship between the two nations and provided for cooperation in defense, security, foreign policy, and economic matters. Many people, especially Lebanese Christians, worry that the treaty is a means for Syria to control Lebanese affairs. Many Lebanese want Syria to end its occupation of their country and to remove its troops, but Syria refuses.

In southern Lebanon 1,500 Israeli troops patrol the area that is known as the Israel Security Zone. Israel claims that the Lebanese Army is still unable to prevent guerrilla attacks against Israel. The Lebanese Army must prove that it can police its borders before Israel will remove its troops.

The Western Hostage Crisis

During the years of civil war there was almost a complete breakdown of law and order in Lebanon. The country became a center for international terrorism.

In 1984, several Americans living and working in Lebanon were kidnapped and held hostage by terrorist groups. The kidnappers demanded the release of 17 convicted terrorists imprisoned in Kuwait. In the following years, other Americans, as well as other Westerners—mainly English, French, and German citizens—were kidnapped and held hostage in Lebanon. These kidnappings were carried out by extremist Shi'ite groups. The most important of these groups was the Islamic Jihad. Most of the groups had ties to the pro-Italian terrorist organization Hezbollah. Each group had its own reasons for taking and holding hostages, and each put forth its own set of demands. In some cases it was to put pressure on Israel to release Shi'ite prisoners held in Israeli jails.

During the early years, the hostages were treated cruelly. They were kept in isolation in tiny cells, blindfolded, and chained. In some cases they were beaten by their guards. Several hostages died or were killed, including William Buckley, who had been an officer at the United States Embassy in Beirut.

For the most part, the United States and other Western nations refused to make any deals with the kidnappers. These nations believed that negotiating or giving in to the kidnappers' demands would encourage them to take more hostages in the future. The Western governments insisted that the hostages be released unconditionally.

The hostage crisis continued for years. Periodically the kidnappers released a few hostages, but almost immediately new hostages were taken. In 1991, political conditions in the Middle East were changing. Syria, a long time supporter of terrorism, was anxious for better relations with the United States. Since Syrian troops were in control of large parts of Lebanese territory, Syria was in a position to put pressure on the groups holding the hostages. More important was the role played by Iran. Most of the groups holding the hostages were Shi'ites with ties to the Shi'ite government of Iran. Therefore, the Iranian government had a great deal of influence over them. Iran, too, was interested in improving relations with the West. It needed trade, technology, and loans from the West to improve its economy. Iranian leaders knew that better relations with the West depended on the resolution of the hostage crisis. With pressure from Syria and Iran, the kidnappers released the remaining Western hostages between July and December, 1991.

The two hostages who were released last were the most famous—the American journalist Terry Anderson and the English clergyman Terry Waite. Anderson, a correspondent for the Associated Press, was kidnapped in March, 1985. He was held for more than 6½ years, longer than any other hostage. Terry Waite, representing Great Britain's religious leader, the Archbishop of Canterbury, had traveled to Lebanon several times to negotiate for the release of the hostages. In January 1987, soon after arriving in Lebanon, Waite disappeared. Nothing was heard of him for more than four years and it was feared that he had been killed. He too was released in December, 1991.

The Resurgence of Islam

The Islamic religious revival that began in the 1970s has had a great impact on the whole Muslim world. Since 1979, with the establishment of the Islamic Republic of Iran, Islam has become extremely militant. This has affected the relations between Muslim countries and the rest of the world. What does the resurgence of Islam or the revival of Islam mean? It is a revival of the strict religious teachings that go back to the earliest Islamic times. It is an attempt to apply these teachings to all aspects of social and political life. Many Muslims today believe that Islam alone as a political system and a religion can provide answers to the problems of contemporary life. The Islamic revival is in many ways a rejection of the West and Western values.

Westernization: A Means of Modernizing

Since the end of the 18th century, Muslim civilization, like other non-Western civilizations, has found itself at a disadvantage in its relations with the West (Europe). The Western (European) nations by this time had achieved economic and military superiority over the rest of the world. Thus, they were able to extend their political influence over the non-Western world.

Muslim leaders saw this as a dangerous threat to their own power and to Islam in general. They began looking for ways to defend themselves. The answer they came up with was Westernization. In the beginning, Westernization involved importing Western weapons and military techniques. However, as the 19th century advanced, it became apparent that the Muslim nations were even weaker in relation to the West than they had been before.

Many educated and patriotic Muslims worried about the weakness and corruption of their backward countries. They came to believe that the real secret of Western superiority lay in its system of representative government, its educational system, and freedom of thought. They believed that if these aspects of Western civilization were adopted, they could bring their countries into the modern world. Westernization remained the ideal well into the 20th century.

Disillusionment with the West

As time went on, however, it became obvious that Westernization had failed to remedy the weakness of the Muslim countries. The Westernizers lost prestige as their reforms failed to bring economic prosperity or military strength. The West also lost prestige in the eyes of many Muslims in the 20th century. World War II was a very important factor. As Japan defeated the British, French, and Americans in the early years of the war, the Europeans did not seem as invincible as they once had.

The Muslim Brotherhood

The Muslim Brotherhood is an Islamic movement that began in Egypt in 1928. Its founder, an Egyptian school teacher, observed the miserable lives of the poor people around him. He believed that the only way they could regain a sense of identity and self-respect was to be instilled with Islamic piety—devotion to religious duties and Islamic brotherhood. The movement grew rapidly and gained many followers. The Muslim Brotherhood taught that society in Egypt and in other Muslim countries was being destroyed by Western godlessness. The only remedy was to overthrow the Westernized political and social institutions and replace them with an Islamic governmental organization such as had existed at the time of the Prophet Mohammed and his immediate successors.

The Revival of Islam

As time passed there were deep feelings of discontent in the Muslim world. Western ways had not solved their problems. The common people had never really been touched by Westernization. The Muslim countries had no great accomplishments to show since independence. Therefore, why not return to Islam?

Several events reinforced this renewed interest in Islam. In 1969, Muammar al-Qaddafi came to power in Libya. Under his leadership the government became increasingly Islamic, using its growing oil profits to spread its beliefs both inside and outside Libya. The rise in oil prices brought power and prestige to Saudi Arabia, a religious fundamentalist state. The 1979 revolution in Iran brought the Ayatollah Khomeini and his religious followers to power. They set up a theocracy—a government run by religious leaders. All three countries share the same vision of a return to a pure Islam and the same desire that all aspects of life be ruled by Islamic law. Khomeini's teaching was similar to that of Muslim Brotherhood. He denounced the West for its exploitation and imperialism. They said that Western constitutional democracy is a deception and a fraud.

The vision that these leaders offered their followers is that of a society modeled on what is thought to have existed in the first century of Islam. This vision is contrasted with present discontents: injustice, oppression, poverty. Khomeini was able to arouse the masses in Iran and elsewhere in the Middle East to a fervor and frenzy unseen in recent years. The fact that his message found such a receptive audience showed that there was a deep feeling of discontent within the Islamic world.

Islam and Politics

One of the most important ideas upon which the American system of government is founded is the separation of church and state. This means that government and religion are two totally separate areas. Religious leaders cannot influence government decisions and the government can in no way interfere in religious matters. It also means that no official religion can be established in the United States. This same separation exists in many other countries today. But the idea is relatively new—a little more than 200 years old. Throughout history, in almost all societies, religion and government were closely connected.

Islam from its very beginning had a close association between religion and politics. Islam, more than other religions, is a political religion. Mohammed, the prophet of Islam, founded a state and governed it. Mohammed was a ruler—he made laws, collected taxes, raised armies, made war and peace, and dispensed justice. Thus politics, government, law, war, and peace are all part of the Holy Law of Islam. In Islam, God is the head of the state. The state is God's state, the army is God's army, the treasury is God's treasury, and the enemy is God's enemy.

Over the last few centuries there was some separation between political and religious matters in the Muslim world. However, at the present time there is a reassertion of this association between Islam and politics. One of the main arguments of Khomeini and other fundamentalist leaders is that the removal of religion from politics and public life has led to all kinds of evils. They desire to return to an Islamic society governed by Islamic law.

A Revolution in Iran

Iran, with 36 million people, is the third most populated nation in the Middle East. Iran has strategic importance because of its location on the Persian Gulf, where the world's greatest concentration of oil reserves are found. (Iran is also one of the world's largest producers of oil.)

Iran has a long political history and also a long history of unity in its cultural traditions. As we have already learned the early Persian Empire was strong (Iran is the modern name for Persia).

Iran developed into a modern nation under Riza Shah Pahlevi. Pahlevi was an army officer who made himself Shah in 1925. He tried to use Iran's oil revenues to modernize his country.

During World War II (1939–1945), the British and the Russians, fearing German control of the Middle East, took over oil-rich Iran. The Allies forced Riza Pahlevi to give up the throne. In his place his young son, Mohammed Riza Pahlevi, became the new Shah.

After World War II, Iran became strongly nationalistic. In the early 1950s, the Iranian government nationalized the oil fields. However, Iran found it difficult to operate the fields, so in 1954 Iran made agreements with the Western nations to develop the oil. Under the agreements, half the profits went to Iran.

Investing money from the large oil profits, the Shah began a program of reform and industrial development. He built factories, schools, and superhighways. He gave women greater freedom, including the right to education and the right to vote. Over 100,000 students were sent to colleges in Europe and the United States.

Large areas of land that had belonged to the Shah and the clergy were given to the peasants. The income of the ayatollahs (religious leaders of Iran) was reduced. The clergy also feared that traditional values and customs were being destroyed. Most shocking was the sight of bars, gambling casinos, and women without the traditional veils and wearing Western styles.

The Shah moved quickly in trying to bring Western technology and lifestyles to Iran. The bazaar merchants worried about competition from foreign imports. The riches from the oil and economic development were divided unequally. The royal family's use of public monies for personal use was much criticized.

The Shah used dictatorial and brutal methods to promote modernization. Those who opposed or criticized the Shah were arrested and then tortured by the secret police. Many who criticized him were members of the newly educated middle class that the Shah's own modernization had created.

Islam and Freedom of Expression: The Case of Salman Rushdie

In February 1989, British author Salman Rushdie published the novel *The Satanic Verses.* Rushdie, a Muslim, had been born in India but was living in Great Britain and was a British citizen. Religious Muslims immediately denounced the book. They called it "blasphemous" and "an insult to Islam." They said that references in the novel to Mohammed, his wives, and events in the Koran were offensive and dishonored the faith. Ayatollah Khomeini, leader of Iran, publicly condemned Rushdie to death and called on all Muslims to seek out and kill Rushdie and those responsible for the publication of the book. Rushdie apologized publicly, saying he meant no insult to Muslims. He went into hiding under the protection of the British government.

Demonstrations and riots broke out in many Muslim countries. In India and Pakistan the rioting involved tens of thousands of people, resulting in several deaths and many injuries. Most of the people who denounced the book had never read it because copies were banned in most Muslim countries. In Britain, Muslims paraded and burned copies of the book. There were threats against bookstores and bomb threats against the publishing company, Viking Press. In New York, bomb threats caused many bookstores to temporarily remove the novel from public display, fearing that employees or customers might be injured.

After repeated threats from the Ayatollah Khomeini, Western governments took action. Led by Great Britain, many European countries, as well as Canada, withdrew their top ranking diplomats from Iran in protest. President Bush called Khomeini's death threat "deeply offensive to the norms of civilized behavior."

In the West, the Rushdie affair was seen as a case of freedom of expression versus censorship. Westerners defended Rushdie's right to express his views. They said freedom of speech and press must be upheld, that censorship is wrong, and that governments do not have the right to silence authors. Religious Muslims saw the issue differently. As expressed by Iran's president, the West had made the mistake of confusing "freedom of expression with the freedom to insult one billion Muslims."

Since 1989, Rushdie has apologized many times. In early 1991, Rushdie announced that he would not publish the book in paperback. He hoped that his announcement together with his apologies would pacify Muslims and make it possible for him to come out of hiding and return to a normal life.

Yet Khomeini's death threat remains in effect and Rushdie is still in hiding. His Japanese translator was stabbed to death and his Italian translator was wounded in a knife attack. The Iranian government still refuses to remove the death threat.

In the mid-1970s, the Shah also began a program of military expansion. Millions were spent to make Iran the strongest power in the Persian Gulf. Inflation and high prices became a problem. Unrest began to grow.

The strongest opposition came from the Muslim religious leaders, the ayatollahs. In Iran, the Muslim religious leaders saw their authority being taken away by civil courts that had been set up to replace the religious courts. The religious leaders felt the Shah's program of national modernization and emancipation (the act of setting free) for women threatened traditional religious values. The religious leaders also resented the Shah's land reform program. It was their lands that were to be given to the peasants. Without the money from the rents collected the power of the ayatollahs would be weakened.

Violent rioting, strikes, and demonstrations broke out in late 1978 and continued into 1979. Finally, early in 1979, the Shah fled Iran, and an Islamic republic was set up. Ayatollah Ruhollah Khomeini became the power behind the new government. He and his followers did not reject all forms of modernization; they rejected the Shah's way as modernization that would destroy Islam.

The new government was anti-Western and viewed the United States with particular suspicion and hatred. This was due to the close ties that had existed between the Shah and the United States.

In October 1979, the Shah was allowed to enter the United States for medical treatment. Two weeks later, in November, Iranians violently invaded and took control of the U.S. embassy in Teheran and took 52 American diplomats hostage in violation of international law. The Iranians said they would release the hostages when the Shah was returned to Iran to stand trial for his "crimes" against the Iranian people. Both the United Nations and the International Court of Justice demanded the release of the hostages. The Iranians refused. Finally the American hostages were released in January 1981 after almost 15 months of imprisonment.

The Iranian Revolution left Iran in an unsettled and unstable condition. Iran's oil production dropped as its economy was disrupted by the revolution, and has not fully recovered years after the revolution. The ethnic minority groups in Iran—Kurds, Baluchis, and others—have become more active in their search for independence.

The War Between Iraq and Iran

In September 1980, Iraqi troops invaded Iranian territory. Within days Iraqi pilots flying Soviet-built MIGs were bombing military targets and oil facilities in Iran. Iraq's president, Saddam Hussein, was convinced that Iran's revolution had left the country divided and its military forces weak. He believed that he could overthrow Iran's revolutionary government "in days."

Iran and Iraq are neighbors, but the differences between them are great. Both are Muslim nations; however, Iraq's population is Arab and Iran's people are Persians. Religious differences also exist. Iran is predominately Shi'ite Muslim; Iraq is made up of Shi'ite and Sunni Muslims. Over the centuries, differences in language, culture, religion, and history resulted in a great deal of enmity. When the Shah ruled Iran, efforts were made to resolve some of the problems dividing the two.

The Ayatollah Ruhollah Khomeini.

Women, many in traditional Iranian garb, march in support of Khomeini in
a 1979 demonstration in Teheran.

Causes of the War

After the Khomeini government came to power in Iran in 1979, tension between the
two nations increased. Clashes along the border began and escalated into an all-out war.
The immediate cause of war was a territorial dispute. Saddam Hussein sent Iran a list of
demands. He claimed the Shatt al-Arab waterway that separates the two nations and
demanded the return of three small islands in the Persian Gulf. Iran rejected Iraq's
demands. The real reasons for the conflict, however, were much more complex.

1. Iran's frequent declarations that its Islamic revolution should be exported to other
   countries in the region aroused fears in the Arab states, including Iraq.
2. Iran began to meddle in the affairs of Shi'ite communities in Iraq and other countries. This caused much concern to the Iraqi government, which is dominated by
   Sunni Muslims though the Iraqi population is mainly Shi'ite.
3. Khomeini had spent 14 years living in exile in Iraq during the Shah's reign. But his
   dislike for Iraq's government was intense and he openly criticed it.
4. Iraq wanted to gain control of Iran's Khuzestan province. This province is rich in oil
   and has a predominantly Arab population. Khomeini accused Iraq of creating

unrest among the Arabs in the region. Khomeini in turn called on Iraq's Shi'ite Muslims to overthrow the "godless" regime of Saddam Hussein.

5. It was widely believed that Saddam Hussein hoped to make Iraq the most important power in the Persian Gulf region and perhaps in the entire Middle East. A quick victory over Iran could make this possible.

The War: A Danger to the Whole World

From the beginning the war posed a threat to the West and other countries. A war fought amid the oil fields and across the oil routes of the Persian Gulf could at any time cut off vital oil supplies as 60 percent of the oil used in the West passes through the Strait of Hormuz, at the entrance to the Persian Gulf. Supertankers carrying oil from Saudi Arabia, Kuwait, and the other Gulf States pass through this strait. If the Strait of Hormuz were closed to shipping due to a blockade or mining, the whole world could be affected. For this reason the United States was determined to keep the strait open. Another danger was that the war could spill over and involve other countries—the Gulf States or even the United States and the former Soviet Union.

The Key Targets: Cities and Oil Facilities

Iraq's initial blitz failed to produce the quick and easy victory that was anticipated. The military experts who predicted that the war would be over in a few weeks were wrong. The war lasted eight years. There were hundreds of thousands of casualties and enormous destruction.

What surprised everyone was the strength of the Iranian resistance. After getting over the initial shock, the country rallied enthusiastically behind the government's war effort. Khomeini told the Iranian people to fight until the "infidels" had been driven not only from Iran but from Iraq too. Iran also possessed superior weapons, mainly U.S. phantom jets that had been purchased by the Shah.

From the beginning cities and oil facilities were key targets for bombing raids. There were air strikes against Teheran, capital of Iran, and attacks on Baghdad, Iraq's capital. Iraq began a systematic bombardment of Abadan, Iran's largest oil refinery. Iraq continued to bomb Kharg Island, Iran's main oil exporting terminal. The Iranians hit at Iraqi oil installations at Basra and Kirkuk. There was severe damage to the oil refining and shipping facilities of both countries. This for a time sharply reduced the amount of oil exported by both nations. Efforts were made by the United Nations and the Conference of Islamic Nations to end the fighting. These efforts failed. Despite concessions from Iraq, Iran said it would not end the struggle until the government of Saddam Hussein was overthrown.

Attacks on International Shipping

A dangerous development began in 1984: attacks on international shipping in the Gulf. Each side tried to prevent oil tankers and ships from approaching the ports of the other. Vessels were hit by missiles or bombed from the air. Mines were placed in the Gulf. Several hundred ships were hit in the Gulf with the loss of hundreds of seamen. In May 1987, the U.S. frigate *Stark* was hit by an Iraqi missile; 37 American sailors died.

During 1987, there was a dangerous escalation of the war in the Persian Gulf. Iran placed more mines in the Gulf, which caused considerable damage to shipping. After a

Kuwaiti tanker was struck by a mine, the United States began a mine-sweeping operation. In July 1987, U.S. warships began escorting Kuwaiti oil tankers through the Gulf. The Kuwaiti tankers were flying the American flag because Iran had threatened to bomb Kuwaiti tankers in retaliation for Kuwait's help to Iraq. Iranian attacks on Kuwaiti oil tankers led to U.S. attacks on Iranian oil installations. By the middle of 1987, there was a full scale naval confrontation between the United States and Iran in the Gulf. There were many incidents of Iranian gunboats and U.S. naval vessels firing at each other. A great tragedy occurred in July 1988 when a U.S. warship shot down an Iranian airliner over the Gulf, resulting in the death of 290 people.

Taking Sides

The Arabs

When the war broke out, most nations declared their neutrality. Most of the Arab states also proclaimed their neutrality, but all, except Syria and Libya, sided with Iraq. The Arabs were frightened by Khomeini's Shi'ite Muslim fanatacism. This was especially true of the Arab Gulf States. Most of the Gulf States are ruled by Sunni Moslems. These nations however have Shi'ite minorities that could be influenced by Khomeini. Among the Arabs there was also the feeling of solidarity with their "Arab brothers" in Iraq.

As the war continued the Arabs began to help Iraq openly. By 1981, Kuwait was providing Iraq with financial aid and allowing it to use Kuwaiti ports. Iraq's economy was in serious trouble. Its oil exports had fallen and it was running out of foreign currency. The war effort cost Iraq approximately $1 billion a month. Arab aid to Iraq became vital to Iraq's survival. During the last years of the war a substantial part of Iraq's war bill was paid by the other Arab countries, mainly Kuwait and Saudi Arabia.

The Soviet Union

The Soviet Union was officially neutral at the beginning of the war and hoped to remain on good terms with both sides. In 1984, however, the Soviets moved solidly behind Iraq and began providing them with enormous amounts of new weapons, spare parts, and financial aid.

The United States

The main interest of the United States in the conflict was to keep the Persian Gulf open to international shipping so that vital oil supplies would reach the West. The United States soon began to side with Iraq, selling it weapons and advanced technology.

The Cease-fire—August 20, 1988

During 1988, the tide of war turned against Iran with Iraqi successes on the battlefield and in the air. Iran had suffered great losses of armor, aircraft, and missiles during the war. Its troop losses were enormous.

Iranian Losses

Moreover, Iran was losing in its confrontation with U.S. warships in the Gulf. The U.S. Navy had destroyed Iranian offshore drilling platforms and oil fields in the Gulf. Iran was also losing "the war of the cities." Beginning in February, Iraq bombarded Teheran, the Iranian capital, Qom, and other cities in Iran with intermediate range missiles on a scale that Iran could not match. The Iranian economy had been crippled by the war. Oil exports had fallen greatly as a result of Iraqi air attacks on Iranian oil installation and oil tankers in the Gulf. There were problems of inflation, unemployment, low production, and enormous war damage.

U.N. Secretary General Perez de Cuellar tried for some time to bring an end to the war. Finally in the summer of 1988, Iran indicated that it was ready to accept a cease-fire. In August both nations agreed to end hostilities and start direct talks to resolve their conflict. The Secretary General was to act as mediator. The cease-fire in August 1988 ended the eight-year war which had resulted in almost 1 million deaths on both sides.

Peace talks began in Geneva but there was little progress. The major problem was the status of the Shatt al-Arab waterway. (Saddam Hussein demanded that Iran give up this waterway.) Iraq refused to withdraw its troops from approximately 965 square miles of Iranian territory unless Iran agreed to give up joint sovereignty (rule) over the waterway. Iran insisted that a 1975 agreement between Iraq and the Shah of Iran had provided that both countries would control the waterway. The issue remained unresolved and in September 1989 Iran's President Rafsanjani threatened to renew fighting to drive Iraqi troops from Iran.

Following Iraq's invasion of Kuwait in August 1990, Saddam Hussein informed Iran that he was ready to make peace on Iran's terms. Iraqi troops would withdraw from Iranian territory and the disupte over the waterway would be resolved according to Iran's conditions.

War in the Gulf: Iraq, Kuwait, and the U.S.-Led Coalition

Iraq's Invasion of Kuwait

On August 2, 1990, Iraqi troops invaded Kuwait. Thus began a series of events that led to the Gulf War known as Operation Desert Storm (January 16 to February 27, 1991).

The reason for the Iraqi invasion was to gain control over Kuwait's large and valuable oil fields. Iraq's economy was still in decline after eight years of war with Iran. By annexing Kuwait, Iraq's petroleum reserves would be doubled. Iraq would also gain better access to the Persian Gulf through Kuwait's longer coastline.

Saddam Hussein, the ruler of Iraq, expected no opposition from Kuwait. After the invasion, it was suspected that Saddam was preparing his forces for an attack on Saudi Arabia. If this happened, Iraq would control almost 40 percent of the world's oil reserves.

The United Nations Imposes a Trade Embargo

To stop Iraq from invading Saudi Arabia, the United States called for a meeting of the U.N. Security Council. The Council met on August 6, 1990, condemned the invasion of Kuwait, and passed a resolution calling for Iraq's withdrawal from Kuwait, and the restoration of the government of Kuwait. Another resolution called for an **embargo** (ban) on all trade with Iraq. This meant that all member nations were forbidden to sell anything to Iraq or to buy Iraqi oil. It was hoped that the embargo would weaken the Iraqi economy and force Iraq to leave Kuwait.

The Military Buildup

At the same time, President George Bush quickly organized a multinational force to send to Saudi Arabia. The first American troops, including air force units and marines, arrived in Saudi Arabia in August. Navy units were deployed in the Persian Gulf. Within weeks British, French, Italians, and others joined the effort.

The allies then began the long process of building up their forces, which took more than five months. By December, 500,000 troops from 29 countries were in Saudi Arabia. U.S. forces numbered 450,000. This was the biggest development of U.S. forces since World War II. The military buildup gave the allies an overwhelming advantage in airpower and complete naval superiority in the Gulf.

Iraqi Actions in Kuwait

After the invasion, Iraqi soldiers began a campaign of rape, pillage, torture, murder, and theft of Kuwait's economic assets. Iraqi soldiers tortured and killed hundreds of Kuwaitis and took several thousand prisoners. The soldiers looted shops and private homes. They removed art treasures from the Kuwait National Museum. Library books, scientific equipment, medical and hospital equipment, machinery, and other valuable items were sent back to Iraq. Gold and cash worth $1.6 billion was taken from the central bank in Kuwait.

The Hostages

Thousands of Americans, Europeans, and other foreigners lived and worked in Iraq and Kuwait. After the invasion these foreigners were forbidden to leave. The Iraqis placed the foreign hostages at strategic sites (places of military importance) to be used as "human shields" in the event of an attack. This caused an uproar in the West and after some weeks the women and children were allowed to leave. Later some of the men were let go and most of the remaining male hostages were released in December.

Arab Reaction

At first, the Arab response to Iraq's invasion of Kuwait was that it was an Arab dispute that should be resolved peacefully among the Arabs themselves. President Mubarak of Egypt invited Arab leaders to a summit meeting in Cairo on August 10th. They passed a resolution condemning the invasion and supporting the Saudi decision to invite international forces, including Arab troops, to protect Saudi Arabia. Not all the Arab countries agreed with this position. Jordan, Yemen, Sudan, Tunisia, Algeria, and the PLO sided with Iraq.

As time passed the split became deeper. Troops from Saudi Arabia, Syria, and Egypt joined the anti-Iraq coalition. Syria's President Assad, who had long hated Saddam Hussein and wanted him removed from power, joined the coalition. (During the Iran-Iraq war, Syria sided with Iran.) Jordan's King Hussein was caught in the middle. Fearful that a war against Iraq would eventually involve Israel and might be fought on Jordanian territory, he took the role of mediator and traveled back and forth hoping to resolve the dispute. Nevertheless, while King Hussein claimed that he was neutral, his actions supported Iraq. During the embargo, supplies, equipment, and even arms were transported over Jordanian territory to Iraq. The PLO enthusiastically supported Iraq because of Saddam Hussein's threat to destroy Israel and create a Palestinian state.

Efforts to Resolve the Crisis Peacefully

On August 28, Iraq annexed Kuwait and declared that Kuwait no longer existed as an independent country. It was now part of Iraq, Iraq's 19th province. During the following months, intense efforts were made to get Iraq to leave Kuwait peacefully. U.N. Secretary General Javier Perez de Cuellar, as well as other important leaders, repeatedly appealed to Iraq to leave Kuwait. Saddam Hussein refused.

President Bush insisted that "this aggression will not stand." On November 29th, the U.N. Security Council approved a resolution authorizing the coalition to use force to liberate Kuwait if Iraq did not pull its troops out by January 15, 1991.

Efforts to find a peaceful solution continued. In the United States and Europe many people urged that sanctions be given time to work. However, most experts doubted that the trade embargo would weaken Iraq enough to force it to withdraw from Kuwait. In December, President Bush proposed that Iraq's Foreign Minister Tariq Aziz meet with him in Washington after which Secretary of State James Baker would travel to Baghdad to talk to Saddam Hussein. But Saddam Hussein refused to meet with Baker by the date set as a deadline—January 12th. A compromise was reached. Tariq Aziz and James Baker met in Geneva on January 9th. At this meeting, Aziz insisted that Iraq would not withdraw from Kuwait and that all Middle Eastern conflicts must be solved simultaneously—namely, the Arab-Israeli dispute.

In the days before the January 15th deadline, France and several other nations offered peace proposals to Saddam Hussein. U.N. Secretary General Perez de Cuellar traveled to Baghdad to seek peace but Saddam Hussein refused to pull out of Kuwait.

The War

On January 16, 1991, coalition forces began a massive air attack over sites in Baghdad and throughout Iraq and Kuwait. At the same time, U.S. warships in the Persian Gulf fired Tomahawk cruise missiles at targets in Iraq. This massive aerial campaign continued around the clock for five weeks—the entire duration of the war. President Bush told the world that the coalition would destroy Iraq's offensive military machine (all the weapons and equipment used to make war) so that Iraq would never again be a menace to its neighbors. It was most important to destroy Iraq's nuclear weapons potential and its chemical and biological weapons production facilities. During the first days the bombers knocked out Baghdad's electricity and water systems and its central telecommunications.

Allied strategy was carefully planned by Secretary of Defense Dick Cheney, Chairman of the Joint Chiefs of Staff Colin Powell, and Army General Norman Schwarzkopf who was commander of the coalition forces. The goal was to use air power to cause great destruction to Iraq's military. This would greatly weaken its military forces and once the ground war began would result in a minimum of allied casualties. American military leaders believed that an air war alone would not force the Iraqis to leave Kuwait. They felt that a ground war was also necessary and that the fighting could last months and result in thousands of allied casualties.

The five-week air war succeeded in destroying a great part of Iraq's military might. The success of the air strikes was largely due to the use of "smart bombs." (These bombs guided by lasers or TV cameras allowed crewmen to follow the images relayed from the bomb and keep it on its course toward its target.) U.S. superiority in high-tech weaponry crippled Iraq's ability to fight back.

Although Iraq could not defend itself in the air war, it could still cause a great deal of destruction. Iraq sent its SCUD missiles against civilian targets in Israel. For months Saddam Hussein had threatened to destroy Israel, even though Israel was not involved in the conflict. Israel wanted to fight back, to send its experienced Air Force to seek out and destroy the SCUD launchers. But the United States feared that if Israel entered the war against Iraq, Arab members of the coalition such as Egypt and Syria might break away. The United States persuaded Israel to stay out of the conflict and sent Israel Patriot anti-missiles to intercept the SCUDs. Iraq also launched many SCUD missiles against Saudi Arabia.

Iraq caused a great deal of damage in other ways. It released an enormous amount of petroleum into the Persian Gulf, which almost destroyed the ecology of the Gulf and killed birds, fish, and marine life. Iraq also set most of Kuwait's oil wells on fire. Thick, black, oily smoke covered the skies over Kuwait.

The ground war against Iraq began on February 23, 1991 and lasted 100 hours. The war was short, allied casualties were light, and the victory was overwhelming. The war was over on February 27, 1991. Kuwait was liberated.

The Middle East After the Gulf War

To understand the events that took place in Iraq after the war, it is important to know the following: Iraq, like every other nation in the Middle East, is an artificial creation. It was created by the British after World War I. The British drew up boundary lines and put together different peoples who never wanted to be together in one nation.

During the Gulf War, President Bush repeatedly called on the Iraqi people to overthrow Saddam Hussein. Within days of the war's conclusion, two separate uprisings broke out, one in the Shi'ite areas of southern Iraq, the other in the north where the Kurds live. The Shi'ites, who make up 53 percent of Iraq's population, have long been discriminated against and persecuted by the Sunni Muslims who control the government. The Kurds, who make up approximately 19 percent of the population, have been brutally treated by the Iraqi government for years.

The Kurds

The Kurds are an ethnic group numbering about 23 million people. The majority live in Turkey, Iraq, and Iran, the rest are in Syria and the former Soviet Union. The northern part of Iraq, where the Kurds live, contains some of Iraq's richest oil fields.

The Kurds have long desired an independent nation of their own. After World War I, Britian and its allies promised the Kurds independence. But the Treaty of Sevres (1920), which provided for an independent Kurdistan, was never ratified. Since then there have been Kurdish rebellions in Iran, Iraq, Turkey, and Syria; these have been brutally crushed. The governments of these countries have tried to destroy Kurdish culture and ethnic identity. They have forbidden the use of the Kurdish language; Kurdish schools, associations, and publications have been banned. But Kurdish nationalism survived and the revolts continued, mainly in Turkey and Iraq.

During the Iran-Iraq War (1980–1988), Iraqi Kurds received help from the Iranian government and made important military advances. Saddam Hussein decided to use chemical weapons against the Kurds. In March 1988, 5,000 Kurds, mainly innocent civilians, died when Iraqi planes bombed the town of Halabjah and released poison gas. In August and September, Iraqi troops launched a massive attack against the Kurds, causing 60,000 Kurds to flee across the border into Turkey. In August 1988, Iraqis again used chemical weapons against the Kurds. The Iraqi government began a "resettlement" program for the Kurds. Approximately 1.5 million Kurds were removed from their villages, which were then destroyed. Most of the Kurds were resettled in other parts of the country, but thousands "disappeared."

The Shi'ite and Kurdish Rebellions—March 1991

The Shi'ite and Kurdish rebellions achieved some early successes before being crushed by Saddam Hussein's forces. The Shi'ites had captured a number of towns in the south. Saddam sent two Republican Guard divisions, Iraq's best trained and armed troops, against the Shi'ites. They rapidly overwhelmed the weak and poorly equipped Shi'ite rebels. Thousands of Shi'ites fled to the U.S. held zone in southern Iraq. They begged for food and water and pleaded with the Americans to protect them from Saddam Hussein's terror. They related horror stories about the massacres and mass executions that Iraqi troops were carrying out in their villages.

After the Shi'ite uprising was crushed, Saddam moved his troops north, against the Kurds. The Kurds had achieved many important victories. Much of the Kurdish territory, including the rich oil-producing Kirkuk area, was under their control. However, they were no match for the military might of Saddam Hussein. Saddam used tanks, helicopter gunships, heavy artillery, rockets, and ground-to-ground missiles to attack Kurdish strongholds and villages. In less than five weeks the Kurdish rebellion was over.

Although President Bush had called on the Iraqi people to overthrow Saddam Hussein, the United States did not aid the Shi'ites and Kurds in their rebellion. Consequently, the Kurds and the Shi'ites felt betrayed by the United States. The United States refused to aid the rebels because it was feared that if the rebellions succeeded, Iraq would be partitioned. The Kurds would then control the north, the Shi'ites would take over the south, and Sunni Muslims would have the area in between. This in turn might cause Turkey, Syria, and Iran to seize parts of Iraq for themselves. The United States was especially determined not to let the Shi'ite area come under the control of Iran (ruled by a fundamentalist Shi'ite government). The United States was anxious to avoid the breakup of Iraq because it might lead to even more instability in the Middle East.

The United States also feared that a Kurdish victory in Iraq might encourage Kurds in neighboring countries to revolt. Turkey was especially concerned, since a Kurdish guerrilla struggle had been going on there for years. The United States also did not want to upset Turkey, which was an ally and was part of the anti-Saddam coalition.

Hundreds of thousands of Kurds fled to the mountains seeking safety from Saddam's troops. Iran opened its borders. It claimed that 1 million Kurds had entered Iran. Turkey's borders remained closed, and Turkish soldiers used force to keep the Kurds out. The suffering of the Kurds in the freezing mountains received world-wide coverage. It was estimated that 1,000 people a day died of hunger, dehydration, cold, and disease. International relief organizations moved in to help but their efforts were insufficient. After many weeks,

President Bush ordered American planes to air-drop food, blankets, clothing, and other supplies to the refugees in the mountains. The British and French did the same.

But a more permanent solution had to be found. In mid-April, American, British, and French troops moved into northern Iraq to create "safe havens" for the Kurds. These were tent-cities, built by the allies, each housing up to 100,000 people. The Kurds were brought down from the mountains and relocated to these refugee camps where they could receive food, water, and medical care. The camps were policed by soldiers from the United States, Britain, France, and the Netherlands. Iraqi troops were warned not to come near them. At the end of April the United Nations took over the administration of the refugee camps. At the same time Kurdish leaders began negotiations with Iraqi officials in the hope of gaining some form of autonomy.

U.N. Weapons Inspections

In April 1991, the United Nations Security Council set down the terms for a permanent cease-fire with Iraq. It stated that Iraq had to comply with these terms before the economic embargo (in effect since August 1990) would be lifted. The Iraqi government grudgingly accepted.

The most important part of the agreement called for the elimination of Iraq's weapons of mass destruction. Iraq was to be stripped of all its nuclear, chemical, and biological weapons as well as its ballistic missiles and the plants and equipment used to make them. Iraq was also prohibited from developing weapons of mass destruction in the future. U.N. inspectors and experts from the International Atomic Energy Agency were given the authority to search, find, dismantle, and destroy the weapons, missiles, and manufacturing sites.

Since then, many international inspection teams have gone to Iraq. Their reports revealed two important facts: (1) that Iraq's weapons program was far more advanced than had been supposed; and (2) that the Iraqi government did everything possible to conceal its weapons from the inspectors and to obstruct their efforts.

Secret documents obtained by U.N inspectors revealed that when the Gulf War began in January 1991, Iraq was only one or two years away from producing an atomic bomb. In July 1991, Iraq finally admitted that it had built and tested a "supergun." Experts believe that this giant cannon was developed to fire nuclear, chemical, and biological warheads against Israel.

Since most of Iraq's weapons were produced and stored at secret locations, Iraq was supposed to provide the inspectors with a full inventory (an itemized listing) of its chemical, biological, and nuclear weapons and its missiles. It was also to provide the locations of its research and manufacturing sites. But from the beginning, the Iraqis refused to cooperate. The Iraqis lied about what weapons they had and refused to destroy the weapons and equipment that were discovered.

Iraqi actions led to repeated confrontations with the United Nations. On several occasions during 1991 and 1992, Iraq was severely criticized for continuing to obstruct efforts to find and destroy all its weapons of mass destruction. The United States threatened military action if Iraq did not reveal the full scope of its weapons program. Each time Iraq backed down and promised to comply. But as the threat of military action passed, Iraq returned to its earlier tactics. In the months after the Gulf War, some of Iraqi's weapons and weapon-producing facilities were destroyed, but many more remain.

The Gulf War in Retrospect

What the Gulf War Did and Didn't Do

When the Gulf War ended there was a feeling of great optimism in the United States. President Bush spoke of a "new world order" and many hoped that peace and stability would come to the Middle East. Experts predicted that Saddam Hussein would soon be overthrown. Some claimed that Saudi Arabia and Kuwait would soon take steps toward democracy.

As the months passed, however, it became obvious that little in the Middle East had changed. Despite his defeat, Saddam Hussein was still in power and in command of a powerful army and a large arsenal of weapons. Saudi Arabia and Kuwait were no closer to democracy than they had been before. The Arab-Israeli conflict continued and the Middle East was still the most unstable region in the world.

What did the Gulf War accomplish? What has changed in the Middle East? Kuwait was liberated. Iraq was prevented from invading Saudi Arabia and being in control of 40 percent of the world's oil. Enough of Iraq's arsenal was destroyed to prevent it from becoming the dominant power in the Middle East and being a threat to its neighbors.

The successful outcome of the Gulf War gave the United States enormous prestige in the region. At the same time the collapse of the Soviet Union left the United States as the only superpower in the world. These two events created new opportunities for the United States in the Middle East. The United States was able to use its new position to get Israel and its Arab neighbors to attend a Middle East Peace Conference. Jordan and the Palestinians, isolated because of their support of Iraq during the war, were more willing to compromise. Syria realized that better relations with the United States were essential to achieve its goals. Several months later Syria helped to secure the release of the United States hostages in Lebanon. It must be remembered, however, that these changes resulted as much from the collapse of the Soviet Union during 1991 as they did from successful outcome of the Gulf War.

The Middle East in World Affairs

As we have seen, the Middle East is one of the most important areas in the world. For this reason, outside nations have often tried to dominate the Middle East or to extend their influence over the countries in the region. From 1945 to 1991, the United States and the Soviet Union, the world's two superpowers, were involved in a rivalry to gain influence in the Middle East. This rivalry greatly influenced what happened in the Middle East and contributed to the instability of the area.

The Middle East Between East and West

Until 1945, the Middle East and North Africa were controlled by France and Great Britain. After World War II with the decline of France and Britain, the Soviet Union and the United States became involved in the Middle East. The Soviet Union saw an opportunity to gain greater influence in the area and perhaps even to spread Communism. The

United States moved in to limit Soviet advances. The leaders of the Middle Eastern nations took advantage of the rivalry between the Soviet Union and the United States and played one side against the other for their own benefit.

Soon after World War II the Soviet Union supported a guerrilla movement in Greece, which almost succeeded in setting up a Communist government there. In Turkey, the Soviets asked for military bases, territory, and guaranteed passaged for Soviet warships from the Black Sea to the Mediterranean. If the USSR had succeeded in these demands, they would have obtained a position of great importance in the Middle East. But the United States came to the aid of these two countries with the Truman Doctrine of 1947. The doctrine provided for economic and military aid to countries threatened by Communism. The aid strengthened both Greece and Turkey, and they successfully resisted the Soviets. Turkey became a strong supporter of the West and received billions of dollars of economic and military assistance from the United States. Turkey became a member of NATO in 1952, and the United States built military bases there.

Soviet Influence Grows

In their relations with the Arab countries, the Soviet Union was far more successful than the United States. Until World War II the Soviet Union had practically no direct contact with the Arab world. After the war the Soviets saw the possibility of replacing the West and becoming the most important power in the Middle East. The Soviet Union hoped to be able to limit the West's use of the oil resources of the Middle East. The USSR also hoped to be in control of the important waterways of the Middle East.

Although the Soviet Union did not establish control over any Middle Eastern nation, it did make great gains in the area. Through large scale economic and military aid to Arab countries, the Soviet Union made many friends in the Middle East. Billions of dollars worth of planes, tanks, missiles, machinery, and technical aid were given to Egypt and Syria. In 1958, the Soviet Union agreed to provide the money, equipment, and engineers to build the high dam at Aswan in Egypt. In diplomacy, the Soviet Union consistently backed the Arabs in their conflict with Israel. Before, during, and after the June War of 1967, the USSR supported all the demands made by the Arabs.

Hundreds of young Arabs went to the USSR to study science and technology. Hundreds of Soviet engineers, pilots, and army officers came to Egypt and Syria to train the Arabs.

United States Interests

Between the Arabs and Israel

After 1945, the United States had two major interests in the Middle East: to safeguard the vital oil supplies and to limit Soviet expansion. The United States hoped that its relations with the nations of the Middle East would promote these goals. However, America's relations with the Middle Eastern nations were complicated because the United States tried to have friendly relations with both Israel and the Arab states.

The United States regarded Israel as a strategic ally and a nation with whom it shared a democratic tradition. The United States was committed to Israel's survival and pledged not to allow Israel to be destroyed by the Arabs. At the same time, the United States sought to maintain friendly relations with the Arabs because of their enormous oil resources.

This situation often caused problems. When the United States sold weapons to Israel to balance the weapons sent to the Arabs from the Soviet Union, the Arabs complained bitterly. When the United States sold weapons and aircraft to Jordan and Saudi Arabia to keep them from turning to the Soviet Union, the Israelis were unhappy.

During the 1970s and 1980s, the United States cultivated friendlier relations with the Arabs. While maintaining its long-standing ties to Saudi Arabia and Jordan, the United States developed a new relationship with Egypt in the mid 1970s. Since the Camp David Accords of 1979, Egypt has received about $3 billion in U.S. aid annually. During the Iran-Iraq war (1980–1988), the United States supported Iraq. The United States regarded Iraq as a counter-balance to Iran. The United States sold Iraq millions of dollars worth of advanced weaponry and high technology.

America's New Role in the Middle East

After Iraq's invasion of Kuwait in 1990, the United States began organizing an anti-Iraq coalition. For the coalition to be effective, the United States needed Arab involvement, and therefore cultivated friendlier relations with the Arabs. The United States moved closer to Syria, a nation that had long been on the State Department's list of terrorist nations. President Bush met with Syria's President Assad. Relations with Saudi Arabia and Egypt became even closer than before.

As you read, after the Gulf War, American prestige in the Arab world was at an all-time high. By the end of 1991, with the breakup of the Soviet Union, the United States was the world's only superpower. The United States has tried to use its new influence in the area to resolve the Arab-Israeli conflict and to bring peace to the region. With the fall of the Soviet Union and the end of the Cold War, the United States now regards regional conflicts as the greatest threat to peace and stability in the world. While the United States is still committed to the survival of Israel, since the Gulf War, U.S. policy has been seen as more pro-Arab than before.

Summary
of
Key Ideas

The Middle East and North Africa

A. The location of the Middle East has made the region important in world affairs.

1. Its location at the crossroads of three continents and the existence of the Suez Canal make the Middle East a strategic area.

2. This region forms a land bridge that connects Europe, Asia, and Africa. Historically, it has been a crossroads for traders going from Europe to India, and from Asia to North Africa.

3. The location of the Middle East has led to significant cultural diffusion and cultural blending.

B. Geography has played an important role in the development of the Middle East.

1. Deserts are a major feature of the topography of the Middle East.

2. Scarcity of water is a major problem.

3. Climatic and soil factors would be favorable to agriculture if adequate and cheap water resources could be found.

4. Large populations are concentrated in flood plains and deltas of the major rivers (Nile, Tigris-Euphrates).

C. Cultural factors have served both to unite and separate the peoples of the Middle East.

1. Most of the people of the Middle East belong to the ethnic group known as Arabs (exceptions: Israelis, Turks, Persians).

2. The people of the Middle East can be divided into three groups: e.g., farmers, nomadic herders (bedouins), and city dwellers.

3. Islam is the major influence in the area. It influences the values, thoughts, and actions of most of the people.

4. Ideas from the West have greatly influenced the cultural development of the region.

5. Nationalism has influenced developments in the Middle East and has tended to divide the Arabs.

6. Pan Arabism is a political movement with the aim of uniting all Arabs, but such forces as local tribal loyalties and rivalry among national leaders have prevented its success.

D. The history of the Middle East has been marked by great accomplishment, then steady decline and foreign domination.

1. The Middle East contains the longest span of recorded history.

2. Discoveries and inventions made in the Middle East have helped shape cultures throughout the world.

3. Various ethnic and racial groups contributed to the cultural development of the area.

4. The river valleys of the Nile and the Tigris-Euphrates were cradles of early civilization.

5. Three great world religions were born in the area (Judaism, Christianity, and Islam).

6. The Arabs have made significant contributions to world civilization in the fields of religion, science, art, literature, and mathematics.

7. Arab empires ruled the Middle East and North Africa for centuries.

8. From the 15th century to the middle of the 20th century, Arab areas remained under control of non-Arab rulers. Progress remained at a standstill.

9. World War I and World War II led to a growth of nationalism and finally to independence.

E. The economy of the area is based on farming and oil.

1. Most of the people of the Middle East are farmers and herders. Many of them do not own the land they work on.

2. Farming methods are unscientific, outdated, and primitive.

3. Except for the oil-rich countries and Israel, the Middle East is a region of economic underdevelopment, low standards of living, and low levels of production.

4. Oil is king. The Middle East has vast known oil reserves.

5. Strong desires for complete freedom from foreign influence conflicted with dependence on Western technology in operating the oil fields.

6. Income from oil sales has transformed several of the Middle East countries.

7. The United States and the Soviet Union had been engaged in rivalry to control the rich oil resources.

8. Arab socialism is the economic idea followed by the developing nations in the Middle East.

9. Most governments regulate industrial development and supervise many aspects of economic life.

10. The Middle East faces all the economic problems of developing nations.

F. Conflict between Israel and the Arab nations adds to the problems of the area.

1. Israel is an island of Judaism in a sea of Islam.

2. Israel bases it claim to Middle Eastern land on historical and Biblical grounds.

3. Israel has been an independent state since 1948.

4. Israeli society and economy differ from those of the other countries of the Middle East in religion, language, science, farming, government, and methods of development.

5. Many Arab nations are still pledged to the destruction of Israel.

6. Wars were fought in 1948, 1956, 1967, and 1973. Israel emerged victorious, and now occupies territory of Jordan, Egypt, and Syria.

7. Arab refugees who left Israel in 1948, and their children, present a difficult problem to the solution of the Arab-Israeli conflict.

8. The United States has tried to play a role in the settlement of conflicts in the Middle East. The former Soviet Union has followed a policy of close support and aid for the Arabs.

9. The most difficult peace issues include the security of Israel, Palestinian nationalism, and the future of the occupied territories.

10. State supported terrorism has become a significant factor in the Arab-Israeli conflict.

11. Efforts by the United States in the last decade of the 20th century to achieve a peaceful settlement have resulted in only limited success.

UNIT II

Exercises and Questions

Vocabulary

Directions: Match the words in Column A with the correct meaning in Column B.

Column A

1. caliphs (j)
2. Islam (d)
3. Muslim (e)
4. Hegira (a)
5. mosque (h)
6. Koran (c)
7. Allah (g)
8. pilgrimage (i)
9. monotheism (f)
10. sultan (b)
11. wadis (k)
12. oasis (l)

Column B

(a) Mohammed's flight from Mecca to Medina
(b) Turkish ruler
(c) holy book of the Muslims
(d) submission to God
(e) follower of Islam
(f) belief in one God
(g) Arabic for God
(h) place of worship
(i) religious journey
(j) rulers of the Islamic empire
(k) seasonal streams found in deserts
(l) a part of the desert where water and vegetation can be found

Column A

1. bedouins
2. sheik
3. fellahin
4. bazaar
5. rabbi
6. Talmud
7. kibbutz
8. Zionism
9. pharaoh
10. Pan-Islamism

Column B

(a) collective farm in Israel
(b) marketplace
(c) ancient Egyptian ruler
(d) desert nomads
(e) idea of a single state for all Muslims
(f) book containing Jewish teachings
(g) Arab peasants
(h) Jewish religious teacher
(i) tribal leader
(j) belief in a Jewish state in Israel

THE MIDDLE EAST: POPULATION, DENSITY, AND INCOME

Country	Area (thousands of square miles)	Population (millions of people)	Density of Population (people per sq. mi.)	Income Per Person in U.S. Dollars (per capita)
United States	3,615	251.3	68	19,780
Egypt	386	53.1	138	650
Iraq	173	17.7	105	2,420
Israel	8	4.6	584	8,650
Jordan	37	3.1	92	1,500
Kuwait	6	2.1	312	13,680
Lebanon	4	2.9	751	690
Saudi Arabia	870	14.1	16	6,170
Syria	72	12.1	169	1,670

Source: *Encyclopedia Britannica Book of the Year 1991*

Chart Interpretation

Directions: Select the statement that best answers the question or completes the sentence. Use only the information given in the chart and graphs.

1. The number 386 next to Egypt in the *area* column stands for
   - (a) 386 square miles
   - (b) 3,860 square miles
   - (c) 38,600 square miles
   - (d) 386,000 square miles

2. The number 17.7 next to Iraq in the *population* column stands for
   - (a) 177 people
   - (b) 177,000 people
   - (c) 17,700 people
   - (d) 177,000,000 people

3. The Middle Eastern country with the largest area is
   - (a) Saudi Arabia
   - (b) Egypt
   - (c) Iraq
   - (d) Kuwait

4. The Middle Eastern country with the smallest population is
   - (a) Saudi Arabia
   - (b) Lebanon
   - (c) Israel
   - (d) Kuwait

5. The Middle Eastern country whose per capita income is closest to that of the United States is
   - (a) Saudi Arabia
   - (b) Israel
   - (c) Jordan
   - (d) Kuwait

6. The column that tells us about standard of living is
   - (a) Income Per Person
   - (b) Population
   - (c) Area
   - (d) Density

7. The population of Lebanon is closest to that of
   - (a) Jordan
   - (b) Kuwait
   - (c) Iraq
   - (d) Saudi Arabia

8. The density of population of Israel is greater than all of the following *except*
   - (a) Lebanon
   - (b) Kuwait
   - (c) Iraq
   - (d) Jordan

9. This chart would be of great value to
   - (a) an anthropolgist
   - (c) a psychologist
   - (b) an historian
   - (d) an economist

10. Which of the following statements is true according to the information given in this table?
   - (a) Most of the people in the Middle East live in Lebanon.
   - (b) Iraq has a larger per capita income than Saudi Arabia.
   - (c) Much of Saudi Arabia has a low density of population.
   - (d) The population of Kuwait is three times that of Jordan.

Multiple Choice

Directions: Select the letter of the correct answer.

1. The lands of the Middle East can be studied as one region because they are similar in all of the following ways _except_
   - (a) they all have the same kind of climate.
   - (b) most of the people are Muslims.
   - (c) they are all ruled by the same government.
   - (d) they have similar problems.

2. Much of the world's trade passes through the Middle East because
   - (a) the people of the Middle East are among the world's best traders. ✓
   - (b) the Middle East connects three continents. ✓
   - (c) the best harbors are found in the Middle East. ✓
   - (d) all of these.

3. The Suez Canal connects the
   - (a) Atlantic Ocean with the Pacific Ocean.
   - (b) Atlantic Ocean with the Black Sea.
   - (c) Mediterranean Sea with the Red Sea.
   - (d) Mediterranean Sea with the Black Sea.

4. Most of the land of the Middle East is
   - (a) jungle.   (b) steppe.   (c) desert.   (d) savanna.

5. Only about 15 percent of the land of the Middle East is suitable for farming. Eighty-five percent is unsuitable because
   - (a) it is too dry.
   - (b) it is too hilly.
   - (c) there are too many factories.
   - (d) none of these.

6. The longest river in the world is the
   - (a) Tigris.   (b) Euphrates.   (c) Nile.   (d) Congo.

7. The best land for farming is found in
   - (a) the mountains.
   - (b) the river valleys.
   - (c) Turkey.
   - (d) all of these.

8. Which of the following is true of the nomads of the desert?
   (a) They are always moving in search of water.
   (b) Their animals supply them with most of their needs.
   (c) Many have come under the control of governments in the cities.
   (d) All of these.

9. All of the following are true about farmers in the Middle East *except*
   (a) farmers make up 75 percent of the population of the area.
   (b) most of the farmers use tractors and other machinery.
   (c) most farmers own small plots of land.
   (d) many farmers rent land from rich landlords.

10. Farming in Israel is very different from farming in the rest of the Middle East because
   (a) there are no rich landlords in Israel.
   (b) all the farmers together own the land, tools, and animals.
   (c) Israeli farmers use modern methods.
   (d) all of these.

11. Cities of the Middle East are very interesting because
   (a) there are no slums or poor people.
   (b) old Arab towns exist alongside modern cities.
   (c) most of the people are factory workers.
   (d) all of these.

12. All of the following are true of the marketplace *except*
   (a) every item has a fixed price.
   (b) beautiful jewelry, rugs, and leather goods can be found.
   (c) workshops are often located behind the booths in the market.
   (d) craftspeople pass their skills on to their children.

13. Craftspeople earn a living by
   (a) making goods by hand.
   (b) using modern machinery.
   (c) selling goods to the farmers.
   (d) importing goods from other countries.

14. All of the following are true about Islam except
   (a) Mohammed was the founder of the religion.
   (b) Mohammed was influenced by the teachings of the Jews.
   (c) Mohammed believed that there is only one God.
   (d) Mohammed's ideas were very popular among the people of Mecca.

15. A good Muslim does all of the following *except*
   (a) believes that Mohammed was God's prophet.
   (b) goes to church on Sunday.
   (c) reads the Koran.
   (d) fasts during the month of Ramadan.

16. The Hebrews made their greatest contribution to the world in
   (a) architecture.   (c) religion.
   (b) government.   (d) science.

17. The Prophets were very important in ancient Israel because
    (a) they condemned the worship of other gods.
    (b) they said that God demanded righteousness from his people.
    (c) they criticized the rich and powerful people who were unjust.
    (d) all of these.

18. The main reason that civilization first developed in the Nile Valley and Mesopotamia was that
    (a) there were excellent harbors for trade.
    (b) the soil was fertile for farming.
    (c) many industries developed.
    (d) cities provided many jobs.

19. In the river valleys the need for water led to
    (a) wars among the different people.
    (b) crop failures.
    (c) growth of government.
    (d) none of these.

20. Hieroglyphics and cuneiform were
    (a) ancient systems of writing.
    (b) ancient Babylonian art.
    (c) warfare methods practiced by the Sumerians.
    (d) forms of architecture.

21. The Egyptian pharaohs built huge pyramids because
    (a) they wanted to show that they were good architects.
    (b) they wanted to preserve their bodies for the life after death.
    (c) they wanted to provide jobs for thousands of people.
    (d) all of these.

22. Probably the earliest people to use iron were the
    (a) Lydians.   (b) Hitties.   (c) Phonenicians.   (d) Hebrews.

23. The Muslims made great contributions to the world in
    (a) medicine.   (b) mathematics.   (c) literature.   (d) all of these.

24. All of the following are true of Muslim culture *except*
    (a) the Muslims were influenced by the learning of ancient Greece and India.
    (b) the writings of Greek philosophers were translated into Arabic and later passed on to Europe.
    (c) the numbers that we use today were first developed by the Arabs.
    (d) knowledge of mathematics came to the Arabs from India, but the Arabs added to this and passed it on.

25. Omar Khayyám was famous as
    (a) a Persian poet.
    (b) an Arab scientist.
    (c) an Egyptian general.
    (d) a Muslim priest.

26. The Crusaders were
    (a) Arabs who became Christians.
    (b) European Christians who tried to reconquer the Holy Land.
    (c) Muslims who visited Europe.
    (d) Christian soldiers who defended Europe against Arab attacks.

27. The nomads who invaded the Middle East in the 13th and 14th centuries and caused much destruction were
    (a) Crusaders.   (b) Persians.   (c) Mongols.   (d) Indians.

28. All of the following statements about the Ottoman Empire are true *except*
    (a) the Turks were good soldiers and conquered vast territories.
    (b) the Turks forced all the people in their empire to become Muslims.
    (c) important contributions were made by the Turks in literature and architecture.
    (d) the most intelligent Christian boys were converted, assigned to military units, and trained to rule.

29. The Ottoman Empire declined when
    (a) the rulers became more interested in pleasure than ruling.
    (b) Europe began to make great progress in science and industry.
    (c) Russian fought many wars against Turkey to capture territory.
    (d) all of these.

30. A famous Ottoman ruler was
    (a) Ferdinand de Lesseps.
    (b) Suleiman the Magnificient.
    (c) Mohammed.
    (d) Salah-al-Din.

31. The engineer who built the Suez Canal was
    (a) Turkish.   (b) French.   (c) Egyptian.   (d) English.

32. The Suez Canal was important because it made it easier for
    (a) Russia to trade with the Mediterranean countries.
    (b) European nations to trade with Asia.
    (c) the United States to trade with Latin America.
    (d) the United States to trade with Europe.

33. Until the end of World War II the most important decisions affecting the Middle East were made by the
    (a) Russians and Americans.
    (b) Egyptians and Syrians.
    (c) British and French.
    (d) Germans and Italians.

34. A mandate is related to which of these areas?
    (a) Egypt   (b) Palestine   (c) Morocco   (d) Saudi Arabia

35. Approximately how much of the world's oil reserves is the Middle East believed to contain?
    (a) 30 percent   (b) 50 percent   (c) 66 percent   (d) 85 percent

36. The oil fields of the Middle East were developed by European and American oil companies for all of the following reasons *except*
    (a) the nations of the Middle East did not have enough money.
    (b) the nations of the Middle East did not have the necessary equipment.
    (c) the nations of the Middle East did not have enough engineers.
    (d) the nations of the Middle East were not very interested in their oil reserves.

37. Which of the following is the cause of the other three?
    (a) Desert nomads work for wages.
    (b) New towns are built.
    (c) An oil company begins to drill for oil.
    (d) Many people receive technical training.

38. A very important reason why the nations of the Middle East find it difficult to improve the living conditions of their people is that
    (a) the population continues to grow faster than the rate of food production.
    (b) these nations have no important source of income.
    (c) the former Soviet Union has been charging the countries of the Middle East high interest rates on loans.
    (d) heavy rainfall has destroyed many crops.

39. The Balfour Declaration stated that
    (a) the British intended to take over Palestine for themselves.
    (b) the British Government favored a national home for the Jews in Palestine.
    (c) Palestine should be an Arab state.
    (d) the British and French would rule Palestine together.

40. Which of the following was not a result of the first Arab-Israeli War?
    (a) An Arab state was set up in Palestine.
    (b) Israel defended its independence.
    (c) Thousands of Arabs left their homes in Palestine.
    (d) Israel proved its military strength.

41. Which of the following was true of the 1956 Arab-Israeli War?
    (a) The Arabs captured the Suez Canal.
    (b) The United Nations set up a force to try to keep peace.
    (c) Israel was defeated.
    (d) Egypt was able to blockade the Gulf of Aqaba.

42. Since the Six Day War of 1967
    (a) the Arabs have gained control of Palestine.
    (b) peace and recognition of Israel have been achieved.
    (c) Israel and the Arabs have been unable to reach a settlement.
    (d) Arab refugees have been resettled in Israel.

43. The Truman Doctrine was important because
    (a) it promised American aid to countries threatened by Communism.
    (b) it helped Greece and Turkey resist Soviet demands.
    (c) it won friends for the United States.
    (d) all of these.

44. Soviet interests in the Middle East included all of the following *except*
    (a) to limit the West's use of the important oil resources of the Middle East.
    (b) to make sure that Israel remains strong.
    (c) to win friends among the Arabs.
    (d) to control the important waterways of the Middle East.

45. The United States policy in the Middle East has been
    (a) to win the friendship of the Arabs.
    (b) to win the friendship of Israel.
    (c) to be friendly with both Israel and the Arabs.
    (d) to stay neutral and not take sides.

46. Which of the following statements is *not* true about the 1973 Middle East war?
    (a) Syria and Egypt launched an attack against Israel.
    (b) The United States provided Israel with vast shipments of arms.
    (c) The Soviet Union remained neutral during the conflict.
    (d) The cease-fire went into effect as Israel was about to win a decisive victory.

47. Which of the following statements is true?
    (a) The Arabs used oil as a weapon during the 1973 war and later.
    (b) Western Europe and Japan were hard hit when the Arabs cut back their oil production.
    (c) The Arabs announced a total oil embargo against the United States and Holland.
    (d) All of these.

48. The best known American in the Middle East during the 1970s was
    (a) Ronald Reagan.
    (b) Henry Kissinger.
    (c) Gerald Ford.
    (d) Nelson Rockefeller

49. Which statement is *not* true about the Palestinians?
    (a) The Palestinians want to return to Israel, which they call Palestine, because they consider it their homeland.
    (b) The Palestinians are ready to make peace with Israel at any time.
    (c) Many Palestinians are involved in acts of terrorism.
    (d) The Palestinians often find themselves in conflict with other Arabs.

50. Which of the following statements is true about the Israeli-Egyptian Agreements?
    (a) The Arab nations praised the agreement as a great step toward peace.
    (b) Both sides had to make compromises.
    (c) Egypt did not get back any of the land captured by Israel.
    (d) Israel agreed to withdraw from all Arab territories occupied in the 1967 war.

51. An important result of the Camp David Accords was
    (a) that Israel agreed to remove all its setttlements in the West Bank.
    (b) the establishment of a nation for the Palestinians.
    (c) the recognition of Israel by all Arab nations.
    (d) that Israel and Egypt agreed to negotiate a peace treaty to end the 30-year state of war between them.

52. The role of the PLO in Lebanon has been to
    (a) support and strengthen the Lebanese government.
    (b) act as a peacemaker between Israel and Syria.
    (c) use Lebanon as a base from which to attack Israel.
    (d) support Christian groups against Muslim groups.

53. Which of the following is a cause of civil war in Lebanon?
    (a) distrust and hatred between Christians and Muslims
    (b) the inability of the Lebanese government to control the various warring groups
    (c) fighting between various political groups to gain control of the government
    (d) all of the above are correct

54. Which of the following men tried to modernize Iran?
    (a) the Shah   (c) Ayatollah Khomeini
    (b) Yasir Arafat   (d) Muammar Qaddafi

Thought Questions

1. Why is it very important for us to know about the Middle East today?

2. Why is water a problem to the people of the Middle East?

3. How do the lives of the desert nomad, village farmer, and city dweller differ from each other?

4. What are some of the things a Muslim believes?

5. Why has the Jewish religion had a great influence on other religions and civilizations?

6. Why did civilization develop in the Nile Valley and Mesopotamia?

7. How were the Arabs able to spread Islam to many different parts of the world?

8. Why have historians used such words as "brilliant" and "magnificient" to describe Muslim civilization from 700 to 1200 A.D.?

9. Why did the civilization of the Muslims decline after 1200?

10. Why did the Arabs feel that Britain and France had betrayed them after World War I?

11. (a) What are some of the ways in which the Arabs hoped to unify the lands of the Middle East following World War II?
    (b) Why have these hopes not been realized?

12. Why has oil been called "king" in the Middle East?

13. What are some of the problems Middle Eastern nations face in trying to erase poverty and build up their industries?

14. If you were the leader of one of these nations, how would you try to solve these problems?

15. Why have many Jewish people always hoped to return to Palestine and to set up a Jewish state?

16. Why are the Arabs opposed to a Jewish state in Palestine?

17. What are the main issues that have divided Israel and the Arab countries since 1967?

18. Why was the former Soviet Union successful in winning much influence in the Middle East?

19. Why does the United States face many problems in its relations with the countries of the Middle East?

20. What affect have the Palestinians had on stability in the Middle East?

21. How did Lebanon go from being one of the most advanced nations in the Middle East to one of the most devastated?

22. How did the goals of the Shah of Iran clash with those of religious Muslims?

23. Why did Iraq invade Iran in 1980?

24. Compare the status of Muslim women in the Middle East with the status of women in the United States.

25. Discuss the effect Iraq's invasion of Kuwait had on each of the following: a) Iraq; b) Kuwait; c) United States; d) Israel; e) Palestinians.

Chart Interpretation

Directions: Answer the following questions by indicating whether the statement is *True* or *False* or *Information Not Given*. Base all answers on information given in the chart.

1. All the nations of the Middle East increased their imports from the United States between 1988 and 1989.

2. Israel is the leading trading partner of the United States in the Middle East.

3. Oil is the leading trade product between the United States and the Middle East.

4. The greatest increase in exports between 1988 and 1989 was made by Egypt.

5. We may conclude that trade increased between the United States and the countries of the Middle East between 1988 and 1989.

UNITED STATES TRADE WITH THE MIDDLE EAST AND NORTH AFRICA (SELECTED AREAS)

Country	Exports*		Imports*	
	1988	1989	1988	1989
Algeria	733	756	1,972	1,829
Egypt	2,340	2,612	243	227
Iran	73	55	9	9
Iraq	1,156	1,169	1,605	2,415
Israel	3,248	2,827	3,068	3,239
Saudi Arabia	3,799	3,574	6,297	7,157

*Value in Millions of Dollars
Source: *The World Almanac*, 1991

THE MIDDLE EAST

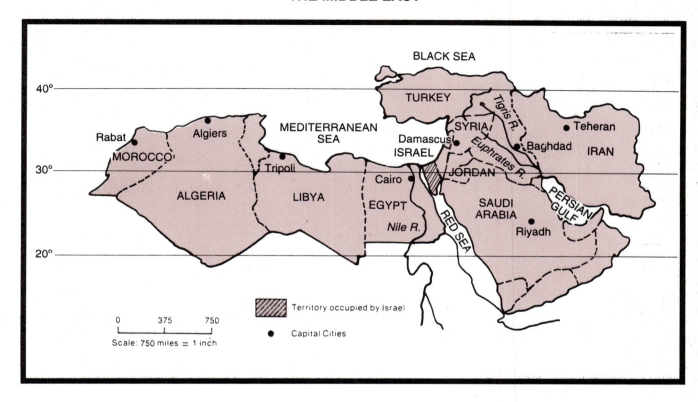

Map Exercises

Directions: Tell whether the following statements are *True* or *False*. Correct the false statements.

1. The distance from Algiers to Cairo is about *1600 miles.*

2. Most of the Middle East is located *south* of the equator.

3. *Baghdad* is located on the Nile River.

4. Territory occupied by Israel is located near *Algeria and Morocco.*

5. Rabat is located on the *east* coast of North Africa.

6. *Turkey* is probably the largest country of the Middle East.

7. The Tigris and Euphrates rivers flow south into the *Red Sea.*

8. The capital of Syria is *Damascus.*

9. Libya is located to the west of *Algeria.*

10. Turkey can be described as an *island.*

Completion

Directions: Complete the following sentences by selecting the correct word or phrases below.

OPEC	disengagement	terrorism
petrodollars	oil embargo	non-belligerence
shuttle diplomacy	Golan Heights	Suez Canal
Sinai Desert	PLO	West Bank

1. The agreement to separate Israeli and Arab troops is known as _____ .

2. The money accumulated by the oil rich countries is known as _____ .

3. The weapon used by the Arabs against the United States during the 1973 war is _____ .

4. The trading route that was once very important to world commerce is _____ .

5. The organization that represents most Palestinians is _____ .

6. Former Jordanian territory that is presently occupied by Israel is _____ .

7. The term that refers to Mr. Kissinger's traveling back and forth between Israel and the Arab countries is _____ .

8. Israel would like a promise from the Arabs not to use force. This is known as _____ .

9. The organization that represents the oil producing countries is _____ .

10. Syrian territory that is held by Israel is called _____ .

11. Methods used by many Palestinians against Israel are termed _____ .

12. A vast territory that had been taken by Israel from Egypt during the 1967 war is _____ .

Developing Answers to Regents-Type Essay Questions

Helpful Hints

In developing your answers to the essays be sure to:

1. Include specific factual information and evidence whenever possible.

2. Answer the question being asked; do not go off on tangents.

3. Keep these general definitions in mind:
   (a) *discuss* means "to make observations about something using facts, reasoning, and argument; to present in some detail."
   (b) *describe* means "to illustrate something in words or to tell about."
   (c) *show* means "to point out, to set forth clearly an idea or position by stating it and giving data that support it."
   (d) *explain* means "to make plain or understandable; to give reasons for or causes of; to show the logical development or relationship."

Sample Essay Questions

1. Geographic factors have greatly influenced the development of nations and cultures.

Geographic Characteristics

Rivers	Natural Resources	Large Bodies of Water
Deserts	Location	Climate

Select *three* geographic characteristics from the list and for each characteristic:

   (a) Discuss how *that* characteristic influenced the development of the history and culture of a specific nation selected from *Egypt, Israel, Iraq, Saudi Arabia, Iran.* (Select a different nation for each characteristic chosen.)
   (b) Explain *one* way in which the nation has adapted to or tried to modify the effects of the geographic characteristic.

2. Leaders have influenced events within a nation and also have influenced world affairs.

Leaders

Saddam Hussein	Ayatollah Khomeini
Anwar Sadat	Mohammed
Menachem Begin	

Select *two* leaders from the list. For *each* one selected:

(a) Identify the nation in which the leader acted.
(b) Discuss one policy—domestic or foreign—of the leader.
(c) Discuss how that leader put his policy into effect.
(d) Explain how that policy affected the leader's nation or the Middle East.

3. Human interaction has often resulted in conflict between groups and cultures.

Groups—Cultures

European Christian Crusaders and Muslims of the Middle East
Shi'ite Muslims and Sunni Muslims in the Middle East
Israelis and Arabs in the Middle East
Muslim Fundamentalists and Modern Middle East Progressives
Ottoman Turks and Eastern Europeans

Select *three* of the groups or cultures from the list. For *each* one selected, discuss a major cause of the conflict and the effect of the conflict on the groups involved.

4. Many factors influence the economic success of cultures and nations.

Factors of Economics

| Natural Resources | Skilled Labor | Markets |
| Availability of Capital | Government Policy | Corruption |

Select *three* of the above factors of economics and describe how *each* of the three influences economic developments in the Middle East.

5. Islam and Judaism have strongly influenced the culture of the peoples of the Middle East.

Aspects of Culture

| Architecture | Art | Role of Women | Music |
| Education | Literature (including the Bible and Koran) | | |

(a) Select Islam or Judaism and discuss how that religion has influenced *three* aspects of culture within Middle Eastern society.
Note: You must use each religion for at least one aspect.
(b) Describe how *two* of the aspects selected have influenced peoples and societies throughout the world.

6. Many nations have similar problems that hinder their economic growth and political stability.

Problems

Lack of Water	Religious Differences
Terrorism	Lack of Natural Resources
Rival Nationalisms	Lack of Peace and Stability

(a) Choose *two* of the problems listed. For each problem selected: Describe how *each* of the problems has affected economic growth or political stability.
(b) Write an essay explaining how the problems of the Middle East have hindered the economic growth and stability of the nations of the Middle East.

Puzzle

Directions: Place the words below in their proper place in the puzzle.

3 LETTERS	**5 LETTERS**	**6 LETTERS**	**7 LETTERS**	**8 LETTERS**
ISM	LACKS	DEMAND	MANDATE	CONFLICT
IST	UNITY	PREFIX	PIONEER	CREATION
		REGION	REFUGEE	INCIDENT
		STRAIT	TACTICS	OCCUPIED
		SUFFIX		PROPOSAL

9 LETTERS	**10 LETTERS**	**11 LETTERS**	**13 LETTERS**
GUERRILLA	IRRIGATION	AGRICULTURE	INDOCTRINATED
INJUSTICE	PROPAGANDA	IMMIGRATION	
PREVENTED	RESTRICTED	IMPERIALIST	
		NATIONALISM	

POLITICAL MAP OF AFRICA

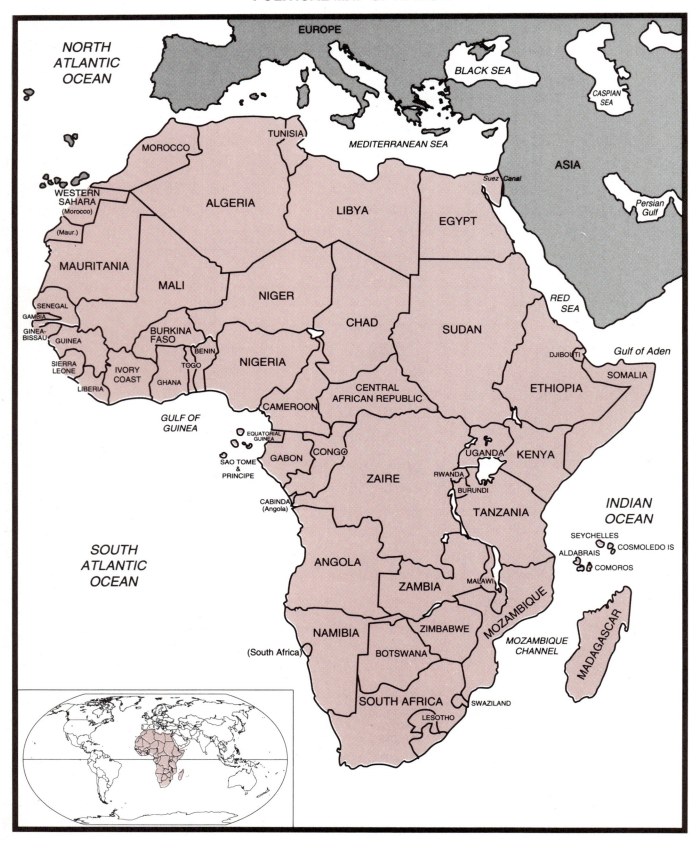

NORTH
ATLANTIC
OCEAN

EUROPE

BLACK SEA

CASPIAN
SEA

TUNISIA

MOROCCO

MEDITERRANEAN SEA

ASIA

WESTERN
SAHARA
(Morocco)

ALGERIA

LIBYA

EGYPT

Suez Canal

(Maur.)

Persian
Gulf

MAURITANIA

MALI

NIGER

RED
SEA

SENEGAL

CHAD

SUDAN

Gulf of Aden

GAMBIA

BURKINA
FASO

GINEA-
BISSAU

GUINEA

BENIN

NIGERIA

DJIBOUTI

SIERRA
LEONE

IVORY
COAST

TOGO

SOMALIA

LIBERIA

GHANA

CENTRAL
AFRICAN REPUBLIC

ETHIOPIA

CAMEROON

GULF OF
GUINEA

EQUATORIAL
GUINEA

SAO TOME
&
PRINCIPE

GABON

CONGO

UGANDA

KENYA

ZAIRE

RWANDA

BURUNDI

CABINDA
(Angola)

TANZANIA

INDIAN
OCEAN

SOUTH
ATLANTIC
OCEAN

ANGOLA

SEYCHELLES

COSMOLEDO IS

ALDABRAIS

COMOROS

ZAMBIA

MALAWI

NAMIBIA

ZIMBABWE

MOZAMBIQUE

MOZAMBIQUE
CHANNEL

MADAGASCAR

(South Africa)

BOTSWANA

SOUTH AFRICA

SWAZILAND

LESOTHO

UNIT III Africa—South of the Sahara

Geography and Isolation

Isolation

Africa has been called the "Dark Continent," a land of mystery and the unknown. To describe what Europeans knew of Africa, we can look at a poem written over 250 years ago:

> So geographers, in Afric maps,
> With savage pictures fill their gaps,
> And o'er uninhabitable downs,*
> Place elephants for want of towns.
>
> *Jonathan Swift*

Little was known of Africa south of the Sahara because, for most of its long history, it was isolated to a great extent from the rest of the world. Geography is largely responsible for this. One of the major causes of sub-Saharan Africa's isolation is the Sahara Desert.

The Sahara

The Sahara is the world's largest **desert**. It covers an area greater than that of the United States. It extends from the Red Sea in the east to the Atlantic Ocean in the west. The desert is more rocky than sandy. It has been an obstacle (block) to travel between North Africa and Central Africa. It has also limited the exchange of ideas between the heartland of Africa and the Mediterranean coastlands.

---

*grassy, rolling uplands

Mt. Kilimanjaro, in northern Tanzania, rises 19,565 feet above sea level. Its peak is snow covered all year round.

The Sahara was not always as dry as it is today. During the last part of the Ice Age (7,500 years ago), people and the animals they hunted lived comfortably in the area. As the ice melted, the climate of Africa changed. The Sahara became drier and warmer, and the people who lived there were forced to move to the south. The region began to dry out about 6,000 years ago. This was about the same time that civilization was beginning to develop in Egypt and Southwest Asia. The Sahara seems to have reached its present desert condition about 4,000 years ago.

Other Factors

Other factors have helped to cause Africa's isolation. Sub-Saharan Africa has an almost unbroken and regular coastline. Because of this, there are few natural harbors for ships to anchor in, for trade and exploration. It is also difficult for ships to sail northward along the west coast, because the winds and ocean currents are always from the northeast.

As if these disadvantages were not enough, Africa has a very narrow coastal plain. Not far from the sea, dense jungles or deserts in the west and an **escarpment** (sharp, steep cliffs) in the east appear. Where they drop down from the inland plateau on their way to the sea, Africa's rivers have falls and rapids. These rapids were another obstacle to opening Africa to the world.

Topography

Size

Africa is a huge continent. From east to west, at its widest point, the distance is almost the same as that between Moscow and New York (4,000 miles). The north-south distance is almost the same as the distance between northern Alaska and the Panama Canal (5,000 miles).

Plateaus

About 90 percent of sub-Saharan Africa is 500 feet or higher. In the eastern half of the area a plateau rises 5,000 to 6,000 feet. The plateau does not level off gradually to the sea. It drops off sharply (escarpment). As a person travels westward, however, the plateau drops more slowly to sea level.

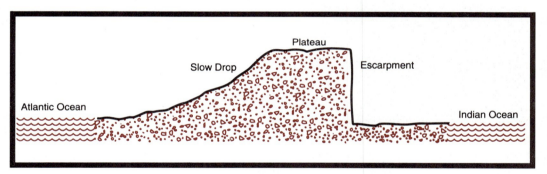

Rivers

The plateau is not completely flat. It is broken by mountains and rivers. In West Africa we find the Zaire (Congo) and Niger Rivers; in East Africa, the Zambezi River; in South Africa, the Limpopo River. The Nile River, with its two major branches, has it sources in Central Africa (Blue Nile—Lake Tana; White Nile—Lake Victoria). The history of Africa, in many ways, is the story of the rise, growth, and fall of civilizations along the river systems. It is also the story of the attempts of outsiders to climb the plateau and control it.

Mountains

On the eastern coast there is a string of mountains that extend from South Africa northward to Ethiopia. In this range the main mountains are Mt. Kilimanjaro, Mt. Kenya, and the Ruwenzori (Runsoro or Kokora) Mountains. These mountains are located almost on the equator, yet they are covered with snow and ice. Most people of European descent live in the highland areas near the mountains because it is cooler.

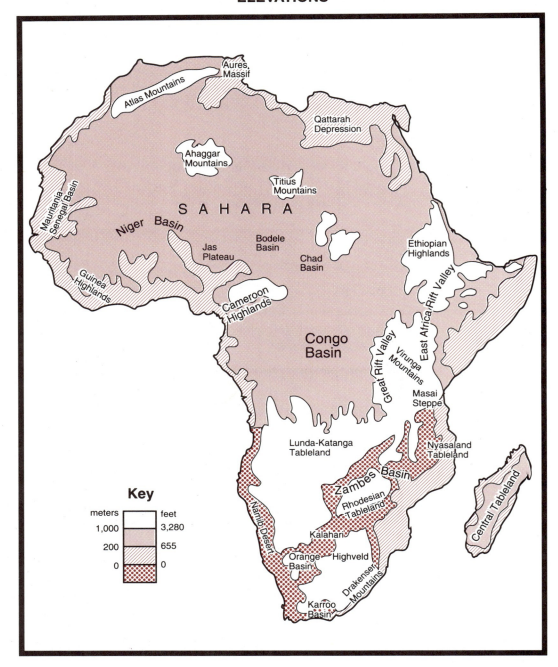

The East African Rift System and the Lakes

In East Africa, the highland plateau is cut by the East African Rift System. This is a series of gigantic **canyons**, which are fissures or breaks in the earth's surface. These canyons were formed millions of years ago by volcanic activity.

The **rift valley** extends for about 4,000 miles from the Zambezi River through eastern and northeastern Africa into the Red Sea. The southern, eastern, and western branches of this rift system are known as: the Southern Rift Valley, the Western Rift Valley, and the

Eastern (Great) Rift Valley. The depth and width of the valleys vary. In some places the valley is more than 20 miles wide and in some places the valley is 1 mile deep.

The majority of East Africa's lakes lie within the East African Rift System. One of them, Lake Victoria, is the largest lake in Africa and the third largest lake in the world.

Where the valley is very deep, the climate and vegetation on the valley floor is often different from the surrounding plateau. Rich soil from the upper plateau has been washed down into the valleys for hundreds of years. As a result, these valley areas of East Africa have very fertile farmland.

The Rift Valley is also rich in minerals and metals. Development of these resources has been made difficult by the area's topography. The escarpments, high mountains, and deep valleys make the building of roads and railroads difficult and costly.

AFRICA: RIVERS, MOUNTAINS, DESERTS, AND LAKES

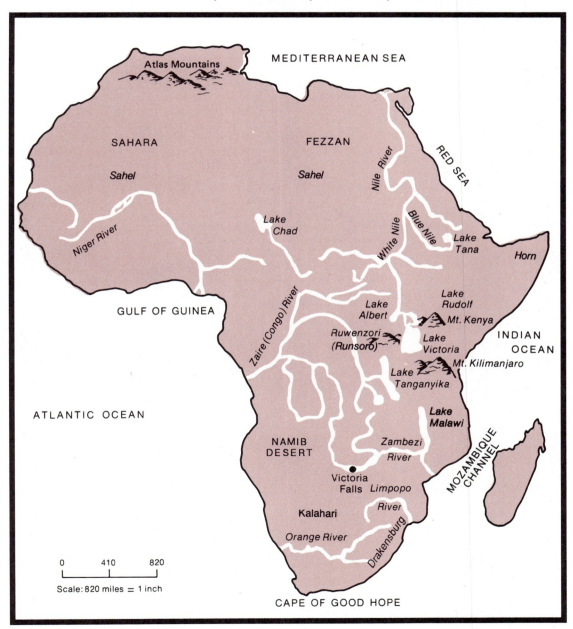

Animals such as this giraffe are found on the savannas of East Africa.

The Rain Forest

Many people imagine that Africa is a jungle or rain forest continent. Actually, there is less true tropical rain forest in Africa than in either Asia or South America. In addition, the African forest is not uninhabited. Many sections of the African forest are thickly populated by farmers, who cut down the trees for farmland.

Savanna

The area around the tropical rain forests is open woodland or **savanna**. In some places, the savanna country is mainly grass with only a few large trees. In other places it looks more like a park, with high grass in place of the usual forest underbrush.

Deserts

Africa has three large desert regions—the Sahara in the north and the Kalahari and the Namib in southern Africa. Other sizable deserts are found in Somalia, Ethiopia, and northeastern Kenya.

The Sahara has often been thought of as a great wasteland and barrier. This idea is not completely true. People, although few in number, have lived in the desert throughout history. Caravans have crossed the desert for thousands of years. In the same way, the other African deserts have provided a place for humans to live. The Somali people raise sheep and goats on the "Horn," as the northeastern desert is often called. For long periods of time people have hunted and gathered food in the Kalahari.

Within the African deserts there is a great variety of topography. We can find rocky, waterless wasteland and mountains and plateaus with some vegetation. Also, constantly shifting sand dunes can be found. During the day the desert is hot. At night temperatures can fall below freezing.

The Climate

Factors Affecting Climate

It is important to remember that the equator runs through the middle of Africa. **Latitude** (distance north or south of the equator), therefore, helps to explain much about the climate of sub-Saharan Africa. The area extends about 20°N to 35°S latitude. Thus, we can always remember the climate of Africa south of the Sahara with the following statement: "Africa is warm, but some places are warmer than others."

Another factor that determines climate is **altitude** (height above sea level). The Kenya highlands, for example, lie on both sides of the equator. Yet temperatures are far lower than in the lowlands, and the air is less humid. Europeans preferred this cooler climate, since it was more like the climate in their homelands.

The cold winds in the highlands and the warm winds that blow from the northeast have an effect on the climate. These winds tend to modify (change) climate in unexpected ways. The cold winds on the equatorial plateau serve to further cool the land. The warm, dry winds from the Arabian Peninsula serve to make the lowlands in part of East Africa warmer and drier.

The cold ocean current (Benguela), flowing north toward the equator on the southwest of Africa, cools and dries the climate of the coastal zones and for miles inland. In the east, warm ocean currents flow south from the equator and bring warm, humid air, which moves far inland.

Rainfall

A great problem faced by Africans is the lack of water. The amount of rainfall and where it falls vary greatly. About 60 percent of the continent does not receive enough rain to support a farming population. An important fact to remember is that the rainfall has a seasonal character. Almost everywhere, apart from the lowlands near the equator, there are wet and dry seasons, not the summer, autumn, winter, and spring we have in North America.

Climate Zones

Near the equator is a large **tropical rain forest**. The climate is always hot, rainy, and unhealthy. (The rain forest is full of mosquitoes, which carry malaria and yellow fever.) North and south of the tropical rain forest are the grassland savannas. Here summer is the rainy season, and winters are dry and dusty. It is always hot. North and south of the savannas are the **steppe** and deserts. Here it is usually hot and dry. Altitude is the main cause of difference in temperature. The steppe (**veld**) gets between ten and 20 inches of rain. It rarely rains on the desert, where it is hot during the day and cold at night.

In southwestern Africa, near Capetown, we find still another climate region. Since Capetown's latitude is 35°S, the climate is sunny and temperate (mild). The summers are almost rainless. Whatever rain there is falls during the winter months. This climate is very similar to the lands that border the Mediterranean Sea and Crimean Russia. This type of climate is called Mediterranean.

On the southeastern coast is an area of humid-subtropical climate. This area is also about 35 degrees from the equator. The climate is much like that of Florida. The summers are hot and the winters are mild. Rain falls throughout the year, with a slightly greater amount falling in the summer.

The People and Their Languages

Africa is a continent of 625 million people. (About 500 million people live in sub-Saharan Africa.)* There are perhaps a greater number of different peoples living in Africa than on any other continent. The African people differ from each other physically as well as culturally. There is no such thing as a typical African or an African way of life. This is because over thousands of years Africans intermarried with people of different races and cultures. Also, because of geography, Africans were often separated from other Africans and therefore developed separately. The common factor is that most of the people of sub-Saharan Africa are Negroid. This means that they exhibit in varying degrees physical characteristics associated with the Negroid race.

---

*Approximate 1990 figures

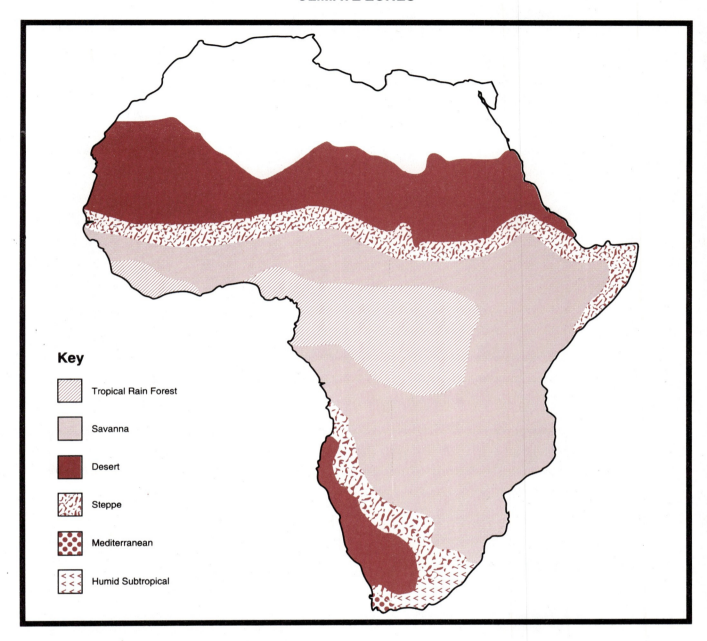

Key

- ⫽⫽⫽ Tropical Rain Forest
- ▦ Savanna
- ▰ Desert
- ⫶⫶ Steppe
- ⬢ Mediterranean
- ⋘ Humid Subtropical

Differences Among Africans

Many people have the false idea that all Africans look alike. This is not so. There are short Africans like the Pygmies, who are a little over four feet in height. There are also tall Africans like the Watusis, who are between six and seven feet tall. Skin color among the African people ranges from almost black to dark brown, gray brown, tan, to the very light skin tone associated with the people of the Mediterranean area. Hair varies from dark and curly to hair that is light in color and straight. Most Africans have dark eyes, but there are people with blue eyes and blue-gray eyes as well. Along the east coast of Africa there are people who have eyes that are usually associated with Asia.

Tanzanian warriors with their brightly decorated shields. Decorating shields is a skilled art.

A young Xhosa girl of South Africa.

Africans also differ from each other culturally. There are differences in language, religion, customs, ways of earning a living, house types, dress, methods of farming, and others. There are also many other peoples who have made Africa their home.

Europeans

About 5 million people of European origin live in sub-Saharan Africa. They live mainly in the Republic of South Africa, Zimbabwe, and Kenya.

Arabs

Hundreds of years ago people from Arabia settled along the coast of East Africa. In recent years many Arabs from Syria and Lebanon settled in West Africa. It is estimated that there are about 1 million Arabs in Africa south of the Sahara.

Asians

Hundreds of thousands of Indians and Pakistanis live in the cities of southern and eastern Africa. They are shopkeepers, traders, and factory workers. Most have kept to their own customs and refused to become citizens of the new African nations in which they live. For this reason the African governments have put pressure on them to give up their foreign citizenship or leave the country. Many have chosen to leave.

Languages

There are many languages spoken in Africa. It is estimated that there are about 800 languages. The actual number may be even greater. These languages can be divided into four major language groups.

Niger-Congo Family

The largest of the language groups and the one that covers the largest geographic area is the Niger-Congo family. This group is divided into seven subfamilies. One of these subfamilies is the well known Bantu. Bantu languages cover most of Central and South Africa. These languages are closely related to one another.

Sudanic Family

The languages spoken in the western Sudan and the area of the middle Niger River belong to the Sudanic family.

Afro-Asian Group

The Afro-Asian group includes ancient Egyptian, Cushitic, and the languages spoken in Somalia and around Lake Chad. The most important language in this group is Hausa.

Click Languages

The Click languages are spoken by the Hottentots and Bushmen.

With so many different languages, it is difficult for Africans to communicate with each other. In Nigeria there are 250 languages. An African leaving his own village may not be able to speak to people living in the next village. Therefore, European languages are used by many Africans to communicate with each other. The two most important European languages that have become the official languages of many countries are English and French. Two African languages are used in the same way. Swahili (a mixture of Arabic and Bantu) is spoken by several million people living in East Africa. Hausa is spoken in northern Nigeria and in other parts of West Africa.

African Families

There is an African proverb that says, "A man or woman without kin is as good as dead." This indicates how important the family is to an African. Family life is important in all societies. The family satisfies the most basic human needs—the need for companionship, for food, for reproduction, and for teaching and training the young. But Africans are far more closely tied to their families than are Americans or people in Western countries. In a number of ways African family life is different from that of American families.

Marriage and the Family

In America when a young couple marries, they move into a home of their own. In Africa the wife goes to live with her husband's family. In our country young people choose the husband or wife whom they wish to marry. In Africa the marriage is usually arranged by the parents. This means that the parents may actually pick the mate for their son or daughter to marry. More often, however, a young man meets a girl whom he likes. He then reports this fact to his father and must get his approval. His father and several other members of the family than arrange to visit the girl's parents to get their approval and to discuss the marriage. Part of the discussion involves the payment of what is known as "bride price" or "bridewealth." The young man has to make some kind of payment to the girl's father before he is allowed to marry her. This payment is usually in the form of cattle or sheep or another type of currency. This does not mean that the man is buying his wife. The bride price is a symbol that the union of the two people is legitimate. It is also a form of compensation for the father of the bride who is not only losing a daughter but a worker as well.

An African man may have several wives at the same time providing he is able to support them. This is known as polygyny. Although polygyny is found throughout Africa, it has been estimated that not more than 10 percent of African men have more than one wife. There are several reasons for polygyny. By having more than one wife a man can be certain of having many children. In this way his name and spirit, as well as that of the whole family, will live on. Also the more wives a man has, the more workers he will have to help him in the fields. While jealousy often does exist, in most cases the co-wives learn to get along and to work together quite well. The children of several wives live together as sisters and brothers. Children can depend on another "mother" if their own is busy.

The Extended Family

Most African families are known as **extended families**. An extended family consists of several generations living together in the same household or group of houses. This includes the oldest male, his wives, their unmarried daughters, the married sons, and their wives and children.

The extended family provides for the social security of its members. There is no need for old age homes or orphanages in Africa because the family takes care of its orphans, widows, and old people. In many cases when a man dies his widow marries her husband's brother. Loneliness is not a problem in Africa. In case of illness the family can be relied on for support. When crops fail, what little there is will be shared. When money is needed to pay for a child's education, relatives will often assist the parents. When relatives request help, it is considered an obligation to provide it. People do not undertake these duties out of the goodness of their hearts—they know that they will be able to demand help from the kin when they need it.

Development of educational facilities is one of Africa's most pressing needs. Here children are studying the Koran at an outdoor school in Lagos, Nigeria.

Children ground millet from sunrise to sunset after harvest. Millet is a relatively good source of protein.

Family Life in the Cities

The family system described here is found in the traditional villages of Africa. In the cities, however, family life is similar to that found in large cities all over the world. Living in apartments makes it difficult for a man to have more than one wife. The city family (nuclear family) consists of the father, mother, and children, rather than the extended family. Young people have greater opportunities to choose their own mates. But people who have moved to the cities still maintain close ties with those relatives remaining in the village.

African Tribalism

A tribe may be defined as a group of people who share the same customs and language, and who believe they have descended from a common ancestor. The people also have a special feeling of belonging together. Many anthropologists today prefer to use the term "nation," "ethnic group," or "people" in place of "tribe."

It has been estimated that there may be from 600 to 1,000 different tribal groups in Africa. Some tribes are quite small and consist of only a few thousand members. Other tribes are very large and have as many as several million people. Some of the most important African tribes are the Ashanti, Fanti, Kikuyu, Ibo, Masai, Watusi, Zulu, Yoruba, and Hausa.

We in America, as well as many people in other Western countries, generally believe that the individual is most important. We believe that the individual has a right to do what he or she alone wants to do, providing that no one is hurt. In other cultures the individual is less important than the group. This has always been true of Russia and China, and it is true of Africa as well. According to the African view of life, a person can only achieve happiness by being part of a group. From birth to death the African is always part of a group. First there is the extended family living together in one household or group of houses. Then there is the clan, a group of related families. And finally there is the tribe, made up of many related clans.

The Individual and the Tribe

Beginning at a very young age a child learns to become a good member of the tribe. From the parents the child learns the laws and customs of the tribe. Tribal customs cover all the important aspects of life from birth to death. As a result people know what they are supposed to do on all occasions and how to do it. They are taught the penalties that result from not following the customs of the tribe. Each member is supposed to make a contribution to the tribe by doing his or her share of the work and obeying its customs.

At the same time the tribe provides its members with security. A person who belongs to a tribe does not feel alone. In bad times he or she can turn to the other members of the tribe and feel confident that they will help. For this reason Africans feel great pride in belonging to a tribe and believe that the customs of their tribe are the best. This pride is shown by a tribal mark, which is usually a cut made on the face in a particular pattern. Although this custom is going out of style, many of today's African leaders still have the tribal marks from their childhood.

A young Masai warrior. The Masai are a tribe of nomadic herders who inhabit the grasslands of Kenya and Tanzania. The Masai rely almost completely on their herds of cattle for subsistence. Milk and cheese are very important in their diet as well as blood from their cattle which is an important source of protein. Since a family's wealth is measured in terms of the number of cattle owned, the Masai do not slaughter their cattle for food, but wait until they are too old to graze.

When a boy or girl reaches puberty, he or she has to go through a complicated ceremony known as initiation to be admitted into the tribe. As part of the ceremony, the boy must show that he has reached manhood by proving that he is brave and skilled. The girl must also show that she has reached womanhood.

Each tribe has its own chief to whom the members of the tribe owe complete loyalty. Decisions for the tribe are made by the chief assisted by a Council of Elders. These people are selected from the different families of the tribe. The tribe provides the law and order needed by an organized group of people. There has been very little crime and almost no juvenile delinquency in African tribes. To kill or steal from another member of the tribe is considered shameful and is severely punished. The punishment is to be thrown out of the tribe.

Tribalism in Modern Africa

To many Africans today, the tribe is more important than the nation in which they live. Africans think of themselves as Yoruba or Ibo rather than Nigerian. This is because the nations that exist in Africa now did not exist before the coming of the Europeans. When the Europeans took over Africa and divided it up among themselves, they drew many boundaries separating their territories from each other. The present nations of Africa came into existence with those boundary lines. As a result many tribes were split up and found themselves in different countries. In other cases many different tribes were grouped together in the same nation.

There are many problems resulting from this situation. Where many tribes find themselves in the same country there is a problem in communication. In Nigeria 250 different languages are spoken. People in one village often do not understand people living in the next village. No tribe wants another tribe to dominate the government of the country. In elections, people often support those candidates from their own tribe rather than voting for the person best suited for the job.

An example of how tribal feeling can affect events in an African nation is the selection of a name for the nation. Until November 1971, the former Belgian Congo, which became independent in 1960, was known as the Democratic Republic of the Congo. The present government felt this name paid too much honor to the Bakongo tribe which lives along the lower part of the river. Most of the people of the country are not from the Bakongo. In November 1971, the name of the country was changed to Zaire to please the non-Bakongo peoples. Zaire was the old name of the great river (Congo) before the Europeans came. Zaire is also the new name that was given to the Congo River.

Today the influence of the tribes and the tribal chiefs is slowly decreasing. As education is spread, more roads are built and more people move away from the tribal lands to the cities, loyalty to the tribe is gradually being replaced by loyalty to the nation.

Religious Beliefs

Although many Africans today are Christians or Muslims, most people still believe in the traditional religions. They continue to cling to the old beliefs and rituals. Tribal religion is an inseparable part of tribal culture. Although religious practices vary from tribe to tribe, there are certain beliefs that almost all the African religions have in common.

Gods and Spirits

Nearly all the African religions believe in a Supreme Being or God who created the earth and all humanity. God then withdrew and left the affairs of the world to humans. God is remote (far away) and not often prayed to. Only in case of major crises do people seek God's help. This is usually when the entire tribe (not the individual) is threatened by drought, epidemic, or some other catastrophe.

Between God and people are the lesser gods and ancestor spirits. These gods are believed to live in rivers, caves, mountains, and trees. Africans do not worship rivers and mountains. They worship the spiritual forces that these things represent. These spirits are of great importance in daily life and are always close to people. Since Africans live close to nature, if the rains fail or the crops are flooded or eaten by pests, people may be threatened by starvation. Therefore, it is best to keep the gods on your side.

It is believed that the ancestral spirits watch over the fortunes of their descendants. These spirits can punish the living if they are forgotten and not honored. Therefore, on all important occasions—such as births, deaths, initiation ceremonies, weddings, planting, and harvesting—prayers and offerings are made to the departed ancestors. Even on lesser occasions, for example, the building of a new house or the judging of a person accused of wrongdoing, the spirits of the ancestors are appealed to for guidance and are offered beer or some other offering. In their prayers, Africans ask for health for themselves and their families, for the welfare of the tribe as a whole, and for the fertility of their fields. Africans do not worship their ancestors; they communicate with them. We have learned how important the family is to African people. This includes both the living and the dead members of the family. Therefore, Africans consider it only right to involve the spirits of the dead ancestors in the affairs of the living.

The Medicine Man

When misfortune strikes, Africans turn to a diviner, or medicine man, to discover the cause of the misfortune. The diviner is believed to have special powers that enable him to find out the cause as well as the cure for whatever has happened. The African may know the scientific cause for the calamity, for instance, that malaria is caused by a mosquito bite. When tragedy occurs, people usually ask the question "why me?" The diviner tries to find out why a certain misfortune has befallen a particular person or group. Often the reason is the anger of an ancestor whose spirit has been neglected and is therefore punishing the descendent. Through the use of many techniques, such as throwing animal bones or palm nuts on the ground to form certain patterns, the diviner tries to find out which spirit has been offended and what must be done to satisfy it. Sometimes an offering of beer to the ancestral spririt is enough. In most cases, however, it is necessary to sacrifice an animal. Sacrificing an animal, which is the symbol of life to one's ancestors, is believed to be a means of communicating with them. Many Africans believe that in case of illness, medical treatment alone is not enough. This may cure the symptoms but not the basic cause of the disease. Thus, although Africans may go to a clinic for treatment, at the same time they will follow the ritual prescribed by the diviner. For this reason the diviner has great influence in most African tribes.

Magic

In many cases magic and religion go hand in hand, and sometimes it is not easy to separate the two. Magic may be used to protect the individual against illness or misfortune; to guarantee success in agriculture, hunting, and even love; and sometimes even to bring harm to another person. This last type of magic can bring severe punishment to the person who practices it. In general, the purpose of magic is to give people confidence in difficult situations. Many people carry a charm with them to protect them from danger.

While many aspects of African religions may seem strange to us, it must be remembered that our religious practices may very well seem strange to them. If we are able to understand why people believe and do certain things, these beliefs will make much more sense to us.

African Arts

African Art Was Unknown in the West

The great qualities of African art and music were not appreciated, recognized, or understood by people of the West until fairly recently. There are many reasons for this. African art and music were quite different from what Westerners were used to seeing and hearing. Our knowledge of African culture was very limited. Westerners did not realize that the art works were part of the religious and cultural life of the Africans. The music seemed to be without rhythm, and the sculpture seemed almost childish. These art objects did not fit into the ideas of what Westerners considered "art."

Only in the last 60 or 70 years have artists begun to recognize that the African forms and creations are related to their own experiences and efforts. Moreover, our knowledge of African art, sculpture, and music is still limited. We do not have many objects that date back to much earlier than the 19th century. Recently, discoveries have been made that give us information about earlier times. Although early artists used stone, bronze, and terra-cotta, the favorite material used was wood. Unfortunately, the moist climate and insects have destroyed all but the most recent wood carvings.

Early African Art—The Bushmen

The first artists were among the earliest inhabitants of Africa. Bushmen artists left a record of striking rock paintings and engravings in limestone. These paintings tell us much about the Bushmen's nomadic life, which was based on hunting and food gathering. The drawings of buffaloes, rhinos, and lions in reds, browns, and ochers, are realistic and lifelike. This rock art was probably begun about 8,000 years ago.

Nok Culture

Some 2,500 years ago, where the Niger and Benue Rivers join in northern Nigeria, lived a highly skilled people. They made pottery, figurines, and life-sized heads from **terra-cotta** (baked clay). By means of trade, these art objects moved throughout West Africa. Archeologists refer to the culture as the **Nok culture** because it was in the town of Nok in Nigeria in 1931 that some tin miners first found these terra-cotta pieces.

Ife Art

Not far from Nok is the holy city of **Ife**. A number of sculptured heads were found here. They date from the 13th century. The heads of Ife were made of bronze. The method used to make them was called the "lost wax" process. This was a difficult and complicated method that only highly skilled artists could use. This method is still used today.

The "lost wax" method consists of modeling the piece of wax, covering it with clay, then baking it. After the wax has melted and run out, being "lost" through holes at the bottom of the clay, the holes are then stopped up and liquid bronze poured in.

The faces of the pieces seem almost alive. The lines found on many of the faces are similar to marks still found on the people of Nigeria. These skin patterns are called scarifications. Such scars often showed the rank of the person and the tribe into which he or she was born.

Benin Art

The bronzes of the Benin also show the great skill of the West African. Their pieces are so beautifully made that art experts today often compare them to the finest works by Western artists. The Benin artists also made sculptures in ivory, a material reserved for the king. The ivory elephant tusks were carved and hollowed out to serve as cups for water, combs, serving spoons, and ceremonial knives, as well as for pendants and small statues or figurines.

Characteristics of African Sculpture

Wood sculpture is a favorite activity of many African tribes. There are different styles. Each group, tribe, or section has its own favorite form of expression. However, most African sculptures show certain common characteristics:

1. The sculptor tried to make the piece as beautiful as possible. This did not mean that the statue necessarily had to resemble the ancestor, god, or spirit. Naturalism that was too great was not considered proper.
2. Much of the sculpture is abstract. The sculpture simplified the most important features of the figure, and then exaggerated these features for emphasis.
   (a) The increase of population (fertility) was the most important concept of life. The symbols of fertility used by the sculptor were the male and female reproductive organs and the female breasts, and he often exaggerated them to show their importance.
   (b) Artists also showed the navel as large and sticking out, as a symbol of continuity of life.
   (c) The head was made oversized. It was carved with great care, as it was the seat of intellect and the origin of power.
   (d) Artists preferred to show still poses, instead of poses showing movement.
   (e) Artists also preferred front views of figures, rather than profiles and side views.
3. Few portraits were carved or painted because Africans felt it was undesirable and lacked humility to make things too realistic. Some figures, like the wood statues of the kings from Benin and Ife, were carved. They were usually idealized (godlike).
4. The different tribes also carved statues to be used as **fetishes**. A fetish is an object thought to have magical powers. It can be protective or threatening.

5. Figures of animals were also carved or cast in bronze to express certain admirable qualities. For instance, speed was often characterized by the antelope, and strength was symbolized by the crocodile. The lizard signified life, the tortoise old age, the snake swift movement or death. Birds were often thought of as intermediaries between the earth and heaven.

Masks

Tribal masks are probably the most familiar kind of African art. Their use goes back to the very early times. For example, some of the figures on the prehistoric rock paintings are wearing elaborate masks.

Masks were worn mainly in religious ceremonial dances related to the growing of crops, celebrations of births, deaths, and important tribal and secret society ceremonies. Masks were based on human or animal forms, or a mixture of both.

Many masks were thought to be sacred, and were kept locked up when not in use. Women were not permitted to wear them and, in many cases, not even to see them. Some masks were deliberately terrifying so as to frighten women away from secret ceremonies. Colors were often used as symbols. To some tribes black meant the earth, and stood for strength and vitality. White meant the supernatural.

Types of Masks   The basic type of tribal mask is the face mask. Often a stick was placed across the back of the mask and the man wearing the mask held it in place by holding onto the stick with his teeth. A costume of some sort was usually attached around the edge of the mask; few of the costumes remain today.

Some tribes used ivory to make miniature masks. Such masks were often given to young boys to show their future rank in the tribe or society. They were prized and worn by each boy under his clothing until he finally passed the initiation rituals. Then he proudly wore them on his belt or arm, where they could be seen.

Another type of mask is the helmet, which may partially or completely cover the head. Still another type of mask sits on the top of the head. When this type of mask is worn, the face is usually covered by a costume.

African Art and the West

At the beginning of the 20th century, African carvings appeared in Paris, France, and influenced the work of a number of European artists. Pablo Picasso, for example, began to experiment in what is now called his "African phase," and produced *Woman in Yellow*, *Young Woman of Avignon*, and *Head*, to name just a few. Amedeo Modigliani carved *Head of a Woman* and painted many canvases that show that he was influenced by African art.

The artistic work of the people of Africa is now recognized as being the artistic equal of anything produced by any other civilization.

Oral Literature

Much of the history, the culture, the folklore, and the music of Africa has been passed along from generation to generation orally (by word of mouth). Certain members of each community would memorize the stories, legends, and family histories learned from their elders. They, in turn, would pass them on to the next generation.

Some African peoples south of the Sahara did develop written languages. But the writings were often on materials such as wood or leather (animal skins) and were lost as the moist, hot climate caused the materials to decay. Therefore, African peoples have had to rely on storytellers and the oral tradition.

All over sub-Saharan Africa the storytellers used the poems, stories, proverbs, and myths as a teaching tool. Storytelling was an activity in which everyone in the village took part. The storyteller, usually an elder of the village, would act out all the parts of the story. Sometimes sound effects or music were used, too. Very often the audience sang any songs that were part of the tale. Often, listeners made comments on the action in the story. The tale is, after all, a part of the past and the present for the villagers.

Creation Legends and Epic Tales

Legends about the creation of the world and the origin of human beings are recited by storytellers. The Ashanti people of West Africa, the Masai of East Africa, and the Bushmen and Hottentots of South Africa all have their oral traditions of creation. *Epic* tales of the bravery of ancestors and local heros are passed on by word of mouth.

Fables and Folktales

Other African tales are about small animals who outsmart bigger and stronger enemies. Fables of the clever spider are found throughout West and Central Africa. There are also

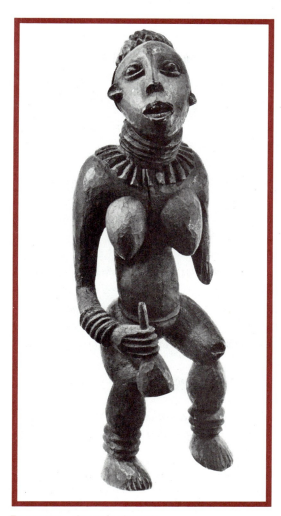

Bangwa—female figure.

Ogoni mask.

tales about the hare and the tortoise. It seems that Africans have long admired intelligence that enables people to overcome the greater physical strength of others. Listeners learn the lesson that intelligence and cleverness can outwit injustice and evil. It is very possible that the Greek Aesop, whose *Fables* are known throughout the world, originally came from Ethiopia.

How Mountains Came to Be

Long, long ago the earth was smooth and flat and even all over. But one day, she arose and wanted to talk to the sky. When the two of them were finished talking, the earth took leave of the sky and started to return to her home. But she did not reach home everywhere. Some parts of her became tired on the way and she had to stop where they were without completing the descent. These are the hills and the mountains.

A fable from Tanzania

Tortoises, Men, and Stones

God created the tortoise, men, and stones. Of each he created male and female. He gave life to tortoises and men, but not to the stones. None could have children and when they became old they did not die but became young again.

The Tortoise, however, wished to have children. And he went to God. But God said:

"I have given you life, but I have not given you permission to have children."

But the Tortoise came to God again to make his request and finally God said:

"You always come and ask for children. Do you realize that when the living have had children, they must die?"

But the Tortoise said:

"Let me see my children and then die." Then God granted the Tortoise his wish.

When Man saw that the Tortoise had children, he too wanted children. God warned Man as he had warned the Tortoise, that he must die if he had children. But Man also said:

"Let me see my children and then die."

That is how death and children came into the world. Only the stones did not want to have children, so they never die.

A fable from West Africa (Nigeria)

Nature Cannot Be Changed

One day, a rabbit and a monkey were engaged in conversation. However, while talking, each of them constantly indulged in his own bad habit. The monkey, of course, kept scratching himself with his paw, while the rabbit, constantly fearing an attack by an enemy, kept turning his head about in all directions. The two animals were unable to keep still.

"It's really amazing," said the rabbit to the monkey, "that you cannot stop scratching yourself even for a moment."

"It's not more amazing than to see you turn your head constantly for no good reason," replied the monkey.

"Oh, I could easily stop doing that," said the rabbit, "if I only wanted to."

"Very well! Let's see if you can. Let's both try, you and I, to keep still. The one who moves first will lose the bet."

The rabbit agreed. And so they both watched to see if the other moved.

Soon the situation became unbearable for both of them. The monkey itched all over. Never in his life had he itched so badly. The rabbit, on the other hand, was sure that some enemy was going to jump on him from behind.

Finally, when he could stand it no longer, the rabbit said, "Our bet did not provide that we could not tell each other stories to pass the time, did it?"

"It did not," answered the monkey, forseeing some ruse (trick) on the part of the rabbit but intending to use some trickery himself.

"All right then, I'll start," said the rabbit. "Imagine, one day when I was in an open field, I was in terrible danger." "Curiously enough, the same thing happened to me one day." interrupted the monkey. "Oh really?" continued the rabbit. "I saw dogs jumping through the field in all directions. They came from the left, from the right, from the front, from behind. I turned my head this way, that way. . . .you see? Like this." And, as if to illustrate (show) his point, the rabbit turned his head in all directions as he had indicated in the story.

Of course, the monkey too had a story to tell. "That day," he said, "I was tormented by a group of children who kept throwing stones at me. They threw one here, and another there, and another there..." and with each place he mentioned in the story, he gave himself a good thump with his paw to stop the itching.

The rabbit, who well understood the subterfuge (misleading act) burst out laughing and said to his companion. "Let us be frank. As much as would like to, we cannot change our natures. This proves it. Neither of us won the bet, nor lost it."

A folktale from Sierra Leone

African Proverbs

"No one tests the depth of a river with both feet." (Ghana)

"Two small antelopes can beat a big one." (Ghana)

"Since he has no eyes, he says that eyes smell bad." (Nigeria)

"Only a monkey understands a monkey." (Sierra Leone)

"If you climb up a tree, you must climb down the same tree." (Sierra Leone)

"Do not tell the man who is carrying you that he stinks." (Sierra Leone)

"Even flies have ears." (Tanzania)

"He who hunts two rats, catches none." (Uganda)

"Do not leave your host's house, throwing mud in his well." (Zululand)

"Do not call to a dog with a whip in your hand." (Zululand)

"Copying everybody else all the time, the monkey one day cut his throat." (Zululand)

"Others' ornaments tire one's neck." (Kenya)

Modern African Literature

Modern African literature developed first in the colonies of West Africa ruled by the French. Writing in French, the authors tried to show the injustices of the colonial system. They wrote about an idyllic African past which they felt the Europeans had destroyed. This movement was called "negritude" and its leading author was Léopold Sédar Senghor of Senegal. Senghor defined *negritude* as, "the sum total of the cultural values of the Negro-African world." In the 1930s Senghor went to study in Paris where he began writing poetry that won him world-wide acclaim. Besides being a poet, Senghor was also a professional politician who led his nation to independence and was president of Senegal from 1960 to 1980.

Senghor believed in the importance of African cultural values. He opposed the French policy of assimilation, that is, encouraging the Africans to adopt French culture in place of their own. Senghor and other negritude poets drew their inspiration from their African heritage and wrote about the African people, their customs and beliefs.

In recent years, many African writers have made important contributions to world literature. Many of their works have been translated into English and other European languages. Their writings present a vivid picture of traditional African life as well as life in contemporary Africa. One well known writer is Chinua Achebe of Nigeria whose novel *Things Fall Apart* is read in many American schools. Another well known writer, Nadine Gordimer of South Africa, was awarded the Nobel Prize in literature in 1991. Her novels deal with race relations in South Africa and the effect of apartheid on individual lives.

Some of the themes that concern contemporary African writers are: traditional village life before the coming of the Europeans; the African encounter with colonialism and Christianity; how European colonialism led to the destruction of old ways of life; and life today in Africa's large cities.

The writers explore the conflict between the old and new values. They portray the dilemma of individual Africans who are torn between two worlds—the traditional world of the village where they grew up and with which they retain strong ties and the modern world of the city in which they live and work. They show the struggle of Africans to understand and adapt to the new ways. For many Africans, life is changing so quickly that it is difficult to keep pace with it. Many of the writers feel compassion for the uprooted Africans and regret the disappearance of the old customs and values. Some encourage Africans to go back to the old values.

Another favorite theme of contemporary African writers is politics in the new African nations. They attack greed and corruption and criticize politicians who are more interested in their own economic benefits than the welfare of the nation. The writers express the frustrations of educated and idealistic Africans who are distressed by many things that are happening in their countries.

African writers also deal with universal themes: the conflict between generations; relationships between family members and between friends; and the importance of human communication.

Agriculture

Agriculture is the life blood of the African economy. Over 70 percent of Africans depend on agriculture for a living. Most Africans are **subsistence farmers** who only grow enough for themselves and for their families, and rarely sell or trade any part of the harvest.

However, African leaders have encouraged the production of **cash crops**. These crops are not used at home, but are sold to cities or to other countries. Most African states depend upon the export of agricultural goods to pay for the development of industry and a modern economy.

The many climates of Africa allow a great variety of farm products to be raised. Because the grasslands of the savannas make good pastures, cattle raising is important. Cattle provide the Africans with milk, meat, and hides. In the highlands of Tanzania and Kenya, sheep and goats are raised. These animals are well suited to the hilly lands and low rainfall.

Corn is an important crop in South Africa. Wheat, peanuts, rice, beans, and peas are also raised. The Mediterranean climate area of South Africa is small, but it is important to agriculture. It is about 200 miles long and 40 miles wide. Peaches, plums, grapes, and citrus fruits are raised here. These fruits ripen during Europe's winter season, when prices are highest. Because of this, fruits make a valuable export to Western Europe. Cereals, such as wheat, oats, and barley, are also raised.

The world depends on Africa for many important products. About 60 percent of the world's **cacao** is raised there. Nearly every chocolate candy bar eaten in the world has an African coating. Palm oil and vegetable oils, used in making soap and salad oil, and sisal, used for making rope and sacking, are also produced in Africa in large amounts. In addition, Africa produces large quantities of tea, coffee, cotton, tobacco, peanuts, and natural rubber. These crops are raised for export.

Basic Problems of African Agriculture

Poor Soil

The African nations face many problems in improving agricultural production. First, most of Africa's soil is poor. Most African soil is tropical laterite. This type of earth, usually reddish in color, is damaged by heavy rains. The rains **leach** the soil, that is, they wash away the minerals in the soil. As a result, most African lands are not very fertile. Even when modern agricultural methods are used, crop yields per acre are low. The best agricultural areas are found in the higher plateau regions. These areas have rich, volcanic soils. The river valleys are also fertile.

Irregular Water Supply

Second, there is the problem of insufficient or irregular water supply. The seasonal character of rainfall does not allow Africans to make full use of the land. The great fear of the African farmer is that rain may not fall. When this happens, the earth dries and crops will not grow. The result is famine. On the other hand, if too much rain falls, it may wash away the newly planted seeds and cause floods. Africa has a great need for both large and small dams and irrigation facilities to control and store the water.

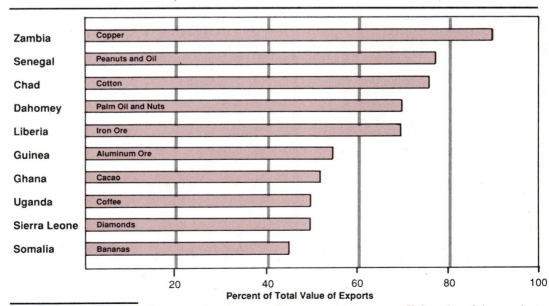

MONOCULTURE—("SINGLE EXPORT" ECONOMY) IN SUB-SAHARAN AFRICA

Zambia	Copper
Senegal	Peanuts and Oil
Chad	Cotton
Dahomey	Palm Oil and Nuts
Liberia	Iron Ore
Guinea	Aluminum Ore
Ghana	Cacao
Uganda	Coffee
Sierra Leone	Diamonds
Somalia	Bananas

Percent of Total Value of Exports

Many African nations depend on one mineral or crop for export to earn money. If the price of that product drops a few cents, these nations will have economic problems.

Because there is often not enough land to support everyone in the village, many Africans go to work on farms or plantations that grow crops for export. These export crops are important to countries without mineral wealth. For example, peanuts make up over 90 percent of Gambia's total exports, cocoa makes up 70 percent of Ghana's sales, while coffee and cotton together are about 87 percent of Uganda's exports.

Disease

The tsetse fly still remains a problem in Africa. The tsetse fly carries sleeping sickness to humans, cattle, and horses. The existence of the tsetse fly has closed some areas of Africa to human settlement. The form of the disease called "nagara," which cattle and horses suffer from, is also a serious problem. Much land that could be used for raising cattle cannot be developed, since animals cannot survive because of the tsetse fly.

New Methods vs. Traditional Methods

Africans must be trained to use new equipment and new methods. They have to be shown that in many cases new methods are better than the old. Africans have often been criticized for their custom of burning grassland in the dry season. However, we know now that the ashes produce minerals that are a good substitute for expensive fertilizers. African farmers in many areas still clear the bush by hand, and then burn the trees they have cut down to provide ash seed beds for their crops. This method, called **slash-and-burn**, also fertilizes the soil.

In the same way, bush-fallowing, the traditional method of farming an area of land for a few years, then moving on to a new stretch and allowing the old plot to lie **fallow** (unused), is a way of allowing the soil to regain its fertility. When land is plentiful, bush-fallowing is as

SLASH-AND-BURN AGRICULTURE

1. Trees were killed by slashing their bark.

2. Ground was cleared by fire. Ashes were mixed with the soil.

3. Crops grew on the cleared ground.

good a way as most to use land properly. It is now a problem because, as the population increases, land becomes less available, and people have to settle down on one plot of land.

Landowning Systems

The landowning system also creates some problems. The land in many African societies is often owned by a group of people, not by one person. Individuals can use what they need, but they cannot sell the land. It always remains the property of the group. Farmers are therefore discouraged from using new methods or spending money to develop the land, because the land is not their own. They are not sure that they or their children will receive the benefits from improvement.

Poor Distribution

Marketing the products raised is the final problem. Poorly developed road and railway systems are part of the difficulty. In addition, storage facilities are lacking. Besides this, distribution of food from farmer to consumer is poorly organized.

Much needs to be done to solve the problems of agriculture in Africa. It is necessary to build dams, irrigation systems, and modern transportation systems. Distribution and marketing must be improved. More agricultural research and farmer eduction is needed. More crops have to be planted to feed the people, not just crops intended for export. The U.N. Food and Agricultural Organization (FOA) concluded that with radical reform in agriculture and economic policies, many African countries could significantly increase their food production.

Famine in Africa

Since the 1970s, Africa has experienced several very severe droughts. A **drought** is a long period of dry weather with little or no rainfall. These droughts have caused famines in which millions of people died, millions suffered the severe effects of malnutrition, and millions more were left homeless. But drought alone was not responsible for the widespread famine. Many other factors were involved.

The Sahel Drought (1970–1974)—A Major Disaster

The Sahel (from an Arabic word meaning shore) is a large area in West Africa directly below the Sahara. The Sahel stretches from the Atlantic Ocean on the west through Mauritania, Mali, Upper Volta, Niger, and Chad to the center of the continent. Parts of Senegal, Ghana, Cameroon, Niger, the Central African Empire, and Ethiopia can also be considered part of the Sahel because of similar geography, ecology, and climate.

The people of the North Sahel are nomads. They raise camels and cattle. In the south there are thousands of villages that depend on the raising of subsistence crops such as millet, maize, and sorghum.

During the early 1970s, this area experienced a severe drought. Millions of people of the Sahel starved. The cause of the problem went back many years. In the 1960s, rains were plentiful, new wells were built, and the cattle population grew. In addition, a great population explosion took place.

However, after 1965, weather conditions in the Sahel and other parts of Africa began to change. These changes caused severe droughts in many parts of Africa. In many places grasslands turned into desert. In some areas, the Sahara is spreading its sands southward at the rate of 30 miles a year.

In 1968, bad weather with very little rainfall gave the first warnings of trouble. Few people or cattle died, but there were vast areas of dead land, without grass or trees. Cattle and goats would never again find grass there. The governments of the Sahel countries did not take the warning and did little to protect their people or prevent the coming disaster.

Between 1969 and 1972, almost no rain fell. Food production in each of the Sahel countries declined sharply. Local food crop production—yams and rice—dropped. So did production of export crops—cocoa and coffee. These reductions affected the economy of each country. Millions of cattle died—Mauritania's herd loss was 70 percent, Mali's 55 percent, Niger's 80 percent, and Chad's 70 percent. But the real problem was that nearly 3 million people were faced with starvation and death from disease and hunger. Disease multiplied the effects of the drought. In the villages of northern Niger, half the school children died from measles. In Mauritania, influenza and chicken pox were the killers. In Chad, diphtheria was widespread.

In Niger, the civilian government was overthrown by army leaders. In Ethiopia, the drought brought about great unrest and led to Emperor Haile Selassie's downfall.

Finally, in late 1974, the rains came. These rains broke the drought that had lasted for six years.

Famine 1980–1985: Africa's Hungry Millions

During the 1980s, many parts of Africa again experienced drought and famine. In November 1984, the United Nations issued a report stating that 150 million people in Africa were facing hunger and malnutrition. The worst-hit countries were Chad, Ethiopia, Mozambique, Ghana, Mali, Somalia, and Senegal. The immediate cause of the famine was the worst and most prolonged drought in recent history.

The drought began in 1980 and affected 44 percent of the total land area of the continent. Other causes for the severe food shortages were insects that damaged many crops, infectious diseases that killed thousands of cattle, and brushfires that scorched the earth in West Africa. Many thousands of Africans died of starvation. Millions left their homes in search of food and became refugees in other countries. Many millions more showed the signs of starvation and malnutrition—emaciated bodies, distended bellies, and stick-like limbs.

In 1985, heavy rainfall in many parts of Africa broke the five-year drought and food production increased. But the food situation remained serious and in several countries famine conditions remained. This was because the famine was also the result of other very serious problems. Until these problems are solved it is predicted that Africa will continue to face serious food shortages. The two most serious problems are a decline in food production and civil wars in many parts of Africa.

Causes of the Famine

Declining Food Production and Growing Population

Between 1965 and 1985, food production in Africa decreased by 20 percent. At the same time, the population increased substantially. Africa's population grew at the rate of 2.9 percent a year after 1960. It reached 439 million people in 1980. In the 1980s, the population growth was 3 percent a year, greater than that of any other continent. During the early 1960s, farm output in 39 African countries grew between 2 and 3 percent a year. Thus, food production kept pace with the increase in population. In the 1970s, food production increased only half as fast as population growth. In the 1980s, the situation was even worse. In 1980, Africa had 12 percent less home-grown food than in 1970. Most of the African countries had to import large amounts of food.

There are many reasons why Africa is producing less food than before.

Shortages of Fuel and Fertilizers

There are shortages of fertilizer, insecticides, and fuel that are necessary for agricultural development. Most African governments do not have enough money to buy them. The shortage of funds is partly due to higher oil prices since 1975. Countries in Africa that have to import oil have had to pay much higher prices. This has left them with less money to buy other necessary things. Africans have also received less money for their exports, such as coffee, cocoa, cotton, peanuts, and sugar.

Poor Transportation

Poor transportation has held back agricultural development. Also, a number of African governments have promoted the growth of industries and neglected agriculture.

Urbanization

Another factor is urbanization. In recent years, more and more Africans have been leaving the countryside and moving to the towns and cities. This has left fewer people on the land to grow food for the exploding urban population. If the income of farmers continues to decline, this trend is likely to increase.

Civil Wars and Military Conflicts

In many parts of Africa, civil wars and military conflicts have been going on for years. These wars have greatly damaged African agriculture. They have also displaced rural people and turned them into refugees. The most severely affected areas are Chad, Ethiopia, and the Sudan in the Horn of Africa and southern Africa.

Ethiopia. In 1985, 7.5 million Ethiopians were on the brink of starvation. Tens of thousands had already died of hunger. There were almost 2 million Ethiopian refugees. The refugees traveled on foot for up to eight weeks to reach refugee camps in neighboring countries. Thousands died along the way. Occasionally Ethiopian government planes bombed the columns of refugees. These refugees were not only fleeing the drought, they were running from civil war and the policies of the Communist government of Lieutenant Colonel Mengistu (see page 216). Mengistu's armed forces bombed villages and mined agricultural land as a way of smashing the rebellions. These tactics contributed to the famine. People were uprooted, and those who remained were not able to plant or store grain. The 1977–1978 war between Ethiopia and Somalia (Ogaden War) created 700,000 refugees who fled to Somalia. It also caused the slaughter of huge herds of camels and the destruction of thousands of acres of grain.

In 1984 and 1985, foreign governments, churches, and international agencies undertook a huge relief effort to save the Ethiopian people. The United States sent grain, water tanks, blankets, medical supplies, and other equipment to Ethiopia. Much of this aid never reached the victims because the Ethiopian government refused to transport it. In 1985, heavy rainfall resulted in increased food production. But more than 5 million Ethiopians still needed aid.

Sudan. Since 1983, there has been fighting between government forces and rebels in the southern Sudan. The rebels have resisted government efforts to force them to accept Islamic law. The war has disrupted planting and harvesting. Harvests have been stolen by soldiers. The drought and the presence of more than half a million refugees have aggravated the situation. In 1986, 2 million people in the southern Sudan were facing starvation. For months relief shipments of food could not reach the victims in the south. Thousands of people traveled on foot across the desert country in search of food, many dying on the way.

Mozambique. The drought that hit Mozambique in 1980 was the worst in recent history. It was estimated that 170,000 people died of hunger during the first three years. However, the famine was in part the result of guerrilla war that has been going on since the mid-1970s. Rebels of the Mozambique National Resistance, supported by South Africa, helped ruin the economy of the country. They destroyed power lines, cut off roads, burned down health centers and clinics, destroyed centers used to distribute food and fertilizer, and kidnapped and murdered government officials and civilian relief workers.

Angola. In 1986, 1 million people in Angola were facing starvation. The civil war that began in 1976 has contributed to this situation. The rebels have planted mines among the crops and practically destroyed the countryside. Since the war began, food production in Angola has declined by 80 percent.

The Refugee Problem

It is estimated that there were over 5 million refugees in Africa in 1990, the largest number of any continent. Approximately 300,000 Somalis fled to Ethiopia and 30,000 Sudanese entered Ethiopia as well. The civil war in Liberia caused 150,000 people to seek refuge in neighboring countries. More than 810,000 people from Mozambique are in Malawi.

The refugee problem is very serious. The refugees live in refugee camps in tiny huts made of paper, sticks, and straw. Their small food rations come from the United Nations and other international organizations. The people suffer from malnutrition and a variety of diseases, and the death rate is high. At the same time, they are a drain on the resources of the countries in which they live. Countries like Somalia and the Sudan are poor and have problems providing for their own populations. The presence of hundreds of thousands of refugees adds to their burden.

End of Drought

The heavy rainfall in 1985 broke the five-year drought. Good harvests together with large-scale relief operations brought substantial improvement in the food situation. After 1985, several years of good weather and decent rainfall resulted in increased food production in many parts of the continent. But problems remained and new problems developed. The rains of 1985, which ended the great African drought, also caused a rapid multiplication of locusts and grasshoppers that threatened the food supplies of 30 countries. This was the worst locust plague in 30 years. African governments and international organizations acted quickly to protect crops. The FAO coordinated these efforts. There was large scale ground and aerial spraying of insecticides. These actions prevented widespread crop losses in much of Africa. The locust problem was brought under control in 1990.

During this same period, a renewal of drought conditions in some parts of the continent as well as civil wars continued to create severe food shortages in a number of countries. Large scale emergency food relief was needed in Ethiopia, Sudan, Mozambique, Angola, and several other countries.

Ethiopia: Continuing Food Emergency

Despite improvements in agriculture in many parts of Africa after 1985, the food emergency in Ethiopia continued. From 1985 to 1991, millions of people were threatened by large scale famine caused by drought and civil war. Ethiopia also experienced the worst locust infestation in 30 years which seriously threatened its limited food supply. Soil erosion was also contributing to famine—2 percent of Ethiopia's land was being lost annually due to soil erosion while the population was increasing at the rate of 2.9 percent annually. In 1990, approximately 5 million people in Ethiopia required massive food assistance from

What It Means to Starve

We see the women of Africa hold their children up to you, pleading for their lives...a woman clasps her empty breasts which can no more keep milk for the little baby, sucking and sucking in vain. Or the old man who points to his blind eyes, because his right to decent food had been taken away from him a long time ago. The children who put their hands on their big bellies to show that it hurts to be hungry...a family showing the little wooden bowl which when filled with food is their whole meal that day for all of them— however many family members there are. And then there are those who had to flee in such a panic from their homes that they did not even have a wooden bowl to put the ration of water and food in.

These lines were written by the internationally acclaimed actress Liv Ullmann. In 1980, Ms. Ullmann was appointed "goodwill ambassador" by UNICEF, the United Nations Children's Fund. She wrote "What It Means to Starve" during her trip to the famine-afflicted countries of the Horn of Africa in December 1980.

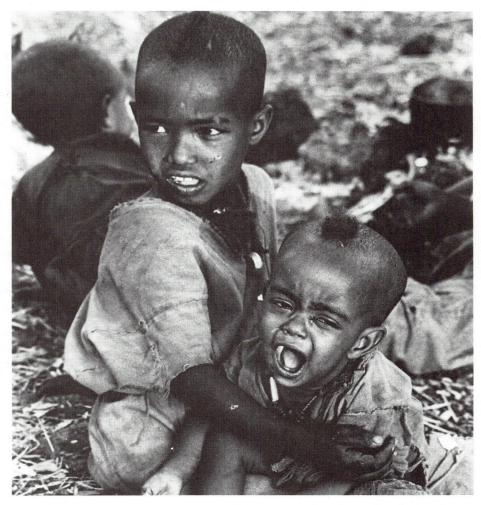

Ethiopian children who fled war and famine in their homeland wait for food in a refugee camp.

abroad as well as medical supplies, blankets, fuel, trucks, and spare parts. However, the continuing warfare often prevented the relief food aid from reaching the starving people.

Conditions in the Horn of Africa remained bleak during 1990–1991. With no letup in the fighting in the Sudan, Somalia, or Ethiopia, millions of people became victims of famine, disease, and homelessness. United Nations estimates indicated that famine in the Sudan put 9 million people at risk.

Natural Resources and Industrial Development

Minerals and hydroelectric power are the muscles of industry. Fortunately, Africa has great sources of both. Africa has about 40 percent of the world's water power resources. This is more than any other continent. However, less hydroelectric power has been developed in Africa than in any other continent except Australia. The reasons for this are: first, most of the waterfalls are far from the cities; second, Africa's industries are so few that there is little demand for electric power.

Almost half of the world's gold is mined in Africa, mainly in the Republic of South Africa. The mining and processing of gold gives jobs to thousands of people. Diamonds of high quality, also mined in South Africa, are used to make jewelry. The Katanga area of Zaire (the Congo) produces much of the world's supply of industrial diamonds. These diamonds are used in factories for cutting and grinding because diamonds are the hardest mineral known.

Large deposits of uranium are found in Zaire and the Republic of South Africa. Uranium is used in the making of atomic energy. Uranium is also mined in Zimbabwe, Zambia, Malawi, Tanzania, and Namibia.

More copper is mined in Africa than anywhere else in the world except for the United States. Cobalt, used in the manufacture of steel, is mined in Zambia. Ghana has large deposits of manganese, gold, diamonds, and bauxite (used in making aluminum). The small nation of Guinea has the world's largest supply of bauxite. Nigeria has rich supplies of tin. Iron ore deposits are found in Guinea, Liberia, and Sierra Leone. Zinc, radium, chromite, asbestos, and manganese are found in Katanga and Zambia.

Great forests still cover about one-third of sub-Saharan Africa. From certain trees come the raw materials for many waxes and medicines. In the rain forests are valuable hardwood trees (mahogany, ebony). African forests can supply the world with by-products of wood, including cellulose, plastics, and industrial alcohol.

However, fuels used to supply power are scarce. There is little coal, except in the Republic of South Africa. There is very little oil in most of sub-Saharan Africa. The greatest oil deposits are found in Nigeria. Some oil is found in South Africa. This presents a serious problem. Since modern industry depends on oil, most African countries have to import oil. The high price of oil has contributed to Africa's serious debt problems.

Most of Africa's riches are not fully used. The main reason for the slow development of resources is the lack of capital. The production of hydroelectric power needs large amounts of capital, with little hope for profit during the early years. Power is necessary for the development of Africa's minerals. Money is also necessary to build roads and railways and to improve transportation and communication. Roads are needed to get to where the minerals are located, and to get the minerals to where they can be used or sold.

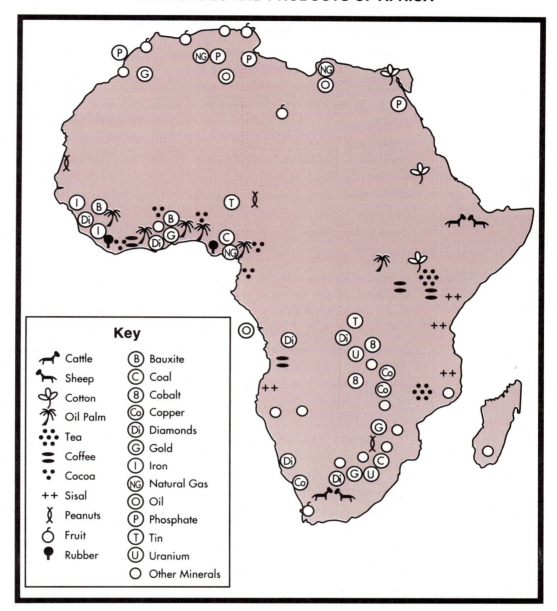

Key

🐎 Cattle	Ⓑ Bauxite
🐏 Sheep	Ⓒ Coal
🌿 Cotton	⑧ Cobalt
🌴 Oil Palm	Ⓒⓞ Copper
Tea	Ⓓⓘ Diamonds
Coffee	Ⓖ Gold
Cocoa	Ⓘ Iron
++ Sisal	Ⓝⓖ Natural Gas
Peanuts	Ⓞ Oil
Fruit	Ⓟ Phosphate
Rubber	Ⓣ Tin
	Ⓤ Uranium
	Ⓞ Other Minerals

Industrial Development

The Desire for Development

The Africans want to modernize. They believe the road to modernization must follow the path of industrialization. They believe industrialization is the key that will unlock the door to wealth and power. However, factories, as we know them, have never been seen by most Africans. Large steel plants, airplane factories, automobile factories, and shipyards do not exist in Africa. In some African countries we find the beginning steps toward building industry.

Accomplishments

As yet, there are few large factories in Africa that can produce heavy machines, cars, tractors, or locomotives in great quantities. However, there is an increasing number of light industries that make goods for the consumer.

In many cities and towns, there are factories that make soap, canned vegetables and fruits, and cloth. There are also some meat packing plants, furniture factories, sugar refineries, and flour mills.

Africans have also developed industries to process and refine the raw materials of their countries. Mills and factories have been built to press the oils from the oil palm fruit, the cottonseed, and the peanut. Latex from the rubber trees is made into sheets of crepe rubber. Logs are cut into lumber, and some of the wood is used in making furniture. Ores such as copper and chromite are processed at smelters close to the mines.

Africans for centuries have been skilled craftspeople. By hand they have made tools, household goods, and other items. These handicraft skills are still being used today. Skilled Nigerians make high quality Morocco leather goods. In Ghana gold thread is woven into cotton goods to make them more attractive. Woven blankets, beautiful rugs, and wood and ivory carvings are other handicrafts of the people. Often these skills are handed down from generation to generation.

Problems of Development

Africa's industrial development has been slow for many reasons.

First of all, for industry and manufacturing to grow, there must be people who want to buy and can pay for what is made. Most Africans are subsistence farmers. They produce much of what they need themselves and have little money to buy manufactured goods.

Second, to build industry there is a great need for capital. Money must be saved by the people to invest, or to be given to the government in the form of taxes. When a new nation starts with very little in the form of capital, development is slow and difficult. The average yearly income in Africa, south of the Sahara, is often not higher than $200 per person and, in some countries, is as low as $50. Because of this, little money can be saved or taxed to make industry grow.

Climate also has held back industrial development. The high temperature and humidity are harmful to both workers and machines. Workers find it difficult to work in the heat, and machines rust and break down more quickly. In drier climates sand and dust get into machinery and cause breakdowns.

Industrial development needs skilled workers. Most Africans have not had the opportunity to learn the skills necessary for industrial development.

Without a good system of transportation and communication there can be little industrial and economic development. Africa's present road and rail systems are clearly not good enough for modern industry. Most of the rail lines are old and in poor condition. They were built in colonial times to meet military, not economic needs. There are few rail connections between African countries. Africa also lacks good harbors because of its regular coastline. A great deal of money is needed to build ports. Money is also needed to improve inland water and land routes. In many parts of Africa roads and rail systems were no better in 1990 than they had been in the 1950s soon after independence. In some places, the situation was worse. In Zaire, there were 80,000 miles of good roads at the time of independence. Now there are less than 5,000 miles of good roads.

Finally, economic development can only take place when there is peace and stability. As we have seen, tribal rivalries and tensions exist in many nations. Rival political leaders are fighting for power. This situation does not lend itself to the foreign investment necessary for development, nor does it allow for continuous planning and development.

Foreign Aid

The success of African development plans depends to a great extent on foreign aid. Loans or gifts from other nations and from international organizations must continue to flow into Africa, or development cannot progress. The United States has given millions of dollars in aid to Africa as have France, Great Britain, and the former Soviet Union. The World Bank is also a source of low interest and interest-free loans to Africa. Foreign aid is a help, but it cannot solve the many economic and developmental problems facing Africa.

Continuing Problems

In the 1980s, the economy of Africa south of the Sahara slipped to its lowest point since the independence movement began after World War II. The combined impact of years of drought plus the world economic recession, heavy debts, rapid population growth, and political instability threatened many African countries with the possibility of economic collapse. The economic problems resulted in higher prices and increased unemployment. This situation, in addition to the famine, created instability in many countries.

In 1985, the World Bank warned of "the specter of disaster" facing Africa and, as a result, the global community. Although good rainfall in 1985 broke the five-year drought in the sub-Saharan region, many countries were not expected to produce sufficient crops to feed the people of the area. Food production in sub-Saharan Africa decreased by 20 percent over the past twenty years. Moreover, per capita income was barely rising because of increased population and in many countries per capita income was dropping. In 1990, 60 percent of Africa's population lived in poverty. Africa's population growth remains a major concern. Africa's average annual growth rate is 3 percent compared with a world average of 1.8 percent. If this growth rate continues, Africa will find it exceedingly difficult to solve its many problems.

Early History

Birthplace of Humans

Most scientists now believe that Africa was the birthplace of humans. In 1959, Dr. Louis Leakey, an anthropologist, discovered the fossilized bones of a skull in northern Tanzania. This, he claimed, was the "oldest example of man on earth," born over 600,000 years ago. It is now thought that this humanlike creature lived as far back as 1,850,000 years ago. What this creature looked like, what color his skin was, and how much hair he had are impossible to know. But Dr. Leakey called this creature a human because it was found together with chipped pebble tools. The ability to make tools is one of the things that distinguishes humans from the apes. Over the years, anthropologists have found other bones in Kenya and other parts of East Africa dating back almost 5 million years. Some of the most important discoveries have been made by Mary Leakey, wife of Louis Leakey, and their son Richard Leakey. On the basis of the evidence, it is believed that human beings began in Africa and from there migrated to other parts of the world.

"Lucy" and the Story of Human Evolution

The knowledge of human evolution was advanced in the 1970s when the paleoanthropologist, Dr. Donald Johanson, discovered hundreds of fossilized human-like skeletons in Ethiopia. These bones were exceptionally well preserved due to the dry weather. In 1974, the most important find was made: the skeleton of a four-foot-tall female. This prehuman who lived over 3 million years ago walked on two legs. It was the oldest and most complete skeleton of a two-legged human ancestor ever found. The skeleton was named Lucy, and 40 percent of her bones were found.

The discovery of Lucy and other similar skeletons caused many changes in the accepted theories about the early stages of human evolution. For example, anthropologists had long believed that brain enlargement came before bipedalism (the ability to walk on two legs) or that both evolved together. The discovery that Lucy's brain was ape-sized proved this theory inaccurate. Anthropologists had also believed there was a connection between tool making and walking on two legs. Yet Lucy walked fully erect and the earliest known stone tools were made 2 million years after Lucy lived. Lucy revealed that bipedalism was fully evolved 2 million years before the earliest known specimen of homo—the first true human—appeared.

Much of human evolution remains a mystery. Why did prehuman primates begin to walk on two legs? One theory suggests that global climate changes resulted in food supplies being less available than before. Bipedalism arose because it allowed prehumans to carry more food. This theory may be linked with the origin of "pair bonding" and the nuclear family. With pair bonding the male began to help gather food for the family.

Many different scientists (anthropologists, geologists, biologists, biochemists, and others) are now pooling their efforts to try to understand how humans evolved. Some scientists suggest that a large number of people migrated to other continents from Africa about 200,000 years ago. Their study of human DNA in different parts of the world has led some scientists to suggest that all human beings alive today are the descendants of these African people.

Changes in the Sahara—African Migrations

Until about 6 or 7,000 years ago, the Sahara was not the dry area that it is today. Cave paintings found in the Sahara are evidence that people and animals lived there. These people earned a living by hunting, gathering, and fishing. Then dryness set in and the area became desert. The people who had lived there moved either north or south. The people who moved north intermingled with the peoples of the Mediterranean area. This accounts for the physical and cultural similarities between Europeans and Africans. Those who moved south intermarried with the people living between the desert and the rain forest. They became the ancestors of the African people. Gradually they spread out over the entire continent. The Bushmen who had inhabited most of south and central Africa were pushed to the southwest by these people.

Beginnings of Agriculture

The first Africans hunted, gathered, and fished for food. A great step forward in civilization was the introduction of agriculture. Once people started farming, they had to settle down and live in one place, villages grew, and governments were set up. Farming was probably first practiced in Egypt around 4000 B.C. or earlier. But the Egyptian crops of wheat and barley were not suited to the conditions of tropical Africa. A few hundred years before the birth of Christ, people from Indonesia settled on the island of Madagascar. They brought with them crops that grew in the tropical climates of Southeast Asia, such as yams, bananas, and plantains. These crops were quickly adopted by African farmers. The African people also learned to domesticate animals, and the use of cattle spread to the interior. Farming and herding became the basis of African life.

Introduction of Iron

Another great advance came when the African people learned how to take iron from the ground and turn it into tools and weapons. This happened about 2,000 years ago along the Nile River. From there the use of iron spread to the west. With iron tools is was possible to hunt and farm better. Iron weapons made it easier for people to defend themselves. In this way it was possible to build strong communities and governments.

Early Trade

Trade was very important to the people of Africa. Trade between different tribes was common. In some places there were market days set aside and metal bars were used as money. Trade was carried on with Egypt. Africa supplied gold, precious stones, ivory, slaves, ostrich feathers, hides, and animals to Rome. It is believed that the Romans introduced the camel, which has been called the "ship of the desert," to Africa. Trade brought wealth, new ideas, and the growth of cities. The trade between East Africa and Asia that was carried on across the Indian Ocean was also very important. We have already mentioned that Africans learned how to raise yams, bananas, and other crops from the people of Southeast Asia. Trade also existed with China. Chinese porcelain as well as ancient Chinese coins have been found along the east coast of Africa. Chinese paintings from the 5th century show giraffes, and giraffes are not native to any area but Africa. African ivory, gold, slaves, and iron ore were important items in the trade with India, China, and other Asian countries. Wealthy trading cities grew up along Africa's east coast.

The Ancient Kingdom of Nubia

In 1960, archaeologists from all over the world joined together to save the monuments, tombs, and **artifacts** (objects made by human skill) of the Nile Valley. These ancient treasures were in danger of being destroyed by the rising waters of the Nile after the construction of the Aswan Dam in Egypt. Between 1960 and 1968, archaeologists excavated thousands of artifacts created by a people known as Nubians. These included jewelry, weapons, tools, pottery, statues, and clothing. The excavations revealed that a remarkable civilization existed in Nubia almost 6,000 years ago.

Ancient Nubia was a black African kingdom of enormous influence and power located in what is today southern Egypt and northern Sudan. Long and narrow, the kingdom stretched 1,000 miles along the Nile from Aswan to Khartoum (see map).

Little was known about Nubia before these excavations because scholars generally overlooked Nubia's accomplishments and focused their attention on Egypt. Also, the Nubians developed their writing system much later than the Egyptians and it is still largely undeciphered. Therefore, information about Nubian culture was derived mainly from Egyptian art and documents. As a result, the world saw the Nubians from the viewpoint of the Egyptians who considered themselves superior to other people.

It is now known that Nubia, long overshadowed in history by Egypt, was an important civilization. The Nubians built cities, roads, and palaces rivaling those of Egypt. They developed a writing system that is the second oldest in Africa, after Egyptian hieroglyphics, and one of the oldest in the world.

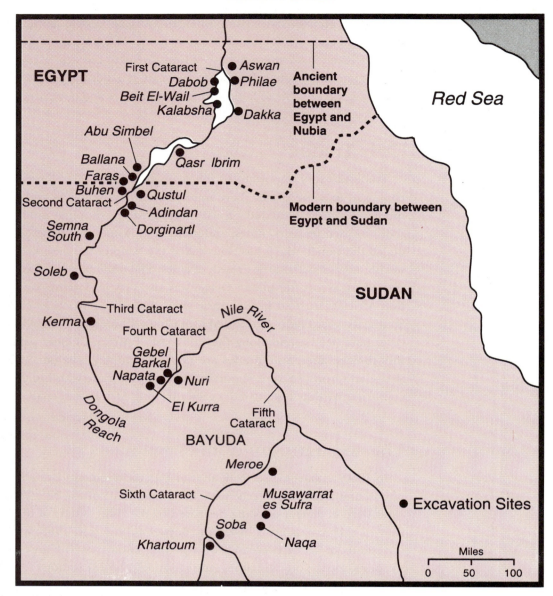

Artifacts excavated at the sites indicated on the map reveal that a remarkable civilization existed in ancient Nubia.

The artifacts provide evidence that Nubian civilization may have had important influences on Egyptian civilization. Scholars believe that kingship (a system of government whereby a king rules over a united country) originated in Egypt about 3100 B.C. As a result of the excavations, scholars now think that kingship may have developed in Nubia at the same time or even earlier. If so, Nubia may have influenced the rise of pharaohs in Egypt.

Evidence suggests that Nubian civilization began about 3800 B.C. By 3100 B.C. Egyptians and Nubians were in close contact through trade in ivory, gold, animal skins, and ebony. Nubian kings ruled from their capital at Qustul (see map). Between 2000 B.C. and 747 B.C., Egypt dominated Nubia. Many aspects of Egyptian culture, including mummification, the pyramid tomb, and artistic styles were adopted by Nubia's upper class. For part of this time,

Nubia was a colony of Egypt, used as a source of gold, silver, ivory, and slaves. The gold that adorned Cleopatra came from Nubia.

In 747 B.C., a Nubian king led his troops north and seized the ancient Egyptian capital of Memphis. He united Nubia and Egypt under his rule and for almost a century Nubian kings ruled Egypt. These Nubian kings are pictured in Egyptian temples and tombs as black pharaohs. During this period there was a great cultural flowering in Egypt. The Nubian kings promoted art and built grand temples. Nubian rule over Egypt ended in 656 B.C. when Egypt was conquered by Assyria.

In the following centuries the Nubian kings ruled from their capital at Meroë (see map). Meroë was farther south than the earlier capital at Qustul and a long distance from Egypt. Egyptian influence was no longer strong. The Nubians developed a more distinctive African culture and their land came to be called the Kingdom of Kush. In the 2nd century B.C. powerful queens ruled the kingdom. Nubia's trade in elephants changed the nature of warfare in the ancient world. Some historians think that the elephants used by Hannibal against Rome came from Nubia.

Kingdoms of West Africa

We have very few written records of African history. Most of what we know about Africa's past is based on oral history—stories handed down from generation to generation. For a long time, it was believed that if a people had no written records they had no history. However, history exists wherever people exist. It is only now that we are beginning to discover Africa's rich past.

Although tribalism has been important from earliest times, Africa has a long history of organized political states. Much of West Africa was the setting for a series of great African empires. The three most powerful ones were the kingdoms of Ghana, Mali, and Songhai. Each of these grew rich because it was able to control the important cross-Sahara trade in salt from North Africa that was exchanged for gold from tropical Africa. This trade resulted in the exchange of ideas, the growth of cities, and the accumulation of wealth. Arab visitors to the West African kingdoms were amazed at the order and prosperity in those lands. A 14th century Arab writer wrote that, "The Negroes are seldom unjust. . . . There is a complete security in their country. Neither traveller nor inhabitant in it has any fear from robbers or men of violence."

These kingdoms had the following features in common: they were headed by kings who were looked on as divine (appointed by God); these rulers had great power; they appointed many officials to carry out their orders throughout the kingdoms; the king and government were supported by taxes collected throughout the kingdom; trade was usually controlled by the king; women of the royal family had much power; the strength of these kingdoms was based on the use of iron; most of the people were farmers; many earned a living by herding; there were many cities and huge armies.

Ghana

Possibly the earliest kingdom in West Africa was Ghana, founded in the 3rd or 4th century A.D. Archaeologists have uncovered examples of a fine civilization. Such iron products as nails, farming tools, knives, scissors, and lances have been dug up. The windows of the king's home were made of glass, a product that had not come into use in Europe at that time.

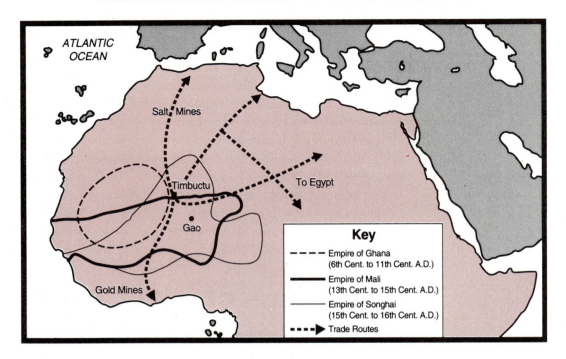

The kingdom's name comes from the title of its king, the Ghana, or ruler. The boundaries of present day Ghana do not in any way correspond to the old empire of Ghana, which stretched from the Atlantic Ocean to the Niger River.

Ghana reached the peak of its power in the 9th and 10th centuries. Ghana's ambassadors were welcomed in European courts; this period in European history was the "Dark Ages," a time during which there was little advance in knowledge. The power of Ghana was based on two things. The kingdom lay between the salt mines of the north and the gold mines of the south. The Africans needed the salt, and gold was in great demand in Europe. By controlling this trade Ghana became very rich. The people of Ghana were able to expand their territory and conquer their neighbors because they had learned to make iron weapons while their enemies still used wood. The use of iron tools helped Ghana to produce more food—another way in which they were stronger than their neighbors.

People living in Ghana were able to obtain many products because of their far-reaching trade. From North Africa came wheat, raisins, and dried fruits; from Spain and Morocco came clothing; and from the countries south of Ghana came cattle, sheep, and honey. African craftspeople produced fine leather. Ghana's goldsmiths, coppersmiths, and ironsmiths contributed their handiwork in jewelry, utensils, tools, and weapons.

This trade was a major source of income for the government. All traders had to pay a tax. The tax money was used to pay for the court, army, and government. The king had a splendid palace decorated with fine sculptures and paintings. Law and order was maintained with the help of a large army.

In the 11th century, Ghana was attacked by armies from Morocco. In the beginning, the army of Ghana was able to fight back and defeat the invaders. But the attacks broke down the gold-salt trade. Agriculture was also damaged and never recovered. Thus Ghana's economy weakened. Many people moved on in search of a better home. At the end of the 11th century,

Ghana was conquered by the North Africans. Although it became independent again later, it continued to decline. By the end of the 13th century, Ghana no longer existed as a country.

Mali

The empire of Mali was even larger than Ghana. In the 13th century, a prince and warrior named Sundiata destroyed what was left of Ghana and united his own people under his rule in the empire of Mali. Sundiata encouraged people to become farmers and before long Mali became one of the richest farming regions in West Africa.

The most famous ruler of Mali was Mansa Musa who came to the throne in 1312. During the 25 years of his rule, Mali's prestige increased greatly. Musa made sure that the splendor of Mali became known far and wide. A 14th century Arab wrote that of all the Muslim rulers of West Africa, Mansa Musa was "the most powerful, the richest, the most fortunate, the most feared by his enemies, and the most able to do good to those around him."

The strength of Mali was based on the income that the government obtained by placing a tax on trade. Musa encouraged this trade by opening up new routes and exchanging a wider variety of goods. He saw to it that travel over the caravan routes was safe. The greatest income came from the gold-salt trade, but Mali also profited from the trade in copper.

Mali was also prosperous because the people raised sufficient quantities of food. The chief food crops were sorghum (grain), rice, yams, beans, and onions. Poultry, cattle, sheep, and goats were raised for their meat, eggs, milk, and skins.

Mali's government was efficient and maintained law and order throughout the kingdom. Legal cases were examined by Mansa Musa himself. Mali also had a large standing army.

The most outstanding event of Mansa Musa's reign was his famous pilgrimage to Mecca. What stands out is the style in which he traveled. There were 12,000 slaves dressed in silks and brocades. Five hundred of these preceded Mansa Musa. Each carried a staff of gold weighing six pounds. Behind him were 80 camels, each carrying 300 pounds of gold dust. In Cairo and the holy city of Mecca, Mansa Musa distributed gifts of gold. This made a tremendous impression on the people of Africa, Asia, and Europe.

When Mansa Musa came back from his journey he brought with him a famous Arab architect who designed a great mosque at Gao and a mosque and palace for Mansa Musa at Timbuctu. Muslim scholars and traders began to come to Timbuctu, and in later years it became an important center of learning.

After Mansa Musa died in 1332, the empire began to decline. Invaders from the south burned down Timbuctu. The people of the Songhai city of Gao were not happy about being ruled by Mali, and soon after its people refused to pay taxes and rebelled. At the same time, people from the Sahara attacked the northern towns of Mali. Another important reason for Mali's decline was that the farmers of the countryside lived a very different life from the city people. Jealousy and suspicion divided these two groups and created instability. In time of crisis the empire fell apart.

Songhai

The empire of Songhai centered around the commercial city of Gao near the Niger River. Songhai's beginnings seem to go back to the 7th century, but its expansion into a great empire came during the 15th century. This was because of its great leader Sunni Ali. Ali was a powerful warrior who drove out all the foreign invaders and created a unified country under his rule. He also set up an efficient government with many officials to rule his vast empire.

The most important king of Songhai was Askia Mohammed. Askia's pilgrimage to Mecca rivalled that of Mansa Musa in magnificence. Askia fought many battles and conquered a great deal of territory. He was determined to make the whole empire a Muslim community. Muslim judges were appointed to all the districts of the empire, and justice was administered according to Muslim principles.

During Askia's reign, the city of Timbuctu became famous as a center of learning in Africa. Medical operations were performed here that were not attempted in Europe until 200 years later. A historian who wrote at the time said, "At Timbuctu sit numerous doctors, judges, and clerks, all are appointed by and receive good salaries from the king. More profit is made from the book trade than from any other line of business." The large cities, fine buildings, and well-administered government were proof of the advanced civilization of Songhai.

Askia was overthrown by his own sons. Following this event, there was a struggle between many people to take over the throne. The trouble lasted for several years and greatly weakened Songhai. At the end of the 16th century, an army from Morocco was able to invade Songhai and capture its important cities. Normal trade was disrupted and a great empire came to an end.

East Africa—Cities of the Coast

In the 14th century, a Muslim traveling down the long coast of East Africa passed through many important trading cities and some small towns. He described the peace and prosperity that he saw along the way. The famous city of Kilwa impressed him the most. He wrote, "Kilwa is one of the most beautiful and well-constructed towns in the world." In Kilwa could be found many palaces, mosques, and large houses.

More than 2,000 years ago, small trading villages grew up along the east coast of Africa. The Arabs called this area Zanj. The settlements were marketplaces for the goods traded between East Africa and other countries along the Indian Ocean, especially Arabia. About 1,200 years ago, many people from Arabia moved to islands along the east coast of Africa. They brought the Muslim religion with them and intermarried with the Africans. Between the years 1000 and 1500 the Arabs had the greatest influence on the settlements of East Africa. The Arabs controlled most of the East African trade, which increased during this period. Goods made in China began to reach Kilwa, and East African ivory was sent to China. Trading was also carried on with India, the countries of the Persian Gulf, and Arabia.

Then the African people of the interior began to offer gold for things they needed from other countries, the most important of which was cotton for clothing. The cities of the coast took the gold and sold it to other countries. Gold from Mozambique and Zimbabwe had begun to leave the seaports of East Africa in the 10th century. A few hundred years later, the traders of Kilwa had charge of this gold trade. They became very rich and made all traders from other countries pay heavy taxes. Kilwa grew and became a large and powerful city.

There were many other big trading cities. Some could even be called city-states because they controlled large areas. Some of these were Sofala, Pemba, Mogadishu, and Mozambique.

These cities began to decline in the 16th century when Portuguese sea captains attacked them. The Indian Ocean trade was taken over by the Portuguese, depriving East Africa of its greatest source of wealth. The cities on the southeastern coast of Africa, especially Kilwa, never really recovered from these attacks.

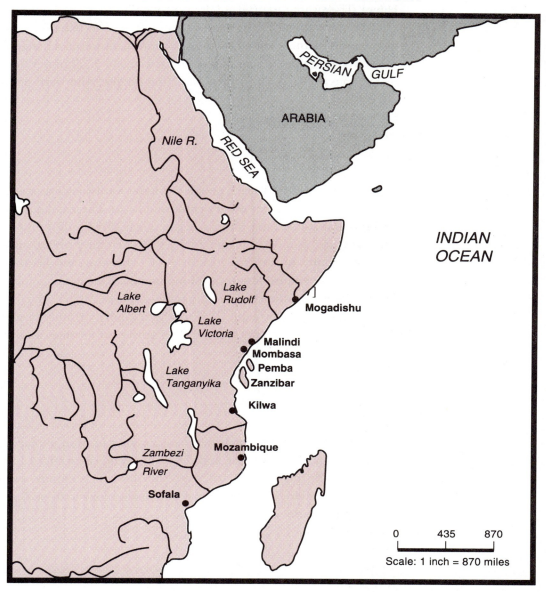

East Africa—Kingdoms of the Interior

In the country that is now known as Zimbabwe, great stone ruins have been found. The largest of these, Great Zimbabwe, had walls that were 30 feet high and 20 feet thick. These walls were built without any kind of cement. It is believed that the stone ruins may have been forts, burial places, a temple, and royal palaces. About 500 years ago an advanced civilization existed here. Historians think that this civilization was based on mining, trade, and stone building. From objects that have been excavated (dug up) here, it seems certain that Zimbabwe was an important center of trade.

Sometime between the years 1000 and 1200 A.D., new groups of people came to Zimbabwe. They were Bantus from the north looking for new lands on which to live. The people who were already living in the area knew how to mine for gold and other metals and also exported these metals. The newcomers, however, changed the way these people lived. They set up a system of government in which all power and wealth were held by a few people at the top and the rest of the people, who were poorer and weaker, had to obey them.

Monomotapa Empire

After a few hundred years, people from the southern part of what is now known as Zimbabwe set out to conquer other people and lands. These conquerors were known as Rozwi. In 1440, the Rozwi king Mutota began a war of conquest and within ten years he had gained control of most of the gold mines between the Zambezi and Limpopo Rivers and of the trade routes to the East African coast. This king and his son Matope, who followed him, built the empire known as Monomotapa. This name comes from the title given to Matope by one of the conquered people—Mwene Mtapa, which means "lord of the conquered lands." They brought all of southern Zimbabwe and Mozambique under their rule. In the empire of Monomotapa, the chief sources of income came from farming, cattle raising, gold, copper, iron, and ivory.

Changamire Empire

About 1485, war broke out between the king of Monomotapa and one of his biggest chiefs, Changa. The king lost, and the leaders who came after Changa set up an empire of their own with their capital at Great Zimbabwe. This empire was known as Changamire and it prospered for about 300 years. The strong stone walls of Zimbabwe were constructed by the Changamire.

The Effect of Outside Forces

Thus there were two empires in the interior of East Africa—that of Monomotapa in the northern part of Zimbabwe, and that of the Changamire in the southern part and in Mozambique. The Monomotapa was taken over by the Portuguese who came up the Zambesi River in small bands. Armed with guns called muskets, the Portuguese gained control by siding with some of the Monomotapa rulers against the others. In 1628, fighting broke out between the Monomotapa and the Portuguese. The Portuguese won, and after that, the Monomotapa empire disappeared.

The empire of the Changamires with its capital at Great Zimbabwe was never really threatened by the Portuguese. They continued to live in peace and to progress. The people earned a living by raising animals, mining for metals, and trading with the cities of the coast. Peace lasted until 1830 when Ngoni Bantus from South Africa entered the cities and stone palaces, robbed and ruined them, and took some of the land for themselves. Less than 100 years later Europeans took over the whole country.

Arabs, Islam, and Africa

In the 7th century A.D., a new religion began in the Arabian Peninsula, the religion known as Islam. In the centuries that followed, Arab traders and conquerors spread their religion to millions of people in different parts of the world. Africa was no exception and today Islam is one of the most important cultural influences in Africa.

Islam Spread to Africa in Various Ways

Conquest

In the 8th century, the Arabs conquered North Africa and converted most of the people to Islam.

Trade

During the 7th century, many Arabs settled in the port cities of eastern Africa and on the islands off the east African coast. From here they controlled the trade between Africa and the Far East. Iron ore, ivory, slaves, and gold from Africa were exchanged for cotton cloth from India and porcelain from China. This trade brought great prosperity to the cities along the east African coast. Arab control of this trade lasted until the Portuguese took over 800 years later.

In West Africa, Islam was spread by the Arabs who controlled the trans-Sahara trade. They brought salt from the Mediterranean and exchanged it for the gold of sub-Saharan Africa.

Intermarriage

The Arabs who settled along the east coast married African women and spread their culture. As a result, there are many Muslims in East Africa.

Political control

When the ruler of an African kingdom converted to Islam, the entire country officially became Muslim. This was true of Mali, Songhai, and the Hausa kingdoms.

There were many reasons why the Africans were able to adopt Islam as their religion. Islam makes no distinction between people on the basis of color. All Muslims are considered brothers, whether black or white. Islam did not interfere with many African customs. It was possible for Africans to be Muslims and still continue to worship the forces of nature. Islam permitted men to have four wives, and Africans had often followed the custom of marrying more than one woman. Other Islamic ideas such as divine kingship, the absolute power of the ruler, and the importance of the family and the community, corresponded to African ideas and customs. African rulers found that by converting to Islam, they could maintain good trade relations with the Arabs, whose trade was so important to Africa.

The Arab Role in Africa

In the 15th and 16th centuries, cities in West Africa such as Gao and Timbuctu became important centers of learning for Muslims. Scholars came from foreign lands to study these places.

The Africans who converted to the Muslim religion took over other aspects of Islamic culture as well. They learned how to write Arabic, and this provided them with a means of keeping records and developing a literature. It also led to a growth of a class of educated people who could help run a stable government. Eventually a new language arose, Swahili, which was a mixture of Arabic and Bantu languages. Swahili today is one of the most important languages in Africa.

The Arabs were also important because of the descriptions that they published about African life. Much of our knowledge about Africa before the arrival of the Europeans comes from Arab geographers and travelers such as Leo Africanus.

In one way, however, the Arab role in Africa was destructive. The Arabs are generally considered to have been the originators of the African slave trade. Arab traders reached into Central Africa, carrying away masses of slaves, who were then sold to India, China, and other places in the East. When the Europeans came to Africa they continued and enlarged a practice that had been begun by the Arabs.

Today there are between 50 and 60 million Muslims in Africa. The Islamic religion as well as the Arabic language, provides a link between sub-Saharan Africa and the Mediterranean area.

The Arrival of the Europeans

Africa south of the Sahara was almost completely unknown to the people of Europe until the late 1400s. In the 15th century, Europeans wanted to find an all-water route to the East Indies and Asia for the purpose of obtaining silks, spices, and precious stones. They realized that by sailing around Africa they could reach the Indies. In addition, the Europeans believed that somewhere in Africa there was a Christian kingdom of Prester John. They were anxious to find this kingdom and also to obtain the gold and ivory for which Africa was famous.

Portugal Becomes Interested in Africa

The Portuguese were the first to set out. They sailed along the west coast of Africa each time going farther and farther south. They traded with the African tribes along the coast and returned to Europe with shiploads of gold and ivory. In 1487, Bartholomew Diaz reached the Cape of Good Hope at the southern tip of Africa. Finally in 1498, Vasco da Gama rounded the tip of the continent, turned north, sailed up the east coast, and on to India.

Portugal's main interest in Africa at the time was trade. For this purpose the Portuguese established trading posts along the eastern and western coasts of Africa.

At this time, the relationship between Africans and Europeans was one of mutual respect. In 1487, the Portuguese landed at the mouth of the Zaire (Congo) River bringing rich presents for King Nzinga, the Congo ruler. King Nzinga was so impressed that he asked King John of Portugal to send him missionaries and builders to instruct the people of the Congo in the new European techniques. King John responded by sending three ships of priests, skilled workers, tools, and religious objects. King Nzinga, the royal family and most of the nobility became Christians. Between 1506 and 1512, the Congo ruler Affonso I (son of Nzinga) tried to convert his whole nation to European ways. The Portuguese were asked to send more teachers, priests, and technicians and young Congolese were sent to Portugal for an education. But efforts to convert the Congo people to European ways failed mainly because of Portuguese greed and their involvement in the slave trade.

Portugal Gains Control of the East African Trade

Following Vasco da Gama's voyage, Portugal controlled the trade between East Africa and Asia. Portuguese ships carried slaves and ivory from Africa to India where they were exchanged for spices, cloth, and glassware. The ships then sailed back to East Africa for repairs and for gold and then returned to Portugal. When some of the African cities along the coast, such as Kilwa and Mombasa, tried to resist Portuguese control, they were defeated and burned. Portugal's control of this trade greatly affected the kingdoms of East Africa. The wealth that trade had formerly brought to Africa's east coast now went to Portugal. As a result, the civilizations along the east coast of Africa gradually declined.

By the middle of the 16th century, other European nations became interested in the profitable African trade and began to challenge Portugal. The English, French, Dutch, and others came to the West African coast for gold and ivory. In the 17th century, Portugal's control over the East African trade declined as other Europeans and Arabs began to take over this trade. At the same time, the trade in gold and ivory was becoming less important to the Europeans and being replaced by another type of "gold."

PRINCIPLE SOURCES AND DESTINATIONS OF SLAVES—1526–1870

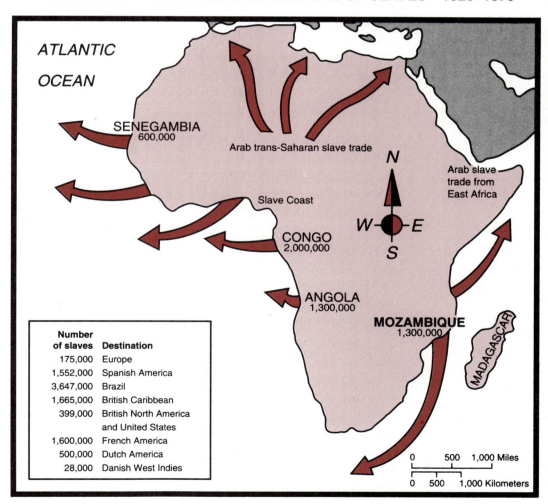

Number of slaves	Destination
175,000	Europe
1,552,000	Spanish America
3,647,000	Brazil
1,665,000	British Caribbean
399,000	British North America and United States
1,600,000	French America
500,000	Dutch America
28,000	Danish West Indies

The Slave Trade

Slavery Before the Arrival of the Europeans

From the beginning of history, slavery in one form or another existed in many parts of the world. Slavery had existed in Africa hundreds of years before the arrival of the Europeans. Enemies captured in battle, criminals, and debtors were often forced into slavery. But this type of slavery existed only on a small scale and was not necessarily hereditary. It was also different from the type of slavery that developed later because Africans did not regard slavery as the total ownership of another human being. The slave trade also existed long before the arrival of the Europeans. Africans were captured by Arabs and sold in the markets of the East—in India, Indonesia, Egypt, Turkey, and Persia.

In 1441, a Portuguese ship returned to Lisbon, bringing back, among other cargo, 12 men, women, and children from Africa. These were the first African slaves to be sold in Europe. But there was not much need for slaves in Europe and so the slave trade was not very important to the Europeans in the beginning.

The Need for Slaves in the New World

It was not until the European planters in the West Indies discovered that they could make fortunes by growing sugar with the labor of African slaves that the trade in human beings became important. By the mid 1500s, the slave trade had grown tremendously. As the European demand for sugar and tobacco grew, the need for slaves in the New World grew as well. The profits of the slave trade for the Europeans were enormous. These profits and the labor of millions of African slaves in part made possible the industrialization of Europe and the development of the Americas.

How the Slave Trade Operated

Slave trading posts were set up on the west coast of Africa by the Europeans. The Europeans did not go into the interior to get the slaves. The slaves were captured by Arab slave traders and by stronger African tribes who raided the villages of other tribes. Africans living in the coastal villages were given guns by the Portuguese and were encouraged to attack the tribes living in the interior. The slaves were then brought to the coast.

After buying the slaves, the Europeans kept them in stockades—sometimes for weeks—until the slave ships arrived. On the ship the slaves were packed in so tightly that there was barely room to lie down. The more slaves jammed into a ship the larger was the profit. Many died of beatings, disease, and lack of food and water.

Results of the Slave Trade

The slave trade had tremendous effects on Africa.
1. The population of the area was greatly reduced. About 15 million of the healthiest and most intelligent young men and women of Africa were removed from the continent. Thus, Africa was deprived of future leaders at a time when they were most needed.
2. There was an increase in tribal warfare. Crops were burned and entire villages destroyed during the slave raids. Millions of Africans died in those wars and on the

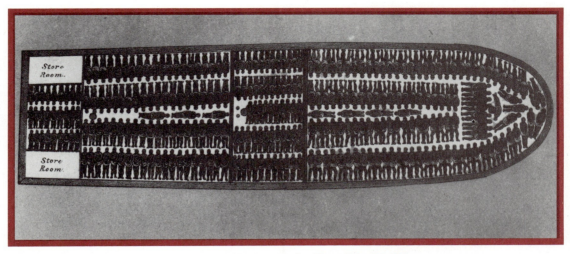

Diagram of a ship carrying African slaves to the New World. What can you tell from the diagram about the conditions aboard this ship?

way to the coast during the three centuries of the slave trade. Insecurity and fear were created. The slave trade broke down respect for tribal laws and customs.

3. The trans-Sahara trade was destroyed. The sub-Saharan peoples stopped raising crops and producing goods that they had formerly traded. Contact with the people of North Africa ended. As a result, the sub-Saharan kingdoms, whose wealth and power had been based on this trade, declined.

4. The coastal states became rich asnd strong from the profits of the slave trade. European products such as iron, guns, gunpowder, rum and brandy, cloth, brass, and other goods came to be regarded by the coastal people as necessities. These products could only be purchased in exchange for slaves. So the people of the coastal states undertook to enslave their neighbors. Some states, such as Ashanti and Dahomey, became powerful and wealthy. When the slave trade was finally ended, these kingdoms lost their most important source of wealth, and economic problems grew.

The slave trade was a major factor in holding back the progress of Africa for centuries. Between the 16th and the 19th centuries, Europe's main interest in Africa was obtaining slaves. There was very little communication between Europeans and Africans, and no exchange of culture and knowledge. No missionaries or teachers visited Africa during this time. The Europeans rarely went inland. Thus, during 300 years of contact with the Europeans, the Africans had no opportunity to learn European techniques so that they could modernize their way of life.

The Slave Trade Comes to an End

A strong antislave movement sprang up in Great Britain and other countries by the end of the 18th century. In 1772, the British abolished slavery in England, and in 1807 it became illegal for British subjects to take part in the slave trade. British pressure forced Spain and Portugal to officially end their participation in the slave trade in the early 1800s. The United States abolished the slave trade in 1808. For more than 50 years the British navy hunted down slave ships in the Atlantic Ocean. But as long as there was a demand for slaves on American plantations, slave boats tried to get past the British patrols. Only after the defeat of the South in the American Civil War in 1865 and the abolition of slavery in Cuba and Brazil in 1880s, did the slave trade finally come to an end in the West. However, even today the United Nations estimates that some 30,000 blacks are still kidnapped each year to be sold as slaves in the Middle East, mainly in the villages of Saudi Arabia.

Africa Is Opened to the Western World: Explorers and Missionaries

European Explorers

Until the 19th century, the only contact Europeans had with Africa was limited to the coastal areas. This situation changed during the 19th century. The antislavery movement had made Europeans curious about the land and people of Africa. European explorers come to Africa and explored the interior of the continent. Missionaries followed and soon businesspeople came. By 1880, most of the interior of Africa was known to the Europeans.

1. <u>James Bruce</u> was the first major European explorer of Africa. In 1770, he sailed up the Nile River and discovered Lake Tana in Ethiopia, the source of the Blue Nile.
2. <u>Mungo Park</u> was the first European to explore the Niger River in 1796. His explorations aroused British interest in Africa.
3. <u>Dixon Denham and Richard and John Landers</u> navigated the entire length of the Niger River (1822–1834). These explorations made West Africa known to Europeans and made it easier to travel into the central part of West Africa.
4. <u>René Callié</u>, a Frenchman, was the first European explorer to enter Timbuctu and return alive. This took place in 1828. His descriptions of his explorations and of Timbuctu stimulated great interest in the exploration of Africa. Callié was also the first European to cross the Sahara from south to north (1827–1828). These explorations gave France its claim to ownership of West Africa.
5. <u>Johann Rebmann</u>, a German missionary, was the first European to see Mt. Kilimanjaro (1848), a great snow-covered mountain located on the equator. Rebmann kept a careful record of his journey through East Africa. His explorations gave Germany its claim to ownership of the area.
6. <u>David Livingstone</u> did more than anyone else to open up Africa to the Europeans. Livingstone first came to Africa as a doctor and missionary in 1840. Until his death in 1873, Livingstone attempted to do the following:
   (a) explore and map the area
   (b) expose the evils of the slave trade
   (c) cure the sick
   (d) translate the Bible into several African languages
   In 1849, Livingstone reached Lake Ngami in what is now Botswana in southern Africa. He surveyed the area and put his observations into writing. In Europe, this account aroused great interest. Following this, Livingstone explored the Zambezi

River. In his search for the source of the river, Livingstone traveled across Africa to the west coast and then turned east again. In 1855, Livingstone saw the world's greatest waterfall, which he named Victoria Falls, in honor of Britain's queen. By 1868, Livingstone had stopped corresponding with the outside world. In 1869, a New York newspaper sent one of its reporters, Henry Stanley, to find the missing Livingstone. Stanley found Livingstone two years later near Lake Tanganyika. Together they explored the northern shore of Lake Tanganyika and other parts of East Africa.

7. <u>Richard Burton and John Speke</u> were two Englishmen who were determined to find the source of the Nile River. They were the first Europeans to visit Somaliland. In 1858, they reached Lake Tanganyika, never before visited by Europeans. Some time later Speke discovered Lake Victoria, which he claimed was the source of the Nile. Their explorations were the basis of British claims to control most of East Africa.

8. <u>Sir Samuel Baker and Florence Von Sass</u>, his wife, discovered a great body of water in 1864, which they named Lake Albert. This is the source of the White Nile. The river, which comes out of Lake Victoria, is known as the Victoria Nile. The Victoria Nile flows into Lake Albert, and when it flows out of the lake, it is known as the White Nile.

Henry Stanley, a newspaper reporter from New York, greeting David Livingstone in 1871 near Lake Tanganyika.

9. <u>Henry M. Stanley</u> remained in Africa after Livingstone's death and continued exploring on his own. Stanley was the first European to explore the Zaire (Congo) River. In 1888, he arrived at a snow-capped mountain peak in central Africa and named it Ruwenzori. (The Africans call this mountain Runsoro or Kokora). Stanely's explorations and actions gave control of the Congo region and the area around Ruwenzori to Belgium.

10. <u>Cecil Rhodes</u> explored Zimbabwe (Rhodesia) and eventually gained control of the area for Great Britain. Among his many ideas was that the British should build a railroad from Cairo to Capetown. His activities were the basis of British claims to control southern Africa.

Accomplishments of the Explorers

In this way, the four great African rivers were explored. The explorers wrote books and drew maps, making it easier for others to follow. But new land and rivers were not all that the explorers of Africa found. Mungo Park found a highly developed civilization in the Sudan. Speke found African kingdoms on the banks of Lake Victoria. The explorers are important not only for their discoveries but also for the picture of the African peoples and their cultures that they provided to Europe. By reporting these things to the people in Europe the explorers aroused interest in Africa and paved the way for the coming of more Europeans to the continent.

The Missionaries

The missionaries followed the explorers into the interior of Africa. The missionaries came to Africa to spread the Christian religion and to wipe out the slave raids which were still being carried on. The missionaries built schools, hospitals, and churches. They also worked out systems of writing for many of the African languages. While the missionaries helped the African people in many ways, they also hurt them in other ways. Many of the reports sent back to Europe by the missionaries were filled with bias and errors. To justify their attempt to spread the Christian religion, the missionaries looked down upon many African customs as "savage" and "primitive." Many of the myths about Africa originated with the missionaries.

European Imperialism in Africa

By 1875, European possessions in Africa consisted of some forts and trading posts along the coast and a few tiny colonies. Between 1880 and 1910, however, Africa was divided up among the Europeans. For the next 50 years, decisions affecting Africa and its people were made not in Africa, but in Europe.

France acquired a huge empire in North and West Africa. Algeria, Tunisia, Morocco, Ivory Coast, Dahomey, Mali, and other areas in West Africa came under French rule. Britain's colonies were scattered throughout the continent. Although the French controlled the most territory, Britain ruled the greatest number of people. Gambia, Sierra Leone, Gold Coast, Nigeria, South Africa, Rhodesia, Uganda, Kenya, Egypt, the Sudan, and others were taken over by Britain. Belgium acquired the Congo, an area 35 times as large as Belgium. Portugal annexed the interior areas of Angola and Mozambique. Italy took over Eritrea, a large part of Somaliland and Libya. Southwest Africa, Tanganyika, Togoland, and Cameroon were ruled by Germany until Germany's defeat in World War I. By 1914, there were two independent countries left in Africa—Liberia and Ethiopia. And even Ethiopia was taken over by Italy in 1935. (Italy controlled Ethiopia until 1942 when the British drove the Italians out.)

EUROPEAN CONTROL OF AFRICA—1914

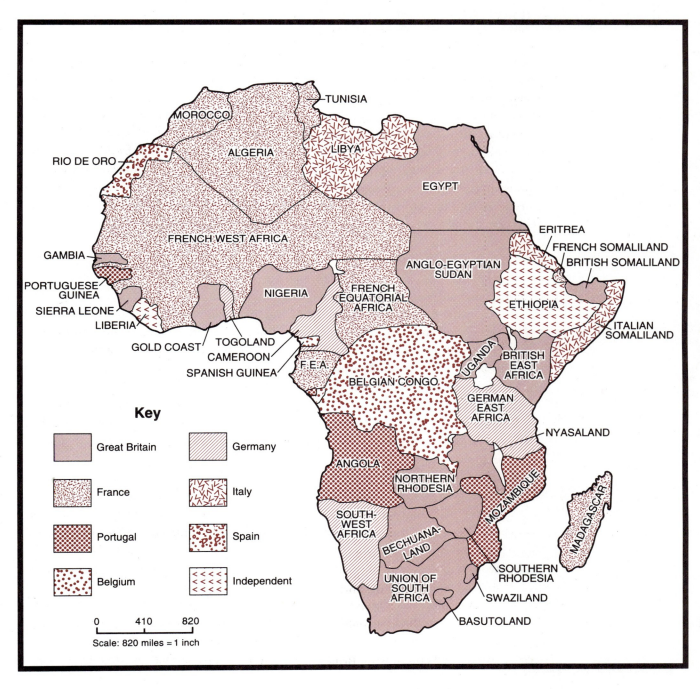

Key

Great Britain	Germany
France	Italy
Portugal	Spain
Belgium	Independent

0   410   820

Scale: 820 miles = 1 inch

Reasons for Imperialism

The European nations competed with each other to gain colonies in Africa for several reasons. They all wanted to gain power and prestige. The more territory that they were able to control in Africa the more powerful and important they became. Africa was tremendously rich in natural resources, which could be brought to Europe and turned into manufactured goods. Europeans also needed markets for the manufactured goods. These goods could be sold in Africa for large profits. Often a European nation would take over territory in Africa simply to prevent another European country from taking it.

How Imperialism Spread

European rule came to Africa in many different ways. Sometimes a European trading company made agreements with African chiefs permitting the company to trade and keep order in the area. The traders then put pressure on their government in Europe to take over that area in order to protect them. In a few cases tribal chiefs voluntarily asked for the protection of one European nation in order to avoid being taken over by another European nation. Sometimes the Africans even asked for European protection against other African tribes.

Treaties were signed by the African chiefs in which they gave the European company or government the right to govern and to take over the land and resources in their area. Thousands of treaties were signed by African rulers giving away most of their rights to the Europeans, but the Africans never really understood these treaties and did not realize what they were giving away.

How Imperialism Changed Africa

European rule brought about great changes in Africa.

1. When the Europeans divided up Africa, they made deals with each other over who was to get what. Boundary lines were drawn that had nothing to do with the needs of the African people. Many tribes were divided and found themselves under the rule of two or three different foreign nations. Other tribes who had nothing in common with each other were grouped together in the same territory. Some of the problems that the African nations have today are the result of this situation.

2. The Europeans did not want to spend large sums of money governing their African colonies. Therefore, the Africans were forced to pay taxes for the cost of ruling the colony.

3. The Europeans were interested in exploiting Africa's natural resources. Using various methods, the Europeans forced the Africans to work for them in the mines and on the plantations and farms that the Europeans now owned. In the Belgian Congo the system was the cruelest of all. Forced labor was introduced and those Africans who did not produce the required amount of rubber were brutally beaten. Rubber from the Congo came to be called "red rubber," because of the thousands of Africans who died tapping it and bringing it to the coast.

4. In such places as Rhodesia (now Zimbabwe) and Kenya, where large numbers of Europeans settled, the best farming land was reserved for the Europeans.

5. European conquest did not bring about the immediate destruction of traditional African governments. The Europeans did not have enough manpower to rule the

Africans directly. Also, they wanted to avoid the costs of setting up new governments, so in many cases they allowed the tribal chiefs to keep some of their power. The British, especially, did this. However, the Europeans were the real masters and told the Africans what they could do and what they could not do. This is known as "indirect rule." The French, on the other hand, removed local rulers and governed through the Africans they appointed or through French officials.

6. Africa's traditional political system was completely changed. The chiefs lost the power and respect that they formerly had. In the past it was believed that the chiefs had been given their power by the tribal god. Thus the African's religious beliefs required support for the tribal chief. However, under European rule many Africans converted to Christianity and they no longer believed that their chiefs were appointed by God. Many Africans who went to work in the cities and gained some wealth did not accept the authority of the chiefs when they returned to the villages. In some cases, wealthy people were actually more important than the chief.

7. The Europeans provided some Western education for the Africans. This was because the Europeans needed people with at least some training to fill the minor government jobs and also to work as semiskilled workers and clerks for the trading companies. Britain also believed that the colonies would one day become independent and so some attempt was made to train Africans for leadership. This group of Western-educated Africans rejected the tribal chiefs' powers, but at the same time they demanded a greater voice in the rule of their countries. These were the first "nationalists," the people who led the struggle for independence from the Europeans.

8. In order to reach Africa's resources more easily, the Europeans improved both transportation and communication. They also built hospitals and improved sanitation among the Africans. However, these improvements were not carried out because they were good for Africans, but because they were good for Europeans and made the colonies easier to control and more profitable.

Nationalism and Independence

Nationalism may be defined as the strong devotion to one's nation that puts the nation above all other things. World War II (1939–1945) was a turning point in the development of African nationalism. Before the war, only a small number of educated Africans were nationalists. Their main demand was that Africans have a greater voice in the running of their governments, which were controlled by the Europeans. By the end of the war, nationalism had spread to the masses. Now they demanded complete independence from the Europeans.

The first African nationalists were those people who had received a Western education. They left their tribes and went to the cities to study in the schools set up by the Europeans. Many of them later went to Europe and America to complete their university education. Kwame Nkrumah, who became the President of Ghana, spent many years working and studying in New York. Jomo Kenyatta, who led Kenya to independence and was Kenya's president until his death, studied in London. In Europe and America, they saw that people had liberty and rights that had been unknown to them—freedom of speech, press, and assembly; the right to vote and hold office; and trial by jury. The Africans felt that they, too, were entitled to the same rights as the English, French, and Americans.

Jomo Kenyatta (wearing white suit) led the people of Kenya in their successful struggle for independence from Britian. He became Kenya's first president.

Dissatisfaction with European Rule

When these Africans returned to Africa they found that despite their university education, they could only get the lowest paying jobs as clerks in European companies or minor officials in the government. The best jobs with the highest pay as well as all the highest positions in the government were reserved for the Europeans. The Europeans looked down on the Africans as primitive and regarded Western civilization as superior. This they believed was due to their own racial superiority. In those parts of Africa where many Europeans had settled there was strict segregation in housing, education, and social life. Africans had the lowest standard of living and they had very little to say about how their government should be run, because all the final decisions were made by the Europeans. Under these circumstances it is little wonder that African nationalists began to demand a better life for their people and finally complete independence.

World War II and the Growth of Nationalism

Why did World War II strengthen African nationalism to such a great extent? During the war years many Africans left their villages to work for high wartime wages in the cities. Others spent years in the army fighting alongside the Europeans. For the first time they were free from their tribal rulers. In the cities, they learned new skills and were exposed to new ideas. They began to read newspapers, to listen to the radio, and to become aware of what was going on in the world and in Africa. Some joined clubs and labor unions that were led by educated nationalists. Many Africans got important positions in the governments, and thus acquired some of the necessary experience and training to lead their people later. In the cities, they met other Africans with different languages and cultures. They realized that they shared many of the same interests and problems. Gradually the loyalty they had felt to their chief and tribe was weakened and replaced by a new loyalty to the ideal of a modern, independent African state.

The war left many problems such as inflation and unemployment. The Europeans were unable to do anything about these problems because they had serious postwar problems at home too. So the Africans showed their discontent in boycotts, strikes, and riots.

After the war, a number of countries in Asia such as India, Pakistan, Burma, and others obtained their independence from the Europeans. The success of the Asians in gaining independence encouraged the Africans to demand the same thing for themselves. The ideas of peaceful resistance and noncooperation practiced by India's nationalist leader, Mohandas K. Gandhi, made a deep impression on the Africans.

The United Nations was established near the end of the war. The preamble to its Charter spoke of "faith in the fundamental human rights, in the dignity and worth of the human person, in the equal rights of men and and nations large and small. . . ." The Africans understood this to mean that they had the same rights as anyone else. The U.N. Charter also called upon all United Nations members "to develop self-government, to take due account of the political hopes of the people and to assist them in the progressive development of their free political institutions. . . ."

The young educated Africans now began to speak out for their people. They organized the discontented masses and led them in making demands on the European governments. They rejected the old promises made by the Europeans that in time they would have greater participation in their governments. They demanded immediate and complete independence. Workers in the cities and even in the villages supported the new leaders in their demands for independence.

Independence Comes to Africa

Faced with this pressure, the European governments had to give in. In 1957, Ghana gained its freedom from Britain. It became the first black nation in sub-Saharan Africa to win its independence from the Europeans. During the next 12 years, 35 other nations became independent. France had hoped to make its African colonies part of a Greater France with the Africans having the same rights as the French. But in 1958, French President de Gaulle gave the French colonies a choice. They were to vote whether they wanted complete independence and separation from France, or self government in their own territory with France in charge of foreign affairs, defense, and finance. Guinea, led by Sekou Touré, voted for complete independence. In 1960, the other 14 French colonies requested and were granted complete independence.

INDEPENDENCE COMES TO AFRICA*

Country	Year of Independence	From
South Africa	1931	Britain
Sudan	1956	Britain & Egypt
Ghana	1957	Britain
Guinea	1958	France
Cameroon	1960	France
Central Africa Empire	1960	France
Chad	1960	France
Congo (People's Republic of)	1960	France
Zaire (The Congo) (Democratic Republic of)	1960	Belgium
Benin (Dahomey)	1960	France
Gabon	1960	France
Ivory Coast	1960	France
Malagasy Republic (Madagascar)	1960	France
Mali	1960	France
Mauritania	1960	France
Niger	1960	France
Nigeria	1960	Britain
Senegal	1960	France
Somalia	1960	Italy & Britain
Togo	1960	France
Burkina Faso (Upper Volta)	1960	France
Sierra Leone	1961	Britain
Burundi	1962	Belgium
Rwanda	1962	Belgium
Uganda	1962	Britain
Kenya	1963	Britain
Malawi	1964	Britain
Tanzania**	1964	Britain
Zambia	1964	Britain
Gambia	1965	Britain
Zimbabwe (Rhodesia)	1965	Britain
Botswana	1966	Britain
Lesotho	1966	Britain
Equatorial Guinea	1968	Spain
Mauritius	1968	Britain
Swaziland	1968	Britain
Guinea Bissau	1974	Portugal
Mozambique	1975	Portugal
Angola	1975	Portugal
Cape Verde Islands	1975	Portugal
Comoro Islands	1975	France
Sao Tomé e Principé	1975	Portugal
Djibouti	1977	France
Seychelles	1976	Britain
Namibia	1990	South Africa

*Liberia and Ethiopia already independent.
**Tanzania was formed by the union of Tanganyika and Zanzibar. Tanganyika gained independence in 1961 and Zanzibar in 1963.

Most of the countries in Africa gained their independence without bloodshed or violence. But in the highlands of East Africa where many Europeans had settled, independence was achieved only after a long period of struggle and violence. The settlers put pressure on the European government not to place the government in the hands of the African majority. In Kenya, members of the Kikuyu tribe formed an organization known as the Mau Mau, which used terrorism against Africans and Europeans to drive out the Europeans. Rebellion broke out in 1952. There was considerable bloodshed and many more Africans died than Europeans. In 1963, Kenya finally became independent.

Portugal was the last European country to give up its colonies in Africa. In 1974, the government of Portugal was overthrown and new rulers came to power. They set about making many changes in Portugal's policies. One of the most important changes was the decision to grant independence to Mozambique and Angola. In 1975, these two African nations became independent.

Today, the African nations play an important role in world affairs. Representatives from the more than 40 countries have a great deal of influence in the United Nations. Over the years, the former Communist nations and the Western nations offered military and economic assistance to the African states in the hopes of gaining their support.

Africa Today—Problems of Independence

After they gained independence, most African nations faced serious problems. Some of these problems were rooted in tribalism and the need to build a feeling of nationalism. Others were caused by the shift to black majority rule, as in Rhodesia. Economic disaster and political instability created turmoil in Uganda and threatened many other new countries. And, finally, the rise of Soviet-Cuban influence in Africa led to additional problems in many countries. In many African countries political instability is still a problem.

Tribalism and Nation Building

The modern nation requires each person to consider himself first and foremost a citizen of that nation. But the nations of Africa are relatively new creations. For centuries, Africans considered themselves to be members of a particular village, clan, or tribe. To transfer one's loyalty from the village or the tribe to the nation requires education and a change in a person's thinking. It cannot be done overnight. Almost all the African nations face the problem of uniting people who differ greatly from each other in language, culture, religion, and levels of economic development. For the new nations to survive, the Africans must learn to think of themselves as Nigerians rather than Yorubas, as Ghanaians rather than Ashanti. Most of the African nations are made up of many different tribal groups. In many of these nations there is rivalry among the various tribes, and each is afraid of being dominated by the others.

Civil War in Nigeria

Nigeria offers a good example of this situation. It has been estimated that there may be as many as 150 different ethnic groups in Nigeria. The most important of these are the Hausa, Fulani, Ibo, and Yoruba. Some of the smaller tribes have resented the fact that they are dominated by the larger ones. And among the larger tribes there is rivalry over who will have the most important positions in the country. Over the years, many Ibos left their area in the eastern region of Nigeria and went to live in the north, the area that is mainly inhabited by the Hausa and Fulani. The Ibos were disliked by the Hausa and Fulani because their education and skills gave them the best jobs in government and business.

In 1966, there was an army rebellion. General Ironsi, an Ibo, proclaimed military rule and made plans for a stronger central government. The Hausa, fearing Ibo domination, overthrew the government several months later. The new leader, General Gowon, tried to limit Ibo power in the central government. At the same time there was a massacre of Ibos living in the north. The Ibos then attempted to **secede** (separate) from Nigeria in 1967, proclaiming their region as the independent republic of Biafra. A bitter civil war followed that lasted into 1970. Most of the African nations supported the government of Nigeria against Biafra. They felt that if Biafra were allowed to secede then other ethnic groups in Africa would try to break away and set up their own states. Biafra and the Ibos were defeated and Nigeria became united once again.

Following the Civil War, a series of coups occurred. Governments changed often. Some were elected civilian governments, others were military dictatorships. As a result of the lack of a stable government and as a result of the drop in the price of oil (Nigeria's main export), Nigeria suffered severe economic problems.

In 1985, General Ibrahim B. Babangida came to power and he reestablished order. At the same time, a series of economic reforms were begun in order to restore stability to the economy. Babangida also promised political reform and set in motion a plan to restore an elected civilian government within 10 years.

Tribal Conflict in Rwanda and Burundi

Another example of tribal conflict in Africa took place in the two small East African nations of Rwanda and Burundi.

In Burundi, the Hutu tribe forms the majority of the population. But the Tutsis, who are a minority, control the government. In 1972, the Tutsi-controlled government conducted nationwide massacres that resulted in the death of 50,000 to 100,000 Hutus. Thousands of Hutu officials, civil servants, soldiers, teachers, students, and others who might hold leadership positions were among those put to death. All were accused of treason and of plotting to exterminate the Tutsis. More than 150,000 Hutus left Burundi and moved to neighboring countries. Thousands of them went to Rwanda, where Hutus controlled the government.

In Rwanda, Hutus are said to have killed more than 1,000 Tutsis between December 1972 and March 1973. Tutsis fled their homes and more than 25,000 went to Burundi in 1973. Between 1959 and 1962, 100,000 Tutsis left Rwanda when the Hutus took control of the government. It is believed that 20,000 Tutsis lost their lives at that time.

The Hutus, a Bantu people, came to this region many centuries ago from the southwest. They settled down and became farmers. About a thousand years ago the Tutsis began drifting into the area from the north. The Tutsis are a Hamitic people—tall and slender, with sharp features like the people of Ethiopia and Somalia. The Tutsis, who were cattle raisers, established the practice known as "ubuhake"—an agreement whereby they provided the Hutus with cattle in exchange for the Hutus' services. This resulted in a feudal system under the Tutsis that lasted until modern times. When the Germans ruled the area and later the Belgians, both of these countries maintained Tutsi supremacy. The Tutsis believed that they were superior, and they treated the Hutus as inferiors.

Both the Hutus and Tutsis are intensely nationalistic. Each group greatly fears and distrusts the other. If they are to live together in peace they will have to overcome these fears and suspicions. Each will have to give up its dreams of dominating the other.

After being free of major ethnic violence for several years, Rwanda again faced a Hutu-Tutsi confrontation in 1990. Thousands of exiled Tutsi, calling themselves the Rwandese Patriotic Front (FPR), crossed into Rwanda from Uganda. The invasion of Hutu-dominated Rwanda was clearly an attempt to restore Tutsi control.

The Rwanda government appealed for international assistance. Belgium, France, and Zaire sent troops to assist the government. After a month of fighting, a cease fire was declared. However, periodic outbreaks of fighting occurred throughout the rest of 1990 and into 1991.

In order to create a more peaceful situation, a new constitution was introduced in June 1991. It provided for multiparty politics and separate legislative, executive, and judicial branches of government. There was to be a prime minister and the powerful office of president was to be limited.

Politics in Sub-Saharan Africa

In most of the countries of Africa only one political party is allowed. Very few African nations have opposition parties or free elections as we know them in the West. Therefore, many Americans have claimed that the new African nations are undemocratic. This is not necessarily true and many Africans give good reasons for the existence of one-party systems.

Many Africans believe that the greatest need at present is for unity. The people need the firm leadership of one party or one individual to hold the nation together and set it on the road to economic development. In some countries, the opposition parties are seen as a danger to the nation, representing groups wishing to break up the nation into smaller units. Some of the African nations owe their existence to the abilities of individual leaders, such as Sekou Touré in Guinea and Jomo Kenyatta in Kenya. There is a strong feeling among many that opposition to such leaders and their policies is the same as disloyalty to the nation. In addition, democratic elections as we know them in the West are difficult when the majority of the population is illiterate, and not used to voting for leaders and representatives.

In recent years, the governments of many African nations have been overthrown by the army which has substituted military government in place of the civilian government. In 1984, the military took power in Guinea, following the death of President Sekou Touré. Military leaders rule in the Congo (Zaire), Dahomey, Togo, Upper Volta, Nigeria, Sierra Leone, Ghana, Burundi and others. In many cases, army leaders have claimed that they felt compelled to take over because the government was not successful in solving the nation's problems. They have promised to return power to the civilian leaders when the nation is ready. Nevertheless, armies will probably continue to play an important role in African politics for years to come.

Uganda in Turmoil

In January 1971, General Adi Amin seized power in Uganda and overthrew President Milton Obote. At that time, many Ugandans regarded Amin as a savior. There had been much opposition to Obote whose government was accused of being corrupt. Obote's tribal policies had aroused fears among army officers who were not members of Obote's Lango tribe. People of the important Baganda tribe were hostile to Obote for having overthrown their traditional leader in 1966. Obote fled to Tanzania where he had the backing of President Nyerere.

Uganda, an independent country since 1962, had many problems that Amin promised to solve. He released many political prisoners and broke up the secret police. He promised the people elections and political freedom. Amin appointed a cabinet that was made up almost entirely of civilians. In a short time, however, Amin went back on these promises and began a reign of terror.

Uganda's 80,000 Asian residents were among those who suffered the most. Centuries ago their ancestors had come to East Africa from India and settled in the countries that are now Kenya, Uganda, and Tanzania. In 1962, these three nations became independent from Britain. The Asians were given the choice of accepting British citizenship or becoming citizens of the countries in which they were living. Most of the Asians chose to become British citizens while they continued to live in East Africa.

Almost all the business and commerce of Uganda was in the hands of the Asians. In November 1971, Idi Amin criticized the Asians for isolating themselves from the African people. In August 1972, Amin ordered all Asians who were not citizens of Uganda to leave the country within three months. Amin claimed that their presence prevented the Africans from playing their rightful part in the economy. Although this order was only supposed to apply to those Asians who were not citizens of Uganda, many Asians who had Ugandan citizenship were also forced to leave the country. The Asians who were expelled were only allowed to sell their property to Africans (who bought the property at rock-bottom prices) or abandon their property altogether. Each expelled family was permitted to take with it the equivalent of $140 in cash and $1,400 in goods. What actually happened was that the government seized most of the Asians' property. By the November 8 deadline, all of the Asians of non-Ugandan citizenship had left the country. Most of them went to Britain, but some went to Canada, India, the United States, and a few other countries.

Economic Problems

Much of Uganda's African population was pleased with the expulsion of the Asians because it gave them the opportunity to take over their property and wealth. But the expulsion had a serious effect on the economy and on the country. Many schools that were staffed mainly by Asian teachers closed. In Kampala, the capital city, 80 percent of the shops closed and many Africans were left jobless. The skills of the Asians had been essential to the economy of the country and for a time there was no one to replace them. At the same time, the Amin government nationalized many European-owned companies. Since most of these firms had been British owned, Britain retaliated by canceling a credit of 24 million pounds sterling (about $58 million).

By 1975, the Ugandan economy was on the brink of disaster. There was a serious decline in the production of many crops, including cotton and sugar, the export crops that brought in foreign currency to pay for imports. As a result, with very little foreign exchange, there were severe shortages of many basic necessities, such as salt and soap. This was accompanied by a sharp rise in the cost of living. Another reason for the acute shortage of cash was that approximately one-third of the country's budget was spend on the army. Uganda received considerable aid from Libya, Egypt, and Saudi Arabia, but this did not stop the economy from continuing downhill.

A Reign of Terror

In September 1972, an attempt was made to overthrow the government of Idi Amin. Soldiers loyal to former President Obote invaded Uganda from Tanzania, but the invasion was poorly planned and it failed. Soon after the invasion Amin's reign of terror began. Thousands of people lost their lives during the next few years. Many of them were government officials who were accused of plotting to overthrow the government. Many foreigners were arrested and a few were murdered. There were attacks against members of the Acholi, Lango, and Baganda tribes and many were killed. Soldiers were allowed to roam free and they committed atrocities. The army became feared and hated throughout the country. Thousands of refugees left Uganda. Many nations, including the United States, broke off diplomatic relations with Uganda in protest. In July 1976, Arab terrorists hijacked an Air

France jetliner and landed it at Entebbe Airport in Uganda. For several days they held the Israeli and Jewish passengers hostage. It was widely believed that the terrorists had the support and cooperation of Idi Amin.

The Overthrow of Idi Amin

Idi Amin managed to survive many army mutinies and assassination attempts. A steady flow of arms from the Soviet Union helped him to remain in power. In 1978, a mutiny planned by three regiments of the Ugandan Army was averted by Palestinian troops flown in from Libya.

In January 1979, Tanzanian troops joined by Ugandan exiles invaded Uganda. They were supported by guerrillas inside the country. Libya sent soldiers and money to help Amin, but the Ugandan Army was disunited. The invading forces captured Entebbe and its airport in April and Kampala fell. Idi Amin fled and took refuge in Libya. Tanzanian troops remained in Uganda to restore order, but for many months there was a great deal of lawlessness.

Uganda Under President Obote

In May 1980, former President Milton Obote returned to Uganda after a nine-year exile in Tanzania. In December, Uganda held its first national elections since 1962. Obote's party won and he was inaugurated president for a five-year term.

When Obote took office in December 1980, the economy was in a desperate state. The production of coffee, an important export crop, was at an all-time low. The people were in a state of shock after years of insecurity and corruption. Obote took many steps to improve this situation. During the next few years, thousands of detainees were released from prison. Obote urged Ugandans in exile, including his critics, to return, and he promised them freedom of speech. Parliament passed a law guaranteeing the return of their property to those Asians who had been forced to surrender it in 1972.

There was a steady improvement in the economy with the help of money from the World Bank, the International Monetary Fund, Great Britain, and other countries. The government made efforts to rehabilitate agriculture and restore communication. There was an increase in the production of coffee and tea.

But economic recovery was threatened by the activities of the guerrillas opposed to Obote's government and the reprisals of government troops. The guerrillas engaged in many acts of violence, and the army retaliated with great brutality. The troops were accused of indiscriminate cruelty during these military operations—setting fire to houses, stealing property, and killing. Thousands of Ugandans left the country and became refugees in the Sudan.

Military Coup

In July 1985, the government of President Obote was overthrown by a military coup. The coup resulted from the discontent felt by soldiers of the Acholi tribe. They were angered by the special treatment given to soldiers from the Lango tribe, Obote's own tribe.

A group led by General Yoweri Museveni continued fighting because it had not been included in the new national government. In 1986, his forces captured the capital city of Kampala. He declared himself President of Uganda. Slowly his forces extended his government's control over the entire country.

Since then, efforts are being made to rebuild and reform Uganda's economy. However, the country and its people are suffering greatly from past governments' instability and mismanagement of the economy.

In the area of political reform, General Museveni agreed to set up a commission to write a new constitution, but declared his opposition to a multiparty system.

The Horn of Africa—Ethiopia

The Horn of Africa is located in the northeast corner of the continent and is bounded by the Red Sea on the north and east. The Red Sea is an important waterway, especially for the transportion of oil from the Middle East to the rest of the world. Ethiopia, Somalia, and Djibouti are the three nations located in the Horn of Africa. Ethiopia, the largest, was ruled by Haile Selassie from 1916 to 1974, when the army revolted.

Ethiopia is a poor country. For about ten years before the revolt, the people showed their unhappiness with strikes and demonstrations. They wanted a fairer division of the land, higher wages and, most important, a greater say in the ruling of the country. In 1974, the army overthrew Emperor Haile Selassie; Ethiopia was no longer a kingdom.

The army ruled Ethiopia and began to make many socialist reforms. Land was taken over by the government and given to peasant associations. These associations were to decide how the land should be used. But, the army did little to increase civil rights or to raise wages. In 1977, Mengistu Haile Mariam, one of the leaders of the army revolt of 1974, emerged as the strong man and became sole ruler of Ethiopia.

The Problem of Eritrea

Eritrea is located in the northeastern part of Ethiopia along the Red Sea. A former Italian colony, Eritrea was given to Ethiopia at the end of World War II. It provided Ethiopia with a coastline; before 1945, Ethiopia was a landlocked country. The people of Eritrea are mainly Muslims and they are not related ethnically to the Ethiopians. Since 1945, opposition to Ethiopian rule has existed and fighting has continued for over 40 years. In the past few years, the rebels have been aided by Muslims in Djibouti and Somalia. The rebels want independence but would probably settle for autonomous rule for the area.

Continued Instability in the 1980s

Conflicts in the Horn of Africa continued in the 1980s. Somalia complained that Ethiopian troops, using Soviet arms, crossed its border to aid Somali rebels who wished to overthrow the existing government. Meanwhile, the Ethiopians made repeated military attempts to destroy the liberation movements in Eritrea and Tigre. These attempts failed. The Ethiopian rebels accused the Soviets of direct involvement in the campaigns to destroy them. Sudan accused both Libya and Ethiopia of giving support to the rebel Sudan National Liberation Movement in Southern Sudan.

Army Rule and Civil War

During his 14 year rule. Mengistu Haile Mariam destroyed the economy of Ethiopia. He used torture and murder to force the people of Ethiopia into following his Marxist and Communist ideas. In one experiment with collectivization in farming, he relocated 700,000 farmers. Production decreased, and as a result, made the famine of 1984 worse. It is estimated that about a million people died in that famine. Mengistu spent about 60 percent of Ethiopia's income on the armed forces. The result was that his army was the largest in Africa south of the Sahara and his country became one of the poorest in the world.

The Ethiopians soon rebelled against Mengistu's harsh rule. Mengistu received more than $10 billion in Soviet military aid to help put down the rebellion among his own people: Eritreans, Tigreans, and Oromos.

The Eritrean People's Liberation Front (EPLF) was formed in 1970 to win independence for Eritrea. The Tigre People's Liberation Front, formed in 1985, was originally created to fight for the autonomy of Tigre Province. However, at present they favor a unified Ethiopia. They support the Eritrean demand for a referendum on independence for Eritrea.

The Oromo Liberation Front (OLF) was established in 1975. Its main objective is to gain independence or at least autonomy for the southern provinces of Ethiopia. These are the homelands of the Oromos or Gallas as they are sometimes called. The Oromos are the largest ethnic group in Ethiopia numbering about 20 million. However, they feel they have been oppressed by the historic rulers of Ethiopia who come from the Amharas.

The three rebel groups used guerrilla tactics. They attacked small groups of government troops; temporarily occupied key points in the country; and avoided large battles with the better armed government forces.

By the end of 1990, the rebels controlled the important port of Mossawa (Mitsiwa) on the Red Sea. Asmara (Asnera), the capital and main city of Eritrea, was completely surrounded. Rebel forces began a steady advance toward Addis Ababa, Ethiopia's capital. At the end of May, Mengistu resigned as president and fled to Zimbabwe.

In July 1990, a charter was drawn up for the new Ethiopian government. Power was to be shared by the rebel leaders and elections were to be held sometime in the future. In this charter, the Eritreans, as well as any of Ethiopia's dozens of other nationalites, have the right to self determination (autonomy) and also the right of secession. An agreement was reached that Eritreans and other nationalities would vote by referendum in two years on whether or not to break away from Ethiopia.

Soviet-Cuban Influence in Africa

Africa has always been a continent where foreign powers competed with each other to gain influence. In the 1970s and 1980s, the Soviet Union made great efforts to expand its influence throughout Africa. In this effort the Soviet Union was assisted by Cuba. To a lesser degree other Communist countries, mainly in Eastern Europe, sent special units to Africa to serve Soviet foreign policy interests. These countries were East Germany, Czechoslovakia, Hungary, Poland, and Bulgaria. In 1978, there were over 40,000 Cuban troops in Africa—20,000 in Angola, 17,000 in Ethiopia and about 4,000 scattered in places like Mozambique, the Congo, Equatorial Guinea, Guinea-Bissau, Libya, and Tanzania.

There were several reasons for the Soviet Union's new interest in Africa. Africa was an excellent location for Soviet air and naval bases. These bases could help the Soviet Union extend its control to the Indian and Atlantic Oceans. The Soviet Union and China were engaged in a worldwide competition to win developing countries to their own form of communism. The Soviet Union hoped the African nations would follow the direction of Moscow rather than Peking. Africa, with its wealth of natural resources, is very important to Western Europe, which lacks many of these resources. This made Africa valuable to the Soviet Union as well. Since the Soviet Union did not have a history of colonialism in Africa as Western nations did, it was in a position to support African liberation movements such as the one in Angola. The United States, because of its close ties to the former colonial rulers and because of its association with South Africa, was looked on with favor by African revolutionaries. While the Soviet Union supplied economic and military aid to a number of African countries and revolutionary movements, there were several areas where the Soviet Union made an all-out effort.

Angola and Mozambique

Angola, which was a Portuguese colony for nearly 500 years, received its independence in November 1975. Before Angola became independent, fighting broke out among three Angolan liberation groups, each of which hoped to lead Angola when the Portuguese left. Following independence, the fighting increased and soon the country was involved in a civil war. The three Angolan liberation groups were: the MPLA (Popular Movement for the Liberation of Angola) supported by Marxists; the FNLA (National Front for the Liberation of Angola) supported by black nationalists; and the UNITA (National Union for the Total Independence of Angola) supported by the majority of Angola's white population.

Because of Angola's vast oil and mineral wealth, a number of foreign countries became involved in the conflict. The Soviet Union and Cuba supported the MPLA. The FNLA was supported by the United States, France, and Zaire. The UNITA was supported by Portugal, China, and South Africa.

By 1976, the MPLA achieved victory in the civil war. The FNLA withdrew from the fighting, but UNITA forces continued to fight.

Mozambique gained independence from Portugal in 1975. Problems in Mozambique resulted when it helped black nationalists try to overthrow the white governments of Rhodesia and South Africa. In the 1970s, the Rhodesian government responded by aiding guerrilla groups trying to overthrow the government of Mozambique.

In the 1980s, instability and problems with South Africa dominated the politics of Angola and Mozambique. Both nations allowed anti-apartheid guerrilla groups to set up bases on their territory. Moreover, Angola allowed the Southwest Africa People's Organization (SWAPO) to carry out raids against South Africa from Angolan territory. In response, South Africa gave military aid to guerrilla groups that opposed the existing governments in Angola and Mozambique. These guerrilla groups were allowed to operate from bases in South Africa.

In 1984, agreements were reached between the three nations. South Africa agreed to withdraw troops from southern Angola and to stop aiding the guerrilla groups. The Angolans promised to stop SWAPO's guerrilla raids from Angolan territory and to get the withdrawal of Cuban troops from Angola. A cease-fire went into effect. South Africa and Mozambique agreed that each nation would prevent the use of its territories for attacks against the other.

In spite of these agreements, the situation did not improve. Guerrilla attacks against Mozambique increased. Mozambique accused South Africa of failing to live up to the agreement. Moreover, in late 1986, the President of Mozambique was killed in a plane crash. The Mozambique government blamed South Africa for the crash.

The agreement between Angola and South Africa also failed to achieve peace. Although South Africa's armed forces finally withdrew from Angola in April 1985, their attacks against guerrilla bases on Angolan territory continued. In addition UNITA, which was receiving support from South Africa, increased its guerrilla activity. Soviet support for the Angolan army and the Cuban combat troops stationed in Angola increased. Negotiations over Namibia's (South-West Africa) independence reached a stalemate over the problem of the withdrawal of all Cuban troops from Angola. This situation continued for the next six years.

The push to end the 16 years of savage civil war took place in February 1991. The Marxist government of Angola agreed to a peace plan that included a ceasefire with the FNLA—the U.S.-backed rebels. UNITA, the main rebel group, quickly agreed to the plan. The agreement called for a new constitution and the establishment of a multiparty government. The United Nations was to make sure the agreement was put into affect fairly.

Zaire

In 1960 Zaire, formerly known as the Congo, gained its independence from Belgium. Almost immediately, there was bloodshed and rebellion. Moïse Tshombe led a rebellion against the central government of the Congo. The goal of this rebellion was the secession of Katanga Province from the Congo. Katanga province (now known as Shaba) in southeastern Zaire is very rich in copper and other materials. Katanga is the homeland of more than 1,500,000 people of the Lunda tribe. There are other members of the Lunda ethnic group in northwestern Zambia and in eastern Angola. Tshombe's followers wanted to preserve their mineral wealth from their enemies—the government and the Bakongo tribes. The rebellion was crushed, but Tshombe's followers fled to Angola. In Angola, the Katangese, as these refugees are known, have considerable autonomy in their region in the northeast. The Katangese helped Agostinho Neto and the MPLA come to power in Angola, and Neto allowed them to use Angolan territory to prepare for invasions of Zaire.

In May 1978, Katangan rebels based in Angola invaded the copper mining province of Shaba (Katanga) in southern Zaire. The rebels brutally massacred several thousand blacks and whites living there. A force of French and Belgian paratroopers, assisted by United States jets, prevented the invasion from succeeding. French and Belgian troops forced the Katangan invaders to retreat back to Angola. They also rescued more than 2,500 Europeans trapped in Shaba. The goal of the invaders was to disrupt Zaire's economy and bring about the downfall of President Mobuto Sese Seko. The copper mines in Shaba province are the main source of Zaire's wealth. One-half the world's annual supply of cobalt comes from this region as well as large quantities of zinc.

Immediately following the invasion, Zaire charged that Cubans were involved in the fighting on the side of the rebels. The United States sharply criticized the Soviet Union and Cuba. However, Premier Fidel Castro of Cuba stated that his country had no part in the invasion of Zaire. The fact remains that over the years, Cubans and Angolans had armed and trained the Katangese. Cuba had troops in Angola, and there were Cuban troops stationed along the Angolan border, the area from which the Katangans launched their invasion.

Under pressure from the United States, Angola signed a treaty with Zaire in 1985. The agreement stated that both nations pledged not to allow or support rebels within their borders.

After 1985, Mobutu tried to reform Zaire's economic situation. His attempts to use a free market economy to cure the ills of the weak economy were not successful. Inflation was the most serious problem. Another problem was Zaire's growing international debt as well as the inability to pay even the interest on the debt.

In the political area, objections to Mobutu's dictatorial rule grew. The U.S. Congress, concerned over corruption and human rights violations, voted to cut off all direct military and economic aid to Zaire (September 1990).

In January 1991, Mobutu called for a dialogue between the state and the people. The purpose of this dialogue was to give the people an opportunity to present their views on how the government was being run. These views led Mobuto to announce in April 1991 that he would allow multiparty democratic activity.

Mobutu's most important opponent was Etienne Tshisekedi who, while in exile, stated that Mobuto had to step down before any progress toward democratic government in Zaire could be made.

Mobutu responded by allowing Tshisekedi to return to Zaire in February 1991. Tshisekedi's party, the UDPS (Union pour la Democratie et le Progress Social), has become the most important political party in Zaire.

Rhodesia—Zimbabwe: The Transition to Black Majority Rule

In the middle of the 19th century, the first white settlers arrived in the land that is now known as Zimbabwe. They were British and Afrikaner (descendants of the Dutch in South Africa) hunters, traders, miners, and missionaries who had moved up from the south. In 1889, the British South Africa Company was formed by Cecil Rhodes, Britain's great empire builder. The company was to bring colonists to the region and promote trade. The land came to be known as Southern Rhodesia in honor of Cecil Rhodes.

During the 1890s, many European settlers arrived. They laid claim to large areas of land and to mining rights in the area. This resulted in uprisings by the Ndebele and Shona tribes, but by 1897 the region was pacified by British troops. The country was governed by the company until 1923, when it became a self-governing British colony.

In Southern Rhodesia, as in South Africa, the white minority ruled the black majority. Although 95 percent of the population was black and 5 percent white, the whites owned half the land. All urban, mining and industrial areas were designated as white, so no African could acquire a permanent home there. There was discrimination against blacks in job opportunities, in education, and in many other ways. The government, the army, and the police were entirely in the hands of the whites.

At first, the black nationalists tried to improve the lives of blacks by nonviolent means. They concentrated their efforts on trying to end discrimination in education and employment. They demanded equal voting rights for blacks. Their methods were strikes, demonstrations, and appeals to Britain. By the 1950s and 1960s, the nationalist movement became more militant and they demanded black majority rule.

Independence from Britain

In November 1965, the white government of Ian Smith declared Southern Rhodesia independent from Britain. The country was now called Rhodesia. In March 1970, Rhodesia declared itself a republic. The purpose of these actions was to prevent an orderly transfer of power from the British to the Africans. (This kind of orderly change to black majority rule had been achieved in the other former British colonies in Africa.) It was at this point that many black nationalists decided that armed struggle was the best way to achieve their goals.

Struggle for Black Rights

Two leading groups in the struggle for black rights were the Zimbabwe African People's Union (ZAPU), led by Joshua Nkomo, and the Zimbabwe African National Union (ZANU), led by Ndabaningi Sithole and later by Robert Mugabe. (Zimbabwe is the ancient African name of Rhodesia.) These groups established bases in Zambia and Tanzania and later in Mozambique after it became independent in 1975. From these bases both organizations launched many guerrilla attacks against Rhodesia. Another important group was the African National Council (ANC) under the leadership of Bishop Abel Muzorewa, a moderate. Although he demanded black majority rule, he believed that that goal could be achieved by negotiating with the government of Ian Smith.

In 1975, after more than a year of negotiations between Smith and Muzorewa, Smith rejected black majority rule. The guerilla attacks intensified and by the end of 1978, more than 12,000 people had been killed. There were attacks on the road and rail communications between Rhodesia and South Africa. This presented a great danger to Rhodesia. Since Rhodesia is a landlocked country, it depends on South Africa's ports to receive its imports and ship its exports. If it were cut off from South Africa, the damage to the economy could be severe. The Rhodesian government retaliated against the guerrillas by launching air strikes and ground operations against the guerrilla camps in Mozambique and other countries. There was danger of war between Rhodesia and its neighbors. Also Rhodesia was cut off from many nations around the world that refused to recognize Rhodesia's independence. When the United Nations called for economic sanctions against Rhodesia, many countries stopped trading with and investing money in Rhodesia. The sanctions hurt Rhodesia's economy in the 1960s and 1970s, but the country was able to survive with the help of South Africa. Another very serious problem was that many whites left Rhodesia during the 1970s. The white population declined from 277,000 to fewer than 100,000 by 1979.

Peace Plans for Black Majority Rule

Britain and other nations put great pressure on Ian Smith and his government to reach an agreement with the blacks. In 1976, Britain presented Smith with a peace plan. The major points included acceptance of the principle of majority rule and elections to be held in 18 months to two years. A few months later, U.S. Secretary of State Henry Kissinger visited Africa and announced that the United States was committed to majority rule in Rhodesia. Smith and the black leaders refused to accept the British and United States proposals.

Formation of the Patriotic Front

Black nationalist leaders had been divided among themselves. However, they realized that it was necessary to agree on a common political strategy. This led to the formation of the Patriotic Front (PF). The most important groups that joined to form the Patriotic Front were ZAPU and ZANU. The Front was led by Robert Mugabe and Joshua Nkomo. However, Smith refused to deal with the PF.

The situation in Rhodesia deteriorated further in 1977 and 1978. There were more guerrilla attacks and more retaliatory raids by the Rhodesian armed forces against bases in Mozambique. More whites left the country. Agriculture and industrial output declined. The collapse of the Smith government was just a matter of time. Still, there were many people in Smith's party who were totally opposed to any negotiations that might lead to black majority rule.

The "Internal Settlement"

At the end of 1977, Prime Minister Smith announced that he was prepared to accept majority rule. But he insisted that he would only meet with black leaders inside Rhodesia and not with the guerrilla organizations that were banned. This excluded Mugabe and Nkomo from any talks. Smith met with Bishop Muzorewa, Ndabaningi Sithole, and Jeremiah Chirau of the Zimbabwe United People's Organization. In March 1978, an agreement was signed. This agreement, known as the "internal settlement," stated that the country would be governed by its black majority. The name of the country would be changed to Zimbabwe Rhodesia. All citizens over the age of 18 would vote to elect a Parliament of 100 members: 72 seats would be reserved for blacks and 28 for whites. The agreement was condemned by Nkomo and Mugabe, as well as by the presidents of Tanzania, Zambia, Botswana, and Mozambique. Guerrilla attacks increased.

In February 1979, Smith dissolved the Rhodesian Parliament, bringing to an end 88 years of white rule. Elections were held in April. Although the guerrillas tried to disrupt the elections, 64 percent of the electorate voted. This resulted in an overwhelming victory for the United African National Council of Bishop Muzorewa.

The First Black Government

In May, Muzorewa was sworn in as the first black prime minister. He appointed Smith as a minister without portfolio. However, the Muzorewa government was opposed by many. The Patriotic Front insisted that it represented the only authentic voice of the black people, and it had the support of the other African nations.

Britain again invited all the parties concerned to a conference in September 1979. This time each side yielded enough so that a settlement was reached. Smith agreed that the whites should no longer be able to block legislation while the Patriotic Front agreed that 20 percent of the seats in the Parliament should be reserved for whites. In December, a ceasefire was accepted by all sides. This marked the official end to the civil war which had begun in 1972.

Beginnings of "New" Zimbabwe

In January 1980, Robert Mugabe, Joshua Nkomo, and many other black leaders returned to Rhodesia after having lived in exile for several years. Elections were held in February, resulting in an overwhelming victory (63 percent of the total vote) for Mugabe's ZANU party. Nkomo's party was second. In April 1980, the country proclaimed its independence and was named Zimbabwe. Robert Mugabe became prime minister. Joshua Nkomo and several members of his ZAPU party were included in the cabinet.

Economic Problems

The new country faced many problems. After years of civil war the economy was in very bad shape. The country had once been an exporter of corn. Now it had to import large quantities of corn. Tobacco had always been the main export crop and the chief source of foreign currency. In the early 1980s, however, tobacco was bringing in less money, due to world over-production. There was also a problem in exporting the tobacco caused by a shortage of railway locomotives. The economy of Zimbabwe also suffered from an acute shortage of fuel. Oil had to pass through South Africa, making the country economically dependent on South Africa. The situation was further aggravated when rebels blew up an oil pipeline from Mozambique, which provided a major source of Zimbabwe's petroleum. Drought, which affected many African countries in the early 1980s, also contributed to Zimbabwe's problems. Many whites continued to leave the country. Another very serious problem that held back economic recovery was the lack of foreign investment. Foreigners were unwilling to invest in Zimbabwe as long as there was insecurity and political instability.

Efforts were made to deal with these problems. Mugabe urged the white farmers to remain in Zimbabwe, promising them security in return for their contribution to the country's prosperity. He appealed to foreign countries for economic aid. Britain, the United States, Canada, France, Germany, and many other countries responded with promises of money. A trade agreement was signed with South Africa.

Political Instability

Political instability was a major problem that held back economic recovery. From the beginning, relations between Mugabe and Nkomo and their ZANU and ZAPU parties were uneasy. As time passed, relations between the two deteriorated. In 1982, Mugabe announced that only policies approved by his ZANU party would be adopted by the government. He also stated that he wanted a one-party state. Nkomo denounced these statements and rejected Mugabe's plan to merge (join) the two parties. When large quantities of armaments were discovered on farms belonging to Nkomo's supporters, Nkomo and three others belonging to his party were dismissed from the government; they were accused of plotting to overthrow the ruling party. Acts of violence began to spread across the country. In June 1982, the government launched a large-scale attack against its opponents.

During 1984, there was an increase in anti-government violence by guerrillas. The government sent large numbers of troops to crush the guerrillas. The troops were accused of excessive brutality and committing atrocities against civilians. By the end of the year, Mugabe said that the time had come for ZAPU to be declared an enemy of the people. The situation worsened in 1985. Nkomo found it increasingly difficult to address public meetings because of the violent intervention by supporters of ZANU. Elections were held in June 1985. In many places, ZANU supporters threatened people, forcing them to vote for the government party. The results of the election showed an overwhelming victory for Mugabe's ZANU party. Mugabe was well on his way to achieving a one-party state where there would be little or no opposition.

The power struggle between Mugabe and Nkomo continued, but Mugabe was victorious. Nkomo's party was absorbed into ZANU in December, 1989. The only opposition party that remained was Edgar Tekere's Zimbabwe Unity Movement (ZMU).

In elections that were held in 1987, Mugabe took office as the first Executive President of Zimbabwe. This was another step leading Zimbabwe away from a parliamentary democracy toward a one-party state.

While Mugabe remains committed to a one-party system, it seems that many members of ZANU do not agree with him. Mugabe has agreed to make no moves against the existing multi-party system in the near future.

South Africa and The Problem of Separate Development (Apartheid)

In the southernmost part of the continent of Africa is the Republic of South Africa. It is the homeland of over 30 million people: Africans (Bantus–blacks); Europeans (whites); coloreds (mixed European or Asian, Hottentot and Bantu); and Asians. The whites of South Africa are made up of two groups of people—the Afrikaners, who are descendants of the original Dutch settlers and the English descendants of the original British settlers.

POPULATION OF SOUTH AFRICA

Official Catagory	Number of People (millions)	% of Total Population
Black	21.0	68.2
White	5.5	18.0
Colored	3.2	10.5
Asian	1.0	3.3

Source: *Britannica Book of the Year, 1991*

Of all the independent countries in sub-Saharan Africa, only one, the Republic of South Africa, is ruled by a white minority. Since 1948, the government of the Republic has followed a policy of separate development, or **apartheid**, as it is called in other nations.

Policy of Separateness

The Nationalist Party Program

In the years before 1948, governments containing Afrikaners and the English ruled the Republic. Social and economic separation between the whites and the Bantus, Asians, and coloreds had existed for a long time. In 1948, the Nationalists, an all-Afrikaner party, won the election.

The Nationalists passed laws to put their program of "separateness" (apartheid) into effect. The Group Areas Act of 1949 provided for segregated residential areas for each race. In 1950, a population register classified the entire adult population according to race. Laws were passed forbidding mixed marriages. Other laws reserved skilled jobs for whites. Separation of facilities for whites and non-whites was put into law. (This was similar in many ways to the separate facilities that existed in the United States in the years before 1960.) It should be noted that the Nationalists put into law customs and traditions that had existed for over 50 years. The Nationalists did not introduce segregation into South Africa because segregation had existed long before they took over. But the Nationalists did make separation of the races the official policy of the government.

Education

In the field of education, the Nationalists passed laws that further separated the races. The Bantu Education Act of 1953 made the local Bantu communities responsible for the education of Africans. The Extension of University Education Act of 1959 forbade all non-Europeans to attend the English-speaking universities. This law also provided for the creation of separate "university-colleges," not only for each of the four racial groups, but even for each of the three main African language groups.

General Law Amendment Acts

Various laws were passed by the Nationalists forbidding practically any form of opposition, by peaceful means or otherwise. The General Law Amendment Act of 1962 provided for a minimum sentence of five years of prison and a maximum sentence of death for sabotage. Sabotage includes any attempt to promote disturbance, to disrupt any industry, to hamper the maintenance of law and order, and to promote hostility between the different sections of the population. Illegal possession of explosives or illegal entry into any building was considered sufficient evidence of an intention to carry out acts of sabotage. The law also extended the government's powers to ban newspapers, organizations, and gatherings, and to imprison any person for any length of time without due process of law. The General Law Amendment Act of 1963 allowed repeated detentions of persons for 90 days at a time for questioning; refusal to allow anybody, including legal counsel, to see the detained persons; indefinite imprisonment without trial; and the death penalty for receiving training in the use of violence outside South Africa.

The Bantu Authorities Act

In 1951, the Bantu Authorities Act was passed. It set up a blueprint for the development of the Bantu (African) peoples and attempted to set up separate "tribal states." The Nationalists felt that Africans should develop within their own tribal groups under tribal laws and traditions instead of trying to achieve equal political rights with whites. When Africans became capable of self-rule, they would rule themselves. The areas or so called homelands set aside for blacks would become "Bantustans" or semi-independent Bantu states. In 1956, the Transkei Territorial Authority was set up and in 1961 the Transkei was given self-government. The Transkei is located on the east coast of the Republic of South Africa and contains the largest single Bantu population group in the republic.

The Homelands Program

The creation of the homelands program was a basic part of the government's long-range plan for the survival of South Africa's whites. This policy called for dividing the country's blacks and whites into ten states. Nine would be for the blacks and one for the whites. The white state would hold 87 percent of the land, which would include all 17 major cities.

Eventually all black South Africans would be given citizenship in one of the tribal homelands. Seventy percent of the population of South Africa would be packed into 13 percent of the land. Only one of the planned homelands would be established with a single piece of land. The others were broken into two or more parts surrounded by white South Africa.

Under the homelands program, when a black person's homeland became independent, he automatically became a citizen of that "nation," and lost South African citizenship. Black workers who were needed to run South Africa's mines and industries would be permitted to continue on their jobs. Without them, South Africa's economy would collapse. However, the wives and children of all those workers had to "return" to live in the homelands most of them had never known. This policy caused much hardship for black families in South Africa.

Establishment of Homelands

Four of South Africa's nine homelands became "independent." In October 1976, Transkei became independent. It was a united area located on the Indian Ocean with a deep-water port. The people of the Transkei depend mainly on agriculture and livestock to earn a living. Cattle, sheep, goats, and horses are raised.

In December 1977, the second of the homelands became independent within the Republic of South Africa. The new republic is called Bophuthatswana. It consists of seven patches of territory scattered in northeast South Africa. It is completely landlocked with no coastline. The area is rich in platinum, asbestos, chromium, and maganese. Little of the land is good for agriculture.

As in the case of Transkei, the nations of the world did not recognize the Bophuthatswana Republic. However, Lucas Mangope, the first president of the Republic, felt it was a good start to freedom. He said, "We cannot take the humiliations of the South African system any longer. We would rather face the difficulties of ruling a fragmented territory and the wrath of the outside world. It is the price we are prepared to pay for being masters of our own destiny."

The Struggle Against Apartheid (1960–1984)

The Sharpeville Massacre—1960

In March 1960, thousands of Africans gathered in the township of Sharpeville to demonstrate against the hated pass laws. The purpose of the demonstration was to get the government to abolish the pass laws. These laws required blacks to carry passbooks that indicated where they could live, work, and travel. They were passed to control and limit the movement of blacks into white cities. If a black person did not carry a passbook, he or she could be fined or imprisoned. It was to be a nonviolent protest. The participants were told to surrender their passbooks and invite arrest. The police opened fire on the unarmed demonstrators and 69 blacks were killed. On the same day, there were large demonstrations in Cape Town. Black workers went on strike for three weeks. The government declared a state of emergency and drastic regulations were put into effect. Meetings were prohibited and police were authorized to detain people without trial. Publications (newspapers, magazines, and books) that were considered subversive (antigovernment) were banned. The African National Congress and the Pan-African Congress were outlawed. Thousands of Africans were jailed.

Many people inside and outside of South Africa were outraged. South African business and financial leaders, churches, and other groups called on the government to modify the race laws. In other countries people boycotted South African goods.

Soweto Riots—1976

The Soweto riots of 1976 were the worst race riots in South African history. Soweto is a township near Johannesburg with a population of 1 million blacks. It was built by the government to house blacks who work in the factories and businesses of Johannesburg. The riots began in June 1976 over what seemed to be a minor issue. The government had insisted that black high school students take some of their courses in Afrikaans, the language spoken by the Afrikaners who control the government and politics of South Africa. To blacks, Afrikaans is a symbol of oppression, the language of apartheid. To protest the requirement, Soweto students boycotted classes, staged demonstrations, and clashed with police. Soweto became the scene of almost daily rioting. The rioting spread to other black townships, to some of the Bantu homelands, and to several universities.

The Soweto riots marked a turning point for South Africa. They were the strongest assertion of black power in the history of the country. Young blacks, unwilling to tolerate apartheid any longer, were accepting violence as the only solution. It was recognized by many in South Africa that the real cause behind the riots was the terrible conditions under which blacks lived. For the first time, criticism of apartheid was heard from Afrikaners. There were growing demands inside and outside the country for radical changes in South Africa's race policy.

Government Reform

During the next few years, the South African government took steps to improve the living conditions of blacks. Apartheid signboards were removed in many public places. These were the ugly signs that kept blacks from using the same fountains, bathrooms, and restaurants as whites and from sitting in the same sections on trains and buses. Blacks were permitted to participate in many sports together with whites. Black residents in Soweto and other black townships were given the right to acquire or build their own houses. This right had long been denied to them. Blacks received permission to open supermarkets and other small businesses in black urban areas.

A number of important advances were made by black workers because there was a serious shortage of skilled labor in the country. More facilities were provided to train black workers. Wage gaps were narrowed in many industries. This meant that black and white workers would receive similar pay for similar work. Job reservation, the practice whereby certain jobs were reserved for whites, was practically abolished. In 1979, black workers were given the right to join or form legally recognized trade unions. In 1980, some unions admitted black members for the first time.

However, the policy of apartheid, or separation of the races, remained basically unchanged. Separate schools and universities for each race continued as before. Blacks were still not permitted to live in the white cities or to move about freely without a passbook. The government claimed that blacks working in the cities of South Africa were still connected with their own "homelands." Therefore, blacks could not have any political rights or citizenship in South Africa.

Reaction and Riots: 1977–1984

The reforms raised the expectations of blacks and many whites. They looked forward to greater and more radical reforms. But the government of President Botha was caught in the middle. On the one hand, there were greater demands for change. On the other, there was pressure from white extremists not to change the traditional racial policies and to preserve white supremacy. There was an open split in the ruling National Party. Those who thought that President Botha had gone too far seceded from the National Party and formed the Conservative Party. Several ultra-conservative groups joined in an alliance that they called "Action to Save White South Africa." Many engaged in acts of violence against people who cooperated with blacks.

The government's slowness and hesitation in bringing about greater reforms led to unrest and violence in the black communities. The violence led to police crackdowns, arrests, and detentions, which in turn led to more violence. Parliament passed the International Security Act in 1977, giving the police greater power to detain persons whose activities were considered a threat to the state. Hundreds of people of all races were detained without trial under the security laws. In 1977, Steven Biko, a former student leader, died in jail in Pretoria while being detained by the Security Police. An inquest into Biko's death found that he died from head and brain injuries received while being questioned by the police.

In the 1970s and 1980s, the outlawed African National Congress (ANC) stepped up its terrorist acts. On several occasions, South African forces attacked ANC bases in Mozambique and Besotho in an effort to destroy the organization.

South Africa Since 1984

Internal Turmoil

The New Constitution

In 1983, a new constitution was approved by South Africa's white voters. The new constitution provided for a Parliament with three separately elected chambers—a white House of Assembly, a colored House of Representatives, and an Asian House of Deputies. Each chamber would be responsible for its community's "own affairs": education, social welfare, housing, local government, arts, and culture. For the first time the colored and Asian people were given the vote and the right to participate in a limited way in the political process. But South Africa's 23 million blacks remained completely excluded from the new Parliament. Many South Africans of all races condemned the constitution, saying that it entrenched (strengthened) apartheid.

Rioting and Violence

In September 1984, on the day the constitution went into effect, rioting broke out in the black residential areas outside of Johannesburg. During 1985 and 1986, there was no letup in the violence. Outbreaks occurred in different parts of the country. Blacks set buildings on fire, threw stones at police, looted stores, and attacked buses and trains. Angry young people, many of them teenagers, took over the leadership of some communities. They organized school boycotts and boycotted white businesses. Thousands were arrested and detained. Crackdowns by the South African government led to more violence.

At the same time, foreign countries began to put a great deal of pressure on South Africa to end the system of apartheid.

Much of the violence by blacks was directed against blacks who were regarded as "collaborators" with apartheid: black police officers, blacks regarded as police informers, and black officials in the local community councils. In many townships, the local police force, although commanded by white officers, is made up almost entirely of blacks. Some of them come from distant regions and hostile tribes and are hated by the local people. Moderates like Bishop Tutu (see page 240), who opposed the government's racial policies, condemned the violence and warned that it would only hurt the black cause.

Government Crackdown

The government reacted to the violence harshly, and at times brutally. The police were reinforced by units of the South African Defense Force (army). They used whips, tear gas, truncheons, and shotguns to break up crowds. They fired on demonstrators, killing many people. The government put a ban on all indoor meetings in black urban areas. Outdoor meetings had long been banned. But blacks defied these bans, coming together for memorial services for the dead and at huge outdoor funerals. The police broke up these gatherings and arrested many of the people. Thousands of people were detained without charge for weeks and months. Most of the detained were eventually released. There were widespread reports of torture. The Security Police raided the homes and offices of opponents of the government, especially members of the United Democratic Front, an organization made up of more than 700 non-white community groups, trade unions, and church groups. A number of its members were arrested and detained, and several were charged with treason.

The South African government also attacked bases of the African National Congress in some of the neighboring countries. It accused the ANC of carrying out dozens of terrorist acts in South Africa from these bases. In June 1985, army commandos attacked ANC bases in Angola and Botswana. In May 1986, South African armed forces attacked ANC bases in the capital cities of Zambia, Zimbabwe, and Botswana.

The State of Emergency

In July 1985, after 11 months of mounting violence, the government declared a "state of emergency" in 36 districts. It was South Africa's first declared state of emergency in 25 years (since the Sharpeville massacre). Police were given much greater power to enter homes, seize property, make arrests, detain suspects indefinitely, impose curfews, and restrict press reporting. During the following weeks there were thousands of arrests, violent clashes between blacks and police, and many deaths. In August, the government banned mass outdoor funerals in the areas where the state of emergency existed. Blacks reacted with outrage. In African tradition, funerals are occasions when the whole community participates to express feelings of sorrow and sympathy. In South Africa, where blacks cannot hold political meetings of any kind, funerals had become the one place where large numbers of blacks were able to express their anger publicly. Funerals for the victims of violence often attracted as many as 50,000 mourners. The government ordered that funerals were to be held indoors; there was to be no talk about the political system, police actions, or the state of emergency; and there was to be no display of flags, banners, or posters.

Limited Reforms

The actions of the South African government were denounced all over the world. The government of President Botha faced tremendous pressure from all sides to begin to make serious reforms. Rioting by blacks continued despite the state of emergency. More and more white South Africans, especially business leaders and church groups, demanded that

Mass funeral for black victims of one of South Africa's violent clashes between police and demonstrators.

An anti-apartheid demonstration in South Africa.

the government begin negotiating with black leaders. Other countries, including the United States, pressured the South African government to make changes or face economic sanctions. But President Botha hesitated. He spoke of reforms, but then did very little.

In June 1985, the government repealed (cancelled) the Mixed Marriages Act and sections of the Immorality Act. These laws prohibited marriage and sexual relations between whites and non-whites.

Repeal of the Pass Laws

In September, Botha announced that the government would grant citizenship to blacks who lived in urban areas but who were considered citizens of the four "independent homelands." Blacks, however, would still not be allowed to vote in South Africa. A most important change was announced in April 1986, when the government said it would abolish the pass laws that required blacks to carry passbooks. Instead, all South Africans would carry identification cards in the future and no one would be punished for failure to carry them.

International Response

Disinvestment

In the 1980s, Western nations, including the United States, put greater pressure on South African leaders to end apartheid. In 1984 and 1985, there were anti-apartheid demonstrations on college campuses in the United States. Students demanded disinvestment, that is, that the universities sell all their investments in companies that do business with South Africa. Pressure was also put on state and local government to divest the billions of dollars they had invested in companies dealing with South Africa. The hope was that if enough U.S. companies stopped doing business with South Africa, it would suffer economically and be forced to make changes. As a result of this pressure, many universities as well as state and city governments took steps to sell their South African investments.

Sanctions—1985

Many Americans demanded that the U.S. government impose economic sanctions, or penalties, on South Africa. This means to punish South Africa economically by not buying or selling vital things. There was a great demand for sanctions in Congress, but the Reagan Administration opposed sanctions. President Reagan preferred to follow a policy of "constructive engagement." This was an attempt to persuade rather than pressure the South African government to make changes. This policy, however, did not produce results.

Many black leaders including Bishop Tutu called on other nations to impose economic sanctions on South Africa. Tutu declared, "I have no hope of real change from the government unless they are forced. We face a catastrophe in this land, and only the action of the international community by applying pressure can save us." Many people in the United States and South Africa who opposed sanctions claimed that sanctions would also hurt black Africans, that many would lose their jobs. Tutu's answer was, "We know we'll lose jobs, but in the long run it is good for us."

In 1985, the United States decided to impose limited sanctions. These sanctions restricted new bank loans to South Africa, banned the sale of computer systems to government agencies that enforce apartheid, banned the sale of nuclear technology, and prohibited the importation of Krugerrands (gold coins from South Africa). France banned any future investments in South Africa. Canada, the other nations of the British Commonwealth, and many European countries also announced that they were imposing sanctions on South Africa. For a long time Britain had condemned apartheid, but the British government was opposed to sanctions. However, Britain also went along with the other nations of Europe and the Commonwealth, although it imposed milder sanctions.

Violence and unrest in South Africa continued. In June 1986, the government declared a new nationwide state of emergency. (The earlier state of emergency had lasted eight months and had ended in March.) The security forces were given greater power to make arrests without charge, hold detainees without hearings for unlimited periods, search any home or office without warrant, ban meetings, and to use whatever force necessary to break up "illegal" gatherings. Many new restrictions were put on the press.

Countries around the world denounced this action and demanded stiffer sanctions. In September 1986, the U.S. Congress voted for sanctions against South Africa. These stronger new sanctions banned all new public and private loans to South Africa, as well as new investments. These prohibited importing uranium, coal, textiles, iron, steel, arms, agricultural products, and Krugerrand gold coins from South Africa. They also prohibited the export to South Africa of crude oil, petroleum products, munitions, nuclear energy equipment, and computers. Direct air travel between the United States and South Africa was cut off. At the same time, the 49 nations of the British Commonwealth voted for sanctions, as did the nations of the European community.

Although the sanctions voted by Congress prohibited new investments in South Africa, they did not affect investments already made by U.S. companies. However, in 1986, a number of companies announced plans to sell their investments in South Africa and leave the country. These included Coca-Cola, General Motors, IBM, Warner Communications, Honeywell, and Eastman Kodak. In 1985 and 1986, more than 70 big U.S. companies left South Africa.

South African leaders claimed that their country was strong and would not be greatly affected by the sanctions. South Africa produces most of what it needs, including arms and 50 percent of its oil needs. At the same time, South Africa produces a number of things that are vital to the rest of the world. South Africa is the world's leading exporter of gold, platinum, and diamonds. Besides being used for jewelry, platinum and diamonds have great industrial importance. South Africa has 71 percent of the world's manganese, which is vital in making batteries, steel, and cast iron. It has 84 percent of the world's chromium, a material essential in defense, aerospace, and other industries. South Africa would have no problem selling these materials to the rest of the world. But many Americans and Europeans claimed that even if the sanctions did not have any real practical effect, they made a political statement. They are saying that until South Africa ends apartheid, it will be treated as an outcast.

Movement Away From Apartheid

De Klerk Becomes President of South Africa

In January 1989, South African President P.W. Botha suffered a stroke and then resigned his office in August. Frederick W. de Klerk was elected leader of the National Party (NP) and he replaced Botha as the head of the government. A national election held one month later in September gave the NP a majority in the all-white House of Assembly. However, the NP suffered its most serious loss of seats since 1950 because the supporters of apartheid felt that de Klerk would not continue these policies. Both the Conservative Party and the Democratic Party gained seats.

The Formation of the Mass Democratic Movement

Despite the restrictions placed on political and economic activity, black South Africans continued to defy the government through rent strikes, hunger strikes, and boycotts. To protest the exclusion of the black majority from the September election, black opposition groups set up a new organization called the Mass Democratic Movement (MDM). It included all groups opposed to apartheid and the white government.

The MDM called for a two day general strike in which 3 million South Africans took part on the day elections were held. The strike resulted in the death of 28 demonstrators who were shot by riot police. South Africa depends on the labor of its 6 million black workers who now have the power to bring the economy to a stop.

De Klerk Removes Some Apartheid Laws

Under de Klerk's leadership, the South African government began to move away from complete apartheid. Although the idea of majority rule was still rejected, the de Klerk plan called for the right of minorities to retain control of their own affairs.

De Klerk legalized mass demonstrations. This was followed by the release from prison of Walter Sisulu, former secretary general of the ANC, and seven other political prisoners. All beaches were opened to all races. Four previously segregated areas near Johannesburg were also opened to all races.

The Release of Nelson Mandela

In February 1990, de Klerk announced the lifting of the ban on the ANC, the South African Communist Party, and 33 other anti-apartheid organizations. The long awaited release of Nelson Mandela (see page 236), who had been imprisoned since 1962, took place in February 1990.

A series of meetings took place between de Klerk and Mandela. In the first meeting, the ANC agreed to assist in curbing violence, and the government agreed to end the four-year old state of emergency. In the second meeting, the ANC agreed to suspend the policy of armed struggle that began in 1961. The government agreed to release more political prisoners to allow the return of all political exiles and to ease the security laws.

Repeal of Many Apartheid Laws

During 1990, the de Klerk government repealed the Separate Amenities Act which opened formerly white-only public facilities such as libraries, pools, and parks to people of all races. The government also said it would no longer push for the setting up of independent black "homelands" in South Africa. Apartheid was abolished in state hospitals. The death penalty for certain offenses of a political nature was also abolished. The government promised to establish a nonracial state education system as soon as possible, to repeal the Land Acts, and to amend the Group Areas Act. These last two laws were the cornerstone of the official government policy of apartheid. Membership in the National Party was opened to people of all races.

In June 1991, the South African government repealed the Land Acts, which had set aside 67 percent of all property in South Africa for whites only. At the same time the Group Areas Act, which told South Africans where they could and could not live, was also repealed. The South African Parliament also repealed the Population Registration Act which had ordered the classifying of all South Africans by race.

Despite these actions that seemed to do away with much of the apartheid system, a new Local Governments Act was also passed. This law gave local governments the right to set qualifying standards for those people who lived in their communities. It enabled local communities to exclude blacks and coloreds. Futhermore, all people born before February 1, 1991, had to retain their racial classification. This made the repeal of the Populations Registration Act meaningless.

The Proposed New Constitution

In September 1991, de Klerk presented a proposed constitution that would give black South Africans the right to vote. However, the power of black voters was greatly limited by a feature of the plan that would set up an executive council that would have to ratify acts of the president and the legislature. This executive council would be made up of members of the three largest parties in Parliament. Since the National Party was certain to finish at least second or third in any general election, this feature would give the white-dominated National Party veto power over any law. De Klerk included the executive council to protect white South Africans. He has said, "Black domination is as unacceptable as white domination."

The ANC opposes de Klerk's plan because they feel that it cheats blacks of the right to rule South Africa. Another problem is the question of decentralization. De Klerk wants to establish a federation form of government that will give a great deal of power to local governments. The ANC favors a strong central government with enough power to enforce its ideas after apartheid is ended.

The ANC strongly objects to giving great powers to local areas in the field of education. They fear that a white town council could easily deny blacks access to local schools because they do not speak Afrikaans well enough.

However, there are some issues on which there is agreement. Both sides are in favor of a two-house legislature, an independent court system, and a bill of rights. The government has agreed to end the black homelands program. The ANC is prepared to drop its idea of nationalization of key industries such as mining. Both sides agree that all South Africans should have the right to speak their own language and follow the religion of their choice. They also recognize South Africa's tribal and culturally diverse society. (There are 10 major languages.)

Both blacks and whites realize that negotiations will be long and difficult. However, many decisions will have to be made before 1994 when a new constitution will go into effect.

The Dispute Between the ANC and Inkatha

Despite some movement toward winning political rights for blacks in South Africa, mass protests have continued against high rents, poor housing, inferior black education, unequal wages, and poor working conditions.

Violence by black South Africans against one another has become a serious problem. This has resulted from the lack of agreement between the ANC and the Inkatha Freedom Party. The Inkatha movement, led by Chief Gatsha Buthelezi (see page 238), was set up in 1984 to represent the interests of the 7 million Zulus of South Africa. (The Zulus are the largest ethnic group of South Africa.) Inkatha believes that the ANC, which has few Zulu members, does not pay enough attention to Zulu concerns. Since 1984, almost 11,000 blacks have died in the fighting between the ANC and Inkatha.

Soon after Nelson Mandela was released from prison in February 1990 he appealed to both sides to stop the killing. Chief Buthelezi rejected the appeal and the violence continued. Throughout the early months of 1991, attacks by the ANC and Inkatha on each other continued. The ANC repeatedly accused the police and security forces of working closely with and supporting Inkatha.

Not only is an agreement between ANC and the white South African government essential, an agreement between the ANC and Inkatha must be worked out to assure a stable future in South Africa.

Historic Vote in South Africa

In December 1991, President de Klerk began constitutional negotiations with the ANC and 17 other parties to discuss plans to end apartheid and grant full citizenship to blacks. Amid growing opposition from conservative whites, de Klerk called for a **referendum** (a vote by the people on a proposal or law) on the issue of a new constitution.

The referendum, in which only whites were allowed to vote, was held in March 1992. A total of 85.1 percent of the 3.3 million white voters cast ballots in the referendum, which asked "Do you support the reform process begun by the State President of February 2, 1990, which is aimed at reaching a new constitution through negotiations?" The results showed that 68.6 percent of the voters answered "yes" and 31.2 percent voted "no" to the question. The vote was seen as giving de Klerk a decisive mandate to end apartheid and negotiate a new constitution.

Many whites voted for the proposal for a number of reasons. Many white South African businesspeople and workers have been hurt by the worldwide boycotts. They believe that the end of apartheid would bring an end to the economic boycotts. Others wanted South Africa to again be accepted as a member of the world community. Some feared that a "no" vote would mean increased violence by militant black South Africans. It also appears that many whites are ready to accept blacks as citizens of South Africa.

The result of the referendum was hailed worldwide. Some countries called for an end to economic boycotts against South Africa. However, black leaders were more guarded. Nelson Mandela, who had urged white support of the negotiation process, welcomed the result but warned that apartheid was not yet over. He said, "Apartheid is far from over. Above all, I still cannot vote in my own country." Both de Klerk and Mandela said they would move quickly to negotiate an end to apartheid.

The African National Congress (ANC)

The African National Congress has become the most important political organization for black South Africans. It was outlawed in South Africa between 1960 and 1990. This was because the ANC advocated a policy of armed struggle to end apartheid and achieve equal rights for blacks. From its bases in neighboring countries, the ANC engaged in acts of sabotage and terrorism inside South Africa. As the situation in South Africa worsened after 1976, and especially after 1984, more and more blacks identified themselves with the ANC. At the same time the ANC became more militant. In 1985, the military wing of the ANC, of *Umkonto We Sizwe* (Spear of the Nation) called for a full-scale "people's war" against the white rulers of South Africa.

Nelson Mandela

Nelson Mandela is South Africa's best known black nationalist leader. In 1964, he was sentenced to life imprisonment for his political activities and he remained in prison until 1990. During this time, he became a hero to black South Africans. His resistance to apartheid and his struggle for equal rights for blacks has been an inspiration for all.

Mandela joined the African National Congress in the 1940s. Since then he has struggled against the ruling National Party and its policy of apartheid. After the Sharpeville Massacre of 1960 and the banning of the ANC, the ANC gave up its policy of nonviolent resistance. Mandela was one of those who pressed for armed struggle. In 1962, he was arrested and sentenced to five years in prison for subversive activity. In 1963, police raided the headquarters of *Umkonto We Sizwe*, the military wing of the African National Congress. They discovered quantities of weapons and equipment. Mandela, who was in jail at the time, was linked with the organization and charged with seeking to overthrow the government by violence. Mandela pleaded guilty and admitted responsibility for having started the *Umkonto We Sizwe* to wage an armed struggle. In June 1964, he was sentenced to life imprisonment.

Mandela achieved worldwide fame despite the fact that he was in jail for almost 30 years. He has received many international prizes as well as a number of honorary doctorates from universities. Many of his writings and speeches have been collected and published.

Part of the reason for Mandela's importance was the great effort made by his wife, Winnie Mandela, to promote his cause. Winnie Mandela endured arrests and solitary confinement as a result of her struggle against apartheid. In 1977, she was forbidden to travel and to make public appearances. She was restricted to a black ghetto near the town of Blandfort, 250 miles southwest of Johannesburg. After August 1985, as violence increased in South Africa, Winnie Mandela defied the ban. She traveled around the country without permission and met with reporters.

For many years, very little was heard from Nelson Mandela. In 1984, the South African government relaxed many of the restrictions against him, including visiting rights. Soon after, President Botha declared that he was prepared to release Mandela if the black leader promised not to "plan, instigate, or commit acts of violence for the furtherance of his political objectives." Mandela, who was 67 years old, rejected the offer, saying he would not give up violence until blacks in South Africa achieved equal rights. Mandela sent the government a message stating his own demands: the South African government must renounce violence, end apartheid, end its ban of the African National Congress, free those who are imprisoned or banished because of their opposition to apartheid, and guarantee blacks the right to choose their own leaders.

Nelson Mandela was released from jail in 1990. Since then Mandela has traveled to many countries, including the United States, to win support for his cause. Mandela was received as a hero in all the countries he visited. Mandela is now president of the ANC and has frequent meetings with South African leaders to try to bring peace and justice to South Africa.

Nelson Mandela addressing the United Nations. Mandela has achieved international fame for his leadership in the struggle to end apartheid.

Chief Buthelezi

Chief Gatsha Buthelezi is the political leader of South Africa's largest ethnic group, the 7 million Zulus. He rules KwaZulu, the poor mountainous territory that the South African government set aside for the Zulus in 1973. KwaZulu is the largest of the ten "homelands" set aside for blacks.

Buthelezi is one of the most important black leaders in South Africa at present. He differs with many of the other black leaders, however, in that he rejects the use of violence against the government. Buthelezi believes in compromise and negotiation as the best way to bring about an end to apartheid. "There are no prospects either now or in the forseeable future of toppling the South African government by violent means. The harsh reality...is that we do not destroy the foundations of the future by what we do now." Buthelezi also differs with other black nationalists over the issue of economic sanctions. Buthelezi frequently said that sanctions against South Africa would hurt blacks more than anyone else. Therefore, many black activists call him a "puppet" of the South African government.

Buthelezi insists that all South Africans must have their share of political power. In 1982, he proposed a plan for KwaZulu Natal (one of the four provinces of South Africa) to be governed by an executive body composed of equal numbers of whites, blacks, Indians, and coloreds. The South African government rejected the proposal. But in 1986, Buthelezi organized a historic meeting between blacks and whites to discuss the creation of a multiracial government in Natal. Buthelezi has resisted the South African government's efforts to grant KwaZulu "independence." He said "independence" would deprive the Zulus of their South African citizenship and of participating in the political affairs of the country.

As a student, Buthelezi had joined the African National Congress and became good friends with Nelson Mandela. Even though he differed with Mandela and the ANC over the use of violence, Buthelezi repeatedly called for Mandela's release from prison and for lifting the ban on the ANC.

Buthelezi talks of future cooperation between Afrikaners and Zulus for the "common good." He is respected by many white South Africans. He also has great prestige outside his country and has met with Pope John Paul II, President Reagan, Prime Minister Thatcher, and other world leaders. All agree that Chief Buthelezi will play a very important role in the future of South Africa.

Bishop Desmond Tutu

For much of the world, Bishop Desmond Tutu symbolizes the struggle of black South Africans against apartheid. In October 1984, Bishop Tutu received international recognition for his efforts when he was awarded the Nobel Peace Prize. Bishop Tutu declared that the award was not personal. "It belongs to all the black people of South Africa who have suffered, to all who have left and lived with the evil of apartheid and are trying and striving for peace."

Tutu, the son of a schoolmaster, was born in 1931. He was educated in schools headed by his father, and after graduating from one of South Africa's segregated colleges, became a teacher. At the age of 25, he began his studies for the ministry and was ordained as Anglican minister in 1960.

In 1978, Tutu was appointed general secretary of the South African Council of Churches, an organization strongly opposed to apartheid. In the same year, Tutu became assistant bishop of Johannesburg. In November 1984, he was elected bishop of Johannesburg and in 1986 Tutu became Archbishop of Cape Town and primate of the Anglican Church for all of Southern Africa. In this position, Tutu is the spiritual leader of 2 million Anglicans—black and white—in South Africa, Botswana, Mozambique, Namibia, Swaziland, and Lesotho.

For many years, Tutu has used his respected position to call on the South African government to abandon apartheid and improve the lives of its black citizens. He has encouraged blacks to struggle for their rights in a peaceful, nonviolent way. When Columbia University awarded Tutu an honorary degree in 1982, the president of the university compared him to Martin Luther King, Jr.

Tutu's foreign travels have been his greatest service to his black countrymen. More than any other black South African, Tutu has dramatized to the world the injustices of apartheid. During his frequent travels abroad, Tutu has urged other governments to support the cause of blacks in South Africa by exerting political and economic pressure on the South African government to force it to bring about change. Tutu's winning the Nobel Prize was seen by many as evidence of international sympathy for the cause of peaceful change with which Tutu was identified.

As the situation in South Africa began to deteriorate in 1984, Tutu was effective in calming angry crowds in black townships. But he admitted that "young blacks are becoming increasingly committed to using violence, despite my calls for peaceful change." In January 1985, Tutu called on the outside world to impose punitive economic sanctions on South Africa if conditions of black workers did not improve in the next two years. Tutu pleaded "I am calling for political, diplomatic, and above all economic pressure as our last chance to avert the bloodbath."

Bishop Desmond Tutu was awarded the 1984 Nobel Prize for his crusade against South Africa's racial segregation system (apartheid), and his attempts to find a peaceful solution to South Africa's problems.

The African National Congress was founded in 1912. For many years it fought apartheid through nonviolent means, mostly labor strikes and boycotts. In 1955, the ANC joined several other South African civil rights organizations in signing a document called the Freedom Charter. The charter declared, "South Africa belongs to all who live in it, black and white." It called for a unified, democratic state governed along color-blind lines. The ANC still adheres to this program.

The ANC gave up its policy of nonviolence after the Sharpeville Massacre in 1960. It was soon after this event that Nelson Mandela and Oliver Tambo, who were friends and law partners, became the leaders of the ANC. During the months of unrest following the massacre, the South African government outlawed the ANC. The ANC then began carrying out armed attacks from its hiding places. Nelson Mandela and other ANC leaders were captured and jailed. Oliver Tambo escaped arrest because he was out of the country raising money for the organization. Tambo was president of the ANC from the 1960s until 1991 when Nelson Mandela took over after Tambo suffered a stroke.

After the 1976 riots, thousands of young blacks fled South Africa to avoid detention. Most of them joined the ANC. With new blood and new fighting spirit, the ANC became more militant. Guerrillas armed with Soviet rifles began to escalate their attacks on South Africa from bases in Angola, Zambia, and Mozambique. South African troops in turn attacked ANC bases in neighboring countries. President Botha declared in 1986 that "South Africa has the capacity and the will to break the ANC. I give fair warning that we fully intend doing it."

In an interview in 1986, Tambo stated, "Violence is one of the tools we use. It is not the first we thought of. For 48 years we had a policy of nonviolence. This is a difficult policy if you are being hit and cannot hit back. Every act we committed that was nonviolent produced more violence from the other side. We reached a dead end after the Sharpeville Massacre in 1960. Only after that did we decide to embrace violence—to remove a violent system." Tambo insisted that the ANC would not disarm. He said that even if the South African government agreed to negotiations, the armed struggle would continue during the negotiations.

For many years, the United States and other Western countries were uneasy about the ANC because of its ties with the Soviet Union and with the South African Communist Party. In 1963, the Soviet Union became an important supplier of money and military equipment to the ANC. Tambo said, "No country in the West would give us weapons so we went to the Soviet Union." He insisted that the ANC was not a Soviet puppet.

It is now recognized by many whites in South Africa and in other countries that there can be no solution to South Africa's problems without the participation of the African National Congress. In 1986, a number of white South African businesspeople, churchleaders, and others traveled to Lusaka to meet with ANC leaders. Western governments began talking with the ANC. In September 1986, the British Foreign Secretary met with Oliver Tambo. In January 1987, Tambo visited Washington and held talks with Secretary of State George Shultz. This was an indication that the United States considered the ANC to be very important in any future settlement of the South African problem and was willing to engage in discussions with the organization.

In 1990, the 30 year ban on the ANC was lifted by President de Klerk. Exiled ANC members, including Oliver Tambo, returned to South Africa. Since then, the South African government has been meeting with Mandela and other ANC leaders to work out a solution to South Africa's problems.

Summary of Key Ideas

Africa—South of the Sahara

A. **Size and diversity of geographic features have greatly affected Africa's past and present.**

1. Deserts have to some degree isolated sub-Saharan Africa from the outside world.

2. The narrow coastal plain, jungles, and a steep escarpment have prevented greater contacts between Africa and the world.

3. The rivers serve as centers of development and population, but, by their nature, have not been useful for transportation and communication.

4. The Great Rift Valley has divided Africa from itself.

5. Africa's vast size has led to the development of varied cultures and civilizations.

6. The regular coastline has retarded the development of harbors, trade, and a seafaring tradition, thus furthering isolation.

7. There are at least five distinct climatic regions: tropical rain forest, savanna, steppe, desert, and Mediterranean.

B. **African cultures and societies are varied and complex.**

1. People of many races, religions, languages, and cultures live in Africa.

2. Tribal society is central to the social structure, political organization, and economic activity of Africa.

3. Tribal structure is based on family and kinship relationships.

4. Tribal societies have played an important role in Africa's history.

5. African art is rich and varied in terms of form, style, and technique.

6. The transition from tribal to modern, industrial society is changing African traditions and institutions rapidly. Great problems have also resulted.

C. **The history of sub-Saharan Africa has been a long and continuous process.**

1. European and American awareness of African history is filled with myths, such as their "backwardness."

2. There is some archeological evidence that the earliest humans made their home in Africa.

3. Much of the story of Africa and its heritage has been transmitted orally.

4. Ancient Egyptian civilization influenced, and was influenced by, the rest of Africa (religion, government, economy, technology, language).

5. Ancient empires flourished in Africa (Kush and Axum).

6. Outside influences have had great effects on African culture and society (Islam, as a religion and way of life; the impact of Western imperialism on African culture and development).

7. Empires such as Ghana, Mali, Songhai, and Zimbabwe flourished in Africa.

8. The European slave trade reduced the population of the continent and weakened the economic, cultural, and political institutions. It greatly speeded up the decline of African kingdoms.

9. The scramble for African colonies by the Europeans in the 19th and 20th centuries led to a partition of Africa among these Europeans.

10. Nationalism in Africa resulted from Western influences, and led to the development of independence movements.

11. World War I and World War II speeded up the movement toward independence.

12. Since World War II, European nations have given up all their colonies in Africa.

D.   Economic development is the key to the future of Africa.

1. Agriculture is the most important economic activity in Africa. Mining is the most important industry.

2. Few areas in Africa possess good soil.

3. Agriculture is divided between subsistence and plantation (cash crop) farming.

4. Natural resources are varied and in excellent supply. Only coal and oil are lacking in great quantities.

5. Resources have not been developed to their greatest potential.

6. Soil erosion and lack of sufficient rainfall have caused famine in Sahel, Ethiopia, and Somalia.

E.   Sub-Saharan Africa faces all of the problems that developing nations have.

1. African expectations are rising from a life of mere survival to expectations of a modern life of abundance.

2. Modern political patterns of Africa reflect colonial rule by Europeans. Political divisions were made with little understanding of or regard for local conditions, customs, and traditions.

3. Tribalism and nationalism have caused conflicts in many African states (e.g., Nigeria, Ghana, Sudan, Ethiopia).

4. Political life in many African nations is controlled by one political party.

5. The lack of political stability is a grave problem for African nations.

F. African nations play a vital role in world affairs.

1. The many nations of Africa have great influence in the United Nations.

2. The nations of the West and the former Communist nations tried to gain the support of African states by giving economic and military assistance.

3. Apartheid has become an international issue resulting from the subjugation of a majority, black African group by a minority, white African group in South Africa.

4. Draught and famine in the Sahel and East Africa (Ethiopia and Somali) have created the need for international efforts to relieve the situation.

UNIT III

Exercises and Questions

Vocabulary

Directions: Match the words in Column A with the correct meaning in Column B.

Column A

1. fetish
2. ethnic group
3. terra-cotta
4. missionary
5. polygyny
6. clan
7. imperialism
8. nationalism
9. anthropologist
10. literacy
11. secede

Column B

(a) the ability to read
(b) a person who tries to spread a religion
(c) a group of related families
(d) when a strong nation takes over a weaker nation
(e) a person who studies the human past
(f) a group of people who share the same customs and language and believe they have descended from a common ancestor
(g) an object thought to have magical powers
(h) having several wives at the same time
(i) baked clay used to make art objects
(j) love of country above all else
(k) to leave or break away; separate

Column A

1. escarpment
2. isolation
3. plateau
4. latitude
5. topography
6. altitude
7. canyon
8. sisal
9. tropical
10. source
11. reserves

Column B

(a) area that is near the equator
(b) used in making rope
(c) measures distance from sea level
(d) sharp, steep cliffs
(e) description of the earth's surface
(f) deep cuts in the earth's surface
(g) where the river begins
(h) cut off, separated from other people
(i) fairly flat land high above sea level
(j) measures distance from the equator
(k) land set aside for Africans in South Africa

Who Am I?

Directions: Select the name of the correct person.

Mansa Musa   Vasco de Gama

Henry Stanley   Dr. Lewis Leakey

David Livingstone   King Nzinga

Jomo Kenyatta   Mungo Park

Sekou Touré   Kwame Nkrumah

1. I was a European missionary and explorer. I hoped to end the slave trade. _____ .

2. I was famous for reaching India by sailing around Africa. _____ .

3. I am an African nationalist. I was president of Kenya. _____ .

4. I explored the Niger River. _____ .

5. I found some of the oldest human bones in Africa. _____ .

6. I was famous for my pilgrimage to Mecca. I impressed everyone with my wealth in gold. _____ .

7. I was the newspaper reporter who found Livingstone. _____ .

8. I ruled the Congo nation at the end of the 15th century. I admired the culture of Portugal. _____ .

9. I was an African nationalist. I became the first president of Ghana. _____ .

10. I led my nation to independence from the French. I was president of Guinea. _____ .

Sources of Information

Directions: Which of the below sources would be the best place to find information about the following.

DICTIONARY   ATLAS   INDEX   TABLE OF CONTENTS   ENCYCLOPEDIA

1. The distance from Cape Town, South Africa, to Nairobi, Kenya.

2. A chapter in your Social Studies book dealing with the Land and People of Africa, South of the Sahara.

3. The meaning of the word *culture*.

4. A detailed account of the life of Jomo Kenyatta.

5. The pages in your Social Studies book discussing David Livingstone.

6. The pronunciation of the word *escarpment*.

7. The capital of Zaire.

8. The different units that are covered in your Social Studies textbook.

9. Pictures of the different peoples who live in Africa.

10. How many pages in your book deal with the minerals of Africa.

Pictogram Exercise

Directions: Study the pictogram entitled "A Kikuyu Homestead." Tell whether you agree or disagree with the followintg statements. Give reasons for your answers.

1. The Kikuyu are farmers and herders.

2. Water for the crops comes from irrigation ditches.

3. Kikuyus have little to do with other tribes.

4. Kikuyu men and women have different jobs to do.

5. Kikuyu women move to their husbands' families' homestead after marriage.

6. The Kikuyu are religious people.

7. The Kikuyu live in buildings made of brick.

8. The main crop of the Kikuyu is wheat.

9. The Kikuyu use all of their fields for raising crops.

10. The land belonging to the Kikuyu is mainly rocky and desert.

A KIKUYU HOMESTEAD

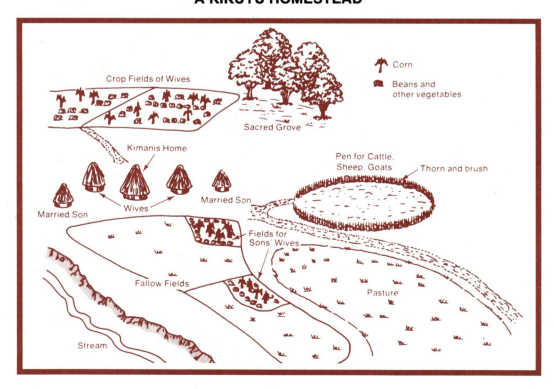

True or False?

Directions: Tell whether the following statements are true or false. Correct the false statements.

1. All of Africa is hot and humid.

2. Most of Africa is jungle.

3. The Sahara Desert is larger than the United States.

4. In most of Africa when a young couple marries they move into an apartment of their own.

5. Africans are usually very proud of their tribal mark.

6. Members of a tribe obey the decisions of the elders whether they like them or not.

7. African art shows the human body the way it actually is.

8. Most African sculpture was made of marble.

9. Africa was never civilized before the Europeans came.

10. Africans traded their gold in exchange for salt.

11. European traders raided African villages to obtain slaves.

12. Africa continued to progress despite the slave trade.

13. Africa was known as the Dark Continent.

14. The purpose of the Mau Mau rebellion was to drive the British out of Kenya.

15. Africa depends on foreign aid for industrialization.

16. Most African farmers can be called subsistence farmers.

17. Cacao is used in the making of soap.

Multiple Choice

Directions: Select the letter of the correct answer.

1. Which of the following statements are true about the Sahara?
   (a) The Sahara is the world's second largest desert.
   (b) Most of the Sahara is a sandy, dry wasteland.
   (c) The Sahara was not always as dry as it is today.
   (d) The Sahara extends from the Atlantic Ocean to the Arabian Sea.

2. Which of the following does *not* describe the topography of sub-Saharan Africa?
   (a) Most of sub-Saharan Africa is 500 feet or lower in elevation.
   (b) There is a large plateau in the eastern part of Africa.
   (c) Sub-Saharan Africa has very narrow coastal plains.
   (d) The coastline of Africa is regular.

3. Which of the rivers of Africa has its source in Lake Victoria?
   (a) Niger   (b) Nile   (c) Zambesi   (d) Zaire

4. The Rift of Africa is a
   (a) large lake.   (b) deep canyon.   (c) deep sea.   (d) plateau.

5. Traveling is often difficult on Africa's rivers because
   (a) most of the rivers flow inland.
   (b) most of the rivers are frozen part of the year.
   (c) many rivers have rapids and falls.
   (d) there is a lack of boats.

6. Most of the Europeans settled in the highland areas of East and South Africa because
   (a) the climate is cooler.
   (b) the people were friendlier.
   (c) trading opportunities were greater.
   (d) the land was unsettled.

7. The Benguela current
   (a) brings plenty of rain to West Africa.
   (b) warms the coast of East Africa.
   (c) affects the climate of North Africa.
   (d) cools and dries the land on the southwest side of Africa.

8. Which of the following statements is true about rainfall in Africa?
   (a) About 60 percent of Africa does not receive enough rainfall to support a farming population.
   (b) Rainfall in most of Africa is seasonal.
   (c) It rarely rains in the desert.
   (d) All of the above.

9. West Africa has been called "The White Man's Grave" because
   (a) many wars were fought here in which white men were killed.
   (b) Africans living here attacked all foreigners.
   (c) the rain forest is hot, rainy, and unhealthy.
   (d) none of these

10. All of the following are true about African people *except*
    (a) there are great physical differences among the Africans.
    (b) Africans are different from each other in culture.
    (c) most Africans look alike.
    (d) Africans have intermarried with other peoples.

11. Most of the people living in sub-Saharan Africa
    (a) belong to many different ethnic groups.
    (b) have the same religion.
    (c) live in a typical African way.
    (d) none of these

12. Swahili is
    (a) the main language spoken in West Africa.
    (b) the main language spoken in East Africa.
    (c) the language spoken mainly by Pygmies.
    (d) all of these

13. Which of the following is true about language in Africa?
    (a) There are hundreds of different languages spoken in Africa.
    (b) Often Africans living in the same country find it difficult to communicate with one another.
    (c) English and French are often used by Africans to speak to each other.
    (d) All of these.

14. An "extended family" consists of
    (a) several generations living together.
    (b) the father, mother, and their children.
    (c) the bride, groom, and their in-laws.
    (d) all the people of the tribe.

15. African men may have several wives because
    (a) they want to have many children.
    (b) they want the family name to live on.
    (c) they will have more workers to help them in the fields.
    (d) all of these

16. All of the following are true of the "bride price" *except*
    (a) it is usually in the form of cattle or sheep.
    (b) it is a symbol that the marriage is legitimate.
    (c) it is proof that African men buy their wives.
    (d) it compensates the father of the bride for losing a worker.

17. As more people move to the cities the importance of the tribe is expected to
    (a) increase.   (b) decrease.   (c) remain the same.   (d) disappear.

18. Many of the new African nations are having difficulty uniting their people because
    (a) many people are more loyal to their tribes than they are to the nation.
    (b) there are many disloyal Europeans.
    (c) most African nations are still ruled by the Europeans.
    (d) all of these

19. All of the following are African tribes except
    (a) Ashanti   (b) Kalahari   (c) Kikuyu   (d) Yoruba

20. Which of the following is true of African religions?
    (a) Africans do not believe in a Supreme Being or God.
    (b) Africans worship rivers, trees, and mountains.
    (c) Africans worship their dead ancestors.
    (d) Africans believe that the spirits of their ancestors can protect or harm them.

21. The *diviner* (medicine man) is important in most African societies because
    (a) he is responsible for maintaining law and order in the tribe.
    (b) it is believed that he can find the cause and cure for many misfortunes.
    (c) he is in charge of educating the young to be loyal members of the tribe.
    (d) all of these

22. All of the following are true of African art *except*
    (a) exaggeration of the head and reproductive organs was common.
    (b) poses showing movement were preferred by the artists.
    (c) much of the sculpture was what we would call abstract.
    (d) Africans painted few portraits.

23. Which of the following are correctly paired together?
    (a) Ife—Rock paintings
    (b) Benin—Bronze heads
    (c) Nok—Last wax process
    (d) Bushmen—Terra-cotta figurines

24. Anthropologists believe that humans originated in Africa because
    (a) Africa probably had the best climate for farming.
    (b) there are many African folk tales that talk about the beginning of the human race.
    (c) the oldest known human bones have been found in Africa.
    (d) all of these

25. Cave paintings found in the Sahara are evidence that
    (a) thousands of years ago the Sahara was not a desert.
    (b) people and animals once lived in the Sahara.
    (c) the Sahara was very different from what it is today.
    (d) all of these

26. The very first people earned a living by
    (a) farming and hunting.
    (b) mining and trading.
    (c) hunting and gathering.
    (d) herding and weaving.

27. Pictures of giraffes found in China and dating from the 5th century are evidence that
    (a) China had many giraffes at that time.
    (b) the Chinese were good artists.
    (c) trade existed between China and Africa.
    (d) none of these

28. Trade was very important in early African history because
    (a) the Africans learned how to grow crops such as yams and bananas from the people of Southeast Asia.
    (b) trade brought wealth and new ideas to Africa.
    (c) important trading cities grew up.
    (d) all of these

29. All of the following are true about the kingdoms of West Africa *except*
    (a) glass was used in Ghana before it was used in Europe.
    (b) the kingdoms became wealthy from the gold-salt trade.
    (c) the governments were poorly run—there was injustice and insecurity.
    (d) the kingdoms grew powerful because they used iron weapons and tools.

30. Timbuctu was famous as
    (a) an important center of learning.
    (b) the scene of a famous battle.
    (c) the headquarters of the slave trade.
    (d) a legendary city.

31. The earliest kingdom in West Africa was
    (a) Songhai.   (b) Ghana.   (c) Mali.   (d) Ethiopia.

32. Islam spread to Africa in all of the following ways *except*
    (a) the Arabs conquered South Africa and forced the people to convert.
    (b) Arabs married African women and spread their culture.
    (c) Arabs spread their religion by controlling much of Africa's trade.
    (d) the rulers of Mali and Songhai became Muslims and converted many of their subjects.

33. Which of the following is *not* true about the Arab role in Africa?
    (a) The Arabs probably began the African slave trade.
    (b) Arab geographers left many records providing much information about African life.
    (c) The Arabic language and Bantu language were combined to form a new language—Swahili.
    (d) The Arab influence on Africa was not great.

34. The Europeans became interested in Africa in the 15th century because they
    (a) wanted to settle in Africa.
    (b) were interested in African culture.
    (c) were looking for a new route to the Indies.
    (d) were looking for markets for their manufactured goods.

35. The first European nation to set up trading posts along the coast of Africa was
    (a) Spain.   (b) England.   (c) Portugal.   (d) France.

36. The trading cities of East Africa declined during the 16th century because
    (a) they fought many wars against each other.
    (b) their trade and wealth were taken over by Portugal.
    (c) bad weather conditions resulted in poor crops.
    (d) all of these

37. Which of the following statements is *not* true?
    (a) Slavery never existed in Africa before the arrival of the Europeans.
    (b) Long before the Europeans came African slaves were being sold in India and other places of the East.
    (c) Africans raided the villages of other African tribes to capture slaves for the Europeans.
    (d) On a slave ship the slaves were packed in so tightly they barely had room to move.

38. The slave trade became very important to the Europeans because

    (a) they needed slaves to work on the plantations in Europe.

    (b) they needed slaves to work in the factories of Europe.

    (c) fortunes could be made by using slaves on the sugar plantations of the West Indies.

    (d) all of these

39. The slave trade was finally ended when

    (a) the Africans threatened to declare war on the Europeans.

    (b) slavery was abolished in the United States, Brazil, and Cuba.

    (c) the United Nations demanded an end to the slave trade.

    (d) the Europeans realized they were doing the wrong thing.

40. The explorers of Africa were important because

    (a) they explored the four great African rivers.

    (b) they wrote books and drew maps of the places they explored.

    (c) they provided the Europeans with much information about Africa and its people.

    (d) all of the above reasons

41. Europeans became interested in Africa after 1880 because they

    (a) were looking for a new route to the Indies.

    (b) needed slaves and ivory.

    (c) wanted raw materials and markets.

    (d) wanted to help the Africans.

42. By 1914, most of Africa was controlled by

    (a) Spain and Portugal.

    (b) Britain and France.

    (c) the United States and the Soviet Union.

    (d) Germany and Holland.

43. Which of the following statements is *not* true?

    (a) By 1914, there were only two independent countries in sub-Saharan Africa.

    (b) African rulers signed treaties with the Europeans to come in and protect them.

    (c) African rulers sometimes asked the Europeans to come in and protect them.

    (d) Belgium was the only European country without colonies in Africa.

44. Under the Europeans the tribal chiefs lost much of their power because

    (a) Africans realized that the chiefs no longer made all the decisions and so they did not feel that they had to obey them.

    (b) Africans who became Christians didn't believe that the chiefs were appointed by God.

    (c) wealthy people became more important than the chiefs.

    (d) all of these

45. The first African nationalists were

    (a) the people who had received a Western education.

    (b) the tribal chiefs.

    (c) the farmers and herders.

    (d) none of these

46. Which of the following statements is not true?
    (a) Nationalism spread greatly among the African people after World War II.
    (b) By 1969, most of the countries in Africa were independent.
    (c) The Europeans fought long and bitter wars to hold on to their African colonies.
    (d) Most of Africa became free without bloodshed or violence.

47. The majority people of the Republic of South Africa are
    (a) Bantus.   (b) Europeans.   (c) Asians.   (d) coloreds.

48. The policy of racial separation as practiced in South Africa is referred to as
    (a) integration.   (b) segregation.   (c) apartheid.   (d) imperialism.

49. A leader in the fight against apartheid in South Africa is
    (a) Jomo Kenyatta.   (b) Nelson Mandela.
    (c) Kwame Nikrumah.   (d) Mungo Park.

50. The Sharpeville Massacre occurred in South Africa when
    (a) armed demonstrators attacked police.
    (b) opposing African tribes attacked each other.
    (c) rioting students demanded an end to apartheid.
    (d) police fired on unarmed demonstrators.

51. The Soweto riots were called a turning point for South Africa because
    (a) demands for changes in apartheid laws arose both in and out of South Africa.
    (b) the South Africa government ended its apartheid laws.
    (c) Black leaders decided that violence was the only way to end apartheid.
    (d) the government put further restrictions on blacks in South Africa.

52. International pressure has been placed on South Africa to end apartheid through the use of
    (a) an international force to police South Africa.
    (b) international support of civil war in South Africa.
    (c) economic sanctions imposed on South Africa by many nations.
    (d) all of the above

53. The type of industry one would most likely find in Africa is
    (a) steel factories.
    (b) airplane factories.
    (c) food packing plants.
    (d) missile plants.

Thought Questions

1. How did geography isolate Africa from the rest of the world?

2. (a) What are the factors that cause the different climates of Africa?
   (b) What effect does climate have on the people of Africa?

3. "If you have seen one African you have seen them all." Do you agree or disagree with this statement? Give reasons for your answer.

4. How does the African family differ from the American family?

5. How does the African family take care of its members?

6. How is an African's whole way of life influenced by belonging to a tribe?

7. Why have the accomplishments of Africa in art and music not been appreciated or recognized until recently?

8. Why can we say that masks served a vital function in African life?

9. Why can it be said today that Africa's accomplishments in art are the equal of art produced by any other civilization?

10. A careful study of African history shows that Africa was never completely isolated from the rest of the world, but merely less accessible. Give evidence to prove or disprove this statement.

11. Cultural diffusion has been as important to Africa as it has been to other parts of the world. What evidence of cultural diffusion do we have from African history?

12. What are some of the things anthropologists use to study the human ancient past?

13. Why can we say that the kingdoms of West Africa reached a high level of civilization?

14. Why was it not difficult for Africans to become Muslims?

15. How did the slave trade affect Africa?

16. How did the missionaries affect developments in Africa, south of the Sahara?

17. How did European nations gain control of African areas?

18. Why did the European nations divide up Africa among themselves?

19. How did European imperialism affect Africa?

20. Why did Africa's nationalists want independence from the Europeans?

21. Why did World War II greatly strengthen African nationalism?

22. Why is agriculture "the lifeblood" of the African economy?

23. (a) What problems are faced by African farmers?
    (b) If you were an African leader, what solutions might you suggest?

24. Why have Africans not made the best use of their large supply of natural resources?

25. (a) What problems do Africans face in trying to develop their industries?
    (b) What solutions might be suggested to solve these problems?

26. As a reporter, describe the changes that have taken place in Africa during the past five years.

27. (a) Why can we call the Sahel drought a major disaster?
    (b) How did the drought in Sahel come about?

28. How is the South African Homelands program similar to the United States' creation of Indian reservations in the 1800s? How is it different? (Clues: forcible removal, citizenship)

Developing Answers to Regents-Type Essay Questions

Helpful Hints

In developing your answers to the essays be sure to:

1. Include specific factual information and evidence whenever possible.

2. Answer the question being asked; do not go off on tangents.

3. Keep these general definitions in mind:
   (a) *discuss* means "to make observations about something using facts, reasoning, and argument; to present in some detail."
   (b) *describe* means "to illustrate something in words or to tell about."
   (c) *show* means "to point out, to set forth clearly an idea or position by stating it and giving data that support it."
   (d) *explain* means "to make plain or understandable; to give reasons for or causes of; to show the logical development or relationship."

Sample Essay Questions

1. The geographical features of a region affect its development.

   Geographic Features

Africa's regular coastline	Africa's Great Rift Valley
Africa's escarpment	African Rain Forest
Africa's great deserts	Africa's Rivers

   Select *three* geographic features from the above list and for *each* one explain how that feature influenced African cultural, economic, and historical development.

2. The ideas or actions of individuals have often changed the course of a nation's or a region's history.

   Individuals

Mansa Musa	Kwame Nkrumah	Desmond Tutu
Jomo Kenyatta	David Livingstone	Nelson Mandela

   Select *three* of the individuals listed above. For *each* one chosen describe how each individual's ideas or actions affected the course of history in the nation or region in which the person lived.

3. Many factors influence a region's economic strength.

Factors

Availability of natural resources	Government policy
Availability of skilled labor	Cultural
Availability of capital	Markets
Historical	Transportation and communication

Choose *five* factors from the list above, and for *each* one chosen, discuss how it influenced the development of African economic strengths or weaknesses.

4. Issues or problems in one part of the world often have an impact on other areas of the world.

Problems

Famine in Somalia	Apartheid in South Africa
Civil war in Nigeria	Uganda's struggle for stability
Civil war in Ethiopia	Namibia's struggle for independence

Select *three* of the problems listed above. For *each* one selected:
• Define and describe the problem.
• Discuss how the problem affected or affects other parts of the world.

5. United States policies and attitudes toward South Africa are influenced by South Africa's policy of apartheid.
   (a) Define the policy called "apartheid."
   (b) Identify three features of the apartheid policy as they were practiced in South Africa.
   (c) Describe how South Africans reacted to the policy of apartheid.
   (d) Describe how American policy toward South Africa has been influenced by the policy of apartheid.
   (e) Discuss the most recent developments in the apartheid situation in South Africa.

6. Nations have achieved their independence in a variety of ways.

Nations

Kenya	Namibia	Ghana
Zaire	Zimbabwe	Tanzania

   A. Select *two* of the nations listed above. For each one chosen, describe how the nation achieved independence.
   B. Base your answer to part B on your answer to part A. Write an essay showing the different way nations can achieve their independence.

Puzzle

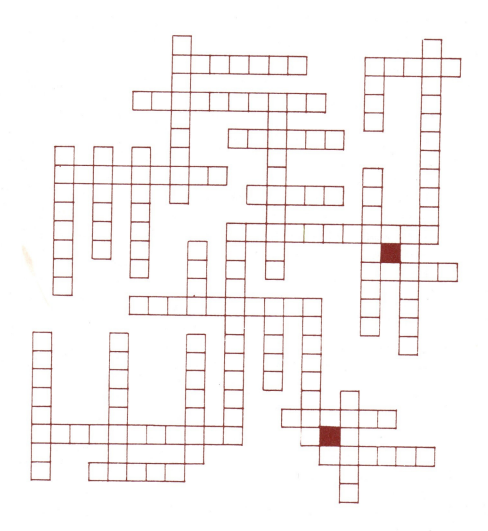

Directions: Place the words below in their proper place in the puzzle.

4 LETTERS	5 LETTERS	6 LETTERS	7 LETTERS	8 LETTERS
CLAN	CACAO	EMPIRE	MARKETS	DIAMONDS
GOLD	IVORY	FETISH	PLATEAU	EXTENDED
	SLAVE	JUNGLE	SWAHILI	LITERACY
	TRADE	KIKUYU	URANIUM	TROPICAL
	TRIBE	SOURCE		

9 LETTERS	10 LETTERS	11 LETTERS	12 LETTERS
APARTHEID	BRIDE PRICE	AGRICULTURE	INDEPENDENCE
ISOLATION	TERRA-COTTA	IMPERIALISM	
SCULPTURE	TOPOGRAPHY	NATIONALISM	

Crossword Puzzle

Directions: Using the map and the clues below, complete the crossword puzzle.

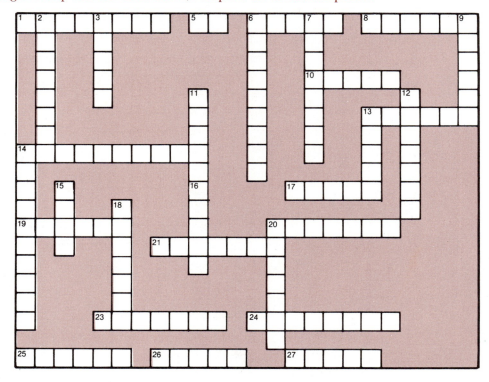

Across

1, 5, 6, 8 The country of apartheid. *Country W.*

10 The area once called the Belgian Congo. *Country L.*

13 Sekou Touré led this country to independence. *Country K.*

14 Island nation off east coast of Africa. *Country Z.*

17 Jomo Kenyatta led this country to independence. *Country M.*

19 "Land locked" country of East Africa. *Country V.*

20 A Sahel country on Africa's West Coast. *Country B.*

21 An African country completely surrounded by South Africa. *Country X.*

23 Independent nation on the southwest coast of Africa. *Country U.*

24 Once called Rhodesia. Now independent. *Country S.*

25, 26 A former Brtitish colony "Lion Mountain." *Country J.*

27 A northeast African country, a Nile country. *Country C.*

Down

2 Civil war and famine have caused great suffering in *Country D.*

3 The name of this country is the same as an African culture. *Country F.*

6 An independent nation in East Africa. *Country Y.*

7 Julius Nyerere led this nation to independence. *Country N.*

9 A former Portuguese colony of West Africa. *Country R.*

11, 16 A country on the Gulf of Guinea. *Country H.*

12 Country settled by freed American slaves. *Country I.*

13 Kwame Nkrumalh led this country to independence. *Country G.*

14 A former Portuguese colony in East Africa. *Country Q.*

15 A country of West Africa named after an ancient kingdom. *Country A.*

18 A civil war nearly destroyed this nation. *Country E.*

20 A country on the Horn of Africa. *Country O.*

COUNTRIES IN AFRICA

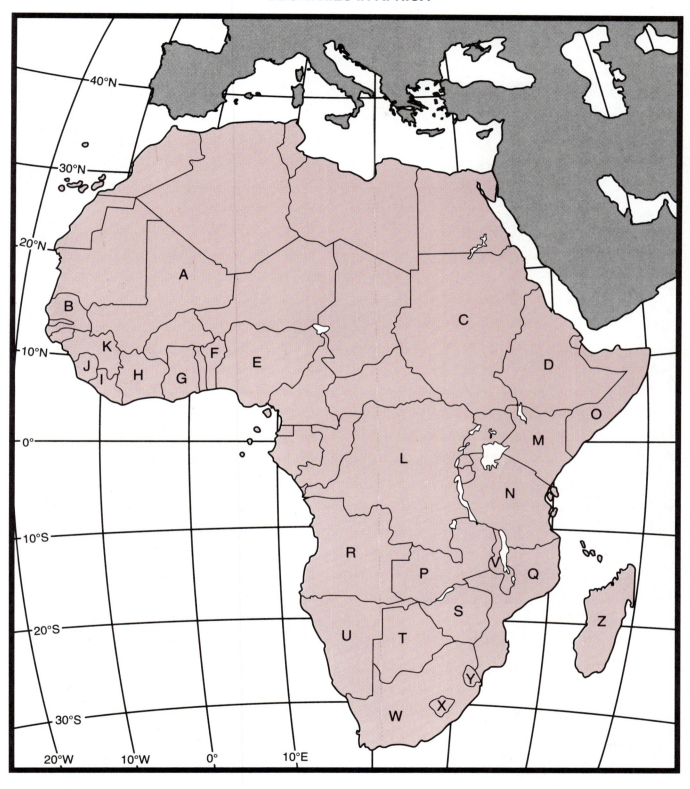

CHINA

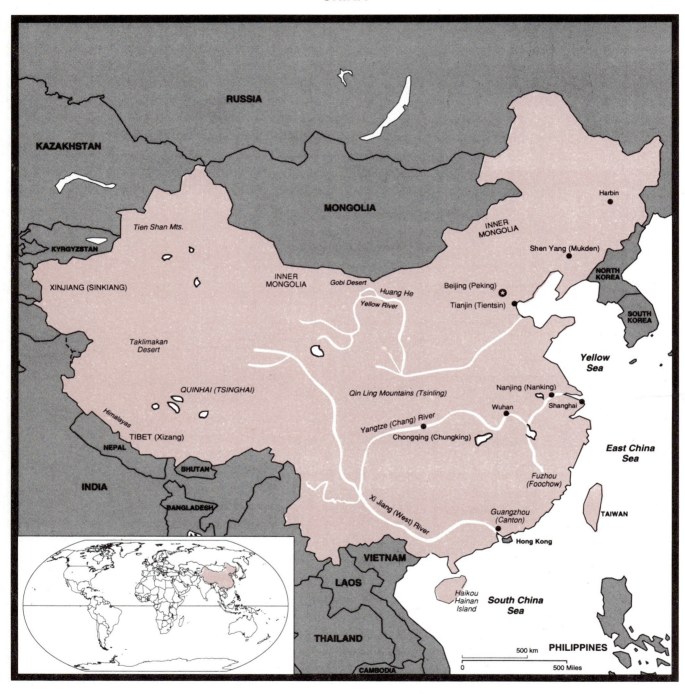

UNIT
IV   China

Topography of China

Geography and Isolation

China, like most other regions, has been influenced by geography. Probably the most important of these geographic factors has been **isolation** (separation). Chinese civilization began and grew in the easternmost part of Asia. It is an area far from other centers of civilization. High mountains and wide deserts isolated this area from other parts of Asia. These natural and protective barriers allowed the Chinese to develop their culture without constant interruption from outside. China also enjoyed conditions favorable for the development of a great culture. Wide plains, fertile soil, great rivers, and coastal harbors were used to support a high level of civilization. Geography explains why Chinese civilization turned out to be **unique** (one of a kind). It developed with only minor contacts with other major cultures, and therefore, only minor instances of cultural diffusion occurred. Where cultural diffusion did take place Chinese culture was diffused into Vietnam, Korea, and Japan.

The Chinese call their country *Zhongguo* (*Chung-kuo*) 中國 , which means the "Middle Kingdom." To the Chinese, their country is the center of the universe. The name China came from the Qin (Ch'in) Dynasty (royal family), which created the Chinese Empire more than 2,000 years ago.

Rivers

China is a huge country. In area, it is the third largest in the world (after the former Soviet Union and Canada). China was not always as large as it is today. About 3,500 years ago China was located in a small area on the banks of the Yellow River (Huang He). The Yellow River flows across the North China Plain. Tracing the river's course in reverse, about 400 miles inland, the river turns sharply north. It then turns west again, and then south to Qinghai (Tsinghai). Geographers call the shape that the Huang He forms the great "Horseshoe Bend" of the river.

Here, at the southern, open end of the Horseshoe Bend, Chinese civilization was born. This area was chosen because of its rich, **loess** soil. Loess is the German word for fertile soil deposited by the wind. This topsoil is renewed every year by rich, new soil brought by winds. In the Horseshoe Bend the loess is sometimes 400 feet thick. With so much fertile topsoil delivered each year, it is no wonder the Chinese have been farmers for 40 centuries. It was here, in the rich loess highlands of the Horseshoe Bend, that the Chinese built their first capital, An-yang.

The heartland of China has always been located in the eastern section, often called China Proper. The three great rivers—Huang He (Yellow), Chang (Yangtze), and Xi (West)—have shaped China's history and life. They are the arteries of China Proper.

The Huang He (Yellow River), the second largest river in China, originates in the mountains of Xizang (Tibet). It flows 3,395 miles in an eastward direction to the Yellow Sea. The Yellow River takes its name from the color of its waters. As the river flows across the North China Plain, it picks up silt (small pieces of earth) from the loose soil that muddies its waters. (The Huang He is the world's muddiest river.) The Yellow River is not very useful for navigation because its many rapids and sandbars (deposits of silt at the bottom of the river) prevent large boats from traveling on it. However, its water is important to millions of farmers. The Huang He waters the North China Plain, making it one of China's richest agricultural areas. While the Yellow River is a source of life, it also brings death and destruction. It often overflows its banks, flooding large areas of the surrounding countryside. Because of these floods, the Chinese people call the Yellow River "China's Sorrow."

The most important river of China is the Chang (Yangtze). It is the fifth largest river in the world. It is navigable for almost a thousand miles inland from its mouth. For centuries the Chinese have used this river for travel and transportation. Many of China's most important cities are on the Yangtze (Shanghai, Nanjing, Hangzhou, Chongqing). The annual flooding of the Yangtze brings rich soil to the farmland of the river valley.

Located in the far south, the Xi River flows through rough lands for almost 1,700 miles. Guangzhou (Canton), an old and famous seaport, lies near the mouth of the river. Since the lower part of the river is navigable, the river serves as a major transportation route.

Coastline

The coastline of China is long and irregular. Along this coast there are many good harbors, such as Dairen, Qingdao, Tianjin, Shanghai, Fuzhou, and Guangzhou (in order from north to south). The irregular coastline also serves as a highway for coastal trade from city to city.

Mountains and Plateaus

Mountains and plateaus are another feature of China's topography. In the southwest are the Himalayas, which separate China from India. The cold plateau of Xiang lies in these mountains. North of Tibet is Xinjiang (Sinkiang), mountainous and difficult to live in. East of Xinjiang is the dry plateau of Inner Mongolia. In the western part of this area is the Gobi Desert. These dry, mountainous lands in which few people live make up about a third of China's land area.

Most of South China is made up of low hills. Between these highlands are fertile river valleys and flat plains. It is in the coastal plains, river valleys, and hills of the eastern one-third of China, known as China Proper, that most of China's population is located. In the far north of China is the Manchurian Plain. This plain is almost completely surrounded by mountains.

Climate

The climate of China can be discussed by comparing its differences in North China and South China. The Qin Ling (Tsinling Mountains) divide the country.

CHINA LANDFORMS

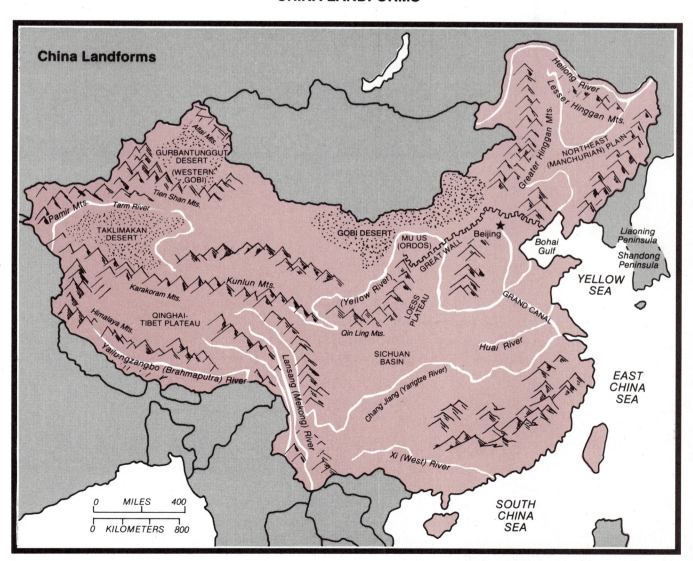

POPULATION PER SQUARE MILE IN CHINA

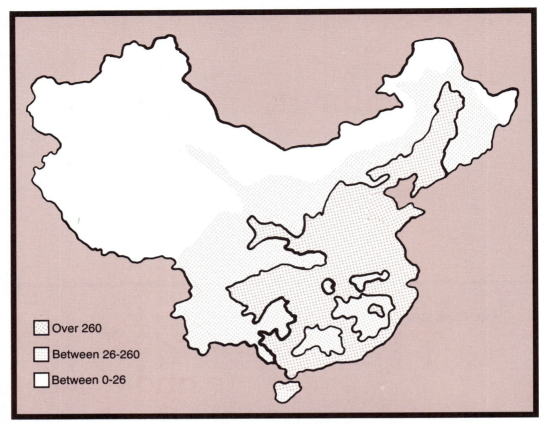

Over 260

Between 26-260

Between 0-26

Why is China's population heavily concentrated in the eastern part of the country? (see map page 265)

North China

Summer on the North China Plain is warm and, at times, hot. During the winter fierce northern winds whip across the area, and snowfalls are common. North China has little rainfall. Consequently, the farmers in this part of China have irrigated their lands since ancient times. When the water supply fails, famine results.

South China

The south is very different from the north. Mountains and dense forests cover much of the south. (The north is practically treeless.) This area is warm during most of the year, and the southernmost parts are hot. Winters are much milder than in the north and, in some parts of the south, snow has never fallen. The Qin Ling Mountains block the cold northern winds from blowing into the south. Because of the high temperatures and the many forests, the people of South China build wooden houses that can be easily ventilated. (In the north, houses are made of mud or mud-brick.)

The Monsoons

In the summer, from June through September, the southeast **monsoon** (seasonal wind) and **typhoons** (storms like hurricanes) may bring heavy rains to southeastern and central China. Some areas have so much rain that rivers overflow and flood the land. Again, the Qin Ling Mountains play an important role. In the summer, they serve as a barrier preventing the moisture-bearing southeast monsoon winds from reaching the North China Plain. In the winter, they prevent the cold, dry winds of the northwest monsoon from reaching the southeastern hill region. The mountains divide the dry wheat lands of the north from the wet rice lands of the south. Rainfall ranges from 10 to 25 inches in the north to between 40 and 90 inches in the south. While northerners can count on a growing season of only five to eight months, crops are grown the year round in most of South China.

The West

As you move west in China, the land becomes drier. About half the land is steppe and the other half desert. It becomes drier for two reasons. First, the mountains block the rainfall carried by winds blowing from the ocean. Second, western China is far from the ocean, in the middle of the vast land area of Asia. The winters here are bitter cold and the summers very hot.

Agriculture and Natural Resources

Agriculture

Shen-nung, whose name meant "divine farmer" and "holy laborer," was a great king of ancient China. The Chinese believe that he taught people to raise crops and that he invented farm tools for them to use. Although the story of Shen-nung is a myth, about the time he was supposed to have lived—4,700 years ago—farmers were raising grain in the Yellow River Valley. The Chinese have been planting and harvesting for perhaps 5,000 years. By patient work, they can make each acre give a surprising amount of food. Farming is the best way of living for at least 80 percent of the Chinese people.

For centuries, China has been one of the world's greatest producers of food. Because of the uncertainty of the water supply in North China, the principal crop of the North has been wheat. The annual wheat crop of China is the largest in the world, ahead of both the former Soviet Union and the United States. Other important crops are also raised, including barley, millet, and sorghum, all cereal grains. From cereal grains the Chinese make food such as noodles, porridges (cooked cereal), dumplings, and pancakes. In southern Manchuria, the main crops are **kaoliang**, a kind of cereal grain, wheat, and soybeans.

South China is rice country. Rice **paddies** (fields) are part of every farm found in the south. The farmers flood the paddies many times during the year, and then transplant young rice plants, which have been grown from seeds in nursery beds. South China has a long growing season because of its warm weather. Often, the farmers can grow two or three crops a year.

Rice is grown throughout South China in flooded paddies such as this one.
Water buffaloes are often used for plowing.

Picking tea in Sichuan (Szechuan) Province, central China north of the
Chang (Yangtze) River.

Central China is tea and silk country. China's finest teas grow here, for the hilly country south of the Yangtze River is well suited for raising tea bush. Conditions are also favorable for the growth of the white mulberry. This tree has leaves that are used as food for silkworms. Thus, China's world-famed silks are produced in this area.

A number of other crops that are important to the Chinese diet and economy are also grown. Enough cotton is grown to meet China's needs. Flax and jute are also raised. China is a major producer of soybeans, sweet potatoes, peanuts, and oil-bearing seeds. The Chinese farmer also raises green vegetables, apples, oranges, and watermelons.

The small amount of protein in the Chinese diet comes mainly from fish, pork, or chicken. People living near the seacoast eat fish. Although China is one of the world's major fishing nations, there is not enough fish to meet the demand of the Chinese people. The Chinese eat pork and chicken rather than beef because pigs and foul can be raised in small spaces. Raising cattle requires more land which would be taken away from the production of grain. The Chinese can feed a lot more people with grain raised on the same number of acres than they can with cattle raised on those acres.

Despite the tremendous amount of food raised in China, the people have often gone hungry. Even today, the Communists face the great problem of feeding the Chinese people adequately.

Natural Resources and Industry

China is very rich in natural resources. It has more raw materials for industry than any other nation in Asia.

Coal
Coal is China's most abundant natural resource. Since the 1980s, China has been the world's leading producer of hard coal. Huge coal reserves are found in northeastern China, in the region known as Manchuria. However, coal is also found in nearly every province in China.

Oil
China is an important producer of oil. The total amount of China's oil reserves is still uncertain, but it is estimated to be about 20 billion barrels. More exploration needs to be done before total reserves are known. Recently, new oil reserves were discovered in the South China Sea. Some of the most important oil fields are found in Manchuria and Xinjiang (Sinkiang) Province. Oil fields are also found throughout northern and central China.

In recent years, China has modernized its methods of producing and refining petroleum. As a result, there has been a great increase in oil production. Most of this oil is used for China's own industries, but there is enough petroleum left for export. Japan is the leading importer of petroleum from China. The money China receives from its oil exports is used to pay for machinery and equipment imported from Japan.

Iron
China has large deposits of iron ore in Manchuria, in the area northeast of Beijing, in Xingiang, and in the area north of the Yangtze River.

Tungsten
China is one of the world's leading producers of tungsten. It is estimated that China has 75 percent of the world's supply of tungsten. Tungsten is used in making steel and in the filaments in light bulbs as well as in high-tech industrial products.

Antimony
China is the world's fifth largest producer of antimony. Antimony is used to harden metals and in printing.

AGRICULTURAL PRODUCTS OF CHINA

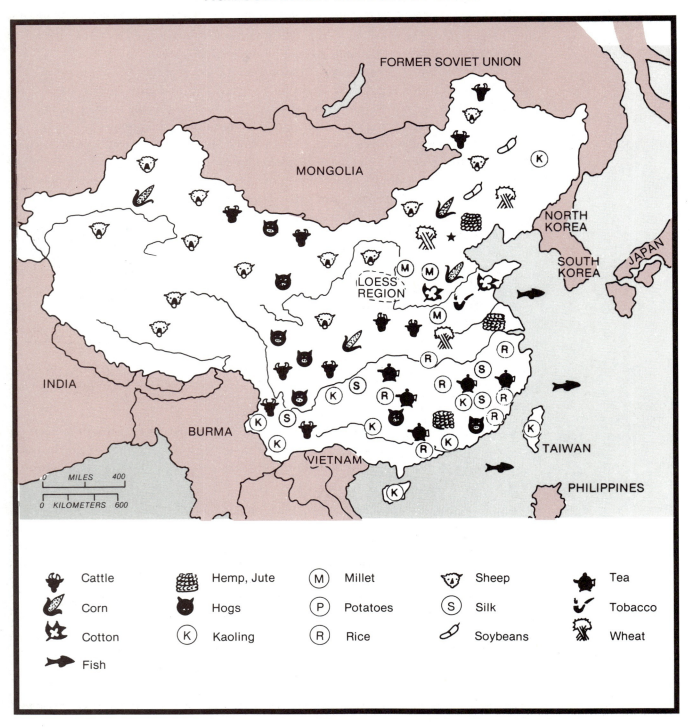

FORMER SOVIET UNION

MONGOLIA

NORTH KOREA

SOUTH KOREA

JAPAN

INDIA

BURMA

VIETNAM

TAIWAN

PHILIPPINES

LOESS REGION

MILES 0 400

KILOMETERS 0 600

Cattle	Hemp, Jute	(M) Millet
Corn	Hogs	(P) Potatoes
Cotton	(K) Kaoling	(R) Rice
Fish		

Sheep	Tea
(S) Silk	Tobacco
Soybeans	Wheat

CHINA'S NATURAL RESOURCES AND INDUSTRIES

Natural Resources

- Coal
- Copper
- Tin
- Gold
- Lead
- Petroleum
- Tungsten
- Iron

Industries

- Agricultural Machinery
- Aircraft
- Aluminum
- Cement
- Chemicals
- Engineering Tools
- Railroad Cars
- Shipbuilding
- Steel
- Textiles

| Tin | There is an abundance of tin in Yunnan Province. Tin is used in making steel and in food containers. |

Tin   There is an abundance of tin in Yunnan Province. Tin is used in making steel and in food containers.

Uranium   Uranium, an essential element in making atomic bombs, is found in Xinjiang (Sinkiang) Province where China's nuclear testing sites are located.

Hydroelectric Power   China's greatest source of energy is hydroelectric power. This means that water power from China's rivers is used to produce electricity. China's two largest rivers—the Yellow River and the Chang—are the main sources of electricity for many cities.

Industries and Industrial Areas

A nation's industries are usually found in areas that have important natural resources and are linked to the rest of the country by good transportation. In China, such an area is Manchuria. An abundance of coal and iron, rich forest resources, and important oil fields in addition to an extensive rail system have made Manchuria the most important industrial area in China. The enormous deposits of coal and iron ore have made possible the development of a large iron and steel industry. Other industries in this region include shipbuilding, chemicals, locomotives, paper, textiles, and food processing.

Another important industrial area is located along the Chang River in and around the cities of Wuhan and Nanjing. Many of these industries are based on local iron ore and coal deposits. One of the largest steel complexes in China is found near Wuhan. New heavy industries are being developed there that will manufacture machinery, engineering tools, aircraft, and ships.

Near the mouth of the Chang is Shanghai, a major port and China's largest commercial and industrial city. Shanghai is a leading textile center. Its other industries are food processing, metals, rubber goods, chemicals, machinery, and shipbuilding.

China has a large and important textile industry. Cotton, silk, and flax produced in China provide the raw materials for this industry. China is a leading world exporter of cotton and silk clothing.

In recent years, many new factories have been set up in the countryside. These factories produce textiles, chemicals, cement, rubber, and other products.

Despite its great wealth in natural resources and its many factories and industries, China is still considered a "developing nation." China lags behind the major industrial nations in science and technology and faces many problems in catching up. Moreover, China has a serious shortage of capital to invest in new industries and new technology. The majority of Chinese people still work in agriculture, not in industry, and the capital to invest in new industries must come from the sale of agricultural products. But with its enormous population, China often has to import food to feed its people. Although China has encouraged foreign companies to invest in new industries in China, in the last few years foreign investment has declined. China's transportation system is inadequate and cannot meet the needs of a growing industrial nation. Huge investments are needed to modernize and enlarge the transportation system.

The Peoples of China

China is made up of a variety of peoples. About 94 percent of the people of China are known as the Han Chinese. Their ancestors created the civilization we know as Chinese. The name Han comes from the Han dynasty, one of the greatest dynasties in Chinese history. The Han Chinese originally lived in China Proper, the area that lies along the seacoast and inland along the valleys of the Huang He and Chiang (Yangste) Rivers. Today, the Han Chinese inhabit almost every part of China.

The other 6 percent of the population is made up of "minority peoples." There are 55 legally recognized minority groups in China today and they number about 60 million people. For the most part, these people live in the outlying areas, the areas that surround China Proper. These areas are Xizang (Tibet) in the west, Xinjiang (Sinkiang) in the northwest, Inner Mongolia in the north central part of the country, and Heilongjiang (Manchuria) in the northeast. Among the more well known of the minority groups are the Tibetans who inhabit Xizang, the Uygurs, Kazaks, and Kirgiz of Xinjiang, the Mongols of Inner Mongolia, and the Manchus of Manchuria. Much of the land inhabited by these ethnic minorities is desert, steppe, and mountains. Therefore, for centuries, many of these people have earned a living herding their sheep, goats, and yaks. Some are farmers who raise fruit, wheat, cotton, and rice.

The minority peoples differ from the Han Chinese in one or more of the following: language, religion, race, customs, and history. For example, a large number of the people of Xinjiang (Sinkiang) are Muslims and speak Turkish languages. The people of Tibet are Buddhist.

Relations between the Han Chinese and the minorities have often been tense. Even though centuries ago the Mongols and later the Manchus were able to overrun China and rule it, the Han Chinese have generally looked down on the minority groups and discriminated against them.

After the Communists came to power in 1949, the minorities were allowed limited autonomy in their own regions. They have been given freedom to use their own language in the schools and government of their areas, to practice their customs, wear their native dress, and observe their holidays. But in recent years, these rights have often been restricted. As a result, rebellions broke out in Xiziang in 1959 and in Xinjiang in 1962. The Chinese government crushed the revolt in Tibet by forcing the Tibetan leader, the Dalai Lama, to flee the country and by closing down most of the Buddhist monasteries.

Minority rights have been restricted since 1989, especially in Xizang and Xinjiang, and there is a very strong anti-Chinese feeling in these regions. In Xinjiang, rioting broke out in April 1990 and about 200,000 troops were needed to suppress the rebellion. Some of the minorities feel that Chinese culture and majority values are being imposed on them.

China will probably never loosen its control over the regions inhabited by the minorities because most of China's mineral resources are located in their territories. These areas also have great military importance to the Chinese. Some of these regions lie along the border with the former Soviet Union. A large part of the Soviet Union's military forces were deployed in this area that the Chinese regarded as a grave threat to their security. It is still too soon to know what China's relations will be with the Commonwealth of Independent States (CIS) which has replaced the Soviet Union.

Some Characteristics of the Chinese People

The Chinese people have always believed that they have the longest history and the most civilized culture of any people in the world. They developed an **ethnocentric** attitude, believing that their way of life was superior to all other people. As a result, they are a self-confident people, proud of their heritage.

Family life is very important to the Chinese people. Family ties among the Chinese are much stronger than in the West. A person is seen as a member of a family first and only secondly as an individual. Individualism as it exists in the West is frowned upon by the Chinese.

The Chinese have always placed a great value on education. Scholars and educated men had the highest place in Chinese society. Teachers were held in very high esteem. This respect for education has carried over into the present.

Over the centuries, many Chinese people have emigrated to other countries. These people are known as the Overseas Chinese. In their new countries, these Chinese have established businesses in all areas of modern life. They have become bankers, plantation owners, mine operators, merchants, money lenders, and leaders in other types of businesses in Singapore, Hong Kong, Rio de Janeiro, San Francisco, and New York.

The majority of Chinese people have always lived in villages, and often spent their entire lives in their local district. In the past only a very small number left their homes to work, to trade, or to serve in the government. The need to take care of the parents as well as respect for ancestors also kept the Chinese at home.

For centuries, the Chinese people accepted nature as it was. Unlike Westerners, the Chinese people had little interest in using science to change nature to meet their needs and wishes. The secrets of the universe and discovering what controlled the universe did not interest them. Their aim in life was to live in peace with nature, out of respect and fear. Chinese art often shows tiny humans overshadowed by great mountains and other natural features. The Chinese believe humans are only a small part of a great universe.

The Chinese people have had the ability to wait, not to be impatient or in a hurry. Peoples in the West, especially Americans, find it difficult to understand this about the Chinese. An old Chinese proverb says, "If a solution to a problem is not found now or in our lifetime, it will be found in the lifetime of my son or grandson." This is a sense of time that comes from 50 centuries of history.

Above all, the Chinese people have a sense of history. They call history a "mirror," in which they can see the past, the present, and the future. No Chinese man or woman sees himself or herself apart from other people. He or she is an important part of the history, tradition, language, and culture of China. Thus, the Chinese people attach great importance to historical writing. No other people have so long and continuous a record of the past as the Chinese.

Like any other culture, Chinese culture did change over a long period of time. But the changes in the 20th century have probably been greater than all the changes in the centuries before.

Acupuncture

Traditional Chinese medicine is very different from Western Medicine. **Acupuncture**, which plays an important part in Chinese medicine, is the ancient Chinese practice of stimulating certain nerve points with needles. Developed thousands of years ago, it is used throughout China as a means of anesthesia and as a treatment for illnesses such as appendicitis, asthma, migraine headaches, and even deafness. There are 500 to 800 nerve points in the body that are used in acupuncture.

Western doctors and other visitors to China have witnessed major operations where needles were used as the only anesthetic, while the patient remained fully conscious. These patients showed no pain and after their operation many were able to walk out of the operating room with no help. Many Americans have become interested in this practice in the last few years and have gone to China and to Taiwan to learn how acupuncture works.

Population Growth and Population Control

With over 1 billion people, China is the world's most populous country. According to the 1990 census, the population of China was over 1,133,000,000. Although it has about 20 percent of the world's population, China has only 8 percent of the world's food-producing land. As a result, China has to constantly struggle to feed its people. There are also severe shortages in educational facilities, housing, and health care.

When Mao Zedong became ruler of Communist China in 1949, he encouraged the Chinese people to have more children even though China had over 540 million people. Mao believed that more people meant more workers to produce more food and strengthen China's economy. However, by the early 1970s, Mao realized that China would not be able to feed its rapidly growing population. Consequently, he agreed to plans calling for a two-child limit to each family. This policy helped reduce China's growth rate from 2.85 percent to 1.6 percent (the rate in the United States is 0.7 percent).

Deng Xiaoping, Mao's successor, realized that China would not be able to modernize or raise its standard of living if it did not limit population growth. Thus, in 1979 Deng announced his "one-couple, one-child" policy. Deng's goal was to limit China's population to 1.2 billion by the year 2000. Local officials distributed contraceptives and educated couples on birth control. Posters were distributed throughout the country to preach the benefits of one-child families. People were told that having only one child was good for China.

To enforce Deng's program, the government used a system of rewards and punishments. Couples who agreed to have only one child got better housing, free medical care, and pay increases. Those who did not comply were fined, had their salaries reduced, and even lost their jobs. Local officials in charge of population control sometimes forced women to have abortions and undergo sterilization if they exceeded the one child limit.

The "one-couple, one-child" policy met with much resistance because it conflicted with the Chinese tradition of having many children, especially many sons. Rural families argued that sons were needed to work in the fields to produce the food demanded by the government. In 1984, the government eased its restrictions by allowing rural families to have a second child if the first child was female.

China's population control policy has had mixed results. It has lowered China's birthrate to about half the average for the world's 50 poorest countries. However, China's population will exceed the 1.2 billion goal set for the year 2000. It will probably be closer to 1.28 billion or even 1.3 billion.

The policy has had a serious effect on female children. There has been a large increase in female infanticide (the killing of female infants) and in the number of abortions of female fetuses. Although the Communists teach equality, the Chinese still prefer male to female children.

Although China has one of the world's most vigorous programs to reduce population growth, its population will continue to grow at a tremendous rate. Population control will remain one of its leading problems throughout the 1990s.

In recent years, the Chinese government has been encouraging people to have only one child.

Life and Society in Traditional China

Chinese Philosophy: Confucianism, Legalism, and Daoism

The philosophies of Confucianism, Legalism, and Daoism originated between the 5th and 3rd centuries B.C. during a period of civil war and great unrest. It was also a time in which the old ideas and values seemed to have lost their importance, and new ones had not yet taken their place. The people of China had two basic needs: to end the bloody wars between the states and to set up a new social order. Confucianism and Daoism are considered philosophies and not religions because they were not concerned with God or life after death. They were mainly concerned with ways of improving society and achieving a better life on earth.

From the 5th century to the 2nd century B.C., these two philosophies as well as a number of others competed with each oher. About 100 B.C., Confucianism was adopted by the government as the official philosophy. For the next 2,000 years, that is, until the 20th century, Chinese life and society were based on the ideas of Confucianism.

Confucianism

Confucius, the Latinized form of the name of Kung Fu-tzu, was born in 551 B.C. and died in 479 B.C. The philosophy that is known as Confucianism comes mainly from the speeches and writings of Confucius. Disciples (followers) of Confucius, such as Mencius, made important contributions to Confucianism as well. The ideas of Confucianism are found in nine works: the "Four Books" and the "Five Classics."

Confucianism is an ethical system rather than a religion. (Ethics deals with human behavior and conduct.) Confucius was mainly concerned with how human beings behaved toward each other and paid little attention to such matters as sin, salvation, and the soul. He developed a system of government, society, and justice which we call Confucianism.

Confucius believed that people, because of their nature, desire to live in the company of other people, that is, in society. It is only in society that people reach their fullest development. Therefore, it is important for people to know how to behave in society, that is, in their relations with other people.

The Five Basic Relationships   According to Confucius, each person had a specific place in society and certain duties to fulfill. Confucius hoped that if people knew what was expected of them they would behave correctly. Therefore, he set up five principal relationships in which most people are involved. These relationships were (1) ruler and subject; (2) father and son; (3) elder brother and younger brother; (4) husband and wife; and (5) friend and friend. All, except the last, involve the authority of one person over another.

Power and the right to rule belong to superiors over subordinates; that is, to older people over younger people, to men over women. Each person has to give obedience and respect to "superiors"; the subject to his ruler, the wife to her husband, the son to his parents, and the younger brother to the older brother. The "superior," however, owes loving responsibility to the inferior.

The earliest printed text in the world, dated May 11, 869 a.d., this is a part of the Diamond Sutra, a prayer to Buddha.

Bronze ritual vessel from the Chou Dynasty, 11-10th century b.c.

The Family and the State

Confucius placed great importance on the family. Family life was seen as a training ground for life in society. It is at home in the family that the child learns to deal with problems that he or she will face later in the world. The family is responsible for educating the child to be a good member of society. Confucius emphasized the importance of education, the aim of which is to turn people into good family members, responsible members of society, and good subjects of the emperor.

The state (government) was regarded as an extension of the family in many ways. The emperor and his officials were referred to as the parents of the people. Subjects owed the same loyalty to their rulers that they owed to the senior members of their family.

However, the emperor had duties to fulfill as well. Confucius believed that for society to be well ordered and for people to live in peace and prosper, it was necessary to have a good government and a virtuous ruler. It was the duty of the emperor and his officials to set a good example for the people. The good example of the ruler would transform the people and make them better. Confucius believed that only the wisest and most humane men should rule. He further believed that if the emperor was not morally perfect, heaven would cause the world to suffer.

The emperor also had to maintain the proper relationship betwen himself and heaven. Heaven was regarded as the governing authority of the universe and the final judge of right and wrong. The Chinese believed that a dynasty ruled as long as it held the "Mandate of Heaven," that is, the right to rule. The people felt they had the right to say whether or not the ruler had the Mandate. When the Emperor did not see to it that there was water for irrigation, that canal barges could transport rice, that rivers did not flood, and that roads were safe for traveling, the people suffered. When the people suffered, they were sure that Heaven had taken away its protection of the Emperor, so they rebelled. When the rebellion was successful, the Mandate of Heaven was given to the leader of the rebellion. He became the emperor of a new dynasty.

The Importance of Confucianism

For 2,000 years Confucianism was the official philosophy of China. The only way a person could achieve an important position in the government or in society was by having a good knowledge of Confucianism. To become a government official it was necessary to pass a difficult civil service examination based on the ideas of Confucius. Since it was Confucianism that kept the leaders in power, they were opposed to any changes.

The Confucianists believed that they were the only civilized community in the world and they looked down on the beliefs and cultures of other people. This attitude made the Chinese unwilling to change their way of life when they were first exposed to Western culture. This unwillingness to adopt Western ideas and techniques in the late 19th and early 20th centuries proved to be disastrous for the Chinese.

Confucius himself was not very interested in the ideas of a God, an after life, heaven, and other ideas that we associate with religion. However, when Confucianism became the official philosophy of China, religious functions were incorporated into it. Confucius, together with his ancestors and famous followers, became objects of worship. Confucian temples were built all over China and sacrifices and rituals were performed.

Legalism

Legalism is a philosophy that became important during the period of civil war in China (the period of warring states from 475–221 B.C.). Legalist philosophers served as advisers to the leaders of the warring states. In 221 B.C., Qin (Ch'in), the most powerful of the warring states, conquered the others and unified China. This required harsh methods and absolute control by a single leader. The first Qin emperor, Shi Huangdi, used the idea of legalism to achieve this control and to unite China. Legalist ideas formed the basis of the Qin dynasty, which ruled China from 221–206 B.C.

The Legalist philosophers believed that government and laws had to be based on the realities of human behavior. They believed that people by nature were selfish and not good. Therefore, to maintain order in society, people had to have a strong ruler who governed by harsh laws and threats of punishment. The Legalists believed in strong government control and absolute obedience to authority on the part of the people. They rejected the Confucian ideas that a ruler could influence people by his virtuous conduct and good example. They believed that only harsh laws, punishments, and rewards would insure order, not good examples.

The Qin emperors feared that the other philosophies might undermine their power. Therefore, they outlawed Confucianism and all philosophies other than Legalism. The emperor ordered that the books of other philosophies be burned and their scholars buried alive.

The harsh rule of the Qin dynasty led to its overthrow in 206 B.C. The Legalist philosophy was discredited. The new dynasty, the Han, returned to Confuciansim and made it the offical philosophy of China. However, some of the ideas of the Legalists became rooted in China and have influenced the action of Chinese governments ever since.

Daoism

The philosophy of Daoism (Taoism) takes its name from the Chinese word *Dao* (*Tao*) meaning "The Way." The three principal teachers of this philosophy were Lao Tzu, Tang Chu, and Chuang Tzu. According to tradition, Lao Tzu (meaning "Old Master") was the founder of Daoism, but modern scholars have questioned his existence.

The philosophy of Daoism stated that people should live naturally. People are happiest when they live according to their own nature. However, society does not permit people to live naturally. Society forces human beings to live according to rules which are not natural. This results in suffering and problems. To escape from this unhappiness, people must free themselves from all the rules that are forced upon them by society. They must find the Dao, or "Way" of the universe.

It is very difficult to say what Dao is. The early Daoists never defined it because they believed that language could not give its exact meaning. "Those who know the Dao do not speak of it; those who speak of it do not know it." The Dao is the unseen power beneath all the life and movement in nature. The Dao is present everywhere in all things. It has no beginning or end. The Dao is the force that gives life and a particular nature to all things. It is the nature of a fish that it cannot live out of water. It is the nature of man that he must breathe air. It is because of Dao that this is so. To act contrary to the Dao or nature, for example, to deprive a fish of water or a man of air, can only be harmful.

The Daoists spoke of a golden age in the past when people lived naturally. They wore the clothes they had woven and ate the food they had grown. All the creatures of sky and earth lived together in peace and harmony. People were not restrained by rules or codes of behavior. They lived and acted spontaneously. But as civilization advanced, this situation changed. People stopped acting naturally. The Daoists believed that society corrupted people and separated them from their true nature. To live in society and obey its rules of behavior is contrary to human nature and harmful. People can be truly happy only when they are able to express themselves freely.

Since the Dao exists in everything, Daoists feel that they possess all things. They do not fear or desire anything. Because of their union with the Dao, everything is part of them and they are part of everything. Daoists have no fear of death. To them, death is merely a change of form and has no significance. Being at one with the Dao puts one in complete control of all the things of the universe. Daoists, therefore, feel that they are masters of the world.

In later years, Daoism came to be associated with spirits which the Chinese would turn to in times of need. Daoists were called upon to select lucky days for weddings and funerals, to choose sites for housing, and to do other things of this nature.

Daoism had a great influence on the Chinese people and their culture. This can be seen in Chinese literature and painting. Because of its ideas about nature and the universe, Daoism has fascinated scholars for more than 2,000 years.

Social Classes in Traditional China: The Gentry and the Peasants

The Gentry

The **gentry** and the **peasants** were the two main **classes** of traditional Chinese society. The gentry were at the top of Chinese society. They were the landowners who possessed vast landed estates and the officials who administered the government of China. The gentry were a leisure class who looked down on any kind of physical work. Because of their wealth and comfort they had time to engage in social activities and political affairs. They devoted a great deal of time to cultural activities such as poetry, painting, writing, and the art of **calligraphy** or brush-writing.

Economic Life

The gentry received most of their income from the land that they owned and rented out to tenants from whom they collected rent. The gentry did not cultivate or live on their land. Instead, they lived mainly in the towns, which were the political and cultural centers. With the money from the rents they collected they were able to buy luxuries such as paintings, musical instruments, jewelry, clothing of fine silk, and different art objects. The towns provided them with amusements and entertainment such as teahouses, restaurants, and theaters.

Gentry families often added to their incomes by opening shops, usually pawn shops and rice shops. Since the Chinese people frequently lived through periods of economic crisis and needed ready cash, the pawnshops served as banks and lending agencies. The gentry kept the interest rates high. The rice shops also brought the gentry high profits. They would buy the rice immediately after the harvest when it was cheap and store it until it was in short supply. Then they sold it at a high price or made loans at high interest rates.

Those gentry families who stayed in the countryside and lived solely off their land soon became quite poor. In each generation, the family property was divided among all the sons, and after a few generations, instead of one large landowning family there were many small landowners.

Family Life

The gentry lived in large, extended families that sometimes included four or five generations. The head of the family ruled over the family, had complete authority in all matters, and was not questioned about anything he did. There was a specific code of behavior that the members of the family followed in their relationships with each other. A great deal of time and care was spent training the younger members of the family in the proper behavior.

Large families gave the gentry power. Marriage was a way of increasing the power of gentry families. Marriages were arranged to establish alliances among important families. All the family property and wealth were preserved as a unit. The individual members strove to maintain the power and important position of the whole family. However, since there were so many people living together, there was often jealousy and arguments among the family members. While the head of the family was alive, he was able to keep the entire family together as one unit. After his death the property was often divided, and the large family was broken up into smaller, independent groups.

The Scholar-officials

To become a government official in China it was necessary to pass a difficult civil service examination which required years of study. Since the gentry were the people who had the money and leisure to devote to education, they became the scholar-officials who administered the government of China. Since most Chinese peasants lived in great poverty, they were unable to spend years studying Confucian philosophy. As a result, very few of them ever became part of the ruling group.

As government officials, the gentry were able to protect their own interests. By filling all the government posts with their own people, they were able to check the power of the emperor.

Political Functions

The gentry carried out many important political functions. Their services were needed by both the government and the peasants. The gentry assisted the central government in dealing with local matters. They helped the government collect taxes, construct public works, and preserve the peace. When the peasants felt that their taxes were too high or that the government required too many soldiers from their district, they turned to the gentry for help in getting the government to moderate its demands. In cases of land quarrels and feuds, the gentry acted as arbiters. In this way, the gentry carried on an informal government in the countryside. This kept the central government from interfering too much in local matters.

The gentry maintained their important position well into the 20th century. In modern times, they became lawyers, doctors, engineers, and professors. Many found employment in industry, commerce, and banking. However, when the Communists came to power in 1949, one of their first steps was to break up the power of the gentry and take away their wealth.

The Peasants

The majority of Chinese people were peasants. They made up between 80–90 percent of the population of China. The life of the peasants was very different from the life of the gentry.

One basic difference was that the peasants earned a living doing physical work. Their income came mainly from cultivating the land. Some peasants were the owners of their small piece of land. Others were tenants who cultivated the land for landowners. And some were farm laborers who received a salary for farming the land. But in all cases, the peasants worked very hard to produce enough food to feed their families. The peasants also found it necessary to add to their incomes by handicrafts. At night and during the slack season the whole family would weave, embroider, work with silk, or make baskets and other goods. They sold these products in the nearby towns. Most often the additional money was used to buy the necessities of life, not luxuries.

The peasants rarely left their villages. On occasion, the peasants did go into town, but this was only to buy the few things they could not produce at home or to sell the surplus crops or handicrafts they had made. The peasants had no time or money for the entertainment or luxuries of the towns. Only rarely did they enjoy any form of enterainment. Sometimes, storytellers who roamed from village to village arrived and spent a few days reciting various kinds of tales. On special occasions, theatrical companies came to the villages. The peasants tried to make their festivals, especially New Year, as happy as they could. Weddings were another time for celebrating.

The peasants generally lived in small families. They were often a nuclear family consisting of parents and children. Some peasant familes consisted of two generations—the parents residing with their oldest married son. Their tiny pieces of land could not support many people. To preserve this small piece of land, they often permitted only one son to inherit the property. (The gentry usually allowed all the sons to inherit the property equally.) The peasants offered sacrifices to their ancestors when they could, at least once or twice a year. In choosing a wife, the peasant placed the greatest importance on obtaining a strong helpmate. What was looked for in a wife was a strong back, sturdy legs, and firm hands, not a pretty face.

Chinese peasants were independent individuals. They relied on their own labor and physical strength. They solved their problems by themselves and with the help of their sons. When problems arose that they could not handle alone, the peasant turned for help to the gentry or the village elders, but not to the government.

The peasants regarded the government with deep suspicion. They associated it with evil things, such as taking their scarce food for taxes, taking their strength for public works, taking their sons for the army, and often also taking their land away. In general, the peasants felt that the less they had to do with the government the better.

Life for the Chinese peasants was difficult. They worked from sunrise to sunset, yet most of their life was lived in poverty. Malnutrition and disease were common. During periods of drought, famine, or floods, the peasants suffered more than any other group. Yet despite their hardships and suffering, the peasants were conservative by nature. They were content to live out their lives in their accustomed way, rather than try to change the political system. Throughout Chinese history, when life became unbearable for them, the peasants rose up and helped overthrow the government. But they were mainly interested in throwing out the unjust rulers, not in changing the political system. Once the rulers had been changed and the injustices remedied, the peasants returned to their traditional way of life.

It was the hope of those in the peasant class to become members of the gentry class. One way in which peasants could move into the gentry was through education and government service. Bright peasant boys were often helped by relatives to get an education. If they passed the examination and became government officials, they became members of the gentry class. Peasants who became wealthy educated their sons and set them up in government careers. In this way, the sons joined the ranks of the gentry. Sometimes a gentry family might lose its wealth and descend into the peasant class. Thus a certain degree of mobility between classes existed in China.

The Chinese Family

The Importance of the Family in China

The Chinese people have always considered the family to be the most important part of society. The individual thought of himself as a member of a family, and others saw him in the same way. If the individual was successful, the prestige of the family was increased. If the individual was a failure, that brought shame on the whole family. The family was held responsible for the acts of its individual members. Confucianism emphasized the importance of the family. It was in the family that the individual learned his role in Chinese society. Of the five basic social relationships necessary to the right functioning of Chinese society, three were family relationships—the relationships between father and son, elder brother and younger brother, and husband and wife.

Family Size

In traditional China three types of families existed: the small, the middle-way, and the large family. The small family usually consisted of the parents and their unmarried children. The middle-way family was made up of the parents, their unmarried children, and one married son with his wife and children. The large family included the parents, the unmarried children, and the married sons with their wives and children. Sometimes, other close relatives, such as grandparents, uncles, aunts, cousins, and nephews, might live in this family. The head of the family was usually the father, but sometimes it might be the elder brother. He supervised the common property and watched over the moral life of its members.

From ancient times until very recently, the large family was the ideal family. However, only certain wealthy families were able to achieve this goal. The majority of the Chinese people lived in small and middle-way families. There are several reasons why most Chinese were not able to achieve the ideal of a large family. Malnutrition, disease, and famine were very common in China. Many children died at a young age and many mothers died in childbirth. The small amount of land that the poor people possessed was not enough to support a large family. In present-day China the small family, consisting of the parents and their children, is typical.

Family Relationships

Until recently, the parents had almost complete authority over their children. Chinese fathers were regarded by their sons with a great deal of fear. Since untrained and undisciplined sons gave the community a bad impression of the father, Chinese fathers were very strict in training their sons. Relationships between fathers and daughters were usually warmer and closer. The relationship between the mother and her children was generally one of love and affection. She was often the one who protected the children, especially the sons, from the anger of their father. When the grandfather headed the family, he often protected his grandchildren from the father and mother. Children would run to their grandparents to escape from their father's punishment. Often, children received more love from their grandparents, uncles, and aunts than from their own fathers.

Social Training

Parents were supposed to train their children to fulfill their proper role in Chinese society. For each generation, for each age, for each sex there was an accepted form of behavior which had to be learned. From the age of four to 16 children were taught their future duties. The boys of gentry families were sent to schools or to private tutors. The boys of peasant families were taught field work at an early age. All boys were taught the ancestral rituals. Both peasant and gentry girls had to learn many household duties. Peasant girls, in addition, learned to help in the fields.

Marriage

Marriage was very important in China because only through marriage could the family line be continued. Arranging marriages was the responsibility of the parents. The bride and groom had little to say about the choice of their mate or the marriage arrangements. In fact, they rarely saw each other before the wedding. There was no question of love in arranging marriage in China. Of great importance in choosing a mate was the social and financial position of the family. This was carefully checked before the marriage contract was signed.

A middle man always negotiated the marriage. He or she did the talking and bargaining and carried the messages back and forth. One of the most important questions to be settled was the size of the dowry to be paid by the family of the bridegroom to the family of the bride. The girl's family used part of the dowry money to buy the bridal outfit. If there were unmarried sons in the family, part of the money was used to obtain wives for them.

On the day of the wedding, the bride was taken to the home of her bridegroom. Here the bride faced a completely new environment. In most cases she had not seen any of the family members before, including her husband. The most difficult adjustment was to her mother-in-law. The mother-in-law was responsible for training and disciplining her daughter-in-law. The husband and wife were not supposed to show affection in public. The young bride spent most of her time in the company of her mother-in-law. The son could not interfere with his mother's treatment of his wife, because both he and his wife were subordinate to his mother.

Old Age

Old age and childhood were thought of as the happiest times in life. The Chinese looked forward to old age and growing old was pleasant. Age was respected. It was a time of leisure and little responsibility. Children had to do everything to provide for the comfort and happiness of their parents. They were required to support their parents in their old age and to carry out the ceremonial rites after their death.

Women also achieved respect and importance as they grew older. As the years passed, the timid bride became a mother-in-law and head of her own household. Once she had sons and daughters-in-law of her own, all owed her respect, obedience, and support.

The Family in China Today

After the Communists came to power in 1949, they set out to transform Chinese society. This affected family life as well. In China today, people are taught to think in terms of loyalty to the state first and the family second. While families are still held responsible for teaching the young their roles in society, there are now other places where the young person can learn this. Nurseries, schools, clubs, factory committees, and party groups serve the function that the family did in the past. Young people in China today are no longer dominated by their elders as they were in the past. In fact, young people are placed in many positions of authority. The role of women is also totally different from what it used to be. However, in places with large Chinese populations such as Taiwan, Hong Kong, and Southeast Asia, many Chinese people still retain the old customs and traditional family patterns.

The Clan

A clan is a group of people who can trace their ancestry back to a common ancestor. Descent is traced on the father's side. Some clans have thousands of members. Included in the clan are all those people having the same surname who can trace their descent to the common ancestor who first settled in the area.

Since the Chinese people place such value on the family, their dead ancestors are important to them as well. The Chinese kept genealogies—charts and written histories tracing the clan's descent from the common ancestor and showing the relationship among the members.

Every clan usually had a center where the ancestral hall was built and where most of the ancestral graves were located. Once or twice a year the clan met to honor their common ancestors. The memorial service was to show their respect and reverence. The Chinese believed their ancestors continued to live as spirits. These spirits had the power to help their descendants if they were given the proper rites. If they were neglected, the descendants would suffer misfortune. One reason that the Chinese considered it so important to have sons was that they would have descendants to carry out the proper rites to their spirits after their death.

Clan leaders met periodically to discuss clan matters. Special funds were set aside to take care of orphans, widows, and the sick. In times of crises, such as floods, famine, or war, the clan helped its members. Funds were also used to help educate the promising children of the poorer members. Civil and criminal cases affecting clan members were judged by the clan instead of the government. For serious offenses the punishment was expulsion from the clan.

The Role of Women

Women in Traditional China

An old Chinese proverb states "A wife married is like a pony bought; I'll ride her and whip her as I like." This proverb shows how low a woman's position in China was. There are a number of examples in Chinese history of women becoming empresses and ruling with great power, but women were never considered to be equal to men. The ancient Chinese custom of footbinding was supposed to keep a woman's feet small and beautiful. At the same time it made it very difficult for a woman to walk, thereby keeping her at home and dependent on her husband. (Footbinding was not practiced among the poor because women had to work in the fields alongside their husbands.) When there was famine, girls were often sold by their parents who regarded them as just another mouth to feed. These girls were usually used as slaves by the families who bought them. Also during times of famine, people would sometimes kill their newborn baby girls. Children as young as six were often betrothed (promised in marriage). If the girl's parents experienced bad times, she would be sent to work in the house of her future husband. Young brides were very frequently mistreated by their mothers-in-law. Chinese literature is full of stories of women throwing themselves down wells or hanging themselves. When a woman's husband died, it was considered unacceptable for her to remarry.

Women in China Today

All this has been changed. Women are now regarded as equal to men and they work and fight side by side with men. In 1950, the Communists passed a new marriage law. This law made husbands and wives equal in the marriage relationship, outlawed dowries and forced marriages, forbade mistreatment of children and infanticide, permitted divorce for women, and gave women property rights. The Communist government also outlawed foot-binding. All over China women's study groups were set up to discuss the new law and inform women of their rights.

Women in the Work Force

Women today feel proud of the useful role they have in building China. The government encourages women to do productive work outside the home. Women receive equal pay for equal work. Today they drive heavy trucks and bulldozers and fly planes in the air force. Half of the doctors in China are women. Chinese women, as well as men, consider their work to be a very important part of their lives. Often women and men leave their families for weeks or months if their jobs require them to go to the countryside, the army, or another part of the country.

Marriage and Divorce

Young people today choose their own marriage partners. The government discourages early marriages. This makes it possible for a woman to get the education she needs. If a woman works for several years before she is married, she will be more independent of her husband. Divorce is discouraged. The court first tries to help the couple work out its problems. Only after many failures to work things out does the court agree to grant a divorce.

"One child per family"

In the past, Chinese women had many babies. Today couples are told that they should have only one child. At study groups, local clinics, and their places of work, people can learn about family planning. Birth control is encouraged and abortions are readily available.

Child Care

After giving birth, a woman worker gets 50 to 60 days off with full pay. If a woman has to stay away from her job longer, she is paid for the days she is out. To make it possible for the woman to return to work as quickly as possible, children can be left in special child care centers. Between the ages of six weeks and 18 months a child is looked after in a "feeding station" in the same place where the woman works. The mother is given time during the day to feed and hold her baby. From 18 months to 3½ years, children are left in nurseries. (If there is a grandmother at home, children are left with her.) At the age of 3½ the child enters kindergarten and stays there until old enough to start school. Sometimes, children are left in the centers overnight if their parents work the night shift or have meetings in the evening.

Women in China have not reached complete equality yet. The great majority of leaders in the government, the Communist Party, the army, and industry are still men. But more and more leadership positions are being taken over by women.

A natural gas worker at a Takang oilfield. Chinese women play an important role in industrial development.

Language and Writing System

Language

Chinese belongs to the Sinitic or Sino—Tibetan language family (Tibetan, Burmese, Siamese, Chinese). Most Chinese speak *Kuo-yo* (meaning national language), also known as Mandarin Chinese. This language and its dialects are spoken in the northern and western parts of China. Throughout the southern part of China many other dialects are in common use. Educated people in the south usually learn the national language, in addition to the dialects of their area.

All words in Kuo-yu, as well as in all Chinese dialects, are made up of single syllables. For this reason the language is called monosyllabic. For example, *chop suey* means "mixed small pieces"; *chow mein* means "fried noodles"; *kow tow* means "bow the head"; *typhoon* means "big wind"; *ting hao* means "very good"; *tasi chien* means "see you again." The city Shanghai is a combination of *shang*, meaning "above" and *hai*, meaning "sea." The name Mao Zedong like most Chinese names is made up of three parts. The family name, which comes first, is Mao. (Mao was a place in ancient China.) Zedong, the given name, consists of two parts meaning "east marsh," the same as the first and middle names in America.

The Chinese langauge uses many homonyms, or words that are pronounced alike but have different meanings, like *to*, *too*, and *two* in English. Communication between speakers would be difficult without a way of making clear differences in the meaning of words pronounced the same way. Context, or the position of the word in a sentence and its use, is one way of making meanings clear. But still another method is the use of tone.

The national language generally uses four tones. In learning a new word in Chinese, it is necessary to know both its sound and its tone. A word pronounced with a rising tone may mean something different from another word with the same sound, but said in a falling tone. The tones give you the feeling that Chinese is sung, and not merely spoken.

Contact with the West has added many words to the Chinese language. The Chinese express their ideas by putting two or three syllables (words) together like *ting hao* (very good). Today, with new and strange terms having to do with science, technology and ideas, the Chinese have borrowed and pronounced foreign words as much like the originals as possible. Sometimes new combinations have been made like *fei chi* ("flying machine"—airplane); *huo ch'e* ("fire wagon"—train); *yuan tzu tan* ("primary unit egg"—atom bomb).

The Chinese Writing System

The Chinese began developing their writing system more than 3,500 years ago. Chinese writing began with the drawing of rough, but recognizable pictures of things. Even today it is possible to guess the meaning of some of the ancient Chinese pictographs. The Chinese have developed a means of expressing ideas in writing by combining pictographs to suggest it.

日	+	月	=	明	女	+	子	=	好
JIH (sun)		YUEH (moon)		MING (bright)	NU (woman)		TZU (child)		HAO (good)

Other characters in Chinese writing are composed of a "meaning" symbol and a "sound" symbol. The meaning symbol gives a clue to the meaning, and the sound symbol suggests the pronunciation. Most of the characters in present-day Chinese writing are of this kind.

Chinese writing includes more than 50,000 characters. A great many of these are rarely used, but a knowledge of 1,000 to 1,500 characters is necessary for even elementary reading and writing. This need to memorize so many written characters resulted in widespread illiteracy among the Chinese people.

The writing system has served to unify the Chinese. The same written characters were used throughout China, even though the dialects and therefore, the pronunciation may have been different.

Some words written in Chinese:

Numbers (HI):

一	二	三	四	五	六	七	八	九	十
1	2	3	4	5	6	7	8	9	10

子	女	筆	食	行	朋	友	光	人
boy	girl	pen	eat	walk	friend	(PONG-U)	light	man

Pinyin: The New Chinese Spelling

Early in 1979, a new way of spelling Chinese words was adopted by many newspapers, magazines, and books. At the request of the Chinese government, writers began using Pinyin, which is a new way of "spelling the sounds" of Mandarin Chinese by means of the Latin alphabet. Pinyin was adopted by China in 1958, but English-speaking countries continued to use the older system of writing Chinese words, known as the Wade-Giles system.

It is very difficult to reproduce many Chinese sounds using our alphabet. In the 19th century, Thomas F. Wade, a British scholar, tried to do so. He devised a way of writing Chinese words and names using the Latin alphabet. This system was later modified by H.A. Giles and became known as Wade-Giles. For almost a century, writers everywhere used Wade-Giles as the standard way of writing Chinese words. The Chinese government changed to Pinyin in 1958 because it is supposed to be more accurate in reproducing Chinese sounds.

This change is sometimes very confusing to readers. Books and articles written before 1979 use the traditional spelling. Those written after 1979 use Pinyin. Some use both. A person accustomed to the traditional spelling often does not recognize the same word written in Pinyin, and vice versa.

In many cases, the Pinyin and Wade-Giles spellings are identical. The city of Harbin is spelled the same way in both. In other cases, Pinyin has no resemblance to the traditional spelling. Peking becomes Beijing in Pinyin and the city of Canton changes to Guangzhou. Pinyin makes frequent use of *x* and *q* and gives them sounds that can be confusing to English-speaking people. The hyphen used between two personal names disappears in Pinyin because personal names are run together. Thus Mao Tse-tung becomes Mao Zedong.

Some examples of the changes in spelling:

	Wade-Giles	Pinyin
Sounds	hsi	xi
	ch'ing	qing
	chiang	jiang
	chang	zhang
	ta	da
	pai	bai
	kang	gang
People	Mao Tse-tung	Mao Zedong
	Chiang Ch'ing	Jiang Qing
	Chou En-lai	Zhou Enlai
	Teng Hsiao-p'ing	Deng Xiaoping
	Liu Shao-ch'i	Liu Shaoqi
	Hua Kuo-feng	Hua Guofeng
	Lin Piao	Lin Biao
Cities	Peking	Beijing
	Foochow	Fuzhou
	Kiangsi	Jiangxi
	Nanking	Nanjing
	Szechuan	Sichuan
	Sian	Xian
	Tsingtao	Qingdao

Education

Education plays a very important role in a Communist nation. In China, education has had two main goals—one practical: to educate enough people to be engineers, technicians, and skilled workers to build up China; the other political: to remake society by instilling the ideas of communism in every child and adult. The Chinese discovered that education was more effective than force in changing the Chinese way of life.

In 1949, when the Communists took control of China, only about 10 to 20 percent of the people could read and write. The new government began a campaign to improve this situation. Schools were built. The difficult Chinese writing system was simplified. As a result of these changes, more than 80 percent of the Chinese children now attend school. A larger percentage of the Chinese people are now able to read than at any other time in Chinese history. Education in China has not been limited to children. Programs in adult education are carried out after working hours.

For many years China's rulers have used the educational system to indoctrinate the people in communism. Teaching people to be loyal Communists began as early as nursery school. Such plays as "The Little Truck Driver Goes to Peking to See Chairman Mao" were presented. In kindergarten, children climbing over chairs and crawling through hoops were told that this represented the hardships of Mao's Long March. A typical elementary school math problem was: "If 473 students out of 500 volunteered to go to the countryside to do farm work, what percentage volunteered?"

The basic Chinese curriculum includes math, geography, art, literature, politics, the Chinese language, and foreign languages—with English the most common foreign language. Yet in these subjects too, politics was brought into the curriculum. Every school child and adult spent hours memorizing the writings of Mao Zedong. The Chinese people were taught that capitalism was evil, that communism was superior, and that work was dignified. In addition, newspapers, motion pictures, ballet, opera, radio, and art were used as part of the process of educating the people.

In 1966, during the Cultural Revolution, the universities were closed. They did not reopen until 1969 and 1970. It was felt that university students were losing contact with the masses and developing a feeling of superiority. After 1970, universities only accepted students from the masses—workers, peasants, and soldiers. The emphasis in all course work was on communism. Many courses were purely vocational.

After 1979, much greater emphasis was placed on the study of math, science, and foreign languages in the curriculum. Emphasis was also placed on vocational subjects and many vocational schools were established. This was in keeping with the new economic reforms that were taking place. Much less time was spent on the study of communism.

The History of China: Ancient China

Early Civilization

Chinese civilization began about 4,000 years ago in a river valley in northern China. The first people were wandering hunters and fishermen. After they learned to farm (sometime before 1800 B.C.), they settled down, built homes, and worked the land. Even more important, they developed cities and government, religion and writing, coined money, and made a calendar. These early Chinese learned how to raise cattle, horses, and sheep. They learned to make pottery from clay and to shape it on a wheel. They made jewelry from shells, played music on whistles, and learned to make silk. The Chinese mined copper and tin, and mixed the two metals together to make bronze. The tools and weapons made of bronze were better shaped and sharper than stone tools, which had been used before. Since bronze was used a great deal, this period of human history is called the Bronze Age.

The Shang Dynasty

According to legend, the Xia (Hsia) was China's first ruling dynasty. Archaeologists have never discovered its location, nor have they found any objects that they can prove were made by its people. The first dynasty for which archaeologists have found actual evidence is that of the Shang (1766 B.C.–1122 B.C.). In 1929, archaeologists discovered the remains of a Bronze Age city near the present day city of Anyang, just north of the Huang He. This city was one of the capitals of the Shang Kingdom. The Shang kings seem to have been very wealthy, for they built large palaces. The people of the Shang were mainly farmers, but some were highly skilled craftspeople who made beautiful jewelry and other articles out of bronze. Shang bronzes are considered the finest the world has ever seen. The people of the Shang also left behind the oldest form of Chinese writing yet found. It was mainly carved on cattle bones and on tortoise shells ("dragon bones").

The Zhou (Chou) Dynasty

The Shang Dynasty was replaced by the Zhou (Chou) (1122 B.C.–221 B.C.), the longest lasting dynasty in Chinese history. Few of the Zhou kings were strong rulers. As a result, China was divided into small states whose rulers spent a great deal of time fighting each other. The Zhou kings ruled a feudal empire and for the first 300 years were able to control the feudal lords. As they lost power, conflicts between the states grew worse and the last 400 years of Zhou rule is known as the time of "Warring States."

Art in the Zhou Dynasty

The artists of the Zhou Dynasty continued to work in bronze and made bronze bells, mirrors and cups. On their bronzes they carved birds and animals, dragons, and other symbols. Other cultures and nations have never made better bronzes than these ancient Chinese.

Many of the Zhou buildings had curved roofs which overhung the walls. Roofs were made with tiles of various colors, mostly blue and green. The tiles of the royal palace were of yellow, the royal color. The Chinese liked bright colors and used them a great deal. The wooden beams and pillars of buildings were carved and brightened with gold, lacquer, and inlays of different kinds.

Artists of the Zhou Dynasty (as well as the Shang) also did beautiful work in jade. Zhou artists made rings, bracelets, and buckles of jade. Other jade items were made for use in temples. The government used jade for seals, medals, and badges of high office.

The Hundred Schools

The scholars of Zhou times are called the "Hundred Schools." The Zhou Dynasty is known as a time when freedom of thought existed, because scholars of the Hundred Schools discussed their ideas and argued with each other.

It was during the Zhou Dynasty that the first sections of the Great Wall of China were built. The wall was built to protect China from the people of the north, who raided Chinese land. Later emperors added to the wall until it reached a length of 2,000 miles.

Because of the many accomplishments of the Zhou Dynasty, the Chinese felt it was one of the greatest periods in their long history.

Imperial China

The Qin (Ch'in) Dynasty

The fighting and wars among the states during the Zhou period ended when one state, called Qin (Ch'in), defeated all the others. The ruler of this state took the name Shi Huangdi (Shih Huang-ti), meaning the First Emperor, and made China an empire (a large territory ruled by an emperor). Europeans get the name China from Ch'in.

Shi Huangdi did many things to unify China. He established a uniform system of coinage (money) and of weights and measures. He also ordered that the same writing system be used by all. He angered the people by forcing them to read books that only agreed with his ideas. All books which did not agree with his ideas were burned. Several hundred scholars who disagreed with the Emperor were said to have been buried alive. Some books were saved by burying them under ground and by hiding them in walls. Chinese scholars memorized others.

The Great Wall of China—a Chinese architectural wonder. Note the mountainous topography typical of North China.

The Chinese revolted against the Qin because they felt the "Mandate of Heaven" (the right to rule) had been taken away. The revolt was led by a peasant who organized the farmers into a strong army. When the revolt was successful, the Mandate of Heaven was given to the leader of the rebellion. This dynasty, which was called the Han, lasted for over 400 years, until 220 A.D. (The Qin had lasted only 15 years.)

During the over 2,100 years of Imperial China, there were only nine important dynasties and 23 minor ones. The nine important ones cover 1,800 years, whereas the weaker dynasties cover only 300 years. For most of China's history a stable government was maintained.

The Han Dynasty

The Han emperors did a great deal during their rule. They set up a system of government under which China was ruled for 2,000 years. They made the ideas of Confucius the law of the land and established civil service exams to choose government officials. They extended China's land to the west and south. Under the Han, the Chinese invented paper and porcelain. They also developed a rich trade with the far-off Roman Empire. China's first and greatest historian, Ssu-ma Ch'ien, lived during the Han period. Han rule was so great that many Chinese today call themselves "Sons of Han."

The Time of Troubles

The 400 years after the fall of the Han Dynasty was a time of great troubles. During this period, China broke up into several independent states. Life became difficult for the Chinese people, and many turned to a new religion, Buddhism, for hope and peace of mind. China became a stronghold of Buddhism after its influence in India, the country where it originated, weakened.

There were many wars among the independent states. The commanders and soldiers of the wars became great heroes to the Chinese. Their acts of bravery were told over and over again in homes and teahouses. After hundreds of years, these stories were written down in *The Romance of the Three Kingdoms*, one of China's greatest novels.

The Tang (T'ang) Dynasty

After a time, the Empire was again united by the Sui Dynasty. The Sui Dynasty ruled only for 30 years. In 618 A.D., a dynasty as powerful as the Han was set up. This was the Tang Dynasty which ruled for the next 300 years. This period is one of the greatest times in Chinese history. This greatness was caused in part by the expansion of China to the west and south. China's influence extended westward into Central Asia and southward into Southeast Asia and beyond.

The Tangs excelled in many ways. It is in art and poetry that they are most remembered. Their appreciation of beauty was the center of their artistic skill. Little remains of the paintings of the Tang Chinese—but we know that they painted scenes from nature and drew horses, flowers, and birds in fine, exact detail. But they especially liked to paint landscapes.

The Chinese did not often paint pictures of people. Sometimes people were put into landscapes. In those paintings people were very small and *insignificant* in the middle of the greatness and marvelous works of nature. These paintings were not framed. They were painted on scrolls that could be hung or rolled up and stored.

The Chinese also created a vast literature. They wrote essays, fiction, and beautiful poetry. They wrote a great deal about history, mainly about their own past.

Among the great poets of the Tang period were Li T'ai-po, Tu Fu, and Po Chü-i. It is during this period that one of China's most famous tales of love and tragedy began—the drama of the great king Hsuan Tsung and the beautiful Yang Kuei-fei.

Under the Tangs, trade and commerce grew. Gunpowder and the techniques of printing from wood blocks were invented in Tang China. One of the oldest printed books we have comes from this time. It is a Buddhist text printed in 868 A.D.

The Song (Sung) Dynasty

The Song (Sung) Dynasty, which followed soon after the Tang, made contributions in art and scholarship. Song landscape paintings are now national treasures. The Songs also developed the use of paper money in trade and commerce. During the Song period, Mongols invaded from the north and slowly took power away from the Songs.

The Yuan and Ming Dynasties

The Mongols were nomads who herded sheep. They were excellent horsemen. In 1280 A.D., the Mongol leader, Kublai Khan, became China's ruler. The Yuan Dynasty, or Mongol Dynasty, lasted for about 90 years. Marco Polo visited China during this time and wrote a book about his experiences in China. This book sparked interest in China by European traders.

The Mongols lost the Mandate of Heaven to the son of a poor worker. The new Dynasty was called Ming, and was the last dynasty in China controlled by native Chinese. It lasted about 300 years. It is most famous for its great trade with other nations and for its fine porcelain. A Ming vase has become a symbol of beauty and refinement. The Mings were great architects, and made Beijing (Peking) their capital, one of the most beautiful cities in the world. They also set up many schools and libraries for the education of the people.

The Mings, in their turn, were overthrown by invaders from the north, the Manchus.

Maritime Expeditions During the Ming Dynasty

Between 1405 and 1433 the Chinese carried out seven major maritime expeditions, the most ambitious sea voyages of the time. Chinese ships, led by the Admiral Zheng He (Cheng Ho) sailed across the Indian Ocean reaching Hormuz on the Persian Gulf and Arabia. Later the ships sailed down the eastern coast of Africa. The first fleet, which sailed between 1405 and 1407 and reached India, was made up of 62 ships and 28,000 men.

These voyages were made possible by Chinese advances in shipbuilding and in the techniques of navigation. The ships were of considerable size, larger than the ships used by European explorers almost a century later. Their crews had detailed sailing directions and used compasses. It is believed that the voyages had several purposes: (1) to trade; (2) to bring foreign countries into China's tribute system (see p. 306 for an explanation of the tribute system); and (3) to show off China's wealth and power.

However, in 1433 the voyages stopped and never resumed. No one knows why. One possible reason is that the voyages were very expensive and Ming officials considered them wasteful at a time when China was already spending a great deal of money fighting the Mongols. Another, and more important reason has to do with the values and nature of Chinese society. Despite its seapower, China was not interested in commerce or in setting up colonies overseas. China was an *agrarian* (farming) society and it was believed that Chinese civilization rested on its peasants. Merchants were held in low esteem because they did not create anything and commerce was not valued. In addition, the scholar-officials who ruled China felt that China was **self-sufficient**—that it had everything it required and did not need anything from other countries. They also believed that Chinese civilization was superior to all others. Consequently, the Chinese turned inward, placing their emphasis on self-cultivation rather than expanding their power overseas. The great commercial revolution that was sweeping over Europe did not touch China.

China and Europe: A Comparison

In the 15th century, China was wealthier and more cosmopolitan than Europe with cities of over 1 million people, which did not exist in Europe at the time. The Chinese people enjoyed a higher standard of living than the Europeans. Ming China was greater in size than all of Europe, and the volume of its commerce was greater than that of Europe. At the time that Zheng He's ships were sailing across the Indian Ocean, the Portuguese were

MARITIME EXPEDITIONS OF ZHENG HE

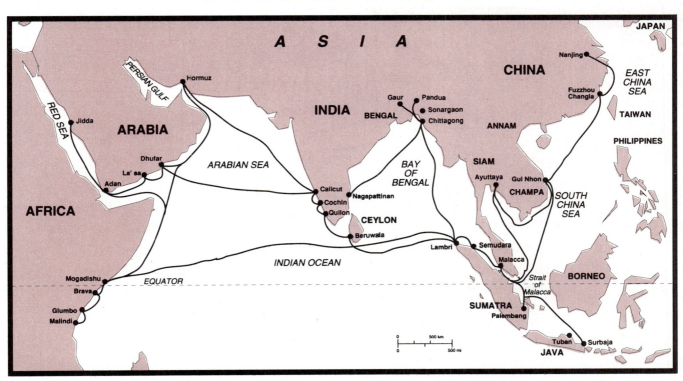

carrying out expeditions down the coast of Africa. The Chinese fleets were larger than the Portuguese and sailed farther. In the technical skills of navigation, the Portuguese and Chinese were equal.

Yet within a century, the Portuguese navigator Vasco da Gama reached India and soon after Portuguese merchants and missionaries arrived in China. Portugal became rich and powerful from its Asian trade. Enormous changes were taking place in Europe which placed great emphasis on commerce and navigation. These would lead to Columbus discovering the New World and Spain gaining a huge empire in the Americas. French and English explorers and sea captains would follow, bringing great wealth to their countries and laying the foundations of empires for Britain and France.

China, unlike Portugal and the other European nations, had no real interest in navigation, in foreign trade, or in expanding its power overseas by conquering other lands. This was the marked contrast between China and Europe of the 15th century. While China was turning inward, the Europeans were expanding overseas. Ming China had no understanding of the possibilities of seapower and failed to become a maritime power. In time, the eastern seas and even the Chinese coast came to be dominated by the seafaring Europeans—the Portuguese, Spanish, Dutch, and finally the British and the Americans. This domination later contributed to the breakup of the Chinese Empire.

THE ANCIENT PROCESS OF PAPERMAKING

Processes in papermaking as shown in drawings from the Tiangong Kaiwu, a comprehensive encyclopedia on traditional technology written by Song Xingchu and first published in 1637.

Cutting bamboo and washing it in a pond.

Boiling pulp.

Straining the pulpy solution through a fine screen.

China's Contributions to World Civilization: Achievements in Science and Technology

China has contributed a great deal to the world in both science and art. A British scientist has written that China's technological discoveries and inventions were "far in advance of contemporary Europe, especially up to the 15th century."

Paper

According to tradition, paper was first made by Cai Lun, a Chinese government inspector, and presented to the Emperor He Di in 105 A.D. Tree bark, pieces of hemp, linen rags, and fish nets were boiled and then pounded into a loose pulp. After water and plant gums were added, the solution was strained through a fine screen on which the pulp dried to become sheets of paper. The sheets were then dried on a heated wall. Papermaking flourished in China during the Tang and Song dynasties. A great variety of paper for different purposes was made.

Although Cai Lun is usually credited as the first papermaker, recent excavations have discovered even earlier examples of paper. The earliest dates back to the period 140–87 B.C.

At the beginning of the 3rd century, Chinese paper was introduced to Korea and Vietnam and from Korea to Japan. By the end of the 7th century the technique of papermaking reached the region that now includes India, Nepal, Pakistan, and Bangladesh. In the

Pressing it dry to form a sheet of paper.

Drying the sheets on a heated wall.

12th century, Spain learned papermaking from the Arabs, and in 1150, Europe's first paper mill was built in Spain. From Spain the technique spread to France, Italy, and other European countries. In 1575, papermaking reached Mexico, the first place in the Americas.

Printing and Paper Money

Before the invention of printing, books and documents were handwritten. The technique of printing with carved wood blocks appeared about the 7th century, early in the Tang Dynasty. This technique was used for copying manuscripts and illustrations. Block printing reached its golden age during the Song Dynasty when the imperial government encouraged the publication of large numbers of books.

Movable type was invented between the years 1041 and 1048. The method was based on the same principles of typesetting used today. Movable metal type printing began in China in the 13th century. Printing techniques invented in China spread to Japan and Korea and later westward to Persia. Their influence was felt in Egypt and Europe.

The first paper money used in the world was printed in China early in the 11th century. The plates used to print the money were made of copper. They were engraved with intricate designs to discourage counterfeiting.

Gunpowder

The discovery of gunpowder in China resulted from experiments to produce longevity (long life) pills. As early as the period of the Warring States (475–221 B.C.), alchemists were brought to the imperial court to prepare drugs that would ensure immortality. The experiments did not produce the desired results, but many important discoveries were made.

During the 8th century, alchemists discovered that combining sulphur, saltpeter, and charcoal produced an explosive mixture. This was gunpowder, or *huoyao* (fire medicine) as the Chinese still call it, because its three ingredients were used separately as medicines.

Firearms

It is not known exactly when gunpowder began to be used for military purposes. Some historians believe this dates back to the late Tang Dynasty. A military encyclopedia written sometime between 1010 and 1063 described in detail the making and use of gunpowder. In the year 1000, rockets and fireballs were used. Arrows bearing gunpowder near the tip were also in use at that time. True rockets were used in battle for the first time by Kublai Khan, the first emperor of the Yuan Dynasty, in military expeditions against Japan in 1274 and 1281. The first gun to discharge arrows fired by gunpowder also appeared during the Yuan Dynasty. In 1332, the world's first bronze cannon was made. Powder-propelled firecrackers were invented between 1127 and 1194 during the Song Dynasty and led to festival fireworks.

The use of gunpowder and firearms spread to Europe along the trade routes and the westward march of the Mongol armies, arriving in Europe in the 13th century.

The Compass

Lodestone, which has magnetic north-south pointing properties, is believed to have been used for direction-finding in the 3rd century B.C. or even earlier. The earliest written

A copy of the world's first compass.

reference comes from the 3rd century B.C.: "When the people of the State of Zheng go out in search of jade, they carry a south-pointer with them so as not to lose their way in the mountains." The world's first compass, the "south-governor" was made in China during the Qin (Ch'in) Dynasty. A piece of lodestone carved in the shape of a ladle was balanced on a round bronze plate. This was set within a square plate and engraved with directional points. When the ladle was spun, it always came to rest with its handle pointing to the south. During the 11th century, advances in technology led to the use of magnetic iron needles and the creation of very sensitive instruments.

The invention of the compass had an enormous impact on navigation. Sailors established ocean routes, which they called "needle routes." By the 13th century, China was trading with many countries in Asia and Africa.

Silk

The raising of silkworms and the production of silk is one of China's great contributions to the world. Silk comes from the cocoons that silkworms spin around their bodies after they have eaten the leaves of the mulberry tree. By means of a very difficult process, the tiny threads are removed from the cocoons and spun into silk thread. The thread is then woven into silk cloth.

Silk was woven in China more than 4,000 years ago. We have evidence for this from excavations made by archaeologists in recent years. Silk was highly valued and it was often placed in people's tombs after they died. Some of these ancient silks are being discovered now. In many places, farmers had to pay taxes in the form of silk.

For many centuries silk was the chief item in China's foreign trade. Beginning in the 1st century B.C., silk was carried over the Old Silk Road, which started in Xi'an in Central

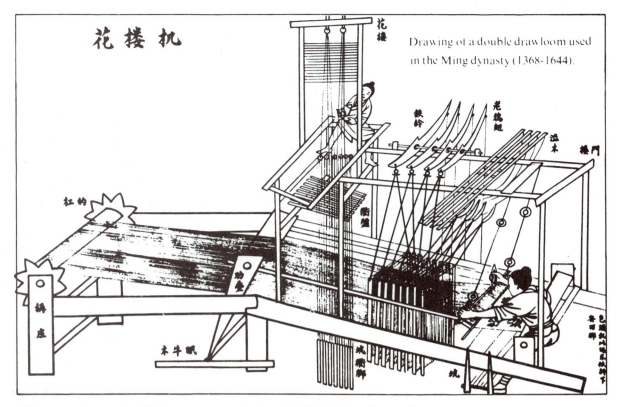

花楼机

Drawing of a double drawloom used in the Ming dynasty (1368-1644).

Weaving brocade: Of the many varieties of silk fabrics, brocade woven in raised patterns with gold and silver thread was considered the most beautiful. The invention of the double drawloom seen in this picture made it possible to weave brocade with the most elaborate patterns.

Old Silk Road

There was a great demand for Chinese silk in the Roman Empire. So much silk was exported from China to the West that it contributed to a harmful drain of gold and silver from Rome. The route by which the silk was transported is known as the Old Silk Road. This was the same route taken centuries later by Italian merchants. Marco Polo and his father and uncle traveled to China over this road.

China and continued for 7,000 kilometers to the Mediterranean. Merchants from Europe and the Middle East traveled to China to obtain silk and other precious goods. In early modern times, these voyages were to change the course of world history.

Ceramics: Pottery and Porcelain

Pottery was made and used in China as early as 7,000 or 8,000 years ago. Throwing pottery on a wheel gradually replaced the earlier method of building it up by hand. About 3,000 years ago, during the Shang Dynasty, it was discovered that coating the surface of the clay with a glaze prior to firing would give it a smooth and brilliant finish. During the Zhou, Chin, and Han Dynasties, glazes appeared in more colors. Pottery was no longer used only for making household utensils, but to create works of art.

Porcelain is generally finer and more translucent than other kinds of pottery. It was first made in China during the Tang Dynasty and reached a high degree of perfection during the Yuan Dynasty. The word *porcelain* is derived from "*porcellana*," used by Marco Polo to describe the pottery he saw in China. Chinese porcelain was of such high quality that it was described as having "the brightness of a mirror, the thinness of paper, and the resonance of a chime-stone." It was highly valued in other countries and was exported overland via the Old Silk Road or by sea to be sold in countries of Asia, Africa, and Europe. European potters tried to imitate this translucent porcelain for centuries, but it was only in 1575 that the first porcelain was made in Europe—in Florence, Italy.

Manchu China—The Qing (Ch'ing) Dynasty

In the 17th century, peasants began to rebel against the Mings. In 1644, the rebels entered Beijing and the Mings fled southward. The Ming commander of the Great Wall defenses united his forces with nomads from the Manchurian plains, the Manchus.

The Chinese have a saying, "Never call in a tiger to chase out a dog." By allowing the Manchus into China, the Chinese commander had not followed these wise words. The Manchus, once allowed in, refused to leave. The Manchus took over the Empire and set up a new dynasty, the Qing (Ch'ing).

The Manchus, or Qings, were few in number, but ruled China for almost three centuries. They respected and encouraged the development of Chinese culture. They permitted the Chinese to take part in ruling the government and rarely interfered in village affairs. The villagers themselves handled most of the problems of government.

During the Manchu Dynasty, the population of China grew. The Manchus provided good government, kept law and order, and operated public works well (irrigation canals, roads, bridges). They introduced new crops, such as kaoliang (a cereal), potatoes, corn and peanuts, and more land was used for farming. These efforts increased the food supply. But, as usable farm land become scarce and population grew, and the government began to neglect law and order and public works, peasant rebellions began to break out.

The Manchus had succeeded in extending the power of the Chinese Empire throughout East, Central, and Southeast Asia. The Manchus increased trade with the West. However, Europeans found it difficult to carry on trade with China, since the Chinese had many restrictions. European merchants could only trade in the city of Guangzhou (Canton) in South China.

Chinese silks and porcelain found good markets in Europe. The Chinese also exported brocades (silk textiles), sugar, ginger, and tea. The Chinese, however, were not interested in European goods. Western textiles were too expensive and not as good in quality. To trade with China, Europeans had to ship large amounts of silver to buy Chinese goods.

China's Relations With Foreigners: The Tribute System

Since ancient times China's relations with foreigners were based on the tribute system. Tribute is money paid regularly by one ruler or nation to another as an acknowledgment of an inferior-superior relationship between the two. The tribute system developed from Confucian doctrine. According to these ideas, Chinese civilization was superior to all others and those people who lived outside of China were considered barbarians. Therefore, it was only natural that the foreign barbarians should acknowledge the superiority of Chinese civilization by presenting tribute to the Emperor and *kowtowing* (kneeling) before him. The kowtow was intended to show great respect and obedience. It was a series of three long kneelings, each one involving three long prostrations, nose and forehead upon the floor. Kowtowing was an important part of Chinese tradition. The Emperor kowtowed to Heaven and to his parents; the highest officials kowtowed to the Emperor. Foreigners were expected to do the same.

All foreign nations that had relations with China were required to send regular tribute missions (official representatives bringing tribute) to Peking (now Beijing). There were very specific rules covering every aspect of these missions. Also, when foreign merchants came to China seeking trade, their ruler had to send tribute to the Emperor. Without tribute there could be no trade. When the first European merchants arrived in China they were immediately put on the tribute lists. All the formalities of the tribute system were required of them, including the kowtow. The Europeans, with the Western ideas of equality, regarded the tribute system as highly offensive. As time passed, the European governments began to pressure the Chinese to do away with it.

The Opium Problem

Since ancient times, **opium**, a drug which is made from the seed pod of poppy plants, had been used by the Chinese in making medicine. However, in the 17th century the Chinese people began using opium as a narcotic. "Smoking" opium brought temporary relief from pain and misery, but it was also habit-forming. People became slaves to their habit and their lives were destroyed. Most of the opium used by the Chinese was grown in India and brought to China by British and Indian traders.

The British Opium Trade

During the 18th and 19th centuries, the smoking of opium in China increased and the opium trade grew. In the late 1700s, about 1,000 chests of opium were shipped from India to China each year. (A chest usually contained 133 pounds of opium.) From 1800 to 1821, an average of 4,500 chests were imported annually. In 1838, 40,000 chests of opium were imported. This great increase in the opium trade was due to several factors. In the 19th century, China was experiencing many economic and social problems. A large increase in population resulted in a decline in the standard of living for most people. Corruption, lawlessness, and discontent were widespread. This atmosphere was conducive to drug smuggling and drug use. Another reason was that the opium trade brought enormous profits to everyone involved: the foreign merchants, the Chinese traders, and Chinese government officials. The British government in India had become dependent on the opium trade, receiving 5 to 10 percent of its revenue (income) from it.

Chinese Efforts to Wipe Out the Opium Trade

The Chinese government tried to stop the opium trade but was not successful. The selling and smoking of opium were prohibited by imperial edict (by order of the Emperor) in 1729 Its importation and domestic production were prohibited in 1796. However, government officials accepted bribes from the opium smugglers and the trade continued. Opium addiction grew; smuggling and official corruption increased.

Finally in the 1830s, with millions of Chinese addicted and faced with an economic crisis, the Chinese government acted to wipe out the opium trade. China's silver supply was being drained by the trade. This outflow of silver upset the currency system and brought hardship to many. The government concluded that most of the silver was going to British India to pay for the opium. During 1837 to 1838, the government tried to suppress the opium trade at Canton (now Guangzhou). But smuggling continued along the coast and opium imports increased. In 1839, the Emperor ordered that anyone involved with the opium evil—cultivators, distributors, consumers, and foreign importers—would be subject to the death penalty.

In 1839, the Emperor appointed Lin Zexu (Lin Tse-hsu) commissioner and sent him to Guangzhou to wipe out the opium evil. Lin demanded that the foreigners surrender their opium stocks. When they refused, he detained the foreign community in Guangzhou releasing them six weeks later after they had agreed to give up their opium stocks. He then publicly burned the opium.

The Opium War 1839–1842

War between Britain and China broke out in 1839. China's attempts to suppress the opium trade and the detention of British subjects gave Britain an excuse to go to war. But other, more important, reasons had been building up over many years. At the same time that China was acting to end the opium trade, Great Britain was engaged in a struggle to gain trading privileges from the Chinese. Britain also demanded that relations between the two nations be carried out on the basis of equality and not according to the tribute system. The refusal of the Chinese to accept the Western ideas of unrestricted trade angered the British and other Western nations. The Westerners felt the tribute system was insulting and believed that relations between nations had to be based on equality.

The Opium War which began in November 1839 and lasted until August 1842 ended in a humiliating defeat for the Chinese. This was due to Britain's military superiority on land and at sea. China's armed forces were technologically backward and no match for the British.

The Treaty of Nanjing (Nanking)—1842

The Treaty of Nanjing (Nanking) between England and China was the first in a series of treaties which opened China to the Western world. They were called the "unequal treaties" by the Chinese because of the one-sided privileges they gave to the Europeans. China, in a helpless position, was forced against its will, to accept what it had so long resisted. The Treaty of Nanjing provided for the opening of five Chinese ports to British traders to "reside and to carry on trade." It ended the old Chinese system of controlled trade. The British were now free to trade with anyone they wished instead of only with licensed Chinese merchants. It also forced China to pay an **indemnity** to Britain (money to pay for the confiscated opium and to reimburse Britain for the cost of the war) and the island of Hong Kong was given to Britain. Britain took away from China its freedom to regulate its own **tariff** (a tax on imports). Britain was to be treated as an equal, not as a tributory state.

In a supplementary treaty signed in 1843, Britain introduced the "most favored nation" clause. This stated that any privileges which China might grant to other nations in the future would automatically apply to Britain. After this, all treaties between the Western nations and China contained this clause. The Treaty of Nanjing did not mention the opium trade, which continued until the end of the 1900s.

In 1844, the United States signed a treaty with China that gave Americans the same rights as those gained by the British. The treaty also provided that if American citizens committed a crime in China, they would be tried and punished only by officials of the U.S. government according to the laws of the United States. This practice was called **extraterritoriality**.

The privilege of extraterritoriality was immediately granted to the British and French. The Chinese did not realize that by giving the Western nations this privilege China was giving up its right to control the foreigners living and doing business in China.

War With Britain and France: 1857–1860

The British expected that the Treaty of Nanjing would greatly increase their trade with China, but this did not happen. British merchants complained that the reason trade had not developed the way they had hoped was that there were still too many obstacles to trade. They argued that there were not enough open ports and said that as long as they were not allowed to go into the interior of China, trade would remain low. British and other merchants put pressure on their own governments to gain more trading privileges from the Chinese.

At Guangzhou, Chinese officials ignored the treaties and put many obstacles in the way of the foreigners. The Chinese tried to continue the practices that had existed before the treaties.

The British, French, and U.S. governments wanted to revise the treaties in order to remove all the remaining obstacles to trade and diplomatic relations. The Chinese government naturally resisted. Two incidents occurred which gave Britain and France excuses to force the issue by going to war. In the first incident, Chinese officials boarded a ship flying the British flag whose registration had expired and removed some members of the crew. The dispute over their return caused British troops to occupy Guangzhou in 1857, but the incident was soon settled. However, Britain then decided to settle the issue of treaty revision by force and sent naval and military forces to Tianjin (Tientsin). In the second incident, a French missionary was executed by Chinese officials for traveling in the interior, which was forbidden by the treaties. To punish China, French forces joined the British in the fighting at Guangzhou and Tianjin.

The United States refused to cooperate with the British and French in going to war. The United States wanted to play the role of China's defender. At the same time, the United States agreed with Britain and France in demanding that the treaties be revised to remove all obstacles to trade.

In 1858, the Treaties of Tianjin were concluded between China and Britain, France, the United States, and Russia. They provided for the opening of 11 new treaty ports. The

Chang River, China's most important river for trade, was opened to foreign commerce. Foreigners also gained the right to travel inside China. China's tariff was set by the Europeans at 5 percent and could not be changed without their permission. The importation of opium was legalized. Foreign missionaries were allowed to travel and carry on their activities all over China. The diplomatic representatives of the four nations were allowed to live in the capital Beijing. This last privilege would have ended the ancient tradition of China's superiority. Therefore, the Manchu government became determined not to grant it, even though it had accepted it earlier.

When British and French negotiators arrived at Tianjin in 1859 on the way to Beijing to ratify the treaties, the Chinese tried to prevent their passage. Fighting broke out and in 1860 the British and French defeated the much larger Chinese forces and then occupied Beijing. In 1860 at Beijing, the Chinese government was forced to ratify the Treaties of Tianjin. They had to sign additional agreements in the Treaties of Beijing (Peking) giving the Europeans more privileges.

Effects of the Unequal Treaties

The treaties of Nanjing, Tianjin, and Beijing took away from the Chinese government control over its own economy and its own affairs. Foreign merchants were now free to travel and do business all over China. Missionaries were able to travel into the interior and teach the Christian religion. The privilege of extraterritoriality meant that the foreigners would not be subject to Chinese laws. Foreign communities sprang up in newly built sections in all the treaty ports. They were governed by their own officials according to the laws of their own country. Foreign troops and gunboats were stationed at the treaty ports to back up the demands of their own citizens. Foreign goods could now be distributed all over China. The 5 percent tariff was so low that foreign goods were cheaper than Chinese goods. The treaties were a great blow to the Manchu Dynasty and undermined the traditional order.

By the middle of the 19th century, China was carved up into **spheres of influence**. These were areas where foreign nations exercised control and had special economic and political privileges. Britain, France, Russia, Germany, and Japan each had a sphere of influence in China.

Because of the unequal treaties in the years after 1860, China was not really an independent nation. It was not until the end of World War II that China regained its full **sovereignty** (control over its country's affairs). The treaties imposed on China by the Western nations became a symbol of national humiliation. Twentieth century Chinese leaders regarded the Opium War and treaties as examples of Western imperialism.

The Fall of the Manchus

Population Growth   As China entered the 19th century, powerful forces were being set in motion which were to shatter the old order and destroy the glory of the Manchu Empire. As you read, China's population had grown without an equal increase in agricultural production. The official estimates showed a population increase from 142 million in 1741 to 432 million in 1851. However, land used for farming was about eight million *ching* (about fifteen acres) in 1701, but was not more than ten million *ching* in 1850. This had never happened before in Chinese history.

SPHERES OF INFLUENCE IN CHINA

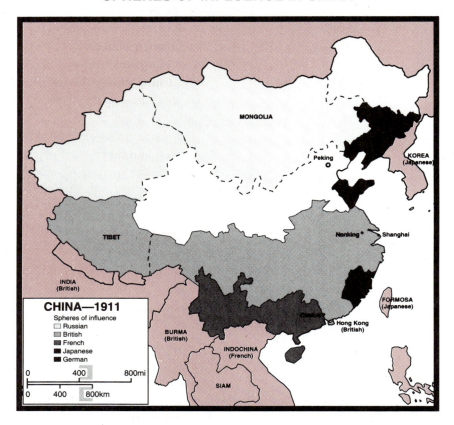

CHINA—1911
Spheres of influence
☐ Russian
▨ British
▦ French
■ Japanese
▩ German

Peasant Revolts

At the same time, the Manchus were faced with the same type of opposition that dynasties had faced many times before in Chinese history. The peasants who were unhappy and did not trust the Manchus as rulers felt that the Manchus had lost the Mandate of Heaven. A series of peasant revolts broke out in northern and western China. From 1850 to 1865, the worst of these revolts, the Taiping Rebellion, almost succeeded in toppling the Qing Dynasty. Many peasants joined the rebellion because its leaders promised land, equality, and brotherhood. The Manchus were not able to defeat the rebels and they asked the Europeans for soldiers and money. With this help, and after much fighting, the Manchus crushed the Taipings.

European Imperialism

Another powerful force that tore apart the Manchu Empire was Western **imperialism**. Imperialism takes place when a strong country uses a weaker, less developed country to its own advantage. China's troubles in the 19th century made it easier for European imperialism to succeed.

Japanese Imperialism

The Japanese also decided to take advantage of China's weakness. Japan's victory in the first *Sino* (China)-Japanese War was a disaster for China and the Manchus. The great weaknesses of China were obvious, and encouraged the Western powers and Japan to press for even more rights and privileges in China.

In the late 19th century, the Chinese Empire was ruled by a boy whose aunt, the Dowager Empress Cixi, controlled the government. She allowed some reforms to be made. However, her main interest was to keep the Manchu Dynasty and her own power intact. She used the Chinese resentment of the West to try to get rid of the Westerners and the Japanese. In 1900, a group called the Boxers attacked the foreigners, but were defeated.

By the opening of the 20th century, it seemed that China was to be divided by the Western powers and Japan. The United States wished to protect its own trading interests in China. Therefore, the United States asked other nations to stop looking for special privileges in China and to respect China's independence. The American government proposed equality and an "open door" for China's trade and privileges. However, no one paid attention to this plea.

Weak from rebellions and wars, the Manchus were doomed. They could not fight the West, they could not keep order, and they could not reform China. Therefore, they had to be overthrown, for they had obviously lost the Mandate of Heaven.

The Chinese Republic (1911–1949)

A revolution happens when important changes are brought about in the form of the government, the economy, or the society of a country. Revolutions can be peaceful or violent. The causes of a revolution may develop over many decades, but the revolution itself usually occurs in a short period of time. This was true in the American and Russian Revolutions.

The years of preparation for revolution in China took many decades. The revolution itself has lasted for over 80 years, and still seems to be going on. It is interesting to note that in the past, when the Chinese revolted against their rulers, the revolutions also lasted for long periods of time and went through many stages.

The Ideas of Dr. Sun Yat-sen

The Chinese Revolution started when a bomb exploded in the city of Wuchang, in Central China, on October 10, 1911. A republic was set up in Nanjing with Sun Yat-sen as its first President. Dr. Sun is known as "the Father of the Chinese Revolution." He was a thinker and a planner. He was trusted by the people, and he had trust in the people's ability to run the government. For years he spread the idea that the Chinese people should have a government "of the people, by the people, and for the people." He spoke all over China, and wrote about his ideas, which he called *Three Principles of the People,* in Chinese, San Min Chu-I (Sahn min jooee).

The three principles were **nationalism**, **democracy**, and **livelihood**. Nationalism meant love and sacrifice for China; democracy meant government of the people; and livelihood meant economic equality, for all the Chinese people would share in the wealth of China equally.

These ideas were difficult to put into practice. Dr. Sun gave the Presidency to Yuan Shih-kai, the general who helped the revolutionaries overthrow the Manchus. However, he betrayed the ideas of San Min Chu-I, became a military dictator, and drove Sun out of the country. Yuan was not powerful enough to rule the whole country. Consequently, generals and leaders of bands of soldiers became independent rulers in their own provinces. They were given unlimited power and were known as warlords. The warlords cared little for

China, and fought each other for power. China became badly divided, civil war broke out, and the central government broke down.

Dr. Sun returned to China in 1916 after Yuan's death and formed his Kuomintang (KMT), the Nationalist Party, to work for the unity of the country under the Three Principles. The KMT received important help from Soviet Russia. The Russians sent an advisor to aid Sun. He helped to organize the KMT and form it into a powerful revolutionary party. The Russians also helped the Nationalists set up a military academy where officers devoted to the ideals of the Chinese Revolution were trained for a new revolutionary army. In 1923, Dr. Sun brought the Chinese Communist Party (CCP), which had been set up in 1921, into the KMT.

Dr. Sun died before his ideas were fulfilled. His spirit and dream lived on. He soon became the symbol of the Chinese Nationalist Revolution and of the Communist National Revolution.

Chiang Kai-shek Rules China

After Dr. Sun's death, there was a power struggle. Chiang Kai-shek, the president of the military academy and an important leader of the KMT, took over the leadership of the Nationalist Party.

In 1926, Chiang led the new KMT army in a military expedition against the warlords in the north and united much of China. He interrupted this expedition in 1927 and turned on the Communists because he did not trust them. Fearing they would seize power, he expelled them from the KMT. The main communist centers in Hankow (now Hangzhou) and Shanghai were attacked and many communist leaders were killed or forced into hiding. Mao Zedong, a young communist leader, escaped. He and his followers went into hiding in the hills of southeastern China where they set up their own government and built an army. Chiang then returned to his conquest of the warlords. When Beijing was conquered by Chiang, the second revolution had occurred, and the Second Republic was set up. Chiang renamed Peking, *Peiping*, which means "northern peace." He also moved the capital to Nanking (now Nanjing) in the Chang Valley because of its central location. Chiang made himself leader with unlimited powers. (When the Communists came to power in 1949 they returned the traditional name of Peking, meaning "northern capital," and made the city their capital.)

Chiang faced a number of problems. The warlords still controlled a large part of China. The Communists, although greatly weakened, still blocked national unity. Finally, the Japanese continued to cause problems for the Chinese.

Japan Invades China

In 1931, the Japanese invaded Manchuria. This was a deadly blow to Chiang's government. Japan took Manchuria and made it an industrial and military base. Chiang's difficulties with Japan gave the Chinese Communists a chance to recover their strength.

After repeated attacks by Nationalist forces in 1934, the Communists, led by Mao, fled to Yenan, in Shaanxi (Shensi) Province near the Yellow River. This retreat known as the Long March covered over 5,000 miles. Of 130,000 people who started out, fewer than 25,000 survived. In the caves of this northwest province, the Communists were safe from Chiang's army and closer to the Russian border. The Russians sent some aid to the Chinese Communists, but not very much. Here, the Communists formed a peasant army, and trained it in guerrilla warfare.

In 1937, the Japanese again invaded China and quickly gained control of the eastern coastal areas. Hundreds of thousands of Chinese fled westward. Chiang and the other members of the government fled to Chongqing (Chungking), in southwest China near the Chang River, where a new capital was set up. Both the Nationalists and Communists refused to fight each other while the Japanese took over China. Chiang and the Communists agreed to join forces to fight the Japanese. Mao's soldiers were successful in using guerrilla tactics against the Japanese.

During the eight years of war, Chiang's Nationalists were severely battered. Not only was the country exhausted, but the morale of the people was low. Help from the United States allowed Chiang to survive the war, but not to solve the many economic and social problems.

Civil War and the Success of the Communist Revolution

When the Japanese surrendered in 1945, the Communists were not yet strong enough to take over all of China. They agreed to work together with the Nationalists to rebuild China.

The United States was very anxious to bring peace to China. In December 1945, President Truman sent General George Marshall to visit China and to try to set up a lasting peace. Unfortunately, Marshall was not successful. As a result, the United States decided to help the Nationalists. Between 1945 and 1948, the United States poured more than $2 billion worth of arms into China. This was in addition to the $1.5 billion loaned to the Chinese during the war.

Full scale civil war between the Nationalists and the Communists broke out in 1947. In 1949, the Communists won a smashing victory over the Nationalists and set up a Communist government to rule all of mainland China. They have been in power ever since. Chiang Kai-shek fled from China to the island of Formosa (Taiwan).

Reasons for the Communist Victory

Why did the Communists win? In 1945, Communist forces numbered only about 1 million, while the Nationalists had over 3 million. The money which the United States sent to China went to the Nationalists. How could they lose? There are many reasons for the Communist victory:

1. The Nationalist government of Chiang Kai-shek failed to use its power well. Many officials in his government were corrupt. They were more interested in becoming rich than in doing anything for the Chinese people. The Chinese people were poor and tired of war. All they wanted was a little land to farm and a chance to live in peace. Chiang did not pay any attention to what the people wanted. As a result, the people were unhappy and did not have confidence in the government of Chiang.

2. The Communists lived for many years under very difficult conditions. Many of the Communists had been killed by Chiang. For years they lived in caves in Yenan, where they were protected from attacks. During this time, they built up their strength and discipline so they would be ready for the final battles when they came. They became tough and fearless, and ready to die for what they believed in.

3. The Communists had many good generals. In 1948, the Communists won one battle after another. Nanjing (Nanking), Hangzhou (Hankow), Shanghai, Guangzhou

(Canton), and Chongqing (Chungking) fell into their hands. In many places thousands of Nationalist soldiers surrendered without firing a shot, or deserted to the Communists.

4. Another important reason that the Communists were successful was their policy toward the Chinese peasants. In October 1947, the Communists called on the Chinese people to get rid of the Chiang government and build a new China. At the same time, they carried out a land reform, which Chiang had promised for many years, but had never done. In the land reform, the Communists took land away from the rich landlords and gave it to the poor peasants. It was for this reason that the peasants supported the Communists.

5. In addition, the Communists received aid from the Soviet Union. At the end of the war in 1945, the Russians turned over large amounts of captured Japanese arms to the Communists. The Russians also helped the Communists take over Manchuria. With its industry and natural resources Manchuria became a base for the Communists.

In 1949, Chiang Kai-shek fled from China to the island of Formosa (Taiwan). With complete control of the mainland, the Communists took control of the government.

Mao Zedong and the People's Republic of China (1949–1976)

When the Communists led by Mao Zedong, came to power in 1949, they officially named their country "The People's Republic of China." The years after 1949 were a time of great change in China. The Communist Party set out to create a new society and to modernize the country. They tried to remake society by remaking the people. By means of government-sponsored campaigns and movements, they involved the whole population in these tasks.

The Importance of One Man—Mao Zedong

During this period of great change, the Communist Party and the nation were influenced by one man—Mao Zedong. Mao wanted to transform Chinese society and destroy much of what had gone before. Mao's early experiences had made a lasting impression on his personality. Much of what happened in China reflected the tastes and beliefs of this man.

Mao was born into a peasant family, and he never got over his peasant origins. His tastes remained simple all of his life. He never used his position of power to live a life of luxury or comfort. Mao had great concern for the common peasant and great faith that the will of the masses could conquer all. He shared the peasants' ancient hatred of the landlord class and distrusted the educated elite. He also disliked city life. His ideal was the self-sufficient man of the soil—farmer, craftsman, militia soldier all in one.

Mao was more interested in achieving social equality than in achieving practical results. His great concern was that a new ruling class would rise in China—either a new class of rich peasants or a new class of educated professionals, or even a class of privileged party members. Mao's method to prevent this was "continuing struggle" and "continuing revolution." Periodically in vast campaigns affecting the whole country, people in important positions were removed from power and sent to the countryside to be in touch with the masses.

Former Chairman Mao Zedong

Former Premier Zhou Enlai

Quotations from Mao Zedong

Mao's quotations have been read by millions of Chinese, in the so-called *Little Red Book*. The *Little Red Book* is also the handbook for revolutionaries and guerrilla movements throughout the world. Below is a selection of Mao's ideas from the book:

On Power: "Political power grows out of the barrel of a gun."

On Victory: "Just because we have won a victory, we must never relax our vigilance (watchfulness) against the mad plots for revenge by the imperialists and their running dogs."

On Revolution: "A revolution is not a dinner party, or painting a picture; it cannot be leisurely, gentle, kind, courteous, and restrained. A revolution is an insurrection by which one class overthrows another."

On Ignorance: "It is to the advantage of despots (rulers with unlimited power) to keep people ignorant; it is to our advantage to make them intelligent. We must lead all of them gradually from ignorance."

On Youth: "The world is yours as well as ours. China's future belongs to you. You young people, full of vigor and vitality, are in the bloom of life. Our hope is placed in you."

On Women: "Enable every woman who can work to take her place on the labor front, under the principle of equal pay for equal work. Genuine equality between the sexes can only be realized in the process of changing society as a whole."

On Guerrilla Warfare: "The enemy advances, we retreat
The enemy camps, we harass
The enemy tires, we attack
The enemy retreats, we pursue."

Mao, like most Chinese peasants, had a deep distrust of foreigners. This greatly affected China's relations with other countries.

Mao became a godlike figure in China. His posters and statues were everywhere. "Mao thought" became an important part of the curriculum in schools. This later came to be known as the "cult of personality"—treating Mao and his ideas as a religion.

Setting Up a New Government

The Communists established their new government at Beijing in September 1949. Mao Zedong, as chairman of the Communist Party and chief of state, became China's top ruler. Zhou Enlai (Chou En-lai) was named prime minister and foreign minister. Zhou had been an early member of the Communist Party and Mao's right-hand man since 1931. He had great diplomatic skill, which would serve him well as foreign minister. Zhou remained the second most important leader in China until his death in 1976. The two other top leaders were General Zhu De (Chu Teh), who helped bring Mao to power, and Liu Shaoqi (Liu Shao-ch'i).

At first, the Communists needed the broadest possible support. They also needed the skills and ability of the upper class and the intellectuals. Therefore, many prominent positions were given to non-Communists and many local officials were left in office. This, however, was only temporary.

Power in the People's Republic is divided between the Communist Party (CCP), the government and the army, but real power is in the hands of the top leadership of the party. These top leaders form a small group known as the Politburo. Several of these people belong to an even smaller group, the Standing Committee. It is in the Standing Committee and the Politburo that all important decisions are made. The government agencies simply carry out the decisions made by the party.

Economic Recovery

One of the first tasks the Communists had to deal with was the terrible destruction resulting from years of war. The transportation and communication systems were badly destroyed. Production in agriculture and industry was down. Inflation was high. It was necessary to restore the economy and raise production to pre-war levels. The Communists were able to accomplish most of this in the first three years. By the middle of 1950, inflation was brought under control. By 1952, railway tracks had been rebuilt and even expanded and highways reopened. Agricultural production improved, and there was an increase in the production of steel.

During this period the state took control of most of the economy—banking, most heavy industry, railways, and foreign trade. Private enterprise still continued, but it was brought increasingly under state control.

The Social Revolution

The Communists soon turned their attention to remaking Chinese society. Their goals were to destroy the old ruling classes—the landlords, capitalists, and the educated elite; to change the values of the Chinese people and turn them into loyal Communists, and to pave the way for a socialist economy. Various means were employed to achieve these goals.

The Agrarian Reform Act of 1950

This law proclaimed under the slogan "Land to the Tillers" set the maximum amount of land that it was legal to own. Land was taken away from the rich landlords and distributed to the peasants. It soon became evident that the Communists were determined to destroy the landlords as a class. A period of "class struggle" began in 1951 during which peasants denounced the landlords. The landlords lost their property and in many cases their lives. When it was over the landlord-gentry had been wiped out—either in person or in status. The new people in authority in the villages were those committed to the Communist *regime*.

The Marriage Law of 1950

This law, which is discussed in greater detail on page 287, provided for the emancipation of Chinese women. At the same time it was a death blow to the old family system. The ancient Chinese virtue of filial piety (respect and obedience for parents) was done away with. A person's primary loyalty was to the state, not the family.

Counter-revolutionary Suppression Campaign

This campaign, started in 1951, was aimed at all "war criminals, traitors, bureaucratic capitalists, and counter-revolutionaries." The campaign called for patriotic spying on relatives and neighbors and public denunciations. Since "traitor" or "counter-revolutionary" was never defined, anyone who stood in the way of the regime could be denounced. Mass public trials were held to whip up hatred against the "enemies" and to promote loyalty to the regime. The number of people executed was in the hundreds of thousands; some estimate it was in the millions. Thousands were sent to forced labor camps. At the same time, there was an intense propaganda campaign against "American imperialism." Foreign missionaries were denounced as spies and were jailed or expelled.

The Five Anti-Movement

This campaign lasted from 1951 to 1952 and was directed against "tax evasion, bribery, cheating on government contracts, theft of economic intelligence, and stealing of national property." In reality it was directed against the businesspeople of the cities who were described as exploiters and enemies of the working class. Thousands of businesspeople were imprisoned, executed, or sent to labor camps. Many committed suicide. Their property was confiscated, and they were forced to pay huge fines. The business soon became government controlled. Private enterprise was eliminated by the Five Anti-Movement.

Thought Reform

In 1951, the movement for "thought reform" or "thought control" began on a large scale. It started in the schools and universities. The purpose was to impose a general acceptance of Communist **doctrine** (ideas). It began with "reforming the teacher's mind" and was soon extended to the students. Independent thinking was out. The program involved learning the revolutionary theories of Marx, Lenin, and Mao. It also involved regular meetings where people had to admit their own feelings to the group. There was criticism, self-criticism, and confessions. People were made to feel guilt and shame. Finally there were promises to accept the truth of Mao's teachings. This intense emotional experience lasted for months. The result was submission to authority and identifying with the party.

Control of the Arts

In 1949, Mao stated, "In the present world, all culture or literature belongs to one class, to one party, and follows one fixed political line. Art for art's sake . . . does not exist in reality." This meant that artists and writers would not be free to express themselves as they liked. Their art and writings were to serve the interests of the revolution and the Communist Party.

Mass Organizations

To carry out their goals, the Communists believed they had to reach every individual. A vast network of mass organizations was set up. In the villages, the peasants joined peasant organizations. In the cities, there were organizations for factory workers, teachers, students, employees, women, and children. Among the most important groups were the New Democratic Youth League and the Young Pioneers. These two groups were the training ground for future party members.

The mass organizations were controlled by the Communist Party. Orders were transmitted from the top of the local level. The local groups, called "cells," met constantly to discuss topics assigned by the party. The meetings were used to check on the attitudes and "thoughts of the masses." An important function of the mass organizations was to apply a great deal of public pressure on each individual so that he or she would think and act as the party directed.

The individual in China, therefore, lived in a world that was completely controlled. The news he or she read in the newspaper was carefully selected. In school, he or she was indoctrinated in Maoist thought. In the mass organizations people were watched and their thinking was controlled. Part of the control was the threat and use of force. There were militia units in each district. Street committees engaged in mutual surveillance and reported individuals to the local police stations. Serious cases were passed on to "people's courts," where the accused, without the benefit of a lawyer, had to confess their "crimes" and denounce others. The laws were unwritten and changeable and protected the interests of the state, not the individual.

The Economic Revolution—Efforts to Create a Socialist Economy

By 1953, the Communists had removed all resistance to the regime and had broken up the old social order. Vast numbers of people in the villages who had formerly enjoyed wealth, authority, and respect had been killed. The business and industrial groups in the cities were ruined. Freedom of thought of the intellectuals had been destroyed. The dominant group in the new society was the Communist Party. Its members were tightly disciplined by the party leaders. By 1953, the Communists were ready to move ahead toward a socialist economy in agriculture and industry.

Industry

The Five-Year Plan

The aim of China's first Five-Year Plan (1953–1957) was to industrialize China as rapidly as possible using the Soviet Union as a model. Some of the goals were to quadruple the production of steel and to double the output of power and cement. The government invested most of its capital in heavy industry. Increasing agricultural production was less important.

Soviet aid. Thousands of Chinese party members had been trained in the Soviet Union since 1921. They hoped to copy what the Russians had done in industry and agriculture. In the 1950s, thousands of Chinese went to the Soviet Union to learn about the economy. Large numbers of Soviet technicians and advisers came to China. A Sino-Soviet Agreement of 1953 provided for Soviet assistance in the establishment of over 100 industrial projects—mainly in the fields of electric power, mining, chemicals, and metal. China received essential help in the form of technology loans and equipment.

Agriculture. The money to pay for China's industrialization had to come from its agricultural products. The Agrarian Reform Law of 1950 and the campaign against the landlords had given the peasants their own land. Most peasants now farmed small plots of land using primitive methods and tools. This did not produce enough food for China's enormous population of nearly 600 million people. It did not provide the government with enough crops to sell to pay for the new industries and the imports of machinery.

The Communist leaders believed that the best way to get more crops from the peasants was to organize them into collective farms (very large farms run by the government). The Five-Year Plan prepared the way for the collectivization of agriculture. It was to be done in stages. During the first stage, peasants were organized into mutual-aid teams. These teams shared their tools, animals, and fertilizer and helped each other by joint planting and harvesting. But the land still remained in individual hands. In the next stage, producers' cooperatives were set up where the small plots of 30 or 40 families were combined into a large cooperative farm. The members shared the equipment and farm animals. Each family owned a share of the cooperative and divided the crops. By 1956, 90 percent of the peasants were reported to have joined the cooperatives.

The cooperative system allowed for greater planning of farm production. Workers could be assigned to plant the crops that were most needed. Modern methods began to be used. By 1955, more food was being produced then ever before.

Between 1955 and 1957, many cooperatives were joined together to form collective farms. The peasants were asked to give up the shares they owned in the cooperatives and to become wage laborers on the collective farms. Soon there were one or two collective farms to a village. They were run by members of the Communist Party who made sure that the state received the required share of crops. Many peasants were unhappy with the situation because they did not like giving up ownership of their land.

The "Hundred Flowers"

By 1956, party leaders believed that they had been successful in basically changing Chinese society. They decided that it was time to allow greater freedom of expression. In May 1956, a campaign was begun using a slogan from China's ancient history: "Let a hundred flowers bloom, let a hundred schools of thought contend." People were encouraged to express their opinions, even to criticize party workers. Mao believed the criticism would be healthy and that it would result in unity.

However, the result was a storm of criticism against the aims of communism and the basic policies of the state. Mao and the top leaders were shocked. In the spring of 1957, the movement was harshly suppressed. Many of the protesters were punished. So were party workers for failing to keep in touch with the people. Party workers and intellectuals were sent to work in the countryside, to be close to the masses.

The Great Leap Forward

The First Five-Year Plan had achieved excellent results. There were new roads, dikes, dams, factories, and cities. Industrial production had increased rapidly. However, the setting up of collective farms had not increased crop production. Between 1952 and 1957, the population in the cities grew by about 30 percent, but the government's grain collections hardly grew. In 1958, a second Five-Year Plan was adopted. It was to be a "Great Leap Forward" in industrial and agricultural production.

The plan set very high goals for increases in production. A basic idea was to use China's abundant manpower to develop the countryside. Millions of people in the villages were mobilized for irrigation, flood control, and land reclamation projects. To encourage the spread of industry throughout the country, small iron furnaces were set up in backyards. Mao believed that spirit and willpower were enough to get economic results.

The first results seemed to show a great leap forward: through sheer muscle power the face of China was changed. There were thousands of new reservoirs, hydroelectric power stations, and hundred of miles of railways, bridges, new canals, and new highways.

But the plan had set unrealistic goals and there was not enough careful planning. The all-out effort at instant growth led to massive errors and wasting of labor. The new factories could not get the raw materials they needed. The transportation system could not handle all the traffic. It became clear that the ambitious goals would not be met.

An important part of the Great Leap Forward was the setting up of **communes**. In each area a number of collective farms were joined together to form a commune. The communes were huge. Some were the size of towns, containing as many as 25,000 people. The people were divided into production brigades and production teams. Each brigade had a specific job to do. It was believed that because of the large size of the commune it would be possible to use labor and resources more efficiently. In this way agricultural production would increase without a huge investment in modern equipment.

Control in each commune was in the hands of Communist Party members who took on the functions of a local government. They assigned members to teams and brigades; paid out wages; ran the schools, health clinics, and day-care centers; collected the taxes; and provided for security.

Many peasants disliked the communes. They disliked being moved about and assigned to jobs against their will. They were exhausted by the long hours of hard work and poor diets. A wage system of paying each person according to need instead of according to work lowered productivity. Soon there were serious food shortages. By 1959, Mao admitted that the Great Leap Forward was a failure.

Economic Decline

The agricultural crisis worsened in the early 1960s as China suffered from drought and plagues of insects. Poor harvests led to widespread malnutrition. There were food riots, and great numbers of people died because of famine.

At the same time, the Soviet Union withdrew its aid and its technicians. Transportation broke down, and industry practically came to a standstill. Production (GNP) declined by about one-third in 1960. The people were exhausted. It was acknowledged that Mao and his followers had made errors on a gigantic scale. Mao removed himself from the day-to-day administration of affairs. He turned over his position as chief of state to Liu Shaoqi (Liu Shao-ch'i), although he still kept his post as chairman of the party.

The Great Proletarian Cultural Revolution

The Great Proletarian Cultural Revolution was launched by Mao in 1966. For the next three years, China was turned upside down. Everything was shaken up—the economy, the education system, the government, and the party. Many important people were publicly humiliated, including the future leader of China, Deng Xiaoping. Thousands lost their lives during this time of chaos and violence. Things did not begin to return to normal until 1969. However, many historians now date the Cultural Revolution from 1966 to 1976 because they include in this period the radical activities of the "Gang of Four."

Causes

The Great Leap Forward had brought China close to disaster. For the first time, there was great opposition to Mao, especially within the Party. There was also opposition from the intellectuals—writers, artists, professional people, and university professors and administrators. From 1962 on, essays appeared in newspapers and journals satirizing (making fun of) Mao's incompetence.

Liu Shaoqi (Liu Shao-ch'i) took over the day-to-day running of China. He and Deng Xiaoping set about restoring the economy. They established production goals for agriculture and industry that were realistic. They gave a great deal of authority to technicians and experts. There were also bonuses and incentives for peasants and factory workers to make them work harder. By 1965, the Chinese economy had recovered.

Mao was very concerned with what was happening. A great debate began within the leadership of the Communist Party over what path to follow. It was a debate over "red versus expert." On one side were Liu and his followers who stressed the importance of economic progress, the need for specialized skills and a technical education, and the need for a class of professionally educated people. On the other side were Mao and his supporters who believed revolutionary spirit and dedication to communism were more important than a technical education. Mao was very suspicious of "experts." He saw in them the making of a new ruling class. In fact, Mao was very concerned that the Party members themselves had become an upper class. In the Party, the government, and the army there were many who had privileges, private property, and an advanced education that the ordinary people did not have. To Mao communism meant equality—equality between town and country, between workers and peasants, and between mental and manual labor. Consequently, in 1966 Mao decided that it was time to renew the class struggle and he launched the Cultural Revolution.

Mao had several goals in starting the Cultural Revolution. Some of these were to:

1. Regain his leadership
2. Rekindle the revolutionary spirit of the nation, especially among the young people
3. Remove from power all those who opposed him
4. Bring about a change in leadership throughout China by removing government and Party officials, university professors and administrators, and factory managers

Mao had to look outside the Party for support. He turned to Defense Minister Lin Biao (Lin Piao) and the army. He called on the young people to organize themselves into Red Guards. Between August and November 1966, approximately 11 million Red Guards came to Beijing to meet with Mao and participate in mass demonstrations. Then they dispersed all over the country, where they violently attacked people and things that represented the "four olds"—old ideology, thought, habits, and customs. The Red Guards grew in numbers and power. Each Red Guard carried a copy of *The Quotations of Mao Zedong*, known as The Little Red Book. Mao's ideas were the guide for all action, and the actions of the Red Guards became more and more violent.

Every part of Chinese society was affected. The top leadership of the Party was shaken up. Liu Shaoqi (Liu Shao-ch'i) and Deng Xiaoping issued confessions admitting their past errors and pledged their loyalty to Mao. But Mao rejected them as insincere. Liu was thrown out of the Party and died in disgrace in 1969. Deng was sent to work in the country-side. Red Guards paraded officials wearing dunce caps through the streets and looted the homes of officials who seemed to lack revolutionary spirit.

Also singled out for attack were the outstanding writers, scholars, and scientists. They were publicly humiliated and sent to the countryside to do manual labor while many of their works were destroyed. The Red Guards also destroyed many precious art works of the past. The entire educational system was affected. University officials and professors were criticized and even denounced. Students went to mass meetings and organized instead of going to class. Then the universities and schools were closed.

The Cultural Revolution spread from city to city. The newspapers urged city residents to seize control of their local governments. The radicals took over factories, banks, newspapers, and police stations. Mao called on the people to set up "revolutionary committees" to take the place of the local party and governments. Chaos was widespread. Clashes between armed groups occurred in many places. The army had to be called on to restore order and it took over many of the functions of the government. In some cases local army commanders ignored the authority of the central government in Beijing. Finally at the end of 1968 Mao called for a halt to the disruptions. He encouraged young people to go to the country-side to help with the farming. In 1969, about 20 million young people went to work on farms. This weakened the power of the Red Guards. In 1969, life in China began to return to normal.

Results of the Cultural Revolution

The Cultural Revolution was a personal triumph for Mao. He was honored in songs, banners, statues, and portraits. The old moderates in the party, like Liu Shaoqi, were gone. Lin Biao, Mao's loyal supporter, became the number-two man and was named Mao's successor. Jiang Qing, Mao's wife, also emerged as an important political leader. The Cultural Revolution hurt China's economy. The damage to agriculture, industry, education, and science set back China's development by 10 to 20 years. Millions of lives and careers were ruined and thousands died.

During the years of cultural revolution, there were mass demonstrations all over China. Here, Red Guards carry banners and photographs of Mao.

The Last Years of Mao's Rule

The bitterness created by the Cultural Revolution lasted many years and resulted in a continuing power struggle. Under circumstances that still remain unclear, Lin Biao and Mao had a falling out. It seems that in 1971, Lin planned to have Mao assassinated. When the plot was discovered he tried to escape to the Soviet Union, but he and a number of senior military officials were killed in a plane crash. Again there was preoccupation with the questions of who would succeed Mao and what path China would follow. Two factions arose—the moderates led by Zhou Enlai and the radicals led by Jiang Qing, Mao's wife. Zhou said that China should concentrate on economic development, with the goal of making China an industrialized nation by the year 2000. He set forth the guidelines for this development which became known at "The Four Modernizations." Zhou sponsored the return to power of Deng Xiaoping. In 1975, when he was very ill, Zhou turned over the day-to-day administration to Deng. Jiang Qing and her three allies, who became known as "The Gang of Four," believed that the Cultural Revolution had been a positive experience and they fought to keep its revolutionary ideas alive. When Zhou Enlai died in January 1976, the Gang of Four convinced Mao to remove Deng from office. Deng was disgraced for a second time. By this time Mao was very ill and the Gang of Four was preparing to take over power. Mao died in September 1976 at the age of 82.

China and the World: Foreign Relations Under Mao Zedong

China and Taiwan: the Problem of "Two Chinas"

A hundred miles off the coast of Southeast China lies the island of Taiwan, also called Formosa, a name given to it by Portuguese sailors in the 16th century. Taiwan became part of the Chinese Empire in the early years of the Manchu Dynasty. Following the war with Japan in 1895, Taiwan was given to Japan but was returned to China 50 years later.

After the Communists took control of China in 1949, the defeated Nationalists, under the leadership of Chiang Kai-chek, fled to Taiwan. There they set up a government that they called the Republic of China. Approximately 2 million Chinese left mainland China and came to Taiwan. Both the Nationalist Government of Taiwan and the People's Republic of China claimed that it was the only legitimate government of China.

The Chinese people have a strong feeling of nationalism that calls for the unity of all Chinese people under one government. Therefore, a principal aim of Chinese foreign policy was, and is, the recovery of Taiwan. The communist leaders in Beijing have always claimed that Taiwan is an integral part of China. As soon as they were firmly in power, Mao and the People's Liberation Army prepared for an invasion of Taiwan. At the same time, the Nationalist government prepared for a counterattack to recover the mainland.

These plans changed as a result of the Korean War. President Truman sent the U.S. Seventh Fleet to patrol the Taiwan Straits, which separate Taiwan from the mainland. This action prevented the Communists from making any attempt to recover Taiwan. It was during the Korean War that the United States began to build up the military power of Taiwan. After the war, the United States recognized the Nationalist government as the legitimate government of China and pressured its allies to do the same. In 1954, the United Sates signed a mutual defense pact with Taiwan, promising to protect it against attack. These moves convinced Mao that the United States would resist any invasion of Taiwan. The United States continued to provide generous military and economic aid, which helped Chiang Kai-shek build up the island's economy. By the mid-1960's, Taiwan's industrialization was so successful that U.S. economic assistance was discontinued.

The existence of "two Chinas" presented a problem to the United Nations. Who was to represent China in the United Nations? Until 1971, the Nationalist government of Taiwan was a member of the United Nations and the People's Republic of China was barred. This was mainly the result of United States's pressure and influence. Year after year, the Soviet

Union and India tried to get U.N. membership for Communist China, but these efforts were blocked by the United States.

For the leaders of China, the question of Taiwan was an issue of national pride. They felt that only U.S. support for Taiwan prevented them from taking over Taiwan and unifying the Chinese people. Thus, the communist leaders of China regarded U.S. policy as a great insult. The United States became the main target of Chinese propaganda and the United States was called an imperialist power.

Over the years more and more nations came to believe that the People's Republic of China should be represented in the United Nations. In October 1971, the United States removed its objection to seating the People's Republic in the United Nations. The U.S. delegation, however, fought to keep both Chinese governments in the world organization. When the vote was taken on October 25, 1971, the Communist Chinese were admitted to the United Nations and the Nationalist Chinese were expelled.

Relations with the Soviet Union

Since the establishment of the People's Republic of China in 1949, China's relations with the Soviet Union, as well as with other countries, have gone through many changes.

"Lean to One Side"

Several months before he took control of the country, Mao proclaimed that China would "lean to one side" to support the Soviet Union in its rivalry with the United States. For a number of years during the 1950s, the two Communist powers were close allies. During the late 1950s, however, serious differences developed between the two, and by 1960 their "unbreakable friendship" had deteriorated.

In 1950, Mao traveled to Moscow and the leaders of the two nations signed a treaty, the "Sino-Soviet Treaty of Friendship, Alliance, and Mutual Assistance." This treaty provided that if either country were attacked by Japan or "any state allied to it" (meaning the United States), the other country would come to its assistance. The treaty lasted 30 years. During the Korean War, China and the Soviet Union drew closer together. Chinese forces in Korea, fighting the Americans and South Koreans, were built up with heavy Soviet weapons.

During the 1950s, the Chinese modeled just about everything on Soviet examples. They modernized their army and created a professional officers corps similar to that of the Soviet Union. Soviet examples guided the Chinese in their economic planning, the organization of their party and government, and in many other ways. In addition, the Soviet Union provided a great deal of economic and technical assistance to China. Thousands of Chinese trainees went to the Soviet Union, and thousands of Soviet technicians came to China to help with hundreds of industrial projects. China received equipment and large loans to help its industrialization. The Chinese Constitution of 1954 was copied in large part directly from the Soviet Constitution of 1936.

The Sino-Soviet Dispute

In the late 1950s, very serious differences arose between the Soviet Union and China. In 1960, there was an open split. Soviet technicians and advisers suddenly left China. Then, in 1969, serious military clashes occurred along the Sino-Soviet frontier. What are some of the causes behind the quarrel that turned the two communist allies into enemies?

1. <u>De-Stalinization in the Soviet Union</u>: Joseph Stalin, who had ruled the Soviet Union for almost 30 years, died in 1953. The new Soviet leader, Nikita

Khrushchev, began a program of de-Stalinization in 1956. He accused Stalin of many crimes and of having made many serious mistakes. In China, Stalin was still regarded as a great communist hero. Mao and the Chinese Communist leadership were embarrassed by Khrushchev's anti-Stalin campaign. Mao even found it a threat to his own leadership.

2. Economic position: For almost 50 years, Soviet leaders worked to build up a powerful, modern industrialized nation. China in the 1950s was still a poor developing country. Thus, the Chinese and the Soviet peoples had very different needs and goals. This made the two countries look at things differently.

3. Differences over ideology: Arguments arose over communist doctrine. Each country accused the other of betraying communist ideas. During the Great Leap Forward, the Chinese claimed that the establishment of communes put them farther along on the road to communism than the Soviet Union. Khrushchev denounced the Great Leap Forward and the communes as dangerous fanaticism. Mao regarded this as an unforgivable insult and accused the Soviets of revisionism (revising Communist theory) and selling out to capitalism.

4. International goals: Under Khrushchev the Soviet Union tried to improve relations with the United States and ease international tensions. Mao saw this as a betrayal. When Khrushchev visited the United States in 1959 and spoke of "peaceful co-existence," Mao felt that Khrushchev was sacrificing socialist unity. He accused Khrushchev of "capitalist collaboration."

5. Attitude toward war: Communists always believed that there could be no lasting peace in the world until all countries had a Communist form of government. As long as there were capitalist nations, they might try to attack the Communists. Therefore, according to Communist theory, it was the duty of Communists everywhere to wage war against capitalists and bring about their downfall. However, with the development of atomic weapons it became obvious that such wars could destroy the world. The Soviets were not willing to take this risk and they began to promote a policy of "peaceful co-existence," that is, living peacefully with other countries. The Chinese criticized Soviet policy for not being revolutionary enough. Mao's statements minimizing the dangers of nuclear war frightened the Soviets. In 1957, the Soviet Union promised China assistance in developing nuclear weapons. In 1959, the assistance was stopped.

6. Rivalry for leadership: In Russia, the Communists came to power in 1917. In China, the Communists took over in 1949. For years, the Soviet leaders felt they were more experienced, and therefore they should determine the policy that Communists all over the world would follow. As the split between China and the Soviet Union widened, China tried to capture the leadership of world communism. China tried to increase its influence with the developing nations in Asia and Africa. The Chinese said that these nations had more in common with China than they did with a powerful, industrialized Soviet Union. Therefore, the Chinese model of revolution should be followed by these countries. China supported "national liberation movements" in Asia and Africa and called for "people's wars" against both superpowers.

7. Territorial disputes: The Soviet-Chinese border extends over 6,500 miles. Under the tsars, Russia expanded into territory that had been part of the Chinese Empire—in northeast China, Mongolia, and Turkestan. The Chinese charged that the Soviet Union was holding over 700,000 square miles of land that once belonged to China.

This land is rich in resources and is sparsely populated while China's land is over-crowded. The Chinese were angered by Soviet statements that they would not give up this territory. The Soviets feared that one day China might try to take back this land for its growing population.

China's relations with the Soviet Union worsened throughout the 1960s. In 1962, a border dispute between China and India developed into war. China defeated India and took a chunk of territory that India had controlled. Both the United States and the Soviet Union backed India's claims. China regarded Soviet support for India as a further betrayal by its former ally. Mutual fear and suspicion between China and the Soviet Union increased. Fear of Chinese fanaticism and expansion grew in the Soviet Union.

In 1969, Soviet and Chinese troops clashed along the border between the two countries. Battles were fought along the Amur River and in central Asia. Each side claimed that the other had attacked first. Hundreds of dead and wounded soldiers on both sides showed the seriousness of the fighting. The growing Soviet military buildup was a serious threat to the Chinese. Despite China's successful testing of a nuclear bomb in 1964, China was still much weaker than the Soviet Union. This led Mao to turn to the United States and other non-Communist countries in the West. A new era in Chinese foreign policy was beginning.

Relations with the United States

For many years China and the United States were close friends. During World War II both nations fought together on the same side against the Japanese. The United States sent China several billion dollars in aid. Then, in 1950, the two nations became bitter enemies.

Years of Bad Feeling

When the Korean War broke out in 1950, U.S. troops fought on the side of South Koreans, while the Chinese sent troops to support the North Korean Communists. From then until 1971, the United States had little to do officially with The People's Republic of China. We had no diplomatic relations with China. That means that we did not recognize the Communists as the legal government of China. For 22 years, the United States kept The People's Republic out of the United Nations. In addition, the U.S. government greatly restricted American businesspeople from trading with China.

In 1950, the Communists began a carefully planned "hate America campaign." In daily broadcasts, in posters, newspapers, and street demonstrations, the Chinese leaders told their people that the United States was their enemy and that an attack by the United States was likely.

Reasons for Bad Feelings

What were the causes of this animosity? One reason is that the United States supported the Nationalist government of Taiwan. The Nationalists and the Communists had fought each other for control of China for many years.

Mao Zedong often said that he was ready to come to terms with the United States if the United States would agree to the following: (1) stop supporting the Nationalist government, (2) remove the Seventh Fleet, (3) remove its troops from Asia, and (4) give up its defense treaties with Asian nations. In other words, the Chinese Communists wanted the United States to get out of Asia and leave Asia to the Asians.

Some Americans favored a change in U.S. policy. They felt that if we offered friendship to the Chinese Communists, they would become more friendly and more peaceful.

The opponents of a change in policy felt that the Communists were warlike and would remain warlike. They said that China was overcrowded and poor, and so the Communist leaders would always try to conquer new lands for their people. They said that the Communists sent troops to Korea, Tibet, and India, and that the Chinese Communists were encouraging the North Vietnamese to attack South Vietnam, Laos, and Cambodia. Therefore, the United States must be prepared to stop the Chinese Communists, by force, if necessary. For a long time the debate continued.

Signs of Change

Early in 1971, in a surprise move, the Communists invited the U.S. Ping Pong Team, which was in Japan, to visit China. The Americans accepted and for the first time since 1949 Americans officially visited the Chinese mainland. The U.S. team was received with great friendliness. U.S. news reporters were allowed to accompany the team into China. Zhou Enlai, the Chinese Premier, greeted the team and said that he would like to visit the United States.

Then in July 1971, President Nixon announced that he would visit China by invitation of the Chinese government. Nixon recommended that The People's Republic of China be admitted to the United Nations, provided that Nationalist China be allowed to remain in the organization. This was a historic change in U.S. policy. In late 1971, the United States began to allow Americans to visit China and to resume trade relations.

What brought the two nations closer together was a common fear of the Soviet Union. Former Secretary of State Henry Kissinger wrote in his memoirs several years later that friendship between the United States and China was born out of "dire necessity"—dealing with the menace posed by the Soviet Union.

President Nixon's Visit to China

For seven days in February 1972, the world's attention was focused on President Nixon's historic trip to China. The Chinese went out of their way to make the visit a big success. Nearly all of China's senior leaders, except Mao Zedong were at the airport to greet the President. A few hours after his arrival, Chairman Mao called to invite the President to his home. For seven days, the President and his aides held meetings with Zhou Enlai and other Chinese officials. The Americans went sightseeing; they were wined and dined and taken to the theater. The Chinese showed in many ways that they were interested in better relations between the two countries. The visit received unprecedented coverage in the Chinese press. Radio broadcasts carried news of the trip all over China. No other foreign leader in recent years had received such coverage in China.

What did President Nixon's journey accomplish? President Nixon repeatedly warned that "no miracles should be expected." Perhaps the greatest miracle was the fact that the leaders of two nations, which for 22 years had shown only outright hostility toward each other, met in an atmosphere of cordiality and friendliness. The trip achieved the goal of breaking a silence that had lasted more than two decades. Both realized that wide differences existed between the two countries and many obstacles stood in the way of closer relations. But the leaders of both nations indicated that despite the differences there are common interests.

At the end of the visit there was a *communiqué* (an official statement summarizing the results of the meetings.) In it, both nations agreed to make it easier for Americans and Chinese to have contacts with each other. The two countries agreed to expand trade and to make relations between the two nations more normal.

February 21, 1972. A new era in Chinese-American relations begins. Chairman Mao Zedong, leader of the Chinese Communist Party, greeting President Nixon in Beijing.

Within the first year after that historic meeting, some 2,000 Americans and many Chinese crossed the Pacific to talk business and exchange ideas. American firms agreed to build earth-satellite stations in China, to sell Boeing 707 airliners, and to train pilots and maintenance workers. Corn and wheat sales to China worth over 40 million dollars were arranged.

In February 1973, Henry Kissinger, President Nixon's special assistant, visited Peking for special meetings with Chinese officials. It was agreed that the United States would establish a mission in Peking and a Chinese mission would be set up in Washington. This was the first step toward full diplomatic recognition. These missions made it possible for both countries to have contact with each other on a regular basis. Soon scientists, doctors, reporters, business people, athletic teams, and cultural groups were visiting each other's countries.

China Under Deng Xiaoping

Deng Xiaoping

The man who has ruled China for most of the years since Mao's death is Deng Xiaoping. After 1978, Deng brought about dramatic economic reforms and political changes. Many observers refer to these changes in China as a "second revolution." Deng's goal has been to pull China out of its backwardness and to push it into the 20th century. A loyal Communist for most of his life, Deng is, above all, a pragmatist (practical person) and will employ whatever means are necessary to achieve his goal. For this purpose Deng took many risks, such as opening up China to Western influences for the first time since 1949, introducing elements of **capitalism** (private enterprise) into the economy, and allowing greater personal freedom for individuals.

Deng Xiaoping was born in 1904 and came to power when he was in his 70s. Deng became a Communist when he was a young man studying in Europe. After returning to China, he spent the next 20 years carrying out important assignments for the Communists. After the People's Republic was established, Deng received various appointments. Deng supported Mao in many of his programs, including the "Hundred Flowers" campaign and the "Great Leap Forward." When it became evident that the "Great Leap Forward" was producing disastrous results, Deng made important economic changes. Mao was furious, and relations between the two began to deteriorate. Mao, who was aging, came under the influence of his wife Jiang Qing and her radical allies. In 1967 during the Cultural Revolution, Mao's wife openly denounced Deng as a counter-revolutionary capitalist (a person who wants to overthrow communism and bring back capitalism). Deng was dismissed from his party and government jobs and was exiled to southern Jiangxi province. There he was forced to perform manual labor in a tractor factory and to wait on tables in a mess hall. Members of Deng's family were also punished. In 1973, Deng was rehabilitated (restored to his former rank). He took over the day-to-day running of the government from Zhou Enlai, who was dying. In 1976, Jiang Qing and her three radical allies, who became known as the "Gang of Four," removed Deng from all his offices. Mao's death in September 1976 and the arrest of the Gang of Four a month later cleared the way for Deng's return to power the next year.

After coming to power Deng brought about enormous political, economic, and social changes in China.

Political Changes

The main political reforms under Deng Xiaoping may be summarized as follows:
1. Bringing to justice the Gang of Four and others responsible for the violence and destruction of the Cultural Revolution
2. De-Maoization—undoing the glorification of Mao as a godlike figure
3. Replacing followers of Mao who were hostile to his reforms with individuals who supported his program
4. Replacing hundreds of thousands of aging Party and government officials all over China with younger, better educated people

Since Mao's death Deng Xiaoping has ruled China. He has brought about dramatic economic and political changes.

Trial of the Gang of Four

The arrest of the Gang of Four came one month after Mao's death in 1976 and their trial began in November 1980. The Group's leader, Jiang Qing, was Mao's widow and a powerful member of the ruling group, the Politburo. The other three were also powerful members of the Politburo. They were accused of the "heinous crimes" committed during the Cultural Revolution: instituting a reign of terror during which thousands of writers, artists, and scientists were viciously persecuted, resulting in the death or suicide of many; framing and persecuting party and government leaders in an attempt to take over power for themselves; and bringing China to the edge of chaos.

The prosecution demanded the death penalty for Jiang and the other three. The final verdict declared Jiang guilty and sentenced her to death. She was given two years in prison to reform and repent of her crimes. The other three received harsh sentences. In 1983, the Supreme People's Court commuted Jiang Qing's sentence to life in prison. Mao was still widely revered in China. To have executed his widow would have dishonored his memory.

One goal of the trial was to punish and permanently discredit the four radicals who were responsible for the suffering of Deng Xiaoping and other leaders of the present government during the years of the Cultural Revolution. Another goal was to discredit those individuals who were associated with them and who still occupied high places in China. A final goal was to lower the public esteem for Mao without discrediting him entirely.

De-Maoization

In order to bring about basic changes in China, changes that Mao would never have allowed, it was necessary to make Mao into less of a godlike figure and to admit that he was responsible for many serious mistakes. This policy has been called de-Maoization. At the same time, China's new leaders had to be careful not to go too far, because in destroying

Mao they could destroy the Communist Party and Communist society as well. Starting in 1978, statues and portraits of Mao, which had been everywhere in China, were removed. In 1981, the Communist Party Congress issued an official document summing up 32 years of Communist rule in China and evaluating Mao's leadership. It said that Mao's early contributions as founder of the Chinese Communist State "far outweigh his later mistakes." His worst mistake was the Cultural Revolution, which "led to domestic turmoil and brought catastrophe to the party, the state, and the whole people."

Changes in Leadership

Within a few years after Mao's death, most of the people who had been removed from office and exiled during the Cultural Revolution were restored to power. Many of those who had died in disgrace were rehabilitated, the most famous being Liu Shaoqi. At the same time, Deng succeeded in getting rid of most of the radical followers of Mao in the Politburo, in the central government, in the military, and in the provinces. In 1980, Deng removed his greatest rival for power, Hua Guofeng, who was Mao's handpicked successor. (Hua had succeeded Mao in 1976 and had been proclaimed Chairman of the Communist Party and Premier.) Deng's closest ally Hu Yaobang was chosen to succeed Hua as chairman, and Zhao Ziyang was appointed Premier. This was a great victory for Deng and put him firmly in control of the Party and government. By 1985, Deng managed to remove most of his opponents from the Party leadership and replace them with younger, better educated, and more pragmatic people. In all government departments, local as well as national, older officials were encouraged to retire. Younger people were moved up to take their places. Deng's hope was that the new people would bring more energy and efficiency to the government and would carry out his ambitious Modernizations program.

Economic Policy

In 1984, Hu Yaobang, the head of the Chinese Communist Party, admitted that communism had failed to bring about a better life for millions of people. The average Chinese peasant or city worker was little better off when Mao died in 1976 than he or she had been in the 1950s. China was backward and needed to be pushed into the 20th century. The top priority of the new leadership, therefore, became economic growth and modernization.

In December 1978, the Communist Party Congress approved a program of "Four Modernizations," for agriculture, industry, science, and technology, and defense. Deng Xiaoping began introducing broad and dramatic economic reforms. The new leaders turned away from Mao's most cherished ideas. They began creating a mixed economy in which socialism was combined with a free market system. Many elements of capitalism were introduced into the economy. Yet Deng insisted that China's economic system would remain socialist. Deng firmly believed that China should learn from the experience of foreign countries, another idea that Mao would not have tolerated. He encouraged greater reliance on foreign technology and foreign investment.

Changes in Agriculture

About 80 percent of China's people live in the countryside and work in the fields. Under Mao, most of the peasants belonged to the 52,000 communes that grew what the government directed and turned the crops over to the government for distribution. Chinese peasants were grouped into production teams that worked the land in common. Each peasant earned "work points," which were exchanged for a ration of grain and a small cash stipend. The work points a person received had no relation to the amount of food produced. There was no reason to work harder and produce more because the peasant did not benefit from it.

The Responsibility System

In 1979, Deng began his economic reforms in agriculture. Communes were abolished and the "responsibility system" was introduced. The idea behind the responsibility system was: produce more, keep more for yourself. Although the state continues to own all of the land, it leases plots to individual families. The peasant decides what to plant and when. Each year peasants sign a contract that obligates them to turn a fixed amount of their produce over to the state. Anything they can produce above the quota they keep for themselves, sell to the state, or carry to one of the free markets and sell. The free markets were made legal in 1978. China's leaders insist that they have not turned away from collective agriculture because the state-owned land cannot be bought or sold by the farmers.

Improvements in Living Standards

The new policy was a great success. Leaders claimed that the peasants worked twice as hard as they used to because they knew that if they worked harder they could make more money. The grain harvest rose from 320 million tons in 1980 to 400 million in 1984, and in many places the average peasant income more than doubled. The new system changed the lives of 800 million people. Many peasants now own radios, sewing machines, alarm clocks, and bicycles, things that were considered luxuries only a few years earlier. Brick and tile houses replaced the old mud and thatch homes. Many peasants began combining farming with other activities that produced an income, such as carpentry. The peasant was allowed to keep all the cash he earned from selling the furniture he made, for example, whereas before he had to turn most of it over to the government. The improvement in living standards in the countryside was visible everywhere and the huge markets were packed with foods. Only a few years earlier meat was practically nonexistent and eggs could only be bought on holidays. In a country that has known periodic famine throughout 4,000 years of its history, for the first time the average citizen finally had enough to eat.

Reforms in Industry

Deng Xiaoping then tried to achieve the same successes in industry. He admitted that bringing about changes in industry was a much more difficult task and faced greater opposition than making changes in agriculture. Therefore reforms in industry were introduced later, on a more limited scale, and were only gradually extended.

Government Control of Industry Under Mao

Under the old system (which Mao had copied from the Soviet Union), the central government had complete control over everything that was produced in the country. There were almost no private businesses, and the government owned everything. The government decided how much to invest in each industry and assigned the raw materials to each factory. It told every factory manager what and how much to produce, where to sell it, and at what price. The government assigned workers to their jobs and decided on their wages. If the factory made any profits they were turned over to the government. If there were losses, the government subsidized them (made up for the loss.) Since managers and workers had very little to gain if factory production was high and not much to lose if production remained low or of poor quality, they did not work as hard as they could. As a result, production in most of China's industries remained low and the Chinese economy remained backward.

In 1978, the first small changes were made. Small-scale private enterprise became legal for the first time since 1949. Private individuals were allowed to own small businesses, such as restaurants, inns, tailor shops, barber shops, and beauty parlors. Some doctors and dentists opened private practices. It became legal for owners to hire up to seven workers and later this was extended to 15.

Gradually the government began to loosen its control of industry. Managers were given greater freedom in running their factories. In 1984, a program was approved to extend the reforms to the whole country. The goal of the new program was to create a more modern and efficient economy by moving away from central planning and allowing greater freedom

Local street scene in Wuhan, China

and incentives to managers and workers. The government retained a great deal of control over industry. It still owned the factories and raw materials, set broad production goals, and required that the factories produce a certain amount of goods that must be sold to the government at fixed prices. Beyond that, however, managers were given a great deal of autonomy. They were allowed to obtain their own supplies, decide what to make beyond the goods that must be sold to the state, and find buyers for their merchandise.

Workers' Bonuses

Instead of turning over all of their profits to the government, they paid a tax to the government and kept the rest of their profits. This money was used for reinvestment and to provide bonuses for their workers, as well as housing, medical care, and recreation for the workers. Managers were given greater power to hire and fire workers on the basis of job performance. Workers were encouraged to work harder by means of bonuses, which often amounted to 40 percent of their annual salary.

In October 1985, the government approved a new Five-Year Economic Plan. The plan called for major development projects in transportation, communication, energy, and resources. It also called for increased exports to earn the foreign exchange needed to finance purchases of advanced technology from abroad. It called for the economy to grow at an annual rate of 7 percent. Deng did not push for rapid economic growth because it would create too many problems. He said it would take five years for the reforms in industry to be successful.

New Open Door Policy

In order to modernize the economy Deng encouraged foreign companies to invest in Chinese industries. This is called the *New Open Door Policy*. But the door is not that open and the Chinese government only lets in carefully selected foreign investments. Since 1979 billions of dollars have been invested in China by foreign companies. Many of these companies are owned by Chinese living overseas. The others are mainly U.S., Japanese, British, West Germany, and French companies. The most important U.S. companies doing business in China are Citibank, 3M, Exxon, Atlantic-Richfield, McDonnell-Douglas, and IBM. An agreement signed between Armand Hammer, the head of Occidental Petroleum, and the Chinese government in 1983 gave the American oil company the right to drill for oil in the Yellow Sea and the South China Sea. This is one of the largest unexplored basins in the world. If large quantities of oil are discovered the contract will run for 15 years and China will receive 51 percent of the proceeds.

A growing trend was for business ventures to be jointly owned by the Chinese government and foreign firms. American Motors Corporation and the Chinese Automotive Industry Corporation jointly produced Jeeps in China, which are called "Jipu." In 1985, 2,300 joint ventures were registered.

Special Economic Zones

To make it more attractive for foreigners to bring their capital, technology, and management methods to China, the Chinese set up Special Economic Zones. Here the foreign investors have unusual privileges. They can set up factories, import raw materials, hire and fire workers, and earn profits. Originally, four Special Economic Zones were set up; in 1984 another 14 were established.

The Chinese want to learn everything they can from the advanced industrial nations. They are spending billions to import advanced technology and equipment. Hundreds of Chinese delegations have traveled to the United States to learn about U.S. technology, skills, and ideas. There are now several hundred joint research projects involving Americans and Chinese.

Continuing Economic Problems

Despite the improvements in the Chinese economy after 1979, very serious problems remained.

1. <u>Shortage of capital</u>: On several occasions the Chinese have had to postpone or cancel major development projects in order to save money. In 1981, more than 1,500 projects were affected, including the giant Baoshan Iron and Steel Works near Shanghai

2. <u>Inadequate infrastructure</u>: China's transportation system is very underdeveloped for a nation of its size. Its factories, power plants, and machinery are outmoded and inefficient. There are severe energy shortages.

3. <u>Shortage of skilled labor</u>: There is a very serious shortage of engineers, technicians, scientists, computer programmers, and skilled personnel of all kinds.

4. <u>Natural disasters</u>: From time to time, China suffers from drought, floods, earthquakes, and famine. For example, in 1981 central Hubei province suffered severe flooding, making it impossible to cultivate much of the land. At the same time, the northern province of Hebei and its neighboring areas were affected by a two-year drought. Since Hubei and Hebei are usually areas of agricultural surplus, the food supply of theentire country was affected. China was forced to import millions of tons of grain and to appeal for international help.

5. <u>Unemployment</u>: Unemployment in China is a serious problem that has developed in recent years. During the years that China's agricultural system was organized in communes, there was work for everyone. After the changes, millions of workers were no longer needed on the farms. They came to the cities, were unable to find work, and added to the high unemployment rate.

6. <u>The problem of "red eyes"</u>: One of the most serious problems that resulted from the reforms was the growth of inequality. Under Mao, equality was the number-one goal: communism meant an equal society. With the reforms, harder and better work was rewarded by bonuses. In the countryside some peasants became rich while others were left behind. The "red eyes" are those who have watched their neighbors get rich while they themselves have not benefited. These people resent the changes, and some have even gone so far as to wreck the property of their richer neighbors.

7. <u>Inflation</u>: Before the reforms, the price of just about everything in China was fixed by the government. The costs of basic items such as food, clothing, rent, and even haircuts and public baths, were kept very low because they were *subsidized* by the government. This cost the Chinese government about $55 billion a year, or about half the national budget. In 1985, a policy of price reform went into effect. The government allowed the prices of many items to rise to respond to the market forces of supply and demand. A wave of panic went through the country as people rushed to buy and hoard things. Many Chinese feared that the costs of rice, clothing, and other essential things would skyrocket. Foreign economists estimate that during 1985 prices rose between 10 and 15 percent.

8. <u>Corruption</u>: The new freedom brought with it many instances of corruption. There are government and party officials who have demanded bribes and used funds for purposes other than those for which they were intended. Some people became involved in tax evasion, selling on the black market, and setting up illegal businesses.

9. <u>Problems faced by foreign investors</u>: With the exception of the companies mentioned earlier, many U.S. and other foreign companies held back from major investments in China. There are several reasons for this. Initially foreigners saw China as a huge market of 1 billion people and a chance to make enormous profits. These high hopes turned to disappointment. Foreigners complained that doing business in China was not easy. They said that Chinese officials often made up new taxes, rules, and regulations instead of sticking to the contract. One month the tax on a shipment of imported parts might be 20 percent and the next month 60 percent. Because so many workers must be trained in high-technology methods, each project takes very long to complete and this reduces the profits. McDonnell-Douglas, which began assembling twin-engine MD-80 airplanes in Shanghai, had to allow three months to produce each fuselage compared with one week in the United States. In many instances, the Chinese government suddenly cancelled contracts with foreigners or cut back on imports that were necessary to keep a project going. Another important reason that foreigners did not invest more in China was the concern that, after Deng is gone, the reforms could disappear and China could return to the anti-Western attitudes of the past.

Opposition to Deng's Policies

There was serious concern about the survival of the economic reforms of Deng Xiaoping. There were important people in the Communist Party and the government who were very critical of these reforms. They said that the changes went too far in the direction of capitalism and had resulted in corruption and other evils that are inherent in capitalism. They opposed the Open Door Policy, saying that Western influences were causing "spiritual pollution" among the Chinese people. They feared that China was moving away from Marxism. Most important of all, they feared that less central control over the economy would mean a loss of power by the Communist Party.

Deng assured his critics of his own devotion to socialism. Deng often stressed that only socialism could eliminate the greed, corruption, and injustice that are inherent in capitalism. But Deng insisted that China must "adopt the useful things from the capitalist system." Progress for China depended on "combining the market economy and the planned socialist economy. This is the only road China can take. Other roads will only lead to poverty and backwardness."

The Chinese People and the Communist Party

Western Influences

From 1979 to 1989, China under Deng was in many ways very different from the China of Mao Zedong. The Communist leadership under Deng Xiaoping allowed a greater degree of freedom and choice than was possible before. Most people were more concerned with having a better life than worrying about revolution and communism. More people began to dress in stylish Western clothing, buy refrigerators and televisions (which until recently were considered luxuries), and choose from a great variety of products in their supermarkets.

Under Mao, Western products and ideas were considered decadent and were banned. After 1979, billboards advertised a whole array of Western goods—Kodak film, Coca-Cola, Marlboro cigarettes, and Sanyo cassettes. Radio Peking carried a weekly program of contemporary Western music. In 1985, the British rock group Wham gave a concert in Beijing. American movies, including *Star Wars*, were shown in China. In 1986, Chinese National Television began broadcasting Walt Disney cartoons.

Party Control

Still, China remained a one-party dictatorship. It was less oppressive under Deng than it was under Mao. Yet rights taken for granted in the United States, such as freedom of speech, press, and assembly were strictly controlled in China. The right to criticize the government and the party was very limited. The Party did not find a comfortable balance between freedom and control, and since 1978 periods of greater freedom were followed by crackdowns.

China's Economy After a Decade of Reform

Until the mid-1980s it seemed that China's economic reforms were succeeding. Agricultural output had doubled since 1979 and industrial production was increasing. There was a new prosperity in the countryside and much of the poverty in the cities was being erased.

At the same time, however, serious problems were developing. By 1986, it became evident that the industrial reforms were more difficult to carry out than the agricultural reforms begun in 1979. Large investments in industry had greatly reduced China's foreign exchange reserves and inflation was growing. Hopes for modernizing thousands of inefficient factories and industries depended on the willingness of foreign companies to invest in China. But many foreign firms were unwilling to take the risks and held back. The economy grew rapidly in 1987 and output increased, but this rapid growth added to the problems. The demand for raw materials, energy, and transportation was far greater than the supply available. Also, the production of food slowed down. However, the two most serious problems were inflation and corruption. These aroused a great deal of resentment among the Chinese people and led to the protest movement of 1989.

Inflation and the Rising Cost of Food

Inflation began increasing in the mid-1980s causing the prices of food, consumer goods, and raw materials to rise. Government attempts to control inflation were only partly successful. In 1987, inflation was officially estimated at 20 percent, but was probably much higher. In the spring and summer of 1988, panic buying broke out in many places after food prices increased by 50 percent. In September 1988, the government adopted a retrenchment program (reducing investments in the economy and controlling the money supply) to curb inflation. However, during the first half of 1989 inflation soared. In the major cities the inflation rate exceeded 40 percent. The people who suffered the most were workers and other urban residents with fixed incomes. After 1985, food prices climbed rapidly. By 1988, the share of a person's income spent on food had risen to 60 percent. Thus the benefit of the reforms were completely wiped out for working people. As their living standards declined, the discontent and frustration of urban workers grew.

Official Corruption

As the government loosened some of its control over the economy, many officials in the Party, the government, and the military abused their official positions to enrich themselves and their families. After 1984, two sets of prices existed for most raw materials and finished products—an official price and a negotiated price. People with special connections were able to buy goods in short supply at the official price and resell them at the negotiated price, thus making enormous profits. Many officials and their families formed speculative companies and engaged in illegal activities. This raised the price of all goods and contributed to the inflation. Many officials also accepted bribes and took public funds for their own use. Popular demands to curb these special privileges and end corruption were very strong.

After relations between China and the United States were established in the late 1970s, U.S. industries began to do business with China. Here we see Coca Cola sold in China.

The Massacre at Tiananmen Square

On June 3–4, 1989, the government of China sent heavily armed troops and tanks into Tiananmen Square in the center of Beijing to clear the square of student demonstrators. The students, who were unarmed, had occupied the square for six weeks demanding political reforms that would allow for more democracy. Approximately 1,000 demonstrators were killed and the democracy movement was suppressed.

Background

As you read, in 1979 China began a program of far reaching economic reforms to modernize the country and turn it into a major power. These reforms continued for the next decade and transformed the Chinese economy. However, very little was done to bring about political reform, that is to allow a greater degree of democracy and loosen some of the control of the Communist Party over all aspects of Chinese life. During the 1980s, there was even a struggle within the Communist Party between those people who wanted to continue the economic reforms and those who resisted them. Some feared that the reforms challenged the authority of the Communist Party and threatened the socialist system. During the same period, the Chinese government seemed to swing back and forth between allowing the people greater political freedom and curbing these freedoms.

The success of China's economic reforms created pressure for political reform. The economic reforms had also led to many changes in China during the 1980s. The Communist Party's control over the economy had been loosened. China had been opened to the outside world. Thousands of Chinese students were studying abroad. Intellectuals were freer to express themselves than they had been in years. There was a feeling that China was at last liberating itself from the terrible repression that had existed under Mao.

Student Demonstrations—December 1986

This made many people impatient for more change. Young, idealistic university students led the way in demanding more democracy. In December 1986, student demonstrations took place in nearly a dozen cities, calling for individual rights and freedom of expression. Although the demonstrations were peaceful, China's leaders saw them as a challenge to Party control and feared that other dissatisfied groups would join them. Consequently, the government banned all demonstrations. However, some students ignored the ban and continued their protest. This led to a government crackdown in January 1987. Many students were arrested and many were thrown out of the universities. During the next two years, the government took measures to strictly limit political activity.

The Democracy Movement at Tiananmen Square

Hu Yaobang "Martyr of Reform"

In the spring of 1989, the pro-democracy movement burst forth again. The period between April 23rd and June 4th has been called "the most remarkable six weeks in Chinese history." What triggered these events was the death of Hu Yaobang, who had been chosen by Deng Xiaoping in 1980 as his successor to lead the Communist Party. Hu, a strong advocate of reform, was forced to resign in January 1987 by conservatives in the Party. They blamed him for failing to put down the student demonstrations. Hu became the students' idol and his death turned him into a martyr of reform.

On April 23rd, the day of Hu's funeral, between 100,000 and 150,000 students gathered in Tiananmen Square. Defying a government ban on demonstrations in Tiananmen Square, they demanded greater freedom, an end to corruption, and an opportunity to meet with government leaders to make their wishes known. These students were loyal to the government and the Party. They did not wish to bring about the end of communism. But the Communist leaders saw the demonstration as a serious threat to their own authority and to the Communist system. On April 26, the government threatened to use force to break up the demonstrations but the students refused to back down. During the next six weeks, thousands of students continued to occupy Tiananmen Square and the surrounding streets in the center of Beijing. Students boycotted classes and organized independent student unions. The students printed their own newspapers and used various means to influence public opinion.

There was a great outpouring of public support for the students in many cities. In Beijing, workers, professionals, and ordinary citizens began to organize themselves to support what had become known as "the democracy movement." Soon there were demonstrations in dozens of cities. The students escalated their demands to include the removal of Premier Li Peng. In May, 3,000 students went on a hunger strike in Tiananmen Square to emphasize their determination. The demonstration in Tiananmen Square received world-wide coverage.

For weeks, the Chinese government debated over how to deal with the situation. Some, including the General Secretary of the Communist Party, Zhao Ziyang, were in favor of making concessions to the students. However, hard-liners wanted a military solution. When Deng Xiaoping supported the hard-liners, Zhao was removed from office, and on May 20 the government announced that martial law would go into effect in parts of Beijing. Troops were sent to the city to take control, but the demonstrations continued for another two weeks. Resistance by the citizens of Beijing prevented the soldiers from advancing to Tiananmen Square.

The Government Crackdown

On the night of June 3–4, heavily armed troops and tanks moved into Tiananmen Square. They attacked and killed almost 1,000 student demonstrators. Bloodshed also occurred in other cities as troops put down the democracy movement.

The government called the demonstrations a "counter-revolutionary rebellion," that is, an attempt to overthrow the Communist system. Thousands of people who had participated in the democracy movement were arrested; more than two dozen people were publicly executed. Many leaders of the democracy movement escaped abroad. In the universities and in other institutions where the democracy movement had flourished, the government began a new campaign of repression.

After Tiananmen Square: Human Rights Abuses

Since Tiananmen Square, China is very different. Many Communist party officials who favored reform, especially the supporters of Zhao Ziyang, were removed from office. The hard-liners, who are now in control, have been trying to reassert strict Party control over all aspects of Chinese life.

Students taking part in a pro-democracy demonstration at Tiananmen Square in the spring of 1989.

In June and July 1989, a nationwide hunt for protesters was undertaken. The crackdown continued well into 1990. Tens of thousands of participants in the democracy movement were rounded up and held without any charges. Many have been released, but many, perhaps thousands, are still being held. Reports tell of killings, disappearances, torture, severe beatings, arbitrary arrest, and interference with personal privacy. Basic civil rights—freedom of speech, press, assembly, association, and religion—have all been severely restricted. There has been renewed discrimination against women and China's national minorities.

New laws were passed in late 1989 and early 1990 that restrict the right of citizens to organize demonstrations. A universal population registration system was ordered in September 1989 requiring people to carry identification cards which can be checked at any time. This restricts the movement of Chinese citizens in their own country.

In August 1989, 500,000 college graduates were sent to remote rural areas for one or two years of **indoctrination,** (intense instruction) in Communist ideas. The Party has tightened its controls on education, especially in the universities. **Ideological** (basic concepts) study of communism and military training have been reintroduced in the universities. China also limited the number of university students allowed to study abroad.

The Chinese Economy after Tiananmen Square

The Chinese economy began showing signs of serious weakness in 1988. It was further weakened by the massacre at Tiananmen Square and the subsequent events. The main effects of the massacre were: the suspension of foreign loans; the cancellation of new foreign investments; the loss of tourist revenue; and increased spending on defense. As a result, production declined, unemployment rose, and social tensions increased.

1. <u>Suspension of foreign loans</u>. China's major source of interest-free and low-interest loans was the World Bank, which provided $8.5 billion in loans to China between 1980 and 1989. Following the massacre, the World Bank suspended all new loans. A $6 billion loan from Japan that had been negotiated in 1988 was also put on hold. These losses were a severe blow to China.

2. <u>Cancellation of new investments</u>. Foreign investments, which were an important part of China's economic reform program, had grown steadily during the 1980s. Although most foreign companies did not pull out of China after Tiananmen Square, they suspended or cancelled plans for new investments.

3. <u>Loss of tourist revenue</u>. Before June 1989, tourism was a growing industry and it provided China with $2.2 billion a year. After the massacre, foreign visitors were frightened away causing a sharp drop in tourism.

4. <u>Increased spending on defense</u>. Chinese leaders believed that the support of the army was necessary to remain in power. Between 1979 and 1986, China's defense budget had declined sharply. After Tiananmen Square, the government gave in to military demands for greater defense spending which left less money to invest in the economy.

These new developments added to the very serious problems that already existed; a shortage of raw materials, of electricity, and capital; outdated equipment and backward technology; an inadequate transportation system; and inflation. The government's attempt to control inflation brought on a serious recession.

Production Falls

The Chinese economy went into a deep slump at the end of 1989. Industrial production declined sharply. Every part of the economy was affected. The recession hurt the machine building industry—the backbone of the economy. The production of consumer goods, an industry that had been rising throughout the 1980s, was also hit.

Unemployment   Millions of workers and other employees lost their jobs. Unemployment became a serious economic and social problem. The unemployed traveled from one city to another looking for jobs, creating a "floating population" of millions. They slept in railway stations, parks, and urban slums. There was an increase in crime.

Turning Back the Clock   After 1989, China's new hardline leadership halted many of the reform programs. The government returned to a policy of centralized control over major segments of the Chinese economy. Steps were taken to severely restrict private businesses. During the preceding decade, the number of private businesses had grown from 100,000 to over 14 million. This was one of the most dynamic parts of the Chinese economy. After 1989, the number of private businesses dropped. The "Open Door Policy" was maintained, however, because it served as a means of attracting foreign capital.

Foreign Policy Under Deng Xiaoping

The new Chinese leadership under Deng Xiaoping recognized that a peaceful international environment was essential to its plans for economic development. Therefore, the Chinese continued their efforts to improve relations with the United States, other Western countries, and Japan. They also tried to lessen tensions with the Soviet Union. China is also very active in trying to win friends among Third World nations. At the same time, China saw itself as an independent major power that stood apart from both the United States and the Soviet Union. After many years of isolation under Mao, China has been increasing its participation in international events.

China's Relations with the Soviet Union

Relations between China and the Soviet Union have remained tense since the 1960s. In the early 1980s, the Chinese were still attacking the Soviet Union as the "most dangerous source of war in the world today." The Chinese repeatedly denounced the Soviet invasion of Afghanistan and the Soviet-backed Vietnamese invasion of Cambodia. China was nervous about the presence of 1 million Soviet soldiers and the Soviet missiles along the Chinese-Soviet border. Yet, it was in the interest of both nations to try to improve relations. The Soviets hoped to lure China away from its growing friendship with the United States. The Chinese wanted to reduce the growing Soviet military threat so they could concentrate on economic development.

In 1982, the two nations began talks to explore the possibility of normalizing relations. During the next few years Soviet and Chinese officials exchanged visits. Both sides signed agreements for economic and technical cooperation and scientific exchanges. Soviet and Chinese athletes began participating in competitions in each other's countries. Trade between the two nations grew. By the late 1980s, the Soviet Union had become one of China's leading trading partners.

At the same time, China began to have friendlier relations with the Soviet Union's allies in Eastern Europe. Chinese officials traveled to Romania, Yugoslavia, Hungary, Poland, Czechoslovakia, Bulgaria, and East Germany. In May 1989, Soviet President Gorbachev visited China. Relations between the two nations improved.

China's Relations with Its Asian Neighbors

Vietnam

During the long years of the war in Vietnam, both the Soviet Union and China sent weapons and supplies to the Communists in Vietnam to fight the United States-backed government in South Vietnam. In 1975, two years after the last U.S. troops left South Vietnam, North Vietnam conquered South Vietnam and united the country. Vietnam became the strongest military power in Southeast Asia, especially after it signed a treaty of alliance with the Soviet Union in 1978. Hostility between China and Vietnam grew. In 1979, Vietnam sent its army into Cambodia to overthrow the government of Pol Pot, which China had supported. The Soviet Union backed Vietnam. At the same time there were frequent clashes along the border between Vietnam and China. Vietnam mistreated the Chinese people living in Vietnam, and 500,000 of them fled to China. In 1979, China invaded Vietnam. The war lasted four weeks, but nothing was settled. Border clashes continued during the next few years. China feared that it was being encircled by the Soviet Union in the north and Vietnam in the south. The Chinese were very concerned about the buildup of Soviet naval and air power in Vietnam.

Japan

China and Japan have developed closer relations in recent years. During the 1950s and 1960s, Japan followed the lead of the United States and avoided trading with China. After President Nixon's visit to China, Japan also began to normalize its relations with China. In 1979, the two nations signed an economic agreement. Over the next few years Japan became China's leading trading partner. Japan is playing a very important role in helping the Chinese to develop their economy. Japan has given China billions of dollars in loans for railway, port, and hydroelectric projects. There are joint projects to develop the steel and petrochemical industries. In 1980, Chinese premier Hua Guofeng visited Japan. It was the first visit by a Chinese head of government to Japan in 2,000 years.

Hong Kong—China and Great Britain Reach an Agreement

In 1842, Britain and China signed the Treaty of Nanking ending the Opium War. This treaty **ceded** (gave) to Britain the island of Hong Kong, which has remained under British control for more than 140 years.

In 1842, Hong Kong was a largely uninhabited island. By 1983, its population had grown to 5.5 million people. Hong Kong is now the world's third most important financial capital after New York and London. It is a manufacturing center with exports greater than those of all of mainland China. It is also a tourist site for several million people a year who are attracted by its modern hotels, shops, and restaurants.

Britain's lease on Hong Kong runs out in 1997. In 1982, Britain and China began negotiations and in 1984 an agreement was reached to end British rule and return Hong Kong to China in 1997. Hong Kong will continue under British administration until then.

The agreement leaves Hong Kong basically unchanged, at least until the year 2047. Although Hong Kong will become part of China, its economy will continue to be based on private enterprise for 50 years after the takeover. The Chinese are willing to allow for continuation of capitalism because Hong Kong provides China with 40 percent of its foreign exchange In 1997, Hong Kong will become an "autonomous special administrative zone." It will be allowed to keep its legal, educational, and financial system until 2047. Its residents will be permitted to travel and trade freely. The free port and international banking system will remain intact (untouched), as will the markets for foreign exchange and gold. Hong Kong will have a great deal of autonomy, but China will be in charge of defense and foreign affairs.

Many of Hong Kong's residents, especially those in the business community are very uneasy over this situation. They fear that a future Chinese government might not abide by the treaty. Half of Hong Kong's citizens are refugees who fled from Communist China, and many are not willing to live under a Communist government again.

China and the United States

Relations between China and the United States continued to improve after 1978 despite continuing problems over Taiwan. The friendship between the two countries was based in part on a shared hostility toward the Soviet Union. Fear of Soviet-Vietnamese encirclement drew the Chinese closer to the United States. The United States saw China as a potential partner in checking the growth of Soviet military power in Asia. China also needed U.S. investments and advanced technology to modernize its economy. The United States, for its part, hoped that trade with China would bring large profits in the future. Finally, after 30 years of estrangement, the United States and China announced the establishment of full diplomatic relations on January 1, 1979.

View of Hong Kong from the mainland. Hong Kong is a major financial and manufacturing center. It provides China with 40 percent of its foreign exchange. Hong Kong attracts several million tourists every year.

Trade, Loans, and Other Agreements

During the next few years, many visits by top-ranking officials were exchanged and numerous agreements were signed. In July 1979, China and the United States signed a long-term trade treaty that included a **most-favored-nation** clause. This meant that China would be treated as a favored trading partner and tariffs on Chinese goods would be much lower than before. In 1980, the United States and China signed an agreement providing for U.S. government assistance in building major hydroelectric and flood control projects in China and training Chinese engineers in the United States. Also in 1980, the two countries signed four major agreements covering civil aviation, shipping, consulates, and textile trade. This led to the first regularly scheduled airline service between the United States and China since 1949.

Sale of Military Equipment

Following the Soviet invasion of Afghanistan in December 1979, the United States and China exchanged visits of senior defense officials to explore ways of cooperating in response to the Soviet military threat. The U.S. government then authorized U.S. firms to sell China a wide variety of nonlethal military equipment. China, for its part, agreed to let the United States monitor Soviet missile tests from top secret intelligence-gathering stations in Xinjiang Province. In 1981, the United States announced it had decided in principle to sell arms to China.

Continued Problem of Taiwan

Yet, despite the growing cooperation and friendship between China and the United States, tension continued over the question of Taiwan. During the first two years of the Reagan administration, relations deteriorated sharply. U.S. policy was still being pulled between an interest in good relations with China and long-standing ties of friendship, cooperation, and trade with Taiwan. When the United States and China signed the "normalization agreement" in 1978 to establish diplomatic relations, both countries agreed that Taiwan was part of China. President Carter accepted China's demand that the United States break diplomatic relations with Taiwan and closed the American Embassy in Taipei, capital of Taiwan. The United States insisted, however, that it would continue to maintain commercial and cultural relations with Taiwan and would continue to sell defensive weapons to Taiwan. The United States also declared that it expected the Taiwan conflict to be resolved in a peaceful way.

Close Cooperation

Relations between the United States and China showed a marked improvement in 1983 and 1984. The United States began to supply China's increasing need for high technology (for example, advanced computers). Before this, China, along with other Communist countries, was not allowed to buy various kinds of "sensitive technologies." In June 1983, China was placed in a different category than other Communist nations, making it possible to sell China a much wider range of advanced equipment. There was a great increase in the number of visits between top Chinese and U.S. officials. President Reagan visited China in 1984.

As the Chinese continued to modernize their economy, trade with the United States increased. Trade between the two countries grew from 1.1 billion dollars in 1978 to 8 billion dollars in 1985. For several years, the United States had been China's second biggest trading partner after Japan. The main products that the United States sold to China were wheat, raw cotton, and other agricultural products; industrial equipment, such as oil-drilling gear, mining equipment, and power generators; and computers and other high-technology products. The main U.S. purchases from China were textiles and petroleum products.

Imports of men's and women's clothing from China grew so rapidly after 1977 that U.S. manufacturers were afraid that they would go out of business. The U.S. government tried to get China to limit its textile exports to the United States. However, the Chinese refused because they needed the money from these sales to pay for their imports. When many months of negotiations produced no agreement, the United States imposed quotas on textile imports from China. A compromise agreement was reached in 1983 whereby Chinese textile imports would be allowed to grow by 3 percent annually.

Despite the setbacks over Taiwan and the textile imports, relations between China and the United States continued to improve. Thousands of Americans visited China. Chinese delegations traveled to the United States to learn U.S. technology, skills, attitudes, and ideas. Thousands of Chinese students were enrolled in U.S. universities and technical schools.

Since the Communists came to power, the Chinese government has made a great effort to increase industrial production. Here we see a group of iron workers. China's iron industry is growing rapidly.

China and the World After Tiananmen Square

The brutal crackdown at Tiananmen Square in 1989 received worldwide coverage. The United States and many other countries condemned China. The Chinese government was also criticized for using force in Tibet and for restricting human rights. The United States, the European Community, and Japan showed their disapproval by imposing a number of economic sanctions that seriously hurt the Chinese economy.

In the United States, the issue of China's human rights abuses was hotly debated. Congress and the American people were very critical of the Chinese government and favored strong action against it. President Bush, however, was determined to maintain "normal relations" with China. Soon after the massacre, Congress approved a number of economic sanctions. President Bush announced that all high-level government contracts with China would be suspended. However, one month after the Tiananmen Square massacre, President Bush sent a high-ranking personal representative to meet with Chinese leaders. In December, two of President Bush's top officials visited China. President Bush received a great deal of criticism in Congress and the press for these actions.

Several months later, the question of renewing China's most-favored-nation (MFN) status arose. A country that has most-favored-nation status is taxed at the lowest rate. China's status has to be decided on every year by Congress. Naturally, China is eager to retain its most-favored-nation status.

To improve its image and win Congressional approval for its MFN status, China released several hundred pro-democracy activists from jail. However, many in the United States felt that China's MFN status should not be renewed until there was a substantial improvement in human rights. Under great pressure from President Bush, Congress voted to extend China's MFN status for another year.

Relations between China and the United States remained tense. Chinese leaders denounced the U.S. Congress and others for criticizing China's human rights abuses. They called it "intervention in Chinese internal affairs." China maintained that a government's dealings with its own citizens are its "internal affair" which foreigners have no right to criticize.

The crackdown at Tiananmen Square cost China $2 to 3 billion in loans and assistance from the World Bank and other foreign sources. This loss came at a time when the Chinese economy was experiencing many difficulties. In addition, foreign companies held back on any new investments in China.

Chinese leaders have tried to convince the world that China is a stable country and its leaders are committed to reform. They also offered to release some important political prisoners in exchange for an end to some of the economic sanctions. During 1990, there was a normalization in relations between China and the rest of the world. Japan resumed normal economic relations, and gave China the $6 billion loan package promised in 1988. The European Community agreed to lift its economic sanctions and the World Bank resumed assistance to China. However, as China entered the 1990's, it had lost the international confidence, credibility, and support that it gained during a decade of reform and opening up to the outside world.

China: Arms Merchant for the Third World

In recent years China has become one of the world's leading proliferators of weapons and nuclear technology. For the Chinese this is a way of obtaining needed cash for their economic development projects. Therefore, China sells to any country that is willing and able to pay. Most of its customers are Third World countries. In 1991, China ranked fourth, after the former Soviet Union, the United States, and France, as a major supplier of arms to the Third World.

China's unrestrained sale of arms and nuclear technology to the Middle East, an area that is already very heavily armed and highly unstable is especially dangerous. In the 1980s, during the Iran-Iraq War, China began selling large quantities of weapons to Iran. At the same time, it supplied Iraq with hundreds of tanks. The Chinese also sold Silkworm missiles to both sides. In 1988, China supplied Saudi Arabia with intermediate range ballistic missiles and since then it has sold M-9 missiles to Syria. In 1989, China began providing Iran with nuclear technology, including a reactor. Although the Chinese claim that this equipment is intended for peaceful purposes it also can be used to make an atomic bomb. China has also admitted the sale of nuclear technology to Algeria.

Summary of Key Ideas

China

A. Geographic and physical features have influenced Chinese history and culture.

   1. China is one of the largest countries in the area, and the largest in population.

   2. Pressure of population has made the supplying of food a major and continual problem.

   3. Geographic differences have resulted in different ways of living in North and South China.

   4. Ancient civilizations in China grew in the great river valleys.

   5. Geographic barriers isolated China from the West in the past.

   6. Geographic factors prevented the full development of China's natural resources.

   7. The monsoon plays a vital role in the life of the Chinese people.

   8. The river systems play a life and death role in the lives of the Chinese people.

B. Chinese civilization is the oldest continuous civilization in the world.

   1. Chinese civilization is more than 1,500 years old.

   2. Chinese history and culture has followed a continuous and unbroken road.

   3. The rise and fall of dynasties has occurred over and over in Chinese history.

   4. The idea of the Mandate of Heaven greatly influenced the course of Chinese history.

   5. Confucianism was the model for the value system of the Chinese culture.

   6. The Chinese have accepted and developed parts of many cultural and religious systems (Buddhism and Confucianism).

   7. Chinese contributions in art, architecture, ceramics, literature, religion, theater, and music have influenced civilization in Asia and in the rest of the world.

   8. Chinese fear and dislike of outsiders and the Chinese belief in the superiority of Chinese ways have influenced China's cultural history and its relations with other countries.

   9. The belief in the superiority of Chinese customs and traditions prevented change when the Europeans made the influence felt.

C. During the 19th and 20th centuries, China experienced great changes and upheavals. This led to the end of China's imperial system which had lasted for over 2,000 years.

   1. In the 19th century, the great increase in population put great pressure on Chinese resources.

2. Traditional Chinese society and values were changed by contact with the West, western interference in Chinese life, civil war, and a long war against Japan.

3. Revolutions in 1911 and 1912 overthrew the traditional monarchy and plunged China into a long series of civil wars.

4. After the Communists won the military victory in 1949, a vast program was begun to reshape Chinese political, economic, and social institutions along Communist lines.

5. The Chinese people speak many different dialects; the written language can only be read by the well-educated. The Communists are trying to simplify the language.

6. All media of communication are used to make people think in terms of the Communist idea.

7. Artistic effort must conform to the rigid standards set by the Communist Party and the government.

D. The victory of Communism in China presented challenges to Asian nations as well as to the Soviet Union and the non-Communist world powers.

1. The military victory of the Communists in 1949 was due to many factors.

2. The structures of the government and the Party are modeled after those of the Soviet Union.

3. Two governments, Nationalist (Taiwan) and People's Republic (mainland), claim legal rule over all of China.

4. The People's Republic of China was admitted to membership in the United Nations and the Nationalists were expelled.

5. The People's Republic of China is active in Asia and Africa in support of revolutionary activities for the establishment of communism.

6. Troubles between the Soviet Union and China had historic roots. For many years they were rivals for leadership of the world Communist movement.

E. China's Communist rulers brought about major changes in the economy. Their goal has been to turn China into a powerful industrial nation.

1. The Communists introduced a system of government ownership and control of the land and the means of production.

2. Industrialization has been promoted in a series of Five-Year Plans.

3. Rapid industrialization (Great Leap Forward Program) was not succeessful.

4. Agricultural production still remains a major problem.

5. Chinese scientific and technical potential is great, as shown by the production of atomic weapons.

6. Personal income and the production of consumer goods while rising in recent years remain low in comparison with industrialized countries.

UNIT IV

Exercises and Questions

Vocabulary

Directions: Match the words in Column A with the correct meaning in Column B.

<u>Column A</u>

1. loess
2. traditional
3. unique
4. dynasty
5. opium
6. rebellion
7. imperialism
8. communes
9. kaoliang
10. mandate
11. revolution

<u>Column B</u>

(a) one of a kind

(b) important change in government, economy, or society

(c) a narcotic drug

(d) large farming or factory units set up by the Communists

(e) the control of a weak country by a strong one

(f) order or command

(g) wind deposits of soil

(h) a cereal grain raised in China

(i) open resistance to authority or government

(j) a group of rulers from one family

(k) customs that have been handed down from generation to generation

Directions: Using the words below complete the following sentences:

| Zhongguo | Zhou Dynasty | Song Dynasty | Boxers | Kuomintang |
| Shang Dynasty | Daoism | Taipings | San Min Chu-I | Long March |

1. .... was the first Chinese dynasty for which archaeologists have found evidence.

2. .... was the dynasty famous for its literature and philosophers.

3. .... are the group who rebelled against the Manchus.

4. .... means the Middle Kingdom and is what the Chinese call their land.

5. .... is a view of people and the universe in which people must find "the way."

6. .... occurred when Mao Zedong fled to Yenan with his Communists to escape the Nationalists.

7. .... was the dynasty that made great contributions in art and civilization.

8. .... was the party formed by Sun Yat-sen to work for the unity of China.

9. .... were the three principles of Dr. Sun Yat-sen.

10. .... were a group of Chinese who tried to drive out the Westerners from Manchu China.

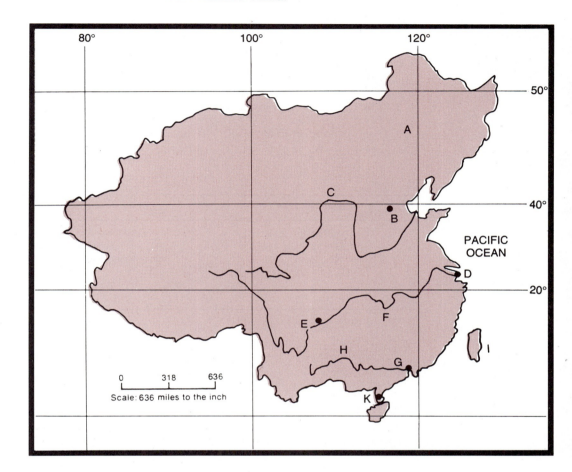

Map Exercise

Directions: Select the number of the correct answer.

1. An *island* is shown by the letter: (1) C   (2) F   (3) K   (4) I

2. A *peninsula* is shown by the letter: (1) C   (2) F   (3) K   (4) I

3. The distance from B to G is about: (1) 250 miles   (2) 500 miles
   (3) 1000 miles   (4) 1500 miles

4. The place located closest to 120° east longitude and 20° north latitude is
   (1) A   (2) B   (3) D   (4) K

5. Which of the following statements is true?
   (1) The climate of A is probably warmer than that of G.
   (2) The climate of I is probably warm and rainy.

(3) As you move from D to E the climate will become warmer.

(4) The climate of B and D will be exactly the same.

6. As you travel from B to G you are going   (1) North   (2) South   (3) East (4) West

7. The rivers shown on this map all flow in a/an   (1) northern direction (2) southern direction   (3) eastern direction   (4) western direction

8. This is a map of China. Which river is indicated by the letter C?   (1) Huang He (2) Chang   (3) Xi   (4) Yalu

9. The Chang River is indicated by the letter   (1) C   (2) F   (3) H   (4) K

10. You would most likely find the delta of the Xi River in   (1) North China (2) Central China   (3) South China   (4) West China

CHINA'S FOREIGN TRADE

Import Source		Export Destination		Main Exports
Japan	21%	Hong Kong	25%	Textiles
W. Germany	8%	Japan	13%	Clothing
United Kingdom	5%	United Kingdom	5%	Metal Ores
				Tea
				Rice
				Coal

Chart Analysis

Directions: Answer the following questions by indicating that the statement is *True* or *False* or that the *Information Is Not Given.* Base all answers on information given in the chart.

1. China's leading trading partner is probably Japan.

2. China sends much of its goods out of the country through Hong Kong.

3. More than 90 percent of the goods China buys are bought from Asian countries.

4. China has no trade with the United States and the former Soviet Union.

5. In conclusion we might say that China mainly sells light industrial products and raw materials.

Multiple Choice

Directions: Find the letter of the correct answer.

1. China's rivers have
   (a) greatly influenced the lives of the people.
   (b) not influenced the lives of the people.
   (c) only recently influenced the lives of the people.
   (d) slightly influences the lives of the people.

2. Which of the following statements is *true* about Chinese geography?
   (a) The mountains of China are along the east coast.
   (b) The rivers of China are navigable for only a short distance.
   (c) Geography has in part isolated China from the world.
   (d) Geography has had little to do with China's unique development.

3. The most densely populated areas of China are found
   (a) near industrial cities.
   (b) in the river valleys.
   (c) in the western mountains.
   (d) on the southern plateau.

4. The irregular coastline of China is important because
   (a) it prevents the development of trade.
   (b) it allows the cold winds from the north to destroy crops.
   (c) it aids the development of trade and harbors.
   (d) it prevents communication between North and South China.

5. The best way to discuss the climate of China is to
   (a) compare the differences between North and South China.
   (b) study the entire country because there are few variations.
   (c) study only the southern area because most of the Chinese live there.
   (d) compare the differences between China and Southeast Asia.

6. Which of the following would have the greatest effect on the lives of the Chinese people?
   (a) the Xi River
   (b) the monsoons
   (c) the North Wind
   (d) the Gobi Desert

7. As a person travels west in China, he or she is most likely to find
   (a) densely populated cities.
   (b) large agricultural areas.
   (c) mountains and desert country.
   (d) large lakes.

8. The main crop of North China is wheat because
   (a) the people do not know how to raise rice.
   (b) there is too much rain for rice growing.
   (c) there is not enough water for rice growing.
   (d) the people like to eat wheat products.

9. China's greatest potential for economic growth is in its
   (a) rate of population growth.
   (b) large areas of fertile farmland.
   (c) huge capital resources.
   (d) vast reserves of natural resources

10. The majority of people in China are known as the
    (a) Tibetans.
    (b) Kazaks.
    (c) Mongols.
    (d) Han.

11. The Chinese people believe in all of the following things *except*
    (a) the importance of history.
    (b) the need to live in peace with nature.
    (c) the right of rebellion.
    (d) the importance of the individual over the family.

12. Which of the following statements is *true* about Chinese culture?
    (a) The Chinese way of life remained unchanged until modern times.
    (b) The Chinese family plays only a small role in Chinese life.
    (c) Chinese art shows the great part human beings play in the universe.
    (d) Great changes in culture have taken place in the 20th century.

13. Which statement best describes China's one-couple, one-child policy?
    (a) It has successfully reduced China's population.
    (b) It was met with the full approval of the Chinese people.
    (c) The government did little to prepare the people for the program.
    (d) It has helped reduce the rate of growth of China's population.

14. Which of the following is *not* an idea of Confucius?
    (a) People should live by their senses and reject knowledge.
    (b) People have a place in society and duties to fulfill.
    (c) Obedience to one's parents is important.
    (d) The family is the foundation of Chinese society.

15. Confucianism is a
    (a) philosophy.
    (b) religion.
    (c) form of writing.
    (d) style of architecture.

16. Confucius was *not* interested in
    (a) how people acted.
    (b) how the government was run.
    (c) heaven and hell.
    (d) family relationships.

17. Which of the following is *not* one of the Five Basic Relationships of Confucius?
    (a) father and son
    (b) husband and wife
    (c) mother and daughter
    (d) friend and friend

18. Confucius believed that the emperor should be
    (a) rich and powerful.
    (b) wise and humane.
    (c) friendly and sociable.
    (d) strong and cruel.

19. Which of the following statements is true about Confucianism?
    (a) Salvation of the soul is a very important part of Confucianism.
    (b) According to Confucianism there is only one God.
    (c) Confucianism was mainly concerned with life after death.
    (d) Confucianism was mainly concerned with achieving a better life on earth.

20. Which of the following is *not* an idea of Daoism?
    (a) People are happiest when they live according to the rules of society.
    (b) Dao is the unseen power that controls all life and movement in the universe.
    (c) People must find out what Dao is and live according to it.
    (d) Society causes unhappiness and problems for people.

21. The gentry made money from all of the following except
    (a) large landed estates.
    (b) rice shops.
    (c) pawn shops.
    (d) hard work.

22. The gentry lived
    (a) in villages.
    (b) on their land.
    (c) in the towns.
    (d) along the coast.

23. In arranging marriages for their sons, it was important to the gentry that the
    (a) bride be beautiful.
    (b) bride be educated.
    (c) bride be capable of hard work.
    (d) bride's family have wealth and social position.

24. The gentry became the scholar-officals of China because
    (a) the Chinese believed that only educated people should run the government.
    (b) years of studying were necessary to pass a difficult civil service examination.
    (c) the gentry had the money and leisure to devote to education.
    (d) all of these

25. Which of the following is not true about the peasants of China?
    (a) The peasants earned a living doing hard physical work.
    (b) The peasants lived mainly in small families.
    (c) The peasants enjoyed many forms of entertainment and luxuries.
    (d) The peasants looked for wives who were capable of doing hard work.

26. Life for Chinese peasants was difficult because
    (a) they lived in great poverty.
    (b) disease and hunger were common.
    (c) they suffered from droughts, famine, and floods.
    (d) all of these

27. Which of the following is *not* true about family life in China?
    (a) The family was considered to be more important than the individual.
    (b) If a person did something wrong the shame was on the whole family.
    (c) Young people became independent only after marriage.
    (d) The oldest male was the most important person in the family.

28. Which of the following *is* true about family life in China?
    (a) Chinese fathers were very strict with their sons.
    (b) Daughters were often sold as slaves.
    (c) Parents had to train children to behave properly in society.
    (d) All of these are true.

29. Which statement is true concerning Chinese marriage customs?
    (a) Young men and women married on the basis of love.
    (b) Mothers helped pick husbands for their daughters.
    (c) Often the bride and groom did not see each other before the wedding.
    (d) The bride's family had to pay a dowry to the family of the groom.

30. In China, old age was
    (a) something to look forward to.
    (b) considered to be a terrible time.
    (c) not respected.
    (d) not considered to be important.

31. Women in China today
    (a) are legally inferior to men.
    (b) often leave their families for months in order to work.
    (c) cannot get a divorce.
    (d) still practice the custom of footbinding.

32. In China today it is believed that
    (a) a woman's place is in the home.
    (b) men have more to contribute to building up China than women.
    (c) a woman's family is more important than her job.
    (d) men and women should get equal pay for equalwork.

33. The Chinese language
    (a) is similar to European languages in the use of vowel sounds.
    (b) uses tone and sound to make meanings of words clear.
    (c) has changed very little despite contact with the West.
    (d) has not influenced other parts of the world to any extent.

34. The Chinese writing system
  (a) has served to unify the Chinese.
  (b) has only a few characters.
  (c) is similar to our writing system.
  (d) all of these

35. Which of the following statements is *not* true about education in China today?
  (a) An important goal in Chinese education is to promote the ideas of communism.
  (b) The Chinese have largely succeeded in wiping out illiteracy.
  (c) Confucianism and communism are the two most important philosophies taught in Chinese schools.
  (d) Most learning is still carried out by means of reciting and memorizing.

36. The earliest people of North China
  (a) developed little culture and lived in a primitive way.
  (b) developed cities and an agricultural civilization.
  (c) used only the simplest tools and weapons made of stone.
  (d) left few records so we know little of the culture.

37. Which of the following is *not* an accomplishment of the Han
  (a) The Han made the ideas of Confucius the law of the land.
  (b) The Han Chinese destroyed the power of the Mongols.
  (c) The Han Chinese invented paper and porcelain.
  (d) The Han Chinese developed trade with the Roman Empire.

38. (a) Yuan Dynasty   (b) Song Dynasty   (c) Ming Dynasty
  In which order did the above dynasties rule China?
  (a) abc
  (b) bca
  (c) bac
  (d) cab

39. The Manchus were able to rule China for all of the following reasons *except* which?
  (a) They outnumbered the Chinese in soldiers and arms.
  (b) They respected and encouraged the development of Chinese culture.
  (c) They allowed the Chinese people to take part in the government.
  (d) They rarely interfered in village life.

40. Invaders of China until the 19th century usually
  (a) adopted Chinese culture.
  (b) destroyed Chinese culture.
  (c) paid little attention to Chinese culture.
  (d) changed Chinese culture.

41. The Chinese sold which of the following groups of products to Europeans?
  (a) brocades, opium, tea
  (b) silk, opium, porcelain
  (c) porcelain, silk, tea
  (d) silver, porcelain, tea

42. The Opium War was fought because the
    (a) Chinese were not allowed to sell their opium in India.
    (b) Chinese wished to stop the British opium trade in China.
    (c) British and Chinese could not agree on how to split the profits.
    (d) British wanted to make China a colony.

43. The Manchus were faced with the problem of
    (a) overpopulation.
    (b) peasant revolts.
    (c) European imperialism.
    (d) all of these

44. Which of the following events was the result of the other three?
    (a) The Opium War breaks out.
    (b) The Chinese begin to smoke opium.
    (c) Rebellions break out against Manchu rule.
    (d) The British try to sell opium to the Chinese.

45. Which of the following nations did not take territory from the Chinese?
    (a) United States
    (b) Japan
    (c) Great Britain
    (d) Russia

46. Which of the following events happened *after* the other three?
    (a) Taiping Rebellion
    (b) Boxer Rebellion
    (c) Sino-Japanese War
    (d) Chinese Revolution

47. Which of the following was *not* an idea of Dr. Sun Yat-sen?
    (a) government of the people
    (b) economic equality
    (c) sacrifice for China
    (d) cultural revolution

48. Chiang Kai-shek
    (a) was successful in his attempt to unite China.
    (b) joined with the Communists to unite China after Dr. Sun's death.
    (c) joined with the Communists to fight the Japanese.
    (d) joined with the war lords to defeat the Communists.

49. The Communists were successful for all of the following reasons *except* which?
    (a) Russian troops were used to fight against the Nationalists.
    (b) The Nationalists were corrupt and were not supported by the people.
    (c) The Communists were given large amounts of captured Japanese arms.
    (d) The Communist army was better disciplined and had better generals.

50. Which of the following events occurred *before* the other three?
    (a) The Long March takes place.
    (b) Chiang Kai-shek flees to Formosa.
    (c) The Cultural Revolution takes place.
    (d) The Japanese surrender at the end of World War II.

51. Which of the following statements is *not* true about the Chinese government?
    (a) There are many political parties in China today.
    (b) Real power is in the hands of the Communists.
    (c) Important decisions are made by a small group of people.
    (d) Young people are not in positions of power.

52. The purpose of the mass organizations and militia units is to
    (a) give people an opportunity in making important decisions.
    (b) train people to participate in the government.
    (c) promote the ideas of the Communist Party and check on the people.
    (d) train people to exercise freedom of speech and press.

53. Which of the following does *not* represent Mao's basic ideas?
    (a) Professors, writers, and other city people had to be sent to the countryside to work alongside the peasants.
    (b) The landlord class had to be eliminated.
    (c) China had to learn from the United States in order to develop its economy.
    (d) Revolution and class struggle is a good thing.

54. The Agrarian Reform Act of 1950
    (a) organized the farmers into huge collective farms.
    (b) took land away from the landlords and gave it to the poor peasants.
    (c) introduced the "responsibility system" to agriculture.
    (d) provided the peasants with modern machinery and scientific methods.

55. The purpose of "thought control" was to
    (a) turn people into loyal Communists.
    (b) get people to accept Mao's teachings.
    (c) get people to give up the ideas and values of the past.
    (d) all of these

56. Many peasants were unhappy with the collective farms because
    (a) they were exploited by their landlords.
    (b) they no longer owned their land.
    (c) the land they received was dry and rocky.
    (d) some peasants became rich while others remained poor.

57. The purpose of the "Hundred Flowers" Campaign was to
    (a) make China more beautiful.
    (b) increase agricultural production.
    (c) produce new varieties of crops.
    (d) allow greater freedom of expression.

58. The "Great Leap Forward" involved

  (a) using China's abundant labor for irrigation, flood control, and construction of new projects.

  (b) setting up small furnaces in backyards.

  (c) organizing peasants into huge communes.

  (d) all of these

59. The "Great Leap Forward" failed because

  (a) it set unrealistic goals and was not carefully thought out.

  (b) China was not able to sell its agricultural products abroad.

  (c) the United States withdrew its technicians from China.

  (d) many Party leaders were opposed to it.

60. Which of the following suffered most from the Cultural Revolution?

  (a) the peasants.

  (b) the landlords.

  (c) the intellectuals.

  (d) the army.

61. The Cultural Revolution

  (a) modernized the Chinese economy.

  (b) spread education to the masses.

  (c) caused chaos and set China back about 20 years.

  (d) spread the ideas of communisim to China's neighbors.

62. The Cultural Revolution involved a(n)

  (a) attempt to bring back capitalism.

  (b) struggle for power between Mao Zedong and his opponents.

  (c) great change in the way of life of the Chinese people.

  (d) attempt to remove the Communists from power.

63. Peasants in China today

  (a) are still exploited by the rich gentry.

  (b) have less land than the large landowners.

  (c) are living better than ever before.

  (d) still suffer from famine and widespread hunger.

64. The ideas of Mao Zedong are presented to the Chinese people

  (a) in school.

  (b) in the newspapers and on the radio.

  (c) in movies and the theater.

  (d) all of these

65. One of the changes in agriculture made by Deng Xiaoping was

  (a) the development of huge communes.

  (b) the introduction of the responsibility system whereby workers who worked more earned more.

  (c) the return of all government owned land to the peasants.

  (d) the system of work points was started as a method of paying workers.

66. Deng's economic plan for China was to
    (a) strengthen and expand the Communist system of ownership in China.
    (b) return all property to individual ownership.
    (c) create a mixed economy in which both socialism and capitalism would exist.
    (d) eliminate all government controls over business.

67. Which of the following is true of Deng's "New Open Door Policy?"
    (a) Foreign companies were encouraged to invest in China.
    (b) The Chinese people were encouraged to emigrate to other countries.
    (c) Foreigners were encouraged to immigrate to China.
    (d) Chinese businesspeople were encouraged to build and run new factories.

68. Which problems continue to hurt the growth of China's economy?
    (a) A shortage of capital to build major projects.
    (b) A serious problem with unemployment.
    (c) A fear on the part of foreign investors to risk money in China.
    (d) All of the above.

69. Which of the following was a result of the other three?
    (a) The Chinese came into contact with foreign businesspeople.
    (b) Chinese students demanded political reforms.
    (c) The Communists allowed Chinese students to study abroad.
    (d) Some freedom of speech was allowed.

70. The group most responsible for the democracy movement in China was (were) the
    (a) peasants.
    (b) military.
    (c) college students.
    (d) Communist Party members.

71. Which statement is true about the demands of the demonstrators in Tiananmen Square?
    (a) They wanted greater freedom.
    (b) They wanted to bring communism to an end.
    (c) They wanted to remove China's rulers from power.
    (d) They wanted to end collective farms.

72. How did the Chinese government deal with the demonstrators at Tiananmen Square?
    (a) About 1,000 demonstrators were killed and many others were arrested.
    (b) They agreed to make sweeping reforms in the government.
    (c) They agreed to the demonstrator's demands for economic changes.
    (d) They praised the demonstrators as loyal Communists.

73. A major problem of China is the lack of enough food to feed the people. This is true because
    (a) little food is raised.
    (b) poor soil covers most of China.
    (c) China has a very large population.
    (d) most food is destroyed by insects.

Directions: Use the words or expressions below to fill in the blanks.

Little Red Book	Five-Year Plan	Young Pioneers	"red versus expert"
communes	class struggle	production teams	
Politburo	Red Guards	the Five-Anti-Movement	

1. Mao's young supporters in the Cultural Revolution were the _____ .

2. The top leadership of the Communist Party is known as the _____ .

3. Turning one group of people against another is known as _____ .

4. _____ was a program to industrialize China rapidly.

5. _____ is a mass organization to train future members of the Communist Party.

6. _____ destroyed the business class in China.

7. The main ideas of Mao Zedong are contained in the _____ .

8. Huge farms, often the size of towns, are called _____ .

9. Peasants were organized into _____ that worked the land in common.

10. _____ refers to the debate over what is most important: a loyal Communist or a technically educated person.

Directions: Use the phrases below to fill in the blanks.

New Open Door Policy	de-Maoization Campaign
Special Economic zones	Democracy Wall
"Four Modernizations"	responsibility system
"red eyes"	"Gang of Four"

1. _____ are areas where foreign investors can set up factories and earn profits.

2. Between 1978 and 1979, posters criticizing Mao and the Cultural Revolution were allowed on the _____ .

3. Allowing Western ideas, products, and technology into China is known as the _____ .

4. Mao's wife and her associates who were responsible for very radical policies were known as the _____ .

5. The program adopted in 1978 to end China's backwardness and push it into the 20th century is called _____ .

6. The policy of criticizing Mao's errors and rejecting him as a godlike figure is known as the _____ .

7. _____ refers to the poor peasants who are jealous of the people around them who have recently become rich.

8. The _____ allows Chinese peasants to make decisions about what to plant and what to sell after the government's quota is met.

Vocabulary

Directions: Match the words in Column A with the correct meaning in Column B.

Column A

1. pragmatist
2. radicals
3. counterrevolutionary
4. quota

5. reforms
6. mixed economy

7. dissidents

8. private enterprise

9. infrastructure

10. socialism

Column B

(a) changes, improvements
(b) people who follow extreme policies
(c) a fixed amount of something
(d) transportation and communication systems, power plants, etc.
(e) a practical person
(f) an economic system in which individuals own the factories and businesses and make profits
(g) a person who seeks to overthrow the Communist system
(h) an economic system in which the government or society owns all of the factories and the means of production
(i) people who disagree with the government's policies
(j) an economic system that combines elements of socialism with private enterprise

Mao Zedong or Deng Xiaoping

Directions: Read the following statements. Decide whether each one refers to Mao Zedong or to Deng Xiaoping. Write the correct name next to the sentence.

1. For 30 years his ideas controlled every aspect of Chinese society.

2. Revolutionary spirit and class struggle were more important than practical results.

3. His main goal has been to end China's backwardness in agriculture and industry and push China into the 20th century.

4. He was one of the victims of the Cultural Revolution.

5. He was always suspicious of landlords, intellectuals, experts, and anyone who could become part of a new ruling class.

6. He encouraged U.S., Japanese, and European companies to invest in China.

7. Under his rule, mass movements and campaigns were frequently used to carry out the policies set by the Communist Party.

8. He led the Communists to victory in 1949 and set up a Communist government in China.

9. He introduced many elements of capitalism into China's socialist economy.

10. Under his leadership, peasants were organized into collective farms run by the Communist Party.

Which of the Following Does Not Belong in Each Group?

Directions: Indicate which of the following does not belong in each group.

1. Problems of Industrialization: lack of sufficient capital, inadequate transportation, lack of iron and coal, oversupply of trained labor

2. Chinese Communist leaders: Mao Zedong, Chiang Kai-shek, Zhou Enlai, Lin Piao

3. Rivers of China: Chang, Mekong, Yellow, Xi

4. Actions of the Communists: Long March, Cultural Revolution, Great Leap Forward, Retreat to Formosa

5. Harbors of China: Chongqui, Shanghai, Tianjin, Guangzhou

Thought Questions

1. How has geography affected the development of Chinese civilization?

2. If you were a sociologist, how would you describe the major characteristics of the Chinese people?

3. How has the Chinese government tried to solve the country's problem of overpopulation?

4. "Confucianism was not a democratic philosophy." Give reasons to prove or disprove this statement.

5. Compare Confucianism and Daoism.
   (a) Show how the two philosophies were similar.
   (b) Show how the two were different.

6. Compare the peasants and gentry in traditional China in *each* of the following ways:
   (a) where they lived
   (b) the type of life each group led
   (c) the economic position of each
   (d) the family structure

7. How was the traditional Chinese family different from the typical American family?

8. "The Chinese language and writing system have served both to unify and separate the Chinese people." Explain this statement.

9. How did each of the following periods contribute to Chinese and world civilization?
   (a) Bronze Age
   (b) Zhou Period
   (c) Han Period
   (d) Manchu Period
   (e) Nationalist Period

10. How is the idea of the "Mandate from Heaven" similar to the ideas of the Declaration of Independence?

11. What were the factors that led to the fall of the Manchus?

12. What were the main ideas of Dr. Sun Yat-sen?

13. (a) What problems did Chiang Kai-shek face when he became leader of China?
    (b) How did he try to solve these problems?

14. How did the war with Japan, 1931–1945, affect China?

15. Why were the Chinese Communists able to gain control of China after 1945?

16. Explain how Mao Zedong and the Communists used mass movements and campaigns to eliminate "enemies of the people."

17. How were mass organizations used by the Communists to reach every individual?

18. How did the Soviet Union help China in the early years after the Communist revolution?

19. Why did the Communist leaders end private farming and organize the peasants into cooperatives and collective farms?

20. Why were Mao and the Communist leaders shocked by the results of the "Hundred Flowers" campaign?

21. How has life improved for the majority of Chinese people since the Communist Revolution?

22. How is the position of women in China today different from what it was in the past?

23. (a) Describe the program that was called "The Great Leap Forward."
    (b) How did this program affect China?

24. Why did Mao unleash the Cultural Revolution?

25. What were some of the results of the Cultural Revolution?

26. In what ways are Deng Xiaoping's basic ideas different from those of Mao Zedong?

27. How has Deng Xiaoping changed Chinese agriculture?

28. What are some of the changes that have been introduced into Chinese industry under Deng Xiaoping?

29. Why is Deng Xiaoping encouraging an "Open Door Policy" and "Special Economic Zones"?

30. What are some of the problems that China faces today in its attempt to modernize?

31. In what way has China remained unchanged under Deng Xiaoping?

32. Why has Taiwan been a serious problem for the United States and China?

33. Describe the causes of the Sino-Soviet dispute.

34. Why were there many years of bad feeling between the United States and China?

35. Why did relations between the United States and China improve during the 1970s?

36. How have relations between the United States and China continued to improve during the 1980s?

37. Imagine you were a supporter of the pro-democracy movement in China. How would you try to convince the government to make political reforms?

38. How has China changed since the crackdown at Tiananmen Square?

39. China claims that other nations do not have a right to condemn China for human rights violations because it is an internal affair. Do you think foreign nations have a right to interfere when another nation mistreats its people? Explain your answer.

40. Explain how the upheaval at Tiananmen Square has hurt the economy of China.

Developing Answers to Regents-Type Essay Questions

Helpful Hints

In developing your answers to the essays be sure to:

1. Include specific factual information and evidence whenever possible.

2. Answer the question being asked; do not go off on tangents.

3. Keep these general definitions in mind:
   (a) *discuss* means "to make observations about something using facts, reasoning, and argument; to present in some detail."
   (b) *describe* means "to illustrate something in words or to tell about."
   (c) *show* means "to point out, to set forth clearly an idea or position by stating it and giving data that support it."
   (d) *explain* means "to make plain or understandable; to give reasons for or causes of; to show the logical development or relationship."

Sample Essay Questions

1. Geographic factors have greatly influenced the development of nations and cultures.

   Geographic Characteristics

Rivers and River Valleys	Mountains	Climate
Size	Deserts	Coastline

   Select *three* geographic characteristics from the list. For each characteristic:
   (a) Discuss how that characteristic influenced the development of the history and culture of China.
   (b) For each of the three geographic characteristics, explain *one* way in which China has adapted to or tried to modify its effects.

2. Individuals often influence the political, social, and economic life of their country.

   Individuals

Confucius	Chiang Kai Shek	Sun Yat Sen
Mao Zedong	Deng Xioping	Zheng He

   Select *three* of the individuals and show how *each* influenced the development of China.

3. Major events or movements in the history of a nation are sometimes described in terms of cause and effect relationships.

Events—Movements

The Opium War	The Communist Revolution
The Boxer Rebellion	The Cultural Revolution
The Chinese Revolution of 1911	Tiananmen Square—Demonstrations & Massacre

Choose *three* of the events or movements listed above. For *each* one chosen:
(a) Describe the major cause of the event or movement.
(b) Discuss the impact or effect of the event or movement on Chinese historical and political development.

4. Culture is made up of many aspects of a people's daily life.

Aspects of Culture

Religion	Social Classes	Language & Writing System
Sex Roles	Education	Family Relationships

Choose *three* aspects of culture listed above. For *each* aspect chosen:
(a) Describe that aspect of culture in the lives of the Chinese people.
(b) Discuss how that aspect influences the lives of the Chinese people today.

5. China has faced many problems that have restricted economic development.

Problems

Shortage of Capital	Natural Disasters
Inadequate Infrastructure	Lack of Development and Capital
Shortage of Skilled Labor	Corruption

Choose *three* of the problems listed. For *each* one chosen:
(a) Describe the specific conditions that each problem has caused China.
(b) Explain how these conditions restrict China's economic development.
(c) Describe *one* specific attempt that has been made by China to overcome that problem.

6. Communist ideas and programs have influenced the economic, political, and social life of China.

(a) 1. Identify *two* ideas or programs of the Communists in China.
    2. State how *each* of these ideas or programs has affected or affects the Chinese people.
(b) Using the information in your Part (a) answer, and any other information you may have, write an essay with the following topic sentence: "Communist ideas and programs have influenced the political, economic, and social life of China."

Puzzle

Directions: Place the words below in their proper place in the puzzle.

4 LETTERS	**5 LETTERS**	**6 LETTERS**	**7 LETTERS**	**8 LETTERS**
RICE	CLASS	GENTRY	DYNASTY	COMMUNES
SILK	LOESS	REFORM	MANDATE	CULTURAL
	OPIUM	SOURCE	PEASANT	DIFFUSED
		UNIQUE	TYPHOON	MONSOONS

9 LETTERS	**10 LETTERS**	**11 LETTERS**	**12 LETTERS**	**13 LETTERS**
DEMOCRACY	COMMUNISTS	ACUPUNCTURE	NATIONALISTS	RELATIONSHIPS
ISOLATION	PHILOSOPHY	TRADITIONAL		
PORCELAIN	PICTOGRAPH			
REBELLION				
SOCIALISM				

14 LETTERS

OVERPOPULATION

Above Qin Shi Huang Di, first Emperor of Qin, fortified his burial site with more than 6,000 life-size pottery warriors. Each figure has different features and is painted with bright colors to indicate rank.

Left Chinese archaeologists carefully excavate the figures originally uncovered in 1974.

INDIA, PAKISTAN, AND BANGLADESH

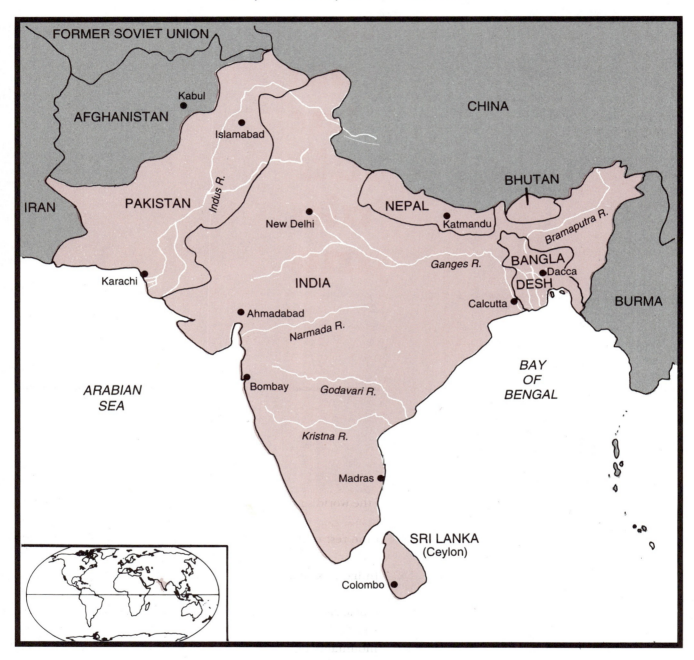

370 The Subcontinent of India and South Asia (Pakistan and Bangladesh)

UNIT V

The Subcontinent of India and South Asia (Pakistan and Bangladesh)

The Land

India, the home of one of the world's great civilizations, is the seventh largest country in the world in size and the second largest in population. Because it covers a vast area, and because it is separated from the rest of Asia by mountains, India, together with its neighbors Pakistan and Bangladesh, is often called a **subcontinent**.

Historic India includes India, Pakistan, and Bangladesh. The Indian peninsula juts southward from the Asian continent into the Indian Ocean. On the east is the Bay of Bengal; on the west, the Arabian Sea. At the southern tip of the peninsula is the island of Sri Lanka (Ceylon), separated from India by a shallow strait. The subcontinent is bounded on the north by the towering mountains of the Himalayas in the northeast, and the great ranges known as the Karakorum and the Hindu Kush to the northwest. In these mountains are some of the highest peaks in the world. Mount Everest in the Himalayas, at more than 29,000 feet, is the world's highest peak.

The high wall of mountains is very hard to cross. However, there are a few places where long passes cut through these mountains. Here, through the Khyber Pass and other passes of the Hindu Kush, great **migrations** (movements) of people, as well as invading armies, pushed down into the lush river valleys of North India.

The Thar Desert lies in the northwestern part of the subcontinent, just south of the Indus River. It is almost impossible to cross this dry wasteland. The Thar has successfully prevented invading armies, customs, and ideas from moving from the northwest into the great interior (inside) of India.

The Rivers of the Subcontinent

What made historic North India so desirable to invaders was its fertile land, watered by two great river systems. The Indus River, which flows down from the northern mountains, is one of the most important in the subcontinent. India takes its name from this great waterway. With its four **tributary** (branching) rivers, the Indus forms a large fertile plain in Pakistan. This region has long been known as the Punjab, which means "five rivers" in Hindustani.

The second great river, the Ganges, rises in the Himalayas and flows for hundreds of miles across northeastern India. The Ganges plain is the most densely populated part of the entire subcontinent. Many of India's major cities, including New Delhi, the capital, and Calcutta, the leading seaport, are located there.

Another great river, the Brahmaputra, flows across Bangladesh in the northeastern parts of the Indian subcontinent. This long river has its source in Tibet and empties into the Bay of Bengal. Near its mouth, it joins the Ganges. The large delta area of the two rivers is densely populated.

The Deccan Plateau

The central part of the nation of India is known as the Deccan Plateau. (*Deccan* means "south.") In this area, there are many flat-topped hills and high, rolling plains. The plateau is divided by deeply cut river valleys, many of which are very wide. On each side of the Deccan are low mountains called Ghats. (The word *Ghats* means "steps" or "a steep place.") These mountains isolated the Deccan from other parts of India for hundreds of years. Today, however, the airplane and railroads connect the Deccan with other parts of India. Many of India's minerals are mined in the Deccan. The population here is the least dense of any part of India. With the development of irrigation projects, parts of the Deccan have become grain-producing areas.

The Coastal Plain

Between the uplands and the sea is a narrow coastal plain, which borders much of the eastern, or Carnatic, coast and the western, or Malabar, coast. The plain is broken in places by hills that reach all the way to the water. In many places these hills end as cliffs.

The Indian subcontinent has a coastline that is long but unfortunately also very straight. As a result, there are few good harbors. Except for one or two river mouths, there are almost no indentations that can shelter oceangoing ships from a storm.

The coastal plains are very fertile and heavily populated. The rich land has been used for centuries for raising rice. The countries that wished to trade with India set up trading posts on these narrow coastal strips, where many of India's largest cities are located. Calcutta,

Typical bazaar. Bazaars are important social and business centers in Indian life.

The Ganges Plain is flat and fertile. It is the center of the production of rice, sugarcane, and cotton. Irrigation makes it possible to grow two crops a year.

India's largest city, is the center of trade on the east coast. Bombay is the most important trading center and second largest city on the west coast. Madras, the fourth largest city, has become the most important port of South India. (Delhi, located in the interior, is the third largest city.)

The South

South India is a separate world in the Indian part of the subcontinent; it is a land of mountains, forests, and jungles. Most of the coastal areas have rich farmland. The inland parts of South India have never been good places to live. Consequently, most of the people live on the narrow coastal plains, which have always been very crowded. Because of the crowding and the nearness to the sea, South India's people have often left India for other places in which to trade and to live. Many of the people of South India have settled in Sri Lanka (Ceylon), Malaysia, Singapore, the islands of the South Pacific, and East and South Africa.

Climate

A Wide Range of Climates

The Indian subcontinent stretches from the latitude of 8° north to 37° north. Although this is a wide range of latitude, temperature does not vary very much throughout the country. (Why do you think this is so?) In the northern mountains we find snow; 2,000 miles to the south, at the tip of the peninsula, there are palm trees and beaches of golden sand near a tropical rain forest.

Seasons and Monsoons

In most of India, the year may be divided into three different seasons. One is hot, another is cool, and the third is rainy. The cool season, from October to February, is winter, when the winds blow from the north. However, the very cold winds from central Asia do not reach India because they are blocked by the Himalayas. Along the coasts the temperature is higher because those lands are heated by warm ocean currents.

During the hot and dry season, from March through June, the land is brown and dusty, the muddy waters of the Ganges are low, and the irrigation ditches are empty. The temperature in many parts of India often rises above 100°F, making it difficult to work very hard. The upland and coastal areas are slightly cooler.

From July to September is the rainy season. India's rainfall is controlled by the seasonal winds called monsoons. The southwest monsoon, beginning in late June, blows across thousands of miles of ocean, and is soaked with moisture when it reaches India. Rain falls when the monsoon is forced to rise over the Ghats and other highlands. The southwest monsoon brings about 90 percent of all the rain that falls. There is less rain from September until the beginning of January. Then the northeast monsoon takes over and blows from the land toward the sea. Since it can pick up very little moisture, except as it blows over the Bay of Bengal, it brings very little rain.

The Effects of Climate and Topography on Indian History

"To know India and her people one has to know the monsoon."* When the monsoons come late or fail to bring enough rain many people suffer. The rivers and wells cannot supply enough water for crops, and the people must go hungry. To the people of India, the monsoons are a source of life.

MONSOON INDIA

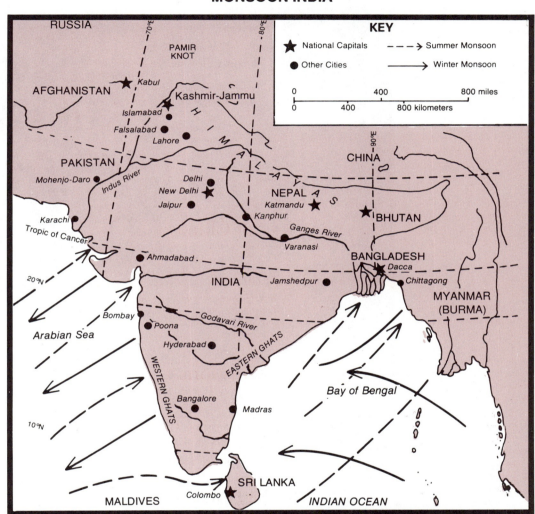

For centuries, the monsoon winds have played an important role in cultural diffusion. As early as the Roman Empire, traders took advantage of the winds to sail the Indian Ocean between India and the Middle East or Africa. They carried goods, such as glass, swords, and textiles, as well as ideas, from one culture to another. Islam moved by way of the trade routes from the Middle East to India and Southeast Asia. Indian mathematics, literature, and science moved along the same trade routes to the Middle East and Europe. Vasco da Gama, the first European to travel from Europe to India around Africa, took advantage of the summer monsoon in his voyage.

---

*Singh, Khuswant. *I Shall Not Hear the Nightingale.* New York: Grove Press, 1959.

Climate and topography have had a great effect on the course of Indian history. In the south, the tropical and subtropical climate provided ideal conditions for the rice, cotton, sugar, pepper, cinnamon, and other spices that make the south a natural marketplace. But the same climate weakened the people. In the north, the more moderate climate and rich soil made for good crops and a hardy people. As a result, northern ideas spread to the south. Hinduism, the main unifying force of modern India, was brought south by its northern followers.

Monsoon India. Heavy rains and flooding occur during the monsoon season.

The south was rich enough to attract northern invaders, and weak enough to be conquered. The rough terrain could not keep northerners out. However, once they had gained control of the area, northerners found it difficult to hold onto, because they could not supply armies or maintain proper communication with the south. (How did geography affect supply lines and communications?)

Agriculture

Influence of Climate on India's Agriculture

Most people of India live today as their ancestors lived for hundreds of years, chiefly as farmers. Most of the farmers live on the North India plain and on the coastal lowlands. The crops are largely determined by the climate. The northeastern part of India near

Calcutta, and most of the southwestern coastal region, receive very heavy rainfall. Even during the dry season a great deal of moisture remains in the soil. Some of the lowland areas near the east coast receive less rain, but streams, wells, and man-made ponds provide water for farming. In these well-watered areas, rice is the most important crop. It is grown in flooded fields called paddies.

AGRICULTURE AND MANUFACTURING IN SOUTH ASIA

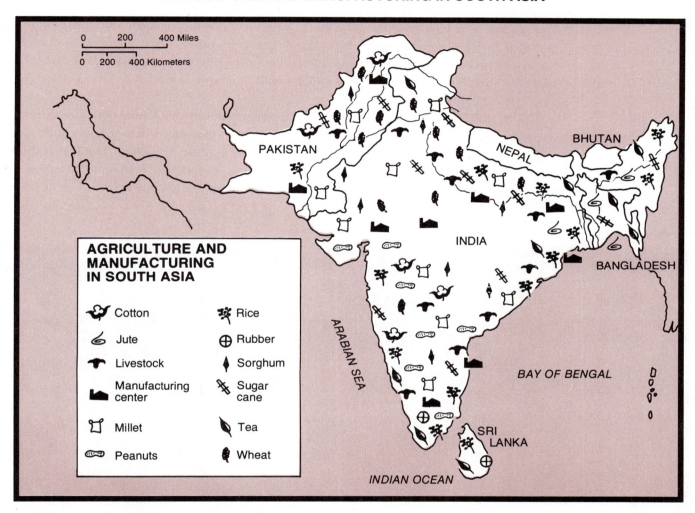

In the warm, wet lowlands that border the western coast, farmers raise coconuts, pepper, ginger, and other tropical crops. Large amounts of **jute** (a plant that provides fibers for making burlap bags, twine, or cord) are grown in the eastern part of India. Toward the middle of the North India Plain, where there is less moisture, farmers often grow corn or sugarcane.

The western part of the North India Plain receives little rainfall. However, here the great Ganges and other rivers provide water for farming. Thousands of miles of canals have been dug to carry water to the fields. Wheat, barley, flax, sugarcane, and cotton are raised in the irrigated fields.

The hilly plateau region has less rainfall, and irrigation is not possible. Here, wells and ponds are dug, and millet and sorghum, as well as large quantities of peanuts, are grown.

Agricultural Production in India

India is a major producer of a number of farm products, but it also has many people to feed. Therefore, many of the over 850 million people do not have well-balanced diets or as much food as they need.

Nearly three-fourths of the Indian people live by farming. Although about half of India's vast area is suitable for agriculture, most of the farms are small and provide only enough for the farmers' own needs. According to tradition, when a father dies, land owned by his family is divided equally among the sons. Often there are many sons, and the death of their father results in division of the land into farms too small to provide enough food for each son's family.

In the period before the 1980s, Indian farmers produced small amounts of grain per acre. For example, the average yield of rice per acre was one-third that of Japan and less than one-third that of China. This has been due to a number of factors. The first is the poverty and illiteracy of the Indian farmer. Many of the farmers have held on to their traditional ways and have resisted change. Another reason for the low yields is the size of the

Animals are sacred in the Hindu religion. They are allowed to roam freely in towns and villages.

farms. They are so small that, even if farmers were willing to improve the land, modern methods would not be economical (worth the money spent).

The Indian government is working hard to overcome these problems. Better use of agricultural resources is a major goal. More land has been put into use through the expansion of irrigation, and laws have been passed opposing high rents for farmers. Since 1980, the government has concentrated on modernizing the thousands of small farms by giving direct aid to individual villages. In addition, the government has sent experts to the farms to teach modern agricultural methods.

Flood control and soil erosion projects are helping to preserve precious soil. Better grain storage facilities reduce losses due to rats and other pests. The introduction of high-yielding rice crops from the Philippines and "miracle wheat" developed in Mexico has resulted in higher production and a shorter growing season. These changes make up what is called the green revolution.

Rice, wheat, and millet are India's leading food crops. India now grows more peanuts, peppers, and tea than any other country and is second only to China in rice production. It is also a world leader in growing bananas, sugarcane, tobacco, cotton, wheat, and jute.

India has about 42 million sheep and 182 million cattle. The Hindus believe it is wrong to kill these animals. However, cattle are used to produce milk and to do farm work.

Although improved agricultural methods have enabled India to feed itself in most years (when the monsoon cooperates), there are still serious problems. Crop yields per acre have improved, but they remain low and have not kept up with the population growth. Fertilizer is still too expensive for most farmers. Although cow dung, which is available in large quantities, could serve as fertilizer, Indians use the dung for heating and cooking because no other fuel is affordable or available. Natural disasters such as droughts, floods, cyclones, locusts, and crop disease have also caused agricultural setbacks and added to the nation's farming problems.

AGRICULTURAL PRODUCTION IN INDIA, 1972–1989

Commodity	Amount (millions of tons)				
	1989	1984	1975	1974	1972
Wheat	53.4	45.1	25.8	22.0	26.4
Rice	70.8	59.8	70.5	60.0	57.9
Barley	2.1	1.8	2.9	2.3	2.5
Corn	9.4	8.0	5.5	5.0	6.2
Potatoes	10.4	10.1	6.1	4.6	4.8
Bananas	5.3	4.5	—	3.2	3.1
Peanuts	8.0	7.3	6.6	5.2	3.9
Sugar (raw)	10.4	5.5	5.3	4.3	3.3
Jute	2.1	1.6	0.8	1.0	0.8
Cotton	9.0	7.4	5.4	—	—
				Number	**(millions)**
Cattle	193	182	180.3	179.9	176.9
Sheep	51	42	40.0	40.2	43.3
Buffaloes	72	63	—	60.0	55.0
Goats	105	78	—	69.0	69.0
Poultry	164	150	—	118.4	118.0

Sources: *Encyclopedia Britannica, Book of the Year*, 1991; United States Statistical Yearbook, 1976.

Peoples and Languages

India Is a Land of Many Peoples

The population of India is more than 850 million, about two-and-one-half times larger than the population of the United States. Since India is about one-third the size of the United States, it is obviously very crowded, especially in the cities.

There are many groups of people in India. They have a common culture, but they are different in many ways. No one description fits all Indians. In the north and central regions, the men and women are quite tall and well built. They have light skin, straight or wavy black or brown hair, and dark or light brown eyes. In the northeast and south, many Indians are short and slight in build. Skin colors range from tan to dark brown or black, and eyes are usually dark. In the hill country of central India and in the far north are still other types of people. In the Himalayan border region of India, there are people who strongly resemble the Chinese or Japanese.

India Is a Land of Many Languages

Physical diversity is matched by the variety of languages. The national language of India is **Hindi**, but 13 regional languages are also recognized. More than 100 dialects are spoken. Some of the languages belong to the Indo-European language family. This means that they are related to Western languages like English and French and are quite different from all other languages spoken in Asia. The language spoken in South India belongs to still another group, the Dravidian language family, which is also unknown in other parts of Asia.

Sanskrit, the ancient, holy language of India, has been in use for over 3,000 years. It is still spoken and written throughout India by the educated *pundits* (intellectuals) and by the upper classes. It was, and still is, the language of the great literature of India, used in such works as the "Upanishads," the "Ramayana," and the "Mahabharata" (see pages 387–388). Sanskrit has influenced almost all the languages of East Asia.

PRINCIPAL LANGUAGES OF INDIA AND PAKISTAN

India		Pakistan	
Language	**Number of People Speaking (millions)**	**Language**	**Number of People Speaking (millions)**
Hindi	331	Punjabi	72
Telugu	68	Pushto	16
Bengali	64	Sindhi	14
Marathi	62	Saraiki	12
Tamil	56	Urdu	9
Urdu	44	Other	12
Gugerati	41		
Kannada	33		
Malayalam	32		
Oriya	28		
Punjabi	23		
Rajasthani	16		
Assamese	10		
Kashmiri	4		

Historically, the difference in languages has raised important political problems. It has contributed to the **fragmentation** (breaking up) of India into hundreds of small states. For modern India, it has hindered the building of a truly national state. Officials in Delhi have difficulty in making their wishes known to members of the National Assembly and to governors in the provinces. Attempts to standardize the nation's schools have been hindered by the unwillingness of the various regions to accept a common language.

Language Diffusion—East to West

Many words from the various languages of India, especially Hindi, have been borrowed by the English. Some of these borrowed words have become part of the English language and are in daily use. Here are some examples:

Brahmin: a wealthy person of the highest class
bungalow: a small cottage—*bungalow* is a Bengali word
calico: a type of cloth developed in India
chintz: another type of cloth developed in India
coolie: a laborer who works at odd jobs for low pay
curry: a highly spiced dish
divan: a couch—usually found in an Indian palace
khaki: another type of cloth developed in India
loot: stolen goods
madras: another type of cloth developed in India
mogul: a rich or important person
pajamas: loose-fitting clothes
pariah: a poor person, an outcast (person not welcome in society)
punch: a drink (originally had five ingredients—from *panch*, Hindi word for "five")
pundit: a teacher or scholar
shawl: a scarf worn over the shoulders
thug: a gangster or cutthroat

(Why have so many Indian words related to clothing and cloth also become English words?)

The Village in Indian Life

The village is the heart of Indian life. This has been true throughout the history of India, and today four out of five Indians live in villages. Most of India's 550,000 villages are small, with an average of 100 families each. The typical village consists of a small group of huts and cottages. The street, if there is one, is usually rutted and narrow, no better than a cowpath. For many Indians, their village neighbors are the only people they ever know because they live out their lives without traveling more than a few miles from their home village.

The well is an important part of village life. Most villages depend on the well for all or part of their water supply. Getting the water from the wall is considered woman's work, and the women of the village go to the well every day. It is a good time to trade news and gossip and to show off new **saris** and bracelets.

The Panchayat

The village is usually ruled by a council of older men. The **panchayat** (*pancha* is five), or "council of five," is the most common type of council, ruling over more than 90 percent of Indian villages. The members of the panchayat are usually elected by the villagers. However, in many cases the richest villagers and members of the highest caste are elected. The panchayats became very important in history because of the failure of India to unite under a single national government, and they are still important today. In general, they are responsible for agricultural production, local industry, and maintaining village streets, ponds, and sanitation. In addition, some village councils set local taxes and make decisions about elementary school education.

Indian Food

India is a country with many different groups of peoples and many religions. One group eats pork but not beef; another beef but not pork. A third group is completely vegetarian. The religious beliefs of each group of people determine which foods may be eaten and which are forbidden. Throughout all of India, however, one ingredient is found in the food—curry.

Curry is a mixture of spices. In India, the housewife buys individual spices and then she grinds and blends them together according to her own recipe. No two curries are alike. Curry dishes vary from village to village, from city to city, and from family to family in any village or city.

Ghee, a form of clarified (skimmed) butter, is used instead of oils and fats in cooking. Yogurt is also important in cooking. The main food eaten by Indians is boiled rice (*chawal*) prepared with herbs and spices, and *chapattis*, which is Indian bread.

Indian Dress

Most village Indian men wear a *dhoti*, which is a simple white cloth wrapped between the legs and around the waist. Hindu women wear a sari, a wide piece of cloth draped in such a way that it covers the body from shoulder to ankle. Indians can tell which region of India a Hindu woman comes from by the way she wears her sari.

Housing in the Indian Village

The climate of an area and the building materials available influence the kinds of houses built by the villagers. Trees were uprooted centuries ago to make room for farming. With little wood, the farmers build houses of sun-dried brick. Often, in times of flood and heavy rain, the houses "melt" away.

In northeastern India and in the south, where wood is available, construction is very different from that on the North Indian Plain. The houses here are built of wood and various kinds of reeds. Houses built in this manner are fairly livable during most of the year. At least they are well ventilated, an important feature in the hot, humid climate. But the houses are not waterproof. They become damp and uncomfortable during the rainy season, and they are often destroyed by floods.

Houses in the various Indian villages do have certain things in common. Most have few rooms, three at most. Often the family lives in one room and the second or third room houses the water buffalo or cow. The floor of the hut is the bare earth. There is little or no furniture and the family takes its meals sitting on the floor. The bed is a mat or blanket. The family's possessions are stored around the room, suspended from pegs or hung from the rafters.

Problems of Village India

Poverty

Village India presents a picture of continuing struggle and poverty. Farms are small. The average size of an Indian farm is five acres, but many farmers must be satisfied with one acre or two. Villagers who do not farm are carpenters, blacksmiths, potters, weavers, or barbers. They earn a living by trading their services to the farmers for grain. The average yearly income of most village farmers is less than the weekly income of many Americans, and many Indians are hopelessly in debt. Often, the debts are inherited from parents, and tradition demands that the debts be paid.

Poor Nutrition

The diet of the villager consists mainly of rice in the south and wheat in the north. Little meat is eaten because the Hindu religion teaches that to eat beef is sinful, and Muslims do not eat ham, bacon, or any form of pork for the same reason. Most Indian villagers die before they reach the age of 45, and many suffer from disease during their lives.

Young Population

Because of the relatively short life span in the Indian villages, most of the people there are young. More than one third of them are under 14 years of age. The chart below shows just how young India's population is.

Age	United States		India	
	1989	1984	1984	1989
55 and over	24%	19%	10%	17%
35–54 years	24%	24%	15%	18%
15–34 years	30%	26%	25%	28.5%
Under 14	22%	31%	50%	36.5%

Illiteracy and Isolation

Most of the villagers are illiterate; that is, they are not able to read or write. Because of poverty and poor transportation, millions of villagers have never had an opportunity to leave their birthplaces. Roads between villages have been little more than dirt paths. Today, however, villages have more contact with the outside world. New roads are being built, and primary schools have been set up in most villages. Also, most villages now have at least one radio to keep people informed about events.

As India becomes more industrialized, many villagers are getting jobs in the cities. These people seldom return, but news of city life gets back to the families they leave behind. Despite these new contacts, however, the Indian villager is hardly part of the modern world.

In spite of all the hardship and lack of possessions, many Indian villagers feel that their present life suits them. They know little about other ways of living, and they prefer the familiar to the unknown.

The Hindu Religion

"Hinduism is much more than a religion; it is a total way of life, including the customs, beliefs, practices, institutions of the people in all parts of the subcontinent [India], developed in all periods of human settlement there. . . . Hinduism is not a single religion, but many religions tolerating [willingness to allow beliefs or actions in which one does not necessarily believe] one another in the shifting framework of **caste** [Hindu social class]."[1]

An example of a Hindu temple built many centuries ago in Madras by the seashore.

---

[1] W. Norman Brown, from S. Fersh, *India and South Asia.* New York: Macmillan, Inc., p. 35.

Main Ideas of Hinduism

Reincarnation

Three main ideas are important in understanding the Hindu religion and the caste system.

The first of these ideas is **reincarnation**. According to this belief, each person and every other living thing has a soul. When a living thing dies, its soul moves into another human being or animal. In other words, when death comes, the soul is reborn in a newly created life.

Karma

The second idea is **Karma**. Karma teaches that every action brings about certain results. If a person behaves badly, the results will be bad. If a person behaves well, the results will be good. There is no escaping the consequences of one's actions. If a person does what he or she is supposed to do, his or her soul will be rewarded in the next rebirth by being reincarnated into a higher ranking human.

Thus, if an **untouchable** (see the next section) does a job well and does not complain, the untouchable may be reborn into a higher caste. Some day, if the untouchable continues to behave well, he or she may reach the highest caste and become a Brahmin.

Dharma

The third idea is **Dharma**. Dharma is a set of rules that must be followed by all living beings if they wish to work their way up the ladder of reincarnation. Each person's Dharma is different. (How have these ideas created a sense of order for the Hindus of India?)

The Caste System

The caste system began in India more then 3,000 years ago. The Aryans, who conquered India, took for themselves the kind of work that they thought was desirable. They became the religious leaders, the rulers, the traders, and the landowner farmers. The other people were forced to become servants for the Aryans, or to do work that was necessary but took more effort, or was considered less respectable, such as the tasks of the barber, carpenter, tailor, potter, or street cleaner.

Lowest of all the jobs was sweeping the streets, handling dead people and animals, and tending pigs that fed on village garbage. No one even liked to come near people who did these jobs that other villagers considered to be unclean. This attitude probably sprang from the idea that disease was carried from person to person, and that it was better to stay away from anyone who touched dead or dirty things.

The Five Orders of Castes

The caste system divides the Indian population into **hereditary** (passed from one generation to the next) social groups (Varnas). There are five general orders, or groups, of castes. The three highest orders are Brahmin (priests), Kashatriya (soldiers), and Vaishya (merchants). The fourth order is Sudras (laborers). The members of the fifth (lowest) group of castes, those who do jobs that others consider unclean, are referred to as "untouchables" or "outcasts." To many Hindus, untouchables rate so low as to be considered outside or beneath the caste system itself. They must live apart from the rest of the people and are not permitted to use the village wells.

The Main Ideas of the Caste System

A major idea of the caste system is that people are born unequal in both opportunity and ability. Thus, while untouchables have few privileges, less is expected from them than from a Brahmin.

The caste system also teaches that a person belongs to a specific caste from birth. His life, marriage, and work are governed by specific caste rules. The son of a laborer becomes a laborer; the son of a teacher becomes a teacher. And, of course, the son of a king usually became a ruler upon the death of his father. Girls are regarded as inferior to boys and are married into families that do the same work as their fathers and brothers did. In this way, a small kingdom or a village is almost certain, year after year, to have all of the kinds of workers it needs.

In other words, the purpose of the caste system is to develop a plan by which villagers can live and work together. Its main goal is to produce enough food and to provide enough labor of all the necessary types so that each family has everything it needs.

Castes are often divided into clan or landowning groups called *jatis*. In the cities, jatis are often in competition with each other for power and access to government funds. In the villages, however, jatis are frequently interdependent and cooperative. Voting is a perfect way to show how belonging to a jati works. With rare exceptions, members of a jati will vote the same way, as will their servants and other workers.

Each caste has its own Dharma, which is carefully taught to the young by the elders. Within the caste Dharma, each person begins to understand his or her own personal Dharma as well.

Relationship Between Hinduism and the Caste System

Can you see how Hinduism and the caste system are related? The caste into which a person is born is determined by the way that person performed his or her Dharma in a previous life. According to the law of Karma, if one is an untouchable, one has no one to blame but one's self. Instead of complaining, that person had better do a good job. If not, he or she will sink to the level of an animal that crawls.

If a person behaves well through an unknown number of reincarnations, that person's soul will reach *Moksha*, the final resting place. To enter Moksha is desirable because the soul will then be free of all the pain that life brings, and it will be able to rest from its long, sad travels on earth. (Why did many Hindus accept their roles as "untouchables" in the past? Why might they be unhappy about that place in society today?)

The Literature of Ancient India

India has a tradition of learning that stretches far back into the past. Much of its culture and writing grew out of Hindu teaching and practices. Many of the stories and traditions were passed on from generation to generation by the village storyteller, usually an elderly person. By hearing the stories over and over, and by seeing them staged at holiday festivals, Indians remained close to their traditions.

Many centuries later, the great literature of the early Indians was written down to be enjoyed not only by the village dweller but also by all the other peoples of the world.

The Vedas

We know something about the customs, institutions, and religious practices of the Aryans from four collections of sacred writings called Vedas. The Vedas are very ancient; in fact, they are the earliest collection of writings in India (1500 to 800 B.C.). The Vedas are a collection of hymns, sacred prayers, and chants that are still recited at weddings and funerals today. The Vedas tell of nature worship. (There were gods of the sun, the wind, and the rain.)

A frieze from the temple at Konarak in Orissa that is a fine example of temple sculpture. The figures portray the pleasures of life.

The most famous Veda is the Rig-Veda, which was written about 800 B.C. and is the oldest known religious document in the world. (*Rig* means "hymn" and *Veda* means "knowledge.") There are 110 Hymns of Knowledge. One of these, called the Hymn of Creation, is in many ways similiar to the creation story told in the Old Testament of the Bible. There is also a belief shown in a universal spirit or Creator.

Of the three other Vedas, the Sama Veda is a collection of hymns; the Yajur Veda is a manual used by priests in the performance of their religious duties; and the Atharva Veda contains many magical spells.

The Vedas were passed by word of mouth from one generation to the next for many centuries before being written down. In the Vedas may be found the roots of Hindu beliefs and ideas.

The Upanishads

The Upanishads, a collection of rituals and ceremonies written about 2,500 years ago, is a valuable source of information about Hinduism. It is written in both prose and verse. The writers discuss the origins of the universe and also the meaning and importance of the soul. The prayers contain messages on religious thoughts and present a way of life for the Indian people. ("Truth conquers ever, falsehood never.")

The Mahabharata

The Mahabharata is the longest poem in the world and contains about 200,000 lines (100,000 couplets). *Maha* means "great," and *Bharat* is the legendary name of India during the ancient Vedic Age.

The Mahabharata tells the story of a war between two Indian families, so savagely fought that few survived its end. Within the poem is a section that has become famous throughout the world, the *Bhagavad-Gita* or *Gita* (the Song of God).

The Gita tells the story of Arjuna, the perfect warrior. Arjuna is unhappy because many of his friends and relatives are in the army opposing him. He does not want to kill them, but he doesn't want to lose the fight either. He asks advice from one of his soldiers, who turns out to be Krishna, one of the gods. Krishna explains to Arjuna that the purpose of life is to know God and that each person must do his or her duty. Good deeds will bring good results and put human beings closer to God; bad deeds will bring bad results. Krishna points out that it is not bad for a person to kill within the line of duty or in self-defense. It is Arjuna's duty to fight and win. One must never forget duty or fear death. The story ends with Arjuna's victory in battle. The moral of the story is that duty should be done without emotion or desire. (Do you agree?)

Over the years of Indian history, scenes from the Mahabharata have been told by the village storyteller, dramatized on the Indian stage, and repeated in many books. There are few Indians who are not familiar with its content and teachings. The great Indian leader Gandhi called the Gita "a dictionary of conduct." This poem is also well known to other Asians in Thailand, Cambodia, Myanmar (Burma), Indonesia, and elsewhere.

The Ramayana

The Ramayana, written about 400 B.C., tells the story of Prince Rama and his wife, Sita. Rama loses his throne to his stepbrother and for 14 years is forced to travel through India. During his travels he has many exciting adventures.

One day Sita is kidnapped by the evil demon Rawana, king of Sri Lanka (Ceylon). After many battles and setbacks Rama, with the help of his loyal brother, Lakshmana, and the brave monkey general, Hanuman, finally traps Rawana on the island of Sri Lanka. The monkeys, led by Hanuman, build a bridge of stones to connect the mainland to the island. Rama kills Rawana in a fierce and bloody battle, and Sita is then rescued. Without the help of the monkeys, this victory would not have been possible. For this reason, it is said, monkeys are considered sacred by the Hindus. Hanuman is looked on as the god of strength and loyalty. He is considered the special friend of athletes.

After 14 years of wandering, Rama returns to his home to become king. The people welcome Rama and Sita with great joy.

According to one of the more popular endings of the Ramayana, Rama and Sita live happily ever after. However, another ending tells that the people come to believe that Sita had not remained true to Rama while living with Rawana. The people insist that Rama send Sita away and he does. The lesson is that Rama places the wishes of his people above his own desire.

To generations of Hindus, Rama, Sita, and Lakshmana have shown how human beings should behave. Their loyalty, love, devotion, obedience, and sense of duty have been held up as a model to Indian children.

Folk dancers from Himachal Pradesh in the northwest part of India.

Early History

The Indus Valley Civilizations

The earliest civilizations on the Indian subcontinent arose in the period between 3000 and 1500 B.C. These civilizations were located in the Indus Valley of the northwest in what is now Pakistan. The most important cities, Harappa and Mohenjo-Daro, were among the most skillfully designed cities in the ancient world. The people who settled there brought with them bronze weapons and the idea of living in cities, both of which may have been borrowed from Middle Eastern peoples.

Although 400 miles apart, these two cities were connected by a navigable (able to sail on) river, the Indus. Discoveries by archaeologists and anthropologists have revealed that the Harappan civilization spread over 1,000 miles.

In each city, a fort was built for protection. Buildings were made of brick. Streets were wide, and houses were comfortable. There appears to have been plenty of water, and many families had their own wells. Drainpipes were used to carry wastewater away from the city.

An efficient irrigation system for farming was built. This suggests that these early Indus Valley civilizations had a well-organized system of government. The farmers grew wheat, rice, peas, barley, and cotton. They may have been the first people to raise cotton, which was used to make clothing. Farmers also raised cattle, pigs, sheep, chickens, and camels. Craftsmen used copper and brass as well as gold and silver. Elephants were used for transportation and heavy work.

Life centered around trade. The people sailed the Indus River and along the coasts of the Arabian Sea to the Persian Gulf to trade with the faraway cities of Mesopotamia.

No written records of the Harappan culture have been discovered. Although a system of pictorial writing was developed in the city of Mohenjo-Daro, no one has been able to understand what was written. Harrapan merchants rolled carved soapstone seals across soft clay to identify property or to sign contracts. These seals may suggest that other Indus Valley people also developed a form of pictographic writing.

Summary of Achievements of the Indus Valley Civilizations

1. They developed the idea of living in cities.
2. They developed the ability to shape cups and bowls on a potter's wheel and then glazed, baked, and decorated the pottery.
3. They used wheeled carts pulled by bullocks (large cattle).
4. Artisans made wooden furniture that was often decorated with inlays of bone, shell, and ivory.
5. Craftsmen made jewelry and other ornaments from gold, silver, copper, bronze, and a reddish clay called terra cotta.
6. Smiths worked copper and bronze to make weapons such as spears and other implements such as fishhooks.
7. Harappan traders used a uniform system of weights and measures to ensure fair trade practices.
8. A pictographic written language may have been developed.
9. Chess, a game for two players, originated in Harappa. Its aim was to capture an enemy king by eliminating his army and allies.
10. Several ancient Indian settlements have been discovered along the northeast coast of the Arabian Sea. These settlements probably began as trading posts for Indus Val-

ley ships sailing to Persian Gulf ports or to Mesopotamia. The ships carried timber, ivory, and crafted goods to those ports before 2000 B.C.

The Decline of the Indus Valley Civilizations

1. The city of Mohenjo-Daro ("the place of the dead") seems to have been slowly over run by mud from a nearby lake. This was probably caused by the earth's shifting surface. The idea that mud covered the city is based on the discovery that houses were repeatedly rebuilt on higher and higher platforms as mud levels rose.
2. Evidence has been found that the mineral salts in the underground water had a destructive effect on the baked bricks of Mohenjo-Daro.
3. A change in the salt content of the underground water could have made agricultural production impossible.
4. There is evidence of major earthquakes and flooding in the period around 1700 B.C. A major earthquake may have blocked the Indus River and caused flooding of Mohenjo-Daro and other cities in the Sind Plain.
5. Beginning round 1500 B.C., Aryan people (see the following section) from the Iranian plateau invaded the Indus Valley. A series of massive attacks by these invaders finally destroyed what was left of the Indus River civilizations in the Sind Valley and at Harappa and Mohenjo-Daro.

The Aryans Invade India

The Aryans were taller and lighter-skinned than the earlier Indus Valley peoples. The Aryans built no cities, and had no art, architecture, or written language. They were nomadic herders who measured their wealth in livestock. Even their word for "war" meant, in Sanskrit, "a desire for more cows."

When the Aryans left their homes in central Asia in search of better land to graze their sheep, the fertile valley of the Indus attracted them. The Aryans conquered the Dravidians (the original people of India). As they advanced eastward into the Ganges River plain, the Dravidians fled southward.

The Aryan tribes decided to settle in India. Although they destroyed the Harappan civilization and culture, they were greatly influenced by it. They became farmers, finding it pleasant to live in India after the hardships they had suffered on the dry plains of what is now southern Russia. In poetry and song they expressed their thanksgiving. In their new surroundings they retained the memories of their conquests, their ideas about human beings and life, and the rituals and ceremonies in the Vedas.

Blending of Harappan and Aryan Cultures

The blending of the Harappan and Aryan cultures was the basis for the development of Indian civilization. Between 1500 and 500 B.C. the Aryans developed the main characteristics of what came to be the Hindu way of life. During this thousand-year period many Aryan tribes moved into northern India. Gradually, small kingdoms began to appear. Each kingdom was ruled by a prince called a **rajah**. Although the Aryans brought new ideas into India, they also became, in some ways, like the people who already lived there.

On the other hand, Aryan language, literature, ideas about government, laws and social classes, as well as religious traditions, became a vital part of Indian life. The Aryan heritage had far-reaching effects on the historical, cultural, and social development of India.

Among the contributions of the Aryans was the Indo-European language called Sanskrit. The religious literature you have already read about—the Vedas—was passed down from generation to generation orally in Sanskrit. Many Sanskrit words are similar to English words having the same meanings.

Sanskrit Words	English Words
matr	mother
bhrata	brother
svasir	sister
duhita	daughter
sunu	son

Sanskrit, you will recall, is still spoken and written by upper-class Indians.

Aryan Society

Aryan society was divided into three social classes: noble warriors, priests, and the common people, who took care of the cattle. The Dravidians, who were conquered by the Aryans, became a fourth class, which was not considered equal to the first three.

A member of the warrior class was chosen to be the rajah or chief. He and a chosen group of nobles were in charge of Aryan affairs. This class system, unlike the Hindu caste system, was flexible since people could intermarry and move from class to class.

Male and female roles were clearly defined. Men were fighters and herders. Women raised crops, wove cloth, ground grain, and took care of the children. Although women were not permitted to help decide tribal policy, they did have the right to choose their husbands and had a voice in household matters.

Changes in Aryan Society

Over a period of 1,000 years, many changes in Aryan society took place. Rules and traditions began to control the behavior of each social class. Class structure became stricter and movement from one social class to another ended. As you have read, a strict caste system developed with Brahmins (priests) at the top. A Kashatriya class of warrior-nobles came next, followed by a Vaishya class made up of the common people (the merchants, traders, artisans, farmers, and herders). The fourth and lowest class was the Sudras, the descendants of the conquered Dravidians, who were not even considered Aryans. They were slaves, servants, unskilled workers, and tenant farmers.

As the Aryans settled down, they established small kingdoms. In each one, the rajah soon became a hereditary king, not simply a leader chosen from the warrior class. The Aryans established kingdoms from the Indus Valley eastward to the shores of the Bay of Bengal. They made northern India their home and spread Aryan culture southward onto the Deccan Plateau in central India.

The Aryan conquest had forced many Dravidians onto the Deccan Plateau and into the extreme south of the Indian Peninsula. In the southern part of India the Dravidians developed languages, customs, and traditions very different from those of the Aryans in the north. As a result, geography and historical developments created two very different Indias. These differences between North India and South India still exist today.

The Persians Invade India

The Persians invaded India in the 6th century B.C. They conquered the Indus River valley and parts of modern West Punjab. Trade developed between India and Persia, and some Indian soldiers fought alongside the Persians when Persia invaded Greece in the 5th century B.C. The written Sanskrit language used by most educated Indians is related to written Persian, and there are many Persian words in Sanskrit.

The Greeks Invade India

In 326 B.C., a Greek king, Alexander the Great, who was determined to conquer the world, appeared in India on the banks of the Indus. His men, far from home, tired, and afraid of the unknown that lay before them, refused to go on.

The Greek conquest of India was brief. Greek culture had little impact on India, except for its influence on Indian art. Early Buddhist art used no human image of Buddha. After the Greek invasion of India, however, sculptors influenced by Greek and Roman art created the first Buddha in human form. This Greco/Roman-style Buddha was the model for later works by Indian, Chinese, and Japanese artists.

The Maurya Empire

An important result of the Greek invasion was its influence on a young Indian leader, Chandragupta Maurya. When Alexander conquered India, he destroyed the small kingdoms and republics in the northwest. In 322 B.C., Chandragupta took possession of the throne of Magadha in northeastern India. This area, rich in timber and animals, served as a base for Chandragupta's expansion to the northwest when Alexander left. Magadha became wealthy and was the most powerful kingdom on the Ganges plain. It formed the center of the Mauryan Empire, which spread into the Indus Valley and the Punjab.

The great accomplishment of the Mauryas was the establishment of good and stable government. Chandragupta set up a postal system, developed roads, and built an extensive irrigation system. Business and trade flourished, and an army of 700,000 soldiers maintained order.

The Wise Rule of Asoka

Great as Chandragupta was, his grandson Asoka was even greater. Asoka, who ruled from about 273 to 232 B.C., is thought by many to have been the greatest king India ever had, and one of the greatest rulers who has ever lived. He is remembered and respected most because, although a powerful and mighty warrior, he did not use force to rule or to extend his kingdom. As a ruler, he followed the principles of Buddhism, and he commanded his officials to be just and considerate.

Under Asoka, the Maurya Empire spread south through the Deccan Plateau to the lands of the Tamils in the extreme south, and west to the Gondhara region near the Persian border and to the Hindu Kush Mountains.

The Rise and Fall of Buddhism

As the Hindu religion developed over the years, many Indians did not approve of the changes that had taken place within it. They felt that the religion had too many ceremonies that did little to increase the goodness of the people. These ceremonies served only to increase the powers of the Brahmins (priests). Moreover, many of the Sudras class and the untouchables were unhappy with the misery and poverty and their lives.

Origin of Buddhism

One who disapproved strongly was Siddhartha Gautama (563–483 B.C.), a prince of a kingdom near the Himalayas in North India. According to one legend, when he was nearly 30 years old, Gautama was given four signs. As he walked in the palace grounds, he saw three men: one very old, one ill and in pain, and one dead. Gautama was very troubled by these signs of age, pain, and death. Then he saw a fourth man—a wandering holy man—and at that moment he realized that this was the way of life he had to follow. Other stories say Gautama discovered the misery and poverty of his people when he made secret trips throughout his kingdom.

Whatever the reason, Gautama left the palace, his easy life, and his wife and son to search for the answer to the question that was troubling him: Why do people have to suffer from pain and sorrow? At first, Gautama tried traditional Hindu ways to find the answer to the question. He studied with Hindu teachers and lived alone in the forest as a hermit. He fasted and denied himself all comforts so that his mind would be free to find the answer.

Then one day, as he meditated (engaged in deep thought) under a sacred fig tree, ideas miraculously began to come to him. After 49 days of meditating, the answer to the question became clear. He had become the Buddha—"the Enlightened One"—and Buddhism was born.

The Four Noble Truths and the Eightfold Path

The basis of Gautama's belief was the "Four Noble Truths of Stopping Sorrow":
1. Sorrow and suffering are part of all life.
2. People suffer because they desire things they cannot have.
3. The way to escape suffering is to end desire, to stop wanting, and to reach a stage of not wanting.
4. To end desire, one should follow the "middle way—the paths that avoid the extremes of too much pleasure and desire as well as too much refusal to have pleasure and desire." There is an Eightfold Path to the middle way:

Right understanding	Right means of earning a living
Right purpose	Right effort
Right speech	Right awareness
Right conduct	Right meditation

These teachings challenged basic Hindu beliefs. Buddhism places more importance on how one lives than on one's caste or class. Among Buddhists today, there is no caste system.

Rules for Right Living

Buddhists believe that there are four Rules for Right Living:
1. Hatred is never ended by hatred; hatred is ended by love.
2. People should overcome anger by love.
3. People should overcome evil by goodness.
4. Everyone trembles at punishment; everyone loves life.

Buddhism under Asoka

The people of India were ready to accept a new religion and a new set of ideals. The rule of the Brahmins (priests of the Veda) was harsh and unfair. Many Indians were unhappy, and opposition grew. Buddhist priests told the people that to gain knowledge and to be just, ethical, and compassionate was the best way to live. They spoke against the caste system and the complicated rites that the Brahmins followed.

Asoka sent people all over India to spread Buddhist ideas. Indians by the millions accepted the teachings of Buddha. After the death of Asoka, however, there were many changes in Buddhism. The religion survived and grew stronger in many parts of Asia, but in India it almost disappeared. Today, there are only about 1 million Buddhists in India.

Reasons for the Fall of Buddhism

The fall of Buddhism had many causes. Hinduism was broad and tolerant, and it accepted many of the teachings of the Buddha. Also, Buddhists in India were quite willing to compromise with the beliefs and customs of Hinduism. In fact, Indian Buddhism eventually became so much like Hinduism that it was regarded as a part of Hinduism. The final blow to Buddhism in India was delivered by the Muslims. Pushing into India from the 8th century on, they destroyed the great Buddhist monasteries, burned the libraries, and killed the monks. Most of the monks who survived left India, and Buddhism was never again important there.

Jainism

Another attempt to reform the Hindu religion was the result of the work of Mahavira ("Great Hero") who lived at about the same time as Gautama, the Buddha. Mahavira believed in many of the same things as Buddha. However, he felt that strict discipline and self-denial were the only ways to purify the soul.

Jains, as his followers call themselves, do not have gods and do not pray. They do not believe in violence. **Ahimsa**, or nonviolence, is their central belief. They do not fight back if attacked. They do not eat meat or do farm work because they believe that farming the soil kills plant and animal life.

Jainism never became a very important religion in India or elsewhere. (Can you think of reasons why this was so?) However, the important concept of ahimsa was adopted by the Buddhists, and in the 20th century Ahimsa became the cornerstone of the Congress Party's struggle for independence under Mohandas K. Gandhi.

The Dravidian Tamils

Soon after the death of Asoka, the Maurya Empire of North India began to fall apart. For the next 600 years invaders swept over the Indian Plains. In time, the invaders were either driven out or became Hindus. Meanwhile, the Deccan Plateau and South India were entering the mainstream of Indian history. People of these regions made important contributions to Hinduism.

The southern area was called the Tamil country, after the main Dravidian language in use there. The people of the Tamil country began to combine the Hindu traditions of the Aryans with their own Dravidian folklore to produce some of India's finest poetry, epics, and music.

The Dravidians who had been pursued to the south during the Aryan invasion, were different from the Aryans in appearance and language. The Dravidian languages, which are still spoken in South India and Sri Lanka (Ceylon), are not Indo-European; in fact, they are unlike any other languages in the world. Today, the main Dravidian language is Tamil.

The Importance of Trade

The Dravidian Tamils were sailors who traded and conquered. Trade was an important part of life in India in the last 600 years B.C. Important trade routes were developed to link India with western Asia and the Mediterranean world. In the Deccan and South India, trade increased as traders from China and Arabia visited Indian ports. Sea trade flourished, and peninsular India, long overshadowed by the states of the north, began to gain in influence and power.

By about the 1st century A.D. there was a profitable trade from Tamil ports in South India to China, Egypt, and parts of the Roman Empire. The Tamils carried cargoes of spices, jewels, perfumes, textiles, and animals for trade in the Asian and Roman world. In return, they received gold from Rome and silk textiles and porcelain from China.

India's contacts with Southeast Asia developed as a direct result of its trade with the West. Southeast Asian lands were largely unsettled and undeveloped. However, they produced spices, which were much in demand in the West. Indian traders sailed to various parts of Southeast Asia, and many settled there. The Indians brought their customs and their religions, Buddhism and Hinduism, to Southeast Asia.

The Gupta Empire

In North India, the period of invasions came to an end when the Gupta family, led by another Chandragupta, united the kingdoms of the north. The Guptas ruled for over 200 years (A.D. 320–550), a period of stable government and great accomplishment. Indian scholars, writers, and artists distinguished themselves by producing masterpieces of art, literature, and architecture.

Gupta Accomplishments

Mathematics

In the field of mathematics, the Indians were the actual developers of so-called Arabic numerals. Arab sailors, merchants, and traders learned of this Indian system of numbers and carried it to the Middle East and then to Europe. The idea of zero, the idea of infinity, and a decimal system were also developed by Indian mathematicians. The value of π was determined to be 3.1416.

Medicine

In medicine, Gupta India was far advanced. Indian physicians had learned to diagnose and treat many ailments. Surgery was quite sophisticated; surgeons set broken bones, performed Caesarean sections, and used plastic surgery to repair mutilations. In addition, Indian doctors were aware of an important fact not understood by Western physicians until modern times—that cleanliness can prevent infection.

Literature

Kalidasa was the greatest of the poets and playwrights of the period. In fact, some of his plays are still performed in India and in other countries. His drama *Sakuntala,* a love story about a king and his beautiful bride, is available in English. The early Hindu storytellers delighted in fairy tales, folklore, and animated fables. In Gupta times, many of these tales were gathered into a collection that passed eventually, by way of the Arabs, into European literature. In this way, many modern European writers are indebted to the Hindus for the forms or plots of their tales.

Art and Architecture

The Guptas spent large sums of money on the building of temples. Painters and sculptors were well rewarded for their work. Gupta palaces were richly decorated and were always showplaces. Nearly all the art and architecture was of a religious nature.

The peak of Gupta art and architecture was reached in the Deccan. The magnificent cave temples at Ajanta and Ellora took nearly 1,000 years to build. All were cut out of solid rock, and the outside walls were decorated with sculptured figures, columns, and fresco paintings. South India has some of the finest freestanding temples in the world.

Influence of the Guptas

The Guptas left a great heritage:
1. Sanskrit was the language of the Guptas. The influence of Sanskrit culture gave India a cultural unity.

2. Hinduism became the main religion of the Guptas. (As already mentioned, Buddhism, which had become important under Asoka, died out in India.) Hinduism gave India a religious unity.
3. The Gupta rulers believed they ruled as the choice of the gods (divine right). They believed they had absolute power to promote "the right way" (Dharma) as set up in the sacred books of Hinduism. The ideas of absolute rule lasted in India well into the 19th century.
4. The Guptas encouraged the setting up of village councils to rule local areas. The council was made up of five elders and was called the panchayat (pancha means "five"). Village life became the basis of the Indian economy and way of life. A headman, usually a wealthy peasant, was in charge and passed the position down to his descendants. This system, including the panchayat, still exists in India today (see page 382). Reliance on local government continued as the Indian people failed to unite into a true national state through the succeeding centuries.
5. The Guptas set up a system of land taxes. Payments were based on a percentage of the crops raised. Today, taxes in India are still collected as in Gupta times.

Destruction of the Gupta Empire

In the 6th century A.D. a series of nomadic tribes (Huns, Turks, and Mongols) invaded India and slowly destroyed the Gupta Empire. By the end of the 7th century, the Gupta Dynasty no longer existed. For the next five centuries there was no unity in India.

The Muslims in India

The Delhi Sultanate

From the 8th century on, the course of Indian history was influenced by the expansion of Islam. The conflict between Islam and Hinduism led to tensions in Indian life. The followers of the two religions were far apart on matters of belief and custom, and for centuries these differences caused many problems between the two groups.

These religious tensions had their origin not long after the Gupta Empire fell apart, when Muslims began to invade India. Their first expeditions were unsuccessful, but by 712, they had taken over the state of Sind. The Muslim kingdoms bordering India gained strength. Mahmud of Ghazni and Muhammed Ghori led armies into India, and their successors set up the Delhi Sultanate. For several centuries most of northern and much of central India was controlled by the sultans. However, the sultans had a difficult time keeping order and resisting attacks from outside India. In the 13th and 14th centuries, the most notable attackers were the Mongols—Genghis Khan, Tamerlane, and Babur.

The Mogul Empire

In the early 16th century, Babur brought an end to the Delhi Sultanate, and a new and powerful Indian Empire was started. The new Muslim rulers set up the Mogul Empire. Akbar the Great, Babur's grandson, who was an excellent organizer and administrator, established a firm basis for the empire. He included capable Hindus in the government and won their loyalty and cooperation. Also, he eliminated the head, or poll tax, placed on Hindus, thus gaining the cooperation of most of them. Although Akbar tried to combine the best teachings of Christianity, Islam, and Hinduism in a new religion, the Divine Faith, he failed in this effort.

Akbar's policies were followed by the next two rulers, but the last of the mighty Moguls, Aurangzeb, reversed some policies, an action that led to the disintegration of the empire. His biggest error was trying to enforce Islamic law and customs, thus driving the loyal Hindus away. Aurangzeb quarreled with the Sikhs and the Rajputs. He wasted wealth and energy in trying to conquer the Marathis, but was never successful.

The Mogul Empire did not end with Aurangzeb's death in 1707. His descendants remained on the throne in Delhi until 1857, but their kingdom shrank until it included only the area around the capital.

Cultural Advances

The Mogul rulers took pride not only in their political and military achievements, but also in cultural advances. Having great wealth, the Mogul kings were patrons of the arts. The new Mogul school of art became known especially for its portraits, pictures of animals, and use of color. The Moguls were also interested in the construction of beautiful buildings. The most famous building of this period is the Taj Mahal, designed by Emperor Shah Jahan as a tomb for his wife.

The Taj Mahal was built by the Mogul ruler Shah Jahan in the 17th century as a tomb for his wife.

The Moguls encouraged the use of the Persian language for both writing and speaking. Little by little, Persian was fused with Hindi, the language of North India. The result was the creation of a new language, Urdu.

Fall of the Moguls

Rajputs

The Moguls were never in contol of all of India. The Rajputs, who are supposed to represent the Kashatriya, or warrior class, ruled most of northwest India. The Rajputs have always been proud of their fighting ability. All Rajput men became warriors since, according to one of their most important rules of conduct, they were never allowed to touch a plow. This rule kept all Rajputs from the most common way to earn a peaceful living—farming. The Rajputs successfully fought off the Moguls and deserve much of the credit for preserving Hinduism in northwest India.

Sikhs

Another people of the northwest who caused trouble for the Moguls were the Sikhs. The founder of the Sikh religion was Guru Nanak (1469–1539), who preached monotheism, the worship of one supreme being (god). He took the idea of monotheism from the Muslims of India. Although Nanak rejected the idol worship of Hinduism, he did not disagree with the main Hindu beliefs of Karma and rebirth. Therefore, the Sikhs, as Nanak's followers came to be called, remained "reformed Hindus."

After Nanak died, his work was carried on by **gurus** (teachers). Ram Das, the fourth guru, undertook to build the city of Amritsar, which became the pilgrimage and religious center of the Sikhs. It was here the Sikhs built the Golden Temple, their holiest shrine.

By the 17th century, the Sikhs were facing religious persecution from the Muslim rulers of the Mogul Dynasty. To protect themselves, the Sikhs set up a military brotherhood known as the *Khalsa* (pure). A member of the Khalsa changed his surname to "Singh" (lion).

For the next 300 years, however, the Sikh and Hindu communities lived together in peace and cooperation.

Marathis

A third people who actively resisted the Moguls were the Marathis, who lived near the western Ghats. Under their great leader Sivaji, the Marathis successfully waged guerrilla warfare against the Moguls. They set up a strong state in central and western India.

After Aurangzeb's death in 1707 one Mogul province after another followed the Maratha plan: they broke away and successfully established their own independence.

Persians and British

The ruler of Persia invaded India in 1739 and carried off the Mogul crown jewels and the famous gold and jeweled Peacock Throne.

Finally, in 1857, the British put an end to the Mogul Dynasty at the time of the Sepoy Rebellion (see page 400). The Moguls were the last independent Indian Dynasty.

The British in India

European Trading Companies

While Akbar ruled from 1556–1605, European ships began to call at Indian ports in increasing numbers. Portugal was the first nation to claim land in India. Vasco da Gama landed on the Malabar coast in 1498, and Portuguese settlements were established almost immediately on India's west coast near Bombay. The Portuguese were followed by the Dutch, French, and British.

Trade was the main reason for the Europeans' voyages. From India, the Europeans hoped to get cotton goods, spices, silk and **indigo**, a plant from which a blue dye is made. The Europeans set up trading companies in rented seaport areas off the mainland of India to handle their business. It was in this way, for example, that the British East India Company founded the cities of Madras, Calcutta, and Bombay.

The Growth of British Control

During the period of Mogul rule, these European companies became more and more involved in Indian affairs. This was especially true of the French and British East India Companies, whose involvement led to wars against each other in India. The rivalry between the French and the British in India was part of a larger clash of interests in Europe and America.

Led by Robert Clive, the British East India Company was victorious. At the Battle of Plassey, in 1757, Clive defeated the ruler of the state of Bengal. This victory, coming after an earlier British defeat of French troops in South India, gave the British control of much of India. The rajahs were unable to unite, and were thus defeated, one by one.

In the late 1700s, the British **Parliament** (supreme legislative body) decided that the British East India Company was not doing its job properly. The British government increased its own role in India, and began social, land, and tax reforms. Some of these reforms did not receive the approval of the Indian people.

The Sepoy Rebellion

Background

The event that is most written about in Indian history is the uprising against British rule in 1857. Throughout the first half of the 19th century, Indian dissatisfaction with the rule of the British East India Company and with the reforms of the British Parliament grew.

1. In 1784, the India Act was passed by the British Parliament. This law limited the British East India Company to trading activities, the British government took charge of military and government actions. However, the company still had great power since it was allowed to keep its army and to raise money from the taxes it collected.

2. Lord Cornwallis, the first governor-general of India appointed by Parliament, made reforms in taxation and landholding. Under Cornwallis, local leaders were strictly controlled, and a civil service of government workers based on ability, not on class, was set up. Most higher level jobs, however, went to the British; only jobs on middle and lower levels were given to deserving Indians.

3. Education reforms were put into effect. The British model became the rule, with the result that traditional Indian education and customs were often ignored or destroyed.

4. Other British reforms also often meant the destruction of Indian practices if they violated British custom or law.

5. In 1829 the British *raj* (government) abolished **suttee**. Suttee was a traditional Indian practice in which a widow (often drugged at the time) was forced to commit suicide on her husband's funeral pyre. The Indians were outraged by this destruction of a "sacred tradition," even though it was a brutal practice that deprived the

woman of her rights. (In 1856, the British raj passed a law that allowed widows to remarry.)

6. The Muslims of the dying Mogul Empire resented their loss of power in government and the replacement of Persian with English as the language of government.

7. Local opposition in the villages also increased as the British East India Company began to interfere with Indian life and customs. Settlement of disputes passed from the village council (panchayat) to British officials and their Indian representatives. Their decisions often followed British custom and law, not local tradition. In addition, village taxes were raised to help implement these changes. Although new roads and ponds were built with part of the tax money, much of it went into the pockets of people outside the village.

8. Most disturbing was the custom of the British of setting themselves apart from the Indians as a new ruling class. The Indians resented the British attitude of superiority.

9. In 1855, Parliament passed an act requiring **sepoys** (Indian soldiers in British service) to serve in other areas of Asia. According to Hindu tradition, Kashatriya warriors could lose their caste position if they left the country.

Outbreak of the Rebellion

In May 1857, the British introduced the new Enfield rifle into the Indian army. To load the rifle, the sepoys had to bite off the tops of the greased cartridges. Rumor spread that the bullets were smeared with a mixture of beef and pork grease. Hindus hold cows sacred, and the Koran (Muslim holy book) forbids Muslims to eat pork.

Even though the bullets were removed from service, the episode became a symbol for all the Indian grievances against the British. The sepoys refused to load the rifles. Some sepoys were dismissed from the army; others were sent to jail. In response, the sepoys **mutinied** (rose in rebellion) against their officers.

On a Sunday morning in May 1857, three sepoy divisions near Delhi, the center of English power in North India, freed their fellow soldiers who had been jailed and moved toward the city. The rebellion spread rapidly across India. The sepoys captured many important cities, including Delhi Cawnpore (Kanpur) and Lucknow. The rebels proclaimed that a new Mogul Empire was to be set up.

By the summer of 1858, stronger and better equipped British forces, aided by loyal Indian troops (mainly Sikhs), defeated the rebels. Many innocent people both British and Indian, were massacred and both sides committed atrocities.

Aftermath of the Rebellion

The 1857 rebellion was a turning point in Indian history. The British called it the Indian Mutiny or the Great Mutiny of 1857. Many Indians, however, called it the First Indian War of Independence. To them it was the beginning of a militant Indian nationalism that sought to overthrow the power of the British raj. Later, Indian nationalists claimed that Indian nationalism could be traced to the events of the Sepoy Rebellion and its aftermath.

Bitterness and resentment lingered for many years on both sides. The immediate results of the Great Mutiny were changes in British government policies toward India. The British East India Company was abolished, and India was ruled by a viceroy appointed by the British government. In 1876, Queen Victoria was declared Empress of India, making the people of India subjects of the Queen and India part of the British Empire. Also the British government promised that it would no longer interfere with Indian religious beliefs or traditions unless they directly violated existing law.

The British began a policy of improving transportation and communication. Between 1850 and 1870, networks of roads and railroads were built. By 1870, India had the best transportation **infrastructure** (basic framework) in Asia. The British also set up an efficient telegraph and postal system.

These improvements made Indians more aware of each other and of the rest of the world. Unintentionally the British were helping the Indian people to unite and to develop a strong national feeling.

Development of Indian National Feeling

After the Sepoy Rebellion, a new type of leader emerged in India to oppose the British. This leader was often educated in British universities, was familiar with the British tradition of political rights, and wanted to share in the governing of his own land. The India National Congress, founded in 1885, was set up to help achieve this goal. Most members did not call for independence, but for a share in a ruling India. Within the group, however, there were many different opinions about how to gain this goal. A small but vocal minority, led by Bal Tilak, called for any means to drive out the British, even revolution.

The Congress was also opposed by Muslims, who were suspicious of the motives of the Hindu-led Congress Party. In 1906, the Muslim League was set up under the leadership of Sayyid Ahmad Khan to protect Muslims from Hindu domination.

During and after World War I, the Indian nationalist movement began to change from a passive, patient movement to an aggressive, demanding one. The nationalists were disappointed by British rejection of their wartime request for more rights. As a whole, the Indian people were angered by the Rowlatt Acts, which restricted the rights of Indians, and by the Amritsar Massacre, in which unarmed Indians were killed by British troops. The British attempted to calm the Indians with the Montagu-Chelmsford reforms, giving Indians a larger share in their government, but the clamor for self-government never died.

It is important to remember, however, that, although the Indian people were united in their desire for independence, religious tensions between Hindus and Muslims continued to cause dissension and conflict.

American Influence on the Indian Independence Movement

A striking example of the close relationship between the American and Indian independence movements is to be found in the following excerpts from the U.S. Declaration of Independence and the pledge taken by members of the Indian National Congress on "Independence Day" (January 26, 1950):

AMERICAN DECLARATION OF INDEPENDENCE

We hold these truths to be self-evident: that all men are crated equal; that they are endowed by their Creator with certain unalienable rights; that among these are life, liberty, and the pursuit of happiness; that to secure these rights governments are instituted among men, deriving their just powers from the consent of the governed; that whenever any form of government becomes destructive of these ends, it is the right of the people to alter it or abolish it.

We believe that it is an unalienable right of the Indian people, as of any other people, to have freedom and enjoy the fruits of their toil and have the necessities of life, so that they may have full opportunities of growth. We believe also that if any government deprives a people of these rights and oppresses them, the people have a further right to alter it or to abolish it.

Mohandas K. Gandhi and Jawaharlal Nehru

The upsurge of nationalist feeling brought the Indians a new and great leader—Mohandas K. Gandhi. He made the nationalist movement a struggle against British rule. His goal for India was **swaraj**, self-rule free of all foreign control. To achieve this, Gandhi believed in ahimsa, the Indian idea of nonviolence. His program called for nonviolent noncooperation against the British. Gandhi is remembered in India both for his success in awakening the people to the need for self-government and for his humanitarian efforts.

The late 1920s and the 1930s were troubled years in India. A new group of leaders, including Jawaharlal Nehru, began to ask for independence. In 1935, the British Parliament passed the Government of India Act, which set up a partnership between India and the British government. However, this law was only partially successful in quieting the unrest.

Mohandas K. Gandhi (right) and his pupil and ally Jawaharlal Nehru.

Independence and Partition

The outbreak of war in Europe in 1939 brought about the final split between the British and the Indian Congress Party. Gandhi, Nehru, and their followers refused to support the British war effort unless their demands for independence were met. Also, the Muslim League, cooperating with the British, was committed to the setting up of a separate Muslim state.

At the end of World War II, the British government left its Indian Empire, having decided to partition the Indian subcontinent into two nations, Pakistan and India. On August 15, 1947, amid and followed by violence involving millions of deaths (including in 1948 the assassination of Gandhi) and great disorder, two new nations, one Hindu and the other Muslim, came into being. This division resulted from the failure of Hindu and Muslim leaders of India to solve their religious differences.

Views on the Partition into India and Pakistan

Both before and after the partition in 1947, various writers expressed their views on the Hindu-Muslim tensions that resulted in the division of India.

The differences which separate Hindu and Muslim are essentially religious.... Purely religious causes explain most of the communal disturbances of which we have record.... It may indeed be claimed with justice that [Hindus and Muslims] have been drawn together, not severed by their century and a half under a common administration, which has given them the same laws,...the same progressive civilization and the bond of a common speech.

Hugh MacPherson, Political India *(1932), pp. 109–116.*

This idea of a Muslim nation is the figment of a few imaginations only, and, but for the publicity given it by the press, few people would have heard of it. And, even if many people believe in it, it would still vanish at the touch of reality.

Jawaharlal Nehru, The Discovery of India *(1946), pp. 237–238.*

More than anything else, there has been no sense of a common history; instead there are two views of such historical happenings as are capable of creating any emotion.... The attitude of the Muslim community toward the idea of Pakistan was, therefore, the logical consequence of its history.
I.H. Qureshi, The Muslim Community of the Indo-Pakistan Community *(1962), pp. 301–304.*

It is necessary first to realize that the Muslim community exists and that it is essentially different in texture and outlook from the Hindu community.

Percival Speal, The Partition of India *(1966), p. xiii.*

The Hindu-Muslim antagonism in its modern form has nothing to do with race, and very little to do with the tenets of religion.... The real basis is economic and social.

G. T. Garratt, The Partition of India *(1966), p. xiii.*

The true cause [of Hindu-Muslim tension] is the struggle for political power and for the opportunities which political power confers.

Simon Commission, The Partition of India *(1966), xiii.*

Lasting Effects of British Rule

Great Britain ruled India for almost 200 years. During that long period the British introduced many institutions and ideas that continue to have a great effect on India today.
   1. The British set up an *educational system* in India that stressed Western culture, history, attitudes, and beliefs. Through this system, India's leaders of today learned about Western ideals of freedom and liberty.

2. The British gave India a *common language*. As we have learned, India is a nation of many local languages so that it was difficult for even educated Indians to communicate with one another. The lack of a common language was the most serious block to national unity. Although this problem still exists, the use of English as a common language has provided a partial solution.

3. The British example of *parliamentary government* resulted in the setting up of a representative government in India. Like Great Britain, India has a cabinet and a legislature (Parliament), elected by the people. The members of the cabinet must be members of Parliament.

   Instead of a queen or king, as in Great Britain, India has a president who is the head of the state. The president of India, like the British queen, has little power. As in Great Britain, the prime minister is the real head of the government and the head of the political party that holds a majority in the lower house of Parliament. In 1991, P.V. Rao became prime minister. The New Congress Party is the largest party in the *Lok Sabha*, the lower house of the Indian parliament.

4. The British brought to India the concept of *rule by law*, which replaced the idea that the king is the only giver and interpreter of law. The constitution of India has many provisions that guarantee the freedom and rights of the individual.

Highlights in the History of India

I. Prehistoric period	**3000–1500 B.C.**	
	Around 2500 B.C.	Advanced civilization develops in the Indus River valley.
	Around 1500 B.C.	Aryans invade India.
II. Hindu period	**1500 B.C.–A.D. 1200**	
	567–518 B.C.	Persians invade India.
	563 B.C.	Gautama Buddha is born.
	326 B.C.	Alexander the Great invades India.
	322 B.C.	Chandragupta sets up Maurya Empire.
	273–232 B.C.	Asoka rules, following policy of religious and racial tolerance.
	A.D. 320–550	Golden Age of Gupta Empire
III. Muslim period	**A.D. 1200–1760**	
	647–1200	Rise of Hindu princely states. Muslim invasions.
	712	Arab-Muslim conquest of Sind in northwest India.
	1000–1026	Invasions by the Muslim Mahmud of Ghazni.
	1175–1192	Invasions by the Muslim Muhammad Ghori.
	1206–1526	Muslim Delhi Sultanate in North India.
	1221	Invasion of Mongols under Genghis Khan.
	1398	Invasion of Mongols under Tamerlane, the "scourge of God."
	1498	Arrival of the Portuguese. Vasco da Gama discovers sea route to India.
	1519–1526	Invasions of Mongols (Moguls) under Babur.
	1526–1857	Mogul Empire in India.
	1526–1658	Mogul-Muslim Golden Age in India.
	1613	Trading post is set up at Surat by the British East India Company.
	1628–1658	Reign of Shah Jahan, who builds the Taj Mahal.

1658–1707	Reign of Aurangzeb. Religious intolerance leads to the fall of the Mogul Empire.

IV. British period 1760–1947

1744–1763	Anglo-French struggle for power in India.
1757	Robert Clive defeats French and their Indian allies at Plassey.
1772–1858	British East India Company controls most of India.
1857	Sepoy Rebellion (The Great Mutiny).
1858	British government takes over British East India Company holdings. Company is abolished.
1876	Queen Victoria is proclaimed Empress of India.
1885	Indian National Congress is organized.
1906	Muslim League is formed.
1919	Amritsar Massacre. Montagu-Chelmsford reforms. Gandhi proclaims passive resistance movement for Indian self-rule.
1940	"Two India" proposal by Muslim League.
1947	India wins independence, is partitioned into two nations: India and Pakistan.

V. Modern independent period 1948–Present

1948	Gandhi is assassinated.
1962	War between India and the People's Republic of China.
1964	Prime Minister Nehru dies.
1965	Three-week India-Pakistan war over Kashmir.
1966	Indira Gandhi becomes prime minister—for the first time.
1971	India defeats West Pakistan in short war. East Pakistan becomes independent Bangladesh.
1975–1977	Indira Gandhi suspends civil and political rights.
1977	Indira Gandhi is defeated in a democratic election; Morarji Desai becomes prime minister.
1980	Indira Gandhi returns to power as prime minister.
1984	Indira Gandhi is assassinated; Rajiv Gandhi becomes prime minister.
1989	Rajiv Gandhi is defeated by coalition of anti-Congress Parties.
1989–1990	V. P. Singh is prime minister.
1991	Rajiv Gandhi is assassinated.
1991	P. V. Rao becomes prime minister.

India and Pakistan after Independence

Independent India committed itself to democracy. Under Nehru's leadership, a constitution was drafted and a new political structure was set up. India's federal system provided the central government with broad political powers. The new state tried to improve the welfare of the people by passing laws to eliminate social abuses, including the caste system. The government also set up five-year plans for economic improvement through the industrialization and modernization of agriculture.

Like India, newly independent Pakistan faced difficult problems after partition. More than ten years passed before a government emerged that was capable of handling the many, nearly impossible, tasks. State planning, backed up by large-scale private investment, resulted in a great expansion of industry. In foreign affairs, Pakistan was concerned with the containment of India, its unfriendly neighbor.

India Attempts to Modernize

Achievements, Assets, and Problems

Introduction of a "Mixed Economy"

When India became independent in 1947, its leaders recognized the urgent need to strengthen the economy. They were determined to raise their country's standard of living, which was among the lowest of the major nations in the world. The leaders of the new India agreed to establish a "mixed economy," which combines the use of private capital and public funds to develop industry, mining, and farming. The government prepared a master plan, set up in a series of five-year plans, for developing the nation's resources.

The Problem of Population Growth

In the first Five-Year Plan of 1951, agricultural expansion was stressed. (See section headed "Agriculture," page 376.) As a result, the output of food was greatly increased. However, a serious complicating factor is India's great increase in population. This is due, not to a rise in the birth rate, but rather to the introduction of modern medicine, improved methods of fighting disease, and the development of an efficient system of famine relief. The seriousness of the population problem can be judged from the chart below:

1948—345 million	1977—615 million
1957—392 million	1985—768 million
1961—439 million	1990—853 million
1967—501 million	2000—1.042 billion (projected)
1971—548 million	2010—1.225 billion (projected)

Sources: *Encyclopedia Britannica*; United Nations *Statistical Yearbook*.

Even in a year free of droughts and floods, the population growth more than offsets agricultural gains.

The Need for Capital

India has also attempted to increase industrialization, but this has not been easy, because the nation lacks capital. In 1961, the government launched its third Five-Year Plan. The purpose was to make an all-out effort to strengthen and build industry. Unfortunately, India soon found itself at war with China, which had invaded disputed territory in North India. Fearing the worst, Indian leaders hurried to strengthen military defenses, a measure that necessitated scrapping plans for industrial development.

In 1965, India experienced the worst drought of the century. Faced with the threat of famine, money had to be used to buy food. By the time the third Five-Year Plan ended in 1966, India appeared to be little better off than when the plan began. The need to spend scarce capital for other purposes had prevented the government from expanding industry.

Resources

India is among the world's leading producers of **bauxite**, an ore used in the making of aluminum. Chromium and copper are also mined in great amounts. Much of the world's mica comes from India; mica is used in electrical equipment. Monazite is also mined. Uranium and thorium, two valuable sources of atomic energy, are obtained from Monazite.

Emeralds are mined in Pakistan, and gold is found near Mysore in South India. Land surveys are being made to learn what other minerals may be found in India.

From India's forests come such valuable woods as cedar and teak. Its rivers can produce large amounts of water power to make electricity.

Although some oil has been found in India, the amount is far from enough to satisfy the needs of the country. Therefore, India is almost completely dependent on the Middle East for its oil. India's other important shortages are in lead, tin, zinc, nickel, and tungsten.

Steel Production

India has very large amounts of such important minerals as coal, iron, and manganese, all of which are needed in the making of steel. In fact, it is estimated that India may have as much as 25 percent of the world's supply of iron. India mines about 70 million tons of coal per year, mostly in the Deccan Plateau. India ranks third in the world in the mining of manganese, which is used to harden steel.

The Tata steel plant in Jamshedpur in North India, west of Calcutta, is the largest in India. Although India produces more than 7 million tons of steel a year, the country needs more steel than it produces and must increase its production. The United States, Germany, and Russia have agreed to help build additional modern steel mills in India.

Industry

At present, as in 1947, the manufacture of textiles is the single largest industry in India. India has contributed to the fashion world such important materials as calico, muslin, cashmere, and madras. Also, India has the world's largest jute manufacturing industry. (Jute is a plant that can be used in making rope, carpets, and burlap bags.) Other large-scale industries include sugar processing, motion-picture making, and cement, leather, glass, rubber, and paper production.

Cottage industries are those in which goods are produced in the home. Hand looms are used in place of power-driven machines. The Indian government believes that cottage industries offer a good use for Indian labor. At present, handicrafts, silk goods, and *khadi* (homespun) are the major products of the cottage industry. In addition, very skilled artisans make artistic brass, copper, silver, and gold objects for export.

Scientific Advancement

In May 1974, India's scientists set off an underground nuclear explosion in the Rajasthan Desert. This nuclear blast was widely criticized by many countries. Critics said that India, a poor nation that could barely feed its people, had wasted valuable resources by developing an atomic bomb. Also, the blast had added to the arms race and opened the way for other nations to become nuclear powers.

The Indian government answered its critics by saying that it had a right to do as it saw fit with its resources. With nuclear power available, India would be less dependent on oil as a source of energy. The Indian government felt that in the future the Indian people would benefit greatly from this advance.

The Indians also launched a space satellite, with the assistance of the former Soviet Union. The Russians supplied materials, and the launch took place from Soviet soil. The purpose of this satellite shot was to look for X rays in space and to detect ultraviolet radiation in the night sky. An unstated purpose was to show that India is a great nation and can do what major nations have done.

Social Problems

India's social needs have been, and remain, tremendous. Education is a prime problem that the government has not yet been able to solve. There are not enough schools, books and other materials, or trained teachers. The dropout rate is very high. On the other hand, competition for admission to university programs is fierce.

MINERAL RESOURCES AND INDUSTRIES

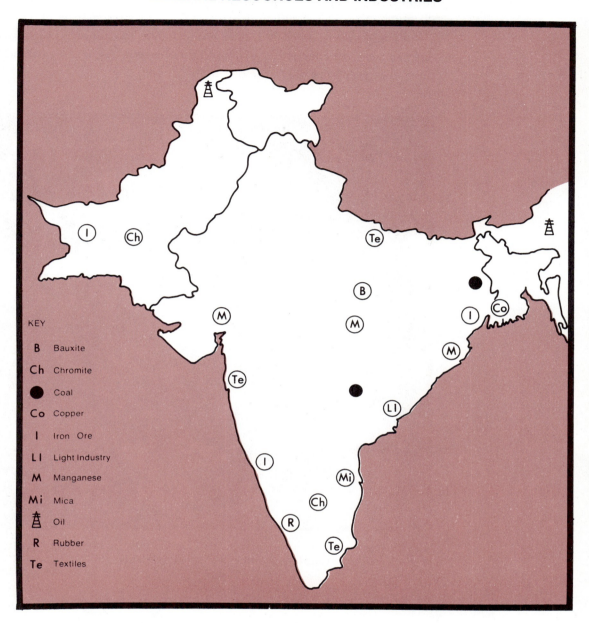

KEY

B	Bauxite
Ch	Chromite
●	Coal
Co	Copper
I	Iron Ore
LI	Light Industry
M	Manganese
Mi	Mica
⚒	Oil
R	Rubber
Te	Textiles

The housing situation has become increasingly serious. Particularly with the growth of cities, the government has not come up with solutions to this pressing problem.

The promotion of good health has become an important function of the Indian government. Campaigns have been launched to get villages to avoid polluting water supplies. The government has subsidized the education of doctors and nurses, built hospitals and clinics, and sponsored medical research. Also, India recognizes the need to limit population growth and has initiated educational programs in birth control to achieve this.

The government has acted to improve the lives of India's millions of untouchables. Untouchability is now illegal and all professions and trades are open to these people. Penalties for discrimination were set up, and laws were passed giving untouchables specific government jobs. Also, since their living conditions were even worse than those of other citizens, the government furnished financial aid to raise their standard of living. Seats in the national and state legislatures are reserved for representatives of their own choice.

Although the condition of India's untouchables has improved slightly since 1948, it has not been easy to change deep-rooted attitudes and customs. Legislation to help is one thing; the acceptance of change by Hindus is another.

An adult education class in Calcutta. The Indian government has tried to increase educational opportunities for all Indians.

Indira Gandhi Rules India (1966–1977)

On June 25, 1975, the prime minister of India, Indira Gandhi, announced that secret groups were planning a revolution. (It has never been proved that a revolt was actually being plotted.) She announced the temporary suspension (ending) of civil liberties and arrested the leaders of all the opposition parties. None of those put in jail were allowed to appeal to the courts for release. In addition, for the first time since India won its independence from Great Britain in 1947, all Indian newspapers and all news articles written by foreign reporters were censored.

Proposed Reforms

What brought about this historic act that ended democracy in India, at least for a time, Indira Gandhi, the daughter of the first prime minister, Jawaharlal Nehru, became prime minister in 1966. She was not expected to be a strong leader. However, she introduced a sweeping ten-point program for remaking India into a socialist democracy. After she had ordered that 14 private Indian banks be nationalized, she was thrown out of the Congress Party. She then formed her own party—the New Congress Party (NCP). In 1971, she called for a national election. The NCP used the Hindi slogan *Garibi hatao* ("Abolish poverty"). The results of the election gave the NCP two-thirds of the seats in the Lok Sabha, the Indian Parliament.

Growth of Problems

But *Garibi hatao* came back to cause problems for the government. Poor crops, poor management of the economy, and the rise of world prices for fertilizers and oil created seemingly unsolvable economic problems. Corruption spread in the government, and Indira Gandhi seemed to ignore it. Java Prakash Narayan, a leader of the opposition and follower of Mohandas Gandhi, accused her of wanting to become a dictator.

A judge in her home city of Allahabad discovered that she had won election to the Lok Sabha ("House of the People") illegally in 1971. The judge said she would have to leave Parliament if a higher court upheld his decision. Since the prime minister of India must be a member of Parliament, Indira Gandhi would be forced out of that office too.

Narayan and other leaders called for Indira Gandhi to resign. When she refused, Narayan announced that a massive *satyagraha* (civil disobedience) campaign would begin. Narayan and other leaders called for the army and police force to mutiny. Then, in 1975, Indira Gandhi decided to act, and at her order the president of India proclaimed a state of emergency. Civil liberties were suspended, and the opposition leaders were arrested.

"Limited Democracy"

In March 1977, Prime Minister Gandhi eased the state of emergency that had existed for 19 months and called for national elections to be held then. She hoped that the people of India would show their approval for her program and the state of emergency that she had declared. She said that with this "limited democracy" she could attack poverty more forcefully. She promised that the peasants' great burden would be lessened and that rural lands would be redivided more fairly. Finally, she promised to attack the problem of India's massive **inflation** (over 30 percent in 1974).

All of this, however, would be achieved at a price. Although Indira Gandhi had said she was acting to protect India's democracy, the facts showed that democracy had been greatly limited. Leaders of opposition groups were put in jail. Newspapers that criticized the government were censored or closed down. Also, charges of corruption and bribe-taking were made against Prime Minister Gandhi's son Sanjay and other members of the government.

Opposition and Defeat

The leader of the opposition was Morarji Desai, head of the Janata Party. He told the Indian people that, if Indira Gandhi was reelected, she would again take away all rights from the people and set up a dictatorship.

Another important issue was sterilization and birth control. Thousands of Muslims who opposed the government's forced sterilization of men voted against Prime Minister Gandhi and her Congress Party.

The results of the election were a great surprise—Indira Gandhi was defeated. For the first time since independence was gained in 1947, India would not be ruled by the leaders of the Congress Party. The Indian people had spoken as a democratic people speak—by the vote. A peaceful revolution had taken place. The Indian people wanted changes and did not trust Indira Gandhi to make these changes; therefore, they voted for candidates of the Janata Party, led by Desai.

India Under Morarji Desai (1977–1980)

Morarji Desai was 81 years old when he became prime minister of India in March 1977. He told the Indian people, "You must not fear the government as you have feared it all these past months. We are your servants, not your masters."

With these words Desai began his rule of India. He released almost all the people who had been put in jail during the state of emergency. He removed most censorship rules and allowed many newspapers to reopen. All constitutional civil rights were returned to the Indian people.

Desai announced that the birth control and sterilization program would now be entirely voluntary. However, he hoped that the program would be continued and that India's population growth could be controlled. Desai also hoped that laws would be passed to give the untouchables greater civil rights and greater legal protection. Land reforms were to be continued to ensure all the Indian people a greater share of the nation's wealth. In short, full democracy was returned to India under the Janata government.

Indira Gandhi Returns to Power and Is Assassinated (1980–1984)

In spite of its good intentions, the Janata government finally collapsed through its own incompetence, and Indira Gandhi was returned to power in 1980. She faced a number of serious problems, the first of which was the beginning of a widespread drought. Grain production fell, and the government was forced to buy grain to meet the needs of the Indian people.

Problems with the Sikhs

The most serious problem, however, was the desire of the Sikhs to have an autonomous state in the Punjab. Only in the 20th century did local political competition begin between Hindus and Sikhs. Early in the century, the British rulers began to set up local democratic elections. In the 1920s, the Sikhs demanded control over their temples, which had been under the control of the local Hindu governments. A specially elected committee set up in 1935 to manage all Sikh shrines, the Shiromani Gurdwara Prodandhak Committee (SGPC), became the center of all Sikh nationalist action. The *Akali Dal,* the major Sikh political party, demanded Sikh separateness and political and economic reforms to improve the lives of Sikhs.

By the 1960s, the SGPC and the Akali Dal had forced the Indian government to set up the separate, Sikh-controlled state of Punjab. Then, in the 1970s and 1980s, Sikhs started to demand the creation of an independent Sikh nation, Khalsa (Khalistan).

In 1984, the Sikhs threatened to withhold the vast food and energy resources of the Punjab from the rest of India. On June 6, 1984, Indira Gandhi ordered the Indian army to storm the Sikh Golden Temple, the holiest shrine to all Sikhs, at Amritsar. The prime minister suspected that the Sikhs were plotting terrorist acts and storing large amounts of guns and ammunition in the temple.

The attack on the Golden Temple resulted in many dead and wounded. The leaders of the suspected terrorists were killed, and large stores of ammunition were found. The Sikhs vowed revenge.

Assassination of Indira Gandhi and Its Aftermath

On October 31, 1984, Indira Gandhi was assassinated by two of her Sikh bodyguards as she walked to her office in New Delhi. The Hindu majority of India then began a series of riots against the Sikh minority. More than 1,000 Sikhs were murdered, and large amounts of Sikh property were stolen or destroyed.

Indira Ghandi served two terms as Prime Minister of India. She was assassinated in 1984.

Rajiv Gandhi, Prime Minister of India from 1984–1989, was the son of Indira Gandhi. He was assassinated in 1991.

Domestic Policies

Indira Gandhi's son, Rajiv Gandhi, became prime minister of India on October 31, 1984, just after the assassination of his mother. In the year that followed, he quickly gained control of the government. In his earliest action he freed many of the Sikh leaders who had been arrested by his mother. Solving the Sikh problem became his most important task.

Gandhi hoped to gain the support of the Sikhs by allowing them to continue to control the government of the Punjab State. He also returned control of the administration of the Golden Temple to the Sikhs and opened meetings with the Sikh **moderates** (people who did not hold extreme views). However, the Sikh extremists were not satisfied, and many acts of terrorism were carried out throughout 1986, including the murder of defenseless Hindus.

For India's troubled economy Rajiv Gandhi and the Indian government adopted a new Five-Year Plan. Major attention was given to the modernization and improvement of agriculture, as well as to industrial modernization, trade development, and programs giving direct assistance to the poor.

Foreign Relations

In the area of foreign policy, Rajiv Gandhi led a conference, held in New Delhi, to consider limiting armaments. The conference asked all nuclear powers to halt tests, stop adding to atomic stockpiles, and engage in talks for the future control of weapons of all kind.

When Rajiv Gandhi became prime minister, he said that he wished to improve relations with the United States. He visited the United States and met with President Reagan and leaders of Congress. He told the president and the American people that a new era in Indian-American relations was about to begin. However, his actions did not match his words. When Soviet Premier Gorbachev visited India in late 1986, Gandhi gave the impression that he was following the Soviet leader on almost all issues. After Gorbachev's visit, the Soviets promised over $1 billion in aid to India, and pledged to continue to support India in its policies in regard to Pakistan.

Singh Government (1989–1990)

In 1987, V. P. Singh, a former minister of finance and later defense minister in Congress Party governments, began an investigation of suspected wrongdoing by Rajiv Gandhi. He discovered corruption and bribery in the awarding of government contracts to the largest companies and to groups in which Gandhi's relatives held important jobs.

In November 1989, an election was held. The Gandhi Congress government, which had enjoyed the largest majority in the Indian Parliament—the Lok Sabha—in Indian history, was upset by a loose **coalition** (united group) of parties called Janata Dal and led by Singh.

Although V. P. Singh became prime minister, he was forced to rely on the help of the Bharatiya Janata Party and the Communist Party. Both of these parties had their own ideas about how to reform India.

The Mandal Report

The constitution of India provides safeguards for the "scheduled castes" (groups earlier considered "untouchables"). Some 22.5 percent of jobs in government and public works are to be reserved for them. Other low-ranking castes had long asked for similar treatment. In 1980, a commission that had been set up in 1979 under B. P. Mandal to look into the matter presented its report. It recommended that an additional 27 percent of jobs be reserved for other "backward classes."

In late 1990, the government, led by V. P. Singh, announced that the Mandal reforms would at last be enforced. This decision sparked riots that continued for several weeks, during which over 150 young men and women set themselves on fire in protest. The Bharatiya Janata Party (BJP), which had been a member of the Singh coalition government, objected and left the government. The BJP, which had already protested government action in the Ayodhya temple situation (see page 415), now felt further threatened. Its main supporters are upper caste, privileged Hindu Indians who would lose the most from government enforcement of the Mandal recommendations.

Collapse of the Coalition

Opposition to Singh's actions led to the collapse of the coalition in November 1990. In elections held in November 1990, Singh's party lost control of the government. An interim caretaker government ruled for four months, and new elections were scheduled for 1991.

India in the 1990s

Threats to India's Unity as the 1990s Began

Ever since India gained its indpendence in 1947, the country had been torn by internal strife.

Separatism in Punjab, Assam, and Kashmir

As a multiethnic country with distinct regional, religious, and ethnic groups, India has been troubled by demands for greater local autonomy from the day of its independence in 1947. The increased centralization of power under Indira Gandhi intensified (made sharper) these demands. Moreover, many ethnic groups increasingly turned to violence to back up their demands. In the Punjab, Assam, and Kashmir, separatist movements strongly challenged India's unity.

The Sikhs in the Punjab

Over the years, the Akali Dal movement of the Sikhs followed a policy of peaceful opposition within India as it attempted to gain autonomy for the Punjab State and greater protection for the Sikh religion. However, successive Indian governments did little to meet Akali Dal demands. As a result, Sikh militants turned to terrorism and demanded an independent Sikh nation, Khalistan. Extremist Sikhs attacked Hindus and the police. In January 1990, the convicted assassins of Indira Gandhi were hanged after the Indian Supreme Court had rejected petitions for clemency. The Indian government also rejected pleas for mercy from foreign governments. The hangings resulted in attacks by Sikhs on Hindus and police and government forces in the Punjab.

The Situation in Assam

The Bodos, a tribal group in Assam in northwest India, have demanded that their region be given special protection through the creation of an autonomous area within Assam State. An even more serious challenge to Indian unity came from the United Liberation Front of Assam (ULFA), which launched a rebellion whose aim is Assam's secession from the Indian nation.

Other Demands for Separation

Another tribal group living in Bihar, West Bengal, and Orissa, located in eastern India, have pressed for the formation of a separate Jharkand State. Also, Buddhist groups in Ladakh in northwest India have demanded separation from the Jammu and Kashmir states.

The Jammu-Kashmir Situation

For over 40 years, Hindus and Muslims have been attacking each other in Jammu and Kashmir. (Kashmir is the only Indian state with a Muslim majority.) However, in 1988 the Jammu and Kashmir Liberation Front, together with an assortment of separatist and Islamic religious groups, started a wave of strikes, bombings, and assassinations. The state governments were unable to stop the violence. Consequently, in early 1990 the central government led by V. P. Singh dismissed the state government and imposed direct rule. This attempt was met with increased and widespread resistance and violence.

Kashmir was not only a domestic problem. India charged that Pakistan was arming and training the rebels in Kashmir. These charges brought India and Pakistan to the brink of war on many occasions during the 40 year period.

The Ayodhya Situation

In late 1990, Lal Krishna Advani, the president of the Bharatiya Janata Party (BJP), launched a *rath yatra* (chariot rally). This was to be a 6,000-mile trip, in a van made to look like a mythological chariot, across the heartland of North India to Ayodhya, located in Uttar Pradesh State. It was here, at the supposed birthplace of the epic hero Lord Rama, that construction of a new temple was to begin.

This site had been disputed between Hindus and Muslims since the 16th century, when the Mongol emperor Babur built a mosque. In 1989, Hindu religious extremists tried to destroy the mosque. In addition, they wished to build a new Hindu temple to "recapture injured Hindu pride." The result was the most serious Hindu-Muslim rioting since the partition of India in 1947.

In October 1990, tens of thousands of Hindu militants, led by Advani, moved toward Ayodhya. On October 23, as they were about to enter Uttar Pradesh, Advani and other BJP leaders were arrested.

At the same time, the arrests and fighting in Ayodhya sparked a wave of Hindu-Muslim violence that left more than 300 dead. At that point, the Hindu militants left Ayodhya with a promise to return.

Sikh Distrust

To this day, the Sikhs believe that the massacres of Sikhs in the Punjab and other areas after the assassination in 1984 of Prime Minister Indira Gandhi by Sikh bodyguards were not motivated by religious feeling. They believe they were political. They feel that the Congress Party inspired the attacks to weaken Sikh opposition and in fact, then placed the blame on the militant Hindu parties. (In many cases, Sikhs were rescued from the massacres by militant Hindus.)

Political Parties

From its independence in 1947 to the middle of the 1980s, India was ruled mainly by the Congress Party, led by Mohandas K. Gandhi, Jawaharlal Nehru, and Indira Gandhi (Nehru's daughter). In the 1980s, Indian voters made their choice by voting for or against Congress candidates. In general, there was little difference between the platforms of Congress and the anti-Congress parties. For the most part, other parties were established to oppose one or more ideas of the Congress Party. The minor parties were not strong enough to remain in power after they won elections. They never remained united long enough to create change.

In the 1990s, however, the situation seems to be different. In the May 1991 elections, the people of India were presented with a clear choice among many political parties, all of which had different proposals for solving India's problems.

1. <u>India National Congress</u>: The India National Congress, widely known as the Congress Party, is made up of many factions (groups) with different objectives and ideas. The main group was led by Indira Gandhi and later by her son, Rajiv Gandhi. Congress is the largest party and held 195 of the 543 seats in the Indian Parliament prior to the election in 1992. Its policy is the traditional one of slow reform but little change in the present social situation.

2. <u>Janata Dal</u>: Janata Dal (National Front Coalition of Parties) arose as a result of the corruption and poor government during the rule of Rajiv Gandhi between 1984 and 1989. Led by V. P. Singh, the coalition campaigned in 1989 for reform and honest government and defeated the Congress Party. Singh and Janata Dal ruled India from December 1989 to November 1990. Janata Dal won 148 seats in the 1989 elections but lost nearly one-third of the seats in the November 1990 elections when the party split.

3. <u>The Bharativa Janata Party (BJP)</u>: One cause of the party split was a decision of the Hindu militants in the BJP to support the building of a Hindu temple on the site of a Muslim mosque (see "The Ayodha Situation," page 415). The BJP opposed government actions to prevent the building of the temple at this site. The BJP is a conservative party and extols the glories of "Hindutva"—the greatness of the Hindu past. It has a large following among religious Hindus and enjoys strong support from small businesspeople and shopkeepers, who make up an important part of the Hindu-Indian middle class.

4. <u>Socialist Janata Party:</u> A small party with little chance of gaining power, it split from the main Janata Dal party in November 1990. Members of this party wish to move swiftly on the issues that have kept India's poorest peoples from improving their lives.

5. <u>Bahujan Samaj:</u> The Bahujan Samaj (Party of the Majority) is another small but significant party. Led by Kanshi Ram, the party wishes to represent low-caste and outcaste Hindu Indians. It has become the natural ally of V. P. Singh's Janata Dal since it also wishes to improve the lives of these groups by reform.

6. <u>Communist parties:</u> There are two Communist parties that would be important only as part of a coalition to set up a new government. The larger of the two is the India-Marxist Party, led by Jyoti Basu. This group holds power only in the state of West Bengal.

The Elections Scheduled for May 1991

Three rounds of parliamentary elections were scheduled for May 1991. The troubled states of Assan and Punjab were to conduct elections separately in June. Jammin and Kashmire, torn by rebellion, would not hold elections.

The main issues of the May elections were related to the caste situation and to religious and ethnic unrest.

V. P. Singh of the Janata Dal Party believed that more self-rule for the Indian states would end secessionist movements and ease religious animosities. He supported the Mandal recommendations (see page 414), which are considered revolutionary by India's uppercaste Hindus. Also, attempts to protect Muslims in the Ayodhya temple situation (see page 415) were hotly debated by Indian Muslims and Hindus.

Rajiv Gandhi and the Congress Party campaigned with proposals that would continue the age-old Hindu social system. This system gives a minority of uppercaste Indians effective control of the government, diplomacy, business, journalism, and the arts. Gandhi accused Singh of dividing the Hindu community and inviting a caste war.

The Bharativa Jamata Party (BJP), led by Lal Krishna Advani, campaigned on the issue of more control of religious affairs by the Hindu majority. The BJP has always felt that Hindu interests have been sacrificed to please Sikh and Muslim minorities. In addition, the BJP offered to aid small-business owners and merchants with low-cost government loans.

Since six parties were involved in the election, no single party was expected to gain a clear majority. However, it was believed that Rajiv Gandhi's Congress Party would win the largest number of seats and thus give Gandhi a chance to form a coalition government.

The Assassination of Rajiv Gandhi

On May 21, while campaigning in Tamil Nadu in southern India, Gandhi, along with 17 bystanders, was killed in a powerful explosion. Experts determined that the assassin was a woman who had detonated a bomb strapped to her body when she bent forward to touch Gandhi's feet in a traditional act of homage. Further clues identified her as part of a conspiracy of Sri Lakan Tamil Tigers (see page 438) to assassinate Gandhi. The Tigers had reason to hate Gandhi because of his role in sending Indian troops to Sri Lanka in 1987 to try to end a guerrilla war there and in pushing for a crackdown on Tamil guerrilla operations from Tamil Nadu.

The May election that could have led to Rajiv Gandhi's return to power was now postponed. Gandhi's death left the Congress Party without a leader.

Election Results of June 1991

The election scheduled for May 20 but postponed because of the assassination of Rajiv Gandhi was completed on June 17–18, 1991.

The results can be summarized as follows:

1. Many Indian people showed their unhappiness by not voting. Only 53 percent of the eligible voters cast their ballots. This was the lowest turnout in modern Indian history.

2. The Congress Party won 225 seats in Parliament. Since the Indian Parliament has 543 seats, this was far short of a majority. P. V. Nershimhe Rao, a Congress Party member from South India, was elected prime minister.

   The 1991 elections again failed to produce a parliamentary majority, and Rao oversees a minority government that depends for its survival, issue by issue, on at least tacit (unspoken) support from members of the opposition.

   The unstable nature of such a government can be transformed through party regrouping. India is evolving an essentially triangular alignment of forces at the national level, with variations among the states. With the left (Socialists and Communists) largely limited to regional strongholds, the battle for power under conditions of realignment will be fought between the BJP and the Congress Party. With the Gandhi dynasty gone, Congress could well reemerge as the majority party.

3. The Bharatiya Janata Party (BJP) made the greatest gain, winning 119 seats. The BJP represents the Hindu Nationalist Party and upper caste privilege.

4. The Janata Dal Party, which had championed government affirmative action for lower castes, lost the most, winning only 24 seats.

5. Denied a majority, the Congress Party will probably have to rely on rule through a coalition government. This type of rule will be very difficult because the Congress Party must depend on new leadership.

Rao's Economic Program

Reasons for the Economic Crisis

Four decades of state-guided economic development in India had resulted in slow growth, rising unemployment, a depreciating currency, and a falling share of world exports. It was apparent that state-planned economic development had not improved the people's standard of living or enabled India to compete successfully for world markets.

When India became independent, there was some justification for a state-planned economy. In the 1950s and 1960s, India's economy grew three times as fast as during the last year of British control. State planning was the main force in transforming India's plantation, agricultural economy into a successful and diversified industrial economy. However, in the 1970s and 1980s, the state-regulated economy was not able to construct a successful economic program. Moreover, the collapse of the state-planned economies of Eastern Europe and the Soviet Union, which purchased one-fourth of India's exports, further strained India's economic situation.

Rao's Reforms

The Rao government's first actions were to correct India's pressing economic problems, including the most serious **balance of payments** (more imports than exports) crisis since independence. The government devalued the rupee and cut **subsidies** (money paid by the government) on staples and to industries. In addition, license requirements were reduced to encourage more foreign investment. These reforms represented a reversal of India's former policies, which were the hallmark of the nation's commitment to socialism.

What Is Different about the 1991 Reforms?

Should we expect the recently instituted economic reforms to be somewhat different from past reforms? Yes, if the statements of Prime Minister Rao, Finance Minister Manmohan Singh, and Commerce Minister P. Chidambaram are to be believed.

Rao's surprising economic initiatives include the following major changes, which are included in a New Industrial Policy:

- Licensing is abolished except for strategic reasons, for overriding environmental concerns, and for hazardous chemicals, and luxury goods. Increases in the capacity to produce steel, for example, no longer require a license.
- Firms no longer need prior approval for new production, mergers, or the expansion of production under the monopoly regulation act.
- The minimum size of a firm that can use the special facilities and concessions for small-scale enterprises is raised for firms producing for export.
- Foreign firms may now own more than 50 percent of a wide variety of their subsidiaries in India and in trading companies in export markets.
- Public-sector enterprises will help private-sector production by providing infrastructure such as power and transportation.

These new policies have been followed by the government's sale of about 25 percent of its 225 public-sector enterprises. These sales are expected to raise 2.5 trillion rupees (Rs) over two years. The central government hopes to use this money to help reduce its 2 trillion (Rs) annual budget **deficit** (an excess of spending over income).

Opposition to Reforms

While Indian and foreign firms have generally approved of these reforms and proposals, actual results have been less positive. There have also been strong objections to the proposals from the opposition in India, especially because of the International Monetary Fund's association with many of the changes.

India's budget deficits, which have amounted to as much as 6 percent of the gross domestic product in recent years, have put strong inflationary pressures on the economy. Eliminating the subsidies to agriculture would yield large budget savings but have caused major protests among large farmers. It is estimated that between 70 and 100 percent of tax revenues in India are lost through subsidies and exemptions.

Reform in agriculture has been a less pressing concern than reforming the regulations on industry, since government policies mainly affect agricultural inputs (for example, power, fuel, fertilizers, and tractors), prices of outputs, and taxes. Prices for farm products have improved since 1980. This has caused a sizeable growth in output between 1980 and 1991: 5 percent per year for food grains and an even higher growth of cash crops. There has been growth despite shortfalls due to monsoons in 1986 and 1987.

Results of the Reform Effort

Although the present leadership has done more in six months to bring about real reform than other governments did in the preceding 45 years, the results have been mixed. **Devaluation** (reduction of the exchange rate) of the rupee has not improved dollar earnings from exports, though many believe exports are underreported. Also, industrial production has fallen in automobiles and other sectors, partly because of declining Indian demand (itself a consequence of reforms). In addition, lack of capital prevents greater reform.

Two positive results are the improvements in India's balance of payments position and in the Indian government's control of debt. It is true that India's economic prospects could be brighter. Nevertheless, the Rao government's efforts must be considered the most serious attempt, since independence was gained, to break up a regulatory system that many believe has kept India's economic performance well below its potential.

India's Economic Future

The key to India's economic revival may lie in a free-market economy. This would make Indian businesses and the Indian economy open to the competitive pressures of market forces at home and abroad. Businesses that could not compete would disappear, and successful businesses would grow.

If government regulation was removed, India might be able to fully use its excellent existing base for rapid and substantial industrial expansion. The country has a large pool of scientists and technicians, as well as an unused reservoir of innovative (doing things in new ways) business talent.

Rao's Responses to Other Problems

The Mandal Reforms

Rao announced that his government would implement the reservations program (Mandal Program) for backward castes. Preference would be given to the poorer segments of the population, and an additional 10 percent of all central government jobs would be reserved for the unemployed and poor in higher castes. The police were alerted for renewed demonstrations. However, the announcement was greeted with a milder reaction from those who had earlier protested. With 52 percent of the Indian population designated as "backward," no political party was prepared to speak out in opposition, and the Janata Dal was robbed of the issue that had become its virtual reason for existence.

The Ayodhya Situation

Ayodhya was another matter. The Congress government made common cause with three other parties against the Bharatiya Janata Party (BJP) to secure passage of an act freezing the status of all religious shrines at the time of independence—except for the disputed Ayodhya case, which was to be decided by the court. The BJP, as you have learned, was committed to the construction of a Hindu temple on the site (Ayodhya) where a Muslim mosque stood.

The BJP was under mounting pressure from its Hindu supporters to demolish and relocate the mosque. To do so, however, would bring it into confrontation with the central government and would probably result in the dismissal of the BJP state government for defying the court order protecting the mosque. Moreover, with desire for power at the national level, the BJP wanted to broaden its support, and it feared popular reaction against renewed turmoil over Ayodhya at a time when most Indians seemed to want stability.

However, on a Sunday in December 1992, teams of young Hindu extremists stormed the Ayodhya mosque. In a matter of hours, the 16th century mosque was totally destroyed.

In the next week over 700 Hindus and Muslims were killed in the rioting which spread throughout India. Not since India's independence and the partition that divided the subcontinent had there been such bloodshed between Hindus and Muslims. In all, over 3,000 Indians have lost their lives between December 1992 and the end of February 1993.

Separatists' Demands

Unrest had not eased in Punjab, Kashmir, and Assam, and the government responded with continued force against terrorism and insurrection. In Assam, the new Congress state government renewed efforts against the guerrilla United Liberation Front of Assam. By December 1991, the guerrilla group had called a cease-fire, and in January 1992, after a secret meeting in New Delhi with Rao, the guerrillas agreed to end their attempts to set up an independent state. Rao then ordered the Indian army to suspend its campaign against the guerrillas.

In Kashmir, with no hope for a political settlement, the military engaged Kashmir separatists. The Indian government, warning of dire consequences, denounced Pakistan for supporting the Kashmiri separatists.

In Punjab, the situation deteriorated further, with more than 5,000 people killed in 1991 by either Sikh terrorists or government forces. Parliamentary and state assembly elections had been scheduled for June 22, but one day before the voting, the election commissioner (thought to be pressured by the Congress Party) canceled the elections, citing the unrest. With elections set for February 15, 1992, the government moved nine army divisions into Punjab, adding to police and paramilitary forces, to ensure that elections were to be conducted with minimal violence and intimidation.

Pakistan

A Muslim Country

As a result of the partition of the Indian subcontinent in 1947, the state of Pakistan was created. The principles of Islam are basic to the Republic of Pakistan. The preamble to Pakistan's Constitution, as published in 1962, begins:

In the name of Allah, the Beneficent, the Merciful; Whereas sovereignty over the entire Universe belongs to Almighty Allah alone, and the authority exercisable by the people is a sacred trust....
And whereas it is the will of the people of Pakistan that...the principles of democracy, freedom, equality, tolerance and social justice, as enunciated by Islam, should be fully observed in Pakistan....
The Muslims of Pakistan should be enabled, individually and collectively, to order their lives in accordance with the teachings and requirements of Islam....

Geography and Resources

Pakistan is a country of mountains, deserts, and the Indus Valley. The word Pakistan was first coined (created) in 1934: "P" for Punjab, "A" for Afghans (Pathans), "K" for Kashmir, and "S" for Sind; "Stan" is a Persian suffix meaning "country." (Some Muslim Pakistanis say the name stands for "Land of Pure.")

As set up in 1947, Pakistan was a divided country. One thousand miles of Indian territory separated East and West Pakistan. Other factors also separated the two regions: West Pakistan is dry and hilly, East Pakistan (later Bangladesh) hot and rainy.

The Karakoram Mountains form Pakistan's northern border with China. Pakistan borders India along the Thor Desert in the east, and borders Iran and Afghanistan in the west.

Only in the river valleys of the Indus and its tributaries is the land useful for agriculture and able to support a large population. The major crops are wheat, cotton, rice, and sugarcane. Nearly all the farmland is irrigated by the Indus River.

Pakistan has some iron ore, coal, and oil. The country must develop hydroelectric power from the Indus in order to make industrial progress. The main industrial products are cotton textiles and foods. There is a steel mill near Karachi, Pakistan's largest city and main seaport.

Islamabad, located in the north, is the capital city. Lahore, in northeast Pakistan, is the second-largest city and is the cultural and historical center of the nation.

The Split Between East and West Pakistan

Differences between East and West

In addition to the geographic differences, there were cultural and historical differences between the two parts of Pakistan. The people of West Pakistan spoke Urdu, a Persian language. Also, they were better educated and had a higher standard of living as a result of British development, which followed Muslim development in the area. Both groups regarded West Pakistan as the gateway to India and therefore put more resources into the region.

East Pakistanis spoke Bengali, an Indian language. Their customs and traditions followed the Hindu religion more closely, although a majority of the Bengalis were Muslim. Floods regularly destroyed homes and farmland in East Pakistan, and famine was a common occurrence. A low standard of living was the result.

For 20 years, West Pakistan dominated the union. Unstable governments did little to improve the lives of the people of either section. In 1958, General Ayub Khan seized power. He became a dictator, ousted corrupt officials, redistributed land, and began industrial development. However, civil rights such as free speech and free press were forbidden. By 1969, Ayub Khan, faced with riots and demands for more freedom, resigned.

Elections of 1970

Ayub Khan's rule by force had kept the people of East Pakistan quiet. When elections were held in 1970, however, the East Pakistanis (Bengalis), with a larger population than the western area, won enough votes to control Pakistan's National Assembly. This meant that the leader of the East Pakistan Bengali Party, Sheik Mujibur Rahman, would become prime minister of Pakistan.

The military leaders of Pakistan refused to accept the election results. Rahman and the other Bengali leaders were arrested, and thousands of East Pakistanis were slaughtered by the army. Civil war broke out, and millions of refugees fled to India. (For a more detailed account, see page 425.)

East Pakistan Becomes Bangladesh

In March 1971, East Pakistan declared its independence as the new nation of Bangladesh ("the Bengal Nation"). With the aid of India, independence became a reality later that year.

Pakistan after the Split (1971–1989)

As a result of the successful attempt by Bangladesh to become independent, President Yahya Khan was forced to resign as Pakistani president. In 1970, Zulfikar Ali Bhutto became the new president.

The Bhutto Government

A new Pakistani constitution was drawn up between 1971 and 1973, and Bhutto became prime minister. In an attempt to reform and improve Pakistan's economy, the nation's basic industries, such as iron and steel, metals, autos, chemicals, and natural gas, were nationalized. In addition, labor legislation, land reform, and agricultural controls were put into effect.

The basic weaknesses of the Bhutto government were the prime minister's excessive use of secret police and the unlimited power of the police. The army was also often used to put down opposition. In addition, Bhutto's attempts to reform agriculture and industry led to opposition by the middle class. Also, many of Bhutto's supporters in the government were involved in corrupt actions.

In 1977, the army again seized control of the government. Bhutto was put in prison and later executed for crimes against the people of Pakistan.

Islamization by Zia

The new government was headed by General Zia ul-Haq, who discarded much of the constitution. Islamic traditional law replaced civil law. Zia hoped to achieve legitimacy by gaining the support of traditional Muslims. In 1980, his government introduced *zakat* (state assistance to the poor). To pay for this, a 2.5 percent tax was placed on bank deposits, life insurance companies, government bonds, and shares of government securities.

Included in Zia's Islamization was the introduction of Islamic punishments such as floggings (whippings) for drinking alcoholic beverages and amputation (cutting off) of a hand for theft. Changes in the laws of evidence stated that the testimony of one man was equal to the testimonies of two women.

The economy of Pakistan did not improve under Zia. In 1986, Benazir Bhutto, the daughter of executed Prime Minister Zulfikar Ali Bhutto, returned to Pakistan from exile to lead an opposition movement.

Benazir Bhutto Becomes Prime Minister

Benazir Bhutto successfully opposed the Zia government. When Zia was killed in a plane crash in August 1988, Bhutto became prime minister and was the first woman to lead a modern Muslim (Islamic) nation.

Bhutto's program centered on local projects to improve health, education, and public works. The economy, however, still suffered from high inflation and high unemployment.

After 20 months of democratic rule, Bhutto was dismissed by the president of Pakistan, Ishaq Khan. The reasons given were based on charges of corruption, power abuse, and favoritism to relatives. Although the president had acted within the constitution, Benazir Bhutto believed that the generals of the army opposed any democratic reform and had engineered her downfall.

The Administration of Mian Nawaz Sharif

In October 1990, the people of Pakistan voted for a new Parliament. Although no party had a clear majority, the Muslim League won the greatest number of seats and formed a coalition government of Islamic parties. The leader of the Muslim League Party, Mian Nawaz Sharif, is the new prime minister. Benazir Bhutto is a member of the new Parliament and the leader of the opposition, the Pakistan Peoples Party (PPP).

By November of 1992, the uneasy truce between Benazir Bhutto and the government came to an end. On November 18, the Pakistani police arrested her and the other leaders of the PPP. Bhutto had charged the government of Nawaz Sharif with corruption, repression, and electoral fraud. She asked for new elections. After her arrest, Bhutto's supporters rioted in the cities of Lahore and Peshawar. More than a dozen people were injured and thousands were arrested.

The choice of Mian Nawaz Sharif as the new prime minister reflected some deep changes in Pakistan's economy and society. By the early 1990s, one-third of the population lived in urban areas. Many of the cities (Karachi, Lahore, Faisalabad, Rawalpindi, Multan) had populations of more than a million. The economy of Pakistan was no longer dependent on farming. Urban Pakistan, thanks to the migration of about 2 million people to the Middle East, Europe, and the United States, was exposed to the outside world and influenced by it.

Sharif's Economic Policy

Sharif has followed an economic policy aimed at rebuilding confidence in privately owned businesses. He rapidly sold off enterprises that had been taken over by the government in the early 1970s. His efforts to reduce bureaucratic paperwork and interference have helped to create an environment in which private enterprise can work more efficiently. This approach has increased foreign confidence in Pakistan.

Kalabagh and Ghazi Gharal Dam Projects

Sharif has shown ability in bringing together opposing parties to deal with some of Pakistan's most serious problems. He used the Council of common interests to reach an agreement on the distribution of the waters of the Indus River system, an issue that had defied agreement for 70 years. The agreement made possible the construction of massive hydroelectric projects as dams on the Indus at Kalabagh and Ghazi Gharal. When completed, these projects will go a long way toward solving Pakistan's serious energy and water problems.

Government Crisis

In 1991, however, two incidents shook public confidence in the Sharif government. In August, it was reported that 40 banks had violated their charters by trading in real estate and giving large unsecured loans to several important leaders of the government and to members of the prime minister's family.

On December 7, Sandar Shaukat Hayat, an old-time politician, alleged that his daughter had been robbed and raped by a gang sent to her house by Irfanullah Morwat, son-in-law of Ishaq Khan, president of India.

On December 19, Benazir Bhutto and her supporters in the PPP staged a noisy demonstration to protest the government's alleged corruption and lawlessness.

Sharif and Foreign Policy

The Sharif government's foreign policy has been almost entirely unsuccessful. When President Bush failed to certify to the U.S. Congress in 1991 that Pakistan's nuclear program is for peaceful purposes, all American economic and military assistance to Pakistan was suspended.

Also, the Pakistani government's unclear position during the Persian Gulf War in 1990–91 did not endear it to the states of the Arabian Peninsula. General Bey, army chief of staff, openly pushed for a pro-Iraq policy, while the president and prime minister offered to station Pakistani troops in Saudi Arabia. This was a costly blunder since the Arab states had come to Pakistan's rescue more than once with loans to solve balance-of-payments problems. When such a situation developed in December 1990, Arab help was not forthcoming.

Bangladesh

When India was partitioned in 1947, many Muslims and Hindus moved from the places where their ancestors had lived for centuries. Muslims moved from India to the new land of Pakistan. At the same time, many Hindus moved from Pakistan into India. In the Indian subcontinent, the Muslims lived mainly in the northwest and in a section of the northeast known as Bengal.

The people of this area, the Bengalis, had lived here for centuries, and they are Hindu and Muslim. To solve the problem of different religions and cultures, Bengal was divided between India and Pakistan. Pakistani Bengal was called East Bengal. Over 1,000 miles of Indian territory separated East Pakistan from West Pakistan.

Discontent and Revolt in East Pakistan

The Muslims of East Pakistan—the Bengalis—were not happy with the situation. Although the people of both sections were Muslims by religion, they were very different in many ways. Bengal is hot, rainy, fertile, and heavily populated; West Pakistan is drier, is less fertile, and has fewer people. The Muslims of Bengal had developed a culture different from that of West Pakistan Muslims. In fact, their ideas, language, and customs were much closer to those of the Hindu Bengalis than to those of the Muslims of West Pakistan.

The leading export of Pakistan was jute grown mainly in East Pakistan. Most of the money received from the sale of the jute, however, was used to improve conditions in West Pakistan. Other resources and capital were also unequally shared. The pressure for greater freedom and even autonomy grew.

As stated earlier, in the general election of 1971 the Bengalis elected enough delegates from the Awami Party to gain control of the Pakistan National Assembly. This meant that the Bengalis would be able to elect their leader, Sheik Mujibar Rahman, known to his followers as Mujib, as prime minister of all of Pakistan. The Bengalis felt that they would then achieve their goals of self-government and justice.

However, the West Pakistanis, led by President Mohammed Yahya Khan, looked at the situation differently. To give East Pakistan (Bengal) greater freedom might lead to the breakup and destruction of the state of Pakistan. Yahya also felt that his government had been fair to the Bengalis, and so he decided to crush the Awami Party opposition and eliminate the threat to Pakistani unity. In a surprise attack the Pakistani army arrested most of the leaders of Bengali Muslims, including Mujib. The army moved into East Pakistan and occupied most of the main areas. Fighting soon broke out between Bengali guerrilla nationalists and the West Pakistan army.

Reports from East Pakistan claimed that hundreds of thousands of men, women, and children—Muslim and Hindu—were killed by the army. Homes were destroyed. Millions left East Pakistan and moved into Indian Bengal. The threat of famine and epidemic, and, worse yet, of war between India and Pakistan loomed.

The East Pakistan Bengali leaders who survived declared East Pakistan independent and set up a new nation called Bangladesh. Since the Pakistani army ruled most of the main part of East Pakistan, Bangladesh guerrillas used Indian territory for bases. The guerrillas attacked Pakistani army outposts and patrols and the army arrested thousands. More refugees fled into India. (It was estimated that there were 10 million refugees from East Pakistan in India by the end of 1971.) Clashes broke out between units of the Indian army and the army of Pakistan. In late 1971, the situation became so serious that many observers felt that war between India and Pakistan was inevitable.

When fighting erupted between Bengalis and Pakistanis in December 1971, Indian troops raced across the border to aid the Bengalis. In 14 days, the Pakistanis were defeated, and the country of Bangladesh was born.

The Turbulent 1970s

In January 1972, the government of Pakistan, now led by Zulfikar Ali Bhutto, released the Bengali leader, Sheik Mujibur Rahman, in an effort to improve relations with the new nation. Mujibur became the prime minister of Bangladesh.

In September 1973, after 21 months of discussion, India and Pakistan agreed, with Bangladesh approval, to a peace settlement. The main points of the settlement were as follows:

1. There was to be a prisoner of war exchange;
2. All Bengalis stranded in Pakistan at the end of the war would be allowed to return to Bangladesh;
3. A "substantial" number of Biharis (non-Bengali Moslems) in Bangladesh would be allowed to go to Pakistan.

With Prime Minister Mujibur in control, Bangladesh came under the influence of India and the Soviet Union, primarily because of U.S. support of Pakistan. (The prime minister of Bangladesh feared that, with U.S. aid, Pakistan might try to regain control of Bangladesh, and he looked to India and the Soviet Union to help prevent this.) Many of the country's industries were nationalized. In 1974, responding to riots and violence, the government instituted emergency powers. Mujibur was assassinated, and the government suffered a series of coups. In addition, Bangladesh's relations with India deteriorated over water rights disputes.

The 1980s and Early 1990s

In the 1980s, Bangladesh continued to be deeply dependent on foreign aid, which, in 1984, made up 40 percent of the nation's total resources. Rice and jute were the chief crops of Bangladesh, and farms were small. Most Bangladeshi farmers were deeply in debt. Many lost their lands; in fact, it is estimated that almost 50 percent of all farmers were landless in 1985.

If enough food is to be produced to feed the people of Bangladesh, nature must cooperate at all times. A late monsoon or extra-heavy monsoon rains upsets the balance, and the vast rural population is never far from famine. In fact, many of Bangladesh's problems have always revolved around its lack of control over nature. Monsoons cause serious flooding problems and in 1970, 1974, 1984, 1988, and 1989 resulted in thousands of deaths and the destruction of farmland and farms.

Cyclones are another natural menace. In 1970, a cyclone caused the death of about 500,000 people. In 1985, a cyclone drove huge tidal waves across the low-lying islands in the Ganges River delta. Crops were destroyed, and about 40,000 people were killed.

The Return of Parliamentary Democracy

From March 1982 until December 4, 1990, General Hussain Muhammad Ershad ruled Bangladesh as a military dictator. All civil liberties were suspended at times "to maintain law and order."

The End of Military Dictatorship

In October 1990, a series of protests and antigovernment demonstrations occurred. These These were led by Sheik Husina Wajid (daughter of the assassinated Sheik Mujibur Rahman) and Begum Khalida Zia, the leader of the Bangladesh Nationalist Party (BNP). The major student parties joined the protest. On November 20, 1990, the opposition joined forces on a "one-point program" to replace Ershad with a neutral president who would hold the free and fair elections demanded by all of the opposing groups.

Nature must cooperate if Bangladesh is to be able to feed its people. Many times since the nation was born, heavy monsoons and floods have destroyed farmlands and left thousands, like this woman and her two small children, homeless and hungry.

The united opposition called for a hartal (general strike) to continue until Ershad resigned, the Parliament was dismissed, and a neutral president was appointed to oversee the election of a new Parliament. Ershad declared a state of emergency, and the demonstrations became more and more violent in response to police action. On December 4, 1990, Ershad announced his resignation.

The Political Parties and Their Programs

The Awami League Party follows a policy based on four pillars: nationalism, democracy, socialism, and secularism. The Awami League spoke of "Bengali nationalism"; the rival BNP, of "Bangladeshi nationalism." The Awami League's socialism was opposed to private investment and privatization programs and movement toward a market economy, which the BNP supported. The Awami League opposed any steps to associate the state more closely with Islam. Thus, in many ways the Awami League appeared to be a party that supported the status quo. The BNP, in contrast, seemed to offer positive programs for change.

The country's third major political party, Jamaat-i-Islam, wanted Bangladesh to become an Islamic state. The party's economic policies were similar to those of the BNP. Its position on Islam as the state religion, with Bangladesh as an Islamic state, was supported by the BNP.

The fourth party was the Jutiya Party of General Ershad. The Jatiya was allowed to participate even though many of its candidates were in jail or in hiding.

The Elections of 1991

In the parliamentary elections held on February 28, 1991, the BNP won 140 of the 300 seats. The Awami League and its allies won 99 seats; the Jatiya Party, 35; the Jamaat, 18. The BNP was short of a majority, but the Jamaat Party agreed to work with it.

In subsequent indirect elections for 30 women's seats, the BNP won 28 seats, giving it a clear majority in Parliament. (The Jamaat won the other two women's seats.)

The New Parliamentary System

Begum Zia, the BNP leader, became prime minister of Bangladesh. The party wished to change the existing system, in which the president had great powers and the office of prime minister was a rather powerless position. In August 1991, the constitution was amended, and in September a popular referendum approved the change. Now the prime minister, Begum Zia, had great power.

Members of Parliament elected their speaker, Abdur Rahman Biswas, the new president of Bangladesh. Begum Zia was now the powerful head of state, and Biswas the ceremonial head.

Natural Disasters of 1991

The new government had barely settled into office when, on April 30, 1991, Bangladesh's southern coast was struck by a major cyclone and flooding. Advanced warnings were issued, and many people took refuge in shelters built since the cyclone of 1970 (see page 426). Others, however, preferred to remain with their property, and between 50,000 and 300,000 of these people were killed. In addition, hundreds of thousands were made homeless. Damage to Bangladesh's only large seaport, Chittagong, was extensive. The efforts of the Bangladesh government to carry out rescue and relief operations were hampered by shortages of equipment and money, but within these limits the new government performed well.

Neighboring India and Pakistan lent assistance, as did many of the industrial nations and other countries in the Middle East. Perhaps most dramatic was the diversion of U.S.

ships and marines from their journey home after the end of the Persian Gulf War. The equipment and managerial skills that the Americans brought proved highly effective in coastal areas, where helicopters and specially constructed vessels were needed.

During the 1991 monsoon season, there was extensive flooding in northern Bangladesh. The sense of urgency that began with the floods of 1988 and 1989 grew stronger. Flood-control programs for the entire Ganges and Brahmaputra river systems became priority items for the governments of India, Nepal, and Bangladesh.

Foreign Relations

A solution to the flood problem requires close cooperation between India and Bangladesh. A related issue is the division of the waters of the Ganges during the low-water season in May and June. India operates a barrage dam to divert water through a canal and two rivers to Calcutta. India maintains that a steady flow is needed to supply fresh water to Calcutta. Bangladesh says that, after India takes what it wishes during the low-water season, not enough water remains for Bangladesh's Khulna district.

During the rest of the year, there is more than enough water to meet the needs of both countries. In fact, Ganges water, coupled with heavy flows from the Brahmaputra and other rivers, often results in heavy floods such as those that Bangladesh suffered in 1988, 1989, and 1991.

If a solution is to be found, an outside agent acceptable to all parties—the World Bank, for instance—must work with India, Bangladesh, Nepal, and China to find a plan to control the waters of the region so that all of the countries involved will receive the maximum benefit.

In foreign policy Bangladesh has developed "a very special relationship with China." China has pledged economic and military aid to Bangladesh; Bangladesh, friendship and cooperation with China.

The Future

Bangladesh remains one of the poorest countries in the world, mainly because economic growth fails to keep up with population increases. In 1989, Bangladesh's population was 111 million; the number will increase to 139 million by the end of the century (a growth rate of 2.1 percent annually).

For many reasons, foreign investment is not attracted. The nation has few natural resources other than natural gas and is always short of power. The transportation and communications infrastructures need improvement. Trained personnel are in short supply; many of the most highly trained workers have emigrated to the Middle East, where higher wages are paid. Political instability is also a concern to potential investors.

Bangladesh has made significant advances in the garment industry. Traditional exports like jute and tea, however, have not been growing and are not likely to show future expansion.

Bangladesh continues to be a major recipient of foreign economic assistance, much of it in grants. Japan is the largest donor, followed by the United States. In 1991, the United States forgave Bangladesh's government-to-government debt.

In fact, Bangladesh will require international assistance for years to come. Improvements in education, health care, and population planning are targets of international donors. Agriculture must also be given high priority; Bangladesh has never produced enough food to feed its people. A healthy, educated population enjoying a nutritious diet is a prerequisite for the expansion of industry and foreign investment that Bangladesh needs.

Economic and social progress must, however, be matched by political stability.

Nepal, India's Neighbor to the North

Three factors make Nepal a part of any study of South Asia.

1. The majority of Nepal's people are ethnically, closely related to the peoples of northern India.
2. The Nepalese are followers of Hinduism as are most of the people of northern India.
3. Nepal's location on India's northern border places it within the scope of any study of the Indian subcontinent.

Nepal, one of the world's most geographically isolated countries, lies between the northeast frontier of India and Chinese Tibet. Most of Nepal is mountainous; along the northern border are some of the highest mountain peaks in the world; including Mount Everest and Kanchenjunga. The *tarai* (or *terai*) is a flat, fertile river plain along Nepal's border with India.

About half of Nepal's people live in the hills and the valley regions; most of the others, in the tarai. A small number live in groups in the mountains. The highest density of population is in the area called the Valley of Nepal, where the people raise wheat and corn. This valley is also the site of the capital, Kathmandu. Most of the higher mountain areas can be used only for grazing. Rice grows on some of the lower, warmer southern slopes. (What are the major factors that affect farming in Nepal?)

Economy

Nepal's economy depends almost entirely on farming. Nepalese farmers attend small fairs and markets to trade their surplus crops for other needed items. Nepal has no railroads and few paved roads, and this lack of transportation facilities makes large-scale trade difficult.

Nepal has deposits of coal, copper, gold, iron, and mica. However, the country has few mines. Nepal's greatest natural resources are its forests and rivers. One of its most valuable trees is the *sal,* from which railroad ties are made. The swift mountain currents produce hydroelectric power.

Gurkha soldiers (see the next section) employed in the British and Indian armies make an important contribution to the economy of Nepal. The salaries and pensions paid to these soldiers total more than $32 million yearly, or about 10 percent of the income of Nepal.

Money spent by tourists has also helped the economy. More than 150,000 foreign visitors cqme to Nepal every year.

History

About A.D. 400 the Kathmandu Valley came to be called Nepal. Until the 18th century, Nepal consisted of a number of small, independent kingdoms. Over the centuries bands of conquerors, nomads, and refugees moved into Nepal. They were the ancestors of today's Nepalese.

Between 1750 and 1775, Prithwi Narayan Shah, King of the Nepalese kingdom of Gorkha, conquered and united all of the territory that makes up present-day Nepal. His descendants rule Nepal today.

In the early 1800s, Nepal fought a war with Great Britain. After very hard fighting in the mountains, the Nepalese were defeated. The British were greatly impressed, however, with the soldiers of Gorkha—the Gurkhas. After the war, Great Britain agreed to maintain the independence of Nepal, and Nepal and Great Britain became allies. Many Gurkha soldiers were recruited into the Brtitish army, a practice that continues to the present time.

In 1846, a local political leader, Jung Bahadur, took control of the government. He assumed the title of *Rana* and served as prime minister. Until 1951, members of the Rana family ruled Nepal. During this period, the kings had no power. A revolution that began in 1950 led to the restoration of the monarchy to power under King Tribhuwan Shah.

During the 1950s, the government made various attempts to create a democracy in Nepal. However, in 1960 a new king, Mahendra, criticized the political party rivalry that had developed. Declaring that Nepal needed a political system that would suit the country's traditions, he dissolved the Parliament and the elected government. In 1962, Mahendra put into effect a constitution that established the panchayat system, in which most power is held by the king.

In 1979 and throughout the 1980s, the Nepalese demonstrated, sometimes violently, demanding more democratic government. In1980, Mahendra's son Birendra allowed a national vote on the type of government the people desired. By a narrow margin, the voters chose to continue the panchayat system.

People

The majority of Nepalese are closely related to the peoples of North India. Other Nepalese are of Tibetan descent. Almost all the people live in small villages that consist of two-story houses made of stone or mud brick.

The Gurkhas, the Nepalese solders in the British and Indian armies, and the Sherpas are known for special skills. The Sherpas, a Himalayan people, have won fame as mountain climbers and as guides for mountain climbing expeditions. In 1953, Tenzing Norgay, a Sherpa, along with Sir Edmund Hillary, became the first to climb Mount Everest.

Hinduism is the official religion of Nepal and of the Gurkhas. However, the Nepalese have combined the beliefs and practices of Hinduism with those of Buddhism. (Buddha, the founder of Buddhism, was born in Nepal about 563 B.C.) The Nepalese people celebrate the festivals of both religions, and Buddhist shrines and Hindu temples are considered equally sacred.

Illiteracy ranks as one of Nepal's most serious problems. In the 1950s, perhaps as few as 5 percent of the people 15 years of age or older could read and write. King Mahendra built schools and set up a program to train teachers. It is estimated that at present the percentage of literate people has risen to between 20 and 25 percent.

India and World Politics

India's Stated Policy of Nonalignment

In the period between 1945 and 1950, just after the end of World War II, most nations became the allies of either the United States and the other Western nations or of the former Soviet Union and the nations of Eastern Europe. When India gained its independence, however, the new government decided to follow a neutral foreign policy toward both the United States and the Soviet Union. This policy, called **nonalignment**, or **neutralism**, meant that India would not develop strong ties to either of the major powers. In other words, India made a decision not to ally itself to the policies and goals of either the United States or the Soviet Union. No military alliances or treaty agreements were to be entered into with the two superpowers.

In practice, however, India has always taken sides in international disputes. Indian leaders have always felt free to support the side whose policy they felt was best for their people and the other peoples of the world.

India and the United States

Relations through the 1980s

Relations between the United States and India were friendly for many years after India gained its independence. Americans felt deep sympathy for India's goals and aspirations. Over the years, as U.S. concerns over Asian affairs grew, the amount of economic aid to India increased. American funds for economic development and technical assistance in India, and credits for the purchase of food, played an important role in India's attempts to solve its economic problems. However, U.S. offers of military aid were always refused because India hoped to keep American influence out of its foreign affairs.

Gradually, India had to change its policy. The Chinese attacks in 1962 (see page 435) exposed weaknesses in India's defenses, and India was forced to turn to the United States for military aid. When Indian and Pakistani troops became involved in border fighting, however, the United States stopped all arms shipments to both countries. Neither nation was pleased with this policy, and India turned more and more to the Soviet Union for military and political assistance.

When fighting ended, the United States resumed aid to Pakistan, which was a member of the Southeast Asia Treaty Organization. India was not happy with this development, and relations between the United States and India deteriorated (grew worse).

When a new quarrel between India and Pakistan developed over the situation in East Pakistan, relations between the United States and India deteriorated further. The United States angered India by continuing to send arms to the Pakistanis. The Indians felt that these arms would be used to fight the Bangladesh guerrillas and would possibly be used against India itself. In November 1971, Indira Gandhi, then the Indian prime minister, visited President Nixon in the United States, hoping to improve relations.

In 1984, when Rajiv Gandhi became prime minister, he said he wished for better relations with the United States, and he met with President Reagan. Scientific and cultural exchanges between the two countries continued throughout the 1980s.

In general, the late 1980s saw improved relations between the United States and India. The United States believed that Rajiv Gandhi was following a more liberal, less state-controlled economic policy. In addition, the United States saw India as a stabilizing force in a very troubled South Asia. The United States openly praised India's role in trying to settle the Sri Lanka problems (the Tamil rebellion; see page 438) and advised Pakistan of the "inadvisability of supporting and supplying Kashmiri militants."

Relations in the 1990s

After the 1991 general election, the Rao government felt the pressure of India's poor economic situation. The fact that the former Soviet Union, which had been India's main supplier of credit and loans, was experiencing even worse economic problems added to an already serious situation. Also, the increased global importance of the United States as a result of the Gulf War was clearly evident.

After the Gulf War, despite India's lack of support for the U.N. action, U.S. support for India continued. The U.S. government dropped its objection to the sale of a Cray mainframe computer to India, and helped India to get $1.8 billion in credits from the International Monetary Fund (IMF). In November 1991, again with a good word from the United States, the IMF approved another $2.2 billion standby loan arrangement. In December, the World Bank cleared a $700 million credit loan and credit package, with the clear approval of the United States. The obviously friendly attitude of the United States will make it easier for India to change its long-standing policy of nonalignment and thereby further improve relations with the United States.

In fact, India's foreign policy of nonalignment, with a leaning toward the former Soviet Union, now has little meaning and is slowly dying. An alternative inclination in policy toward the West will not force India into the role of beggar. The Gulf War showed both the dominance of the United States in international affairs and the limits to the use of **unilateral** (one-sided) power by the United States. Political and economic realities have demonstrated that **multilateral** (many-sided) burden-sharing and regional cooperation are necessary to resolve problems and conflicts.

Although the United States does not seek global dominance, it would like to see regional and global stability resting on regional balances of power. In South Asia, the balance would depend on India.

India needs American capital and technology, and the United States could use the vast Indian market. Given its size and resources, an India firmly integrated into world markets would be a major boost for international capitalism.

For too long, India and the United States have allowed ego and ideological straitjackets to prevent closer relations. Basically, however, there is an underlying harmony of interests between India and the United States. The world's most powerful and most populous democracies should be allies, not enemies.

India and Russia

Relations through the 1980s

For decades, India looked upon the Soviet Union as a friend, and the leaders of the two countries exchanged many visits. The amount of Soviet aid was much less than that from the United States, but India was happy to have help of all kinds from all sources. India also felt it could get military help from Russia to protect its borders from invasion by the Chinese.

The Russians did not disappoint their Indian friends. When India and Pakistan were quarreling over trouble in East Pakistan in the summer of 1971, the Russians signed an agreement with India whereby the two countries agreed to help each other in case of war. The Russians also sent modern arms and jet planes to India.

In December 1973, Leonid Brezhnev, leader of the Soviet Communist Party, visited India. The Russians and the Indians signed a 15-year economic agreement. The Russians agreed to increase trade with India, to help India build new steel mills, and to supply India with fertilizers, chemicals, and crude oil. The Russians wanted the right to dock their Indian Ocean warships in India's harbors, but Indira Gandhi, the Indian prime minister, resisted the request.

In the 1980s, India, under Rajiv Gandhi, seemed to be following Soviet leadership on most issues. When Soviet leader Gorbachev visited India in 1986, he promised large amounts of aid and pledged to support India in its relations with Pakistan. This promise was kept.

In fact, since World War II, the most successful bilateral relationships for both India and the Soviet Union were with each other. Relations between Moscow and New Delhi were dynamic (active), stable (firm), and resilient (quickly repaired).

Relations in the 1990s

The dissolution of the Soviet Union has raised important questions. Efforts will continue to preserve friendly ties with the Commonwealth of Independent States.

Indian Foreign Minister Madhav Singh Solanki visited Russia in November 1991. India and Russia finalized a new friendship treaty on January 15, 1992, and signed memoranda of understanding on trade and supplies of defense and power-generation equipment. President Boris Yeltsin has agreed to visit India, and New Delhi will grant 32 billion rupees (Indian money) of credit to Russia to pay for Indian goods, as well as 150 million rupees in humanitarian assistance.

India has also moved aggressively to establish political ties (the 12 Commonwealth states were granted formal recognition by India on December 16, 1991), military contracts (Ukrainian enterprises are fulfilling long-term agreements between New Delhi and Moscow), and economic agreements (a joint venture for building personal computers in Uzbekistan) with the newly independent republics. In November 1991, the Indian deputy commerce minister said that rupee settlements in India's trade with the Commonwealth states will terminate in 1994–95. After that date, India intends to conduct its economic relations with the sovereign republics on the principles of a market economy. India would now make payments in pounds sterling (British money) or American dollars.

Both India and Russia are struggling to achieve economic success by means of a mixed but market-oriented, liberalizing economy functioning within a multiethnic, multiparty, competitive federal democracy. And because the new Russian government has established good working relations with both China and the United States, India too can seek to improve its bilateral relations with those countries without fear of damaging its relationship with the former Soviet state.

The United States, Europe, and Japan are now better placed than Russia to assist India. In the past, a strategic friendship with the Soviet Union that did not incur a strategic enmity with the United States gave India the best of both worlds. Now New Delhi must deal with the breakup of the Soviet Union and the resulting emergence of an essentially new world order.

India and China

Relations through the 1980s

India hoped to have friendly relations with its giant neighbor to the north, the People's Republic of China. India was one of the first countries to break off relations with the defeated Chinese Nationalist government, and to recognize the People's Republic. Also, India consistently led the attempt to have China admitted to the United Nations. In 1954,

Nehru and Chou En-lai, the Chinese foreign minister, agreed on the "Five Principles of Peaceful Coexistence," a pledge of peaceful, neighborly relations between India and China.

However, when the Chinese occupied Tibet in 1950, the presence of Chinese forces along the borders of India, Bhutan, and Nepal disturbed Nehru. In 1960, the Chinese occupied Longju, an Indian frontier post, an action that led to fighting between Chinese and Indian soldiers. In 1962, Chinese troops made a deep advance into Indian territory, and then withdrew. Clearly, India, a nation dedicated to peaceful coexistence, was no match for the Chinese.

However, after a visit by Rajiv Gandhi to China in December 1988 and a visit to New Delhi, India, by the Chinese vice-premier in October 1989, both nations adopted a policy intended to increase contacts and improve relations.

Relations in the 1990s

History has shown that India and China have little in common except a long and disputed border. In spite of good intentions, three obstacles have prevented the normalization of China-India relations: (a) the Soviet factor; (b) the Tibet problem; and (c) the border dispute.

With the collapse of communism and the dissolution of the Soviet Union, the *Soviet factor* has been transformed from an impediment into a spur to improving Sino-Indian relations. New Delhi's hesitant moves toward Beijing used to arouse suspicion and unease in Moscow; they are now greeted with smiles of encouragement. China, in turn, has become more receptive to Indian overtures, for the closeness of the Indian-Russian relationship is no longer viewed as a threat to Chinese security.

The *Tibet problem,* although not easily solved, is manageable. That both China and India are committed to preventing their feelings over Tibet from damaging their broader relationship was evident when Indian police used uncharacteristic force in dealing with Tibetan demonstrators protesting the Chinese prime minister's visit. In the joint communique issued by the two nations, China expressed concern about the activities of Tibetans living in India, while India reiterated its position that Tibet was part of China. As one leading newspaper stated in an editorial, the red carpet of welcome for the Chinese prime minister was not strained by expressions of dissent over China's misdemeanors in Tibet (Source: *The Statesman,* December 16, 1991).

The most serious and intractable obstacle remains the *border dispute.* While India's approach to the border conflict is historical, China's is strategic. A democratic solution to the border dispute is not possible because of the small population in the regions under dispute. A judicial settlement could cope adequately with the differences in the historical and strategic approaches by India and China.

China's negotiating position is based on the premise that there is a genuine territorial dispute arising out of conflicting interpretations of the authenticity of British-Indian claims in the era of imperialism. India's position is based on historical actions taken by Great Britian in the 19th century.

The benefits to India of a broad compromise are obvious. A settled border with China would make it easier to stabilize India's troubled northeastern region. In addition, it would reduce opportunities for trouble arising in India's relations with Bhutan and Nepal. It would also ease the task of securing Pakistani agreement to convert the line of control in Kashmir into an international border, thereby resolving India's most serious foreign policy problem (see pages 437–438). Nevertheless, influential Indians continue to make any accommodation difficult by insisting that the Chinese proposals "will only legitimize aggression or illegal occupation of another nation's territory."

After months of maneuvering by both sides, Chinese leader Li Peng paid a six-day visit to India in December 1991—the first visit by a Chinese prime minister since the 1962 war. The Chinese leader said during the visit that neither country wished to see the boundary dispute remain an obstacle to the development of improved relations. China and India signed three agreements: one on the opening of consular offices in Bombay and Shanghai, a second on space cooperation, and a third on border trade.

India and Pakistan

Relations through the 1980s

After the partition of India in 1947, mutual suspicion and distrust highlighted the relations between India and Pakistan. The two countries fought three wars and viewed each other as untrustworthy, irrational, and expansionist. Border fighting occurred often, and the two countries were involved in a conventional arms race and also feared each other's nuclear policies. India, which exploded a nuclear device in 1974, accused Pakistan of secretly developing its own atomic weapons.

Contrary to international trends toward cooperation and reconciliation, hostility between India and Pakistan deepened during the 1980s. Pakistan had recovered from its defeat by India in 1971 and had regained confidence in dealing with its neighbor as an equal. The relative calm in the 1970s had been based on a superior-subordinate relationship rather than on Pakistan's surrendering its long-held claims.

The 1980s brought a different set of circumstances. With the Zia regime in Pakistan came some stability and order. By contrast, a number of different separatist movements and rebellions sprang up in India. Within the South Asia region, India was involved in disputes with Bangladesh, Nepal, and Sri Lanka, which seemed to show a lack of stability and order in India.

Internationally, the Soviet invasion of Afghanistan and the Vietnamese invasion of Cambodia affected India-Pakistan relations. For Pakistan, it meant elevation to the status of a frontline state in the superpower rivalry between the United States and the U.S.S.R. This situation resulted in increased economic aid, military supplies, and diplomatic support from the West as well as from the Arab and Islamic blocs.

India, by contrast, was put on the defensive in trying to explain its continuing close ties with the U.S.S.R., Pol Pot in Cambodia, and the Soviet-supported government in Afghanistan.

In 1985, President Zia of Pakistan and Indian Prime Minister Rajiv Gandhi agreed not to attack each other's nuclear facilities. The agreement was never signed, however, and the Indian prime minister never carried out a promise to visit Pakistan. In early 1987, the two countries reached the brink of war when each side massed more than 200,000 troops on their borders because of rumors of impending invasions by the other country.

Relations in the 1990s

Possibilities for conflict between India and Pakistan have existed ever since the partition of India in 1947. Pakistan has been ruled by the military for most of its history. India now has a functioning democracy almost without interruption, although ruled most of the time by the Congress Party. Pakistan's military appear to feel threatened by the democracy of its neighbor and have restricted cultural ties. Successive Pakistani governments seem unhappy with Indian radio and television programs, which are easily received in Pakistan. These programs have stressed cultural ties between the two countries and promoted the benefits of democracy.

Several measures to increase trade, ease travel restrictions, and improve cultural ties have been proposed, but none has been put into effect. A second border crossing point has been pending for more than 15 years. (The only crossing point is in Punjab.) Newspapers have not been freely exchanged since the 1950s. Two-way trade is restricted to government companies and to a list of 42 items.

Kashmir continues to be the main bone of contention between India and Pakistan (see below). India, which controls the strategically vital valley, wishes to maintain the status quo. Kashmir is the only Indian state with a Muslim majority. Pakistan, on the other hand, is dissatisfied with the present situation but lacks the means to change it.

India and Kashmir

The history of Indian control over Kashmir since 1948 has left several harmful legacies for the country as a whole. Indians take rightful pride in being the world's largest democracy, but the forcible occupation of Kashmir has not been an exercise in democracy. Democratic institutions have been corrupted in Kashmir by repeated vote-rigging and rule by a controlled administration. Also, Indian operations in Kashmir in recent years have been dogged by allegations of police and army brutality and have served to damage the image of the Indian security forces.

In 1990–91, the moral, political, economic, and international costs of India's Kashmir policy were only too apparent. The uprising in Kashmir in 1990 saw a near-complete paralysis of the state administration. Initial attempts to treat the uprising simply as a law-and-order problem by the imposition of curfews and strong-arm tactics by police, paramilitary, and military personnel were intended to intimidate and coerce the separatists. Instead, they strengthened separatist sentiment and recruited a broader spectrum of adherents to the cause of liberating Kashmir from Indian control.

India has four options in regard to Kashmir:

1. Invade and annex the part of Kashmir occupied by Pakistan. This course of action is impractical; international condemnation of India and support for Pakistan would be massive and decisive. Also India could not exercise "normal" control over a large and hostile Kashmiri population indefinitely. India has enough insurgency and terrorist problems already without taking on more.
2. Maintain the status quo. This is to persist in an unsatisfactory situation that will simply erode (eat away at) the fabric of Indian society and economy.
3. Submit the Kashmir dispute to international adjudication (judgment) or arbitration. By taking the conflict to the World Court and abiding by its verdict, India would set an invaluable precedent for resolving all of its bilateral disputes with smaller and larger neighbors alike and could lay claim to a high moral ground in world affairs.
4. Withdraw troops from Kashmir, stop treating the problem as a law-and-order issue, and tackle the political roots of the conflict by letting the people of Kashmir vote to decide their own fate.

A resolution on the basis of self-determination would reinforce India's democratic institutions and principles, strengthen its federal structure and practices, and end a financial drain. Also, it would ease the internal tensions between Muslims and Hindus. An unequivocal act of self-determination in Kashmir, combined with a proclamation of the supremacy of India's secular laws and institutions over religious laws in areas such as divorce and maintenance support, would do much to defuse the Hindu backlash that now threatens to destroy tolerance and secularism in the country. In short, an honorable democratic solution to Kashmir would strengthen the Indian state, underline its political values, and increase the cohesiveness of Indian society.

There would also be external benefits. A popular or judicial solution would eliminate a major liability in courting relations with Arab and other Islamic states, eliminate the most potent source of tension in relations with Pakistan, remove the basis for an anti-India security cooperation between China and Pakistan, rid India of its biggest international embarrassment, undermine the basis for a strategic partnership between Pakistan and the United States, and remove a perennial irritant in Indo-U.S. relations.

India and Sri Lanka

In addition to India's longstanding problems, a relatively new one involves Sri Lanka (Ceylon). Over the past 100 years, many Tamils whose traditional home is South India, have settled in Sri Lanka. Since 1975, part of the Sri Lankan Tamil community has been fighting for an autonomous Tamil state in northern and eastern Sri Lanka.

The Sri Lankan government has accused India of aiding and training Tamil terrorists.

The Sri Lankans believe that both Indira Gandhi and Rajiv Gandhi supported the separatists. Some have gone so far as to say that it was Indira Gandhi who gave "teeth" to the most violent group of separatists, the Liberation Tigers of Tamil Eelam. This group, often called the "Tamil Tigers," are dedicated and battle-tested guerrillas, who have become experts in terror bombings.

Although Rajiv and his mother originally supported the separatist movement, in 1987 Rajiv made peace with Sri Lanka. To cement the peace, Rajiv sent 50,000 Indian troops to Sri Lanka to help put down a Tamil rebellion. Refusing to lay down their arms, the Tamil Tigers fought both the Sri Lankans and the Indians with hit-and-run tactics that resulted in extensive Tamil casualties. (It is rumored that in March 1991 Rajiv held a meeting with a Tiger leader and agreed that the guerrillas could resume using hospitals in Tamil Nadu in South India.) The Tamil Tigers were prime suspects in the assassination of Rajiv Gandhi because of the method used and because extremist Tigers resented Rajiv for sending troops to Sri Lanka.

Conclusion: India's Role among Nations

When India gained its independence, Nehru said, "A moment comes, which comes but rarely in history, when we step out from the old to the new, when an age ends" (J. Nehru, *India Foreign Policy, Selected Speeches:* New Delhi, 1961, p. 13).

Since 1947, India has generally seen itself as a world power and has, for the most part, conducted its regional and international relations on this basis. The result has been insignificant internationally and has caused great suspicion and fear of India in the region.

India's neighbors have tended to view it as overarmed and controlling. It is a remarkable fact that in the early 1990s, India finds itself without a network of useful friendships in South Asia. India's **potential** (possibility) for leadership in world affairs lies first and foremost in its own neighborhood. Instead of trying to realize this potential, India has frightened all the surrounding countries.

Indian foreign policy has failed also by neglecting friendships in the Middle East. Efforts to counter Pakistan's influence among Islamic countries of the Arab World have failed to bear fruit. India's only real friend in the Middle East has been Iraq.

Ironically, India's one genuine friendship with a Southeast Asian country, namely, Vietnam, was a diplomatic liability in the 1980s and early 1990s.

The age of the Cold War and nonalignment has ended. Will India remain a prisoner of the past? Or will it bring forth a leader brave enough to break with old traditions? One thing is certain: stability and prosperity at home will increase Indian credibility and prestige, both regionally and internationally.

Summary of Key Ideas

The Subcontinent of India and South Asia (Pakistan and Bangladesh)

A.   India's varied geographic features have helped to shape its culture and history.

1. India, together with Pakistan, Bangladesh, and Nepal is considered to be a subcontinent of Asia.

2. The Himalaya Mountains in the north, jungles in the northeast, and oceans and seas to the east and west have in part isolated India from the rest of Asia.

3. Geographic features have influenced the development of local cultures, and have aided the development of regionalism.

4. The monsoon plays a vital role in the life of the people of India.

5. River valleys and coastal regions are centers of population.

6. Climate has affected the development of culture and history.

7. Most of India has a subtropical climate.

B.   Outside forces have brought great changes to Indian society, culture, government, and religion.

1. The Dravidian cities of Mohenjo-Daro and Harappa show the advanced state of the first Indian civilizations.

2. Aryan invaders from the north brought many changes to the subcontinent.

3. The Islamic religion was brought to India by traders and invaders.

4. The Indian spice trade had a great effect on Indian history and the history of America, Africa, and Southeast Asia.

5. *No* all-India empire existed throughout the history of the subcontinent. Political history was regional.

6. The British gained control after defeating an Indian-French army at Plassey. The British ruled through Indian leaders.

7. The subcontinent became the "brightest jewel in the British crown." Conflicts and challenges to traditional ways of life developed.

8. The Sepoy Rebellion was one of the most important events in the modern history of India. Among its most significant results was the stimulation of Indian nationalism.

9. The 20th century has been marked by struggles between Indian nationalists and Great Britain, and between Hindu and Muslim nationalists.

10. The careers of Gandhi and Nehru exemplify the struggle for Indian independence.

11. In 1947, Great Britain decided to partition the subcontinent into an independent India and an independent Pakistan.

C. The leaders of India face major economic problems.

1. The monsoons dominate economic life in most parts of India.

2. Over 80 percent of the people live in rural areas. There are over 500,000 villages, averaging about 100 families each.

3. Rice is the main food and is important as a money-raising crop.

4. Wheat, millet, tobacco, and cotton are raised in drier areas.

5. Small-scale farming on a subsistence level is the rule for India.

6. Population pressure makes it difficult for people to survive in the face of poverty and hunger.

7. The Indian government has adopted programs to increase agricultural production and encourage birth control.

8. India has a mixed economy. Public and private funds are used to develop the land and industry.

9. India receives aid from both the United States and the former Soviet Union.

10. India faces all of the problems of a developing nation.

11. The Indian government has tried to improve the economic and social position of the scheduled castes (the untouchables).

12. Corruption and unsuccessful state planning have led to the failure of India's economy.

D. Religion is a way of life that influences the social structure, history, economic activity, and political organization of India.

1. Religion often regulates customs, diet, occupations, and other aspects of life.

2. Knowledge of Hinduism is necessary for an understanding of India's past and present.

3. Hindus believe in reincarnation. This is part of the Hindu belief in the holiness of all living things.

4. Religious differences between Hindus and Muslims have historic roots and have greatly influenced the development of modern India.

5. The Buddhist religion began as a protest and as an attempt to reform Hinduism.

6. The Four Noble Truths and the Eightfold Path state the main principles of Buddhism.

7. Ethnic and religious differences led to the assassination of Indian Prime Ministers Indira Gandhi and Rajiv Gandhi.

E. India has played an important role in world affairs since gaining independence in 1947.

1. India's size and differences in religion, language, and ethnic background create political unrest within its borders.

2. The new state of Bangladesh has created a new set of problems for India.

3. Relations between India and Pakistan have been poor since the partition of the subcontinent.

4. India has tried to follow a policy of nonalignment and to maintain friendly relations with all, especially the United States, Russia, and China.

5. Border disputes with China, rooted in past history, have caused war between the two, and a troublesome situation still remains.

6. Problems with Pakistan have led India to closer relations with the former Soviet Union and distrust of the United States.

7. India has been an active member of the United Nations.

F. Pakistan is an important and strategically located nation of South Asia.

1. Pakistan was created by the partition of British India into Hindu India and Muslim Pakistan in 1947.

2. Pakistan is made up of the Indus Valley, mountains, and deserts.

3. Pakistan's economy is based on agriculture and small industries that produce textiles and food products.

4. In 1971, after a brief revolution, East Pakistan broke away from Pakistan and became the independent nation of Bangladesh.

5. Pakistan has been ruled mainly by military dictators. Democratic reforms have been attempted but have not been entirely successful.

UNIT V

Exercises and Questions

Vocabulary

Directions: Match the words in Column A with the correct meaning in Column B.

Column A

1. migration
2. paddies
3. illiterate
4. caste system
5. untouchables
6. annexed
7. ahimsa
8. Dharma
9. reincarnation
10. swaraj

Column B

(a) added to something
(b) self-rule
(c) movement of people or animals
(d) the return to some form of life after death
(e) rice fields
(f) Indian idea of nonviolent action
(g) unable to read or write
(h) people once considered outcasts in India
(i) social division of the Indian people by birth and according to occupation
(j) Hindu rules of life, which control a person's actions

Completion

Directions: Complete the following sentences by using the terms below.

Vedas	Deccan	Himalayas	Moksha	Ghats
Dravidians	Hindi	Harappa	monsoons	Tamil

1. _____ is the language and the name given to the people of South India.

2. _____ was a city of early India.

3. _____ are books of ceremonies and rituals written by the Aryan people of India.

4. _____ is the final resting place of the souls of Hindus.

5. _____ are the original people of India.

6. _____ are the low mountians found on both the east and west coasts of India.

7. _____ is the name given to the central plateau of India.

8. _____ are the mountains of North India.

9. _____ is the language most spoken in India.

10. _____ are the seasonal winds that affect India and much of the rest of Asia.

INDIAN FOREIGN TRADE—1986
PRINCIPLE TRADE PARTNERS

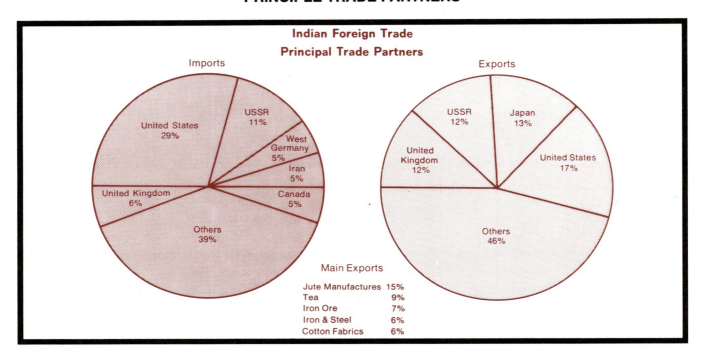

Indian Foreign Trade
Principal Trade Partners

Imports

United States 29%
USSR 11%
West Germany 5%
Iran 5%
United Kingdom 6%
Canada 5%
Others 39%

Exports

USSR 12%
Japan 13%
United Kingdom 12%
United States 17%
Others 46%

Main Exports

Jute Manufactures 15%
Tea   9%
Iron Ore   7%
Iron & Steel   6%
Cotton Fabrics   6%

Chart Analysis

Directions: Select the statement that best answers the question or completes the sentence. Use only the information given in the table and graphs.

1. Each of these graphs is an example of a
   (a) pictograph.
   (b) line graph.
   (c) pie graph.
   (d) bar graph.

2. The leading trading partner of India is
   (a) the United Kingdom.
   (b) the United States.
   (c) the U.S.S.R.
   (d) Canada.

3. Which of the following groups of products are exported from India?
   (a) jute, cotton goods, coffee
   (b) jute, tea, wool
   (c) jute, tea, iron, and steel products
   (d) jute, iron ore, coal

4. Which of the following statements can be proved by information given in the chart and graphs?
   (a) India exports more than 70% of its products to Europe.
   (b) India exports more to the United Kingdom than any other nation.
   (c) India imports more than 70% of its products from Europe.
   (d) The United States and the U.S.S.R. account for 40% of India's import trade.

5. Which of the following statements can be proved false by information from the chart and graphs?
   (a) Jute is India's most important export.
   (b) Japan buys more than 10% of India's exports.
   (c) The United States supplies almost one third of India's imports.
   (d) India has very little trade with her Asian neighbors.

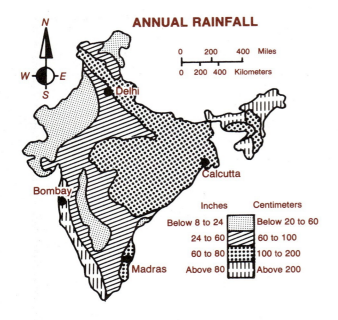

ANNUAL RAINFALL

0 200 400 Miles
0 200 400 Kilometers

Delhi

Calcutta

Bombay

Madras

Inches		Centimeters
Below 8 to 24		Below 20 to 60
24 to 60		60 to 100
60 to 80		100 to 200
Above 80		Above 200

CROPLANDS — INDIA

RICE

Delhi

Calcutta

Bombay

Madras

WHEAT

Delhi

Calcutta

Bombay

Madras

COTTON

Delhi

Calcutta

Bombay

Madras

Map Exercise

Directions: Using the four maps of India on this page, select the answer that best completes each statement.

1. The city with the most rainfall is
   (a) Bombay.   (b) Delhi.   (c) Calcutta.   (d) Madras.

2. The city located in the heart of the wheat-producing area is
   (a) Bombay.   (b) Delhi.   (c) Calcutta.   (d) Madras.

3. Cotton is produced in the areas that have
   (a) the greatest amount of rainfall.
   (b) the least amount of rainfall.
   (c) about 80 inches of rainfall.
   (d) between 24 and 60 inches of rainfall.

4. The distance from Madras to Calcutta is about
   (a) 400 miles.   (b) 800 miles.   (c) 1000 miles.   (d) 1200 miles.

5. An important conclusion that can be reached from studying these maps is that
   (a) wheat needs heavy rainfall for successful growth.
   (b) as you travel from south to north fewer crops are raised.
   (c) rice is mainly raised along the coasts of India.
   (d) rainfall has an effect on the crops that are raised in India.

446 The Subcontinent of India and South Asia (Pakistan and Bangladesh)

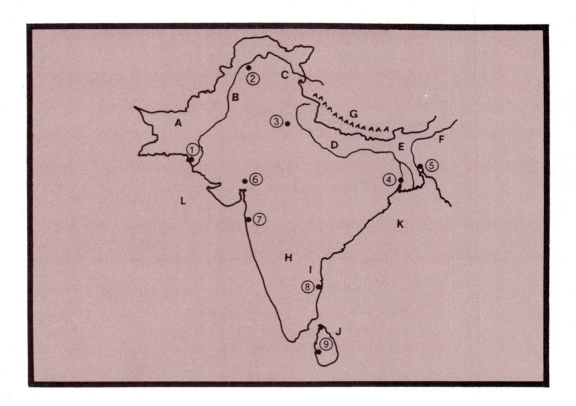

Map Exercise

Directions: Complete the following statements on the map of India.

1. The Himalaya Mountains are shown by the letter
   (a) A.　(b) C.　(c) G.　(d) F.

2. The capital city of India is shown by the number
   (a) 1.　(b) 2.　(c) 3.　(d) 4.

3. The letter "D" represents the
   (a) Indus River.　(b) Ganges River.　(c) Thar Desert.　(d) Ghats.

4. Sri Lanka (Ceylon) is shown by the letter
   (a) J.　(b) K.　(c) L.　(d) H.

5. The letter "H" is located on the
   (a) Thar Desert.　(b) Ganges Valley.　(c) Carnatic Coast.　(d) Deccan.

6. The numbers 4 and 7 represent important seaports. They are
   (a) Madras and Bombay.　(b) Madras and Calcutta.　(c) Bombay and Calcutta.
   (d) Calcutta and Karachi.

7. A delta is found near the group of cities indicated by the numbers
   (a) 1, 4, 5.　(b) 2, 3, 4.　(c) 3, 4, 5.　(d) 1, 6, 7.

8. Bangladesh is shown by the letter
   (a) A.　(b) B.　(c) E.　(d) K.

9. The river indicated by the letter "D" flows mainly
   (a) east to west.   (b) west to east.   (c) north to south.   (d) south to north.

10. The number 8 shows the location of the city of
    (a) Dacca.   (b) Madras.   (c) Bombay.   (d) Calcutta.

Multiple Choice

Directions: Select the answer that best completes the sentence or answers the question.

1. All of the following statements about the geography of India are true *except*
   (a) South India is a land of mountains, forests, and jungles
   (b) the Deccan is isolated from most of India by geography
   (c) mountain passes through the Himalayas have helped people to migrate into India
   (d) the rivers of India play only a small role in the lives of the people

2. All of the following affect the climate of India *except*
   (a) cold winds from central Asia
   (b) the monsoon winds from the south
   (c) the wide range of latitude
   (d) the warm ocean currents along the coasts

3. Which statement about the monsoons is accurate?
   (a) They are mountains that separate India from the rest of Asia.
   (b) They are winds that bring heavy rains to South Asia.
   (c) They form a plateau covering most of the Indian peninsula.
   (d) They form a large land mass smaller than a continent.

4. The major population centers on the Indian subcontinent are generally located
   (a) on the coastline.
   (b) in the temperate foothills of the Himalayas.
   (c) near the major rivers.
   (d) throughout the subcontinent.

5. India leads the world in the production of
   (a) wheat.   (b) tea.
   (c) spices.   (d) jute.

6. Which of the following is true about the population of India?
   (a) Most Indians live in cities.
   (b) More than one-half the population is less than 34 years old.
   (c) There are few racial differences among Indians.
   (d) More than one-half of the people speak Hindi.

7. Indians eat little or no meat because
   (a) the land is too poor for raising cattle.
   (b) the Hindu religion forbids the raising of cattle.
   (c) the Hindu religion forbids the eating of meat.
   (d) all of the above

8. In an outline, one of the following is a main topic and the others are subtopics. Which is the main topic?
   (a) The Hindu Religion
   (b) Beliefs of Hinduism
   (c) Reincarnation
   (d) The Bhagavad-Gita

9. The caste system has survived for centuries in India because it has
   (a) received support from all the rulers of India.
   (b) been subsidized by foreign investors.
   (c) enjoyed the full support of all of the people.
   (d) provided the villages of India with an adequate labor supply.

10. In traditional India, the caste system and the Hindu beliefs in Karma and Dharma most directly resulted in
   (a) a strong belief in the importance of education.
   (b) a strong desire for wealth.
   (c) the rapid industrialization of the economy.
   (d) the establishment of a set of rules for each individual.

11. The concept of caste is based on the assumption that
   (a) money is the root of all evil.
   (b) all people are created equal.
   (c) one's present social class is based on behavior in a previous life.
   (d) one should not eat meat or drink alcoholic beverages.

12. In India, the traditional role of women has changed during the 20th century because of the
   (a) impact of increased urbanization.
   (b) effects of religious persecution.
   (c) use of passive resistance.
   (d) growth of political unrest.

13. The caste system of India has been weakened most by the
   (a) strengthened position of the Hindu religion in India.
   (b) assassination of Indira and Rajiv Gandhi.
   (c) increased production on the farms of India.
   (d) movement of people from the countryside to the towns of India.

14. Which of the following events occurred first?
   (a) Civilization flourished at Mohenjo-Daro.
   (b) The Mongul Empire brought Islamic civilization to India.
   (c) King Asoka proclaimed a new law code for India.
   (d) The Aryans invaded India and introduced Hinduism.

15. The earliest writing system in India was developed in
   (a) Mohenjo-Daro India.   (b) Gupta India.
   (c) Maurya India.   (d) Mogul India.

16. The earliest civilization in India was located in the valley of the
    (a) Ganges River
    (b) Indus River
    (c) Brahmaputra River
    (d) Godavari River

17. All of the following were accomplishments of Harappa and Mohenjo-Daro peoples *except*
    (a) the use of gold and silver.
    (b) buildings made of brick.
    (c) the development of the Vedas.
    (d) drainpipes to carry water.

18. The Aryans
    (a) came to India from the island of Sri Lanka (Ceylon).
    (b) were farmers who settled in Mohenjo-Daro.
    (c) were conquered by the Dravidian herdsmen.
    (d) conquered the Dravidians and settled in India.

19. The Hindu religion was developed in India by the
    (a) Sikhs.
    (b) Jains.
    (c) Muslims.
    (d) Aryans.

20. The Persian invasion of India was important because
    (a) it brought Islam to India.
    (b) it influenced India's language and culture.
    (c) the Persians brought Hinduism to India.
    (d) the Persians destroyed Mohenjo-Daro and Harappa.

21. Alexander the Great's invasion of India was important because
    (a) it brought new ways of thinking and doing things to India.
    (b) it destroyed the power of the Mauryas.
    (c) it prevented the growth of a great Indian Empire.
    (d) it led to the establishment of many small kingdoms and republics.

22. Asoka is remembered as a great king because
    (a) he introduced the Hindu religion.
    (b) he was a just and considerate ruler.
    (c) he conquered new lands for his kingdom.
    (d) he built up the power of the Brahmins.

23. Buddhism did not succeed in India because
    (a) Hinduism accepted many of the ideas of Buddha.
    (b) the Muslims destroyed the Buddhist monasteries.
    (c) Buddhists were willing to compromise with the beliefs of Hinduism.
    (d) all of the above

24. The Maurya Dynasty fell because of
    (a) repeated invasions by Muslims.
    (b) the revolt of the "untouchables."
    (c) the lack of a stable government to defend the kingdom from invaders.
    (d) the failure of the monsoons to bring rain for a ten-year period.

25. Although the founder of a certain religion was born in India and converted many Indians to this religion, it is not important today. This religion is

    (a) Hinduism.
    (b) Islam.
    (c) Buddhism.
    (d) Jainism.

26. The term "Golden Age of Indian History" refers to the

    (a) Maurya Dynasty.
    (b) Gupta Dynasty.
    (c) Delhi sultanate.
    (d) Mogul Dynasty.

27. Current research shows that the decimal system in mathematics was invented by the

    (a) Aryans.
    (b) Muslim Indians.
    (c) Hindu Indians.
    (d) Arabs.

28. The fact that the mathematical concept of zero developed in India is used throughout the world is an example of

    (a) nationalism.
    (b) cultural diffusion.
    (c) imperialism.
    (d) comparative advantage.

29. Wide travel was carried on in the 5th and 6th century between India and

    (a) China and Arabia.
    (b) France and England.
    (c) Japan and Southeast Asia.
    (d) Portugal and Spain.

30. A great poet of India was

    (a) Chandragupta.
    (b) Kalidasa.
    (c) Aurangzeb.
    (d) Muhammed Ghori.

31. The Monguls developed a new language called

    (a) Hindi.
    (b) Punjabi.
    (c) Urdu.
    (d) Marathi.

32. The Rajputs were

    (a) religious leaders of North India.
    (b) Muslims who came to India from Persia.
    (c) Sikhs who fought against the Muslims.
    (d) warriors who helped preserve Hinduism in North India.

33. The Sikhs believed in all of the following *except*

    (a) one god.
    (b) the caste system.
    (c) toleration.
    (d) hard work.

34. An example of cultural diffusion in Indian history would be

    (a) the Sikh idea of monotheism, taken from Islam.
    (b) the Sikh use of Kharma from the Hindu religion.
    (c) the development of the Khalsa for protection against the Moguls.
    (d) the development of Amritsar as a pilgrimage center.

35. The battle of Plassey was important because the

    (a) British were driven from India.
    (b) Japanese were driven from India.
    (c) British gained control of much of India.
    (d) rajahs of India united against the French.

36. The Sepoy Rebellion was caused by
    (a) rivalry between the French and the English.
    (b) the hatred of the Moslems for the Hindus.
    (c) the rivalry between the British East India Company and the British Parliament.
    (d) Indian unhappiness with British rule.

37. The Sepoy Rebellion was important because it
    (a) drove the British out of India.
    (b) was regarded as the first blow struck for independence.
    (c) strengthened the rule of the British East India Company in India.
    (d) destroyed Indian nationalism.

38. An example of Indian nationalism was the
    (a) formation of the Congress Party.
    (b) partition of India.
    (c) formation of the British East India Company.
    (d) signing of the Rowlatt Acts.

39. The government of Great Britain built railroads, schools, and irrigation systems in colonial India mainly to
    (a) prepare India for independence.
    (b) strengthen its political and economic control of India.
    (c) secure favorable trading arrangements with different Indian leaders.
    (d) help India maintain its traditional cultural systems.

40. Which of the following events was the result of the other three?
    (a) The passing of the Rowlatt Acts
    (b) The Amritsar Massacre
    (c) Montagu-Chelmsford reforms
    (d) World War I

41. The Government of India Act of 1935
    (a) gave India its independence.
    (b) was successful in quieting Indian protests.
    (c) was an attempt to quiet Indian protests.
    (d) made India a dominion in the British Empire.

42. At the end of World War II in 1945 the British
    (a) still refused to leave India.
    (b) helped to set up a united India.
    (c) agreed to partition India into two nations.
    (d) assassinated Gandhi.

43. Mohandas Gandhi and Martin Luther King were similar in that both
    (a) fought for the independence of their countries.
    (b) fought for the rights of an oppressed ethnic minority.
    (c) used nonviolent tactics to achieve their goals.
    (d) believed in the violent overthrow of oppressive governments.

44. Which statement best explains why the British partitioned India in 1947?
    (a) The British feared a united India.
    (b) One region of India wished to remain under British control.
    (c) Religious differences led to political division.
    (d) Communist rebellion forced the decision for partition.

45. Which of the following is a result of British colonial rule in India?
    (a) British armed forces still defend India.
    (b) Most Indians follow the Christian religion.
    (c) English is still an official language of India.
    (d) India is still strongly allied to the United Kingdom.

46. The best way to describe the economy of India in the period after independence was
    (a) capitalistic.   (b) socialistic.
    (c) communistic.   (d) mixed.

47. All of the following are true about India's economic development *except*
    (a) private capital is combined with public funds to aid development.
    (b) the government set up a master plan for the development of resources.
    (c) agricultural production now meets the needs of the Indian people.
    (d) the war with China has caused economic development to slow down.

48. The leading industry of India today is
    (a) textiles.   (b) steel.
    (c) automobiles.   (d) electronics.

49. Which of the following groups of minerals are used in steel production?
    (a) copper, iron, coal   (b) iron, coal, manganese
    (c) copper, nickel, bauxite   (d) coal, iron, bauxite

50. The Indian policy of nonalignment meant that India
    (a) did not get involved in international disputes.
    (b) refused to accept aid from the United States and Russia.
    (c) felt free to take any side that helped India.
    (d) did not join the United Nations or other international groups.

51. Which was the result of the policy of nonalignment that India followed for many years?
    (a) India kept its defense spending at a low level.
    (b) The Indian government was successful in limiting population growth.
    (c) The Indian government worked to reduce religious conflict.
    (d) India was able to accept aid from both the United States and Russia.

52. All of the following statements are true about India's foreign relations *except*
    (a) India has followed a policy of friendship toward the United States and Russia.
    (b) India was one of the first nations to recognize the People's Republic of China.
    (c) India did not send troops to the Persian Gulf during the Gulf War.
    (d) China and India have developed strong ties of friendship.

53. Indira Gandhi was assassinated by a group of terrorists who did not agree with her
    (a) trade policy.   (b) religious policy.
    (c) foreign policy.   (d) agricultural policy.

54. The present Prime Minister of India is
    (a) Morarji Desai.   (b) Jawaharlal Nehru.
    (c) Rajiv Gandhi.   (d) P. V. Rao.

55. The basic goal of the latest Sikh rebellion against the government of India is to
    (a) end public discrimination.
    (b) protest against low wages and poor working conditions.
    (c) establish an independent Sikh nation.
    (d) obtain freedom of worship.

56. Which one of the following was the result of the other three?
    (a) Rioting in East Pakistan in 1971
    (b) The partition of British India into India and Pakistan
    (c) The creation of the nation of Bangladesh
    (d) Cultural and economic differences between East and West Pakistan

57. Pakistan's government and economy can best be described as
    (a) a democracy with an industrialized economy.
    (b) a kingdom with an agricultural economy.
    (c) an Islamic republic with an agricultural economy.
    (d) a colony of Great Britain with an industrial economy.

58. Bangladesh can be described as
    (a) an island nation with rich resources.
    (b) a wealthy nation with a plantation economy.
    (c) a poor, overpopulated nation of farmers.
    (d) a large agricultural nation with a small population.

59. The foreign loan programs in Bangladesh have
    (a) provided money for factories.
    (b) helped to build health and recreational facilities.
    (c) provided loans to enable poor students to go to universities.
    (d) provided loans for many agricultural and flood-control projects.

60. Which of the following situations threatens the relationship between India and Sri Lanka?
    (a) An invasion by Pakistan
    (b) The conflict between Tamils and the government of Sri Lanka
    (c) A serious and bloody conflict between Hindus and Muslims
    (d) The Sikh destruction of a Tamil temple in Sri Lanka

61. Nepal is located
    (a) on the Deccan Plateau in central India.
    (b) on a high plateau in the Himalayas.
    (c) near the desert region of Pakistan.
    (d) in the eastern part of the Indian subcontinent.

62. Nepal is a
    (a) democratic republic.   (b) military dictatorship.
    (c) kingdom.   (d) confederation of states.

63. The Ghurkas are well known for their
  (a) musical aptitude.
  (b) mountain-climbing skills.
  (c) religious devotion.
  (d) fighting abilities.

Which of the following does not belong in each group?

1. Rivers in the subcontinent of India: Indus, Ghats, Ganges, Brahmaputra

2. Cities of the Indian subcontinent: Calcutta, Bombay, New Delhi, Yangon (Rangoon)

3. Languages of India: Bengali, Telugu, Jain, Marathi

4. Leaders of Indian nationalism: Tilak, Gandhi, Nehru, Clive

5. Important ideas of Hinduism: Vedas, Moksha, Dharma, Karma

6. Geographic regions of the Indian subcontinent: Deccan, Malabar, Ghats, Malacca

7. Mogul rulers: Asoka, Akbar, Babur, Shah Jahan

8. Indian developments in mathematics: Arabic numerals, the idea of zero, the idea of infinity, geometry

9. Literature of India: Upanishads, Ramayana, Mahabharata, Swaraj

Thought Questions

1. How did geographic features affect the development of Indian civilization?

2. (a) Describe the climate of India.
   (b) How has the climate of India affected the lives of the people?

3. How have differences of race and language affected India?

4. Why might the North Indian Plain be called "the bread basket of India"?

5. Why has India, together with Pakistan and Bangladesh, often been called a subcontinent?

6. Why are the river valleys of India so densely populated?

7. "The monsoons mean life and death to the people of India." Explain.

8. "The growth of population is India's greatest problem." Tell why you agree or disagree with this statement.

9. "Religion in India has served to unite and to drive the people apart." Explain what this statement means. Do you agree? Why?

10. Describe the achievements of the people of Mohenjo-Daro and Harappa.

11. What contributions were made by each of the following groups to Indian civilization?
    (a) Aryans   (b) Mauryas   (c) Guptas   (d) Moguls   (e) British

12. How did the British gain control of India?

13. Why was the Sepoy Rebellion important in Indian history?

14. Why was India called "the most precious jewel in the crown of the British Empire"?

15. "The British both helped and hurt the people of India." Give some evidence to support this statement.

16. Gandhi was called Mahatma, "the Great Soul." Do you think he deserved the name? Why?

17. (a) If you were a member of the Indian government, what would you feel are most important problems of India?
    (b) What suggestions might you make to solve those problems?

18. Why is the village thought to be the heart of Indian life?

19. (a) Describe the caste system.
    (b) Why has the caste system hindered progress in India?

20. (a) Describe the main ideas of the Hindu religion.
    (b) Why is Hinduism "more than a way of life"?

21. (a) Describe India's policy of nonalignment.
    (b) How did this policy affect India's relations with the United States, Russia, and China?

22. Why has Kashmir become a problem between Pakistan and India?

23. (a) Many of the people of India do not have as much food as they need. Why is this so?
    (b) How has the Indian government tried to solve this problem?

24. Why have historians called Gupta India the "Golden Age of Indian History"?

25. How has Islam affected life in India? Why has conflict developed between Hindus and Muslims?

26. What does the Ramayana and Mahabharata tell us about the way the people of India feel about life?

27. How did the British control of India affect the lives of the Indian people?

28. (a) Why did Indira Gandhi decide to suspend civil rights in India?
    (b) If you were a member of the opposition, how would you have felt? Why?
    (c) How did the suspension of civil rights affect the lives of the Indian people?

29. "India has proved it is a modern scientific nation." Explain why you agree or disagree with this statement.

30. "India has made great efforts and is succeeding in solving its food problem." Do you agree or disagree with this statement? Explain.

Developing Answers to Regents-Type Essay Questions

Helpful Hints

In developing your answers to the essays be sure to:

1. Include specific factual information and evidence whenever possible.

2. Answer the question being asked; do not go off on tangents.

3. Keep these general definitions in mind:
   (a) *discuss* means "to make observations about something using facts, reasoning, and argument; to present in some detail."
   (b) *describe* means "to illustrate something in words or to tell about."
   (c) *show* means "to point out, to set forth clearly an idea or position by stating it and giving data that support it."
   (d) *explain* means "to make plain or understandable; to give reasons for or causes of; to show the logical development or relationship."

Sample Essay Questions

1. You have just been elected prime minister of India. The population of India is increasing at a faster rate than the Indian economy.

   Part A: List *two* problems that India faces as a result of the rapid population increase. List *two* recommendations to help solve the problems.

   Part B: Base your answer to Part B on your answer to Part A. Write an essay explaining how your recommendations would slow the growth of population in India.

2. Geography significantly influences the social and economic life of regions and nations.

   Features of Social and Economic Life

   Agricultural Production
   Religion
   Industrialization
   Population Growth
   Standard of Living

   Describe *one* way in which each of the above social and economic features has been influenced by the geography of the Indian Peninsula.

3. Nationalism has been a major force in shaping the development of nations in the sub-continent of India.

Nationalistic Movements and Struggles

Sepoy Rebellion in India	Bangladesh Rebellion
Partition of India	Congress Party Movement in India

For each of the above:
   a. Identify *one* nationalist leader or group involved in the event.
   b. Describe *one* nationalist goal of the leader or the group.
   c. Describe *one* action taken by the leader or group to achieve the goal.

4. Religion has often strongly influenced many aspects of culture within a society.

Aspects of Culture

Painting or Sculpture	Architecture	Dietary laws
Literature	Social classes	

For *each* of the aspects of culture listed above, discuss, using specific examples, how Islam or Hinduism has influenced that aspect of culture in Indian society.

5. The actions or ideas of one person often have great effect on the actions or ideas of another person.

Influential Persons

Mohandas K. Gandhi and Jawaharlal Nehru

Jawaharlal Nehru and Ali Jinnah

Use *two* specific examples to show how the actions and ideas of one person in each of the pairs above affected the actions or ideas of the other.

6. Human interaction has often resulted in conflict between groups and cultures. In India this statement has been true for several groups.

Groups That Have Experienced Conflicts

Hindus and Muslims

West Pakistanis and East Pakistanis

Hindus and Sikhs

Indians and Britishers

For *each* pair listed above, discuss one major cause of conflict and the effect of the conflict on each group involved.

Puzzle

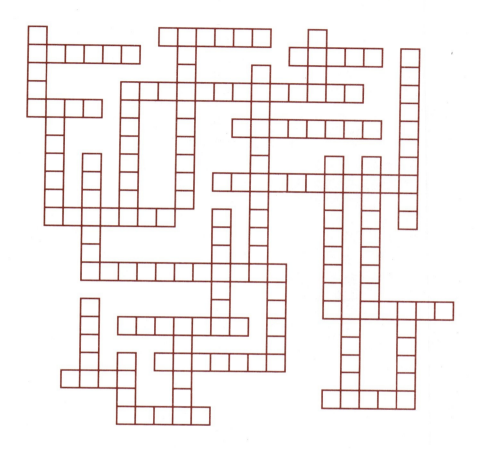

Directions: Place the words below in their proper places in the puzzle.

4 LETTERS	**5 LETTERS**	**6 LETTERS**	**7 LETTERS**	**8 LETTERS**
SARI	HINDU	MUTINY	MONSOON	RAMAYANA
SIKH	KARMA	EMPIRE	PADDIES	CONGRESS
JUTE	ARYAN	BUDDAH	CYCLONE	
JATI	CASTE	MOSQUE	CASSAVA	
GITA	TAMIL	DHARMA	ISLAMIC	
	VEDAS		PASSIVE	
	CURRY			

9 LETTERS	**10 LETTERS**	**11 LETTERS**	**12 LETTERS**	**13 LETTERS**
PARTITION	UPANISHADS	NATIONALISM	UNTOUCHABLES	REINCARNATION
PANCHAYAT	SATYAGRAHA	MAHABHARATA		

SOUTHEAST ASIA

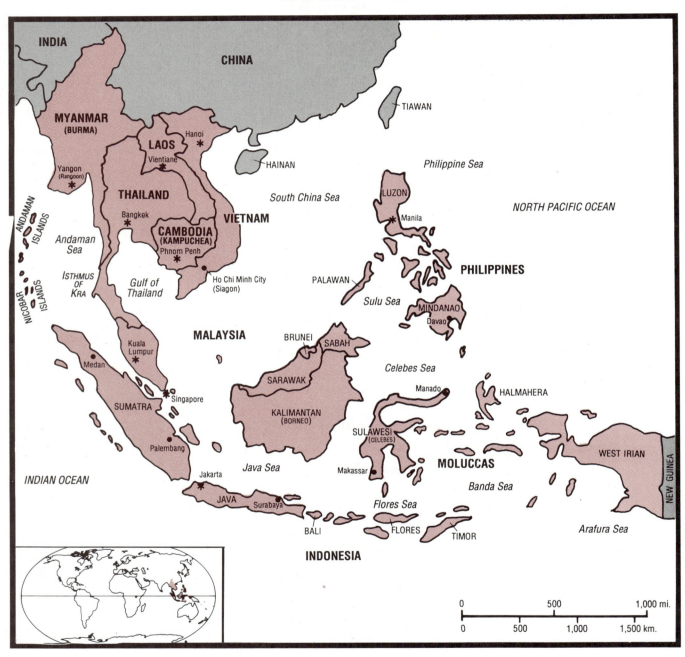

INDIA

CHINA

MYANMAR (BURMA)

LAOS
Hanoi ✳

Vientiane ✳

Yangon (Rangoon) ✳

THAILAND

ANDAMAN ISLANDS

Andaman Sea

Bangkok ✳

VIETNAM

CAMBODIA (KAMPUCHEA)
Phnom Penh ✳

ISTHMUS OF KRA

NICOBAR ISLANDS

Gulf of Thailand

Ho Chi Minh City (Siagon) •

TIAWAN

HAINAN •

South China Sea

Philippine Sea

LUZON

✳ Manila

NORTH PACIFIC OCEAN

PALAWAN

Sulu Sea

PHILIPPINES

MINDANAO
Davao •

MALAYSIA

BRUNEI

SABAH

Kuala Lumpur ✳

Medan •

SUMATRA

Singapore ✳

SARAWAK

KALIMANTAN (BORNEO)

Celebes Sea

Manado •

SULAWESI (CELEBES)

HALMAHERA

Palembang •

INDIAN OCEAN

Jakarta ✳

JAVA

Surabaya •

Java Sea

Makassar •

MOLUCCAS

Banda Sea

WEST IRIAN

NEW GUINEA

BALI

Flores Sea

FLORES

TIMOR

Arafura Sea

INDONESIA

| 0 | 500 | 1,000 mi. |
| 0 | 500 | 1,000 | 1,500 km. |

460 Southeast Asia

UNIT VI Southeast Asia

Introduction and Setting

"When a Thai or Vietnamese farmer is asked where his people *originated*, he is apt to reply that they have always lived in this village because he can, after all, remember his grandfather. Throughout Southeast Asia tradition may be supreme, but time has little meaning. Early Chinese and European travelers who roamed this region kept records, now important sources for Western scholars, but the Southeast Asians themselves were indifferent to history. What they knew or cared about the past came down to them not in any systematic account, but in myths and legends that were, to their ears, just awesome or charming or literary magic."[1]

"Southeast Asia is a green world of islands and peninsulas, so underpopulated and underdeveloped that there is a surplus of raw materials for export. Much of the region has recently emerged from colonialism, with resulting problems of economic and political development."[2]

"Reduced to their essentials the problems of Southeast Asia are: self-protection, self-support, and self-government. They arise out of the strategic importance and untold wealth of the area . . . ., and the determination of the peoples of Southeast Asia to govern themselves."[3]

These are just three views of Southeast Asia. A discussion of them will give you some insight into the people, their land, and the economic, social, and political situations in which they live.

Distances and Diversity

The term Southeast Asia was first used by American military commanders in World War II to give geographical unity to a **region** noted for its **diversity**, and for the distances that separate its peoples from one another.

---

[1] Stanley Karnow, *Southeast Asia* (New York: Time-Life Books, 1967).
[2] G. B. Cressey, *Asia's Land and People* (New York: McGraw-Hill Book Co., 1963).
[3] Carlos P. Romulo, "The Position of Southeast Asia in the World Community," *Southeast Asia in the Coming World*, P.W. Thayer, ed. (Baltimore: Johns Hopkins University Press, 1953).

Almost 450 million people live in Southeast Asia. As a whole, the region has neither cultural nor political unity. The peoples of the independent nations that now exist in Southeast Asia are of many races and religions, and each nation has within its borders many different cultures. Their present differences are a result of these factors.

Shared Experiences

Even though these differences exist, we can, for geographic reasons, study Southeast Asia as a region. In fact, the various peoples who live there share historic and ethnic ties as well as common experiences.

Our study of the area will revolve around five major ideas:

1. Geographic and physical features have greatly influenced the lives of the peoples of the region.
2. Outside forces have affected historical developments in Southeast Asia. Trade and colonial control often changed the course of Southeast Asian cultural and historical development.
3. The peoples of Southeast Asia include a variety of national, ethnic, religious, and social groups. This diversity has created many problems.
4. The nations of Southeast Asia are in the midst of dramatic change.
5. The location and economic potential of Southeast Asia make it a key area in present and future world affairs.

We will begin our study of Southeast Asia by looking at the geography of the region to see how it affects the people living there.

Topography

Southeast Asia is a region of islands and **peninsulas**. In the northwest is the Indo-Chinese Peninsula, which extends off the continent of Asia. Stretching southward from this peninsula is a long, narrow body of land called the Malay Peninsula. The narrowest part of this peninsula is called the Isthmus of Kra. To the south and east are the islands of Indonesia and the Philippines. Together, the islands and peninsulas of Southeast Asia form a land area about half the size of the United States.

Mountain ranges and seas help to divide Southeast Asia into many isolated parts. Some of the seas are connected to the great Pacific Ocean. Others are arms of the Indian Ocean. Along some of the seacoasts are lowlands that are densely populated. Many of the river plains between the mountain ranges also have dense population.

Mountain Barriers

If we looked down from an airplane on mainland Southeast Asia, we would see many mountains. In the north are high ranges that separate most of Southeast Asia from the rest of Asia. Extending southward from these barriers are several other mountain ranges. They reach through the region like giant fingers and stretch on into the sea.

The mountains are forested. These forests are very dense on the ranges that stretch along the edges of the peninsula, for the rainfall here is the heaviest. (Can you explain why?) On the central highlands that receive less rainfall, the forests are less dense.

The rivers of Southeast Asia have always been scenes of activity. Here we see the modern city of Singapore, built along the Singapore River.

Houses are built along the Irrawaddy River, the longest river in Myanmar (Burma). The river is the center of life, used for drinking, bathing, transportation, and exchange of goods.

Rivers and River Valleys

Between the mountain ranges are several great rivers and river valleys. In the western section are the valleys of the Irrawaddy and Salween rivers, which begin in the mountains of Myanmar's (Burma's) northern border and flow southward to the sea. As we look to the southeast, we see the valley of the Chao Phraya (Menam) in Thailand. Farther east is the mighty Mekong River. It flows across Cambodia (Kampuchea) and southern Vietnam. In the northeast part of Southeast Asia is the Songkoi (Red River) of northern Vietnam.

Where the large rivers of the region flow into the sea, they form **deltas**. The deltas consist mainly of sand and silt carried there by rivers from the land through which they flow. The delta of the Songkoi is one of the most densely populated areas of Southeast Asia. Some of the other deltas, such as the Irrawaddy delta, were large swamps until recent times. Now, however, many of these swamps have been drained for rice farms, and in Vietnam the delta of the Mekong is used for rice and rubber plantations.

RIVERS OF SOUTHEAST ASIA

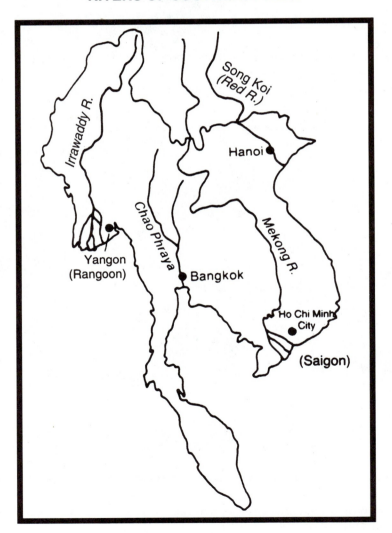

Several of the region's important cities are located on these deltas. Among them are Yangon (Rangoon) in Myanmar (Burma), Bangkok in Thailand, and Ho Chi Minh City (Saigon) and Hanoi in Vietnam.

Coastline

Another feature is the long coastline of the Malay Peninsula, with the narrow Straight of Malacca between Malaya and Sumatra. As a result, Southeast Asian seaports have always been important stopping points on the trade route between China and India. Not only did all sea trade between China and India go through the strait, but also the seasonal pattern of the monsoons made it necessary for early traders from China and India to spend several months in a Southeast Asian port waiting for the winds to change so they could return home or go on. With foreigners living in the ports for long periods of time, the people became thoroughly familiar with alien ways.

The Great Lake

Mainland Southeast Asia has only one large lake, the Great Lake (Tonle Sap) in the central lowland of Cambodia. The Tonle Sap was once an inlet of the sea. Over the centuries, however, the mouth of the inlet has been filled in, and it now forms part of the delta region of the Mekong River.

Climate

Temperature

As we have already noted, dense forests cover much of Southeast Asia. In most of the area the climate is humid and the rainfall is heavy. Temperatures are high and do not change much from summer to winter.

If we look at our maps of the region, we can see the reason for the constant high temperature: the equator passes through the area. In the summer months the temperature frequently rises to 100°F (37.8°C) or more. The upland **plateaus** and the mountains are cooler and may even become quite cold at night. No part of Southeast Asia is more than 15 degrees from the equator.

Seasons, Monsoons, and Rainfall

Though the temperature does not change much throughout the year, the amount of rainfall does. In many parts of Southeast Asia, the year is divided into a rainy season and a dry season.

Summer is the rainy season in Southeast Asia. In some places the rains come every day. Warm ocean winds from the southwest help to bring the rains. These winds, which blow only from the southwest during the summer, are called the summer monsoons.

The winds that blow during the dry season come mainly from across the seas to the northeast. When they reach the mainland, they are forced to rise in order to cross the Annamese Highlands along the coast of Vietnam. The higher altitude causes the winds to cool, resulting in some rainfall. Therefore, by the time they have crossed the mountains, the winds have become drier and warmer. Instead of giving off rain, they pick up moisture from the land. This is the main reason why the land west of the highlands is dry during the winter. These winds are called the winter monsoons.

The people of Southeast Asia could not get along without the monsoons. Without the rainfall produced by the summer monsoons, the rice fields would not be flooded. When the rains are late, or too little rain falls, the crops fail and millions of Asians face starvation.

Some parts of the region are drier than others. One of the drier regions is the central highlands of Myanmar. The dryness there is caused by the location of the valley. (Can you explain why?) In this dry area, farmers grow millet, cotton, and other crops that need less rainfall than rice does.

Peoples, Languages, and Population Distribution

Peoples

Some of the people in Southeast Asia are descendents of settlers who came to the area about 4,500 years ago. They were of average height, with black hair and brown skin. The ancestors of others came to the area from lands to the north and west, over the past 1,000 to 2,000 years. They spoke many languages, had different religions, and followed different ways of life. Even today many new immigrants are making their homes in Southeast Asia. Because of intermarriage and mixed backgrounds, it is difficult to describe the typical Southeast Asian.

Indonesian peoples moved into the Malay Peninsula and the islands of Southeast Asia. The first people to settle on the mainland were the Mons in southern Burma (now Myanmar) and the Khmers in Cambodia. North of them were the Burmese. To the east, in northern Vietnam, were the Vietnamese, who settled in the Tonkin area and the Songkoi (Red River) delta. South of them were the Chams, who were related to the Indonesians. A last group, the Shan, or Thai, began moving into Southeast Asia in the 11th and 12th centuries A.D. after a long time in southern China.

Languages

Many languages are spoken in Southeast Asia; in any one country there may be several different languages. Some of them, such as Burmese, Thai, and Lao, are similar to Chinese. Others are quite different.

A number of European languages are also spoken. English is spoken in every Southeast Asian country, mainly in the cities. It is especially common in the Philippines, Malaysia, Singapore, and Myanmar. Many people in Vietnam, Cambodia, and Laos speak French. Dutch is widely spoken by Indonesians. In the Philippines, some people speak Spanish. In the large Chinese communities all over Southeast Asia, the languages of southern China are spoken. Immigrants from southern India still use Tamil and other Dravidian languages of their homeland.

Students in local dress.

Indonesian weaver. Weaving is an important craft in Indonesia.

Population Distribution

Altogether, there are more than 450 million people in Southeast Asia, more than live in the United States. The number of people inhabiting the area is increasing every year because of better medical care, food, and sanitation. Fewer babies now become sick and die, and adults live longer than they used to. Today, there are more than 20 times as many people living in Southeast Asia as there were in 1800. In many parts of Java and Thailand, and on the Songkoi delta of northern Vietnam, more than 1,500 people live on each square mile of land.

Urban Centers of Population

In the densely populated areas of Southeast Asia there are some large cities, several with 1 million or more people. All of the largest cities are seaports or river ports to which the products of nearby mines, forests, and fields are brought for export. Except for Bangkok, in Thailand, these cities were formerly colonial government centers or trade centers.

Some countries of Southeast Asia have more cities than others. Indonesia has the largest number. Most of Indonesia's cities are located on the island of Java, including the largest city of Southeast Asia—Djakarta. In each country on the Indochinese Peninsula, the capital city is also the largest city; these are Yangon in Myanmar, Bangkok in Thailand, and Hanoi in Vietnam. There are several large cities in the Philippines, but Manila is by far the most important. In the Malay Peninsula the most important cities are Singapore and Kuala Lumpur.

Mountain Tribes

Although the region has large cities, most of the people of Southeast Asia are farmers and live in villages. In areas other than the cities and the lowland farm areas, it is possible to travel for miles without seeing a house or a single person. Large parts of these areas are covered with swamps, forested plains, and mountains. In the **remote** highland areas are tribes whose life-styles might appear backward and primitive to us. Two examples are the Meo and Moi tribes. Some of the tribe members are small and dark-skinned; others have light brown skins like the people of the lowlands. They make their living as hunters and food gatherers. They usually clear small patches in the forests for farmland.

Most lowland villagers in Thailand belong to a group called the Thai. The mountain people, however, are divided into different groups that do not dress alike or speak the same language. In fact, all the countries of Southeast Asia have different groups of people living within their borders. In Indonesia alone, 100 or more different languages or **dialects** are spoken.

In all the countries of Southeast Asia, the lowland people feel superior to the mountain people, resulting in discrimination and prejudice against the mountain dwellers. In Thailand, fighting has periodically broken out in the mountains against the government.

Indians and Chinese in Southeast Asia

Some groups of people are newcomers from other countries who have settled in Southeast Asia. In recent years, many people from China have come to this region to work in the oil fields and mines and on the plantations. Today, there are over 12 million Chinese in Southeast Asia. They now run many of the plantations, shops, businesses, and banks. Most Chinese have kept their own language and customs, instead of learning to live as the people of their new homeland do. As a result, they are not always welcomed by the Southeast Asians. There are also people from India and Pakistan who are in a similar position to the Chinese.

Malay house on stilts. Why has this house been constructed on stilts?

Typical architecture of an Indonesian house.

Village Life

For over 1,000 years the people of Southeast Asia have lived mainly in the countryside, earning their living as farmers. The center of their lives is the village. Each village is usually small but almost always self-sufficient. The villagers try to provide for all of the needs of the people who live there.

Let us imagine a walk through a village in Southeast Asia. We enter the village along a *klong* (canal) or along a narrow dirt road. The village has about 50 small houses, all built on stilts close to the *klong*. The houses are made of bamboo and wood. The roofs are steep and pointed and are thatched with nipa palm leaves. Around each house is a garden, with flowers, fruit trees, coconut palms, and a small vegetable patch.

The work of the village centers around the growing of rice, and the rice fields begin at the back doors of the villagers' homes. The paddy, or rice field, is flooded to aid the growth of rice. In late June or July, the farmers plant their seedbeds. They sow the seeds by scattering a great many by hand. With this method, many seeds are wasted. Five weeks later, the farmers transplant the seedlings by hand with the help of their neighbors. In late November or early December, the crops are ready to be harvested. The harvest is also brought in by hand.

As we continue our walk through the village, there is much to see. The well is always a busy place. A large crowd of women gather there to meet friends and to gossip. Nearby, we see other buildings that are used as toolsheds. All the members of the village use the tools and the toolsheds in a cooperative way. In a grove of trees near the village is a building called the *wat*, or village temple.

The village headman knew we were coming and has prepared a meal for us. His house, like the others, is built on stilts or high posts to protect the floor from floodwaters when the river overflows its banks in the rainy season. The open space under the house serves as a storage place for farm tools. The water buffalo, which is used for plowing and many other jobs, is also kept there.

The first room we enter is a covered porch. Because it is shady and cool, the family spends a great deal of time here. The sleeping rooms are next to the porch and are also cool. Each of these rooms contains a storage chest made of teakwood, and sleeping mats rolled up against the wall. At night the mats are unrolled and used as beds. In most houses in the village, there is no running water or electricity. The village water supply is the well. The members of the family bathe every day in the river. The houses are lit with kerosene or coconut oil lamps.

The dinner is ready. The stove on which the food was cooked is made of clay and looks like a flowerpot. There is a low table in the center of the room, and cushions are placed around the table. Our host asks us to sit on the cushions. The meal begins with coconut and shrimp soup, followed by small bits of broiled meat served on thin bamboo skewers with a spicy peanut sauce. This is called *satay*. Next we are served a delicious spiced chicken curry. Along with the curry we can eat some squash, peas, or beans. There is also a salad. For dessert we have fried bananas and other fruit served in a sweet syrup. Tea is served throughout the meal. We ask our host why the food is so spicy. He tells us that during this time of the year when it is very hot, light but spicy meals stimulate the appetite.

We use a spoon made from a coconut to dip the rice, vegetables, and curry from the serving bowls into our own bowls. Then we eat the food with our fingers.

Terraced rice field in mountainous Java, Indonesia. Rice is the major food and is also an important export.

Thai farmer plowing in a rice field in central Thailand. The water buffalo is used throughout Southeast Asia as a beast of burden.

Most of the people of Southeast Asia live in villages similar to the one described. The only differences are due to the village's location in relation to a canal, river, or road. Although the clothes the people wear and the customs they follow vary greatly from place to place, most Southeast Asians are farmers and therefore their lives are similar in many ways.

Agriculture

The Soil

Southeast Asia is one of the world's important farming regions. In most areas the climate is always warm, so crops can be raised all year. Most of Southeast Asia also has heavy rainfall. Some regions produce large amounts of rice, rubber, and other products to sell to foreign countries. There is enough unused land here to raise even larger amounts of farm products.

Only about nine out of every 100 acres of land are planted in crops. In most of Southeast Asia, the main farmlands are on the river plains and coastal lowlands. The **silt** that the rivers wash down from the mountains helps make these lowlands fertile. On the island of Java, people have made level fields on the slopes of volcanoes by building stairlike **terraces**. Ashes and other materials from the volcanoes help to enrich the soil in these fields. Some mountain slopes in northern Luzon in the Philippines are also terraced.

Swampy lowlands and forested mountains cover much of the rest of Southeast Asia. The soil in many of these wilderness areas is poor; heavy rains have washed out the minerals and other nutrients needed by plants. In addition, mosquitoes carrying malaria and other diseases make some of these areas unhealthy places in which to live. If the mosquitoes were cleared out, the swamps were drained, and the land was cleared and fertilized, Southeast Asia would have more farmland.

Products and Exports

Rice is Southeast Asia's most important food crop. About six out of every ten acres of farmland are planted with rice. It is also an important export crop. Because Myanmar, Thailand, and Cambodia raise more rice than they need, they are the world's largest rice exporters.

People in Southeast Asia raise other food crops to eat. In the drier regions farmers grow corn, sweet potatoes, and other crops that need less moisture than rice does. Most farmers raise vegetables such as beans, which provide protein that people in the United States get from meat. Mango, papaya, and other fruit trees grow around most village houses, and sugarcane is also raised.

Southeast Asia also exports other farm products. It provides nine-tenths of the world's natural rubber and three-fourths of the world's copra. Copra is the dried meat of the coconut. Oil palms grown in the area provide large quantities of vegetable oil.

Coffee, tea, and spices are also grown in Southeast Asia. A medicine called quinine is obtained from the bark of cinchona trees grown in Indonesia. Kapok, used in making pillows and life belts; abaca, a fiber used in making rope; pineapples; and tobacco are other Southeast Asian products.

Agricultural Problems

About three-fourths of Southeast Asia's workers make a living by farming. Most of the farmers use **primitive** farming methods. They plant and harvest their crops by hand and use simple tools, such as hoes and sickles. Water buffalo or oxen pull their plows. Sometimes rats, grasshoppers, or other pests destroy part of the crop. Most of Southeast Asia's farmers should use more fertilizer. In the parts of Southeast Asia that have a dry season, irrigation is needed to help crops grow when there is no rain.

In the highlands and mountains, the people clear away the trees and high grass on the hills in order to farm the land. After the land has been used for a few years, the soil is no longer fertile and the hill people leave. The heavy rains now wash the topsoil from the bare hills and river banks into the river by a process called erosion. Large amounts of rich soil have been washed down the rivers of Southeast Asia. The large deltas at the mouths of the Songkoi, Mekong, Chao Phraya, and Irrawaddy rivers have been formed by the washing away of this rich topsoil. The deltas become rich, fertile farmlands, but much of the upriver land is destroyed for farming.

Heavy rains have another effect on the soil: they wash out minerals by a process called leaching. This loss of minerals ruins the soil for most types of vegetation, except for trees with deep roots.

Farmers also face other serious problems. Better roads are needed so that farmers can more easily transport their products to market. In many countries of Southeast Asia, only one-third to one-half of the farmers own their own farms or are free of heavy debts. Landowners often charge high rents, and those who lend money to farmers or market their goods often ask unfair payment for these services.

Some measures are being taken to help Southeast Asia's farmers. In several countries land reform laws have been passed. These laws are aimed at providing more land and homes for farmers. In some places, **cooperatives** are being started to help farmers market their products and borrow money at lower rates. In addition, farm experts from other parts of the world are helping the Southeast Asians develop ways of raising better crops and livestock in the area.

Religion

Diversity of Religions

Southeast Asia has been a meeting place for the religions of the world. Small groups have worshipped nature (**animism**) since early times. Later, the great religions were brought to Southeast Asia.

Buddhism, introduced from India, today is the main religion of Myanmar, Cambodia, Thailand, Vietnam, and Laos. In these countries, Buddhist temples and statues of Buddha can be seen everywhere.

Hinduism was also brought from India. It existed for many centuries in Southeast Asia, but has largely died out. Today, one of the few places in Southeast Asia where it is still practiced is Bali, in Indonesia.

Left: Young Buddhist monks carrying food received from the local population in Myanmar (Burma).

Below: Major Buddist temple in Bangkok, Thailand.

Islam, the religion based on the teachings of Mohammed, has many followers. It was brought to Southeast Asia about 600 years ago by traders, merchants, and sailors. Islam is the chief religion of Malaya, Indonesia, and the southern Philippines. Indonesia is the most populous Islamic nation in the world.

Christianity was introduced into the Philippines by the Spanish in the 16th century. Today, over 80 percent of the people of the Philippines are Catholic. The French spread Christianity in Vietnam in the 19th century, and there is still a large Christian minority living there.

The Teachings of Buddhism

Because Buddhism is so prevalent in Southeast Asia, this religion merits a closer look. Buddhism had it beginnings in the foothills of the Himalayas in India. Gautama, the great teacher of Buddhism and founder of the religion, was born about 567 B.C. The son of a king and a member of the Kashatriya (warrior) caste, he was a Hindu. As a young man, Gautama became upset over the differences between his own life of ease and comfort and the suffering of most of the people around him. Leaving the palace, he went into the forest to search for wisdom. After six years of isolation from society, and strict, simple living, he had not found the wisdom he sought. In despair, he swore not to move from under a bo tree until he had found the key to free humans from suffering. Finally, after 49 days, Enlightenment was gained. Gautama became the Buddha, the "Enlightened One," and Buddhism was born.

Buddhism is very different from the religions of the Western world and therefore is sometimes difficult for Westerners to understand. In fact, Buddhism is not so much a religion as a way of life, like Hinduism. Buddhism has no gods, or even a supreme being, and no belief in a soul.

Buddha, after gaining Enlightenment, spent the rest of his life spreading his ideas. The four noble truths of Buddha's teaching are as follows:

The Four Noble Truths

1. Existence is suffering.
2. Suffering comes from desire.
3. The cure for suffering is the extinction of desire.
4. To achieve the extinction of desire, there is an Eightfold Path of Conduct:

Right views	Right speech
Right effort	Right conduct
Right mindfulness	Right livelihood
Right intentions	Right concentration

The Five Moral Rules

As a definition of Rightness, Buddha offered five moral rules:

1. Let no one kill any living being.
2. Let no one take what is not given to him.
3. Let no one speak falsely.
4. Let no one drink intoxicating drinks.
5. Let no one be unchaste.

Key Ideas of Buddhism

The most important ideas of Buddhism are as follows:

1. Self-salvation is a person's most immediate responsibility.
2. **Nirvana** is the goal of all Buddhists. Nirvana is a state of extinction or release from the Wheel of Rebirth (reincarnation).

These terms are associated with Buddhism:

1. *Pagoda:* In almost every village of India and Southeast Asia, there is a wat or compound called a pagoda. The pagoda serves as the educational and social center of the community. The people voluntarily support the wat and the monks, for to do so is a way of merit to Nirvana.
2. *Merit:* good works.
3. *Bonze:* Buddhist monk.
4. *Stupa:* large mound of earth, usually covering a relic or relics of the Buddha.
5. *Sutra:* a thread on which the teachings of the Buddha are strung; also a sermon of the Buddha.

Early History of Southeast Asia

Prehistory

Until recently, anthropologists and archaeologists believed that the people of the Middle East were the first to develop agriculture (farming), around 10,000 B.C. However, there is now evidence that a prehistoric group of people, the Hoabinhians of Vietnam, may have been among the first to raise plants. Artifacts and other remains of these people were found in a Vietnam village named Hoa Binh.

Places with similar types of artifacts have been found in Malaysia and Thailand. In addition, there is evidence of plant raising also on the islands of Malaysia and Sumatra. All of these places and the peoples who lived there constitute the Hoabinhian culture.

Hoabinhian Culture

The evidence so far collected seems to show the following about the Hoabinhians:

1. As early as 15,000 B.C., Hoabinhians began to use and grow on a regular basis the wild plants of the area. Domesticated (adopted for human use) seeds of roots plants, peas, and beans found in northern Thailand were proved to be 11,690 years old. Therefore, it is possible that agriculture may have existed in Southeast Asia about 1,000 to 2,000 years earlier than it did in Mesopotamia in the Middle East.
2. Hoabinhians seem to have begun making pottery before 10,000 B.C. By 4000 B.C. they had invented a type of outrigger canoe.
3. Hoabinhians were eating **cultivated** (grown by hand) rice and making copper tools by 3000 B.C.
4. Between 3000 and 2500 B.C., Hoabinhians were working with bronze.
5. According to some evidence, Hoabinhian culture may have spread to Africa.
6. Hoabinhian crops, agricultural methods, and pottery may have been carried to Japan, Taiwan, and the Philippines as early as 3000 to 2000 B.C.
7. Anthropologists have found that the Chinese language has many words that were originally part of Southeast Asian languages. The Southeast Asian words for ax, boat, iron, **kiln** (pottery oven), plow, pottery, and seed were introduced into the Chinese language sometime during the prehistory of East Asia.
8. Sometime in the 1st century a.d., some Southeast Asians may have sailed to Madagascar, an island off the east coast of Africa. Through this contact, Africans may have learned about crops that were suitable to their soil and climate. It is also possible that trade existed between the Southeast Asians and the people of the Middle East.

The borrowing of words usually means the borrowing of the things named by those words. Therefore, some scientists now believe that the Chinese first learned about farming, planting, and pottery making from the Southeast Asians.

The reconstruction of the past by archaeologists and anthropologists seems to prove that certain cultural and economic achievements in other parts of Asia, the Middle East, and Africa may be credited to cultural diffusion from early Southeast Asians.

Early Settlers

Between 1000 B.C. and A.D. 100, tribes from the neighboring lands of Tibet, China, and India traveled into the green valleys of the Indo-Chinese Peninsula, where they decided to settle and begin a new life. Later, some of their descendants settled on the Malay Peninsula and the island **archipelagoes** (groups of islands) of Southeast Asia. The newcomers, who had been forced to leave their own homelands by invading armies of the Chinese emperors, knew how to make better tools and weapons than the people already living in these areas.

After these "foreigners" arrived, many of the original settlers were forced back into the remote mountains and jungles. Today their descendants can still be found living in these areas. Others stayed in the valleys and coastal plains, intermarried, and lived with the newcomers. As time went on, more and more settlers arrived, and the same process occurred again.

By the 1st century A.D., many different groups of people were living in Southeast Asia. Some groups in the remote regions gathered roots and other foods, or they hunted. Other groups used the "slash-and-burn" method of farming. Trees were burned down in order to clear the land for farming, and the ashes were used for natural fertilizer. When the soil in the clearings was no longer fertile, the people moved on and cleared new lands. This type of agriculture is still carried on in the hills of Southeast Asia.

The peoples in the coastal lowlands and river valleys grew rice in flooded fields by a process called "wet rice agriculture." This meant the beginning of settled villages. The irrigation system took a long time to build, lasted a long time, and did not use up the soil. It also meant that people had to cooperate to make the system work. The irrigation system was used by all, and everyone had to agree on when and how it should be used. In this case, rights important to Americans, such as the right to own private property, would have been disruptive. People had to give up their individual rights for the sake of the community as a whole. In return, the village world provided security for the individual. No one had to work or face problems alone, and no one starved while neighbors had plenty.

Another result of this agricultural system was that more rice could be grown than was needed by the community. Only during the planting and harvest seasons did the rice fields need much attention. Consequently, many people were free to do other work, and extra rice was available to feed them. Some stopped growing rice and became priests, **artisans** (craftsmen), merchants, and, later on, rulers.

Although the family became the main unit of society, it was not as important an institution as in Chinese and Indian cultures. People trusted their relatives rather than strangers, but the extended family, with its many social relationships, as existed in China, did not develop in Southeast Asia. This is demonstrated by the fact that in most Southeast Asian countries family names were not used until the Europeans came.

In contrast to the rest of Asia and to most early societies, some of the Southeast Asian cultures gave important roles to women. In fact, throughout the area much of the village marketing and trading is still handled by women.

Indian and Chinese Influence

In addition to the settlers who came overland, Southeast Asia, which is located on the water route between India and China, had visitors who came by sea. Travelers and merchants journeying between these two lands stopped in Southeast Asia. In turn, sailors from Southeast Asia traveled to India and China.

Some of the Indian traders established trading settlements in the area. Later, religious leaders and other people from India also settled in these trading towns. From these Indians the people of Southeast Asia learned about the Hindu and Buddhist religions, and they borrowed Sanskrit as their written language. The Indians also brought with them new ideas about art, government, and architecture. Southeast Asians did not copy their Indian teachers exactly; for example, they did not adopt the Indian caste system. Instead, as in the case of the Africans and Islam, they adapted Indian ideas to their own needs and interests, and created something different and new of their own. Different parts of Southeast Asia made different adaptations, accounting for the differences among these nations that still exist today.

Some of the Indian trading settlements grew into powerful cities that gained control of neighboring areas. Kingdoms were established that fought against each other, often to gain more power and more territory, thereby guaranteeing a larger area from which to gather food and other resources. Several of these kingdoms grew into great empires that at one time controlled large parts of Southeast Asia.

The only exceptions to the general pattern of Indian influence were the Philippines, which were off the main India-China trade route, and Vietnam, which came under Chinese rule in 111 B.C. and remained Chinese for 1,000 years.

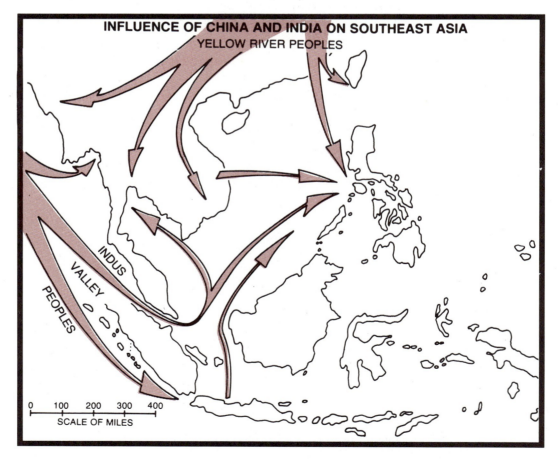

INFLUENCE OF CHINA AND INDIA ON SOUTHEAST ASIA
YELLOW RIVER PEOPLES

INDUS VALLEY PEOPLES

0 100 200 300 400
SCALE OF MILES

The Empires of Southeast Asia

Funan and Srivijaya

As a result of the trade with India and China, small ports at the mouths of rivers along the Malay Peninsula and the mainland coast came into existence. When the Roman Empire and the Han Dynasty of China (200 B.C.–A.D. 200) reached greatness, there was a huge increase in trade between the Mediterranean world and China. Southeast Asian ports grew in power and wealth because of their strategic locations on this trade route.

Funan, at the southern tip of present-day Vietnam, became one of the largest empires in Southeast Asian history (2nd–6th centuries A.D.) Funan was powerful because the earliest route of the India-China trade went across the narrow Isthmus of Kra, connnecting the Malay Peninsula to the mainland. Later, as sailors learned how to cut straight across the China Sea to the tip of Malaya, Funan began to fall. Its place as the most important trading state was taken by the empire of Srivijaya (7th–13th centuries A.D.), which centered on the straight of Malacca.

Khmer Empire

Both Srivijaya and Funan owed their wealth to trade, not to agriculture. However, many inland states also arose, whose wealth was based on rich, fertile soil. The Cambodian, or Khmer, Empire was one of the more important. From the 9th through the 13th century, the Khmer kings gained control of most of the fertile lowlands of the Southeast Asia mainland. The Khmer capital was located at Angkor, near the Tonle Sap, that is, near Siemreap, in modern Cambodia (Kampuchea). Ruins of the magnificent stone temples built in this city still stand today. One temple, the Angkor Wat, is among the largest religious buildings in the world. The temples and other art and writings that still remain not only show a pattern of Indian influence, but also are the best examples of how Indian ideas were adapted to local customs.

The Khmer Empire, having used its wealth and energy on temple building, was too weak by the 13th century to stop attacks from the Siamese (Thai) states to the west. One by one, Khmer border provinces were captured, and within two centuries, the Khmer state ceased to be important. All that remained was what is now modern Cambodia. Today the Cambodians and the Thais still recall the old wars and the destruction that resulted. They have not forgiven each other, and this hostility prevents closer cooperation between these two countries with similar problems.

Kingdoms of the Indo-Chinese Peninsula

From about the 14th to the 18th century, mainland and island history took different paths. More or less continual warfare brought about the outlines of the present mainland countries. Vietnam, which had been under Chinese influence for 1,000 years, gained its independence in the 10th century. Its leaders steadily expanded Vietnam's borders southward from the Songkoi. Vietnam reached its present borders by the 18th century.

Meanwhile, Cambodia (the Khmer Empire) was shrinking under Vietnamese and Siamese (Thai) pressure. One of the many Thai states became the kingdom of Laos in the

14th century. Siam (later Thailand) expanded steadily and by the 18th century was the strongest and most stable of the mainland countries. Burma (now Myanmar) was divided between the Mons in the south and the Shan-Thais in the north.

Islamic Kingdoms

On the Malay Peninsula and the islands of Indonesia a new outside force brought many changes. This new force was Islam, which came by way of India. Followers of Islam are called Muslims, and Muslim merchants from northwest India were among the most active in the Indian Ocean trade. Following the commands of their religion, they preached their faith while carrying on trade.

Islam was accepted by many Southeast Asian states because it gave the rulers many economic and political advantages. It allowed them to trade with other Islamic countries and make money. Also, with a world religion of this kind, the rulers gained a strong set of beliefs to oppose those of Hindu states. Islam provided a reason and a bond for opposing the European Christians who came to Southeast Asia to control trade.

For these reasons, Southeast Asians became Muslims quite rapidly. Wherever Indian influence was weak, Islam became strong. However, Islam merged with existing ways of life, and took on a Southeast Asian flavor.

The Arrival of Westerners in Southeast Asia

Portugal

Five hundred years ago spices such as pepper, cloves, and nutmeg were far more important than they are today. Spices helped to preserve food and made it taste better. The main spice-producing areas of the world were in Southeast Asia. The eagerness of Europeans to obtain spices from this region helped to shape its history.

In 1498, a Portuguese explorer named Vasco da Gama sailed into the harbor of Calicutt, India. From India, ships could sail on to the distant spice lands of Southeast Asia. Vasco da Gama's discovery of an all-water route to the spice lands was very important. The old routes between Europe and the spice lands crossed both land and water. Shipping goods along these routes was expensive and inconvenient because the goods had to be loaded and unloaded many times. Also, the old routes were controlled by the Muslims, who were unfriendly to the Europeans.

With the new route, Portuguese traders were able to transport goods more quickly and cheaply. To make as much money as possible, the Portuguese wanted to control the spice trade completely. They captured many important ports from the Muslims and established fortified posts in Southeast Asia. They patrolled the seas near the spice regions to keep out ships of other nations. Portugal also tried to spread Christianity in the spice lands. Their efforts met with little success, however, for most of the Portuguese who came to Southeast Asia behaved like conquerors and were disliked by the people of the area.

Spain

Portugal was not the only nation that wanted an all-water route to the spice lands; Spain was also eager to discover one. In 1519, Ferdinand Magellan set out to find a sea route to the Moluccas, the islands from which most of the spices came. Magellan sailed west, hoping to arrive eventually in the East. On his voyage he came to the Philippines, making Magellan and his crew the first Europeans to visit these islands. Before long, much of the Philippines was under Spanish control.

Other Europeans

At the end of the 16th century, Dutch ships began coming to Southeast Asia. The Portuguese had made enemies with so many Southeast Asians that the latter welcomed other traders. Before long, British, French, Swedish, and Danish trading ships were also coming to the region.

The Europeans, who came to Southeast Asia, did not want anyone to interfere with their trade. Warships and soldiers from Europe were sent to the region, and Europeans often attacked each other's ships. Sometimes they used force to make the people of Southeast Asia trade with them.

The more powerful European countries gained control of large territories. What is now the country of Indonesia became a Dutch colony. Britain gained control of Burma (now Myanmar), Malaya, and northern Borneo. The territory of Indochina, now occupied by Vietnam, Laos, and Cambodia was taken over by the French. The Philippines were owned by Spain until 1898, when they came under control of the United States. Only Thailand, then known as Siam, remained independent.

Reasons for European Interest

At first, most Westerners who came to Southeast Asia wanted to obtain spices. Soon, however, they discovered that this region could also provide other valuable goods. There were rich mineral deposits, and the climate was suitable for growing tropical plants such as sugarcane and rubber trees. Mines and plantations were built, as well as roads and railroads to carry products to port cities for shipment overseas.

Europeans Brought Progress

The Europeans influenced the region in many important ways. The colonial governments set up by the Europeans provided a framework for the new national states that came after 1945. The Westerners brought peace to a part of the world that had been torn by warfare. Colonialism gave many peoples of Southeast Asia their first feeling of belonging to a national group.

A second result of the presence of Europeans in Southeast Asia was the development in each of the countries of a single major city. These cities became centers of modern life. For example, Rangoon (now Yangon), a small village when the British first came to Burma (Myanmar), grew to be a city of half a million people by 1945. In Indonesia the Dutch set up their capital—Batavia, now called Djakarta—in what were then swamps. Today, Djakarta is the largest city in Southeast Asia, with a population of nearly 8 million. Singapore, Bangkok, Ho Chi Minh City (Saigon), and Manila each became a major city.

A third result was the establishment of modern schools and the introduction of Western learning. Western education opened the minds of Southeast Asians to the possibilities of a better life. The spread of education gave the younger generation ideas and attitudes that differed from those of their parents. Although Southeast Asian women generally had more freedom than other Asian women, increased opportunities to attend school and find employment gave them an even greater degree of economic freedom.

The Europeans also brought about an important change in the economy of the village. The self-sufficient village where the farmers produced only for themselves and their neighbors slowly disappeared. In its place the Europeans encouraged the farmer to grow crops for either the world market or larger urban markets.

Modern hospitals and improved health standards were also established by the Europeans. The result was a population explosion that put great pressure on the customs and traditions of Southeast Asia. The infant mortality rate decreased, and the number of young people increased greatly. For the first time, the importance of youth had to be recognized and accepted.

Western Rule Caused Hatred

Unfortunately, Westerners are remembered by the Southeast Asians more for the ways in which they neglected the region than for the benefits they brought. Most Westerners were primarily interested in making money, and they regarded Southeast Asia as a source of raw materials for their own use. Since the Western nations wished to sell their industrial products in Southeast Asia, little modern manufacturing was established in the region. In addition, people from the Western nations held nearly all of the important jobs. For this reason, only a few Southeast Asians were able to get the kind of experience they needed for self-government.

Nationalism in Southeast Asia

As the years passed, many Southeast Asians became dissatisfied with Western rule and wished for independence. Late in the 19th century, people in several Southeast Asian countries began a movement to end colonial rule. Many leaders of the independence movements were Southeast Asians who had learned about democracy and other political ideas while studying in the West.

Indonesia

In Indonesia the Dutch used Javanese workers (Java is the main island of Indonesia) in the government service, but paid them lower salaries and gave them lower rank than the Dutch received. In addition, the Muslim peasants were disturbed by Dutch interference in trade, farming, and village customs. These situations led to the first signs of nationalism. Groups were formed to set up newspapers and schools, which expressed a desire for independence.

When independence did not come by these peaceful means, a group of Indonesians led by Ahmed Sukarno set up a militant nationalist party in 1927, which used various methods such as study groups, mass meetings, and small strikes in efforts to gain independence. Sukarno was later arrested and sent to a remote island in the Indonesian archipelago. The Dutch were afraid of this nationalist feeling, and did all they could to destroy it.

Thailand (Siam)

Siam (now Thailand), alone of the Southeast Asian countries, never was a colony of a Western power. Its history is evidence that progress can come without colonialism. The preservation of Siam's independence, and the country's modernization, were the work of two rulers, Mongkut (King Rama IV) and his son Chulalongkorn (King Rama V). Nationalism in Siam took the form of preserving independence, and the country borrowed from the West the means to do so.

Myanmar (Burma)

Burma (now Myanmar) fell under the control of the British between 1852, when Lower Burma was conquered, and 1886, when Upper Burma was overcome. The British ended the **monarchy** (rule by the king) which was the center of Burmese national pride and symbolized Burmese culture and history. Under British rule, Indians were brought in as cheap labor, and they were hated by the Burmese. Although rice became a major export crop, few of the profits went to the farmers who grew it. In the late 1920s and 1930s, a series of riots took place. Burmese farmers attacked Indian laborers, the only enemies against whom they could express their anger.

A mild nationalist movement was tolerated. The British promised to give Burma its independence as soon as possible. In 1937, the British allowed a Burmese prime minister to hold office as a step toward independence. This change created a new situation in which a group of younger leaders began to demand immediate independence.

Vietnam

By 1890, the French had gained control over all of the Indo-Chinese Peninsula—the areas now known as Vietnam, Cambodia, and Laos. The French used only a few Vietnamese in the colonial government. They did not offer an opportunity for Western education to many Vietnamese, but educated Vietnamese who tried to adapt to French culture were treated as Frenchmen. On the other hand, those who wanted independence for Vietnam had no way to express their ideas.

Finally, in the 1920s, a number of small nationalist groups were formed, but achieved little. (Seven hundred members of the Nationalist Party were executed in 1929 for trying to oust the French.) The Vietnamese Communist party was formed under the leadership of Ho Chi Minh in 1930, but it too achieved little at that time.

Cambodia

Cambodia's nationalist movement was closely tied to two groups. One was led by Norodom Sihanouk of the Cambodian royal family. He envisioned a slow and peaceful movement toward independence. The other group of nationalists were more violent and were closely tied to the nationalist movement of the Vietnamese Ho Chi Minh.

Thai dancers.

France recognized Cambodia's independence in 1953. Norodom Sihanouk was proclaimed King of Cambodia. In 1955, Sihanouk gave up the throne and became Prime Minister. Between 1955 and 1963, Cambodia received millions of dollars in aid from the United States. However, in 1963, Sihanouk cut off American aid. He charged that the United States supported attempts to overthrow his government. In March 1970, Sihanouk was overthrown by members of his own cabinet. General Lon Nol, who led the coup, abolished the monarchy and made himself President of the new Republic.

During the 1950s and 1960s, Cambodia declared itself neutral in the struggle in Vietnam. This was impossible because Cambodia was useful to the North Vietnamese as a base. The United States would not allow this and repeatedly bombed suspected North Vietnamese bases in Cambodia.

The Philippines

The United States took the Philippines after defeating Spain in the Spanish-American War in 1898. The Filipinos wanted independence immediately. A revolt, led by Emilio Aguinaldo, lasted from 1899 to 1902, but the Filipinos were defeated. The Americans promised self-government and independence as soon as the United States felt the Filipinos were ready for freedom. Within 20 years, a Filipino legislature was running the government. However, the legislature was under the control of *caciques* (chiefs), who were not nationalists and really did not represent the people. Despite this situation, the United States kept its promise.

In 1935, the Commonwealth of the Philippines was set up, with a Filipino president and national assembly (legislature). The United States kept control of foreign affairs and military defense. It was agreed that the Philippines would gain complete independence after ten years.

The Situation in 1941

By 1941, nationalist movements existed in each nation of Southeast Asia. However, except in the Philippines and Burma (now Myanmar), independence seemed to be a distant dream. Events of the next few years, however, were to cause a complete change in the situation.

World War II and Japanese Control

In 1939, war broke out in Europe. France and Holland were soon defeated by Germany, and Great Britain was fighting for its life. Their colonies in Southeast Asia were left on their own. Here the agent of independence entered the drama.

The Japanese Occupation

Soon after World War II began in 1939, the Japanese realized that the conflict provided a good opportunity to gain control of Southeast Asia. Japan required more oil, iron, and other raw materials and also needed markets for its manufactured goods. On December 8, 1941, Japanese bombers moved toward Clark Air Force Base in the Philippines. A few hours earlier on December 7, other Japanese planes had bombed Pearl Harbor in Hawaii. (The bombing of Pearl Harbor and the Philippines brought the United States into World War II.)

By August 1942, almost all of East Asia was controlled by the Japanese. The Germans had overrun the Netherlands and France, and were attacking Great Britain. Of course, these three Western powers could not send warships, planes, or soldiers to defend their distant colonies in Southeast Asia.

The Japanese maintained that they wanted only to drive the Western powers out and to restore "Asia to the Asians," but the people of Southeast Asia soon realized that this claim was just an excuse for Japanese imperialism. The Japanese wanted to **exploit** Southeast Asia for themselves. In many places, the Japanese treated the people more harshly than the Westerners ever had. When bands of **guerrillas** were organized to oppose the Japanese, the British and Americans gave these groups weapons whenever possible, even though some of the guerrillas were led by Communists.

Although Japanese occupation lasted only about four years, its impact on the Southeast Asian struggle for independence was great. First, Europeans were eliminated from top jobs in government and business and replaced by native Southeast Asians. Second, Western prestige was destroyed by anti-Western **propaganda** in the newspapers, on radios, and over loudspeakers. Third, the Japanese granted "independence" to Burma (now Myanmar) and the Philippines. Finally, the Japanese trained native armies to help them maintain control. This trained military leadership was very important in the fight for independence that followed the defeat of Japan.

Japan's Defeat and Its Results

After the defeat of Japan in 1945, nationalist leaders seized control of their governments from local Japanese commanders. All of the countries of Southeast Asia declared their independence. The United States recognized Philippine independence in 1946, and the British granted Burma independence in 1947. However, the French and the Dutch, although weak from the war, did not recognize the independence of Vietnam and Indonesia until after many years of fighting with the nationalists of those countries.

In the span of a few years, about 170 million people who had lived under Western colonial rule for decades or centuries had become independent.

Independence and Its Results

We have seen that World War II furthered the desire of the people of Southeast Asia for independence. Now we will look at the situation that was created after the war, and see how it led to today's events in Southeast Asia.

Myanmar (Burma)

During World War II, Burma (now Myanmar) was a key battlefield; the 800-mile Burma Road was the main supply line from India to China. The Japanese invaded Burma in December 1941. By May 1942, the Japanese controlled most of the country, and the Burma

Road was blocked. After a very difficult series of battles, the British, Indian, and U.S. forces liberated Burma in August 1945.

British and French rule in Southeast Asia was challenged when World War II ended. The British recognized the independence of Burma on January 4, 1948.

Guerrilla Warfare

From the first days of Burmese independence in 1948, many ethnic-based guerrilla groups were established to fight for greater independence (autonomy).

ETHNIC GROUPS OF BURMA (MYANMAR)—1983 (IN PERCENT)

Burman	69.0	Rakhine	4.5	Kachin	1.4
Shan	8.5	Mon	2.4	Other	5.8
Karen	6.2	Chin	2.2		

These guerrilla groups controlled large areas of Burma, especially in the northern and eastern sections. One group, the Karens, have caused great difficulty. For over 40 years, the Karens have fought against every Burmese government, claiming that promises of autonomy for ethnic minorities have not been kept. The Karen National Union (KNU) was the largest of the 12 ethnic groups that joined the prodemocracy National Democratic Front in 1988.

In 1948, the new government of independent Burma was soon faced with a rebellion led by two groups: Burmese led by Socialists and Communists; and the Karen tribespeople of northern Burma. In 1951 and 1952, the Socialists gained control of the Burmese government, and Burma became the first Southeast Asian country to introduce social legislation. These laws were aimed at improving the lives of the Burmese people by giving them land, medical services, and housing. Although the Communists continued to rebel, by 1968 the Socialist government had extended its control over most of Burma and followed the "Burmese Buddhist way to socialism."

Events of the 1980s and Early 1990s

In the 1980s, a strong prodemocracy movement spread throughout Burma. In 1988, all of the prodemocracy groups, regardless of ethnic background, combined to form the National League for Democracy (NLD). In May 1988, the NLD won a landslide election victory—400 out of the 485 seats in the Parliament—over the party of the military rulers (the National Union Party). However, the army refused to turn over power, and in September 1988 a military **junta** (group) seized control and arrested all the leaders of the NLD. The junta said that a new constitution would have to be adopted before power could be transferred to a civilian government.

On May 26, 1989, Burma's military rulers gave the country a new name—the Union of Myanmar. The government's objective was to gain support from the minority ethnic groups for its unpopular policies of limiting democracy. The military junta declared that changing the country's name would "make clear that the country was made up of various ethnic groups, not just the majority Burmans." At the same time, the name of the capital and main city, Rangoon, was changed to Yangon.

The continuing importance of the KNU is shown by its ability to exist against great odds and by its claim to control much of northern and eastern Myanmar (Burma). The Burmese military has repeatedly used the army to try to destroy the movement. However, these attempts have not been entirely unsuccessful. Several times Burmese troops have clashed with Thai troops along the border where the Karens have their bases.

During the last decade, the government has been concerned with putting down various attempts by nonnative ethnic groups to separate their areas from Myanmar. In the highlands and mountains of the north, government troops have battled many minority guerrilla groups. These military actions have consumed much-needed capital and economic resources that could have been used to improve the standard of living in Myanmar.

In September 1992, the military rulers of Myanmar lifted more than three years of martial law, in which all constitutional guarantees of civil liberties had been suspended. This step was a relaxation of a crackdown that had begun in 1988.

It appears that for the last year most opposition has been quieted and most rival leaders have been under house arrest and closely watched.

Even today, the Communists have not given up and continue to fight the government. Several thousand, armed and supported by the Chinese, still operate in northern Myanmar.

The Philippines

Many Influences on Culture

The history of the Philippines for the past 400 years has been one of cultural diffusion. This diffusion has acted upon a population that is mainly Malay in makeup and culture.

For more than 1,000 years, Chinese traders visited the Philippines. Some of them married Malay women and settled in the islands. Then, in the 15th century, mainly because of trade with the Asian mainland, Spain decided to set up a colony in the islands. The Spanish named the islands the Philippines in honor of their king, Philip II.

Also during the 15th century, Muslim sailors from the mainland of Southeast Asia and India began trading and settling in the southern islands of the archipelago. They brought Islam with them. However, with the establishment of Spanish Catholic power in the main city of Manila, Islamic influence was limited to the southern islands of Mindanao and Palawan and to the Sulu Archipelago.

Spanish cultural influence is still obvious in the language of the Philippines, family names, customs, and religion (80 percent of the total population is Roman Catholic). Spanish and **mestizo** (Spanish and Malay mixed parentage) families still have great influence in politics, industry, and agriculture. The Chinese minority also remains important in Philippine business life.

The Philippines were ceded to the United States by Spain in the treaty of Paris at the end of the Spanish-American War in 1898. The United States ruled the Philippines from 1898 to 1942, and American cultural and economic influence was very important. English became the *lingua franca* (language most widely used) of business and government, and American political institutions were introduced (an American-style constitution, a congress, the office of president, and free elections). The United States also influenced economic and social reforms.

In 1942, a brief period of Japanese occupation began. The Japanese set up a puppet republic in 1943, which most Filipinos did not accept. After World War II ended in 1945, U.S. rule returned. On July 4, 1946, the United States granted the Philippines their independence.

Early Days of Independence

From their earliest days of independence, the Philippines have been troubled by social inequities, economic problems, unequal distribution of land, cultural and religious differences, and governmental corruption.

Violent opposition has often existed against the elected government. In 1942, a guerrilla army, calling itself the *Hukbalahaps* (People's Army Against Japan), or Huks, was organized to fight the Japanese. When the war ended, the Huks, who had fought well, admitted that they had connections with the Communists. The Huks continued their guerrilla warfare against the newly elected government of the independent Philippines.

President followed president. These officials could do little to solve the economic problems of rising population and inadequate industrial growth. The wealthy refused to give in to land reform. They bribed officials and bought elections and government leaders. For most of the people, poverty increased.

The Huks were finally brought under control in 1952 when President Ramon Magsaysay made land reforms and adopted other economic measures intended to improve the lives of the Filipino peasants.

The Marcos Era

Ferdinand Marcos became president of the Philippines in December 1965. In his 20 years as president, Marcos did little to improve the lives of the people. He poured hundreds of millions of dollars into 300 government-owned corporations, luxury hotels, and a nuclear power plant. He gave special help to companies owned by friends and relatives, and millions of dollars ended up in Marcos's personal bank accounts in New York, Honolulu, and Switzerland. Bribery was a growth industry in the Philippines. Little was done to improve agriculture, and land reform was not considered.

In 1968, the remainder of the Huks joined with other unhappy groups and set up the New Peoples' Army (NPA). For the next 18 years, the NPA fought against the government. During the Marcos regime, hundreds of millions of dollars were spent to build up an army to fight the NPA instead of improving peasant life. In 1972, Marcos declared martial law and suspended all civil rights, acts that led to an increase in NPA strength and activity. Opposition leaders were jailed without charges or trials. One of those leaders was Senator Benigno Aquino.

In 1980, under pressure from the United States, Marcos freed Senator Aquino with the understanding that he would leave the Philippines. Aquino went to the United States, where he continued the struggle against Marcos. In January 1981, again because of American pressure, Marcos ended martial law.

Despite warnings from President Marcos's wife, Imelda, that Senator Aquino would be killed if he returned to the Philippines, he did return in August 1983. On arrival at the airport in the Philippines, he was shot to death as he was escorted from the plane.

The assassination of Aquino led to huge antigovernment rallies and riots. NPA violence and raids increased and continued throughout 1984 and 1985 and into 1986. In November 1985, Marcos agreed to a presidential election, to be held in February 1986. Corazon Aquino, the widow of Senator Aquino, became the opposition candidate for president.

When Marcos declared himself the winner of the election, most Filipinos objected, believing that Aquino had been cheated. Opposition mounted, and the United States withdrew its support for Marcos. In March 1986, Marcos and his family fled to the United States and Corazon Aquino became president of the Philippines.

Corazon Aquino as President

By the time Aquino became President, the Philippines had become "the basket case of Southeast Asia." Almost one-half of the nation's 21 million workers were unemployed. Per capita income had fallen to about $600, no higher than it had been in 1972. The foreign debt had grown to 27 billion dollars.

Corazon Aquino had two important tasks: she had to negotiate a peace with the NPA, and she had to improve the economy. In December 1986, she negotiated a cease-fire with the leftist-led NPA.

Former Philippines President Corazon Aquino addressing the U.N. General Assembly in September 1986.

After Corazon Aquino became president, the United States promised immediate economic aid, and Aquino traveled around the world looking for additional help. In her visit to Japan in November 1986, she received a pledge of a 250 million dollar aid package. In December 1986, Corazon Aquino was named Women of the Year by *Time* Magazine.

In the first six years of her presidency, Aquino faced six attempts to overthrow her government. Her major opponents and the leaders of several coup attempts were military leaders who objected to her "weak" response to Communist guerrilla activities.

In 1989, industrial and land reform measures put into effect by Aquino's government raised both industrial and agricultural production to their highest levels in 15 years. However, Iraq's invasion of Kuwait in 1990 was a severe blow to the Philippines. Much of the money earned by Filipino workers in Kuwait and the Persian Gulf was lost. At the same time, the Philippines had to pay more than twice as much for imported oil. As a result, economic growth slowed, and poverty tightened its grip on the Philippine people once again.

Anti-American feeling also presented a problem for the Aquino government. Economic aid from the United States was essential. However, the Communist guerrillas who blamed the United States for helping the Aquino movement targeted Americans for terrorist activity. Anti-American feeling was also encouraged by the continued leasing of bases in the Philippines to the U.S. armed forces. In response, the Philippine government announced that its agreement to allow U.S. use of military bases would end in September 1991.

To add to the Aquino government's problems, in June 1991 Mt. Pinatubo, a volcano on the island of Luzon, erupted and covered much of the island with dust and ash. This eruption caused major damage to Clark Air Force Base, one of the U.S. military bases in the Philippines. In late July, the United States announced it was no longer interested in Clark as a base because the cost to repair the damage would be too high. At the same time Corazon Aquino and the U.S. government agreed to extend the American lease on the Subic Bay Naval and Air Base for ten years.

The deal came apart, however, when the Philippine Senate refused to approve the extension. In a referendum called for by Aquino, a majority of the Philippine people rejected an extension of the lease.

The Presidental Election of 1992

In May 1992, the Philippine people voted to elect a new president. In a seven-candidate race, Fidel V. Ramos received 23.5 percent of the vote. His margin over the second-place finisher, Miriam Defensor Santiago, was about 23,000 votes out of 23 million ballots cast. This was the smallest winning margin since the Philippines gained independence in 1946.

The losing candidate protested, claiming that there was a great deal of evidence of illegal voting and other forms of cheating. On June 22, 1992, after a month's debate of the issue, however, a joint session of the Philippine Congress proclaimed Ramos the duly elected president, and he was inaugurated on June 30.

Fidel Ramos, the first Protestant to become president of this country with an overwhelmingly Roman Catholic population, has attempted to gain the support of the groups that opposed him. He has discussed programs endorsed by his campaign rivals and the Catholic bishops who opposed him, and agreed to many of them.

He has proposed peace negotiations with Communist rebels and rebel military officers. By this conciliatory stance, he hopes to gain the support of important segments of Philippine society who remember that Ramos headed the Philippine constabulary, which arrested and sometimes tortured political opponents of ex-President Marcos. (Ramos left the Marcos government in 1986 and led a military rebellion that sparked the "people power" uprising that ousted the dictator.)

Many Problems Remain

Much work is needed to improve the economic situation in the Philippines. In addition, social, cultural, and religious problems abound. For example, the question of a "national language" is still unanswered. For many years English was the *lingua franca* of the rich, the government, and business, a situation that did not satisfy the nationalists. In 1961, Tagalog (now called Pilipino) was selected as the national language. However, only 6.5 million Filipinos speak Tagalog (there are over 54 million Filipinos), and very few in the South use it. Another cultural problem revolves around the 1 million Moros of Mindanao Island. The Moros, who are Muslim and follow the customs and ideas of Islam, believe that they have not been treated fairly by the Catholic leadership in the government.

Indonesia

After the surrender of the Japanese in 1945, bloody and savage fighting broke out in Java, the main island of the Indonesian archipelago. On one side were Indonesians, led by Ahmed Sukarno and armed and trained by the Japanese, who were fighting for full independence from Dutch rule. Opposing them were the Dutch, who wished to regain control of their colony.

In December 1949, after four years of fighting, the Netherlands recognized the independence of the Indonesian Republic, with Ahmed Sukarno as president. At that time, Indonesia had a population of nearly 100 million people, mostly Muslims. The country was rich in such resources as oil, bauxite, copper, rubber, and tin.

The new government under Sukarno said it would be guided by the *Pantjasila* (Pancasila), or five principles: belief in God, humanitarianism, naturalism, democracy, and social justice. However, the new nation faced serious problems in producing and distributing its resources and in uniting a country that consisted of 3,000 islands scattered between Asia and Australia.

In 1957, Sukarno dropped the Pantjasila and in its place introduced "guided democracy." This policy set aside majority rule, and a dictatorship was established. For the next eight years, Sukarno formed closer and closer ties with Communist China and the then Soviet Union. In the process, U.S. property was appropriated, and Sukarno began to follow an anti-American foreign policy.

In 1965, the Communists led a revolt in Indonesia. The Indonesian army charged that Sukarno had approved the revolt as a means of getting rid of military officers who opposed Sukarno's pro-Communist policies. The military defeated the Communists, and Sukarno lost most of his power.

By 1967, all government powers had been taken away from Sukarno, and General Suharto, an anti-Communist army leader, was elected president for a five-year term. He was reelected in 1973, 1978, and 1983. In the 1980s, the Suharto government brought back the Pantjasila program.

In 1988, Suharto was named to his fifth consecutive five-year term in office. The Indonesian people do not vote for the person to become president. Instead, the 1,000-member People's Consultative Assembly (PCA) arrives at a consensus (general agreement of a group) as to who the only candidate should be. The PCA is made up of all the members of Parliament and of regional and sectional delegates; these delegates do not vote.

One of the main reasons that Suharto has been able to remain in power is that Indonesia has not had as many economic problems as its neighbors. Economic progress has been slow but steady. An abundance of oil and gas reserves has contributed greatly to economic stability. Almost 40 percent of all Indonesian exports represent oil and gas sales. Indonesia's forests supply another 10 percent of its exports. Exports are sent mainly to Japan and the United States. The government continues to work toward a free-market economy. It is also trying to diversify the economy and rely less on oil exports.

Two situations must be watched in Indonesia. Politicians both in and out of government have urged that the assembly be allowed to vote on more than candidates. Also, demands for greater freedom are increasing; for example, there have been demonstrations in east Timor, central Java, and northwestern Sumatra. In the late 1980s, the Muslim province of Aceh at the northwestern tip of Sumatra began a serious movement to set up an independent Islamic republic. Armed clashes have erupted between guerrillas and the Indonesian Army.

Vietnam

Even more bloody was the struggle for independence in Indochina. For a brief time in March 1946, Ho Chi Minh and the French in Hanoi agreed to a Democratic Republic of Vietnam, which would keep its economic ties with the French. But Charles de Gaulle, who was president of France at that time, refused to surrender any part of the old French

Empire. War broke out in 1946, and for almost the next eight years the French tried unsuccessfully to defeat the Viet Minh guerrillas.

At a conference held in 1954, France finally agreed to the independence of Vietnam, but the country was partitioned (divided) into two parts. One was controlled by Ho Chi Minh and was Communist; and the other was ruled by a series of weak, unstable leaders, who ruled through the army, and gave little to the people in the way of reform and freedom. Under the Geneva Agreements (1954), the French holdings in Indochina were divided still further by the setting up of the independent countries of Laos and Cambodia (Kampuchea). (See page 000).

Malaya

Malaya was granted its independence after the British and the Malayans had successfully beaten off an attempt by the Communists to gain control of the rich Malay Peninsula. After the Malaysian **Federation** (Malaya, Sabah, Sarawak, and Singapore) was set up, Singapore demanded its independence, and in 1965 this was granted. Singapore wished to be independent because most of the people of Malaysia were Malays and Muslims, while the people of Singapore were mainly Chinese and Buddists.

Thailand (Siam)

Thailand (known as Siam until 1939) had never become a colony of any European nation. During the period of colonialism, the rulers of Thailand ruled without a constitution and with no limitation on their powers. In the 1930s, a revolution took place, and a constitution was written that took much power away from the king. This power was given to an elected leader and elected representatives of the people. However, the experiment in democracy did not last long. The army, which was losing importance under the constitution, was unhappy. Army generals succeeded in taking over the government and for almost 40 years were the real rulers of Thailand.

After World War II, there were succcessful attempts by various rivals in the Thai army to take over the government. There were many changes in leadership, but usually the leader was an army officer. The army rulers did away with the last Thai constitution in 1971. However, late in 1973, the army-controlled government was overthrown by a student revolution.

The revolution was successful because King Bhumibol was in favor of it. Bhumibol had little power, but he was regarded as the symbol of the Thai nation. He joined with student leaders, civilian advisers, and young army officers to force the army generals to give up control of the government.

The constitution of 1974 included land reform, pensions for farmers, and direct election of local government officials. Bhumibol favored these reforms, believing that the people should be given more economic security and a greater voice in the Thai government.

Democracy Thai Style—An Asian Case Study

In May 1992, serious demonstrations broke out in Bangkok, Thailand, against General Suchinda Kraprayoon, who had overthrown an elected government just a month before and declared himself prime minister.

Since the fall of the absolute monarchy in 1932, Thailand has had ten successful coups de état (overthrows of government), a number of failed ones, and 14 different constitutions. But seldom did violence occur. An old Thai joke is that, when a coup is attempted, both sides drive all their tanks into the street and then stop to count. Whoever has the most, wins.

In the May demonstrations, however, a now-affluent middle class refused to accept a coup without protesting. When the army reacted by firing on the demonstrators, a whole new script was written. What caused the change?

Throughout the 1980s, Thai society changed very quickly. An economic boom brought on by Japanese and Western investment in chemicals, textiles, consumer electronics, and other industries gave Thailand one of the highest economic growth rates in the world. Between 1987 and 1990, the country's economic growth rate averaged 11 percent per year. It slowed to 7.5 percent in 1991.

At the same time, Thailand, a nation of 55 million people, has become the world's largest exporter of rice. Thailand is also a leading producer of seafood and is one of Asia's top tourist destinations.

Living and educational standards have risen enormously. In 1965, only about 16,000 Thais were attending college; today the number is nearly 300,000. Bangkok now is an overcrowded (8 million people), traffic-choked city, but in all aspects a thoroughly modern metropolis.

As recently as February 1991, Thais accepted a bloodless military coup that overthrew an elected but very corrupt civilian government. In the coup of April 1992, however, the generals behaved in a manner that greatly upset the rising middle class.

The generals conveniently forgot their pledges to restore popular democracy and forced the acceptance of a new constitution that made military control of the government almost the rule. Then the military forced the Parliament to name Suchinda as prime minister, despite a clear popular preference for an elected civilian in the job.

What made the demonstrations notable was the leadership of Chamlong Srimuang, a former general who quit the army in 1986 to run for governor of Bangkok. He won and was reelected in 1980. Running an exceptionally clean, corruption-free, and democratic administration, he put together a civilian coalition that gained many seats in the parliamentary election of March 1992. To participate in the mass demonstrations, he organized an unusually broad range of society—students, workers, businessmen.

After the soldiers had fired on the demonstrators, the very popular and well-loved king, Bhumibol Adulyadej, mediated a compromise to stop the bloodshed. The compromise provided that Suchinda would resign, and he did. The army would not block amendments to the Thai constitution that would diminish the soldiers' authority. In return, no military personnel would be punished for the crackdown and the bloodshed.

The Future

After Suchinda stepped down, the army's power position was greatly weakened. In the past, however, the generals have proved that they can rule through civilian puppets. After 60 years of holding the real power in Thailand, the military is still the most powerful single group.

These "businessmen in uniforms" own or control hundred of businesses, including two nationwide TV channels, 200 radio stations, and their own bank. Also, the army is very popular among the rural peasants, who are still a majority of the population. In fact, most Thai soldiers are from the countryside of peasant farming families. Because of this military power, many Thais fear another coup is very possible.

However, the situation in Thailand in the 1990s is very different from that in the past. As a result of the economic boon and the business investments of the generals, they have a great deal to lose if violence results from an attempted coup. A major reason why the compromise was reached in 1992 was the fear that continued bloodshed would severely damage the economy by frightening away tourists and foreign investors.

In short, it is not as easy for the Thai military to keep control over the economically successful and educated Thailand of today as it was to wield power in the simpler peasant society that Thailand was in the past, but will never be again.

Problems Following Independence

When independence was granted, few nations of Southeast Asia were ready for it. Most had high levels of illiteracy, low levels of political experience, and unstable economies. Independence did not bring the people the new ease, riches, and importance they dreamed it would. As a result, leaders lost faith in democracy, **dictatorial** governments grew, and many Southeast Asians became disillusioned and bitter.

The Economy of Southeast Asia

Southeast Asia is a storehouse of natural resources. In times past, several Western nations wanted to make certain they could obtain the products of this region. They gradually gained control of all of Southeast Asia except Thailand. Because most Southeast Asians did not want to leave their farms to take jobs in mines or on plantations, Western officials hired many workers from China and India.

When the nations of Southeast Asia became independent, they faced a number of problems. One of the most important was to build economies that would support their growing populations.

Southeast Asia sells large quantities of its raw materials to other parts of the world, as it does not have enough factories to process these materials into finished, manufactured products. In some years, foreign countries pay low prices for Southeast Asian exports. Then many people who have jobs in tin mining or other industries earn less money.

Most nations of the region are working to establish more factories, which will help them to make better use of their raw materials. Increasing the number of factories will also help to provide new jobs for the people.

Myanmar (Burma)

Myanmar (Burma) is located in the western part of mainland Southeast Asia. China lies to the north, India to the west, and Thailand to the east. Myanmar has mainly a mountainous and plateau topography. Most of the people live in the two main river valleys—the Irrawady and the Nu. Myanmar has a long coastline along the Bay of Bengal and the Andaman Sea. The traditions of the people and their economic life are greatly influenced by the monsoon winds. Since Myanmar lies near the equator, the climate is tropical, hot, and wet.

Myanmar is an agricultural country. It is a large exporter of rice and many people work in rice fields and in saw mills. More than half of Myanmar is covered with forests. The lumber industry is based on Myanmar's teak forest. Teak is a hardwood used in shipbuilding and making furniture. Since 1948, a steel mill, spinning and weaving factories, jute mills, and brick factories have been build. The Lawpita hydroelectric power plant supplies inexpensive electricity to the people.

A morning market on a *klong* (canal) in Thailand.

A school in Myanmar. Each class may have 90 students.

NATURAL RESOURCES OF SOUTHEAST ASIA

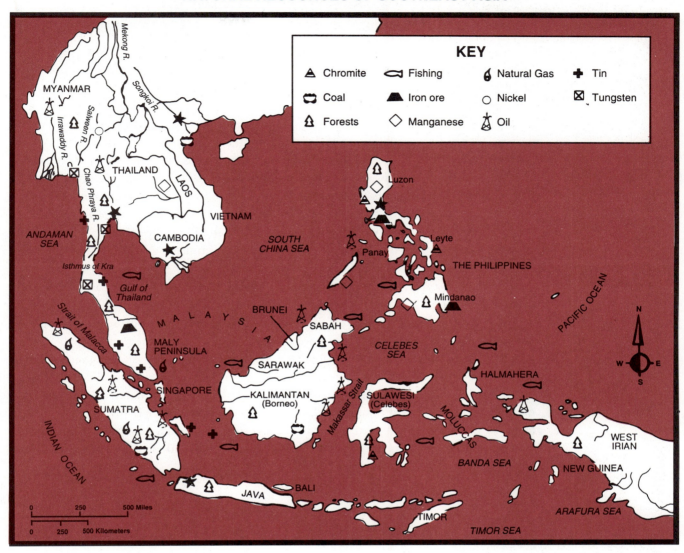

KEY

- △ Chromite
- ◻ Coal
- ⚶ Forests
- ◻ Fishing
- ▲ Iron ore
- ◇ Manganese
- ◖ Natural Gas
- ○ Nickel
- ⧈ Oil
- ✚ Tin
- ⊠ Tungsten

Government policy has not helped the economic development of Myanmar. In 1962, the government created a **Socialist economy** (the government controls key industries and resources), and refused any outside economic assistance. The Chinese and Indians, who had been important in the country's economic life, were driven out, and the government took control of all business and trade. Although this policy was supposed to lead to total economic self-sufficiency, it was a complete failure. To recover from the effects of this economic policy, limited, but increasing, foreign assistance—both technical and financial—in now encouraged.

In the 1980s and early 1990s, the country's economy has changed little. Myanmar is still dependent on agriculture, mainly the exporting of rice, which creates about 60 percent of Myanmar's foreign exchange. However, in 1984 the country changed its policy about accepting loans and agreed to financial assiastance from Japan, Australia, and China. This assistance was used mainly to search for mineral deposits—gold, diamonds, and petroleum—in an effort to end Myanmar's dependence on agriculture and timber products.

Tin is mined in the South, and oil is produced in the lower Irrawady Valley. Lead, zinc, silver, and jade are other mineral products of Myanmar.

Malaysia

Malaysia (formerly Malaya, Sabah [Brunei], and Sarawak) is both an island and a peninsula nation. Its two parts are separated by the South China Sea. Western Malaysia is located on the Malay Peninsula on the mainland of Southeast Asia. Eastern Malaysia consists of Sarawak and Sabah, located on the northern part of the island of Borneo.

All of Malaysia lies near the equator and has a hot, wet, tropical climate. Most of the inner part of the country is made up of mountains and plateaus, and forests cover most of this area. The main population centers are found on the long western coastal plain.

About three-fifths of the people of Malaysia make a living by farming. Many are subsistence farmers, raising enough for themselves and a little more for sale. The production of rubber and tin for export is the basis of Malaysia's economy. Rubber accounts for more than half of the money Malaysia earns from exports. Malaysia is the largest producer of iron ore in Asia; the iron is exported mostly to Japan. There are timber mills and oil refineries on Sarawak. To aid in building up Malaysia's industry, a hydroelectric plant has been built in the Cameron Highlands.

One great advantage Malaysia has had in the building industry is that capital has been available because of a favorable balance of trade. Although Malaysia must import rice to feed its people, the country exports more goods than it imports, and uses the income to build industries.

In the 1980s, however, like many less developed countries, Malaysia felt the economic impact of lower prices for export produced as prices on palm oil, rubber, tin, timber, and petroleum fell. Since these products make up the major part of Malaysia's exports, the country's economic growth was slowed. In the late 1980s and early 1990s, however, prices for these products began to rise slowly. As a result, Malaysia's economy continued to improve. Malaysia's main trading partners are Japan, the United States, Singapore, and Germany.

Thailand

Thailand (known as Siam until 1939) is located in the central part of mainland Southeast Asia and extends from the mainland to the Malay Peninsula in the south. Northern Thailand is made up of the Khorat Plateau and a series of mountains. These areas are covered with forests of teakwood. Myanmar (Burma) lies to the north and west; Laos is to the north and east; Cambodia (Kampuchea) and Malaysia lie to the south. The river valley of the Chao Phraya in central Thailand is the most populated and most economically important area of the country.

The climate is tropical (hot and wet) and in the higher elevations subtropical (warm and drier). (What do you think causes the difference?) In the Malay Peninsula area the climate is hot and rainy. (Can you guess what the topography of this area is?)

Tourism is a very important industry and is the largest source of foreign income. Thailand has attempted to improve its economy with the help of foreign investment. The building of hydroelectric power plants in the north has begun. When completed, these power plants will provide electric power and irrigation for the lightly developed north. Foreign investment has also led to growth in textiles, electronics, and automotive assembly.

Thailand has fertile soil, and most of the people work in agriculture or in processing and transporting agricultural products. Rice is the chief crop and export. The prosperity of

Thailand is due in part to this crop. Manufacturing, though growing, accounts for only18 percent of Thailand's national income. Teak, rubber, and tin are also exported. Thailand imports textiles, petroleum, chemicals, iron and steel, and machinery.

In the 1980s, Thailand's economy suffered from the same problems as the economies of all less-developed nations. Thai dependency on the sale of agricultural and mining products is greatly affected by the price of these commodities on the world market. In the 1980s, the prices of rice, sugar, rubber, and tin—all Thai exports—fell.

This decline led to a period of inflation and unemployment that caused government instability. When prices for these products began to rise in 1988, however, the economy started to grow and prosperity returned to Thailand. New investments poured in from Japan, Taiwan, and Hong Kong, and tourism again became an important industry. Thailand, which suffered from high unemployment in the early 1980s, now has a severe labor shortage.

Despite an improved and growing economy, government stability has not returned. Coalition governments have not been able to remain together long enough to establish a consistent policy. The army is very powerful and greatly involved in the government. It is the army that has prevented the passage of social legislation to improve workers' insurance and other social benefits. Corruption in the government is widespread and has forced the downfall of some coalition governments.

Indonesia

Located southeast of the Asian mainland, Indonesia is the world's largest archipelago. It is also the largest nation, in land and population, in Southeast Asia. The islands have a mainly mountainous volcano topography.

Since all of Indonesia lies along the equator, the entire nation has a hot-wet (tropical) climate. The western islands are usually wetter and have a year-round rainy season. The eastern islands are greatly influenced by the seasonal monsoons.

Indonesia is an agricultural country. Java and Sumatra are the most important islands. Because of the mountainous topography, a variety of crops are raised. Rice, sugarcane, and coconuts are grown along the coastal plain, and tea and coffee on the mountain slopes. Tropical hardwoods are found in the dense forests of the highlands. Timber and lumber products are cut mainly for export to Japan.

Indonesia had not developed economically as fast as might be expected for a country rich in natural resources (rubber, petroleum, tin, and others). The most important industries—shipbuilding, textiles, cement making, and paper production—were small. About three-quarters of the country's exports came from Java. These other islands, however, received only about one-quarter of the imports.

The mishandling of government money under President Sukarno also weakened the economy. Sukarno used all of Indonesia's assets to build his power and glorify himself. By 1966, the country was almost bankrupt. Inflation spread throughout the islands, making money almost worthless. Since 1967, when Sukarno was removed from power, Indonesia has recovered.

The Suharto government, which replaced Sukarno, cut inflation and increased exports. As a result, now more is exported, especially oil, than is imported. Foreign governments invested a great deal of money in industry and mining. Consequently, agriculture has been improved, industry expanded, and more of Indonesia's resources developed.

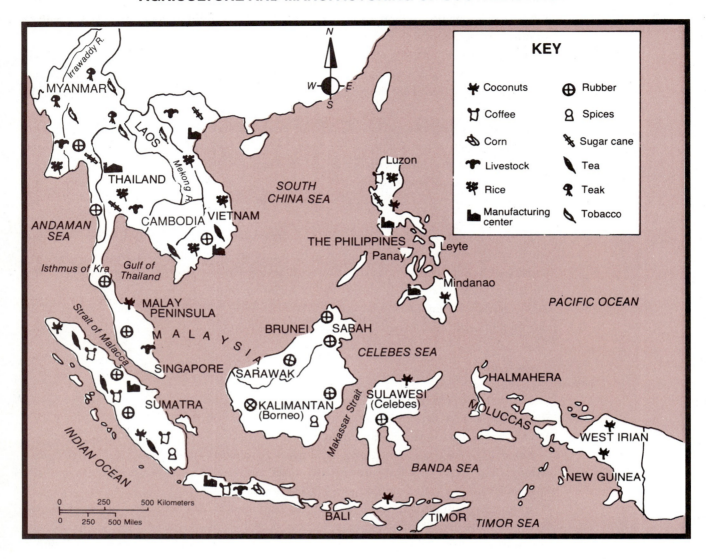

KEY

- Coconuts
- Coffee
- Corn
- Livestock
- Rice
- Manufacturing center
- Rubber
- Spices
- Sugar cane
- Tea
- Teak
- Tobacco

However, serious problems remain. Unemployment is very high, and the island of Java is extremely overpopulated. (Density on Java is 1500 persons per square mile.) The income from the oil industry goes mainly to a few millionaires, while hardly any touches the lives of most of the people. Much of the industry and business is in the hands of Japanese, Chinese, and other non-Indonesians.

Riots in early 1974 showed the hostile feelings of the people of Indonesia toward the Japanese and Chinese. To meet this problem, President Suharto issued an order that any foreigner who wants to do business in Indonesia must go into partnership with a *pribumi* (a native-born Indonesian). At least half of the ownership must be in the hands of the pribumi.

In late 1977, riots again broke out. These riots were led by students who objected to rising food prices, restrictions on political activities, and corruption among leading government officials. To stop the riots, President Suharto ordered the closing of newspapers. Many students were thrown in jail. Protests continue, but President Suharto, using the loyal support of the army, has been able to remain in power.

Despite falling prices on exports, Indonesia made moderate economic growth in the 1980s. This was accomplished by encouraging foreign investment and increasing the productivity of workers.

Vietnam

Vietnam is a long, narrow country located in the eastern part of Southeast Asia, on what was once called the Indochina Peninsula. (Why do you think such a name might be appropriate?) Laos and Cambodia (Kampuchea) are also located on the Indochina Peninsula. China is located to the north; Laos and Cambodia are to the west; the South China Sea is to the east.

In peaceful times, Vietnam has the potential for economic prosperity. In the north, the delta region of the Song Koi (Red River) is a fertile agricultural area. The northern part of Vietnam also has rich coal deposits and other mineral resources. The Mekong Delta in the south is also a fine agricultural area.

However, because of the long period of fighting, first with the French and then with the United States, the economy of Vietnam has been destroyed. The results of the long warfare have made Vietnam one of Asia's poorest nations in the 1990s. Since North and South were united, Vietnam has been totally dependent on the former Soviet Union to keep its economy going.

It is the hope of the current government to get economic assistance from the West. If this is forthcoming, Vietnam has the potential to become a self-sufficient nation.

Laos

Laos is a **landlocked** (not bordering on seas), mountainous nation, surrounded by China, Thailand, Cambodia, and Vietnam. Its climate is hot and rainy. Forests cover much of the highland area.

Rice is the most important crop, and tobacco, corn, cotton, and coffee are also grown. Tin, lumber, and electric power are exported. There is almost no industry.

Laos is one of the poorest nations in the world, with an extremely low standard of living. Laos cannot exist as a nation without large amounts of foreign aid.

Cambodia (Kampuchea)

Cambodia is located on the Indochina Peninsula between Thailand and Vietnam. Laos lies to the north. Cambodia has a limited outlet to the Gulf of Siam on its southwest coast. In the south and around the Tonle Sap, Cambodia is made up of small plains. The rest of the country consists of highland and forested areas. The climate is tropical (hot) and humid (wet).

The main economic area is the fertile rice-growing region along the Mekong River. The only other economic area, located in the northwest, is the Tonle Sap, a large lake region that supports a small fishing industry.

In the 1990s, after years of turmoil and instability, Cambodia faces the problems of reconstruction. Thousands of Cambodians are in refugee camps in Thailand. War will remain an ever-present danger until an agreement is reached between Vietnam and the three Cambodian resistance groups who oppose the Vietnam-supported Cambodian government of Hanj Sen.

Trade continues with Vietnam. Foreign aid comes mainly from the former Soviet Union, but neither the trade nor the aid is anywhere near the amount necessary to improve the very low standard of living of the Cambodian people.

Singapore

Singapore, the smallest nation of Southeast Asia, is located on the southern tip of the Malay Peninsula on the Strait of Malacca. Singapore is the name of both the indepedent country and the capital and main city. Seventy-five percent of Singapore's inhabitants are Chinese. Malay and Indian peoples make up the rest of the population.

Singapore has become one of the "tigers of East Asia," along with Taiwan, South Korea, and Hong Kong. It has a thriving and very active market economy based on free enterprise, individual ownership, and free trade for the exporting of manufactured goods. Singapore specializes in the mass production of goods and the use of a cheap, skilled labor supply for the manufacture of television sets, electrical appliances, radios, and many high-tech products such as computers and computer chips.

The current economic prosperity resulting from this export trade has greatly raised the standard of living in Singapore. (How might this situation affect consumers and workers in the United States?)

TRADE AND COMMERCE IN SOUTHEAST ASIA (SELECTED COUNTRIES)

| Country | Percent of Trade | | Leading Trade Partners | | Major Exports (%) |
	To U.S.	From U.S.	Exports (%)	Imports (%)	
Mayanmar (1988–89)	1	5	Southeast Asia (23)	Japan (40)	Rice (32) Teak (43)
Cambodia (1988)	3	0	Fomer Soviet Union (88)	Former Soviet Union (93)	Rubber (83)
Indonesia (1989)	16	14	Japan (42) USA (16)	Japan (23) USA (14)	Oil (23) Natural gas (12)
Laos (1988)	0	0	China (16) Former Soviet Union (5)	Thailand (11) Former Soviet Union (53)	Timber (33) Coffee (9)
Malaysia (1988)	17	18	Japan (17) Singapore (19)	Japan (23) USA (17)	Petroleum (11) Rubber, palm oil, timber (25)
The Philippines (1988)	34	21	USA (34) Japan (20)	Japan (17) USA (21)	Electrical equipment and parts (21) Textiles (18)
Singapore (1989)	23	17	Malaysia (14) USA (23)	Japan (21) USA (17)	Petroleum products (13) Office machines and electrical equipment (27)
Thailand (1988)	20	14	Japan (16) USA (20)	Japan (29) USA (14)	Food and live animals (34) Basic manufactured goods and machinery (34)
Vietnam (1988)	—	—	Former Soviet Union (51) Hong Kong (14)	Japan (8) Former Soviet Union (69)	Fuel and raw materials (45) Machinery (23)

Source: *Encyclopedia Britannica,* 1991

Economic Problems—A Summary

The nations of Southeast Asia have faced all of the problems that developing nations experience. When they gained their independence, most of the countries were too poor to construct enough dams and factories without outside help, but were too proud to ask for that help. There were not enough trained scientists, engineers, and mechanics, or any schools to train them. There was a lack of railroads and other means of transportation to bring goods to and from the market.

Efforts are being make, however, to tap the tremendous natural resources of Southeast Asia. The most notable of these attempts is the Mekong River Plan. The four countries of Laos, Thailand, Vietnam, and Cambodia are cooperating in the development of the river to provide for hydroelectric power, irrigation, and navigation.

Although the Southeast Asians have made some progress, only peace, stability, and outside aid will create the economic miracle they desire.

Association of Southeast Asian Nations (ASEAN)

In 1967, Brunei (which became independent on January 1, 1984), Indonesia, Malaysia, the Philippines, Singapore, and Thailand formed the Association of Southeast Asian Nations (ASEAN). The purpose of ASEAN is to encourage the nations of Southeast Asia to cooperate with each other in trade, economic planning, and economic development.

In addition to regular discussions of economic matters in the region, ASEAN meetings have been dominated by efforts to solve the problem of civil war in Cambodia. (China, the United States, the former Soviet Union, and Japan also have been involved in efforts to settle the Cambodian situation.) The former Soviet Union's involvement on the side of Vietnam, whose troops invaded Cambodia, has also provided a problem for ASEAN discussion. This Soviet involvement led Thailand, Singapore, Indonesia, and Malaysia to request military and economic assistance from the United States. This assistance was granted throughout the 1980s.

ASEAN's relations with Japan centered on trade problems. Growing trade balances in favor of Japan led ASEAN to charge Japan with "economic colonialism." The economic colonialism charge is serious because it brings back memories of Japan's World War II (1941–1945) conquests and its attempt to colonize the nations of Southeast Asia. ASEAN leaders are upset because the sale of ASEAN raw materials make up the bulk of their exports to Japan. ASEAN claims that the Japanese have closed their markets to Southeast Asian manufacturers and to agricultural and fish products. The association is also disturbed by the refusal of the Japanese to transfer technology and expert assistance to Southeast Asian nations.

Achievements of ASEAN

In 1974, ASEAN acted to play "honest broker" between Malaysia and the Philippines. Malaysia was angry at the way at which the Philippines had handled a Muslim **uprising** (revolt) on the island of Mindanao in the Philippines. ASEAN members tried to keep things from getting worse by giving Malaysia and the Philippines a place to talk about their disagreement. Although no solution was worked out, both nations agreed to continue discussions.

In the energy (oil) crisis in 1973, ASEAN acted strongly. Discussions were held in early 1974. Indonesia, a large oil producer, said it would make every effort to supply oil to its ASEAN neighbors. The ASEAN nations agreed to cooperate to ease each others' shortages. They also agreed to joint industrial planning and development of Southeast Asia.

Agreements were made with the European Economic Community (the Common Market) and Japan. These nations have agreed to consider the needs and interests of the ASEAN nations when setting up their economic policies.

**1976 ASEAN
Summit Meeting**

In 1976, the leaders of the ASEAN nations held their first summit meeting on the island of Bali in Indonesia. Two major agreements came out of the conference: a Declaration of Concord (agreement) and a Treaty of Amity (friendship).

The Declaration of Concord noted the members' desire to continue to expand economic cooperation. In addition, they agreed to set up a trade agreement among the member nations. They also approved plans for large industrial projects, which would use the resources of all the members in common. Special attention was paid to the sharing of food and energy resources in time of need.

The Treaty of Amity looked to establishing a High Council of Ministers to settle disputes among the members. The nations spoke of the need for greater mutual technical aid. Agreements were also reached on improving economic cooperation for the common benefit of the member nations.

Finally, those present agreed that the only real solution to the problem of rebellions in their own countries and in neighboring countries lay in economic progress and improvement of the lives of the people.

The Present Situation

ASEAN conferences were held at least twice a year between 1976 and 1990. Among the achievements of ASEAN was the commitment to *Zopfan* (zone of peace, freedom, and neutrality). In 1989, the ASEAN conference announced that Vietnam had agreed to a complete withdrawal of its troops from Cambodia. This development followed several years of ASEAN diplomatic efforts.

Foreign Relations

The struggle to survive is as important to the nations of Southeast Asia as it is to the rest of the world. After World War II, the Southeast Asian nations, many of them newly independent, knew that they were caught between two powerful forces at a time in history when nuclear weapons had changed the nature of warfare.

The need for survival led different nations to look for different solutions to the problem. The Philippines and Thailand looked to the United States for protection against the Communist countries. Malaysia and Singapore tied their futures to Great Britain. Since the British decided to drop their role as protectors, both Malaysia and Singapore adopted more neutral policies. Vietnam, once aligned with the former Soviet Union, is seeking stronger ties with the West.

Myanmar (Burma)

At first, Myanmar inclined toward communism. Myanmar has now become neutral and leans slightly toward the West because of fear of Communist China.

Indonesia

Indonesia under President Sukarno was pro-Communist. When the Communists tried unsuccessfully to take over the government in 1965, however, Sukarno was replaced as president by General Suharto, and the Communists were wiped out. Suharto took charge in 1967 and was reelected in 1973, 1978, 1983, and 1988, each time for a five-year term.

Under General Suharto, Indonesia has followed a nonaligned policy. However, Suharto leans toward the West on many issues. In 1985, Indonesia hosted an Asian-African Conference to commemorate the Bendung Conference, held in 1958. Of great importance was the presence of Chinese Communist leaders at the meeting. This marked the first contact on such a high level since relations with China were broken off when the Indonesians accused the Chinese of causing the uprising of 1965. In 1990, after 23 years of no diplomatic links, Indonesia and China normalized relations.

Djakarta, Indonesia, one of the largest cities in Southeast Asia.

Thailand (Siam)

Thailand's foreign policy has traditionally leaned toward the strongest nation in the area. The Thais played off the British and the French in the late 19th and early 20th centuries, always allying themselves with the stronger of the two. Mainly for this reason, Thailand was able to keep its independence.

In the 1930s and early 1940s, the Thais supported the Japanese. When it became clear that Japan would lose World War II, the Thais switched their support to the United States and its allies. After the war, the Thais followed American policy. Now, with the United States reducing its power in Southeast Asia, the Thais have tended to seek better relations with the People's Republic of China, while maintaining a strong pro-American policy.

Over the past 15 years, thousands of refugees from Cambodia, Laos, and Vietnam have settled in eastern Thailand. This border area has been the scene of military clashes between Thailand and its neighbors.

Laos

Laos was established as an independent country when the French holdings in Indochina were divided in 1954. As an independent nation, Laos tried to maintain a neutral stance. However, during the Vietnamese conflict, both the Pathet Lao, a Communist group, and the U.S. Central Intelligence Agency (CIA) made serious attempts to gain control of parts of Laos. In April 1974, a coalition government consisting of Communists and non-Communists was set up. Souvanna Phouma, a non-Communist, was premier, and Phoumi Vongvichit, a Communist, became vice-premier and minister of foreign affairs. In July 1974, Premier Souvanna Phouma suffered a heart attack and Phoumi Vongvichit was named acting premier.

By the end of 1974, all foreign troops had withdrawn from Laos. The Laotians said they would be willing to accept economic aid from all nations, both Communist and non-Communist. A Lao People's Democratic Republic was proclaimed in December 1975.

Laos held its first parliamentary election in April 1989. It was supposed to adopt a constitution in December 1990, but agreement on some issues was not achieved. The constitution describes Laos as "a people's democratic state under the leadership of the Lao People's Revolutionary Party." The constitution further states that "the central goal of economic policy is a market economy." Presently the head of state is Prime Minister Kaysone Phomvhan.

Laos continues to survive largely as a result of foreign aid from Japan, China, the United States, France, and Australia. Most of the country's limited trade is with the United States, the former Soviet Union, China, Japan, and neighboring Southeast Asian countries.

Vietnam

The Vietnam Conflict

When Vietnam was given its independence in 1954, it was divided at the seventeenth parallel into North Vietnam and South Vietnam. Under the terms of the Geneva Agreement, an election for the whole of Vietnam was to be held in 1956, but this election was never held. The South Vietnamese government, supported by the United States (neither of which had signed the 1954 Geneva Agreement), refused to take part in any election for fear the Communist North would win.

When it became clear that no election would be held, the North Vietnamese helped organize the National Liberation Front (NLF) to reunite the country. The NLF set up a guerrilla group, the Viet Cong, to fight in the South Vietnam countryside. By 1960 the NLF controlled more than 80 percent of the land. The government of South Vietnam asked the United States to send supplies and technicians to act as advisers.

Gulf of Tonkin Resolution

On August 4, 1964, President Lyndon Johnson announced that the U.S. destroyers *Maddox* and *C. Turner Joy* had been attacked by shell fire and possibly by elements of the North Vietnamese Navy. This alleged attack took place in the Gulf of Tonkin, off the coast of North Vietnam. It has never been confirmed that an attack took place.

On August 7, 1964, at the request of President Johnson, Congress passed the Gulf of Tonkin Resolution. This resolution gave the president the power to take "all necessary measures to repel an armed attack against the forces of the United States and to prevent further aggression."

The United States did not declare war on North Vietnam; however, President Johnson used the resolution as a legal basis for increasing U.S. involvement in South Vietnam. In

March 1965, he sent a group of U.S. Marines to South Vietnam, the first American combat forces to enter the war.

The United States became involved because it hoped to prevent the Communists from gaining complete control of the country. At first, American involvement was restricted to advising, but when the situation did not improve, the United States gradually sent over 500,000 soldiers into Vietnam to fight.

American planes began to bomb North Vietnam. As American raids increased, and more and more Americans poured into Vietnam, the Chinese and Russians increased their aid to the Viet Cong, and North Vietnamese army units began operating in the South.

Why were the Americans in Vietnam? President Lyndon Johnson, who ordered the soldiers into Vietnam, stated on April 7, 1965, "Our objective is the independence of South Vietnam and its freedom from attack. We want nothing for ourselves, only that the people of South Vietnam be allowed to guide their own country in their own way."

Many Americans, however, did not agree that the United States had become involved in Vietnam for these aims. They felt that President Johnson and, later, President Richard Nixon had not been entirely truthful with the American people. Indeed, in the summer of 1971, the publication of U.S. government documents, known as the Pentagon Papers, showed that the American government had not revealed all the facts to the people.

By 1968, Americans in great numbers had begun to speak out against the war, and the U.S. government began to look for ways to get out of it. In March 1968, President Johnson ended the bombing of most of North Vietnam. The North Vietnamese accepted this as an overture for peace, and agreed to begin peace talks in Paris in May. In December 1968, the talks were enlarged to include both the Communist NLF and the anti-Communist government of South Vietnam.

In May 1969, President Richard Nixon proposed a peace plan for Vietnam, one feature of which was a mutual withdrawal of U.S. and North Vietnamese troops. However, in early 1970, the United States launched an attack against the North Vietnamese in Cambodia. The purpose, as stated by President Nixon, was to destroy the North Vietnamese power to attack the Americans while they were leaving South Vietnam.

By that time, American losses in Vietnam had risen to over 55,000 dead. Over 1 million Vietnamese had been killed, and the land in both North and South Vietnam was destroyed.

Peace in Vietnam   Finally, on January 23, 1973, President Nixon announced to a war-weary America that "we today have concluded an agreement to end the war and bring peace with honor to Vietnam and Southeast Asia."

The terms of the agreement were divided into nine parts, or "chapters":
1. All parties would respect the independence and unity of Vietnam as recognized by the 1954 Geneva Agreements.
2. A cease-fire throughout Vietnam, but not in Cambodia or Laos, was to begin on January 27, 1973, with all military units remaining in place. All U.S. troops were to be withdrawn within 60 days, and all U.S. military bases in South Vietnam were to be dismantled (taken apart).
3. All military prisoners were to be released within 60 days.
4. The right of the people of South Vietnam to determine their own political future was specifically recognized.

5. The Demilitarized Zone (DMZ) was recognized as a temporary military boundary between two parts of Vietnam that were expected to be reunited through peaceful negotiation between their two governments.
6. An International Control Commission and Supervision (ICCS) was set up to watch over the truce.
7. Self-determination and neutrality for Laos and Cambodia were agreed to.
8. The United States pledged itself to aid in the reconstruction, specifically of North Vietnam, and also throughout the Indo-Chinese Peninsula.
9. All parties agreed to put the agreement into effect.

However, there still remained the unsolved problem of the other wars in Southeast Asia—in Laos and Cambodia. Although attempts were made to set up a cease-fire in each of these countries, war continued into the summer of 1973.

Continued Problems

In the first year after the signing of the peace agreement in January 1973, nearly 13,000 South Vietnamese soldiers and over 2,000 civilians were killed. According to reports, 45,000 North Vietnamese and Viet Cong also died.

From the start of the cease-fire the four-nation International Commission of Control and Supervision (ICCS) was powerless to halt the fighting. The Canadian members of the ICCS were so unhappy with the commission's lack of power that they quit in August 1973. The Canadians felt that they were sent to observe a peace and remained to watch a war. The other ICCS members—Poland, Hungary, Indonesia, and Iran—were not very active in trying to keep the peace.

The cease-fire agreement also called for the setting up of a council of South Vietnamese and Viet Cong, which would be the beginning of a new coalition government for South Vietnam. But the council was never set up because no one could decide who should be on it.

In addition, economic problems in South Vietnam became very serious. American aid had been cut, and President Thieu was forced to cut exports and raise taxes. Also, South Vietnam suffered from increasing inflation, and prices rose steadily. The price of rice doubled and the price of sugar tripled. The South Vietnamese people were not happy with the economic situation.

In the North, the Communist government made some progress in repairing the damages of war. The government put strict controls on prices and tried to increase production of food and other goods. Although outside aid was limited, peace allowed the North Vietnamese to turn toward efforts at improving the lives of the people.

End of the Conflict in South Vietnam

In late 1974 and early 1975, the situation in Vietnam began to change. Opposition to President Thieu of South Vietnam increased because of corruption in his government and because of Thieu's refusal to allow greater civil rights for the people. Inflation also grew worse. In addition, U.S. military and economic aid was greatly reduced. The Thieu government found it more and more difficult to maintain economic, social, and military stability (balance).

Communist pressure by the Viet Cong and North Vietnamese within South Vietnam grew. South Vietnamese generals were afraid to fight and made serious mistakes. By April 1975, the situation had become extremely serious. Hue, Danang, and Nha Trang, important cities of South Vietnam, were in Communist hands. Only Saigon (now Ho Chi Minh City) remained free of North Vietnamese control.

War as seen through the eyes of these North Vietnamese children.

The Troubled History of Vietnam in a Capsule

Year	Event or Situation
A.D. 1–938	Vietnam was under Han China control. The Chinese had conquered Vietnam 200 years before. This conquest and control is a major reason for Vietnamese fear and distrust of the Chinese even today.
939	The independence of Vietnam was achieved under the leadership of Ngo Quyen.
1000–1800	A Vietnamese state was expanded on the Indo-Chinese Peninsula. At the same time, different Vietnamese families fought each other for control of the government. Vietnam was not unified in this period.
1750	French economic and trading interests and interference in Vietnam affairs began.
1802	Unification of Vietnam's three areas (Annam, Tonkin, Cochin China) was achieved by Emperor Ghia Long.
1881–1885	The French actively colonized Vietnam and all of the Indo-Chinese Peninsula, including Cambodia and Laos.
1930	The Communist party was set up in Vietnam by Nguyen Ai Quoc (Ho Chi Minh).
1940	Vietnam was invaded by the Japanese.
1941	The Viet Minh League (League for Independence of Vietnam) was set up under the leadership of Ho Chi Minh.
1941–1945	Ho Chi Minh led a guerrilla war against the Japanese with American advice and help.
1945	The Japanese proclaimed the independence of Vietnam. A Vietnamese Republic was set up with Hanoi as capital. Ho Chi Minh was leader of the new state.
1945–1954	The French returned and tried to destroy the Viet Minh. With American aid a 10-year war went on.
1954	The French surrendered an important base at Dien Bien Phu in May. In July a cease-fire agreement was made.
1954	At Geneva an agreement dividing Vietnam at the 17th parallel was reached. The United States and the new government of South Vietnam refused to sign.
1960	The Viet Cong National Liberation Front was organized in South Vietnam.
1964	The U.S. Defense Department reported that U.S. destroyers were fired upon by North Vietnamese in the Gulf of Tonkin (later proved untrue). U.S. intervention in Vietnam began.
1964–1973	U.S. troops and planes actively fought Viet Cong and North Vietnamese in Vietnam.
1973	In January, Secretary of State Henry Kissinger and Le Duc Tho of North Vietnam signed an agreement ending U.S. intervention.
1974	Fighting, which had never stopped in Vietnam, in May became much heavier.
1975	Spectacular Communist military successes led to the collapse of the South Vietnamese army and government. In April the Viet Cong set up a Provisional Revolutionary Government to rule South Vietnam.

President Thieu felt that he had been betrayed by the United States. He claimed that Secretary of State Henry Kissinger and former President Nixon had guaranteed aid in case of trouble.

With defeat facing him, Thieu resigned as president. A new government led by General Duong Van Minh (known as Big Minh) was set up. Its objective was to negotiate (work out) a peace with the Communists. On April 30, 1975, the South Vietnamese government surrendered unconditionally to the Viet Cong. Minh handed over all power to the Viet Cong Provisional Revolutionary Government, thus ending the conflict.

Unified Vietnam

In the years since, Vietnam has been united much has occurred. The Vietnamese have followed a strong policy in relation to their neighbors. The Vietnamese opposed the Bali summit meeting of ASEAN (page 504). They felt that the other nations of Southeast Asia were "ganging up" on Vietnam and that ASEAN was being used to oppose the revolutionary and reform movements in Southeast Asia.

At the same time efforts were made to improve relations with their neighbors. Visits were made by high-ranking Vietnamese to Indonesia, Thailand, the Philippines, Singapore, and Malaysia. Hints were sent out that Vietnam wanted peace and might join ASEAN sometime in the future.

Vietnam and China

In December 1991, Vietnam and China opened their joint border for the first time in ten years. Trade blossomed, and the Chinese sent assistance to Vietnam. However, in June 1992, Chinese warships sailed into the South China Sea to renew China's claim to the Spratly Islands. Vietnam also claims these islands, which lie to the southeast of Vietnam and to the northwest of Borneo. The islands are important because it is suspected that large amounts of oil and natural gas lie beneath the sea.

In addition, Chinese troops have moved border markets deep into Vietnam and built compounds. They appear to wish to make this encroachment (advance beyond established limits) a permanent situation.

Cambodia (Formerly Kampuchea)

Involvement in the Vietnam War

Since independence from France was achieved in 1953, Cambodia has faced political unrest and instability. Cambodia would have liked to follow a neutral policy during the Vietnam conflict. However, because of its location near Vietnam, the North Vietnamese used it as a supply base. Prince Sihanouk, president of Cambodia, tried to remain on friendly terms with the Chinese and the Vietnamese. However, as the war continued in Vietnam and more and more Vietnamese entered Cambodia, Sihanouk attempted to strengthen his ties with the United States in order to protect himself from the North Vietnamese. In 1970, while Sihanouk was out of the country, the Cambodian army revolted and made one of its generals, Lon Nol, president.

When the North Vietnamese began to move their army toward the Cambodian capital, Phnom Penh, Lon Nol asked for American aid, which was sent immediately. In late 1970, Lon Nol suffered a stroke, and the government came under the control of military leaders. However, by early 1972, Lon Nol had recovered sufficiently to regain control of the government.

Communist Conflict

Fighting continued in Cambodia throughout the period from 1973 to 1975. The United States sent military equipment in great quantities to the Cambodian army of Lon Nol.

However, this aid did little to help control the Khmer Rouge (the Communist forces). Communist pressure grew, coming closer and closer to Phnom Penh. By April 1975, the situation was hopeless, and Lon Nol left Cambodia for "health reasons." The Communists occupied Phnom Penh, and it appeared that the civil war in Cambodia was over.

The new government was Communist-controlled (North Vietnamese Communists) and anti-American. In May 1975, Cambodian gunboats attacked the unarmed American merchant vessel *Mayaguez* well outside Cambodian territorial waters, capturing the ship and its crew of 39 American sailors. Within a few days American planes bombed Cambodian airfields. American marines attacked an island off the coast of Cambodia where the sailors were thought to be held as prisoners. The *Mayaguez* and its crew were released by the Cambodians.

In an effort to eliminate all opposition, the Communist government of Cambodia, led by Pol Pot, started a policy of repression in 1976. Reports coming from Cambodia stated that thousands of Cambodians had been executed. Many thousands of other Cambodians had been sent to reeducation centers to be made into supporters of the government. The name Cambodia was changed to Kampuchea. (In 1989, the name was changed back to "The State of Cambodia.")

By early 1978, the capital, Phnom Penh, had become a ghost city. In 1975, the population of Phnom Penh had been over 2 million. In early 1978, the population was reported to be about 20,000. The people had been forced to leave and live in the countryside. It is estimated that between 2 and 4 million Cambodians died under the brutal rule of Pol Pot.

War with Vietnam

In December 1977 and January 1978, Vietnamese troops moved into an area of Cambodia called the Parrot's Beak, which juts into Vietnamese territory. Heavy fighting resulted, and both sides admitted that many had died. The Vietnamese took over most of the area and did not seem willing to leave.

The reason for the attack lies in past history. The Cambodians and Vietnamese have hated each other for centuries. When the Khmer Rouge took over Cambodia in 1975, many thousands of Vietnamese living there were massacred. In 1976, the Vietnamese tried to assassinate Premier Pol Pot of Cambodia. In the spring of 1977, Cambodia began to make raids into Vietnam from the Parrot's Beak. By December, the Vietnamese had had enough, and the invasion began.

About one year after Vietnamese troops moved into Cambodia—in December 1978 and early 1979—Cambodian rebels, aided by thousands of Vietnamese soldiers, defeated the Cambodian army. A new government friendly to Vietnam was set up, and the Vietnamese army remained in control of large areas of Cambodia. Then, in an announced attempt "to teach Vietnam a lesson," China attacked Vietnam along its northern border. The former Soviet Union came to the rescue of Vietnam by supplying it with arms. After a brief period of warfare, the Chinese troops withdrew.

In December 1978, Pol Pot and his army were driven out of Cambodia into Thailand. The Vietnamese occupied all of Cambodia and set up a government in Cambodia friendly to Vietnam. Pol Pot asked Prince Sihanouk for his support. Sihanouk agreed, saying, "We have to choose between letting the Vietnamese colonize Cambodia and working with Pol Pot and the Khmer Rouge."

In early 1983, a rebellion broke out in Cambodia against the Vietnamese-supported government. It continued into 1985. In March 1985, the rebels were badly defeated and forced to retreat into Thailand.

When the Vietnamese chased the rebels into Thailand, battles were fought between Vietnamese and Thai soldiers. The Vietnamese left Thailand, but at the end of 1986 the situation in the area was still dangerous. The Vietnamese remained in control of the Cambodian government, and their army still occupied Cambodia.

In the period between 1986 and 1989, the situation improved. The Vietnamese began a slow withdrawal of troops from Cambodia, and by September 1989 Vietnam announced that all its troops were out of the country. Despite this announcement, it has been reported by outside observers that Vietnamese soldiers still aid the existing government.

Recent Efforts to Achieve Peace

As the Vietnamese withdrew, fighting continued between a loose coalition of Khmer Rouge and non-Communist groups led by Prince Sihanouk on one side, and government forces on the other. Results of the fighting have not been decisive. Attempts at a peaceful settlement were made by Thailand (1988), Indonesia and France (1989), and Japan (1990). None was successful.

In late 1990, however, the five permanent members of the Security Council of the United Nations proposed a full settlement. The United Nations would supervise a cease-fire and run the government until elections could be held. In May 1991, limited agreement by all parties was reached at the United Nations and a truce was proclaimed.

In early July of 1991, progress toward the settlement of the 12-year-old civil war occurred. The Vietnamese-supported government of Prime Minister Han Sen and the three rival resistance groups—the Communist Khmer Rouge, the non-Communist followers of former Prime Minister Son Sann, and the supporters of Prince Sihanouk—accepted an unconditional cease-fire and an end to all foriegn arms shipments. A 12-member Supreme National Council made up of the four groups agreed to meet again to begin work on electoral rules and a new constitution.

Summary
of
Key Ideas

Southeast Asia

A.   Geographic and climatic features have influenced the lives of the peoples of Southeast Asia.

   1. Southeast Asia is the area to the south of China and to the east of India.

   2. It can be divided into two regions—the mainland and the islands.

   3. Southeast Asia lies on either side of the equator.

   4. The people of Southeast Asia live mainly in the river valleys.

   5. All of the countries in the area have similar temperatures and climate. Seasons are mainly wet or dry.

   6. Altitude has an important effect on both temperature and climate.

   7. Because of its history and location, Southeast Asia has been a battleground.

   8. Geographic features restrict travel and communication among the various parts of Southeast Asia.

   9. Development of strong tribal and regional consciousness is a result in part of mountainous terrain and dense jungles.

   10. The rhythm of the monsoon determines the patterns of economic activity.

   11. Because of the monsoons, rice agriculture has become the main economic activity.

B.   Outside forces have influenced the history and culture of Southeast Asia.

   1. The history and culture of Southeast Asia have been greatly influenced by India and China.

   2. Southeast Asia has traditionally been part of important trade routes between the Indian and Pacific oceans.

   3. Rich resources have attracted foreign interest in the area.

   4. In different time periods, great kingdoms developed and declined due to outside influences.

   5. With the exception of Thailand, all Southeast Asian countries have been under the control of European powers.

   6. The Europeans found Southeast Asia a culturally advanced area.

7. The Europeans were responsible for certain progress. Their negative accomplishments in the region are also apparent.

8. Nationalistic movements based on anticolonialism and anti-European domination began soon after colonial rule was set up.

9. World War II played an important role in the achievement of nationalist hopes for independence.

10. The Vietnam War focused worldwide attention on Southeast Asia.

C. **The societies of Southeast Asia represent a variety of social classes, ethnic and racial groups, religious faiths, nationalities, traditions, and languages.**

1. Many groups of people have moved from the interior of Asia to settle in Southeast Asia.

2. Muslims, Indians, and Chinese have influenced cultural and social developments.

3. Buddhist and Islamic religious teachings provide systems of values and ways of life for most of Southeast Asia.

4. Art, music, architecture, and the dance have been influenced by Indian and Chinese cultures.

5. Most people live in villages, where society tends to change slowly.

6. The extended family structure is found in most of the area.

7. Serious problems of health, education, and welfare exist.

8. Traditional values, thoughts, and actions are often in contrast and even in conflict with Western culture.

9. In the past 15 years, more and more people of Southeast Asia have moved from the countryside to the cities.

D. **The independent countries of Southeast Asia have been concerned with political stability and economic development.**

1. After independence, some Southeast Asian governments followed Western, liberal ideas. After some disappointments, a swing away from democratic practices occurred.

2. Inexperience in national self-government, economic underdevelopment, and involvement in the Cold War complicated the search for stability.

3. Monarchy, military dictatorship, and dictatorship by Communist groups dominate many Southeast Asian governments.

4. Many powerful nations are drawn into the affairs of Southeast Asia because of its instability, economic underdevelopment, and location.

5. The area has had many political revolutions.

6. Southeast Asia has many important natural resources. However, much of the mineral wealth has been used for the advantage of the colonial powers and little for the people of Southeast Asia.

7. Most people live on a bare subsistence level.

8. Rice has a tremendous influence on the economy of the region.

9. Regional cooperation on such projects as the Mekong River Plan offers possibilities for economic development.

10. The governments of Southeast Asia have used both capitalistic and socialistic methods of developing their nations.

11. Some Southeast Asian countries have developed thriving economies and prosperity by the use of a free-market economy.

12. Vietnam, Cambodia, and Laos have achieved only limited recovery from the devastation caused by the Vietnam War.

13. In Cambodia, civil war and occupation of parts of the country by Vietnam have increased the problems that the nation faces.

14. Struggles to achieve greater democracy and social reform have occurred in Thailand, Myanmar (Burma), Cambodia, and the Philippines in the past decade.

UNIT VI

Exercises and Questions

Vocabulary

Directions: Match the words in Column A with the correct meaning in Column B.

Column A

1. source
2. diversity
3. region
4. stable
5. ethnic
6. potential
7. isolated
8. adapt
9. remote
10. primitive
11. exploit

Column B

(a) characteristic of the earliest times, simple
(b) to change something to meet one's needs
(c) distant
(d) set apart from others
(e) what can be, but has not yet, come into being
(f) area
(g) variety; difference
(h) firm; steady
(i) place where something begins or comes from
(j) of a national or religious group
(k) to make unfair use of other people's things

Completion

Directions: Complete the following sentences:

1. Goods that are sent in trade from your country to another are called _____ .

2. Southeast Asian religious temples are called _____ .

3. The dried meat of the coconut is called _____ .

4. A deposit of mud and loose soil that is washed down a river is called _____ .

5. The winds that greatly affect life in Southeast Asia are called the _____ .

6. The control of a weak nation by a strong one is called _____ .

7. Soldiers who are not part of a regular army are called _____ .

8. A union of a group of states is called a _____ .

9. The method used to farm on the slope of a mountain or volcano is called _____ .

10. In the Buddhist religion, good works are called _____ .

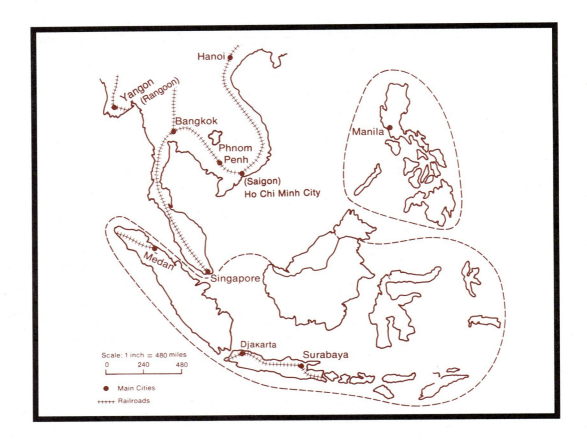

Scale: 1 inch = 480 miles
0   240   480

● Main Cities
+++++ Railroads

Map Exercise

Directions: In each of the following you have four choices. Choose the only correct answer.

1. Which of the following cities is located on a *gulf*?
   (a) Manila   (b) Phnom Penh   (c) Hanoi   (d) Bangkok

2. Which of the following cities is on an *island*?
   (a) Manila   (b) Phnom Penh   (c) Hanoi   (d) Bangkok

3. Which of the following cities is near a *lake*?
   (a) Manila   (b) Phnom Penh   (c) Hanoi   (d) Bangkok

4. Which of the following cities is on a *peninsula*?
   (a) Manila   (b) Singapore   (c) Medan   (d) Djakarta

5. If you went from Hanoi to Ho Chi Minh City, you would probably travel in which direction?
   (a) North   (b) South   (c) East   (d) West

6. Ho Chi Minh City is located to the *east* of
   (a) Hanoi.   (b) Yangon.   (c) Manila.   (d) Djakarta.

7. The distance from Singapore to Djakarta is about
   (a) 250 miles.   (b) 500 miles.   (c) 1,000 miles.   (d) 1,250 miles.

8. Which of the following are over 1,000 miles from each other?
   - (a) Hanoi and Manila
   - (b) Hanoi and Ho Chi Minh City
   - (c) Bangkok and Singapore
   - (d) Djakarta and Surabaya

9. Which of the following cities are *not* connected to each other by the railroad?
   - (a) Hanoi and Ho Chi Minh City
   - (b) Djakarta and Surabaya
   - (c) Yangon and Bangkok
   - (d) Phnom Penh and Ho Chi Minh City

10. From information on the map *only*, which of the following statements is *true?*
    - (a) The distance from Medan to Djakarta is greater than the distance from Yangon to Manila.
    - (b) The railroad lines were built only in a west to east direction.
    - (c) Most of this area is made up of islands and peninsulas.
    - (d) Most of the islands are in the northern section of the area.

Chart Analysis

Directions: Using the chart on page 502, answer the following questions. Of the four choices choose only the correct one.

1. To which of the following nations did the United States export more than it imported in 1988–1989?

   (a) Indonesia   (b) Malaysia   (c) the Philippines   (d) Thailand

2. Which of the following nations is not a major exporter of wood products?

   (a) Myanmar (Burma)   (b) Indonesia   (c) Laos   (d) Malaysia

3. According to the chart, Southeast Asia traded most with
   - (a) the United States
   - (b) Japan
   - (c) other countries of Southeast Asia
   - (d) Western Europe

4. The word *export* means
   - (a) to trade
   - (b) to bring goods into a country
   - (c) to send goods to another country
   - (d) to sell more goods than are bought

5. One conclusion you might make from the information in this chart is that
   - (a) The United States has a favorable trade balance with Southeast Asia.
   - (b) Vietnam has a very serious trade deficit with the United States.
   - (c) Malaysia has a very serious trade deficit with the United States.
   - (d) Thailand exports teak and tea to the United States.

Multiple Choice

Directions: Select the letter of the correct answer.

1. The geographic position of Southeast Asia has influenced its development in that
   (a) it is set apart from the rest of the world.
   (b) it is a natural area for the development of industry.
   (c) it has forced Southeast Asian countries to conquer neighboring lands.
   (d) it has made the area an important trade center between the Indian and Pacific oceans.

2. Rivers are said to have the opposite effect of mountains because
   (a) rivers are great sources of mineral wealth, and mountains are not.
   (b) mountains keep people apart, while rivers bring people together.
   (c) mountains have good soil, while river valleys do not.
   (d) mountains are great sources of natural resources, while rivers are not.

3. Which of the following is *not* true of Southeast Asian geography?
   (a) Southeast Asia has an extremely long coastline.
   (b) Southeast Asia is a region of islands and peninsulas.
   (c) Mountains and seas help to unite Southeast Asia.
   (d) Several important cities are located near the river deltas.

4. To get away from heat in the areas near the equator you would go to the
   (a) low coastal lands.
   (b) highlands.
   (c) river valleys.
   (d) interior flatlands.

5. Houses in the coastal lowlands of Southeast Asia are often built on raised platforms supported by wooden poles for
   (a) prevention of earthquake damage.
   (b) protection from animals and flooding.
   (c) protection from tidal waves.
   (d) proper air circulation.

6. In recent years, the mountain peoples of Southeast Asia have been fighting the governments of their countries because these peoples
   (a) are Communists.
   (b) feel they are not given equal rights.
   (c) believe they are superior to the lowland peoples.
   (d) are not allowed to trade with the lowland peoples.

7. Most of the people living in Southeast Asia today are probably descendants of people who
   (a) came from other places in Asia.
   (b) were the first settlers in Southeast Asia.
   (c) came from the island archipelagos of Southeast Asia.
   (d) were not Asians.

8. The peoples of the hills practice slash-and-burn farming because
   (a) Western advisers said it is the best method.
   (b) the area is cleared, and the ashes provide fertilizer.
   (c) cities can be built on the cleared land.
   (d) these peoples produce too much food to be used by their government.

9. The peoples of the plains tend to regard the peoples of the hills as
   (a) interesting neighbors.
   (b) backward people.
   (c) dangerous enemies.
   (d) crop destroyers.

10. Which of the following is a major concept of Southeast Asian history?
    (a) All Southeast Asian nations have developed the same culture.
    (b) Southeast Asia has felt the impact of many cultures.
    (c) Chinese culture has dominated all of Southeast Asia.
    (d) Southeast Asia has been completely Europeanized.

11. The movement of people from the north to the south into Southern Asia was due to
    (a) the desire to move into a warmer climate.
    (b) the desire to increase trade.
    (c) the direction of the river valleys through the area.
    (d) no apparent reason.

12. The spread of Indian culture in Southeast Asia was accomplished through
    (a) the spread of Buddhism.
    (b) contacts with Indian merchants.
    (c) the use of Sanskrit as the written language.
    (d) all of these

13. Which of the following groups were *not* most influenced by the Indians?
    (a) Khmers   (b) Thais   (c) Cambodians   (d) Vietnamese

14. The Khmer Empire is best remembered for its
    (a) development of mathematic and scientific knowledge.
    (b) conquest of Southeast Asia and Indonesia.
    (c) driving out the Chinese from Vietnam.
    (d) great temple building.

15. Which of the following is *not* an important part of Buddhism?
    (a) reincarnation
    (b) the caste system
    (c) merit
    (d) Nirvana

16. Which of the following is *not* a reason why Europeans became interested in Southeast Asia?
    (a) The Europeans wanted to help extend native dictatorships.
    (b) The Europeans were interested in spreading Christianity.
    (c) The Europeans wanted to gain control of the spice trade.
    (d) The Europeans became interested in the rich minerals of the area.

17. The first Europeans to become involved in Southeast Asia were the
    (a) Portuguese.   (b) Spanish.   (c) English.   (d) French.

18. The French gained control of which of the following areas?
    (a) Burma, Malaya, Borneo
    (b) Indonesia, Thailand, Vietnam
    (c) Laos, Cambodia, Vietnam
    (d) Cambodia, Thailand, Burma

19. One major effect of colonialism in Southeast Asia was the
    (a) introduction of rice cultivation into the region.
    (b) establishment of Hinduism in the region.
    (c) introduction of rubber trees into the region.
    (d) rapid industrialization of the region.

20. Many of the languages spoken in Southeast Asia are the result of
    (a) the work of Spanish missionaries.
    (b) migration and colonial settlements.
    (c) years of French domination of the region.
    (d) centuries of Chinese rule.

21. The only nation that kept its independence from European domination was
    (a) Burma.   (b) Thailand.   (c) Indonesia.   (d) Laos.

22. Nationalists are people who want
    (a) a Communist country.
    (b) to conquer other countries.
    (c) to govern themselves.
    (d) petroleum and other natural resources.

23. Sukarno was the leader of which of the following nationalists?
    (a) Burmese   (b) Thai   (c) Vietnamese   (d) Indonesians

24. The Japanese attacked Southeast Asia because they wanted
    (a) to conquer the United States.
    (b) raw materials and markets for goods.
    (c) to test their military strength.
    (d) "Asia for the Asians."

25. Which of the following was *not* the result of the Japanese occupation of Southeast Asia?
    (a) Western prestige was destroyed.
    (b) Nationalist armies were trained.
    (c) Communists took over the areas.
    (d) Top positions in the government were filled by Southeast Asians.

26. Which pair of countries gained independence peacefully?
    (a) Burma and the Philippines
    (b) Indonesia and Vietnam
    (c) Burma and Malaya
    (d) the Philippines and Indonesia

27. The leader of the Vietnamese nationalist movement was
    (a) Lon Nol. (b) Ho Chi Minh. (c) Mongkut. (d) Sihanouk.

28. The word *partitioned* means
    (a) divided. (b) added. (c) combined. (d) subtracted.

29. Fighting in Vietnam, Laos, and Cambodia has caused millions of people to
    (a) join the army in these countries.
    (b) become members of the Communist party.
    (c) oppose all democratic governments.
    (d) flee to other countries for protection and safety.

30. Almost 65 percent of the labor force in Southeast Asia is engaged in
    (a) agriculture. (b) manufacturing. (c) mining. (d) fishing.

31. Crops most likely to be grown on tropical lowlands are
    (a) rice and sugar.
    (b) tea and coffee.
    (c) wheat and corn.
    (d) soybeans and barley.

32. Which of the following products would most likely be found in a forest?
    (a) teak (b) cotton (c) cement (d) rice

33. In Southeast Asia the continued importance of the monsoons shows that this region is
    (a) becoming a major industrial area.
    (b) dependent on traditional farming methods.
    (c) rich in natural resources that can easily be developed.
    (d) fast becoming an urban society.

34. Subsistence farming means that farmers
    (a) produce more than enough for themselves and their families.
    (b) raise many kinds of crops.
    (c) use scientifically advanced methods of agriculture.
    (d) raise just enough for their own use.

35. Which of the following groups of products is important in Southeast Asia?
    (a) rice, copra, oil palms
    (b) rice, wheat, copra
    (c) rice, mangoes, cotton
    (d) wheat, kapok, tobacco

36. The most fertile soil in Southeast Asia is found
    (a) on high plateaus.
    (b) in the river valleys.
    (c) on mountain slopes.
    (d) near the ocean.

37. Indonesian farmers are unable to grow enough food for the people because
    (a) the country has little fertile land.
    (b) the climate is not suitable for the growing of rice.
    (c) the country has a rapidly growing population.
    (d) the farmers cannot afford to buy modern farm machinery.

38. Most metal ores of Southeast Asia are exported rather than smelted down because
    (a) a higher price is paid for the ores.
    (b) Southeast Asians have never learned to smelt metals.
    (c) there is a scarcity of good-quality coal.
    (d) Southeast Asians are too lazy to build plants.

39. The smallest nation of Southeast Asia is
    (a) Laos.   (b) Cambodia.   (c) Singapore.   (d) Thailand.

40. Since gaining its independence, Singapore has moved from an economy based on rubber plantations and shipping to an economy based on
    (a) electronic products and oil refining.
    (b) rice cultivation.
    (c) handicrafts and tire manufacture.
    (d) military equipment manufacture.

41. Singapore's economic success is based on
    (a) the government's management of all industries.
    (b) the government's control of the banking system.
    (c) the abundance of natural resources found in Singapore.
    (d) a capable work force and government policies that favor business.

42. In recent years Malaysia, the Philippines, Singapore, and Thailand have become more industrialized because they have
    (a) imported skilled workers from China.
    (b) been willing to learn from industrialized nations in other regions.
    (c) refused to accept foreign technology.
    (d) imposed heavy taxes to pay for industrial development.

43. In addition to promoting the lowering of trade barriers in Southeast Asia, the members of ASEAN
    (a) share products during shortages.
    (b) exchange manufactured goods.
    (c) share a common currency.
    (d) work together on defense matters.

44. Travel and transportation are difficult in rural areas of Southeast Asia because
    (a) none of the countries in the region can afford to build roads.
    (b) heavy rains often wash out roads.
    (c) there are few animals to pull the heavy carts used to move goods.
    (d) most countries in the region have laws that limit land travel.

Thought Questions

1. How have differences among the peoples of Southeast Asia affected the situation in the region today?

2. How does topography affect the climate of Southeast Asia?

3. How does climate affect the lives of the people in Southeast Asia?

4. How is life in a Southeast Asian village affected by the environment?

5. "Buddhism is more than a religion. It is a way of life." Explain.

6. How did geography affect the historical development of Southeast Asia?

7. How did spices change the history of Southeast Asia?

8. (a) How did the West aid the development of Southeast Asia?
   (b) Why do Southeast Asians dislike the West?

9. Why was the Japanese occupation (1941–1945) important in Southeast Asian history?

10. How have the governments of Southeast Asia tried to solve their problems of underdevelopment?

11. "Cultural diversity is an important factor in Southeast Asia." Explain.

12. (a) What are monsoons?
    (b) How do the monsoons affect the lives of the people of Southeast Asia?

13. What were the factors that encouraged nationalism in each of the following areas?
    (a) Indonesia   (b) Vietnam   (c) Thailand   (d) Myanmar (Burma)
    (e) the Philippines

14. "The road to survival in Southeast Asia follows many paths in foreign policy." Describe the paths followed by each of these nations:
    (a) Laos   (b) Cambodia   (c) Myanmar (Burma)   (d) Indonesia

15. (a) Why did the United States become involved in Vietnam?
    (b) What were the terms of the peace settlemen?

16. (a) How have the Chinese and Indians influenced life in Southeast Asia?
    (b) What differences in life-styles exist in Southeast Aisa, China, and India?

17. "Europeans made many contributions to improve life in Southeast Asia." Explain why you agree or disagree with this statement.

18. "ASEAN is important to the development of Southeast Asia." Explain.

19. Why were the North Vietnamese and Viet Cong able to take over the government of South Vietnam?

20. How would you describe the situation that now exists in Cambodia and Laos?

Developing Answers to Regents-Type Essay Questions

Helpful Hints

In developing your answers to the essays be sure to:

1. Include specific factual information and evidence whenever possible.

2. Answer the question being asked; do not go off on tangents.

3. Keep these general definitions in mind:
    (a) *discuss* means "to make observations about something using facts, reasoning, and argument; to present in some detail."
    (b) *describe* means "to illustrate something in words or to tell about."
    (c) *show* means "to point out, to set forth clearly an idea or position by stating it and giving data that support it."
    (d) *explain* means "to make plain or understandable; to give reasons for or causes of; to show the logical development or relationship."

Sample Essay Questions

1. The development of an area is often greatly influenced by its geographic or climatic features.

    Geographic and Climatic Features

Rivers	Deserts	Mountains
Natural Resources	Monsoons	Jungles

    (a) Select *two* of the features listed above. State how each feature has affected the history or culture of Southeast Asia.
    (b) Base this answer on your Part (a) answer. Write an essay showing how the development of an area can be greatly influenced by its geographic and climatic features.

2. Geographic factors have influenced the development of many nations. The pairs of nations in Southeast Asia listed below have been influenced by geographic factors.

    Pairs of Nations

Indonesia-Thailand	The Philippines-Malaysia
Myanmar (Burma)-Vietnam	Laos-Singapore

    For each pair, use specific examples to show how geographic factors have had similar or different effects on the economic, political, or cultural development of the two nations.

3. Religions have strongly influenced the political, economic, and social aspects of various societies.

Religions of Southeast Asia

Roman Catholicism	Islam
Hinduism	Buddhism

For *each* religion:
(a) Identify *one* of its major beliefs
(b) Discuss *one* political, economic, or social influence the religion has had on a particular society of Southeast Asia in any specific period of history.

4. Developing nations in Southeast Asia have been faced with many problems that have restricted their economic development.

Problems

Foreign Control	Poverty	Lack of Natural Resources
Overpopulation	Topography	One-Crop Economies

For *each* of the problems listed:
(a) Identify one nation in Southeast Asia that has faced the problem.
(b) Describe how the condition restricted that nation's economic development.
(c) Describe one attempt that has been made by that nation to overcome the problem.

5. A society's beliefs and values are often reflected in its art forms.

Art Forms

Music	Literature	Dress	Architecture
Dance	Theater	Sculpture	Myths and Legends

For *each* art form, describe how it reflects the ideas and values of a society in Southeast Asia. You may choose a different society for each art form.

(Note: Since Southeast Asia has been greatly influenced by India, China, and Europe, you might wish to review those areas' art forms.)

6. Nations have achieved their independence in a variety of ways.

Nations of Southeast Asia

Indonesia	Vietnam	Myanmar (Burma)
The Philippines	Malaysia	Singapore

For *each* of the above nations:
(a) Describe the conditions before the nation became independent.
(b) Describe how the nation achieved its independence.

Puzzle

Directions: Place the words below in the proper place in the puzzle.

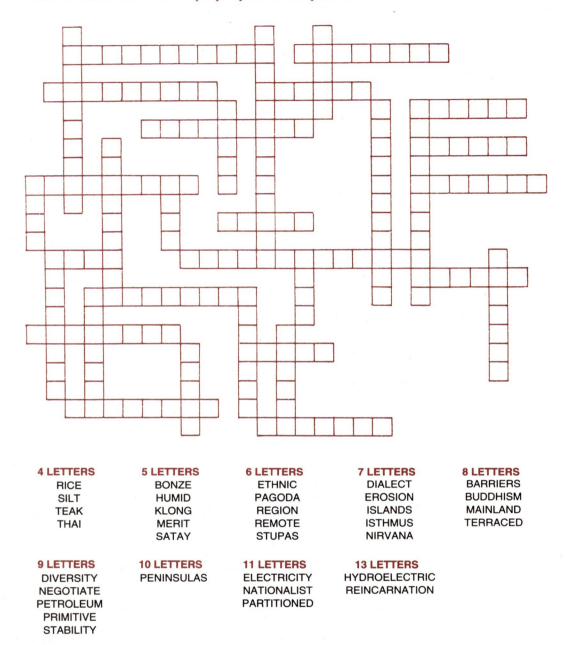

4 LETTERS	5 LETTERS	6 LETTERS	7 LETTERS	8 LETTERS
RICE	BONZE	ETHNIC	DIALECT	BARRIERS
SILT	HUMID	PAGODA	EROSION	BUDDHISM
TEAK	KLONG	REGION	ISLANDS	MAINLAND
THAI	MERIT	REMOTE	ISTHMUS	TERRACED
	SATAY	STUPAS	NIRVANA	

9 LETTERS	10 LETTERS	11 LETTERS	13 LETTERS
DIVERSITY	PENINSULAS	ELECTRICITY	HYDROELECTRIC
NEGOTIATE		NATIONALIST	REINCARNATION
PETROLEUM		PARTITIONED	
PRIMITIVE			
STABILITY			

Shwe Dagon temple in Yangon (Rangoon), One of the largest Buddhist complexes in the world, it is a place for religious and social activities.

One of the about 2,000 remaining Buddhist pagodas in the city of Pagan, Myanmar (Burma).

JAPAN AND KOREA

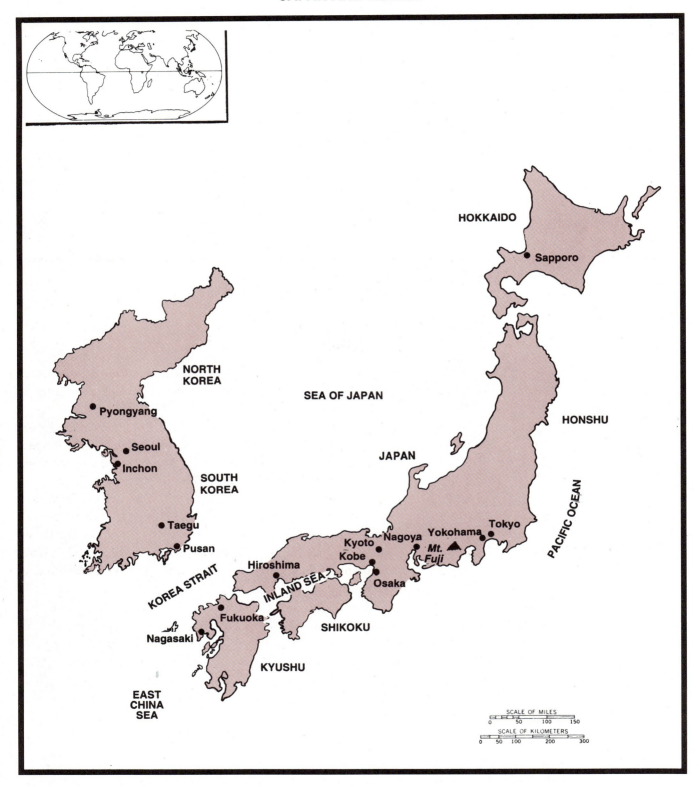

HOKKAIDO

Sapporo

NORTH
KOREA

SEA OF JAPAN

Pyongyang

HONSHU

Seoul

Inchon

JAPAN

SOUTH
KOREA

PACIFIC OCEAN

Taegu

Tokyo

Pusan

Nagoya

Yokohama

Kyoto

Kobe

Mt.
Fuji

Hiroshima

KOREA STRAIT

INLAND SEA

Osaka

Fukuoka

SHIKOKU

Nagasaki

KYUSHU

EAST
CHINA
SEA

SCALE OF MILES

0   50   100   150

SCALE OF KILOMETERS

0   50   100   200   300

530 Japan and Korea

UNIT VII Japan and Korea

Japan—Land and Climate

The name Japan is not used by the Japanese. They call their country Nihon, or Nippon, meaning "Land of the Rising Sun." Their flag, a bright red ball or sun on a white background, is easily recognized.

The Japanese people believe that the god Izanagi stood on the floating bridge of heaven and looked down on the sea below. In his hand he held a jewel-tipped spear. He dipped the sword into the ocean and began to stir the waters. When he removed the spear from the ocean, drops of salt water fell from its tip and formed a group of islands.

The Japanese island group is located off the east coast of Asia. It is part of the "Fire Rim of the Pacific," a great chain of volcanoes lying along the west coast of the Americas and then curving down the eastern shores of Asia. There are about 3,400 islands in all. These islands are scattered over a large area. Japan is shaped like a dragon. The head is the island of Hokkaido, the body Honshu and Shikoku, and the tail Kyushu. The outermost tips of the island chain are separated by almost 1,400 miles.

Most of the 3,400 islands are small and useless. There are four main islands. Hokkaido, in the north, has poor land and a hard winter climate. This island is still Japan's frontier, as the West was to the United States in the 1870s. Just south of Hokkaido is the main island of Honshu. Tokyo and the other great cities of modern Japan lie on its southeastern and southern coastal plains. Southwest of Honshu is the island of Kyushu, which is second in importance to Honshu. Shikoku, the southern island, is separated from Honshu by the calm waters of the Inland Sea.

Topography

Japan is a rugged, mountainous group of islands. The mountains rise from the floor of the ocean, five or six miles deep (25,000–30,000 feet), to a height of over two miles in

Japan is a rugged and mountainous land. Mt. Aso, an active volcano on the
island of Kyushu.

Labe Nojiri on the Josin Etsu Plateau.

some places. Mt. Fuji (Fujiyama) reaches 12,500 feet into the sky. The distance from coast to coast is less than 200 miles anywhere in the islands.

The islands, by their very shape, ensured (made certain) that communication and transportation overland would always be a problem. Almost 80 percent of the land surface is mountainous. Nearly 600 mountains are 6,000 feet in altitude or more. The remaining 20 percent is very **arable** (good for farming) land divided into three main areas. These three great areas of fertile land lie along the eastern coast of the island of Honshu. The largest is the Kanto plain. The others are the Nobi and Kinai plains. The struggle for the control of these lands is the key to Japanese history. (Why do you think this is so?) Throughout Japan's existence these plains have attracted the Japanese people. Today the capital, Tokyo, and other great cities, Nagoya and Osaka, are in the center of these areas.

The Kinai plain, by its position in the center of Honshu, has tended to become the hub (center) of Japan. Until modern times the capital of Japan was found in the Kinai (the former capitals were at Nara and Kyoto). To the Japanese, the Kinai area has been known as the "Home Provinces."

Japan has many short and swift rivers. Hundreds of streams race from the highlands to the sea. The longest river, Shinaino, is only 229 miles long. Because most of the rivers are **navigable** (able to be sailed on) for only a few miles, the streams have little importance for transportation. They have been barriers (blocks) to travel and trade. However, throughout Japan's history the rivers have provided water for irrigating the rice fields. Today the rivers are important for the production of electric power for homes and industry.

WORLD EARTHQUAKE AND VOLCANIC REGIONS

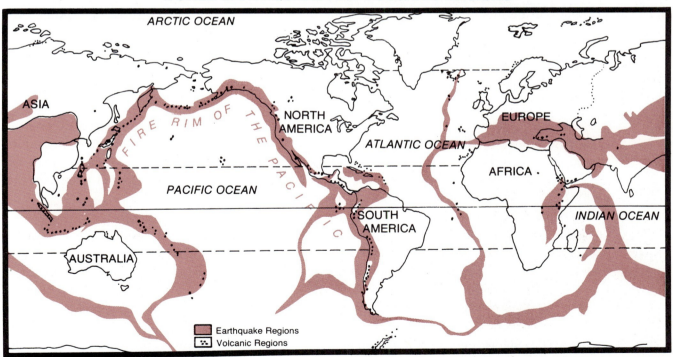

Japan is located in a volcano and earthquake prone area known as the "Fire Rim of the Pacific."

The Effect of Topography

The Japanese, like all other peoples, have been affected in large part by the land in which they live. Japan's location, climate, and natural resources have influenced its culture and history and have helped to give the Japanese culture and history specific direction.

Japan is actually a smaller country in geographic size than the number of square miles would suggest. (The United States is 25 times larger than Japan.) The whole country is so mountainous that less than 20 percent of the land is level enough for farming.

Though the mountains present magnificent scenic views, many of these mountains are active volcanoes. These volcanoes and earthquakes cause a serious problem for Japan.

As we have already learned, Japan is on the western edge of the "Fire Rim of the Pacific." This rim of volcanoes and earthquake-prone areas runs along the west coast of North America and South America to Alaska and then curves southward down the east coast of Asia. The earthquakes are caused by the movement of large plates that lie under the surface of the earth. As the plates move, they slide past each other or bump into each other causing land to rise or sink. Sudden violent movement of the surface of the earth is an earthquake. Movements of the earth can create mountains and make existing mountains grow. Japan's mountains are growing.

Japan is also located near a trench that is one of the deepest parts of the Pacific Ocean. The earth's crust in and around Japan seems to be moving in two directions. The mountains are rising and at the same time the ocean floor is falling. The result is about 1,500 earthquakes a year in Japan. If an earthquake occurs beneath the ocean, it sometimes sets off a tidal wave, called a *tsunami* by the Japanese. Tsunami hit Japan's coastal areas two or three times a year, causing great damage.

It is not surprising that the Japanese look at their mountains with both love and fear. Japanese poets, authors, and painters write and show the beauty, ruggedness and charm of the mountains. At the same time, they write of the destructive force that results from nature.

Fear of earthquakes has greatly affected Japanese architecture. Until the late 1960s there were no skyscrapers in Japan. Since then, however, the Japanese have built skyscrapers that are expected to survive the most severe earthquakes.

The Effect on Culture

Despite its geography, which encouraged disunity and the development of differences, unity and homogeneity (mixed into one) did develop in Japan. As early as the 7th century, the Japanese saw themselves as a single people, living in a unified nation. They were probably influenced by the example of a united Chinese empire already close to 1,000 years old. This view has remained to the present day.

The Effects on Government and Communication

The division of the country caused by its geography led to the development of localized power bases, or a decentralized, feudal pattern of government from the 6th to the 19th century. Topographical factors certainly influenced the division of Japan before the Meiji Restoration (1868) into 68 provinces. These provinces were controlled by local rulers as their own small "countries." It is of interest to note that more than 90 percent of the borders of the 47 prefectures (local government divisions) into which Japan is now divided still follow precisely the mountain ridge boundaries of the earlier provinces.

Until the building of railroads and paved highways in the past 100 years, communication by land within the country was difficult.

The Importance of the Sea

As an island nation, Japan has always relied heavily upon the sea. Its long, irregular coastline makes possible the growth of good harbors, such as Tokyo-Yokohama, Nagoya, Kobe, and Osaka. Smaller harbors serve the needs of hundreds of fishing villages that dot the shores of the islands and that have made possible Japan's development into the leading fishing nation in the world. Fishing is an important industry in Japan and provides many jobs. Fish make up a large part of the diet of most Japanese. The main highway of Japan is the great Inland Sea. In addition to being the main avenue of trade within Japan, the Inland Sea serves as a trade route for foreign trade.

The sea has served Japan in another way—as an effective barrier between the nation and the rest of the world. The Japanese islands are 100 miles across the sea from Asia at the southern tip of Korea. Therefore, it has been easy for the Japanese to adapt from Asia what they wanted and to keep out what they did not want. In the entire history of Japan there was only one case of foreign invasion and, incidentally, only one case of a Japanese attempt to conquer an area outside of Japan before the modern period of Japanese history. Apparently, barriers work both ways.

Climate

Like most parts of the United States, Japan has four seasons. In northern Japan, the climate is a humid continental one. Summers are hot, and winters are cold and long, with January temperatures well below freezing. In the rest of Japan, the winters are usually mild, with many sunny days. Summers are usually mild to warm, with the average summer temperature 60°F (16°C) in Hokkaido, 70°F (20°C) around Tokyo, and in the 80s in Shikoku. In the subtropical south, the heat can be unpleasant because it is very humid and there is a great deal of rain. This heavy rainfall is important for rice cultivation.

Japan has always relied heavily upon the sea. The Inland Sea, shown here, is Japan's main avenue of trade within the country and also serves as a route for foreign trade.

Japan is affected by the **monsoons** (winds). In the summer, the monsoons blow from the ocean and cool the eastern side of Japan. In the winter, the winds blow in the opposite direction, from the Asian mainland. These winter winds bring cold weather to northern Japan. The mountains prevent the cold weather and snow from reaching the eastern and southern parts of Japan.

Another factor that influences climate is ocean currents. The warm Japanese Current, or Black Stream, which moderates the winter climate and warms it in summer, flows as far north as Tokyo Bay. To the north of Tokyo, in Honshu and around Hokkaido, the cold Oyoshio, or Kurile Current, chills the northern coasts.

Japan is often hit by **typhoons**. These storms, which arise far to the south, frequently strike the densely populated eastern coast of Japan with great force. They come annually (yearly) in late summer and early fall. They are identical in nature to the hurricanes that come to the eastern coast of the United States. Typhoons, however, strike Japan more often and with greater destructiveness to life and property. Floods and land slides are often started as a result of the storm. Great tidal waves, which rush in from the ocean, also cause tremendous damage and loss of life.

The Effects of Climate

Japan's climate does not permit year-round growing seasons. To survive the colder months, food surpluses have always had to be built up by hard and concentrated work during the growing season. Of utmost importance is the fact that daytime rest periods or a leisurely work pace have never been necessary to escape the midday heat. (The same situation is true for Japan's neighbors China and Korea.) Climatic and geographic conditions, a century of traditional behavior, and the necessity of supporting a large and continually growing population have combined to produce what may be the strictest work ethic in the world among the Japanese people.

Because of the series of great storms called typhoons, the Japanese have become accustomed to natural catastrophies and they accept them with great resilience (ability to bounce back). This sort of fatalism might even be called the "typhoon mentality," with volcanic eruptions and earthquakes adding to it.

The People and Their Language

The People

Organized human life emerged later in Japan than in other parts of Asia. The Japanese people are a mixture of racial stocks that came from mainland Asia. The descendants of the first group of settlers still live in Japan. They are the Ainu, who are Caucasian and live on Hokkaido.

The first inhabitants were hunters and fishermen. They were followed by people from mainland Asia who knew how to farm rice. These later arrivals are the ancestors of today's Japanese.

Most Japanese have straight black hair and dark, almond-shaped eyes, and are shorter in height than present-day Westerners. Their skin color ranges from fair to yellowish to brown. The Japanese strongly resemble the Northern Chinese and Koreans, since both of these groups are among those who moved from the mainland to Japan.

Japan's population is one of the most homogeneous of any population of the major countries in the world. Japanese leaders have stated that Japan has no minority groups. In fact, all but a very small percentage of the population is of the same ethnic origin. Their ancestors have been in Japan for hundreds of years.

Minority Groups

Ainu

Among the few non-Japanese people in the country are the 12,000 Ainu. As you read, the Ainu are fair-skinned and live mainly on the northern island of Hokkaido. They are slowly becoming a part of the mainstream of Japanese culture.

Koreans

More numerous are the Koreans. In 1990, there were about 70,000 Koreans living in Japan. Most came to Japan during World War II (1941–1945) to work in the factories there. However, some Koreans trace their roots in Japan to the period around 1910 when Korea was taken from China by the Japanese, and some Koreans moved to Japan.

In some ways, the Koreans are almost invisible in Japan. They look like the Japanese, and many second-and third-generation Koreans have taken Japanese names and speak Japanese as their native language. Despite this, Koreans suffer discrimination in housing, jobs, and their social lives.

Koreans must register as aliens and must carry alien registration cards with their fingerprints on them at all times. Koreans born in Japan are not automatically citizens of Japan. Japanese citizenship has always been based on bloodlines and ethnic background, but in 1985 Japan's nationality law was changed and Koreans can now become naturalized citizens of Japan.

Burakumin

Another minority group is known as the *burakumin* (hamlet, or small village, people). The burakumin are ethnic Japanese. Originally, they lived in small villages or hamlets. They worked at tanning leather and as butchers, slaughtering cattle. These jobs are considered unclean by Japanese tradition. As a result, the burakumin are, even today, regarded as outcasts, the "untouchables" of Japan, which means that other Japanese will have nothing to do with them. There are between one and three million burakumin in Japan and they are discriminated against in housing, jobs, education, and their social lives. They live in segregated sections in the slums of the big cities of Japan. Although burakumin can pass as ordinary Japanese, the fact that they live in or travel to and from a "ghetto" neighborhood gives their identity away.

The Japanese Language

The Japanese are united by a common spoken and written language. This has made it easier for the Japanese to achieve political and cultural unity more quickly than other Asian nations.

The Japanese language is mainly polysyllabic (most words are composed of several syllables). But Japanese is not difficult to speak and pronounce, and spelling is simpler than English or French. There is no accent on any syllable in a Japanese word; all syllables are stressed equally, with very few exceptions.

The Japanese borrowed their system of writing from the Chinese, adapting it to Japanese needs. (The knowledge of Chinese writing came to Japan from Korea, not directly from China.) For centuries the Japanese had no way to write down their language. The Japanese people memorized events and traditions and passed them on by word of mouth. After a time, through their contacts with China, they discovered the advantages of writing, and began to adopt the Chinese system. In this system, each character stands for an idea or object, rather than a sound, as in the Roman alphabet. However, the Japanese did not accept the Chinese spoken language. The result is that the spoken language of Japan differs greatly from Chinese. For example, "Japan" is written 日本, in Chinese characters. The Chinese pronunciation is "jih-pen," but the two characters are pronounced "ni-hon" (or Nippon) by the Japanese. (日 meaning origin, + 本 meaning sun, = where the sun has its origin, or "Land of the Rising Sun.")

To the Chinese written system the Japanese later added their own written system, based on syllables or tables of syllables called Kana, unlike the English system that is based on individual letters. Written Japanese is ordinarily formed by a combination of Chinese characters, Kanji, and Kana syllables.

The Japanese also use the Roman alphabet for certain limited purposes. Along the railways, for instance, the names of stations are often shown in three systems of writing—Chinese, Kana, and Roman letters. Since all Japanese schoolchildren study English from the seventh grade through high school, such signs are not at all confusing to most riders. It is also important to note that Japan has the highest rate of literacy in Asia and possesses the best-developed educational system.

Religion

Shrines and temples can be found everywhere in Japan. They are the places of worship of Shintoism and Buddhism, the principal religions of the Japanese people. In the last 100 years thousands of Japanese have become Christians. Freedom of religion is guaranteed by the Constitution of 1947, and no particular religion can receive preference over another. In addition, no one religion can be the state religion. This is an important change because before 1945 Shintoism was the state religion.

Shintoism

Shintoism as a religion developed only in Japan. Shinto means "the way of the gods" from two Chinese words—*shin* meaning "good spirits" and *tao* meaning "the way." Shintoism is based on the worship of nature and good spirits called *kami*. This religion has no bible. It is based on the feelings of human beings toward the world around them.

The kami are powers or spirits loosely referred to as gods but they are actually "superior or extraordinary forces." The kami live in shrines, animals, birds, plants, mountains, waterfalls, storms, and in most natural things. There are thousands of them. The light and heat of the sun and the waves of the sea are caused by the power of the kami. These spirits are never looked on with fear but with friendly closeness, love, and thankfulness.

Shinto has no formal prayer book. *Norito* (prayers), in poetic form, are presented by priests at the hundreds of shrines throughout Japan.

The great Kamakura Buddha was built in the 13th century and is made of copper and gold. Buddhism is the main religion of the Japanese people.

Three-storied pagoda of the Kiyomizu Temple in Kyoto was built in the 17th century.

Great Torii (gate) of Itsukushima Shrine. The torii (in the water) is found in front of all Shinto shrines. Before entering the shrine, one must pass through the torii to become purified. Note the stone lanterns in the foreground.

Shinto has three important symbols: a sword which represents the virtue of wisdom and correct action; a string of jewels which represents kindness, generosity, and obedience; and a mirror which stands for truthfulness and reflects all things good and bad. The Japanese believe that without these three basic virtues—wisdom, kindness, and truthfulness—peace, happiness, and a good life cannot exist for individuals or for the nation.

Buddhism

Buddhism is the major religion of Japan today. More than half the people of Japan are Buddhists. Many Japanese practice Buddhism and also follow Shinto custom and ceremony at life-originating events such as births and marriages. However, a Buddhist priest would officiate at a funeral. Buddhism was founded in India 2,500 years ago. It was brought to Japan by the Chinese about 1,500 years ago, and spread rapidly among the nobles and the upper classes. The common people did not accept Buddhism at first because they found it hard to agree with a religion that prohibited the marriage of priests, and that was not light and happy. As Buddhism was adapted to the needs and feelings of the Japanese, more people became Buddhists. New sects, including Zen, made Buddhism Japanese. As a result, thousands embraced the religion.

Zen Buddhism

The Zen sect of Buddhism came to Japan from China in the Kamakura period (1192–1333). The main idea of Zen is to find self-understanding, called *satori* or enlightenment. Believers in Zen feel that prayer and religious worship are a waste of time. Personal character and discipline are important. **Meditation** (thinking) is the main form of worship. The Chinese who brought Buddhism to Japan came to Japan from Korea, not directly from China.

The goal of Zen is to bring the person to satori—to help people go from thinking to knowing. Satori comes to a fortunate few—often in a sudden flash. To develop the proper frame of mind, one must use *koans* (Zen riddles). Here are some examples of *koans*: "What is the sound of one hand clapping?" "What happens to the fist when the hand is open?" When the Zen believer feels that reasonable analysis and logic do not help in finding the answer (for in reality there are no answers), progress toward satori has been made. Zen followers lead a simple life close to nature.

Zen has influenced Japanese education, literature, painting, foreign affairs, history, theater, and many other parts of Japanese life.

Other Religions

Confucianism, the complicated moral code of China, has strongly influenced Japanese thought and behavior. Christianity ranks behind Shintoism and Buddhism. It first came to Japan in the 1500s, but was banned from 1637 to 1873. Since the ban was lifted, many Japanese have decided to become Christians. Today, about 1.5 million Japanese are Christians.

Although Christians make up only about 1 percent of the population, their influence is important. Many Christians are well educated and as a result, they have gained positions of leadership in government and business. (It is interesting to note that there are many excellent private Christian secondary schools and universities in Japan today. Some of these date back to the late 19th and early 20th century.)

Between 10 and 15 percent of the Japanese people belong to what has become known as the "new religions." (Actually several of the "new religions" are over 100 years old.) Most of these religions are related to Shintoism or Buddhism, but there are elements in each **sect** (group) that make them quite different from the traditional Japanese religions.

All of the new religious movements have "charismatic" (colorful, magnetic) leaders in the style of Fundamentalist Christian ministers in the United States. The new religions promise happiness on earth and deliverance from earthly suffering, if members faithfully follow its beliefs. Most of the members of the "new religions" are lower middle class, or poor. Many of them spent their youth in rural-farming areas and moved to the cities for economic reasons. The "new religions" seem to provide a family-like environment for their members.

The largest of the new religious sects is Soka Gakkai which means "value creation society." The Soka Gakkai is part of the Buddhist Nichirin sect. The main ideas of the sect are that Nichirin (a 12th-century reformer of Buddhism) should be honored above Buddha, and all religions are in error except Soka Gakkai. (Soka Gakkai is quite controversial because of this second teaching.)

Religion plays a positive role in Japanese life and culture. It provides people with a common set of customs and traditions. Historically, there has been peaceful coexistence among the various religious groups. Only during the Tokugawa period was there persecution of Christians. Religion has changed with the times, yet it continues to meet the needs of the Japanese people.

Life in Japan

The Blending of the Old and the New

The most important aspect of life in Japan is the blending of the old and the new. Although willing to adopt better ways of doing things from other cultures, the Japanese retain much that is traditional.

In the past, the Japanese glorified the family and discouraged individual action. There were certain approved patterns of behavior. The father was master of the house and demanded complete obedience. Women had a low position in Japanese society. Many changes in Japanese family life occurred after 1945. The absolute power of the Japanese male as head of the household no longer existed.

The Influence of China on Japanese Culture

After many centuries of isolation from the rest of the world, the Japanese began to expand their borders across the Sea of Japan to Korea. In the late 4th century and early 5th century, the Yamoto emperors set up colonies in Korea. Here, for the first time, the Japanese came into contact with Chinese culture that was more advanced than their own. They sent scholars and diplomats to China to study Chinese customs, traditions, and institutions. Koreans and Chinese were invited to Japan to teach the Japanese new skills and to explain their way of life. Many aspects of Chinese culture were adopted by the Japanese. Weaving, silk making, tanning, and metalwork were introduced. The Chinese calendar was also adopted. More importantly, the Chinese system of writing was introduced.

The Japanese made a conscious decision to learn all they could from the Chinese. This period of cultural borrowing lasted from the 500s through the 700s. The best-known scholar of Japan, Edwin O. Reischaur, describes Japan's efforts to learn from the Chinese as the, "first organized program of foreign study in the world."*

The Yamoto emperors sent the best young men to the magnificent Chinese capital of Ch'ang-an (today Sian). There they studied China's arts, sciences, philosophy, laws, architecture, government structure, and even how cities were organized. According to Reischaur, this period of the Tang Dynasty in China "was a time of unprecedented grandeur, might, and brilliant cultural success. China was the richest, most powerful, and technologically most advanced nation in the world."

Malcolm Kennedy, a British historian, wrote, "The passion for learning, the insatiable thirst for knowledge and the aptitude for choosing, adopting and adapting to their own use the ideas and techniques of foreign countries, which has been so characteristic of the Japanese people in modern times, were equally marked in the 7th century."**

It is interesting to note that the Japanese again adopted many aspects of a foreign culture in the period between 1870 and 1910. During those years, the Japanese studied England, France, Germany, and the United States to learn about Western culture, much as their ancestors had studied Tang China ten centuries earlier.

The Role of Women in Modern Japan

When Japan was mainly a nation of farmers and warriors, the extended family was the norm. In the traditional Japanese family, several generations lived in one house. Wives were subservient to their husbands and mothers-in-law. Most marriages were arranged.

Old Japanese laws and traditions gave Japanese women few if any legal rights. They were supposed to spend their lives taking care of their homes and families.

In traditional Japan, husband, wife, older relatives, and children usually worked together as farmers or owners of small businesses. When a younger son or daughter in a family married, often he or she moved in with the in-laws. Then they were no longer considered members of the original family.

As Japan has become more urbanized and industrialized, family structure has become similar in many ways to the United States and Western Europe. Fewer than 10 percent of Japanese families live on farms in the 1990s.

At present, about 40 percent of the Japanese labor force is made up of women. In addition, women outnumber men working in agriculture. However, the majority of Japanese women who have children still stay at home. Wives have wide decision-making powers regarding family matters. Japanese wives now often control the family finances and budgets. It is not uncommon for Japanese husbands to turn their wages over to their wives and in turn to receive an allowance.

Even though almost half of the women of Japan now work, opportunities for good jobs are quite limited for women. In a recent government survey of 5,000 companies, only 22 percent offered positions to women university graduates. Women earn about one-half the salary of men in similar jobs.

---

* Runkle, S.F. *An Introduction to Japanese History.* New York: Appleton Crofts, 1943.
** Runkle, J.F. *An Introduction to Japanese History.* New York: Appleton Crofts, 1943.

Many working women are young and unmarried. The Japanese have a nickname for them, "office flowers." These young women may work for a corporation for five or six years after graduation from high school or junior college. Then they marry and leave the company. "Office flowers" are never given jobs of importance, but are expected to set up a pleasant environment for the mostly male employees by preparing and serving tea and running errands.

Of course, not all women fit the "office flower" pattern. Many college graduates have pursued professional careers. Still, in a society where it is very difficult for an outsider to be accepted by the group, Japanese women are far too often not considered equals in the workplace, solely because they are women.

On the other hand, today, Japanese women have been given legal equality in marriage and divorce. Also, the law allows equality in property holding and voting rights.

Education

During the Tokugawa Shogunate, (1603–1867) schools were established to serve the educational needs of the various social classes. The *daimyo* (lords) used tutors or set up special schools for their children and those of the **samurai** (warriors). Schools were also set up in rural communities for the wealthier members of the merchant and farmer classes. In the cities, another type of private school was the *terakoya*, where reading, writing, and arithmetic were taught to the children of the common people.

After the Meiji Restoration (1867), a modern national educational system based on the European model (German and English) was introduced in Japan (1872). The government set up elementary and secondary schools throughout the country. In 1886, every child was required to go to elementary school for four years. In 1900, compulsory education was made free of charge and in 1908, the education law required six years of compulsory education. After World War II, compulsory education was extended to the present nine years to cover elementary and lower secondary school education.

The education system is divided into five levels: kindergarten (1–3 years), elementary (6 years), lower secondary (3 years), upper secondary (3 years) and university (4 years). There are also many "junior colleges" that offer courses of study for two to three years. In addition, many universities offer post graduate courses for advanced study.

The two laws that govern the present educational system are: (1) The Fundamental Law of Education and (2) The School Education Law. Both laws were passed in 1947 and were greatly influenced by American standards and principles of education.

A basic principle of Japanese education is equality of education for all. The law prohibits discrimination on the basis of race, religion, sex, social status, economic position, or family background. A central goal of the system is to produce self-reliant citizens of a peaceful and democratic nation who respect human rights and recognize the great importance of truth and peace.

Educational background is an important factor in getting a good job. In order to land a job in a top company, it is necessary to graduate from a first-rank university. To enter a top ranking university, it is necessary to graduate with high marks from top-level upper and lower secondary schools.

Because of the fierce competition in the entrance exams for top-rank schools on all levels, many students attend private coaching and "cram" schools. These schools provide extra, after-school instruction to help students enter schools of their choice. Private coaching exists at all levels from entering nursery school to taking university entrance exams.

Education has played a very important part in the economic progress in Japan.

Kendo is an ancient and traditional activity that teaches the Japanese mental and physical self-control.

In the past decade, a number of problems in the Japanese system of education have become obvious. Among these problems are student violence and bullying. The fierce competition to gain a place in the best school has led to a great increase in mental problems, breakdowns, and suicides among Japanese students. The "cram" schools and the excessive interest in passing tests has made the education system a preparatory one, not an educational one. Learning has become secondary to passing tests. In addition, it has become clear to many Japanese in the government and in business that the current system needs to be changed into one more appropriate for a Japanese society and economy in an age where Japan will play a leadership role.

In 1987, the Japanese National Council on Education Reform offered the following recommendations which are to be carried out by 1997.

1. A more varied selection of subjects should be offered at the lower and upper secondary levels.
2. The university entrance examination system should be revised to allow each university to conduct its own testing.
3. Educational opportunities should be increased for people who are not enrolled in school.
4. The system for accepting foreign students should be improved.

The Young People of Japan

What are the Japanese young people of today like? One thing that can be agreed upon is that they behave so differently from their parents and grandparents that they have been given the title of *shinjinrui* or "the new human race" by the Japanese media.

This generation, which came of age after 1970, has greater affluence (wealth) and has been exposed to greater influences from outside of Japan than their parents. Kentucky Fried Chicken, MacDonald's, and IBM are found in Japanese cities. They are as familiar to the Japanese young people as they are to Americans. There are American movies on Japanese screens and on Japanese TV. Western music is available in stores in all Japanese cities.

In addition to consumer goods, many Japanese young people travel to and study in foreign countries. Many American and European businesses are located in Tokyo and other Japanese cities. A large number of young Japanese men and women with language and technical skills work for these firms. Many of them find the informal work atmosphere and easier opportunities for advancement in Western companies preferable to the policies of Japanese businesses. This is particularly true of young educated Japanese women who are not allowed to take advantage of the best job opportunities in Japanese companies.

It has been observed and documented that the younger generation of Japanese like to have fun, spend more, and save less than their parents and grandparents. In almost all recent studies, Japanese young people showed greater concerns with individual pursuits not found in older Japanese. The younger Japanese look at work as something one must do but not the entire focus of one's life.

This probably does not mean, as many older Japanese think, that young people are extremely lazy and will cause Japan to decline. One Japanese business executive put it best when he said: "Our younger generation is definitely a new breed. They are willing to give only 100 percent at work."

Japanese Diet and Cuisine

The diet and cuisine of the Japanese have been strongly influenced by geography and agriculture. Rice has always been the staple food and until recently was eaten in large quantities at all three meals each day. The word for cooked rice, *gohan*, is also the Japanese word for meal. *Sake*, the traditional alcoholic beverage, is made of rice.

Of the total area of Japan, less than 2 percent, largely in the colder north, is pastureland used for the raising of cattle. In the past, cattle were used to haul carts or to plow fields but not for food. The scarcity of meat, together with the Buddhist taboo against the taking of animal life made the Japanese non-meat eaters for most of their history.

Protein is obtained from the fish caught in great quantities in the sea that surrounds the Japanese islands. Much of the fish is eaten raw, either in small slices called *sashimi* or as *sushi* which combines the fish with seaweed and rice.

Another source of protein is soybeans, which are used to make *tofu* (bean curd), *miso* (bean paste), and *shoyu* (soy sauce).

Of course, Japanese eating habits have changed over the past 50 years. Rice consumption has declined. Cheap imported wheat is baked into excellent European-style breads, which are substituted for rice at breakfast. Meat, either imported or produced in Japan from imported feed grains, has become an important part of the present day Japanese diet. Besides the traditional sake, the Japanese are also developing a taste for German-type beer (pilsner), Scotch-type whiskeys, and other Western beverages. American fast foods such as McDonald's and Kentucky Fried Chicken are very popular in Japan.

The Japanese have also developed many specialty dishes that are not based on traditional menus. *Sukiyaki* is a beef dish mixed with noodles and vegetables. *Tempura* (deep fried shrimp or prawns) is a dish adapted from the Portuguese in the 16th century. Japanese *Kobe Beef*, which is tender and juicy, is known world-wide for its excellence. Kobe Beef cattle are raised in stalls and do not move around on ranges or pasturelands. As a result, their hides, meat, and muscles do not toughen.

The Japanese Home

The "typical" Japanese home is very unlike our own. It is constructed mostly of wood, bamboo, and straw. The rooms are separated from one another by *shoji*, light sliding screens made of paper stretched over a wooden frame. The house has little furniture. The Japanese often use a small charcoal stove called a *hibachi* as a heater.

The floor, which is raised several feet above ground level, is covered by reed mats called *tatami*. Since few homes have chairs, family members and visitors sit crosslegged on pillows. The family sleeps on heavy quilts spread on the matted floor. Bathing is done in a huge wooden vat or tile tub filled with extremely hot water.

The Effect of Cultural Diffusion in the 19th and 20th Centuries

Contact with the West brought changes to Japan. Children use chairs and desks in classrooms, but they sit on the floor while they do their homework at home. The national sport of Japan is baseball. Western style clothing is worn to business, but the traditional kimono and robes are still worn at home. In time, the Japanese might abandon the traditional ways, but now and for many years to come the two syles will exist side by side.

Appreciation of Beauty

Appreciation of the beauty and greatness of nature has been a part of Japanese life since earliest times. This fondness for the world of nature is seen in many aspects of daily life. Holidays and festivals coincide with major changes in the cycles of the seasons. The objects of everyday use, such as clothing, umbrellas, fans, and dishes are decorated with designs from nature, revealing the Japanese awareness of things around them.

Japanese Arts

Tea Ceremony

Japanese art and skills have been influenced by their contact with China and Korea. However, they have been so developed and refined that they have become strictly Japanese. The *Chanoyu* (tea ceremony) is an example.

On special occasions the Japanese transform the drinking of tea into a ceremony that is both a ritual and an art. It is a custom unique to (found only in) Japan. Tea drinking was borrowed from the Chinese during the Ashikaga period (1333–1573) as a substitute for wine. Tea was used in Buddhist ceremonies in which it became the custom to honor the ceremony more than the tea. These traditions merged to become the basis of the tea ceremony as practiced in Japan today.

The Chanoyu takes about four hours and features the serving of *matcha*, powdered green tea. It usually takes place in the *toko-no-ma* (an alcove of a room in the house) or in a *chaya* (tea house in the garden).

The tea is prepared in slow graceful motions and drunk slowly from a bowl. The bowl and other articles used are then admired and discussed. The ceremony is designed to make a person one with nature, to see beauty in simplicity and economy of movement. It is an art, not a means of offering refreshment. Every detail of participation is governed by tradition and the ceremony is both a spiritual experience and a mental exercise.

Ikebana (Flower Arrangement)

Ikebana is the art of flower arrangement. In this art, as in Chanoyu, Zen Buddhism has played an important role. Ikebana uses line, color, and rhythm to create floral designs; branches, stems, and flowers are the materials.

Ikebana tries to show the slow passage of time. This is shown both in materials and types of arrangement. Blossoms in full bloom or dried leaves are used to show the past. The present is shown by half-open blossoms or perfect leaves. Buds are used to show the future.

Curves are used to suggest spring; a full spread of blossoms and leaves to show summer; a thin, square grouping, autumn; and a dark, quiet arrangement, winter. The three stem lines symbolize: Heaven (the tallest stem), Man (the second stem), and Earth (the shortest stem).

The flower arrangements are usually placed in the toko-no-ma, in the most important room in the Japanese home. At first, many scholars believe, the toko-no-ma was the family altar, dedicated to Buddha. Today it is used for scrolls, floral arrangments, and to display art work.

In the 6th century, floral groupings first began to be seen in Buddhist temples. Rigid and large in size, in order to be in harmony with the lofty temple building, these *Rikka* (standing up flowers) towered high above their bronze containers. These containers and other temple ornaments, as well as the idea for decorating the temples with flowers, came from China. These rikka can be called the first Japanese ikebana.

In its beginnings, ikebana was designed to symbolize certain Japanese ideas about Buddhism. However, over the years, much of the religious meaning was lost and more natural-style arrangements were designed.

Bonsai

For centuries the Japanese have developed the art of dwarfing (making small) trees. This art is called *bonsai*. These dwarf trees, which are planted in pots, are used for ornaments in rooms or to decorate a garden.

The growth of the plants is controlled by pruning (cutting) so that the trees are trained into the shapes of ancient big trees. The trunk of the tree, the spreading of the roots, and the spacing of the branches are very important because they are used to give an old appearance to the tree. The empty spaces in the pot are used to suggest plains or distant mountains.

The pot in which the trees are planted plays an important part in the plan of bonsai. The shape and size of the pot is determined on by the kinds of plants it holds. The pots are usually plain but some are highly decorated. However, the pots should blend in with the natural surroundings.

Today many Japanese still learn the art of bonsai as a hobby. This is another example of the Japanese desire to try to understand and remain close to nature.

Theater

Nō Drama

Japanese theatre is unique. During the late 14th century, the Japanese created a new form of drama, the **Nō** play. The Japanese drew upon older traditions of music and dance in the developing of the Nō drama. It was created to entertain the wealthy. The Nō makes use a simple stage setting; for example, the backdrop is often a single pine tree. This simpleness shows the influence of Zen Buddhism on this form of drama.

In Nō plays there are usually three roles—an old man, a woman, and a samurai. Nō plays are usually short. They are presented as a group of plays and single performances may last up to six hours. The groups of plays are about subjects such as: God plays, warrior-ghost plays, women plays, and demon plays. Dancing and chanting accompany the action of the play. Masks and beautifully designed costumes are worn by the actor-dancers.

Nō drama was a significant and original literary development of the Ashikaga period (1333–1573). In some ways Nō is like the drama of ancient Greece. It is performed on an almost bare stage by a chief actor and assistant who both wear elaborate costumes and masks. There may be some other minor actors with a chorus filling in the narrative. Both the actors and chorus chant their lines to the accompaniment of rhythmic, orchestral music. The *librettos* (musical scripts) were written largely in poetry or highly poetic prose. Action is restrained and very stylized and the climax of the play is always a symbolic dance performed by the chief actor.

The leading Nō drama playwrights were Kan'ami (1333–1384) and his son Seami (1363–1443). Their dramas were usually about the actions of Shinto gods or famous people in Buddhist and Japanese history. They often centered on the idea of salvation through faith. An important part of Nō presentations were the comic interludes called *Kyogen* (Crazy World). The Kyogen were burlesques poking fun at contemporary feudal society.

Nō drama is a fine example of the cultural creativity of the Ashikaga period.

Bunraku

A later development in Japanese theater was the puppet play, known as **Bunraku.** This form was developed in the 17th century in Osaka. The foremost writer of Bunraku was Chickamatsu, who is sometimes called the "Shakespeare of Japan."

The Bunraku puppets are nearly life-size and are very lifelike. They are controlled on the stage by a team of three puppeteers who are visible to the audience. The puppeteers' performances depend upon long years of practice and teamwork. The techniques of Bunraku have remained basically the same. Many of the techniques, plays, and music exist only through the memory of the puppeteers since there are no written texts. The art of constructing Bunraku puppets is dead since no living artist is now making puppets. The theater is able to continue only through the use of the remaining puppets—some of which are more than 250 years old. Bunraku performances are given today and the Japanese regard it as a national cultural treasure.

Kabuki

The most popular type of drama for the Japanese is *Kabuki*, which was also developed in the 17th century. It had its beginnings in the puppet play and the Nō drama. Kabuki is made up of drama, dance, music, and singing. (The word *Kabuki* is made up of Chinese characters for music, dance, and singing.)

Kabuki was first presented in specially built theaters for the middle class and poorer people. The stage was very large and many devices were used to provide action. Trap doors allowed actors to disappear from sight and wires could move them through the air. Revolving platforms allowed rapid changing of sets. Fire, smoke, lightning, and ghosts were new innovations of Kabuki.

All roles in Kabuki, both male and female, were, until recently, played by men. In the 17th century a law banned women from the stage and all-male Kabuki became traditional. Actors taking feminine roles were trained from childhood to walk, talk and behave like women. The actors wear brightly colored costumes and wigs that dazzle the eye. Kabuki leaves nothing to the imagination; everything is exaggerated. Color, sound, speech, and dramatic action combine to excite the senses and the emotions.

Chickamatsu, who wrote many puppet plays, also wrote for Kabuki. The stories are somewhat like fairy tales. The favorite subject for both the Bunraku and Kabuki was the conflict between duty and personal desires—duty usually won out in the end. Many of the plays are based on tales and legends of early Japan. Sometimes playwrights poked fun at government officials. The deeds of heroes and villains in Japan's many wars have been favorites year after year. There is little development of characters or the relationship of character to action. However, the skillful and magical combination of color, music, action, and words hypnotizes the audience. Truly one is carried away by the spectacle.

Kabuki is also popular outside Japan; it has been performed with great success in both New York and Chicago. Kabuki today is Japan's most popular and grand theater.

Literature

Japanese literary history is rich. Poetry has been written for over 1,000 years. (Chinese influences are quite noticeable in early poetry.) Good poetry was collected in anthologies. The most famous collection was the *Manyoshu* (Collection of Ten Thousand Leaves). It was completed in 760 and contains more than 4,500 poems and songs. The *Manyoshu* is the most important literary achievement of early Japanese history; the marks the Nara period (710–794) as the Golden Age of Japanese poetry. The great majority of the poems in this collection are called *tanka* (short poems) of 31 syllables, divided into sections of 5–7–5–7–7 syllables. Normally a short poem suggests a natural scene and then changes into an emotional feeling. Most short poems are difficult to translate. The following, from the 9th century, is simple enough, though its simplicity may make it less typical of the style:

<table>
<tr><td>Haru tuteba</td><td>When spring comes</td></tr>
<tr><td>Kiyuru koori no</td><td>the melting ice</td></tr>
<tr><td>nokori naku</td><td>leaves no trace.</td></tr>
<tr><td>Kimi ga kokoro mo</td><td>Would that your heart too</td></tr>
<tr><td>ware ni tokenan</td><td>melted thus toward me.*</td></tr>
</table>

Two hundred years later a second anthology of about 1,100 poems was assembled by order of the emperor. It was called the *Kokinshu* (Ancient and Modern Collection). The preface to this anthology is one of the earliest examples of prose written in Japanese. The author of this preface also wrote a poetic travel diary called the *Tosa Diary*. Many other diaries were written at this time and they tell us a great deal about Japan in early times.

While the Japanese poetic tradition reached a peak in the Heian period (794–1185), earlier poems date back to 300 A.D. The following poem was written by Empress Iwano Hime.

<blockquote>
In the autumn fields
Over the rice ears
The morning mist trails
Vanishing, somewhere....
Can my love fade too?*
</blockquote>

During the Heian Period (794–1185), a purely Japanese literature developed. This literature, which consisted of diaries and novels, was free of Chinese influences. Much of this new literature was written by women because the ladies of the royal court were not taught to read or write in the Chinese style. These brilliant women wrote in the Japanese form (*Kana*).

The Pillow Book of Sei-Shonagon, the most famous diary, was written between 950 and 1000 by Sei-Shonagon, a lady-in-waiting to the empress. In it one can find a day-by-day description of court life with witty comments and deep insight into people and events. Japan's greatest novel was also written at this time. The massive *Genji Mongatari* (*The Tale of Genji*) was written by Lady Murasaki Shikibu. This novel revolves around the adventures and loves of the imaginary Prince Genji. It gives a vivid description of the people, ceremonies, and customs of the Japanese upper class. The *Tale of Genji* has had a great influence on Japanese literature and through Arthur Waley's translation it has become one of the great world classics. (It is quite possible the Japanese were the first people to write novels.)

In the late 11th and early 12th centuries, romantic accounts of the Fujiwara (837–1160) court were written. *Eiga Monogatari* (*The Tale of Splendor*) covers the period 889 to 1092 in chronological order and the *Okagami* (*Great Mirror*) the period from 850 to 1025 in biographic style.

---

* *The Penquin Book of Japanese Verse*. New York: Penguin Books, 1986. p. 13

Maiko, or apprentice geisha, performing the *Miyako Odori* that has been held annually in Kyoto for over one hundred years during cherry blossom time. All the performers are women.

The Japanese have developed several unique sports. Sumo wrestling is one of them.

Stories describing the many wars in the Fujiwara period were a popular form of writing. These stirring war tales are historically accurate in broad outline, but they are also full of imagined and romantic detail. The greatest of these war tales is the *Tale of the House of Taira*.

In the 17th century, a time of peace, more and more Japanese learned to read. The art of printing, which had been known to the Japanese as early as the 8th century, became more developed. These two factors led to a great increase in the number of books published. Many of the early books of this time were on religion or history.

However, many other books dealt with life in the fast growing towns. Special attention was paid to the pleasures of daily life and leisure time activities of the "floating world". (The "floating world" was the term used for the Kabuki Theater and the world of pleasures in the towns).

From this beginning, Ihara Saikaku (1642–1693) developed character portrayals of amusing townspeople. His important works were *An Amorous Man*, *An Amorous Woman*, and *Twenty Examples of Unfilial Conduct in This Land*. His writing was clear-cut and critical as well as humorous.

Haiku

Haiku poetry also developed during this period. One of the earliest and probably the greatest haiku poet was Matsuo Basho (1644–1694), a former samurai who became a poet and traveler. His most famous work, *The Narrow Road of Oku*, is a poetic account of a trip to northern Honshu.

Haiku is the simplest form of poetry. It consists of one verse with 17 syllables, spaced over three lines in a 5–7–5 pattern. A haiku is like a tanka with at least two lines left out. A good haiku sets a mood, then flashes a sudden understanding of life—all in three lines.

In haiku, it is important not to say your real meaning and your feelings directly. The lines do not have to rhyme. The first line usually tells where the poem takes place. The second line tells what the poem is about. The third line tells when the scene takes place. Look for the where, what, and when pattern in the following haiku:

The Pond

The ancient pond
A frog leaps in
The sound of water

                    BASHO

Mist

Above the veil
of mist, from time to time
there lifts a sail …

                    GAKOKU

A Remembrance

Show that we two
looked at together—this yew
Is it fallen anew?

                    BASHO

The Crow

On a leafless branch
a crow has settled:
autumn nightfall.

                    BASHO

Which of these poems do you like? Can you write haiku? Try it—you might like it.

Early Art and Architecture

The earliest known Japanese art forms are the *haniwa* figures of men, animals, and horses of the 3rd century. Architectural examples are not that old. Since most buildings were built of wood they have not survived. However, the Japanese, in rebuilding their many shrines, have always carefully copied the examples of the past. Today, examples of the early-style Japanese architecture can be seen in the holy shrines at Ise.

With the introduction of Buddhism into Japan, art flourished. The full-sized Buddhist images and realistic portrait statues of the Nara period are fine works. The artists used bronze, wood, clay, and lacquer for their work.

The Japanese mastered Chinese architectural and bridge building techniques and many other skills. The Buddhist temples built in Japan during the 7th and 8th centuries are the best remaining examples of classic Chinese Tang architecture. The Golden Hall and the pagoda of the Horyuji are probably the oldest wooden buildings in the world. The Golden Hall has many beautiful statues and its walls are covered by frescoes like the Buddhist cave temples in India.

Influence of China on Japanese Art

There is a close relationship between Chinese and Japanese art. During the Nara Period (710–784 A.D.) and early Heian Period (794–980), China served as a model in art. (Note that knowledge of Chinese styles of painting and other art forms came to Japan through Korea.) A distinctly Japanese style of painting slowly developed from the 10th century on, but the influence of Chinese artists was never completely eliminated.

It is often difficult to tell a Japanese painting from a Chinese painting because many of the same styles and techniques are common to both. For example, both use watercolors and silks rather than oil. Also, the Chinese and Japanese painted on silk screen and paper instead of on canvas or on masonry walls as in Western art.

Another technique that Japanese artists borrowed from the Chinese is the use of "negative space." Large areas of a painting or an ink drawing are deliberately unpainted. The viewer is supposed to fill in these empty spaces by using his or her imagination. The result of this is a free, floating on air feeling. The viewer is assisting the artist in the creation of his or her masterpiece.

The Chinese did not appreciate highly realistic paintings, that is, a painting that looks exactly like the real thing. The Japanese also borrowed this concept. The Japanese artist gave an "impression" of the subject; the artist did not try to paint what it actually looked like. Japanese painters of the Ukiyo-e period were "Impressionists" and greatly influenced the Impressionist painters of Europe in the 19th century.

The Chinese and later the Japanese emphasized brush strokes known as *calligraphy* (art of writing). Calligraphy is a major art form in both China and Japan. Artists use both continuous lines and lines in patterns. At the same time, they use as few lines or strokes as possible. A few curved lines can be used for mountains, several strokes for waterfalls, and some dots and lines represent a field of rice and trees.

Zen Art and Architecture

Zen Buddhism influenced the development of a style of landscape painting. The greatest of the Zen artists was probably Sesshu (1420–1506). The Zen artist wanted to show the main parts of nature by leaving out minor details and by showing with bold brush strokes what was important. In Zen paintings, people, temples, bridges, and boats usually appear as minor details blending into the great pattern of nature.

Traditional crafts still remain a very important part of Japanese life and culture. Here we see an umbrella maker applying the wax finish over the painted paper.

Japanese calligraphy. The Japanese learned the art of calligraphy from the Chinese.

Large heavy-roofed Zen temples were common, but the smaller, lighter Silver (Gin Kakuji) and Golden (Kinkakuji) Pavilions near Kyoto are better examples of the spirit of the times. A more important development of this time was landscape architecture. The setting of the buildings and the surrounding garden became an important art form. The Zen spirit can best be seen in the "rock garden" of the Ryoanji in Kyoto.

Sumi-e

Japanese ink or brush painting with black ink is called *Sumi-e*. This very delicate style began during the 13th century (Kamakura period). The painter hopes to come close to nature. Artists try to paint how they feel about a thing rather than to paint a living quality. During the Kamakura Period a monk painted *The Naichi Waterfall,* which is one of the finest landscape paintings now existing. It shows the artist's love of nature. Scroll paintings which still exist from this period show many things about Japanese life and customs.

In the 15th century, Japanese artists produced some of the finest black and white paintings ever printed. The most famous of these painters were Shuban and Sesshu. They were influenced by the Chinese of that century and by the Sumi-e painters. Most of their paintings are very simple, with only a few brush stokes. The object of the painters is to show the wonders of nature. The painter tries to leave the viewer with a sense of peace and the goodness of the surroundings.

Painting in the Tokugawa Period

During the early years of the Tokugawa Shogunate, a shift from the Chinese influence in art began to take place. Japanese artists used bold, almost abstract effects in landscape painting. The new artistic approach can be seen on lacquer ware and on large folding screens. The greatest artist of this style was Ogata Kōrin (1658–1716).

Other artists, probably influenced by the down-to-earth tastes of the common people of the towns, moved toward greater realism. Hanabusa Itcho (1652–1724), also a Haiku poet, painted in the "Yamato style" going back to the pre-Chinese period. Marayama Ōkyo (1733–1795) adopted Western principles of perspective. Shiba Kōkan (1738–1818) went further in the European style, experimenting with copper plate etchings, oil paints, and even Western subject matter.

Ukiyo-e

The most significant artistic creation of the Tokugawa period grew out of the interest and way of life of the town and its people. This art form was Ukiyo-e. Ukiyo-e is often translated as "floating world." The Ukiyo-e painters were influenced by the colorful theater and the world of pleasure. Ukiyo-e is a kind of wood block-printing. The artist tries to create landscapes and other forms of nature in a realistic way.

"The Floating World"

In the 17th century, townspeople, merchants, business people and well-to-do farmers had to work hard to earn a living. They also had to follow strict rules of behavior and could not show that they had wealth. The Tokugawa government kept close watch to make sure that all laws were obeyed.

To relieve the daily pressures, the people often went to special areas of Tokyo that had been set up by the Tokugawa leader for entertainment and pleasure. Buddhists called this area the "floating world." They believed that the entertainment and pleasure the townspeople enjoyed there were useless and quickly "floated" away.

Block Prints

Japanese artists before the 17th century painted only for temples, palaces, and castles. The Ukiyo-e painters had many more colorful subjects to paint and also had people interested in buying their paintings. At first they painted this floating world of pleasure in bright colors. It was now realistic painting. Each artist painted according to his own imagination. Moronobu was one of the earliest artists of this group.

When the demand for Ukiyo-e paintings became greater, artists began to cut their drawings on blocks of wood. It was now possible to print large numbers of copies or prints. These prints could be sold very cheaply. It was from these penny prints that the country people learned about city life.

Influence on European Art

The earliest prints were done only in heavy black lines on white paper. Late in the 18th century, the Edo (Tokyo) printmakers added rose-red and green. Still later the multi-colored print (*nishki-e*) was developed. The two greatest artists of the Ukiyo-e block-print school were Hiroshige and Hokusai.

The Ukiyo-e had a great influence on European art. In 1865, a Frenchman named Bracquemond who drew designs on French pottery happened to see some Hiroshige prints among the paper wrappings used on a package from Japan. He showed the prints to his friends and to some painters. Many of the French artists were impressed with the bright colors and the flowing lines of movement.

In 1867, Ukiyo-e works were shown at the Paris International Exhibition. These works were the most looked at at the exhibition. They were also inexpensive. Monet, Degas, and van Gogh—all French Impressionist painters—became collectors. Many later works of these Impressionists show the style of Ukiyo-e. There are similiarities in the subjects (seascapes, field scenes, people), the use of color, and the use of line.

Early History of Japan

The First Settlers

Archaeological evidence indicates that humans have existed in Japan for the past 100,000 years. Japan was once linked to the mainland mass of Asia. People traveled from the mainland to what is today the island nation of Japan over a land bridge. Then the oceans, swelled (the level raised) by the melting ice of the glacier, covered the land bridge. Japan was cut off from Asia by the new **straits** (narrow bodies of water between land masses) that have played such a great part in Japan's later history. Japan was also settled by people sailing north from southeastern Asia between 4,000 and 5,000 years ago.

The early settlers were probably hunters and food gatherers. Farming was introduced about 2,900 years ago (9th century B.C.) Archaeological evidence, myths and legends, and the reports of Chinese visitors lead us to the conclusion that Japan's social and political organization remained simple until about 1,500 years ago.

The Gods Create Japan—Legend of Jimmu Tenno

As part of Japanese history, Japanese schools taught that Izanagi, a god, and Izanami, a goddess, were ordered to create a land on earth. They were given a jewel-tipped spear that they dipped into the ocean. When they took the spear out of the water, they allowed drops of water to drip from the point of the spear. These drops formed islands and Japan was created.

Amaterasu, goddess of the sun and daughter of Izanagi and Izanami, inherited all of the earth. She sent her grandson, Ninigi, to rule the islands created by her parents. When Ninigi was about to leave heaven, Amaterasu gave him three things that would make life easier for him: an iron mirror, a necklace of precious jewels, and the "Cloud Cluster Sword." Armed with these objects, which were to become the Japanese crown jewels, Prince Ninigi came to Japan. He married and passed the three objects to his grandson, Jimmu Tenno. This is the legend of the founding of Japan, which many Japanese, even today accept as fact.

The name Tenno means "Son of Heaven." This name has been given to every Japanese emperor since Jimmu. (The name is given when the emperor dies.) According to legend, Jimmu became the first earthly emperor of Japan on February 11, 660 B.C. However, modern historians believe that 60 B.C. is more likely the true date. Therefore, it is possible that Jimmu Tenno lived at about the same time as Julius Caesar.

Jomon Period

Findings of archaeologists show that stone tools were used in Japan in 16,000 B.C. This early period is called the Preceramic (before pottery making) Period. The earliest pottery was probably made about 12,000 years ago.

From about 3000 to 300 B.C., a more artistic type of pottery called *jomon* (rope pattern) was made. This time is known as the Jomon period. During this period, the people built and lived in houses made of thatch. They made tools and weapons of stone and fishhooks and harpoons of bone.

THE PATH OF JAPANESE HISTORY	
3000–300 B.C.	Jomon Culture
300 B.C.–250 A.D	Legendary period
250 B.C.–250 A.D.	Yayoi Culture
250–645 A.D.	Tomb Culture
552 A.D.	Introduction of Buddhism to Japan
604 A.D.	Shotoku Taishi's *Seventeen Article Constitution*
645 A.D.	Taika Reform
702 A.D.	Taiho Code
710–784 A.D.	Nara period
794–1185 A.D.	Heian period
858–1156 A.D.	Fujiwara period
1192–1333	Kamakura period
1274, 1281	Mongol invasions
1338–1567	Ashikaga period
1549	Arrival of Francis Xavier and Christianity
1603–1868	Tokugawa period

Some archaeologists believed that Southeast Asians sailed to Japan between 3000 and 2000 B.C. The Southeast Asians brought methods of agriculture and knowledge of the use of metals to Japan.

Another early people to come to Japan were the Ainu. It is not known where they came from or when they arrived. They settled on the plain of central Honshu.

Following the Ainu, a group of people moved from northern Asia down through Korea. They crossed the sea to Japan and drove the Ainu farther and farther north.

Yayoi Period

The second period of Japan's prehistory is also identified with its pottery-making. The Yayoi period was named after the Yayoi section of Tokyo where remains of a distinctive reddish pottery were first found.

The Yayoi people made their pottery by turning the clay by hand. Delightful pottery and figurines of horses and armored warriors have been found. Tools and weapons made of bronze and iron have also been discovered. These artifacts suggest a society ruled by warriors.

By 200 B.C., the Yayoi people were rice growers. The rice was grown in paddies similar to the paddies found in Southeast Asia and China. (What might this tell us?) A paddy is a field that is flooded when the rice is planted. The people of the Yayoi Culture were assured of a steady food supply because they adopted this "wet field" or irrigated rice farming. Farming of this type allowed these early Japanese to build permanent communities. Also, more time could be devoted to activities other than hunting for food.

As you read, the people of the Yayoi period produced a variety of implements including large jars and urns. The bronze and iron used for making weapons probably came from China as a result of trade. Trade also existed with the Korean Peninsula. Surviving Chinese records show that Chinese officials visited Japan as early as 57 A.D.

In the Yayoi period and in the 200 years that followed, many Japanese political and religious institutions came into being and still exist today. In addition, the adaptation of military technology from the Asian mainland, particularly the skill of horse riding, allowed some families to gain power through alliances.

The Yamoto Kingdom

Our first written view of the Japanese is from Chinese records of the 3rd century A.D. They describe the Japanese as living in a class divided society and earning a living by agriculture or fishing. The Japanese were divided into more than 100 tribal units, each of which was led by a chief. What the Chinese records call the "queen's" country, (a section within the Kanto Plain) had some control and power over the others. The presence of many women rulers fits well within the mythological tradition of the descent of the historical emperor or line from the sun goddess.

By 500 A.D. many small kingdoms were set up in various parts of the islands. Some of them had contacts with the nearby and more culturally advanced states of China and Korea. The most powerful kingdom was that of Yamoto, whose control extended from southern Japan up to Tokyo. The Yamoto introduced Chinese civilization into Japan.

Prince Shōtoku   An important leader of the Yamoto was Prince Shōtoku, who was mainly a statesman and teacher. Realizing that his people had a great deal to learn from the Chinese, Prince Shōtoku built a Japanese state on the Chinese model, and helped to spread Buddhism. He set up landholding, tax systems, law codes, and a military organization based on the Chinese system.

Taika "Great Reforms"

After the death of Shōtoku, a group of Taiki reformers revolted and began a program of change known as the "Great Reforms." The aim of the program was to set up a unified kingdom under one ruler. Although the program was never fully carried out, it brought about lasting changes in Japanese government, society and life. Most important, it established for all time the claim of the Yamoto ruler to the throne of Japan.

To make his claim clear, the Emperor ordered an official history of Japan to be written. One book was called the *Kojiki* (Record of Ancient Matters), and a second was called the *Nihonji* (Chronicles of Japan). The *Kojiki* and the *Nihonji* are the "bibles" of Japan. They record the earliest history of the Japanese people, telling about the sun goddess and her descendants, the rulers of Yamoto. They claim that the emperors were of divine origin (born of gods) and were superior to all other chiefs. No one since has challenged the right of the imperial family to "rule" Japan, if only as puppets.

As we have noted, the Great Reforms never were fully carried out. One idea that was never put into effect was that of national military service. With no national army ruled by the emperor, the emperors of Japan faced many problems up until the Meiji Restoration in 1867.

Samurai and the Code of Bushido

Law and order and the defense of the kingdom was left to the large landowners. Supporters of these powerful landowners called themselves **samurai**. The word *samurai* can be roughly translated as "those who serve." This original meaning, it seems, had little to do with warfare and the military. However, the definition changed a great deal through Japanese history. The samurai as a living institution and as a group died out in the 19th century. However, it is impossible to understand Japanese society and culture today without understanding the samurai and their values.

The samurai were supposed to live by a code of conduct known as *Bushido*, the way of the warrior. Bushido was an unwritten code and many samurai did not follow all its rules. However, it served as a guide for a soldier's behavior. It was in many ways like the code of chivalry for knights in Europe during Europe's feudal period.

According to Bushido, a samurai must be brave, a man of honor, loyal to the Emperor and his *daimyo* (lord), and must not show emotion. To get back lost honor, a samurai must commit *seppuku* (*hara-kiri*). Seppuku is a ritual form of suicide in which the samurai must kill himself by ripping the belly with a special short sword.

Anyone could recognize a samurai. He shaved the crown of his head except for a "top knot" which was "pulled so tight and plastered so firmly with grease that it could not be undone without much difficulty." The samurai wore two swords at his waist. The long one was used in hand to hand combat. The short one could silence an unprepared enemy or could be used if necessary to commit seppuku.

Zen Buddhism

The samurai were devout Buddhists. But it was a different sort of Buddhism than that brought from China and Korea. The samurai were Zen Buddhists. Zen emphasized the ideas of meditation, simplicity, and closeness to nature. It also emphasized a rigid physical and spiritual self-discipline. This type of life produced men of action with strong character and self control. These were useful qualities in a warrior society.

We can learn a great deal about the Code of Bushido and how samurai acted from a famous Japanese story, "The Tale of the Forty-seven Ronin." Ronin are samurai who have lost their daimyo.

Every year, the emperor would send a message of peace to the Shogun. The Shogun chose a daimyo to greet the emperor's messenger. In 1701 the Shogun chose a daimyo named Takumi to greet the messengers. Takumi did not know the proper way to greet them. The Shogun's secretary, Lord Kotsuke, was chosen to teach Takumi how it was to be done. Kotsuke was a greedy, mean, and jealous man. He would not give instruction without pay. Takumi refused to pay. He felt that it was Kotsuke's duty to honor the order of the Shogun and teach him without a reward.

Kotsuke became very angry. He refused to teach Takumi anything and took every opportunity to insult him. One day Kotsuke ordered Takumi to tie the laces on Kotsuke's sandal. Takumi resented the order but he bent down and tied the laces. Then Kotsuke turned to the other nobles who were present and, with a sneer and a laugh, said, "Look at that. This serf can't even tie a sandal correctly."

At this insult, Takumi lost his temper and self-control. He drew his sword and attacked Kotsuke. Kotsuke was not seriously injured but Takumi had committed two crimes: he had drawn his sword in the palace of the Shogun, and he had wounded an official of the Shogun. In addition, he had violated Bushido by showing emotion and losing his temper. For these crimes, Takumi knew he must die. That night, in a shrine in a moonlit garden, he committed Seppuku. All of his loyal Samurai watched the ritual.

Takumi's land and all that he had owned was taken away. Some of his possessions were given to Kotsuke in payment for the wound he had suffered. Takumi's loyal Samurai now became ronin.

Among the Samurai of the dead Takumi was his councillor, a man named Kuranosuke. He and forty-six other loyal Samurai formed a league, The League of Loyal Warriors, to avenge the death of their lord. These ronin felt that Kotsuke was at fault because he had insulted their lord. They believed that Kotsuke had murdered Takumi just as if he had actually stabbed him. The League vowed to seek revenge.

Kotsuke suspected that these ronin would plot against him. He sent spies to watch the ronin and he hired more Samurai to guard his home and family.

Kuranosuke, however, was determined to fool the enemy into a false sense of security. So, for almost two years, the ronin led wild and drunken lives. They seemed to have forgotten their dead lord. When Kotsuke's spies reported this to him, he was very relieved and he began to relax his guard. Then the ronin struck. Dressed in the black silk costume of the ninja, they slipped over the walls of Kotsuke's palace. After a bloody battle, the ronin killed all of Kotsuke's guards. They found Kotsuke hiding in a shed behind some bags of charcoal and firewood. With great respect, they offered to allow Kotsuke to commit Seppuku and die as a true Samurai. But Kotsuke was a coward. He begged them to spare his life and promised that he would give them large rewards.

Kuranosuke, seeing that it was useless to urge Katsuke to die the death of a daimyo, forced him down and cut off his head with the same sword with which Lord Takumi had killed himself. The ronin then placed the head of the dead Kotsuke in a bucket to be taken to the tomb of Takumi.

The forty-seven ronin had proved themselves loyal to their lord and master. Everyone praised their courage and faithfulness. Even so, they knew what they must do now. They had killed one of the Shogun's high officials. They had shown that they were not completely loyal to him. For that crime they must die. Every one of the forty-seven ronin committed Seppuku as Lord Takumi had done. Their bodies were buried in front of his tomb. When news of their deeds spread, people from all over the kingdom of Japan came to pray at the graves of these faithful and brave men.

The Japanese still continue the samurai ideal of personal loyalty and responsibility to an employer. This is found in Japanese industry and trade today. The paternal feeling that managers and owners of the great Japanese industries have toward their workers is based on the relationship of the great landlords to their samurai followers. In recent years, the

Japanese have enthusiastically responded to television serials, movies, and comic books telling of the heroic and swashbuckling exploits of the samurai.

The Taiho Code

The Taika program produced revolutionary changes in Japan and it firmly established the Yamotos as the ruling family of Japan. In addition, upper-class Japanese adapted a great deal of Chinese culture. However, many parts of the program were never put into practice and the basic Japanese culture and common law remained unchanged.

In 702 A.D., the Japanese government issued the *Taiho Code*. This Code described the basic structure of the government and set up the main rules by which the Empire was to be run. The Taiho Code was truly a legal and political document, or in other words, a constitution. The Code set up a highly centralized government with the Emperor at the center of power. The Code reflected the increased strength of the Emperor as well as the influence of the Chinese. However, the Japanese, as has often happened, only borrowed what was useful to them. For example, they never adopted the Chinese system of censors to evaluate government policy and actions. Japanese tradition could not allow a heaven-sent ruler and his selected advisors to be criticized by people of inferior birth. In addition, the Japanese never accepted the Chinese examination system, which would have made it possible for poor but intelligent people to become members of the ruling group. In Japan, government was based on an aristocracy of birth, rather than on learning, as it was in China.

The Nara Period

In 710 A.D., the Japanese emperors moved to a magnificent new capital called Heijo. (Nara is the modern name for the ancient city of Heijo.) Before that time, the emperors had been so afraid of death and disease that the location of the capital had been changed every time a new emperor took the throne. With the increase of money in the royal treasury due to the Taika Reform and the Taiho Code, the emperors decided to live in a new capital that would be safe and permanent.

The Nara period extended from about 710 to 784 A.D. During this time, Japanese art and architecture flourished. Nara artists excelled in sculpture. In much of their work, they used lacquer. The use of lacquer was borrowed from the Chinese, but the Japanese developed it to its highest levels. The lacquer figures of the Nara period were remarkably lifelike.

The Nara period also marked the growth of Buddhist power and influence. Frequent clashes took place between followers of Buddhism and Shintoism.

The Heian Period—The Fujiwara Clan

In 794, the capital was moved to Heian. (Kyoto is the modern name for Heian.) The reason for the move is not entirely clear, but some historians think that it was an attempt to escape Buddhist influence in Nara. Heian was the political center of Japan between 794 and 1185, a period of almost 400 years now known as the Heian Period.

The Heian Period was dominated by the Fujiwara family. The Fujiwaras rose to power by persuading the princes of the imperial family to marry the daughters of their clan. Usually, the Fujiwara father-in-law was also the Emperor's closest adviser. Through Fujiwara pressure, many of the emperors were persuaded to retire at an early age to a life of ease, leaving real power in the hands of a Fujiwara, who took the title of *sessho* (regent) or *Kampaku* (dictator). Under the control of the Fujiwara clan, the central government extended its control over the islands of Shikoku and Kyushu, and the Ainu were pushed farther north on the island of Honshu.

Despite their power, the Fujiwaras never tried to get rid of the imperial Yamato Dynasty. In fact, the right of the imperial family to reign has never really been challenged, even in modern times. The emperors of Japan were stripped of power for centuries, but there never was an attempt to oust the imperial family from the throne. The Japanese rightly boast that theirs is the oldest ruling dynasty.

As its power grew, the Heian court became more and more corrupt. The Fujiwaras were granted the right to own estates and to be free from paying taxes. A large amount of imperial land came under the ownership of the Fujiwaras. These moves violated the Taika program and Taiha Code. Thus both the Emperor's power and his sources of wealth were slowly taken away.

As the court nobility and the warrior families like the Minamoto family gained control of more and more of the imperial land, power began to shift. Central government control became weaker. Violence and disorder increased; the imperial government became weaker; military families grew in power, and feudalism began to be a part of Japanese life.

Literature

The Heian Period saw the development of a native Japanese literature. Chinese characters introduced to Japanese sounds became a new form of writing—*hiragana*. Hiragana used abbreviated Chinese characters to represent Japanese sounds, an innovation which made for greater ease in writing. Poetry flourished; *Manyoshu* and the *Kokinshu* are two famous anthologies of poems.

Heian literature reached its peak with romantic tales called *monogatori*. These stories presented a complete picture of court life and Kyoto. The *Tale of Genji* is a well-known monogatori.

Osaka Castle is in the traditional Japanese architectural style.

Art

Heian art was highlighted for the beauty of its calligraphy. In calligraphy the Japanese artist entered a world of pure and abstract design. Lines were set in a pleasing relationship to other lines. By using a varying range of color tones, ranging from the faintest grays to the deepest blacks, Heian calligraphers produced charming and subtle effects.

During the Heian period, the art of making *makimonos* (colored picture scrolls) developed. Makimonos feature the application of gold paint to the surface of scrolls. Many makimonos were used to illustrate scenes from the *Tale of Genji* and other mongatoris.

Japanese Feudalism

Feudal Japan was in many ways like Europe in the Middle Ages. The Japanese feudal system, like that of Europe, depended on ties of personal loyalty. However, loyalty was the weakest link in both the Japanese and European systems. The medieval history of both Western Europe and Japan is full of cases of treachery, disloyalty, and betrayal.

Loyalty to the ruler was important in the Confucian system brought to Japan. However, the Japanese adaptation made loyalty to the family of greater importance. The fact that three of the five Confucian relationships dealt with loyalty to the family made this adaptation easy.

In Europe, with its background of Roman law, the lord-vassal relationship was seen as mutual and **contractual** (agreed on by both parties)— in other words, a legal relationship. In Japan, based on the Chinese system, the lord-vassal relationship was seen as one of unlimited and absolute loyalty on the part of the vassal. This was based on the lord's superior wisdom and morality. It was not a legal situation or any form of "contract." As a result there was no room for the development of the idea of political rights as in the Magna Carta or of individual liberties for the samurai.

Japanese feudal society differed from the European in other ways. Although the Japanese had a Code of Bushido (*Bushi* is Japanese for warrior), which in some ways was similar to the European Code of Chivalry, it was also very different. Women were not treated as fragile, inferior beings to be sheltered and protected. The Japanese samurai expected their women to be as tough as they were and to accept the rules of Bushido and total loyalty to the daimyo or family. Japanese women were also considered to be samurai.

Moreover, Japanese samurai and daimyo, though warriors like Western knights, did not have the contempt for learning, poetry, and painting found in Western feudalism. Sons of daimyo and samurai, as well as daughters, were taught the Japanese way in writing and in the arts. In fact, the greater daimyo and samurai prided themselves on their fine calligraphy and the ability to paint and write fine poetry.

The political and social organization of Japan today owes much to the feudal period. The warrior spirit and the Code of Bushido were easily taken into the modern Japanese army. The strong spirit of loyalty, duty, and self-discipline still remain from feudal days. These traditions shape the contemporary Japanese character and personality.

Kamakura Shogunate

In 1185, Yoritomo, leader of the Minamoto family, gained military control of all of Japan. The Emperor gave Yoritomo the power to pick his own **vassals** (warriors or agents who pledged their loyalty to the lord) as *shugo* (local high lord-barons) and *jito* (stewards or sheriffs) responsible for maintaining law and order on the local level. This development led to the eventual formation of the Japanese feudal system.

The daimyo discovered the central government did not have enough power to keep law and order. The strongest of the daimyo built castles for their defense and collected taxes from the peasants who needed their protection (taxes were usually in the form of produce or in work-time). The daimyo organized private armies of samurai to protect their holdings and to expand their control over weaker daimyo. As a result, between the 10th and the 17th centuries a feudal system was created. During this period, the Emperors of Japan "reigned but did not rule."

Minamoto Yoritomo established a military government at Kamakura, which ruled most of Japan. He took for himself the title *Shogun*, with the privilege of giving it to his sons. The Emperors of Japan, without control of the army, became powerless puppets. Japan was ruled under a Bakufu, or Shogunate, until 1868.

During the Kamakura period (1192–1333), feudalism, which also existed in Europe at this time, spread throughout Japan. **Feudalism** is a system of landholding and service to a lord. Allies of the shogun, the highest lord, were appointed police officers, tax collectors, and commanders of the army, and were given grants of land. In return, they performed military service for the government.

Feudalism usually had three features:

1. Lords held the land and offered protection to the peasant farmers who worked the land as serfs.
2. People promised to be loyal to their superiors.
3. Local governments took the place of central governments.

All three features appeared in Japan. Slowly, more and more land came under the control of great families or of important temples and shrines. At the same time, small farmers who could not pay high taxes to the Emperor turned over their lands to the great lords (daimyos). In return for protection, the farmers agreed to work the land, to pay rent to the lord, and to be loyal to the lords.

By the 12th century, much of the farmland of Japan was divided into tax-free private estates. As a result of this situation, the power of the Emperor grew weaker and he became poorer. The Emperor continued to be the ruler of the country but the powerful and rich daimyos actually ruled Japan.

In the early days of feudalism, lords divided their land among all their children, so both men and women owned land. However, over the years, the farms became smaller and smaller. Where there had once been one large estate or farm, there were now several smaller ones. Families with more than one child became less powerful. In time, people began to pass on their wealth differently. All the land owned by a family was given to the oldest son. Women were badly hurt by this change. They had once run great estates, had been recognized among Japan's finest writers and artists, and some had even earned fame as samurai. Under feudalism, women lost almost all their power and almost all their legal rights. The only roles open to them were as wives and mothers.

Younger sons were also hurt as feudalism continued: they were left without land or power. Some became samurai who served powerful lords. Others became Buddhist monks. In many cases these monks were not religious men. They lived as soldiers and fought to win land. Buddhism taught people to live in peace, but the Buddhist religion had changed greatly in Japan. Its temples became rich and powerful, and its monks were greatly feared. These monks opposed any effort to unite Japan.

Mongol Invasions

In the 13th century, the feudal samurai met a real test. Japan was invaded twice by the undefeated and seemingly unbeatable Mongols, who had already conquered China. But these wild warriors on horseback from Central Asia suffered defeat at the hands of the samurai. Skilled with bow and sword, the samurai were a match for the Mongols, and typhoons struck the invading fleet, crushing Mongol hopes of conquest. The Japanese called these winds *Kamikaze*, or "winds of the gods."

However, the battles with the Mongols weakened the government to such a great extent that a revolt led by a new military leader of the Ashikaga overthrew the Kamakuras.

Kamakura Accomplishments

The Kamakura Shogunate was a period when painting and sculpture flourished. Japanese armaments reached their peak. For strength and sharpness, Japanese swords of this period have never been equalled in any country.

Ashikaga Shogunate and Civil War in Japan

During the following two and a half centuries (1338–1567), feudalism was steadily extended in Japan. Since the Ashikaga shoguns were unable to control the powerful military lords, warfare was almost continuous. The fighting reached its climax in the 16th century when three great military leaders, Nabunaga, Hideyoshi, and Ieyasu brought unity and peace to Japan.

Nabunaga is remembered for ending the Ashikaga Shogunate. Hideyoshi established a united Japan, and a single ruler dominated the entire country. However, it was Ieyasu, of the house of Tokugawa, who founded the third and last military Shogunate in Japan.

Nabunaga

Nabunaga was only 15 when his father died and left him as daimyo of a small but important estate in central Japan. Even at this young age, Nabunaga proved to be a brilliant general. He defeated neighboring daimyos and brought unity and order to central Honshu.

In the middle of the 16th century, Nabunaga was given the job of bringing order and unity to Japan. He chose Hideyoshi and Ieyasu as his lieutenants.

Nabunaga gave his blessings to the Portuguese traders who came to Japan beginning in 1543. He allowed the Portuguese to spread their religion, Christianity, in Japan. Nabunaga saw this as a way to decrease the power of the Buddhists who resisted the idea of a united Japan. He also wanted the guns and technology of the Europeans for his army. While trying to defeat the armies of his remaining enemies, Nabunaga was assassinated by one of his generals.

Hideyoshi

Born the son of a poor woodsman, Hideyoshi was first a stable boy. He joined Nabunaga's army and rose from the position of common soldier to a commanding general. His soldiers called him "cotton" because he was a soldier whose talents could be put to many uses. His advisors called him *Taiko* (The Supreme Official). At least one of his biographers has called him the "Napoleon of Japan," because of his great ability as a general and conqueror.

When Nabunaga was assassinated in 1582, Hideyoshi took over and completed the unification of Japan by spreading his control over all of the island nation. He made the town of Yedo, near Tokyo, his capital. Hideyoshi never became shogun because of his lowly birth. He persuaded a noble family to adopt him and was therefore able to take the title of *Kampaku*, or Dictator.

Hideyoshi dreamed of conquering China. The Ming rulers of China were having many problems because of the civil wars throughout the country. For the Japanese, the road to China ran through Korea. However, the Koreans refused to allow the Japanese peaceful movement through Korea. Consequently, Hideyoshi was forced to fight his way up the

Korean peninsula. The battles weakened his army and he used up most of his supplies. He therefore had to give up his dream of conquering China.

Hideyoshi died peacefully in 1598. He wanted to leave his son in control of Japan, but the lieutenant of Nabunaga, Ieyasu, did not wish to turn leadership of the country over to a boy. Instead, Ieyasu had himself appointed shogun of Japan by the emperor in 1603.

Tokugawa Shogunate

To establish himself as shogun, Ieyasu was forced to fight rival daimyo and at the battle of Sekigahara, near Kyoto, he won a great victory. This battle marked the end of the feudal warfare that had been part of Japanese life for several hundred years. Two hundred and fifty years of peace were to follow (1603–1868). The daimyo were controlled by the shogun, and a new system of centralized feudalism was set up.

Japanese Isolation

To protect Japan from outside influences, the Tokugawa introduced a policy of national isolation. In 1639, the Tokugawa closed Japan to all foreigners except the Dutch and the Chinese, who were permitted to trade at Nagasaki. This trade was closely watched by the government. About the same time, laws were issued that prohibited any Japanese from going to a foreign country for any reason. The penalty for violating this order was death. Japanese who were not in the country were not permitted to return to Japan. New ideas were considered a threat to the established order.

The cost of this policy of isolation to Japan was great. First, the break with the West came at a time when the Europeans were about to make great advances in commerce, technology, and science. Lack of contact with the West at this time cost the Japanese 200 years of knowledge which would have aided Japanese development, and kept Japan technologically backward. A second great loss was the Japanese trade in East and Southeast Asia, which had proven to be very profitable to the Japanese economy.

Life in Tokugawa, Japan

Japanese society was frozen into four classes: samurai, peasant, artisan, and merchant. The responsibilities of members of each class were fixed by law. Despite the Tokugawa policy of preventing change, some change did take place. As a result of the long period of peace, trade within Japan grew. Towns became important and many cities arose. The city merchants grew rich from trading, and from lending money to the feudal samurai. As the years passed, the position of the samurai was weakened. With no wars to fight, there was no booty to win.

To rule a land at peace, the Tokugawa needed educated administrators rather than soldiers. As a result, the writing brush began to replace the sword as the main weapon of the samurai. They changed from a highly trained fighting force into a city-dwelling class of well-educated bureaucrats and government workers.

Warfare became a matter of theory with little or no practice. Schools were set up to teach the military arts. However, gunnery and the use of firearms were usually ignored in favor of the feudal military disciplines of swordsmanship and archery. (It is interesting to note that Ieyasu was victorious because of his use of cannons and other European supplied firearms.) The use of the sword and the bow were favored for their character building qualities as much as their military value. From this grew the emphasis on other character building martial arts, such as judo and its modern offspring karate.

Despite strong class differences, the Tokugawa system provided peace, law, and order. This stability provided the foundation for people to develop their abilities. The only limitation was that the class people were born into determined their trade or occupation.

The samurai contributed to the development of an efficient government and legal system as well as to the advancement of various areas of scholarship. Farmers, merchants, and artisans had more opportunities to improve their lives. During the 17th and 18th centuries, rice production more than doubled and the raising of commercially (crops for sale) valuable crops began to spread from village to village. Small industries grew and many cities prospered. By the middle of the 18th century, the economic power of the merchants and industrialists overtook that of the samurai class. (Why do you think this happened?)

Various art forms were introduced for the first time. The Kabuki theater and Ukiyo-e woodblock prints became the joy of the common people who now had the leisure time and wealth to enjoy the new art. For the first time, education became available for the common people, and literacy and the knowledge of arithmetic spread.

Opening Up to the West

In the centuries following the establishment of the Tokugawa Shogunate, European influence in Asia and the Pacific increased a great deal. Late in the 18th century, the Russians crossed the vast open spaces of Siberia and reached the Pacific Ocean. Russian efforts to open trade with Japan failed, but the Russians did set up colonies in the Kuriles and in the Sakhalin Islands. These settlements proved a threat to the Tokugawas.

At the end of the Napoleonic Wars in Europe in 1815, Great Britain and other European nations showed new interest in Asian trade. At the same time American merchants also became more interested in trade with Asian nations.

By the mid-1800s, India and much of Southeast Asia had come under the control of European nations. Even China was compelled to great concessions (favors) to the "foreign devils." In fact, before 1850, Western efforts to trade with Asia were aimed mainly at China.

After California joined the United States as a state in 1850, American interest in the Pacific region increased. However, American sailors, if shipwrecked in the area, were often jailed and beaten in Japan. Repeated efforts to end this practice through negotiation were unsuccessful. Both these factors lead to a desire to "open up" Japan.

Commodore Perry's Mission

In 1852, the U.S. government sent a naval expedition to Japan under the command of Commodore Matthew C. Perry. Perry's mission was motivated by:
1. the U.S. view that expansion westward in trade and influence was part of its Manifest Destiny;
2. the fact that many Americans believed that Western culture and progress should be brought to the less-developed areas of the world, including Japan;
3. the desire by Americans to have shipwrecked sailors and all Americans treated fairly and well;
4. the United States wish to expand trade for economic gain and increased political power;
5. the desire by the United States to set up a coaling station for its ships.

The arrival of American ships in Yedo (Tokyo) Bay in July 1853 frightened the Japanese, who had never seen steamships before. The Japanese panicked, and many moved from Tokyo to the countryside.

The Tokugawa were faced with a serious situation. The Emperor and the Tokugawas wished to maintain a policy of isolation. However, they realized that Japan was helpless against the modern military strength of the United States and that it was not possible to maintain Japan's isolation. Consequently, in March 1854, the Tokugawas granted the United States the rights of trade at two ports, the rights of coaling and supplying its ships and the privilege of sending a consul to Japan to represent the United States.

The Fate of the Samurai

City growth hurt the samurai class. By 1850, many samurai had forgotten the military arts since they had not fought a war for over 200 years. Although the samurai still wore swords, they worked mainly as government officials. Their pay was low and, as a result, their standard of living declined. Unable by law to farm or become merchants, some samurai became skilled craftspeople and sold the objects they made. However, their incomes made the samurai more and more unable to live up to their high social status.

By 1850, Japan's economy had changed, but its political and social institutions had remained the same. As a result, the merchants had wealth but no rank; the samurai had rank but little money.

In the nineteenth century, the Tokugawa Shogunate began to crack. The unhappy samurai began to plot against the shogun. The shogun was criticized and blamed for the nation's problems. At the same time, foreign pressure to change the policy of isolation intensified.

End of Isolation

Once the door to the West opened a crack, there was no closing it. Within two years, Japan was forced to sign treaties with Britain, Russia, and Holland similar to the one with the United States. Isolation ended and the weaknesses of the Tokugawas became obvious.

Enemies of the shogunate united under the slogans "Sonno joi" ("Revere the Emperor; expel the Barbarians") and "Isshin" ("Restore the past"). By 1866, the samurai and daimyo of the Choshu, Satsuma, Tosa, and Hizen clans, supported by rich merchants, formed an alliance to get rid of the Tokugawa Shogunate.

Japan Enters the Modern World

Meiji Restoration

By the mid-19th century, great economic problems faced the Tokugawas. The amount of taxes collected had seriously fallen from a century before and the government was forced to cut back as much as 50 percent of the money paid to samurai. Lower ranking samurai were unhappy because higher ranking samurai, regardless of their abilities, were automatically given upper-level positions and higher payments. Many lower ranking samurai were forced to leave the ranks of the samurai in order to survive.

As education became more widespread, many Japanese became unhappy with the rigid class system. Especially unhappy were the merchants, artisans, and manufacturers who, despite their wealth, were still considered socially inferior to the daimyo and samurai.

As criticism of the shogunate grew, many Japanese began to question the idea of the rule of the shogun. Japanese historians became aware that the imperial family, living in Edo (Tokyo), had once led Japan. The idea of an imperial restoration (bringing the emperor back into power) grew. In November 1867, following the death of the shogun, the young Emperor Matsuhito Meiji (*Meiji* means enlightened rule) was given full authority to rule Japan. In January 1868, the Emperor abolished the shogunate.

The new Meiji regime was led by a small group of samurai and merchant-bankers. The old power group of shogun and supporters was replaced with a new group of influential men with military and financial power, who chose to use the Emperor as a symbol of their authority. For the average Japanese it really did not make any immediate difference that the Emperor had replaced the shogun. The real difference was in how the new leaders chose to direct the nation. The direction they picked had a deep and far reaching influence on Japan's future.

The Program of the Meiji

The new leaders wished to set up a modern, centralized nation. To guide their policies, they looked to the great powers of the West. First, opposition to the new government within Japan was ended. A rebellion led by the Satsuma clan was ruthlessly put down. Rebellions would no longer trouble the Japanese. Next, the government set up a commission to draw up a constitution, which was issued as a gift in 1889. The new constitution borrowed a great deal from the Prussian (German) Constitution. The state was greatly strengthened. Great power was given to the emperor, whose position was justified under the Shinto religion and legends. A **bicameral** (two house) legislature, called the Diet, was set up with limited power. A prime minister and his cabinet were to be picked by the Emperor and, in theory, were responsible only to the Emperor. Actual power was concentrated in the hands of the Emperor's advisors. The constitution proclaimed the rights of the people, but with a major restriction: the interests of the state came first. The ministers of the army and navy were very powerful. The army and navy could destroy a cabinet they opposed by resigning from it or by refusing to serve in it. This power had tragic consequences for the Japanese people. It encouraged the growth of **militarism**, which plunged Japan into the fateful war with the United States.

The new government viewed education as a major priority. Educated people were needed for the new factories and government offices. As a result, a national school system was created by the government. This national school system was also used to promote loyalty to the government.

Payments to the samurai were ended in 1876. At the same time, the government ended all samurai privileges including the right to wear swords and to hold government posts. Compulsory military training was introduced for all Japanese men.

Industrialization

Industrialization was viewed by the Meiji leaders as the key to modernization. With state support, tremendous energy and will, many economic innovations were introduced. Textile production became the chief industry. The government needed capital, but refused to borrow from foreign nations because Japan did not want to give any foreign power the slightest reason for getting involved in Japanese affairs. The land and tax system was changed to meet the needs of industry. The peasants were given legal possession of the land. Taxes were placed on the land based upon its value. Often unable to pay their taxes, farmers were forced to borrow money at high interest rates, or to sell their land. Once they lost the land, they became tenant farmers, renting the land they farmed. Rents were high and conditions were difficult, but tenant farming continued. By using cheap labor, and instilling national pride in the workers, the Japanese made slow but steady progress and, within a generation, Japan had succeeded in laying down the basis for a completely modern industrial system.

Nationalism and Imperialism Grow

Japan's desire to modernize was matched by a desire to keep its independence. A cautious policy was followed toward foreign nations, to further Japan's security. The Japanese were successful in removing the "unequal treaties" with Western nations that gave those nations special privileges in Japan. Nationalism was stirred, and the greatness and "divine mission" of the Japanese was proclaimed.

The Japanese began to look outward. Korea, the peninsula that pointed like a knife at Japan's heart, was Japan's chief concern. In 1894, with the idea of gaining control of Korea, Japan attacked China. Within three months the Japanese had completely defeated the Chinese in the Sino-Japanese War. This quick defeat disturbed Russia, France, and Germany, who also wanted parts of China. The Europeans forced a peace on the two Asian nations. Japan was forced to give up its dream of controlling Korea. Russia now moved troops into the area; thus, Japan had a score to settle with Russia. In 1902, Japan signed a military alliance with Great Britain. This treaty assured Japan that France would not join Russia if the latter went to war with Japan.

The war between Japan and Russia came in 1904, and was a strain on both countries. The Japanese attacked the Russian fleet by surprise in Port Arthur, and badly damaged it. A second fleet was destroyed by the Japanese at the Tsushima Straits. On land, the Russians were driven out of Korea, and the Japanese captured Port Arthur and Mukden in Manchuria. Theodore Roosevelt, the President of the United States, brought the two sides together. In the Treaty of Portsmouth, Russia's lease on Port Arthur and its concessions in Manchuria were given to Japan. In 1910, Japan solved its Korean problem by annexing Korea to Japan.

Japan Becomes a Great Power

Japan's rise to a place among the great powers was speeded up during World War I (1914–1918). The Japanese declared war on Germany, and took over Germany's interests in China and the Pacific. The war also gave Japan the chance to build up its industry and trade. As a result of the war, Japan became the foremost power in Asia, and one of the five great powers in the world.

During the 1920s, Japan went through a period of political, social, and economic unrest. Government reforms were introduced. In 1925, all men were given the right to vote. New political parties, often of a radical nature, were founded, and factory workers and peasants were allowed to organize into unions. The conservatives, nevertheless, managed to remain in power.

In international affairs Japan tried to adjust to its new position and to the changing world. Siberia became a target for Japanese ambitions. Worried about Japan's rising naval strength, the Western powers called together all the naval powers to meet in Washington. The purpose of the Washington Conference was to limit the number of warships. This and other issues led to tense relations between Japan and the West.

War with China

In the early 1930s, angry military leaders and nationalist super-patriots decided to act. They blamed the government for the country's economic and social problems. They proposed that territorial expansion at China's expense would solve Japan's problems. Manchuria, a rich and sparsely settled area, interested them greatly. With fertile lands and rich deposits of coal and iron, the area would be of great value to the overpopulated and impoverished Japan. Control of Manchuria would give Japan a source of badly needed raw materials. These officers provoked an incident at Mukden, and war began with China. Manchuria was quickly overrun and taken into the Japanese Empire. Within Japan, the opponents of expansionism and militarism were terrorized and assassinated.

In 1937, Japan went to war with China in an effort to assert its dominance in Asia. Inside Japan, the government moved toward stricter controls of all aspects of life. The war in China and expansion into Indo-China led to trouble with the United States. The United States also wished to have an available supply of raw materials. In addition, the United States opposed the military expansion of Japan as a violation of the legitimate rights of a free China. The key to Japanese dreams was the rich area of Southeast Asia. The area had an abundant supply of raw materials, especially oil and rubber, and its conquest promised to solve many of Japan's economic and military problems. No great resistance was expected, since France, Great Britain, and the Netherlands were deeply involved in war in Europe. Only the United States had the power to block Japan's plans.

War with the United States

On December 7, 1941, the Japanese launched a surprise attack on U.S. bases in the Pacific. The Japanese had taken the supreme gamble. They were to lose.

The Japanese battle plan had been to strike lightning blows at the Europeans in the Pacific, that is, to overrun Malaya, the Philippines, Burma, and the Netherlands East Indies, and then offer peace. They were victorious at first, but soon found themselves in trouble. The United States rapidly recovered from early defeats and losses. What the Japanese feared most was a long war, and this was what they got. The Japanese navy suffered its first defeat at Midway. The Americans went on the offensive, and slowly moved closer to Japan itself. Its armed forces defeated in the Pacific and its home islands blockaded and under attack, Japan prepared for an all-out defense of its homeland.

During the summer of 1945, despite great losses in men and equipment, Japan continued to fight savagely. The leaders of the United States and the other Allies became convinced that only a direct invasion of the Japanese islands would lead to victory. The United States estimated that this invasion would cause over 1 million casualties for the U.S. forces alone.

Potsdam Declaration

In July 1945, soon after the death of President Franklin D. Roosevelt, the new president, Harry S Truman, issued the Potsdam Declaration, calling on the Japanese to surrender or face destruction. The Declaration demanded that:
1. all militarists and nationalists be removed from positions of authority;
2. the Japanese ability to make war be destroyed;
3. Japanese leaders who had committed war crimes be punished;
4. Japanese control would be limited to the four main islands and nearby small islands;
5. all Japanese troops would be allowed to return home;
6. all civil liberties would be reestablished.

Ten days were given for a reply. There was no response from the Japanese government.

Decision to Use the Atomic Bomb

A difficult decision faced the United States. "In all," President Truman said, "it had been estimated that it would be until late in 1946 to conquer the Japanese home islands. We all realized that the fighting would be fierce and the losses heavy." These thoughts convinced President Truman that the use of a terrible weapon was necessary and justified.

On August 6 and August 9, 1945 the first atomic bombs were dropped on Hiroshima and Nagasaki. The Japanese government was now faced with a horrible fate and, on August 15, 1945 the Emperor announced over the radio that he had decided to surrender.

Japan, for the first time in its history, had been completely defeated, and faced occupation by a foreign army.

Japan After World War II

Occupation by the United States

After Japan's defeat in World War II, the American army occupied Japan from 1945 to 1952. The Japanese government was put under the control of General Douglas MacArthur and the American army. As punishment for starting the war and invading various areas, Japan lost its empire and was forbidden to have an army or navy. The occupation government encouraged changes in all phases of Japanese life.

Reform in Government

The core of U.S. reforms in postwar Japan was a new Constitution to replace the old "gift" of 1889. The new Constitution went into force in May 1947. It is one of the most democratic constitutions in the world today.

For the first time, full political power was placed in the hands of the Japanese people. Emperor Hirohito had little power. He announced to the people on January 1, 1946, that he was a mortal human being like themselves, and not godlike. All citizens over 20, both men and women, may vote, and women may serve in the government. The top political body is the two-chamber National Diet. The House of Councilors serves for six years, and the lower, more powerful House of Representatives is elected for four years. The Prime Minister is usually the leader of the strongest party in the Diet. He appoints a cabinet to help him govern. If he is defeated on a bill, or if the Diet votes "no confidence" in the government's policy, the House of Representatives may be dissolved and a new election called.

The Prime Minister and all the cabinet members must be civilians. Military officers may not hold cabinet posts. The Constitution prohibits Japan from waging aggressive war again. The Constitution also guarantees a long list of basic rights. Many of these are like the Bill of Rights of the U. S. Constitution.

The economic gains made by Japan since 1945 have been outstanding. The old industrial system of a few great industrialists has been changed as many new groups have been allowed to open businesses. Today Japan ranks among the three greatest manufacturing and trading nations in the world. Improved economic conditions have caused changes in traditional behavior. In general, the welfare of all the people has been greatly improved.

Restoration of Independence

The Korean War, which began in 1950, revived Japan's economy. It also led to the end of the American military occupation. The United States bought large amounts of military

GOVERNMENT OF JAPAN

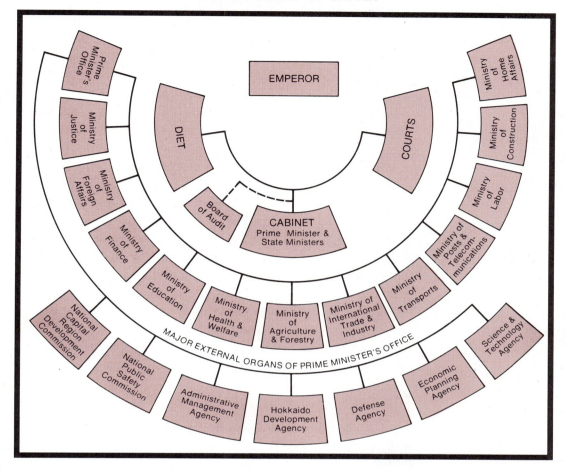

EMPEROR

DIET

COURTS

Prime Minister's Office

Ministry of Justice

Ministry of Foreign Affairs

Ministry of Finance

Ministry of Education

Board of Audit

CABINET
Prime Minister & State Ministers

Ministry of Health & Welfare

Ministry of Agriculture & Forestry

Ministry of International Trade & Industry

Ministry of Transports

Ministry of Posts & Telecommunications

Ministry of Labor

Ministry of Construction

Ministry of Home Affairs

MAJOR EXTERNAL ORGANS OF PRIME MINISTER'S OFFICE

National Capital Region Development Commission

National Public Safety Commission

Administrative Management Agency

Hokkaido Development Agency

Defense Agency

Economic Planning Agency

Science & Technology Agency

goods such as clothing, shoes, and processed food from Japanese manufacturers. At the same time, troops stationed in Japan were transferred to Korea.

In 1951, Japan signed a peace treaty with the United States and 47 other nations (excluding the Soviet Union). The treaty restored full independence to Japan in 1952.

Japan has remained a democracy since the end of occupation in 1952. Several major political parties have competed for leadership, but the conservatives usually have managed to keep power.

For many years Japan did not wish to play a leading role in world affairs. The government was satisfied to improve economic conditions. Japan had the United States to defend it, and followed the American lead in international affairs. However, since the late 1960s, the Japanese have decided to go their own way. Today the Japanese people are split on what course to follow, but Japan is again playing the role of an important power in the world.

Japan's Economy

The Road to Economic Modernization

When Japan entered the modern world after the Meiji Restoration in 1868, Japanese leaders recognized that industrialization was the key to the future. However, the leaders of

Japan saw many existing problems. The lack of trained technicians was critical. Consequently, the government set up technical schools and began the teaching of modern science. Promising students were also sent to Europe and the United States for higher education and special training. The government used foreign engineers as teachers and advisors in the new schools and factories.

Another problem, at the beginning, was a lack of capital. Private capital was in short supply, and the little that existed was invested in banking and domestic trade. The government itself showed the way by building and operating small factories. These factories produced military supplies, iron, textiles, cement, and glass products. The government also set up the first railroad and telegraph, and built a merchant marine.

With this as a basis, and a continued favorable attitude on the part of the government toward industry, private businesspeople began to invest and build. This was the beginning of the huge firms such as Mitsui and Mitsubishi, which still exist today.

Except for the war years (1914–1919), Japan had an unfavorable balance of trade (more imports than exports). Modernization could not be achieved without a great expansion of foreign trade. But Japan had little to export, except for silk, which was in great demand in the West, and ranked for years at the top of Japan's export list. However, neither silk nor cotton textiles earned enough to pay for Japan's growing list of imported goods. Japan's resources were never sufficient to meet the needs of a great industrial power, and Japan was forced to depend on foreign sources for raw materials. Its chief minerals are coal, gold, copper, and sulfur. To keep its factories going, Japan must import oil, cotton, rubber, iron ore, and many other materials.

Japanese Resources

Japan's location has influenced the development of its major resource—the sea and its wildlife. Japan is surrounded by water and it has a long irregular coastline that faces the Pacific Ocean. As a result, Japan has created the world's largest fishing industry. Programs of aquaculture (farming the sea) and developing fish farms on land also supply Japan with fish, shellfish, seaweed, and pearls from oysters. Despite protests from all over the world, the Japanese still hunt and kill whales.

Japan's mountainous topography is heavily forested. However, the forests are not used to a great extent. They serve to control soil erosion and they provide places for leisure activities as national parks. To make up for the limited use of timber from the forest, the Japanese import wood pulp to make paper and plywood.

The largest percentage of Japan's imports are raw materials used for the growing Japanese industries (see page 576). Japan has some coal, but it imports 65 percent of its needs from Australia and the United States. Iron ore comes from Australia. Almost all of Japan's petroleum must be imported, mainly from the Middle East. Repeated attempts at conservation have had a small effect on Japan's dependence on imported oil.

Japan's fast flowing rivers supply about 20 percent of its hydro-electric needs. Another 25 percent of its electrical needs comes from nuclear power plants. The remaining 55 percent of Japan's energy needs are imported.

The Economy at the End of World War II

When Japan surrendered in 1945, its economic situation was desperate. Not only had Japan lost its Asian colonies and, therefore, its main sources of raw materials, but a quarter

Millions of Japanese still live in villages such as this one. Note the thatched roofs made of straw.

Millions more have moved to large cities such as Tokyo where skyscrapers dot the skyline.

of its national wealth had been destroyed by the war. Yokohama and Tokyo, making up one of the most important economic complexes in the world, were in ruins. Close to two million Japanese had been killed, and ten million were homeless.

The Americans poured food, raw materials, industrial equipment, and technical know-how into Japan, and the Japanese began to rebuild. By 1955, Japan was able to export more than it imported, leaving money for expansion of the economy.

Sensational Economic Growth

Since then, Japan's economic growth has been outstanding. Coal, iron, and steel production zoomed to new highs. Machine tools, locomotives, and automobiles streamed off brand new assembly lines. The Japanese created a large electronics industry. Today the Japanese are the leading manufacturers of radios, transistors, television sets, and computers as well as optical goods such as cameras and microscopes.

In the 1990s, Japan's gross national product (GNP) was more than $1 trillion; this was second only to the GNP of the United States. The unemployment rate in Japan was less than 3 percent. Japanese workers earn far more than workers in France and Great Britain, with wages nearing those paid to workers in the United States and West Germany.

JAPAN MUST IMPORT TO LIVE

Wool	100%	Wheat	91.7%
Cotton	100%	Sugar	86%
Crude Oil	99.7%	Coal	65%
Iron Ore	99.3%	Lumber	47%
Soy Beans	96.4%		

Shortly after the end of the Korean War (1953) Japan's economic takeoff began. From the early 1950s until the middle of the 1970s, Japan had the highest continuous rate of economic growth in world history. Annual real Gross National Product (GNP) growth or the money value of the total output of Japan's goods and services averaged 10 percent during these years.[*] During this 25 year period it seemed as if all Japan was dedicated to one objective—spectacular economic growth.

By the end of the 1960s, Japan's economy had grown to the third largest in the world (after the United States and West Germany). Japan's industry was producing about ten times as many goods as in 1941 on the eve of the attack on Pearl Harbor. Through the 1970s, despite the Arab oil embargo and increased world competition, Japan continued to lead all major nations in economic growth.

A most impressive fact of Japanese development has been the huge amount of diversification (various industries). In the mid-1950s, Japan was the world leader in the production of high quality scientific instruments, cameras, and sewing machines. In the late 1950s, electronics and shipbuilding grew rapidly. By 1960, Japan was the world's largest shipbuilder and one of the world's largest manufacturers of radio equipment. In the 1960s, the Japanese ranked among world leaders in production of televisions, petrochemicals, and steel.

Automobiles became Japan's chief growth industry of the 1970s. By the 1990s, Japan had become the world's second largest producer of cars and trucks. (Japan is the world's top producer of passenger cars.)

---

[*]Allen, G.C. *A Short Economic History of Japan.* New York: St. Martin's Press, 1981. p. 190.

Japanese companies today and well into the twenty-first century will be among the world's leaders in robotics, semi-conductors, computers, and fiber optic production. In addition to manufacturing, Japan has gained world leadership in banking, commercial aviation, and insurance.

Myths About Japan's Economic Growth

A number of myths have grown up about Japanese industrial growth in the past 20 years. One common myth is that the growth is based mainly on the use of "cheap labor." It is not. Many parts of Asia have lower labor costs as well as more raw materials. These nations have not achieved what the Japanese have. To be sure, Japan's labor rates are generally lower than those in many Western countries, but in steel and machine production, direct labor rates are at European levels.

Another myth is that Japanese economic growth is the result of exports. In fact, the success of Japanese companies in the export market grows out of high demand at home. In manufacturing, from umbrella frames to motorcycles, the first growth took place to supply a growing home market with the export growth following three to five years later.

A third myth is the view that the Japanese were copiers who were unable to produce original products or technology. Every country has, in the opening states of industrialization, begun by copying. Japan did its copying in the 1930s, and today, the Japanese invest as much in research and development as Germany does and more than Great Britain, France, and Italy do.

A fourth myth is that economic growth is just temporary and caused by good luck. The fact is that the rate of Japanese economic growth has been quite steady since the beginnings of industrialization in the late 19th century.

Reasons for Economic Growth

Instead of relying on myths to explain this growth let us look at some possible reasons. Three key factors in the Japanese system help us to understand the growth: unusual methods of raising capital, a unique (one of a kind) relationship between government and business, and a special way of using labor.

To Western business, the Japanese business structure seems to float on a sea of IOUs (loans). Most Japanese business depends on borrowing from banks instead of raising capital by selling stocks and bonds. The banks that make the loans depend on the Bank of Japan (owned by the Japanese government) for their credit. In fact, the Japanese government is a watchful and skillful partner in everybody's business.

The Japanese factory worker, technician, clerk, or manager is employed for life or at least as long as the company survives. The amount of money earned is set not by the nature of the job or by how well it is done, *but* by age, education, and length of service. The workers identify themselves with their company and its interests. Since pay is related to age, a fast growing company or industry keeps labor costs low by hiring directly out of schools. As a result of this, the skills level of workers remains high. Since status and salary do not depend on types of jobs or how well the jobs are done, rigid work rules and definition of jobs are almost unknown in Japan. This explains in part why the Japanese have been able to adopt the latest labor-saving devices and production methods without the opposition of Japanese labor unions.

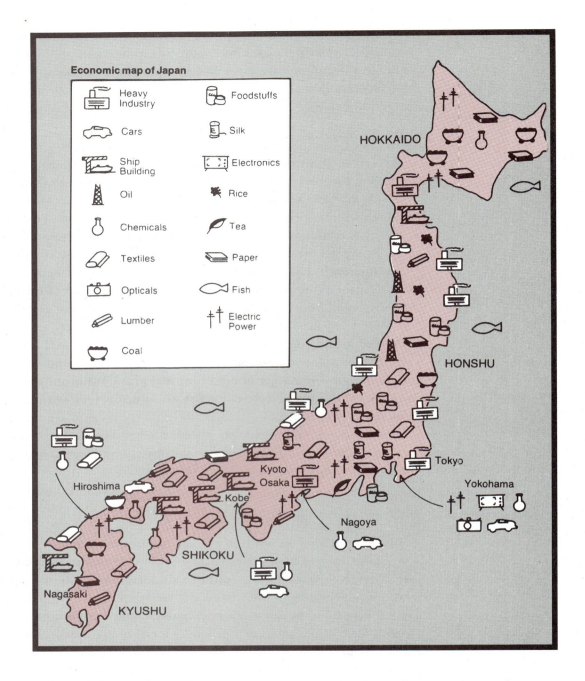

Economic map of Japan

Heavy Industry
Cars
Ship Building
Oil
Chemicals
Textiles
Opticals
Lumber
Coal
Foodstuffs
Silk
Electronics
Rice
Tea
Paper
Fish
Electric Power

HOKKAIDO

HONSHU

Tokyo

Yokohama

Hiroshima

Kyoto
Osaka

Kobe

Nagoya

SHIKOKU

Nagasaki

KYUSHU

Historical factors have also played an important role in Japan's economic growth.

1. A merchant class arose at the end of the feudal period. This rise was encouraged by the Tokugawa Shoguns from the early 17th century to the fall of the shogunate in 1868.

2. Western technology and its adaptation to Japanese needs and interests were accepted early.

3. Powerful industrial and financial family organizations (*Zaibatsu*) developed. In many cases these families were from the merchant class developed under the Tokugawas and from the old samurai class. These people had the capital to help the Meiji survive in the early years of the Restoration. This financial help was not forgotten in later years. A close cooperation in industrial policy developed between the merchants and the government.

4. Japanese culture always valued hard work and cooperation. Achievement for the family or the group is considered more important than individual achievement. The Japanese have the ability to adapt to existing conditions. They are not afraid to tackle new problems and use other people's methods to solve those problems. The Japanese also take the long view. They are willing to lose a great deal of money at the beginning of an operation if they believe they will be able to gain control of a market in the long run.

5. The lack of natural resources has encouraged Japanese business leaders to spend less money on the steel, petrochemical, and shipbuilding industries. Instead, Japan has spent most of its capital in "knowledge-intensive industries," such as electronics and computer technology.

6. Business is helped by the government. When the government decides to help an industry, banks will make low interest loans. Companies working in new areas get a 50 percent **subsidy** (grant of aid). Government help is also given by supplying trade information and by setting up favorable trade agreements with other nations.

7. The military protection given by the United States to Japan has allowed the Japanese to spend more on economic development and less on building a large military.

Agricultural Recovery after World War II

Japan's recovery in agriculture was almost equally outstanding. The occupation government began a land reform program that was very successful. Land held by great landlords was distributed to all Japanese farmers. Two-and-one-half acre plots were sold to several million farm families at very low prices. Within a few years, almost all farmers owned their own land, many for the first time. The percentage of landless and tenant farmers is now lower in Japan than in almost any country in the world.

Inspired by the land reform and generous government subsidies, Japanese farmers rapidly increased their output. By using modern scientific methods, they produced some of the world's highest crop yields per acre, especially of rice. By the 1960s, Japan actually produced more rice than it could use. This is still true today.

Japan has been able to control its population growth to some extent. Realizing that a continuation of the rate of population growth that existed up to 1945 would hamper rather than help recovery, the Japanese government passed laws encouraging family planning. The number of births began to drop. The rate of increase of population fell from over 2 million during the occupation to less than 1 million, annually, during the 1960s.

Historically, the way the Japanese farm the land has depended upon the climate and topography of the area. Although less than 20 percent of the land of Japan can be used for farming, Japanese farmers have achieved the highest crop yields per acre of all the world's farmers.

The success of Japanese farmers is a result of the methods they use. Japanese farmers terrace the steep hillsides and they use the most improved fertilizers and the best farm machinery and farming methods. All Japanese farmers own their own land. The farms are small, about two-and-one-half acres or one hectare.

Climate determines what is raised. In the far south, where the growing season is long, double cropping (two rice crops or rice plus an unirrigated crop are grown each year) is practiced. On Hokkaido in the north, where the growing season is short, a special kind of rice is grown. This rice form developed by the Japanese can be raised and harvested within the short growing season.

About 50 percent of Japan's farmland is used to raise rice. The warm climate of southern Japan allows farmers to raise tea, mulberry trees for silkworms, soybeans, and a variety of fruits and vegetables.

In cooler and drier northern Japan, wheat, barley, potatoes, and vegetables are grown. Cattle grazing and a large dairy industry is found on the island of Hokkaido.

Due to the large Japanese population, Japan must import 30 percent of its food. Grains and meats are among Japan's largest imports. The need for imported food has grown as many Japanese have developed a taste for Western food such as beef and pork. Packaged foods and fast food restaurants, like McDonalds and Kentucky Fried Chicken also have become popular in Japan.

Problems in Japan's Economy

Despite the great success of Japanese industry, there are some problems. Because of its rapid growth and expansion, Japanese industry faces a shortage of skilled workers. The drop in the population growth shows that this shortage may get worse in the future, and the delicate Japanese economy can be easily upset.

Since the end of World War II, Japan has operated on a policy of stimulating industrial growth. At the same time, the Japanese government has not spent as much money on public transportation and communications systems, roads, schools, and housing. The movement of people from the farms to the city has created housing shortages. The average Japanese living in Tokyo lives in four and a half *tatami mats* (tatami are mats on which the Japanese sleep and sit) of living space (81 sq. ft.), while fewer than half of Tokyo's families have a bathtub or are served by sewers.

The Japanese began to protest their situation. Complaints about pollution and lawsuits against corporations have grown. Indeed communities have become so angered over the ill effects of *Kogai*, as the Japanese call environmental upset, that many industries find it impossible to overcome public resistance to the building of new plants.

In the early 1970s, inflation became a very serious problem. Prices went up and the Japanese were forced to devalue the yen (make the yen worth less). The energy crisis in the early 1970s hit Japan very hard because Japan must import all of its oil, mainly from the Middle East. The Arab nations prevented normal shipments of oil to Japan, which created shortages of oil for Japanese industry. There were also shortages of their vital raw materials such as iron ore and lumber. The result of these shortages was a fall in production and an increase in unemployment. The government had to give up its plans to redistribute population and industry throughout Japan.

Prime Minister Kakuei Tanaka was forced to resign from office in early 1976 because of a scandal. Many Japanese government officials, including Tanaka himself, had received money from the American company Lockheed Aircraft. The purpose of the "money gift" was to encourage the Japanese government to buy Lockheed planes for the Japanese Air Force and Japan Air Lines.

Attempts to solve the growing economic problems were made by increasing Japanese exports and productivity. In addition, Japan found new fuel sources in China, while also improving its relations with the Arabs. The Japanese also requested the help of the United States.

Sapporo, on the Island of Hokkaido, is the main city on Japan's frontier. Note the mountains. Hokkaido has very cold winters. Snow and ice sculptures are part of the annual snow festival.

Japan's Economy in the 1980s

In the 1980s, Japan became a serious rival of Switzerland in the manufacturing of watches. The Japanese also made big advances in selling their automobiles in the United States and Great Britain. In 1981, the volume of sales of Japanese cars in the United States reached such a high level that the Japanese were forced to limit car exports to the United States for two years.

Japanese foreign trade continued to grow. In 1981, Japan had a **trade surplus** (exports minus imports) of about $75 billion. In 1984, the Japanese trade surplus was $44 billion. Also in 1984, exports of Japanese goods to the United States reached a record high of $60 billion.

The Japanese government, led by Prime Minister Kaifu, has promised to encourage the Japanese people to import and buy U.S. and European goods. The Japanese government has also promised to make it easier for U.S. companies to set up plants in Japan.

Just imagine, narrow Tokyo streets are lined with McDonald's, Kentucky Fried Chicken, 7-Eleven, and Haagen-Dazs Ice Cream stores. Coca-Cola machines are to be found on every street corner. Small Japanese stores sell Trident chewing gum and Kleenex tissues. In Japanese offices, Scotch Tape, Xerox copiers, and IBM and Burroughs computers are found in great quantities.

A dream for the future? No. This is Japan in the 1990s. This is the flip side of the Sonys, Canons, Hondas, Panasonics, and Toyotas so common in the United States. Coca-Cola has a 60 percent share of all Japanese soft drink business. IBM-Japan is one of Japan's largest exporters. Business machines and computers from IBM-Japan are shipped throughout Asia, Africa, and Europe.

Most American products must be changed to meet the tastes of Japan's consumers. For example, Yamazaki-Nabisco's Ritz Crackers are less salty than the ones sold in the United States; its Chips Ahoy cookies are not as sweet. Ajimoto-General Foods uses a better grade of coffee bean for its Maxim instant coffee. Coca-Cola's Fanta soft drink contains no artificial coloring. Its Sprite tastes less of lime.

Trade Relations

In the 1970s, Japan regularly exported more to the United States and the West than it bought through imports. In the 1980s, this trade balance gap grew larger. In the United States, the auto and steel industries were badly hurt by less expensive imports from Japan and thousands of Americans lost jobs.

The United States and other Western nations felt that Japan was using unfair trade rules and high tariffs to assist their own local industries. For example, the Japanese have forbidden the importation of American rice and other farm products even though rice from the United States is less expensive for Japanese consumers than the local rice. (Japanese farmers have a very powerful influence within the Japanese government.) The European Common Market joined the United States in protesting what it felt was unfair policies restricting imports into Japan.

In the 1980s and into the 1990s, Japan's balance of trade surplus (more exports than imports) reached an all-time high. Due to this surplus, problems with other nations began to grow. How to reduce the surplus and use its economic power to provide greater stability in the international community became important issues for the Japanese.

In May 1987, the Economic Council of the Japanese Government issued the *Maekawa Report*. It claimed that Japan's large balance of trade surplus could not be allowed to continue if Japan was to continue to be in harmony with the rest of the world. The Report suggested that Japan make every effort to reduce its surplus and work closely with other countries to improve trade relationships. The Report also suggested that Japanese economic planning be changed by moving from dependence on exports to a reliance on domestic (local) demand and consumption.

The Report proposed the following steps for the expansion of domestic demand:

1. Improvement of housing, including steps to stabilize land prices and perhaps even to lower them. This could be achieved by increasing the amount of land available for residential (housing) construction.
2. The upgrading of **infrastructure** (road, railroad, and communication).
3. The expansion of consumption by lowering restrictions on foreign imports.
4. The promotion of investment needed to develop new technology and readjust the ideas and structure of industry.
5. The shortening of working hours to allow for more leisure time.

Economic and Political Problems in the 1990s

Since 1989, Japan has faced one of its most serious economic downturns since the end of World War II. The government was reluctant to do anything because it feared inflation would result from any government action. However, in August 1992 after three years of increasing difficulty, the government announced an $86 billion program to improve economic conditions. The money will be used to increase public works programs, assist small and medium businesses, and provide tax incentives for industrial investment.

Scandals Rock Japan's Democracy

Between 1988 and 1992, Japan suffered through four major scandals involving powerful politicians who were caught taking millions of dollars from businesses. In 1989, the scandal was serious enough to force Prime Minister Takeshita to resign.

The scandal in 1992 involved one of Japan's most powerful politicians, Shin Kanemura, the leader of the Liberal Democratic Party that has ruled Japan since 1955.

Mr. Kanemura admitted that he had received $4 million in illegal contributions. It was also charged that Kanemura had asked the leader of a *yakuza* (an organized-crime syndicate) to silence opposition protesters. Soon after this request, the yakuza leader was reportedly lent $2 billion by groups friendly to Kanemura. One of the group who lent the money to the yakuza was indicted by the legal authorities. However, they agreed to Mr. Kanemura's demand that he not be questioned about his part in the deal. Instead, Mr. Kanemura sent a short written statement and paid a $1,700 fine.

The Japanese people usually trust their prosecutors to pursue every law breaker. In this situation, the prosecutors were widely criticized for not pressing Mr. Kanemura more fully and then ending the investigation before discovering what ties existed between Japanese political leaders and the country's underworld. Many Japanese felt this situation presented a major threat to Japan's democracy.

Japan's Place in the World Today

During the years of the occupation, Japan had little to do with the outside world. Most Japanese were involved with the problems of daily survival. Japan's foreign affairs were the responsibility of the occupation government.

Japanese-American Relations

After the occupation, Japan made a new start in the international community. In 1956, Japan joined the United Nations. The Japanese also reestablished diplomatic relations with most governments of the world. Fearing the threat of Chinese Communism, Japan remained dependent on the United States and its military strength for its security. In 1952, a United States-Japan Mutual Security Pact was signed, that gave the United States the major responsibility for defending Japan against aggression. From the beginning, many Japanese opposed this pact, but it is still in effect. Another sore spot between the United States and Japan was the continued occupation of Okinawa and the Bonin Islands by Americans. The Japanese felt that these islands were always a part of Japan, and saw no reason why they should be deprived of lands that were not acquired through imperialist expansion. In 1968, the United States returned the Bonins. In June 1971, the United States promised to return Okinawa as quickly as possible to Japan and in May 1972 the promise was kept. For the most part, the Japanese have followed a pro-American policy, while still holding onto independence of action.

American efforts to improve relations with the People's Republic of China caused some uneasiness in Japan. The Japanese feared that a more friendly American policy with China would be at the expense of Japan. The Japanese decided to protect their interests by following a more independent policy in relation to China and the former Soviet Union. In addition, the Japanese increased their defense budget so that their Self-Defense Forces would be more able to protect an independent policy.

Although relations with the United States remained good in the 1970s, some dark clouds began to form. The United States worried about its trade deficit with Japan and felt that American products were kept out of Japan by government restrictions. The United States wanted the Japanese to lower exports to the United States on a voluntary basis. In addition, the United States did not want the Japanese to "dump" goods (sell them below cost) in the United States (these goods include autos, television sets, and electrical products).

The fall of Vietnam in 1972 caused the Japanese to worry about American plans for Korea. At present, United States troops are stationed in South Korea and large amounts of military aid are sent to South Korea. Since Korea "is a dagger pointing at Japan," the concern of the Japanese is very real. The Japanese look to the United States to help maintain the **stability** (balance) in the eastern part of Asia by remaining strong in that area.

In the 1980s and early 1990s, Japanese-American relations were dominated by trade matters. In 1984, Japanese exports to the United States—about one-third of Japan's total exports—rose 40 percent to a record high of $60 billion. The United States asked the Japanese to increase Japanese imports of U.S. goods and allow U.S. companies to operate in Japan on an equal basis with Japanese companies. The Japanese made small concession on these suggestions but still did not seem to really wish to allow Americans full access to Japanese markets.

When Iraq invaded Kuwait in August 1990, the Japanese were faced with a serious problem. The Middle East supplies Japan with its oil and a disruption of oil deliveries to Japan would create serious economic problems. However, the Japanese Prime Minister Kaifu called Iraq's invasion of Kuwait "unpardonable" and Japan joined the United States and the United Nations in imposing sanctions including a ban on oil imports from Iraq. In October, Kaifu considered sending Japanese soldiers to the Middle East in non-combat roles. However, this idea was dropped because the Japanese Constitution forbids the use of Japanese defense forces overseas. Instead, the Japanese government did agree to share the cost of the allied military buildup in the Middle East. The Japanese pledged $4 billion for this purpose.

Japanese-American relations in the years 1989 and 1990 suffered some serious strains. In 1989, the government of the United States included Japan as an unfair trader. In addition, many Americans were very unhappy when Japanese businesspeople bought Rockefeller Center and Columbia Pictures. Moreover, some Americans criticized the Japanese for apparently stalling on making payments on their $4 billion pledge of cash for the military costs of the Gulf War against Iraq. On the other hand, some Japanese felt that Americans resorted to Japan-bashing (criticizing Japan) to avoid accepting blame for their own economic and political failures.

The United States and Japan will almost surely continue to face problems throughout the 1990s because the economic and financial interests of both nations are at stake. However, the two nations have many common goals and interests and they want to work together to achieve settlements that will benefit both.

Japanese Relations with the Soviet Union

Relations between Russia and Japan have steadily improved. This was caused, in part, by the split between China and the Soviet Union. Hoping to win Japan to its side, Russia began in the 1960s to give Japan a larger share of its trade. Early in 1972, Soviet Foreign Minister Andrei Gromyko was invited to visit Japan. At that time the two governments announced plans to begin negotiations on a treaty formally ending the state of war that existed between the two nations since 1945. They also agreed to discuss their territorial dispute over the Russian-held Kurile Islands. In addition, economic discussions were held in Tokyo about further increases in trade between the two countries and a project to build a $2.5 billion Russo-Japanese Pipeline that would connect a vast Siberian oil field at Tyuman with the Soviet port of Nakhodka, more than 4,000 miles away on the Sea of Japan.

In October 1973, Prime Minister Tanaka went to Moscow to continue discussions with the Russians over the five small islands north of Hokkaido still controlled by the Russians. The Kurile Islands are a volcanic archipelago stretching 180 miles from Japan's northern border. The islands were taken by the Soviets in the last days of World War II. The Japanese still call the islands their Northern Territories and want them back. They are also important to the Japanese fishing fleet. The Japanese offered cash and technical aid to the Russians to help develop Siberian resources. By 1974, the Russians and the Japanese had six major development projects under study or negotiations. These projects involve crude oil development in Tyumen, Siberia; natural gas production in Yakutsk, Siberia; oil and natural gas development in Sakhalin; coking coal development programs south of Yakutsk; forestry development in the Soviet Far East Region; and paper and pulp production in Siberia. However, the Russians still resisted returning the Japanese islands that they control; and there were still disputes over fishing areas.

In February 1978, the Russians offered the Japanese a peace treaty and a good neighbor **pact** (agreement). Japan refused to sign the treaty and the pact because the Russians still refused to return the Kurile Islands.

In the 1990s, Japanese relations with the former Soviet Union continue to hinge on "the islands issue." Annually, on February 7, the Japanese observe "Northern Territories Day," a government-sponsored campaign to publicize Japan's claim to the four islands northeast of Hokkaido (Habomai, Shikotan, Kunashir, and Etorofu).

In the early 1990s, it appeared that the issue of the Kurile Islands might be settled when Russian President Boris Yeltsin was invited to Tokyo to discuss the issue. The Japanese government promised that it would join other industrialized nations in providing direct economic aid to Russia if the Russians returned the islands to the Japanese. Yeltsin was willing to return the islands in exchange for a formal peace treaty never signed after World War II and Japanese financial support for the Russian economy.

However, President Yeltsin was opposed by nationalist groups who threatened to call for his impeachment if he returned the islands to Japan. The nationalists do not want to see any more territory of the "motherland" surrendered. They are allied with the military and are still upset over the loss of Eastern Europe. They also fear that returning the island will threaten the defenses of the Russian Far East (Siberia). Consequently, Yeltsin turned down the Japanese invitation just four days before he was supposed to go. For the time being, the dispute continues.

Japan's sensational economic growth since the end of World War II has created prosperity for the nation but some trade problems with other nations. Here is a modern auto assembly plant.

Japanese Relations with China

Japan's most pressing and difficult decisions in foreign affairs were related to its relations with China. Japan was suspicious and fearful of its powerful neighbor on the Asian mainland. When the Communists came into power in China in 1949, the Japanese were interested in keeping their friendship and establishing profitable trade relations. However, Communist policies and actions worried the Japanese.

When the Chinese exploded their first atomic bomb in 1954, the Japanese became extremely frightened. Many Japanese believed that Japan's safety could be maintained by merely proclaiming and believing in peace, but with China setting off more nuclear devices yearly, the issues of national defense and Chinese-Japanese relations became more vital to the Japanese.

In 1971, the Japanese made direct appeals for discussions on trade to Zhou Enlai, the Chinese Premier. These appeals were ignored by Zhou. However, by improving relations with its neighbors, the Japanese succeeded in changing Zhou's mind. In 1972, Prime Minister Tanaka visited China. This historic meeting ended almost a century of hostility between Asia's two great powers. An agreement was signed to end the "state of war" between the two countries and set up diplomatic relations immediately. Japan's trade with China, which had begun to grow in the 1960s, has grown to over $1 billion as a result of better relations. The Japanese cut off their official relations with the Nationalist Chinese on Taiwan, as a friendly act to the People's Republic of China.

In 1974, Japan and China made an agreement on civil aviation. For the first time in over 40 years scheduled air service between China and Japan operated. Despite some improvement in relations, the Japanese were very concerned and unhappy over Chinese nuclear testing and made strong protests to the Chinese in Peking.

In 1976, the Chinese began to export oil to Japan. The Japanese in return increased their export of industrial machinery to China. Relations between the two nations have improved steadily. Both have common goals in foreign policy and economics. As long as these aims are similar, relations remain good.

In 1978, Japan and China signed a peace treaty ending more than 30 years of unfriendly relations. Along with the peace treaty, the Chinese and Japanese signed a logn-term trade agreement.

In the 1980s, Japanese relations with China continued to improve. In 1984, visits were exchanged by the leaders of the two countries. Trade between the two countries reached record levels. Common policy statements were made showing concern over continued growth of Soviet military power in East Asia. China and Japan expressed their common desire to reduce tensions in the Korean Peninsula. The Chinese have expressed the idea that the U.S.-Japan security treaty was "necessary to strengthen Japanese defense abilities." As a result of the Tiananmen Massacre in China, the Japanese suspended all loans to the Chinese government in June 1989. However, a year later, after an exchange of visits to Tokyo and Beijing, the loans were restored.

ECONOMIC AND SOCIAL PROFILES OF SELECTED COUNTRIES—EAST ASIA

	Population Millions (est.) 1976	1990	Per Capita Income 1989	GNP (billions of dollars) 1989	Literacy Rate % 1976	1992	Doubling Population Time
Japan	113	124	23,730	2920	99	100	exceeds 100 years
Korea (South)	36	43.2	4400	186.5	88.5	96	70 years
Korea (North)	16	21.8	1240	28	NA	95	38 years
China (Peoples Republic)	852	1150	360	393	40	73	48 years
Taiwan (Republic of China)	16.3	20.5	7480	150	86	94	61 years

Source: *Encyclopedia Britannica Book of the Year 1992*

As this table shows, Japan has a higher per capita income, gross national product, and literacy rate than its East Asian neighbors. These factors influence all of Japan's relations with its neighbors.

Japan's Relations with Its Other Asian Neighbors

One of Japan's dreams in the 1960s was to play an important economic role in Southeast Asia. Japan tried to heal the wounds left by invading Japanese armies during World War II, by providing financial and technical aid for the countries of Southeast Asia, the Philippines, and Indonesia. The Vietnam War presented a serious problem to the Japanese. They decided to support the American position. However, in March 1972, the Japanese sent an official trade delegation to Hanoi in North Vietnam. This was the first formal contract ever between the two governments. Relations with Thailand and Burma have been limited to relatively minor trade agreements.

Japan has developed efficient transportation systems between cities and outlying regions. Here you can see the fast Shinkansen (Bullet Train).

Relations with both North and South Korea have improved. In 1965, Japan and South Korea signed a group of treaties that set up formal diplomatic relations between the two nations. Japan agreed to give long term economic aid to South Korea, and trade relations between the two nations increased. The Japanese also made efforts to improve relations with North Korea.

The Japanese made large investments in most Southeast Asian nations, especially Thailand and Indonesia. In Indonesia the Japanese built a $700 million gas project on Kalimantan and Sumatra. Throughout the 1980s and into the 1990s, the Japanese made efforts to improve relations with the nations of South and Southeast Asia. Goodwill visits, exchanges of cultural activities, and economic loans formed the basis of Japanese activities in these areas.

Japan in the 1990s

In the 1960s, former Prime Minister Sato spoke for many Japanese when he announced that Japan wished to have an influence in world affairs equal to its economic power. In the 1990s, the Japanese are fully aware of their power and just as aware of their responsibilities. The Japanese have been developing foreign policy that is more independent of the United States. They are trying to improve relations with all their neighbors. Japan's great trade has had an important impact (effect) on countries all over the world. The Japanese realize they must set limits on export trade or lose the friendship of the United States and the countries of Western Europe. They are making attempts to limit exports by turning their attention to improving life at home. The policies of democratic Japan today stand in sharp contrast to those of the Japanese Empire of the 1930s and 1940s.

Whether the key to the Japanese future lies in a traditional spirit of teamwork or in the attempt to set up individual creativity is difficult to predict. However, it is an almost universally accepted idea that whatever future challenges may face Japan, the Japanese will adapt to them. At the same time they will remain distinct, even unique among the world's peoples.

In his book *The Japanese Mind*, Robert Christopher gives an excellent summation of the Japanese future: "Were I obliged to lay a bet as to which of the world's major societies is most likely to be still functioning in the year 2050 in a form recognizable to its present inhabitants, Japan would be my choice. The Japanese in short, have an uncommon talent for survival."*

Korea—Land and Climate

Koreans call their country a whale's back that has been damaged in battles between prawns (shrimp). Korea's location had made it a highway for invaders from Manchuria and the Chinese mainland. In the late 19th century and into the 20th century, Japan thought of Korea as its stepping stone for control of East Asia. Korea's location and its historical results have given a sense of a common identity and unity to the Korean people.

Korea's location has also made it a link between cultures—especially between the Chinese and Japanese cultures. The Koreans have adapted aspects of both Chinese and Japanese culture.

Location and Topography

Korea is called "The Land of the Morning Calm." It is a peninsula nation that extends off the east coast of Asia between China and Japan. To its east is the Sea of Japan. To its west and south is the East China Sea and the Yellow Sea.

---

*Christopher, Robert. *The Japanese Mind*. New York: Fawcett Columbine, 1983. p. 328.

Korea's northern border with China and the former Soviet Union is the Yalu River and the Paektu-San ("Whitehead Mountain"). The Korean Peninsula is one of the most mountainous areas in the world. Only one-fifth of the land is suitable for farming. The coastline is long but regular and as a result there are few good harbors.

Climate

The climate of Korea is greatly influenced by the sea that surrounds it on three sides. Monsoon winds blow from the southeast in the summer, bringing hot and wet weather. In the winter, the monsoon winds blow from the north and bring cold, dry air from the Asian mainland. The lowland areas of South Korea are less affected by these cold winds.

Although the peninsula is small, there are great differences in the climate of Korea. Highland and lowland temperature and rainfall differ. Since North Korea is attached directly to the Asian mainland, it is influenced by the nearby continental climate regions. In the area bordering China and the former Soviet Union, short, cool summers and bitterly cold winters occur. In the south, the sea a moderating affect. Warm summers and moderate winters are the rule. Rainfall is plentiful on the entire peninsula. The extreme south has a sub-tropical climate.

Korea's People

South Korea is a densely populated country (1,120 people per square mile) with more than 43 million people. About 25 percent live in and around the capital city of Seoul (70 percent of the people live in cities). North Korea has about half the population of the South (23 million) and is much less densely populated (485 people per square mile—65 percent live in cities).

Historians and archaeologists believe that the first people to settle in Korea came from Central Asia about 8,000 years ago. Because of its location near China and Japan, invading armies swept through Korea many times. The invaders settled down and intermarried with the local peoples. As a result, a homogeneous (one type) group was formed (99.9 percent of the people are Korean).

The Korean people were united into one culture group hundreds of years ago. A sign of this was the development of a spoken and written language. Up to the middle of the 15th century, the Koreans used Chinese characters for their writing. In 1443, King Sejong ordered scholars to create a new set of letters or characters with which to write Korean. The result was the current system called *Hangul*. In the Hangul alphabet there are ten vowels and fourteen consonants. The oral language is made of words and ideas from the Chinese, Japanese, Mongolian, and Turkish languages.

Religion

As in Japan, Koreans have accepted and adapted more than one religion into their way of life. Early Koreans believed in nature-spirits. Daoism (Taoism) came from China. Daoists try to simplify their lives and live in harmony with the natural world. Consequently, adapting Daoism to nature-spirit worship was not difficult. Although few Koreans today would call themselves Daoists, Daoism has been very important in the development of Korean culture.

Buddhism, which came to Korea in the 4th century A.D., became the most common religion of the Korean people. As in other things, Koreans adapted Buddhist teachings to fit their existing culture.

Another example of cultural diffusion is Confucianism, which came to Korea from China. This philosophy was of great value to the Korean rulers because it influenced people to respect and obey those in authority. Confucian principles were used to set up a system of education and government administration.

In the 18th century, Christian missionaries came to Korea. At first they were feared and killed by the government. Although the practice of Christianity was outlawed for 100 years, a small Christian community grew. Toward the end of the 19th century, Christian missionaries were allowed to build schools and hospitals in Korea. Many South Korean independence leaders were graduates of these missionary schools.

Today South Korea practices complete freedom of religion. In North Korea, the Communist government discourages people from holding any religious beliefs.

History of Korea

Archaeologists have found evidence that people lived in the southwestern part of the Korean peninsula about 30,000 years ago. About 5,000 years ago, tribes began to migrate into the peninsula from North China and Manchuria. Stone artifacts of pottery, spears, and arrowheads of flint have been found. Evidence of the use of stone plows and sickles have also been found and it is possible these people lived in an agricultural society.

According to legend, Korean history began in 2333 B.C. with the establishment of the ancient state of Chosŏn. It was located along the Taedong River, near present-day Pyongyang in North Korea. The founder of the state was called Tan'gun. Another legend, found in Chinese texts, says that a refugee Chinese noble, Chi-Tzu (Kija to Koreans), led a group of followers from China when the Shang Dynasty fell in 1028 B.C. Kija's descendents ruled Chosŏn for the next 800 years until 194 B.C. In that year General Wiman, either a Chinese or a Korean in the service of the Chinese emperor, seized control of the kingdom in northwestern Korea. This event marks the beginning of Korea's recorded history. Rice farming was the main economic activity (it was introduced in the 8th century B.C.).

Chinese Influence

In the 2nd century B.C., the Han dynasty of China conquered the northern half of the Korean peninsula including the Wiman Kingdom of Chosŏn. The Chinese set up four territories. Korean tribes won back three of the territories over the next 35 years. The remaining fourth territory called Lolong (Nangyang in Korean) remained under Chinese control. Lolong covered the northwestern part of the peninsula near the Chinese border. Through contact with Lolong, the Koreans were able to adapt many Chinese arts and sciences and much of the Chinese system of government. This Chinese contact also led to the introduction of an iron culture and the Chinese ideographic writing system to the Koreans.

Divided Territory

In the 2nd century A.D., the Kingdom of Koguryŏ, the first real Korean state, was set up in the central Yalu River area. By the 4th century, Koguryŏ gained complete control of the Lolong territories.

Meanwhile, the tribes who lived in the southern half of the peninsula had united into three federations called The Three Han. Soon two kingdoms arose out of the three federations. Paekche in the southwestern area (250 A.D.) and Silla in the southeastern area (350 A.D.). The territory of the third Han, which lay in the center of the peninsula, fell to the Koguryŏ in the 5th century.

The Silla

In the wars that resulted, called The Struggle of the Three Kingdoms, Silla conquered the other two kingdoms, and by the middle of the 7th century took control of the entire peninsula.

For the next 200 years (668–892) the Silla monarchs ruled with absolute authority. They continued the process of borrowing and adopting Chinese culture. Silla sailors and traders carried most of the **maritime** (sea) trade in East Asia. Buddhism came to the Korean Peninsula as a result of this trade.

Koryŏ Dynasty

However, a series of disputes among members of the ruling family greatly weakened the Silla. In the early part of the 10th century a warlord, named Wang Kon, took control of the government. He set up a new dynasty and renamed the country, Koryŏ, with its capital in the port city of Kaesong. The name Korea comes from Koryŏ.

The Koryŏ dynasty lasted for over 400 years. It was a period of constant warfare and of economic problems. Late in the 14th century, General Yi Song-gye seized power and set up the Yi or Chosŏn dynasty, which lasted until 1910.

Yi Dynasty

Under the Yi dynasty, Seoul was made the capital. Confucian ideas brought by General Yi from China were introduced. During the Yi dynasty the Korean Hangul alphabet was written. The most productive literary period of Korean history occurred under the Yi dynasty. Scholars of this period wrote encylopedias, histories, and stories in Hangul. Many schools were set up to teach and carry on the ideas of Confucius.

The Yi monarchs ruled with absolute power. They limited trade because they felt that Confucianism, which was followed by the rulers, said it was an evil. Rival factions in the ruling class constantly fought for power and greatly weakened the government.

In the late 16th century, the Japanese invaded the peninsula and captured Seoul. Only the arrival of a Chinese army and brilliant naval victories of Admiral Yi Sun-Sin saved Chosŏn from complete defeat (Yi Sun-Sin was the inventor of the "turtle boat" which was the first iron clad ship). As a result, Korea remained independent but in reality it was under the control of the Chinese as a sphere of influence. In the years that followed, many efforts were made to escape this control. The Chosŏn (Yi) dynasty tried to escape control by closing Korea to all foreign contacts, causing Westerners to call Korea "The Hermit Nation."

The Japanese in Control

In the 19th century, drought and famine futher weakened the Yi dynasty. Peasant rebellions were common. In the last quarter of the century, the Japanese forced Korea to open its gates to trade. When Japan defeated China in 1895 in the Sino-Japanese War, Japan took control of Korea. Over the next 15 years, Korean independence was completely destroyed, and in 1910 Korea was annexed by Japan.

Japanese policy in Korea was based on the needs of the Japanese Empire. Although Japan pushed the economic development of Korea, the Korean people benefitted little from this economic growth. More serious was Japanese cultural policy. The Japanese refused to learn the Korean language. Laws were passed that made Japanese the language of instruction in schools. Newspapers had to be published in Japanese. Japanese policy went so far as to prohibit the use of the Korean language throughout the country.

Korea Seeks Independence

These actions led to the growth of a nationalist movement. Its aim was to gain Korean self-rule. In 1919, a combination of patriotic groups led a nationalist movement called the "Samil Movement" ("Samil" means March 1st). Masses (estimated at over 1 million) of unarmed demonstrators appealed to the conscience of the world to help them gain independence. The Japanese army brutally put down the Samil rebellion. About 7,000 of the Samils were killed and over 20,000 were put in prisons. For the next 26 years, Korean nationalists worked for independence in China, Hawaii, Washington D.C., and in the wild, mountainous areas near the Korean-Manchurian border.

In the 1943 Cairo Conference, the United States, Great Britain, and China proclaimed that, "in due course Korea shall become free and independent." The dream of independence seemed to be fulfilled when the Japanese were defeated and driven from Korea in August 1945.

A Divided Korea

Between 1910 and 1945, the Korean Peninsula was part of the Japanese Empire. In 1945 at the end of World War II, the Soviet Union occupied the northern section of Korea and the United States occupied southern Korea. The dividing line was the 38th parallel of latitude.

The Soviets and the Americans set up governments in each of its zones. A United Nations commission was sent to supervise elections for a government that would rule the entire Korean Peninsula. However, the Soviets would not allow the U.N. commission into their zone. In 1948, elections were held in the south. This resulted in the creation of the Republic of Korea, known as South Korea. At the same time, the Soviets set up the Democratic People's Republic, known as North Korea.

The Korean War

The Cold War that developed after World War II between the United States and the Soviet Union kept Korea divided. In June 1950, thousands of Soviet-trained North Korean soldiers equipped with Soviet-made weapons crossed the 38th parallel and invaded South Korea. A United Nations force made up of troops from the United States and 16 other nations were sent to South Korea to help push the invaders back.

After initial setbacks, the U.N. troops pushed the North Koreans back to the Yalu River, the boundary between North Korea and China. The Chinese warned the United Nations not to invade North Korea, but this warning was ignored. Just before Thanksgiving in 1950, 300,000 Chinese soldiers poured out of mountain hiding places and crossed the Yalu River. The U.N. troops were caught completely by surprise. This surprise attack drove the U.N. forces out of North Korea before the end of December.

The United Nations retreat ended roughly along the 38th parallel, where for over two years, the two armies fought to a standstill. In July of 1953, a truce was signed in the Korean village of Ponmunjom. The agreement left Korea divided. The truce and the division have lasted to this day.

Korea's Economy

Throughout Korea's long history, farming has been the main economic activity of the Korean people. When Japan **annexed** (added to) Korea to the Japanese Empire in 1910, the Japanese took the best farmland for themselves. Many Koreans were forced to move to the cities in order to survive.

Industry began to develop more rapidly in the north than in the south. The main reason for this was the rich natural resources found in the north. Coal, copper, iron, lead, tungsten, and zinc are among the rich mineral depostis found here.

Agriculture

When the Japanese were defeated and driven from Korea, agriculture remained the most important economic activity of the Koreans. In North Korea, on small patches of arable land, farmers grow wheat, barley, soybeans, and millet. The climate and topography of South Korea make farming easier. As you read, the weather is milder and rainfall is more plentiful. Rice is the major crop and in good years it is exported. Barley, millet, soybeans, and sweet potatoes are also grown.

Some Korean farms raise silkworms. These silkworms produce the silk for the very important silk textile industry.

The most important natural resource of Korea is the abundance of water. The sea around the peninsula is rich in fish, shellfish, and seaweed. These foods make up an important part of the Korean people's diet. The rivers that flow rapidly down from the mountains create hydroelectric power. Development of hydroelectric power plants have advanced rapidly in the north. The smaller and slower moving rivers of the south provide irrigation and a means of transportation.

The Growth of Industry

At the time of the division, in 1948, South Korea was economically weak and the best industries were in the north. South Korea depended entirely on an agriculture system that could not support its large population. However, this situation changed greatly. American financial aid and a dictatorial government policy aimed at promoting industrial growth created what seemed to be a miracle. Industries that never existed before were set up, and existing industries were expanded (shipbuilding, steel plants, chemicals, fertilizer, cement making, and glassmaking).

The textile industry was greatly expanded. The latest technology was imported and used to produce wool, silk, rayon, and knitted textile goods. Diesel and petroleum refineries were built. Since the early 1980s, South Korea has become a world class producer of computer technology, automobiles, and television, audio, and electronic equipment.

Korean Industry Today

Today South Korea is regarded as one of the more important industrial powers of the Pacific Rim. This rapid industrialization did not come about without great cost. Japanese rule over Korea disrupted Korean culture by weakening the rural tradition of strong family ties. Moreover, the strong military dictatorship never really allowed for the development of democratic traditions.

In an effort to compete economically with Japan and the United States, the South Korean government encouraged a few families to dominate Korean economic development—the Chaebols. Workers were not treated fairly; wages were low and working condition were not always safe. As a result, large and violent labor strikes took place. Often Koreans demanding greater political freedom joined in these demonstrations. The army and the police used strong measures to control the demonstrations. Many Koreans died or were injured in these demonstrations.

These periodic disturbances have greatly damaged the reputation of the South Korean government. Economic progress also has been slowed. In the early 1990s, it could be truthfully said the economic miracle of Korea had not benefited the majority of South Koreans as much as it should have.

However, a new era in South Korea may be dawning. Elections for president took place in December 1992. This was the first election without army generals running for president. (In the past, it has been said that the army would decide elections by rolling tanks into the street.) By all reports, this election was the fairest South Korea has ever held. There was none of the violence of the 1987 presidential campaign. The president, Roh Tae Woo, a former army general, declared the current government neutral. He moved quickly to assure a fair election by cracking down on suspected violence and abuse of the election law.

The three candidates for president were:

- Kim Young Sam, once a **dissident**, who opposed the government and as a result spent many years under house arrest.
- Kim Dae Jung, South Korea's most famous dissident.
- Chung Ju Young, the billionaire founder of Hyundai. (He might be called the Ross Perot of South Korea.)

All three promised to give more of the benefits of South Korea's economic miracle to the people through economic reform. Mr. Kim Young Sam was elected president in a close election held on December 18, 1992.

The Two Korean Situations in the 1990s

North Korea

For 40 years, North Korea relied on its two giant neighbors, the former Soviet Union and China for political, economic, and military assistance. In 1992, Russia's policy toward Korea changed. It recognized South Korea, stopped supplying arms to the North, and demanded hard currency (gold, American dollars, British pounds sterling) for its oil shipments. In August 1992, against the wishes of North Korea, China also agreed to establish diplomatic relations with Seoul (South Korea).

Isolation is certainly not a new experience for North Korea. The few television sets in North Korea are built so that they cannot pick up telecasts from the South. Radios receive only one North Korean channel that is controlled by the government. Short-wave receivers are illegal for average citizens. The Pyongyang (North Korean) government has forced thousands of young people who were studying in Eastern Europe and in the former Soviet Union to come home. The government was afraid that they might learn new ideas.

North Korea is ruled by its founding dictator, Kim II Sung, who is now 80 and in poor health. The "Great Leader," Kim II Sung's title, has named his son, "The Dear Leader," as his successor. However, this is not a popular choice among other members of the government and a struggle for power over the succession may already have begun.

Some fear the possibility of political turmoil or civil war following the death of Kim II Sung. This is especially disturbing because of North Korea's secret program to develop an atomic bomb. No one knows how close Korea is to having a bomb since Kim has not allowed inspectors access to his facilities or air space.

South Korea's Current Reaction to Possible Unification

Following the death of Kim II Sung, moves to unify North and South Korea would become more possible. German unification presents a powerful example for South Korea. The South Koreans have calculated that based on the size of their economy, it would be ten times more expensive for them to unite with North Korea than it was for West Germany to absorb East Germany.

As a result, the South Koreans hope that communism will die in North Korea and that unification between North and South can be spread over ten or even 20 years. Officials of the South Korean government are hoping that their new friends in Beijing can persuade North Korea to adopt the Chinese model of economic reform and an open door policy toward the rest of the world.

Summary
of
Key Ideas

Japan and Korea

A. **Geographic factors have greatly influenced Japan's history and development.**

  1. Japan is part of a chain of volcanic islands that make up the "Fire Rim of the Pacific."

  2. The islands are mountainous; only one-fifth of the land is usable for agriculture.

  3. There are many rivers, but all are short and not really navigable.

  4. Japan has a long, irregular coastline with many good harbors.

  5. Japan is lacking in all basic industrial raw materials except water power.

B. **Continuity and change are characteristics of Japan's political history.**

  1. Early Japan was greatly influenced by Chinese civilization.

  2. For 1,000 years before 1868 Japan lived in an age of feudalism under the rule of a Shogunate and a Samurai Code.

  3. Japan entered the modern world with the Meiji Restoration.

  4. Rapid modernization and industrialization have been accompanied by social and cultural changes.

  5. Strong nationalism, rapid industrial expansion, and the need for raw materials led to a militaristic foreign policy and wars.

  6. Following World War II, Japan has attempted to establish friendly relations with nations which were once its enemies.

C. **The Japanese have adopted basic political ways of the West.**

  1. The first Japanese Constitution of 1889 gave great power to the Emperor and his advisors.

  2. The Japanese adopted many customs of representative government but power remained in the hands of a small group of military and nationalist leaders until 1945.

  3. The 1947 Constitution set up a democratic limited monarchy. The Emperor is a "symbol of the state and the unity of the people."

  4. A basic part of Japan's foreign policy is to participate actively in the U.N. and keep friendly relations with the great powers.

  5. Japan signed peace treaties with all its former enemies except the Soviet Union.

D. Major changes have taken place in Japanese society and culture since 1945.

   1. The Japanese are racially and ethnically united. (Exception: The Ainu are Caucasian.)

   2. The major religions are Shintoism and Buddhism.

   3. The old family system has been greatly weakened.

   4. The farmers' new position as landowners have given them more status.

   5. Japan has the highest rate of literacy and the most highly developed educational system in Asia.

   6. Japan has a long, rich heritage of artistic creation and appreciation for beauty.

E. Japan has become a modern industrial nation despite its lack of natural resources.

   1. The main problem of Japan's economy is the lack of basic raw materials.

   2. An important asset is the development of Japan's labor force. They include skilled labor, scientists, managers, and technicians.

   3. After World War II, Japan made a spectacular recovery and has become one of the world's leading industrial powers.

   4. Compared with the rest of Asia, Japanese agriculture has a large percentage of owner-farmers.

   5. Japan is the leading fishing nation in the world.

   6. The United States has become Japan's most important trading partner.

   7. Japan's trade and industrial policy have caused serious problems between Japan and its trading partners, including the United States.

F. The Korean peninsula has become an important part of East Asia.

   1. At present the Korean peninsula is divided into two parts with two governments politically opposed to each other.

   2. South Korea is a peninsula nation with a mountainous topography. These factors have greatly influenced Korea's historical and cultural development.

   3. Korean society and culture has been greatly influenced by China and Japan. In turn, Korea has influenced aspects of Japanese cultural development.

   4. Agriculture was the most important economic activity of Korea for many centuries. However, since the 1970s, changes have taken place that caused South Korea to become one of the most important industrial powers of the Pacific Rim.

   5. Korean history has been marked by unstable government and control by foreign powers.

UNIT VII

Exercises and Questions

Vocabulary

Directions: Match the words in Column A with the correct meaning in Column B.

Column A

1. Chanoyu
2. Matcha
3. Ikebana
4. Nō
5. Bunraku
6. Nihon
7. Haiku
8. Manyoshu
9. Kojiki
10. typhoons

Column B

(a) Japanese art of flower arrangement
(b) Japanese puppet plays
(c) Japanese form of poetry
(d) one part of the official written history of Japan
(e) Japanese tea ceremony
(f) famous collection of Japanese poetry
(g) storms which affect Japan
(h) Japanese name for Japan
(i) a form of Japanese drama
(j) powdered green tea

Column A

1. Chickamatsu
2. Basho
3. Lady Murasaki Shikibu
4. Jimmu Tenno
5. Hideyoshi
6. Ieyasu
7. Matthew Perry
8. Mutsuhito Meiji
9. Douglas MacArthur
10. Hirohito

Column B

(a) first Emperor of Japan
(b) established a united Japan in the 16th century
(c) an American sailor who opened Japan to Western trade
(d) a famous playwright of Bunraku and Kabuki
(e) first Japanese Emperor not looked on as a god
(f) Emperor who ended the Shogunate and led Japan into the modern world
(g) author of _The Tales of Genji_
(h) American military commander of Japan after World War II
(i) Shogun who ended the feudal war and established 250 years of peace
(j) a great Haiku poet of Japan

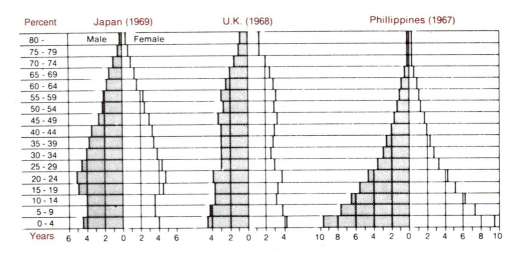

Percent — Japan (1969) — U.K. (1968) — Phillippines (1967)

POPULATION OF JAPAN BY AGE AND SEX (CENSUS OF 1975)
(in thousands)

Age	Total	Male	Female	Age	Total	Male	Female
All ages	111,933	55,115	56,819	40–44	8,210	4,125	4,085
1	1,906	973	933	45–49	7,354	3,658	3,696
1–4	8,059	4,121	3,937	50–54	5,807	2,635	3,172
5–9	8,956	4,587	4,368	55–59	4,647	2,061	2,587
10–14	8,267	4,226	4,041	60–64	4,277	1,922	2,354
15–19	7,904	4,037	3,868	65–69	3,471	1,577	1,895
20–24	9,087	4,569	4,518	70–74	2,548	1,138	1,410
25–29	10,870	5,493	5,377	75–79	1,629	688	941
30–34	9,263	4,627	4,636	80–84	810	310	500
35–39	8,422	4,212	4,210	85+	400	124	276

Source: United Nations *Demographic Yearbook*

Graph Analysis

Directions: Select the statement that best answers the question or completes the sentence. Use only the information given in the graph and chart.

1. The above graph can best be described as a:
   (a) pictograph.   (b) line graph.   (c) pie graph.   (d) bar graph.

2. Most Japanese fell into which of the following age groups?
   (a) 10–19   (b) 20–29   (c) 30–39   (d) 40–49

3. Which of the following conclusions is true?
   (a) The death rate among Japanese below the age of 20 was the greatest of the three countries.
   (b) The birth rate in the Philippines was the greatest of the three countries.
   (c) Women seemed to live longer than men in these three nations.
   (d) About 20 percent of all Japanese were over 70 years of age

4. Which of the following conclusions is false?

    (a) About 35 percent of all the people of the Philippines were below the age of 10.

    (b) There were more Japanese women than men.

    (c) Most Japanese boys were born between 1965 and 1969.

    (d) The Japanese seemed to have the most even distribution of population.

5. The total population of Japan was about

    (a) 102,648.   (b) 50,431.   (c) 52,216.   (d) 102,648,000.

Completion

Directions: Complete the following sentences, using the words listed below:

Ainu	Samurai	Daimyo	Diet	Zen
Shogunate	Feudalism	Kabuki	Kami	Nihonji

1. _____ is a system of landholding and service to a lord.

2. _____ is a form of drama unique to Japan.

3. _____ were the first people who lived in Japan.

4. _____ is one of the official history books of early Japan.

5. _____ are worshiped as parts of nature which arouse fear, awe, or love.

6. _____ is the Japanese lawmaking body.

7. _____ is a new form of Japanese Buddhism.

8. _____ were the warriors of feudal Japan.

9. _____ were the military barons of Shogunate Japan.

10. _____ was the military government that ruled Japan for over a thousand years.

Multiple Choice

Directions: Select the letter of the correct answer.

1. A nation like Japan, made up of many islands, is called

    (a) an inlet.

    (b) an archipelago.

    (c) an isthmus.

    (d) a peninsula.

2. Hokkaido is like the American frontier of the 1870s because

    (a) only Indians are allowed to live on the island.

    (b) it is a dry plain like the American West.

    (c) the climate and poor soil do not attract many Japanese.

    (d) the Japanese government has built many forts.

3. The most important of the main islands is
  (a) Honshu.
  (b) Kyushu.
  (c) Shikoku.
  (d) Hokkaido.

4. Which of the following Japanese cities is likely to receive large amounts of snow in winter?
  (a) Tokyo
  (b) Yokohama
  (c) Hiroshima
  (d) Sapporo

5. All of the following statements about Japanese geography are true *except*
  (a) The Japanese islands are part of a great chain of volcanoes.
  (b) Japan has hundreds of short, swift rivers.
  (c) Japan has a long, regular coastline and few good harbors.
  (d) Japan is made up of thousands of islands scattered over a large area.

6. The mountainous topography of Japan
  (a) prevents a large density of population in any areas of Japan.
  (b) leaves little land for the raising of crops.
  (c) causes Japanese to live mainly on the plateaus of Shikoku.
  (d) gives Japan protection from the monsoon winds.

7. The sea has been important to Japan for all of the following reasons *except*
  (a) It is a source of food and work for the Japanese.
  (b) It is the main route of transportation and communication.
  (c) It has been an effective barrier between Japan and the rest of the world.
  (d) It prevented the development of a unified Japanese nation until 1900.

8. Japan's climate is affected by all of the following factors *except*
  (a) the monsoon winds which blow from the ocean
  (b) the winter winds from the mainland, which blow onto all of Japan
  (c) the Japan Current, which moderates the winter climate and warms in summer
  (d) the similarities in latitude between northern and southern Japan

9. Which of the following is a generalization that can be made about the climate of Japan?
  (a) The entire nation enjoys a mild subtropical climate throughout the year.
  (b) Most of Japan receives little rainfall, less than 40 inches per year.
  (c) Japan is blessed with a climate almost completely without violent storms.
  (d) Japan's climate is similar to that of the east coast of the United States.

10. Which of the following islands would you most likely visit if you wished to go skiing?
  (a) Honshu
  (b) Hokkaido
  (c) Kyushu
  (d) Shikoku

11. Which of the following statements is true about the Japanese language?
  (a) Spoken Japanese is very much like Chinese.
  (b) Most words in Japanese are made up of only one syllable.
  (c) The language has served to unite the Japanese.
  (d) Most words have many syllables, and the stress is very important.

12. The Japanese system of writing
    (a) was borrowed entirely from the Chinese, and is unchanged today.
    (b) was borrowed from China and the West, and adapted to meet Japan's needs.
    (c) is not used today because most Japanese have learned English.
    (d) was a Japanese creation, with no important outside influence.

13. Which of the following statements best describes Japanese life today?
    (a) The Japanese have become completely modernized, and little is left of traditional life.
    (b) The Japanese have rejected modernization, and almost all Japanese customs are traditional.
    (c) The Japanese have blended traditional ways with the new, to meet the needs of modern life.
    (d) The Japanese have rejected Western ideas, and accept Chinese customs.

14. Which value was common in traditional society in Japan?
    (a) pacifism   (b) individualism
    (c) family loyalty   (d) materialism

15. All of the following are examples of cultural diffusion *except*
    (a) the development of the Japanese writing system
    (b) the development of the Shinto religion
    (c) the national sport of Japan is baseball
    (d) the use of desks and chairs in schools

16. All of the following have been important religions of Japan *except*
    (a) Shintoism
    (b) Buddhism
    (c) Islam
    (d) Christianity

17. Which of the following religions is entirely based on the worship of nature?
    (a) Shintoism   (b) Buddhism
    (c) Islam   (d) Christianity

18. All of the following statements are true of the early history of Japan *except*
    (a) The Yamotos used China as a model for forming a Japanese Kingdom.
    (b) For more than a thousand years the Emperor had little or no power.
    (c) The Tokugawas began their rule by encouraging contact with the West.
    (d) Under the Tokugawas, a policy of preventing change was followed.

19. The constitution of Prince Shikōtu was important because it showed the influence of which of the following cultures on Japan?
    (a) Middle Eastern   (b) Christian
    (c) Chinese   (d) European

20. Which of the following events occurred after the other three?
    (a) Kamakura Period
    (b) Fujiwara Period
    (c) Ashikaga Period
    (d) Tokugawa Period

21. The Tokugawa Shogunate in Japan (1600–1867) created a society in which
    (a) social mobility was discouraged.
    (b) militarism was discouraged.
    (c) cultural diffusion was encouraged.
    (d) democratic institutions flourished.

22. The slogan, "Revere the Emperor, expel the Barbarians," was directed against
    (a) the Tokugawa Shogun and the Chinese.
    (b) the Emperor and the Westerners.
    (c) the Chinese and the Westerners.
    (d) the Tokugawa Shogun and the Westerners.

23. The year 1868 is important in Japanese history because
    (a) the age of modern Japan began.
    (b) Matthew Perry opened Japan to the West.
    (c) the Samurai defeated the Mongols.
    (d) a policy of national isolation was begun.

24. A good slogan for the Meiji Restoration might have been
    (a) "Traditional ways and old fashioned ideas are the best."
    (b) "Modernize, but in a Japanese way."
    (c) "Isolation is the best policy."
    (d) "The strong order, the weak obey."

25. Which of the following events was the result of the other three?
    (a) The rebellion of the Satsuma Clan is put down.
    (b) The Meiji Emperor abolishes the shogunate.
    (c) Matthew Perry opens Japan to the West.
    (d) Japan becomes a modern world power.

26. The Meiji ruler did all of the following to modernize Japan *except*
    (a) put down a rebellion of those who opposed modernization
    (b) give the Japanese a new Western style constitution
    (c) establish agriculture as the key to modernization
    (d) stir the nationalism and proclaim the glory of Japan

27. The significance of the Meiji Restoration in Japan was that
    (a) the shogun ruled with supreme power.
    (b) Japan adopted Western customs and technology.
    (c) the Constitution of 1947 was passed.
    (d) it began a period of feudalism in Japan.

28. Japan's attack on China and Russia are examples of
    (a) militarism.   (b) cultural diffusion.
    (c) isolation.   (d) industrialization.

29. Which of the following events happened *before* the other three?
    (a) Japanese invasion of Manchuria
    (b) World War I
    (c) Japanese attack on American bases
    (d) Russo-Japanese War

30. Manchuria was important to Japan for all of the following reasons *except*
    (a) It had fertile soil.
    (b) It had rich deposits of coal.
    (c) It was a good market because of its large population.
    (d) It had rich deposits of iron.

31. The Washington Conference was called because the Western powers
    (a) wished to end the war between China and Japan.
    (b) feared the growing naval strength of Japan.
    (c) wished the Japanese to leave Manchuria.
    (d) wanted Japan to attack Russia in Siberia.

32. Which was a major justification used by Japan for empire building in the 1930s and 1940s?
    (a) revenging attacks by aggressive neighbors
    (b) promoting immigration of foreigners
    (c) spreading the Shinto Religion
    (d) obtaining food and raw materials

33. Since World War II, which development has occurred in the Japanese economy?
    (a) Japan has become self-sufficient since it now has adequate resources.
    (b) Japan has received a favorable balance of trade.
    (c) Japan has returned to an economy based on agriculture.
    (d) Japan has a severe shortage of skilled workers.

34. Which of the following was *not* a problem of Japanese economic development?
    (a) lack of trained technicians
    (b) lack of hydroelectric power
    (c) lack of capital
    (d) unfavorable balance of trade

35. Which of the following events led to the other three?
    (a) Land reform program gives more land to the Japanese farmers.
    (b) Japan is given a new, more democratic constitution.
    (c) Japan is defeated by the United States in World War II.
    (d) Japan creates the second largest electronics industry.

36. After World War II ended
    (a) the Emperor was removed from power.
    (b) full political power was placed in the hands of the people.
    (c) all industry was destroyed and Japan became an agricultural country.
    (d) Japan was forced to become a colony of the United States.

37. The Japanese
    (a) rejected Western technology and skills.
    (b) accepted Western technology and skills.
    (c) use only American raw materials.
    (d) trade only with the United States.

38. Today the Japanese form of government is
    (a) a republic.
    (b) an absolute monarchy.
    (c) a constitutional monarchy.
    (d) a feudal kingdom.

39. In which order did the events listed below take place?
    (a) The Washington Conference takes place.
    (b) Japan joins the United Nations.
    (c) Americans occupy Japan after the Japanese surrender.

    (a) abc   (b) bca   (c) cab   (d) acb

40. A political scientist studying Japan would most likely be interested in
    (a) visiting the Japanese Diet.
    (b) going to a Kabuki play.
    (c) touring Tokyo's museums.
    (d) seeing a high school.

41. Which statement concerning the Japanese Constitution of 1947 is most accurate?
    (a) Women were denied the right to vote.
    (b) The Emperor was stripped of all power.
    (c) The Emperor was declared to hold divine authority.
    (d) Japan placed all power in the hands of a military war council.

42. Which one of the following groups is correctly paired?
    (a) Zen-Satori   (b) Ikebana-Matcha
    (c) Nō-Bonsai   (d) Kabuki-Suim-e

43. Which of the following was an important Japanese painter?
    (a) Chickamatsu   (b) Basho
    (c) Suikaku   (d) Hiroshige

44. Which of the following art forms influenced European art?
    (a) Ikebana   (b) Ukiyo-e
    (c) Suim-e   (d) Nō

45. A study of Japan's music, art, and literature would best help someone to understand its
    (a) foreign policy.
    (b) technological progress.
    (c) cultural values.
    (d) trading policies.

46. Japan's industrial success is based on all of the following historical factors *except*
    (a) the rise of a merchant class in the Tokugawa Period
    (b) the acceptance of Western technology
    (c) the development of powerful industrial and financial families
    (d) American management of Japanese companies

47. An example of a "knowledge-intensive industry" in Japan is
    (a) shipbuilding.   (b) steel.
    (c) textiles.   (d) computers.

48. In Japan, companies working in new areas of technology
    (a) cannot train skilled workers to do the work.
    (b) receive no aid from the government.
    (c) receive a subsidy from the government.
    (d) depend on foreign assistance for development.

49. In Japan workers
    (a) lose their jobs in difficult times.
    (b) have lifetime employment in their companies.
    (c) have little loyalty to the companies they work for.
    (d) earn far less than workers in France and Great Britain.

50. Since the early 1970s, Japan's foreign policy has become more independent of U.S. policies because
    (a) Japan opposed the U.S. policy of ending the Cold War with Russia.
    (b) Japan has grown into an economic superpower.
    (c) The United States has failed to honor its commitments to Japan.
    (d) Japan is so strong militarily that it no longer needs the United States to protect it.

51. Which reason best explains why Japan is one of the world's greatest economic powers?
    (a) It is rich in many important natural resources.
    (b) Its people value hard work and self-discipline.
    (c) It has one of the largest armed forces in the world.
    (d) Its plentiful and fertile lands promote agricultural exports.

52. Which situation would most likely present the greatest danger to Japan's economic health?
    (a) lowering of tariff rates in the United States
    (b) continuing hostilities in Eastern Europe
    (c) rising oil prices around the world
    (d) ending apartheid in South Africa

53. Which Japanese industry would be most severely affected by a maritime disaster such as a typhoon or a tsunami?
    (a) coal mining   (b) electronics
    (c) cameras   (d) fishing

54. Even though Japan has few natural resources, it has a high standard of living mainly because it has
    (a) developed technology that can be exchanged for the resources it needs.
    (b) printed more money whenever living standards have begun to fall.
    (c) imported manufactured goods.
    (d) produced goods and services without obtaining resources.

55. Japanese-American interdependence is characterized most by
    (a) America's wish for Japan's goods and Japan's need for American markets.
    (b) America's need for foreign investment and Japan's need for America surplus goods.
    (c) America's dependence on agricultural imports and Japan's need for electronics.
    (d) America's need for nuclear arms and Japan's ability to supply material for that need.

56. The most accurate description of the economic and political status of women in Japan today is that they
(a) have equal political rights and economic opportunity.
(b) have equal rights under the law, but in fact, suffer from discrimination.
(c) do not have equal rights under the Japanese Constitution.
(d) hold almost half of key government positions on all levels.

57. Which of the following best describes the geography of Korea?
(a) peninsula, extensive lowlands, large lakes
(b) landlocked, mountainous, larger river valleys
(c) peninusla, long coast line, mountains
(d) large coastal plain, mountainous interior, extensive river valleys

58. Which statement best describes South Korea since the end of the Korean War?
(a) The country has suffered a marked decline in its standard of living.
(b) Major industrial development has occurred.
(c) A Communist government has been established.
(d) The population has shifted from urban to rural areas.

59. The strip of land that separates North and South Korea is called a
(a) free trade zone.
(b) combat zone.
(c) demilitarized zone.
(d) truce line.

60. The governments of North and South Korea differ in that
(a) North Korea is democratic and South Korea is Socialist.
(b) North Korea is Communist and South Korea is non-Communist.
(c) North Korea is Socialist and South Korea is Communist.
(d) North Korea is anti-Communist and South Korea is neutralist.

61. North Korea is better suited for industrial expansion than South Korea because
(a) it has more fertile land.
(b) it has rich mineral resources.
(c) it has markets closer to China.
(d) it has state economic planning.

62. Which of the following is not a notable difference which separates North and South Korea?
(a) North Korea is more mountainous and has fewer lowlands than South Korea.
(b) North Korea and South Korea have a common history and language.
(c) Twice as many people live in South Korea as in North Korea and South Korea is much more densely populated.
(d) North Korea has a Communist state-planned economy and South Korea has a capitalist free-market economy.

63. South Korea has been able to gain greater prosperity than North Korea because
(a) it has greater natural resources than North Korea.
(b) government policy has established a free-market economy.
(c) government policy has established Five-year Plans which have been successful.
(d) trade with the Chinese People's Republic has been very profitable.

Thought Questions

1. How does the geography of Japan affect the lives of the people?

2. How has the fact that Japan is made up of many islands affected the lives of the Japanese people?

3. (a) Describe the factors that cause the climate of Japan.
   (b) How do these factors affect the lives of the Japanese people?

4. Why might we call Japan "The Land of the Gods"?

5. If you were an advisor to Shogun Yoritomo, why might you suggest that the position of Emperor be continued?

6. "Japanese society in the feudal period was a military society." How do you think this might have affected this position of women?

7. Why did feudalism grow in Japan?

8. Why were the samurai important in Japanese history?

9. Nobunaga "harvested the rice"; Hideyoshi "cooked the rice": Ieyasu "ate the rice." Explain this statement.

10. How did the Meiji Restoration affect the Japanese people?

11. (a) Why did the Japanese decide to expand their island kingdom?
    (b) Describe the steps taken by the Japanese to reach their dream of expansion and control of Asia.

12. "Japan's recovery from defeat has been a miracle." Give examples to support this statement.

13. The Japanese have been called "copiers of ideas" and "borrowers of ideas." Explain which of the two is more accurate.

14. "An asset of the Japanese is their willingness to learn from others." Explain this statement.

15. Why has Japan been able to become a leading industrial nation despite its small area and few natural resources?

16. How has the life of the Japanese people changed since the end of the war?

17. Describe each of the following forms of Japanese art.
    (a) Nō Drama   (b) Kabuki   (c) Haiku   (d) Ikebana

18. Describe Japanese relations with each of the following since 1945.
    (a) United States   (b) Russia   (c) China

19. Using the rules of haiku discussed in this unit compose a haiku verse.

20. How have myths about Japan influenced what we believe about Japan and the Japanese people?

Explain why you agree or disagree with the following statements:

21. "Japan still has many economic problems to solve."

22. "The languages of the Chinese and the Japanese are the same, yet they are very different."

23. "Exports are the lifeblood of Japan."

24. "Japan's agricultural system has been through a revolution since 1945."

25. "The literature of early Japan gives us little or no information about life in Japan."

26. "Japanese theater is unique."

27. "Japanese art and culture have had little affect on the West."

JAPAN AND KOREA—INDUSTRY AND RESOURCES

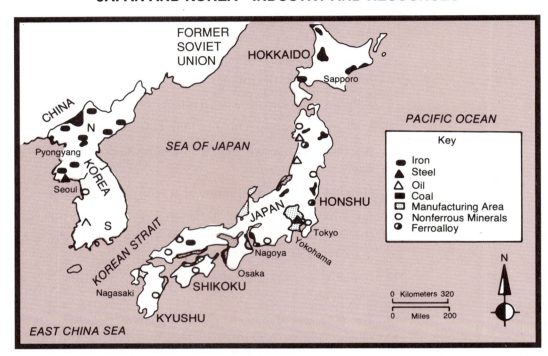

Map Exercise

Directions: Look at the map. Select the best answer for each of the following questions.

1. The archipelago shown on this map is
   (a) Korea.   (b) Japan.
   (c) Hokkaido.   (d) Honshu.

2. "The dagger pointing at Japan" in the form of a peninsula is
   (a) Korea.   (b) China.
   (c) former Soviet Union.   (d) Hokkaido.

3. The distance from Tokyo to Seoul is about
   (a) 300 miles   (b) 600 miles
   (c) 800 miles   (d) 1200 miles

4. The country directly north of Korea is
   (a) Japan.   (b) China.
   (c) former Soviet Union.   (d) Kyushu.

5. An important industrial city is
    (a) Pyongyang.   (b) Seoul.
    (c) Sapporo.   (d) Tokyo.

6. The city which is farthest south is
    (a) Nagasaki.   (b) Nagoya.
    (c) Yokohama.   (d) Sapporo.

7. An important industry shown on this map is
    (a) ferroalloy.   (b) coal.
    (c) oil.   (d) steel.

8. Most of Japan's people probably live on
    (a) the west coast of Honshu.   (b) the east coast of Honshu.
    (c) Shikoku Island.   (d) Kyushu Island.

9. Which of the following is not found in Korea?
    (a) iron   (b) steel
    (c) oil   (d) coal

10. Japan is separated from Korea by
    (a) an ocean.   (b) a sea.
    (c) a bay.   (d) a strait.

Developing Answers to Regents-Type Essay Questions

Helpful Hints

In developing your answers to the essays be sure to:

1. Include specific factual information and evidence whenever possible.

2. Answer the question being asked; do not go off on tangents.

3. Keep these general definitions in mind:
   (a) *discuss* means "to make observations about something using facts, reasoning, and argument; to present in some detail."
   (b) *describe* means "to illustrate something in words or to tell about."
   (c) *show* means "to point out, to set forth clearly an idea or position by stating it and giving data that support it."
   (d) *explain* means "to make plain or understandable; to give reasons for or causes of; to show the logical development or relationship."

Sample Essay Questions

1. Certain people and their ideas have greatly influenced the historical development of a nation or region. Each individual on the following list is paired with a historical development he influenced.

   Individual —Development

   Ieyasu Tokugawa/United Japan in the 16th century
   Matthew Perry/Opening of Japan to the West
   Mutsuhito Meiji/Led movement to modernize Japan
   Hirohito/Led Japan after defeat in World War II

   a. Select *two* of the people listed above. State how each individual and his ideas influenced the development with which he is paired.
   b. Base this answer on your Part A answer. Write an essay explaining how certain individuals and their ideas have influenced the historical development of a nation.

2. Historical, cultural, and economic development of nations are related to geography.

   Geographic Characteristics

Location	Mineral resources
Availability or scarcity of water	Rivers
Climate	Mountains
Landforms	

Select *three* geographic characteristics from the preceding list. For each characteristic, discuss how it affected the historic development, economic development, and cultural development of Japan.

3. Many factors influence the growth of a nation's industrial strength.

Factors

Availability of natural resources	Government policy
Availability of skilled labor	Markets
Availability of capital	Cultural factors
Transportation and communication	

Discuss each of these factors as they influenced the growth of Japanese industrial strength.

4. Nations often adopt ideas and practices from other nations or other regions of the world. Japan and Korea have both experienced cultural diffusion.

Japan from China	Japan from the United States
Japan from Korea	Japan from Western Europe
Korea from China	Korea from Japan
Korea from the United States	

Select *three* of the examples listed and for each example:
a. Describe *one* idea or practice that was acquired by the first nation from the second.
b. Discuss *one* effect of the idea or practice on the nation that adopted it.

5. Throughout history events have had long-term effects.

Events

Commodore Perry's "Opening" of Japan—1854
Emperor Meiji's Restoration of Imperial Power—1868
Japan's Attack on Pearl Harbor—1941
Dropping the Atomic Bomb on Hiroshima—1945
Creating a New Constitution for Japan—1947

For each event:
a. Describe the event.
b. Discuss how the event had an effect beyond its initial impact.

6. Nations have tried many different forms of government in an effort to establish stable and orderly rule.

Issues

Foreign trade	Form of government
Foreign policy	Cultural diffusion
Relation of the military	

In Japanese history, different governments adopted different policies and had different views of the above issues.

For *each* of the following Japanese governments, discuss how their policy affected each issue:
Tokugawa Shogunate
Meiji Restoration
Post W.W. II Japan

Puzzle

Directions: Place the words below in their proper place in the puzzle.

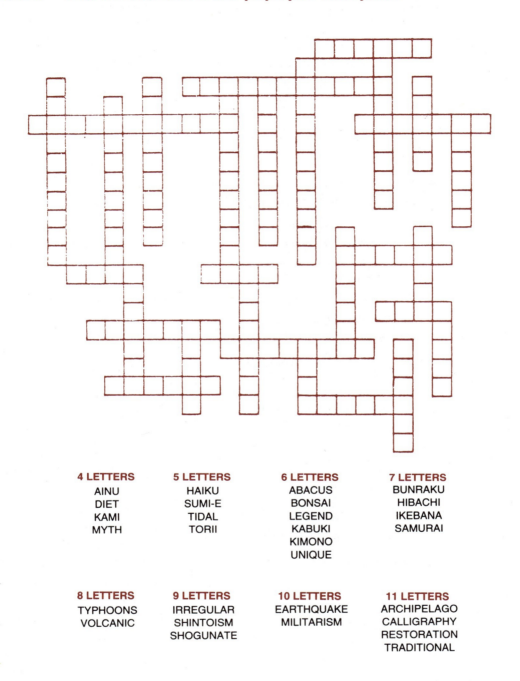

4 LETTERS	5 LETTERS	6 LETTERS	7 LETTERS
AINU	HAIKU	ABACUS	BUNRAKU
DIET	SUMI-E	BONSAI	HIBACHI
KAMI	TIDAL	LEGEND	IKEBANA
MYTH	TORII	KABUKI	SAMURAI
		KIMONO	
		UNIQUE	

8 LETTERS	9 LETTERS	10 LETTERS	11 LETTERS
TYPHOONS	IRREGULAR	EARTHQUAKE	ARCHIPELAGO
VOLCANIC	SHINTOISM	MILITARISM	CALLIGRAPHY
	SHOGUNATE		RESTORATION
			TRADITIONAL

Directions: Complete the following crossword puzzle using the words below. (Definitions are listed after the puzzle.)

CHANOYU   HAIKU   KAMI   OYOSHIYO   TOKUGAWA
CLAN   HIBACHI   KYUSHU   PAGODA   TATAMI
DIET   HOKKAIDO   MEIJI   SHOGUN   ZEN
DIFFUSION   HONSHU   MONSOON   DAO
FUJI   KAMAKURA   NIPPON   TOKYO

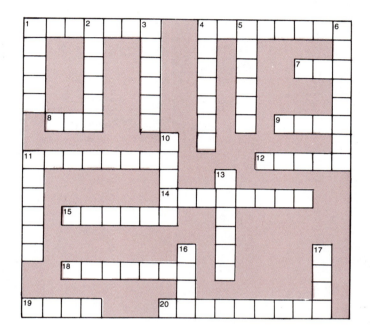

Across

1. An Asian wind that brings a wet season when it blows from the sea
4. The northern island of Japan
7. A Chinese word meaning "the way"
8. A sect of Buddhism
9. Good spirits of the Shinto religion
11. The name of the last Shogunate of Japan
12. The capital and largest city of Japan
14. The name of the first Japanese Shogunate
15. The main island of Japan
18. The tea ceremony of Japan
19. The Japanese legislature
20. The spreading of culture and ideas from place to place

Down

1. The dynasty that led the Restoration in Japan
2. The Japanese word for military leader
3. Japanese for "Land of the Rising Sun"
4. A Japanese charcoal stove
5. The southern island of Japan
6. The cold ocean current off northern Japan
10. A Japanese form of poetry
11. Reed mats of Japan
13. A Japanese religious temple
16. The holy mountain of Japan
17. People within an ethnic group descended from a common ancestor

POLITICAL MAP OF LATIN AMERICA

NORTH

UNITED STATES

ATLANTIC OCEAN

MEXICO

Gulf of Mexico

Mexico City

BAHAMAS
Nassau

Havana
CUBA
CAYMAN ISLANDS (G.B.)
JAMAICA
Kingston

DOMINICAN REPUBLIC
HAITI
Port-au-Prince
Santo Domingo

San Juan
PUERTO RICO
•VIRGIN ISLANDS (U.S. & G.B.)
•ANGUILLA (G.B.)
•ANTIGUA & BARBUDA
•ST. CHRISTOPHER & NEVIS
•MONSERRAT (G.B.)
•GUADELOUPE (Fr.)
•DOMINICA
•MARTINIQUE (Fr.)
•ST. LUCIA
•ST. VINCENT & THE GRENADINES
•BARBADOS
•GRENADA

Belmopan
BELIZE
GUATEMALA
Guatemala City
Tegucigalpa
HONDURAS
EL SALVADOR
San Salvador
Managua
NICARAGUA
San José
COSTA RICA
Panama City
PANAMA

CARIBBEAN SEA

•ARUBA(Neth.)
•NETHERLANDS ANTILLES (Neth.)

TRINIDAD & TOBAGO
Port-of-Spain

Caracas
VENEZUELA

GUYANA
Georgetown
SURINAME
Paramaribo
FRENCH GUIANA (Fr.)
Cayenne

Bogota
COLOMBIA

Quito
ECUADOR

GALAPAGOS ISLANDS (Ec.)

PERU
Lima

BRAZIL
Brasilia

Lake Titicaca
BOLIVIA
Lake Poopo
Sucre

PACIFIC OCEAN

PARAGUAY
Asunción

CHILE

URUGUAY

Santiago
Buenos Aires
Montevideo

ARGENTINA

FALKLAND ISLANDS (G.B.)
Stanley

Strait of Magellan
TIERRA DEL FUEGO

S. GEORGIA ISLAND (G.B.)

UNIT VIII Latin America

Introduction

The term *Latin America* is used to describe a geographic area in which the peoples of many countries share related traditions, heritages, and languages.

Look at the map on the opposite page. The shaded portions show Latin America. It includes parts of North America, all the continent of South America, and the Caribbean islands south and east of Florida. Place a finger on Mexico in the southwestern part of North America, and move it down the map all the way to the southern tip of the continent of South America. Note that a narrow strip of land, called Central America, joins North America and South America. (What is the distance in miles from the northern boundary of Mexico to the southern tip of South America?)

All of this area is known as Latin America. The Spanish and Portuguese who explored and settled this area spoke languages, called "Romance languages," that came from the Latin language. The use of the Spanish and Portuguese languages in most of this area gave the people of Latin America a feeling of unity. In addition, the Spanish and Portuguese brought their customs (way of life) to the New World. Today, the peoples and countries of Latin America show this heritage (background) in their daily lives. However, the term *Latin America* is not wholly accurate. There are groups of people who do not share this Latin American culture. These include the blacks of Haiti, the Aymara in Bolivia, the Maya of Mexico, and about 50 other Native American groups. Also, today Hispanic peoples resent the name "Latin America" because the term *Spain* is not used. Perhaps we might call the area "Indo-Afro-Spanish America"; but, following custom, we will use "Latin America."

The people of Latin America are proud of their heritage. They are proud of being Americans, just as we are. Latin Americans resent people in the United States calling themselves Americans as though the name belongs to them alone. It is common in Latin America to speak of the people of the United States and Canada as "North Americans."

For study purposes, Latin America can be divided into three main sections: South America, Central America and Mexico, and the Caribbean nations. South America, the largest of these divisions, has 13 separate nations. Central America is the narrow strip of land that connects North and South America. It has seven separate nations. Central America is part of North America. Mexico, which is also part of North America, and the nations of the Caribbean make up the third section.

Geography

Location

A look at a map of Latin America tells us a great deal about its location. You will note that South America is actually southeast of the United States. Notice also that most of South America lies east of the North American continent. Locate New York City and then Brazil. You will notice that Brazil is much farther east.

The whole of Latin America stretches from 32° north latitude to 56° south latitude (North America extends from 8° north to 70° north). The area of this vast region is three times the size of the United States. It stretches almost 8,000 miles from the northern border of Mexico to Cape Horn at the tip of South America. Across the continent from east to west, from eastern Brazil to northwestern Peru, the distance is about 3,100 miles.

THE AMERICAS

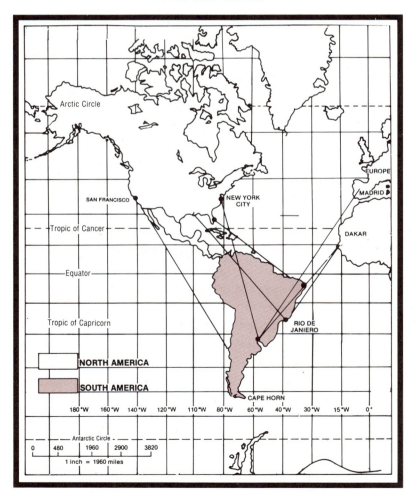

Another fact that should be noted is the distance of Latin America from the United States. Although Mexico borders the United States, and the islands of the Caribbean seem close, most of Latin America is far away. If you look at the map, you will see that Recife, Brazil, is 4,800 miles from Miami, Florida. Another Brazilian city, Rio de Janeiro, is almost 4,800 miles from New Orleans, Louisiana. Actually, the northeast coast of Brazil is closer to Europe and Africa than to any part of the United States. Between New York City and Buenos Aires, Argentina, the distance is 5,300 miles by air. From San Francisco, California, to Santiago, the capital of Chile, it is over 5,900 air miles.

Surface of the Land

Mountains

Latin America has the second highest range of mountains in the world, the Andes mountain chain. This chain is found along the entire west coast of South America. It is made up of several smaller mountain ranges that, taken together, form the longest mountain range in the world. People often call the Andes "the backbone of South America."

The Andes are very high mountains, and many of the peaks are covered with snow during all of the year. Many peaks are over 20,000 feet above sea level. The highest one is Mt. Aconcagua in Argentina (22,830 feet above sea level).

In the northern part of Latin America (Mexico and Central America), the mountain range is the same range as the Rocky Mountains of the United States and Canada. In Mexico the range is called the Sierra Madre Occidental. Here there are still active volcanoes. One is Popocatepetle, the "smoking mountain."

Farther south, in the jungles of Costa Rica, is a mountain, which is also an active volcano, Irazú, that erupted in the 1970s. In the highlands of El Salvador is Izalco. This volcano is known as "the lighthouse of Central America" because of its nearly constant activity since it first erupted in the late 18th century.

Volcanoes

In South America, along the entire length of the Andes, from the north to the south, are hundreds of towering volcanic cones. Some of these volcanoes are **extinct** (no longer active), but many continue to erupt. Ecuador has more volcanic activity than any other Latin American nation. Within 100 miles of Quito, Ecuador's capital city, a traveler passes in view of at least seven great volcanic cones. These cones are almost in a straight line, making up the "avenue of volcanoes." Pichincha, which overshadows Quito, has had five violent eruptions in the past 400 years. Each time Quito was almost destroyed by the lava and earthquakes.

Some of the volcanoes of Central America are also still active. They are all located on the Pacific side of the mountains. Antigua, the old Spanish capital in Guatemala, has been completely destroyed by earthquakes three times since it was first built 400 years ago. (Because Nicaragua has had many earthquakes and volcanic eruptions and Panama has no active volcanoes, the United States built a canal through Panama instead of Nicaragua.) Gigantic volcanoes are also found in Mexico, mostly south of Mexico City.

Eruptions of the many active volcanoes throughout Latin America are frequent and often very destructive. In March and April 1982, El Chichón, a volcano in southern Mexico, erupted several times, killing hundreds, wiping out villages, and destroying many ranches and farms. In 1985, one of the deadliest volcanic eruptions to occur in Latin America took place in Colombia. The Nevada del Ruiz volcano exploded, sending steam and ash into the air. There was only a small lava flow, but the heat inside the volcano melted the snow and ice around the volcano's peak, causing a mud avalanche. Within a short time, the tiny town of Armero was completely covered by mud; other villages were also heavily damaged. More than 20,000 people died or were listed as missing, and over 150,000 were left homeless.

Plateaus

In the eastern part of South America there are several areas of rounded mountains and *plateaus* (flat areas high above sea level). The Guiana Highlands are found in the northeast. Even today much of this plateau, which has both grassland and forests, has not been explored.

The Brazilian Highlands cover a large part of southeastern Brazil. This area is 3,000–4,000 feet above sea level. At some points mountain peaks reach 9,000 feet. The eastern edge of the area is called the "Great Escarpment"; an escarpment is a high, long, cliff-like ridge of land. A large part of the southwest plateau consists of an area of forests and grassland, called the *Mato Grosso.*

To the south, where the continent narrows, is the *Patagonian* region. This is a cool, dry plateau just north of the rugged, dark, and forbidding area of Tierra del Fuego (land of fire). The remains of glaciers that have not entirely melted are also found here.

High in the Andes in Bolivia and Peru, the mountain chain rises to spread into a wide plateau. This tableland is 400 miles wide and from 10,000 to 13,000 feet high. Here on the *Altiplano,* as the plateau is called by the Latin Americans, live 80 percent, or four-fifths, of the Bolivian people.

Highlands are also found in Mexico; in fact, most of Mexico consists of highlands. Some of these highlands make up a large, level plateau in the heart of the country that is the home of more than half of the people of Mexico. Mexico City is located in the center of this plateau. (What does this fact tell us about the effects of land surface on people's lives?)

Plains

Latin America also has large flatland plains; in fact, over 40 percent (two-fifths) of the land surface is covered by plains. One large plain lies east of the Andes.

A much larger plain is located in Venezuela, between the Orinoco River and the Andes Mountains. Called the *llanos,* it covers an area 600 miles long and 200 miles wide. Most of the land is covered with grass and small trees. It makes excellent grazing land for cattle, but during the rainy season the flat areas are flooded. During the floods cattle must be taken to higher ground. In the dry season, the grass burns away because of the heat.

Just south of the llanos is another large, flat area, the Amazon River Plain or Basin. This area is covered with a large rain forest. Much of the Amazon River Basin has not been fully explored.

In the heart of South America lies the *Gran Chaco.* Here are swamps, forests, and grasslands. The land is poor and has little value, except that some oil has been discovered there. For this reason, Paraguay and Argentina are very interested in the area.

The most important plains of Latin America, the **pampas,** are located around Buenos Aires, Argentina. Some of the world's best agricultural and pastureland is found there. Wheat, alfalfa, and corn are grown, and cattle and other livestock are raised, on the fertile pampas.

In Latin America, many coastal areas on the east and west have mountains or plateaus that rise sharply from the sea. Consequently, there is little room for coastal plains, but one coastal plain is the Yucatán Peninsula of Mexico.

SOUTH AMERICA LAND FORMS

GREATER ANTILLES Guadeloupe LESSER ANTILLES
West Indies
CARIBBEAN SEA Martinique Barbados
Curacao
Trinidad and Tobago

Orinoco R. Caroni R. Angel Falls
LLANOS PAXARAUMA MTS.
GUIANA HIGHLANDS Ilna de Morajo EQUATOR 0°

Galapagos Islands Napo R. Rio Negro Amazon River
Cabo do Sao Roque

Nevs Hauscapri Purus R. AMAZON LOWLANDS
SELVA Ucali R. Madeiro SERRA DO PIAUI
Bern. R. Cuapore R. PLANALTO DO MATO GROSSO
Mamore R. BRAZILIAN HIGHLANDS
GRAN CHACO Pilcamayo R. 15°
DO ESPINHACO

TROPIC OF CAPRICORN Salado R. Iguasso R.
ATACAMA DESERT Parana R. Iguasso Falls
Uraguay R.

PACIFIC OCEAN ATLANTIC OCEAN

Cerro Aconoagua
PAMPAS Rio de la Plata

Colorado R.
Chubat
PATAGONIAN PLATEAU

45°

Falkland Is.
Strait of Magellan
Tierra del Fuego
Cape Horn 60°

105° 90° 75° 45° 30°

0 300 600 900 Kilometers
0 300 600 Miles
N

Rivers

Latin America has many long, mighty rivers. The rivers have been used for **hydroelectric** projects that have supplied electric power and light to the major cities. The waters have also served to make more land usable for farming, through irrigation projects. At the same time, rivers, lakes, and oceans have given Latin America an important source (place from which something comes) of food and trade products—fish.

The Amazon

The greatest of all the rivers is the Amazon, which has its source (beginning) in the Andes Mountains. It flows eastward for almost 4,000 miles across the continent to the Atlantic Ocean and is the second longest river in the world. The Amazon flows through the hot, thick **rain forest** (tropical woodland) like an inland sea. At certain points, the Amazon's shores may be 60 miles apart. The **mouth** of the river (where it flows into the ocean) is 200 miles wide. Until airplanes became available, the Amazon was the only means of travel into and out of Brazil for the people along its banks. Today it continues to be an important transportation route.

The Amazon River

The Magdalena

The Magdalena River flows about 1,000 miles through Colombia to the Caribbean Sea. Ships can sail on it for about 600 miles. Even today the Magdalena still carries Colombia's imported goods three-quarters of the distance from the coast to the capital city of Bogotá.

The Orinoco

In Venezuela, the Orinoco is even longer than the Magdelena and is navigable for about 1,000 miles. This river was first discovered by Columbus on his third voyage.

The Rio de la Plata

To the south is the Rio de la Plata ("river of silver"). The two branches of the Plata begin in Brazil and flow southward through the pampas. The Plata empties into the

Atlantic Ocean near the cities of Montevideo and Buenos Aires. The Uruguay, Paraná, and Paraguay rivers are all part of the Plata River system. In fact, these rivers give the land-locked nation of Paraguay an outlet to the Atlantic Ocean.

The Colorado and the Rio Grande

In Mexico, the southern part of the Colorado River brings water to the western part of the country. The Rio Grande flows in Mexico's northeast. These rivers are most useful in **irrigating** (watering) the dry lands through which they flow.

Lakes

Latin America has a few lakes of interest. In Mexico, Lake Chapala and in Central America Lake Managua and Lake Nicaragua, supply fish. In Panama, Lake Gatun is an important part of the Panama Canal System.

Lake Titicaca, in the Andes Mountains between Peru and Bolivia, is the largest and most interesting in Latin America. It is the highest lake in the world (12,500 feet above sea level) and is 1,214 feet deep. The lake's constant (always the same) water temperature keeps the temperature of the air higher than it would otherwise be. Lake Titicaca supplies fish and is an important transportation route.

Islands

The islands in the Caribbean Sea are really the tops of underwater mountain peaks. Cuba, Puerto Rico, Hispaniola (Haiti and the Dominican Republic), and other islands are the tops of mountains that belong to a chain of old volcanoes. The bases of these mountains lie thousands of feet below the sea. One mountain in Puerto Rico is nearly 32,000 feet high when measured from its underwater base.

Geography of Central America

Connecting North and South America is an isthmus. Located on this isthmus are Mexico and the seven smaller republics that make up Central America. The Caribbean Sea lies to the north and east of the isthmus; the Pacific Ocean, to the south and west.

Along the Caribbean coast there is a hot, wet (tropical) plain with dense forests. Mountains rise from the coastal plain. This highland area is where most of the people of Central America live because the climate is mild and rainfall is plentiful.

The Pacific coast of the region has a warm climate with a great deal of rainfall.

Effects of Geography

A Leaning East and South

Most of South America is located east of the United States. Brazil, which bulges out into the Atlantic, is only 1,200 miles from the African coast. Brazil was settled by the Portuguese for trading and lumber. Because of its location, the Brazilian coast could serve as an emergency station for ships on the way to South Africa and India, and Brazilian lumber was used for repairing ships sailing from Portugal.

For several reasons, the major port cities of South America are found on the east, or Atlantic, coast. First, the east coast is closer to the population centers of Western Europe. Therefore, Europe became an important market for South American goods. Second, since most of South America lies east of the Andes Mountains, it is easier to ship goods to ports on the east coast than across the high mountains. Also, the east coastline is irregular, and there are better natural harbors. The Pacific coastline is regular, and the shore areas are much shallower.

Most of South America also leans toward the south, toward Antarctica. In fact, it extends to a point only 1,500 miles from the Antarctic. Since most of the movement of human beings has been north of the Equator and in an east to west direction around the globe, the location of South America has placed it at a disadvantage, off the main shipping centers.

Because of the topography and other factors, the Spanish and Portuguese colonists were able to adapt European crops, livestock, and farming to their New World settlements. They could also *adopt* (take up) Native American crops and farming practices.

Influence of Trade Winds on Travel and Trade Routes

Geography influenced the coming of Europeans to Latin America, and it played an important role in the early Spanish conquest and exploration. Columbus came to the New World through the West Indies because the winds and ocean currents carried his ships there from Spain. (The West Indies are located in the Caribbean sea to the south of the United States and north of South America.) The trade winds, which blow from the northeast, carried Columbus' sailing ships into the Caribbean. In addition, the North Equatorial Current, which flows south from Spain along the coast of the African bulge and then west across the Atlantic Ocean into the Caribbean Sea, helped to carry Columbus to the New World.

Ocean currents and wind directions were also important factors in setting up trade routes between Spain and its Caribbean island possessions. In addition, trade routes were created between Cuba and Florida and between the islands and Mexico and Panama. From Panama the winds and currents led to trade routes across the Pacific Ocean to Asia and the Philippines.

With the West Indies as a starting point, Spanish explorers moved out in all directions around the Caribbean in the early 16th century into South, Central, and North America.

Lack of Regional Unity

Unlike the United States, much of Latin America lacks unifying geographic factors. The United States has a long, irregular coastline with many fine, natural harbors. Close to these harbors flow deep rivers, which gave settlers a route into the rich land of the interior. In this way rivers and the irregular coastline helped to unify the United States.

Great mountain barriers and great distances separate regions in much of Latin America. The nations set up in Latin America in the 1800s after independence were based on four units created by the Spanish (New Spain—Mexico and Central; New Granada—Colombia and Venezuela; Peru—Peru, Bolivia, and Chile; and La Plata—Argentina, Uruguay, and Paraguay). These units soon split into smaller units that more closely fit geographic regions.

In addition, regional differences caused by geography exist between Buenos Aires and the interior parts of Argentina; between north, central, and south Brazil; between coastal and highland Peru and Ecuador; between north and south Colombia; and between northern and southern Mexico. In the life and history of Latin America, these regional forces based on geographic differences have played important roles.

Isolation of Parts

Geography has not only led to a lack of unity but also served to isolate parts of Latin America. The high mountains, **dense** (thick), rain forests, arid (dry) deserts, and parts of rivers that are not navigable have resulted in division and isolation. They cut off travel and communication from one country to another. They reduce trade among the South American nations and have held back economic growth. Even today, partly because of geography, parts of South America are economically underdeveloped.

Transportation is a major problem in South America because of the geography. Overland routes between countries are difficult to create. Rock slides, volcanic eruptions, and earthquakes often block roads and railroads. At present, because of poor transportation and communication, the people of rural areas seldom travel to the big cities. At the same time, education and new scientific methods rarely reach rural farmers. However, the governments of Latin America are making plans to change this situation and expect to see a big improvement during the 1990s.

Geography has also resulted in an uneven distribution of population in many South American countries. People have settled in areas where the land is fertile and water is available. Many population centers are located on or near rivers; others, on lakes or close to the ocean. Almost all of them are within 200 miles of the coast. Many villages and towns remain isolated from the main centers of government and industry. Ignorance about other villages and events in the country and the world often leads to feelings of being left out and of distrust among the rural people. Even in the 1980s, with great improvements in transportation and communication, many Latin Americans knew little of the world outside their villages. As a result, many countries find regionalism a serious problem. **Regionalism** is loyalty by the people to a particular region, rather than to the nation itself.

Climate

Factors Influencing Climate

Many factors affect climate. Some of these factors are (1) latitude, the distance a place is from the equator; (2) altitude, the height a place is above sea level; (3) the nearness of large bodies of water; (4) the presence and direction of ocean currents; and (5) the direction of the main winds. Let us examine how each of these factors affects the climate of Latin America.

Latitude   Latin America spreads nearly 7,000 miles north and south of the equator from 32° north latitude to 56° south latitude. A large part of the area is near the equator. This area is hot, with an average temperature throughout the year of 80°F. As we move away from the equator, the areas become cooler. In the higher south latitudes, in the southern part of South America, the areas are cold.

An important point to remember is that in areas south of the equator the seasons are opposite from those we experience in the Northern Hemisphere. For example, in January, when it is winter in the United States, it is summer in Argentina.

Altitude   Knowing that so much of Latin America is in the tropics (the hot region near the equator), you might think that the entire area is hot. This is only partly true; there are differences in temperature between places only a few miles apart. Parts of Ecuador, Peru, and Bolivia are very cool, although they are located near the equator. How is this possible? These places are high in the mountains. The higher you climb, the lower the temperature becomes. It is estimated that temperature drops one degree for every 350 feet of **elevation** (height). Quito, Ecuador, located high in the mountains near the equator, is cooler than lowland areas farther from the Equator, such as Belem, Brazil.

ALTITUDE INFLUENCES CROPS

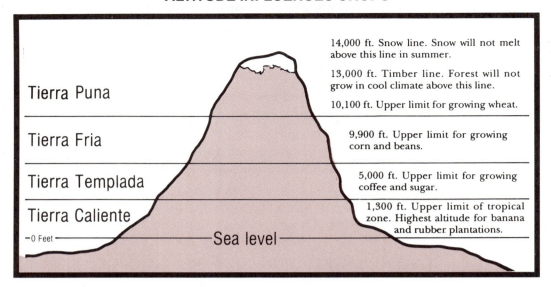

Tierra Puna

Tierra Fría

Tierra Templada

Tierra Caliente

—0 Feet—

Sea level

14,000 ft. Snow line. Snow will not melt above this line in summer.

13,000 ft. Timber line. Forest will not grow in cool climate above this line.

10,100 ft. Upper limit for growing wheat.

9,900 ft. Upper limit for growing corn and beans.

5,000 ft. Upper limit for growing coffee and sugar.

1,300 ft. Upper limit of tropical zone. Highest altitude for banana and rubber plantations.

The influence of height on temperature has led geographers to name four different zones:

Tierra Caliente (hot country)—0–3,000 feet
Tierra Templada (cool country)—3,000–6,000 feet
Tierra Fría (cold country)—6,000–10,000 feet
Tierra Puna, or Helada (cold, dry plateaus of the Andes)—over 10,000 feet

It should not surprise you that the climate of Andean South America is called a *vertical* climate.

Nearness of Large Bodies of Water

Proximity (nearness) to large bodies of water has a great influence on climate. It tends to moderate climate and keep it from becoming extreme. Water heats and cools more slowly than land. In winter, because the oceans usually have a higher temperature than the land, they warm the nearby land. In summer, the nearby lands are cooled by the oceans. Therefore, lands far from large bodies of water have warmer summers and colder winters than lands closer to large bodies of water.

Ocean Currents

Ocean currents also play an important role in Latin American weather. The west coast of South America between the Andes Mountains and the Pacific Ocean is very dry. The reason for this dry climate is the cold Humboldt (Peru) Current, which flows from the Antarctic, north along the Pacific coast of South America as far north as the equator. Winds that blow from the land area push the warm surface waters of the Pacific out to sea. Winds passing over the colder waters of the Humboldt Current pick up very little moisture as they blow toward the coast. As a result the land remains dry along the coast.

The coast of Argentina is cooled by the Falkland Current. Elsewhere around the continent, warm water washes the shores. When the South Atlantic Equatorial Current, flowing west, hits the bulge of Brazil, it divides into the south-flowing Brazil Current and the north-flowing Caribbean Current. On the north Pacific coast, the Equatorial Countercurrent (against the current) sends a warm water stream to wash the shores of western Colombia and Ecuador. Because of the action of these currents, the city of Lima, Peru, on the Pacific is several degrees cooler than the city of Bahia, Brazil, on the Atlantic, although both are at about the same altitude and latitude.

TRADE WINDS

NORTHEAST TRADE WINDS

SOUTHEAST TRADE WINDS

NORTHEAST TRADE WINDS WINDS

SOUTHEAST TRADE WINDS

SOUTHEAST TRADE WINDS

Rainy Tropical

Wet and Dry Tropical

Desert

Steppe

Humid Subtropical

Mediterranean

Marine West Coast

Highlands and Mountains

Winds

OCEAN CURRENTS

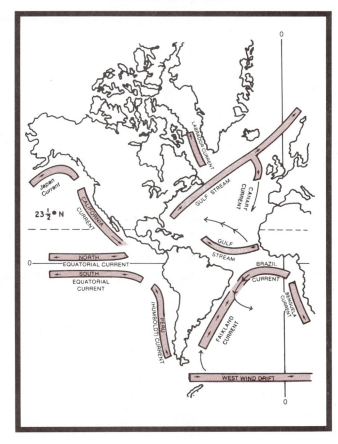

$23\frac{1}{2}°N$

Japan Current

CALIFORNIA CURRENT

NORTH EQUATORIAL CURRENT

SOUTH EQUATORIAL CURRENT

LABRADOR CURRENT

GULF STREAM

CANARY CURRENT

GULF STREAM

BRAZIL CURRENT

PERU (HUMBOLDT) CURRENT

FALKLAND CURRENT

BENGUELA CURRENT

WEST WIND DRIFT

Winds   The trade winds blow from the northeast and southeast across the Atlantic Ocean. These winds carry with them a great deal of moisture, which falls on the eastern and central parts of Latin America as rain. By the time these winds reach the mountains in the west, they have lost much of their moisture; therefore, less rain falls toward the west. From Ecuador in the north to central Chile in the south, the west coast of South America is dry. Winds blowing over the cold Humboldt Current are also cold. These winds are unable to hold moisture; what little moisture they do carry falls as snow in the mountains. Although some rain may fall in this region, which is called the Atacama Desert, there are some places where rainfall has never been recorded. In southern Chile, however, wet west winds blow from the Pacific and bring a great deal of rain. In some places, rainfall averages 220 inches a year. Here the mountains block the winds going east, so the Argentine side is much drier. Some areas have as little as four inches of rainfall a year.

Effects of Climate

In Latin America the people have adapted to the different climates—and the problems presented by the climates. Those living in the Amazon River valley must protect themselves from the heat and learn to live in the heavy, humid air. At the same time, the people of Tierra del Fuego, at the southern tip of South America, must adapt to constant wind and cool weather.

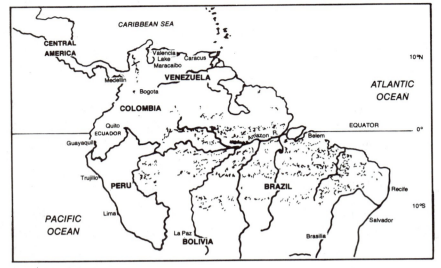

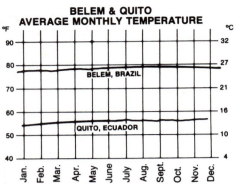

Locate Belem, Brazil, and Quito, Ecuador. What do you think causes the differences in their climate?

The human body makes adjustments so that people can live in reasonable comfort in almost any climate. One striking example is found among the people of the Altiplano of Bolivia. The Altiplano, you will remember, is a high plateau in the Andes. There the people's lungs have increased in size to make up for the lack of oxygen in the air. As a result, the people of the Altiplano can do most heavy work without loss of breath or mountain sickness. You or I, however, would have a difficult time breathing on the Altiplano.

Climate has played an important role in determining which parts of Latin America would become highly developed. The widest part of South America and most of Central America, almost two-thirds of the land, is entirely in the tropical and rainy region, where few people can live because of the unsuitable climate. The Tierra del Fuego area to the south is too cold and windy to offer a good place to live. Therefore, a large part of the land in Latin America is not lived on, and more temperate areas are greatly overpopulated.

Climate also influences the food people grow and the work they do. In the rain forest most food is raised in small clearings. The chief foods are bananas, yams, and tapioca (cassava or manioc). Heavy rains leach the minerals from the soil. Therefore, the farmers must move from place to place. In the savanna, cattle raising is important and sugarcane is the largest crop. In the Tierra Templada area of the mountainside, coffee growing is important.

An interesting example of the effect of climate on human activity is offered by the Brazilian coastal city of Santos and the plateau city of São Paulo. Both cities are located at about the same latitude (22° south). Santos has a population of about 300,000. Except for people involved in the shipping business, the city is quiet, sleepy, and hot. Behind Santos rises a magnificent escarpment, the Sierra do Mar (the "mountain of the sea"), to a height of some 2,500 feet. A road and an electric railway go to the top. On the top lies the industrial city of São Paulo, with more than 8 million people in its metropolitan area. It is a city full of activity, the most important in Brazil. The difference between the two cities is that Santos lies in the tropical lowlands, and São Paulo is on the cooler plateau.

The People and Customs of Latin America

Population Groups

The population of Latin America is growing at a faster rate than that of any other region of the world. As of 1990, almost 400 million people were living in the lands to the south of the United States. (By the year 2000, Latin America will have almost 700 million people.) There are four main groups: (1) Native Americans, (2) Europeans and criollos, (3) blacks, and (4) peoples of mixed origins: mestizos, mulattos, and zambos.

Native Americans

The Native Americans were the first people to live in Latin America. They came from Asia by way of the Bering Sea, over an ice-free land bridge between Siberia and Alaska. Pushed by other groups behind them, the early arrivals and their descendants drifted south. Slowly, over thousands of years, hundreds of Native Americans spread out over North and South America to set up settlements. By the time Columbus arrived, Native Americans were living in all of America, from the Arctic Ocean to Cape Horn.

Today, unlike the United States, Latin America has a large Native American population. Although the exact figure is not certain, there are between 15 and 20 million Native Americans in Latin America. In Ecuador, Peru, and Bolivia, Native Americans account for half of the population. Mexico and Guatemala have more persons of Native American descent than of European origin. Native American culture, therefore, is still important in many of these nations.

Europeans

Europeans make up the second, and largest, group in Latin America. Beginning with Columbus and continuing to the present time, Europeans have come to Latin America. Most came from Spain and Portugal; some, from England, Italy, France, and Germany. The **criollos** are the descendants of the Spanish settlers. Today, the European population of Latin America is mainly Spanish or Portuguese in origin. Of the 20 nations, 18 are offspring of Spain's once-great empire. Brazil was set up as a Portuguese colony, and Haiti once belonged to France.

Blacks

The third group, blacks, originated in Africa. Beginning in the 16th century, Africans were brought to Latin America as slaves. They were the chief source of labor on the large sugar plantations. The blacks of Latin America live mainly on the Caribbean islands and the wet, coastal lowlands of Colombia, Venezuela, and Brazil. About 90 percent of the people of Haiti and large parts of the population of Cuba and the Dominican Republic are of African descent.

People of Mixed Origins

In many parts of Latin America these three groups—Native Americans, Europeans, and blacks—have been mixing for centuries. Whenever two or three different groups have lived together, there has been intermarriage. A **mestizo** is a person descended from Native Americans and Europeans. A **mulatto** is descended from blacks and Europeans. A **zambo** is descended from Native Americans and blacks. Perhaps in no other part of the world has the blending of groups originally from such geographically distant origins taken place. A result of this mixing is that the people of Latin America have not been greatly concerned with the color of a person's skin. Consequently, Latin America has far fewer race problems than any other area of the world.

Languages

The main language of 18 Latin American nations is Spanish. In Brazil the people speak Portuguese, as they have since colonial times. Haitains speak French and also use a **patois** (local speech) that shows an African influence. In almost every country other European and Asian languages are also spoken. A large group of Italian immigrants and their descendants living in Argentina and Brazil speak Italian. German is used in parts of Argentina, Brazil, and Chile. Descendants of many Chinese and Japanese immigrants continue to speak their native languages.

Guatemalan weavers. The women of Central and South America are skillful in weaving, a traditional craft.

All of these languages have been changed through the centuries in Latin America. Many Native American words have been added to Spanish (see page 645). In addition, thousands of people in Central and South America never learned Spanish or any other European language. These Native Americans continue to use the languages of their ancestors; **Quechua**, the Inca language, or *Aymara*, is used by about half of the people of Bolivia, Ecuador, and Peru. In Paraguay, most of the people use Guaraní in addition to Spanish. In Mexico and Guatemala, about one-tenth of the people use only Native American, sometimes with Spanish words mixed in. In other areas, Native American languages survive even though they are spoken by only a few hundred or a few thousand tribal members.

Language	Where Spoken
Spanish	Most countries of Latin America except:
Portuguese	Brazil
French	Haiti, French Guiana
Dutch	Suriname, Aruba, Netherland Antilles
English	Belize, Guyana, Jamaica, Virgin Islands, Barbados, Trinidad, and Tobago
Native American Languages	
Nahuatl	Mexico, El Salvador
Quechua	Peru, Bolivia, Ecuador
Aymara	Bolivia
Guarani	Paraguay, Argentina, Brazil

Marriage and the Family

The family is the heart of Latin American life. Family life is based on a mixture of Spanish, Portuguese, and Native American customs. Ideally the father is the head of the **patriarchal** family. The mother is next in importance, and then the oldest son. The father takes care of business; the mother, of the home. Traditionally, women in Latin America have not been considered the equals of men. They have been kept at home and away from outside influences.

The Latin American family is not like the family in the United States. Latin Americans include cousins, aunts, and uncles in their idea of a family. On holidays, saint's days, and other celebrations, all the members of the extended family (sometimes a hundred or more) celebrate together.

There is a feeling of closeness in the family. Members come home from work at lunchtime to eat together. Family members feel they should do as much as possible for each other. Businesses are often owned and run by a family. If members of a family are in the government, they use their influence to get jobs for their relatives.

Each child has a *padrino* (godfather) and a *padrina* (godmother). *Padrinos* (godparents) are very close to being family members. They take part in the baptismal ceremony and also act as substitute parents. Godparents are expected to care for their godchildren if the parents die.

The family is very much a part of the marriage customs, and Spanish traditions are followed. Close watch and control over unmarried couples are the rule even today. Traditionally, a young man and woman have had dates only when they were accompanied by a *dueña* (chaperone). Although in some areas, mainly in the large cities, this practice is beginning to weaken, generally it remains an important part of the Latin American culture.

When a young man or his family decides he should marry, he or they ask the young woman's parents for their consent. Once permission is given, the woman's parents are responsible for arranging the wedding. Every young Latin American woman would like to have a church wedding followed by a *fiesta*, that is, a time of joy, dancing, and celebration. The size of the marriage and fiesta depends upon the wealth of the family. The poor often have no formal marriage but simply live together.

Although the patriarchal family is the ideal, a large part of the Latin American population does not live in families of this type. Native Americans, in many cases, still follow their old culture. They look to their village or tribe as the important unit. The tribal group works together as a big family, even though the people live together in small families of parents and children. Among the Native Americans the woman is often the head of the **matriarchal** family.

In times of hardship, the patriarchal family has broken down among the poor of Latin America. At such times, sons and daughters have to leave home to find work as servants or workers in the cities. Some fathers have been unable to earn enough to support their families, and the children then grow up without respect for the authority of the father. Also, in parts of Latin America to which a large number of immigrants have come, a great many people live in small families. Where there is good transportation and communication and people can move about easily, the old patriarchal extended family often splits up. In such situations, a man can more often take his own small family unit to a new place where there is a better chance of earning a living.

Social Classes

The people of Latin America can be clearly divided into social classes, or groups.

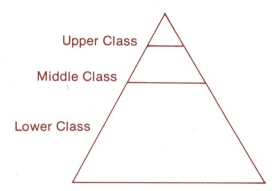

What matters most to the people of Latin America is not racial differences but class differences. The difference is between the rich people who have everything to make life comfortable, and the poor who do not.

The upper class is made up of the old *hacendados* (landowners) and the new group of wealthy industrialists. The hacendados are from families that have owned land since colonial times. Land and what it produces have always been important in Latin America. The landowner hires workers and controls their votes, thereby gaining political power. Most hacendados are European, but a few are Native American.

The middle class, not an important group for much of Latin America's history, is now beginning to develop. The growth of a middle class depends on industrialization. In industrialized countries people are trained to hold skilled jobs and are given supervisory positions. These people make up the middle class, which is usually found in cities. In Latin America foreigners held the skilled jobs and became the supervisors. Only the unskilled jobs were left. This situation is now changing slowly, and Latin Americans are being trained for these jobs. As a result, the middle class is growing.

At the bottom of society are the **peons** (unskilled peasants) and city workers. On the **hacienda** (ranch), the peons work for low wages, producing crops and raising cattle. Despite poor living conditions, they are loyal to the landowner, because their families have worked for the hacendado's family for a long time and been taken care of in difficult periods. The peons feel deep family ties to the hacienda and its owner. In cities, the lower classes work for low wages as unskilled laborers or are unemployed. They are worse off than the poor of the haciendas because in cities they have no attachments to places and no one to care for them in difficult times. They live in run-down, dirty slums called **favelas** in Brazil and **barrios** in other countries in Latin America.

These slum homes, made of shrubbery, stones, corrugated tin, and even cardboard, are often found on hillsides and cliffsides. The contrast between rich and poor is most easily seen where the slum homes are near the homes of the rich, as in Rio de Janeiro. Most favelas and barrios are located on the outskirts of large cities. Bad as conditions are here, they are probably worse in the *sertao* (backlands).

The opportunity to move from a lower to a higher class is rare; Latin Americans usually remain in the class they were born in. Few opportunities exist for the poor to earn money and move up. One reason is that education is limited to the rich. Also, differences in language have caused many Latin Americans to remain in the lower classes. Many Native Americans either cannot speak Spanish or speak it so poorly they cannot communicate. Another block to moving upward in Latin American society is the fact that most nations are agricultural and rural. Few have much industry. Moving upward is easier in an industrial nation, where a middle class can develop. Under present conditions it is difficult in Latin America to earn enough money in agriculture to move into the middle class. In the section on economics (see pages 655–665) more information will be found on moving upward in society.

Religion

More than 80 percent of the people of Latin America are Roman Catholic. Many of the Native Americans were converted (changed) to Catholicism by the missionaries who came with the Spanish and Portuguese during the periods of exploration and colonization. The Catholic church is an important part of the everyday life of the people.

The Native Americans often became Catholics without really understanding the main ideas and principles of the religion. Since they had been defeated in battle, they believed that they must accept the religion of their conquerors. The Spanish built churches on top of the ruins of Native American temples. The Native Americans simply transferred their prayers to the new buildings, and combined their old gods with the god of the conquerors. The Spanish even allowed the Native Americans to join their old ceremonies or religious dances with the Catholic ceremonies. In this way, Catholicism came to have a personal meaning for the Native Americans. Although even today their descendants may not fully understand the beliefs and symbols of their adopted religion, the Native Americans are very religious.

Important as they are, the Native Americans are only one part of the Latin American Catholic population. In most countries, there are many more European than Native American Catholics. Latin Americans are very religious and celebrate a great many religious holidays. When a child is born, he or she is given a patron saint, and a fiesta is held each year on that saint's day. Christmas and Easter are also times of great celebration.

Religious observance in Latin America is different from that in other parts of the world. Mass in **rural** (country) areas is usually attended only by women and children. Young boys stop going to church when they reach ten to 12 years of age. Only girls continue to go to Mass with their mothers. Men enter the church only on special occasions such as christenings and funeral services. This situation may be due to a feeling that the church leaders have often sided with the government, against the wishes of the people. In the past, the leaders of the church usually opposed any reforms that would have improved the people's lives. The men still feel they are Catholics, even though they do not go to church often.

Today, the church in Latin America faces many problems. First, there is a great lack of priests. Also, in the past the church was very wealthy, but now it faces serious difficulty in raising money to finance (pay for) itself.

Political problems also affect the church in Latin America. Political leaders have been very unhappy with the church. Church leaders were criticized for their favoritism toward the wealthy and toward political dictatorships. In many cases, the church had much more money than the governments. Because of this wealth and the poverty of the people, the church has often been under attack.

More recently, some church leaders have inclined more toward political freedoms and social reforms. The church has taken a lead in the solving of social problems and the growth of civil liberties. It is making more and more important contributions toward reducing illiteracy, improving education at all levels, expanding trade unions, encouraging free speech, and resisting (fighting against) the harsh policies of dictators. Some members of the clergy have supported the ideas of liberation theology, a church of the people, and even rebellions against the government in power.

Education

In Latin America's early history the church was in charge of all education. Only a very few public schools were built during this early period. After independence was gained in the 1820s, this situation began to change slowly. The new idea in most countries was that education should become public, to meet the needs of each independent nation.

Today each of the Latin American republics has stated its belief in the ideal of education for all, and each has laws that established free education. Each nation assigns a minister or secretary of education to run the educational program. Education is compulsory (required) for four to six years. The government controls the selection of textbooks, courses of study, and training of teachers. Often there are no local boards of education. Except for church schools and the few private universities, education in Latin America is tax supported.

In spite of the effort to educate everyone, in Latin America only a little more than half of the people can read and write. Until Latin Americans master these educational basics, it will be difficult for them to learn the skills needed to increase their incomes and the knowledge required to use their rights as citizens.

National School Systems Most of the national school systems are set up on a plan of six years in the *escuela primaria* (primary school) and six years in the *escuela secondaria*, or *colegrio* (high school or academy, not college). After these come the technical school, the normal school for teachers, or the university. However, it must be understood that this description is general and that each nation has its own national plan.

Whatever the plan, much remains to be done. Only about four-fifths of all Latin American school-age children are enrolled in schools. Therefore, one child in five gets little or no formal education. Even more serious is the problem of *deserción* (dropouts). At best, only 30 percent of the children complete all six grades of primary school.

At the secondary level, fewer than one of every four students of high school age is going to school. Most of those who do enter high school never graduate. About five of every 100 students of college age are in the universities of Latin America. (In the United States the number is 35 out of 100.)

Most students avoid subjects such as agriculture, industrial arts, and the commercial subjects, yet these subjects teach the skills most necessary in Latin America. In the universities, too few specialize in natural sciences, mathematics, agriculture, and teaching. Too many—four of five—take up engineering, law, the social sciences, and the humanities. (Suppose you were a Latin American student. Why might you want to study one of those subjects?)

Reasons for Problems

Why is the educational situation in such trouble? First, there is the great growth of population. The cities are growing so fast that new housing, new roads, new hospitals, and other necessary services are more important than new schools. At the same time, there is little money left to improve older schools.

Second, textbooks and teaching materials, such as desks, blackboards, and chalk, are not always available. Where the people use one of the Native American languages, textbooks in Spanish and Portuguese are of little use.

Third, teachers are scarce, partly because salaries are very low. Few teachers educated in city schools are willing to go to the rural areas. As a result, poorly trained teachers have to be used there.

The attitude of many poverty-stricken parents provides a fourth reason. They are uneducated, distrust the teachers, and feel that a child should help out at home.

Finally, at the root of all these reasons, is the shortage of money.

Pre-Columbian Latin America

The Earliest Native American Groups

When Columbus came to the New World in 1492, he thought he had landed off the coast of India, in Asia. Therefore he gave the name "Indian" to all the people living in Latin America. They were not Indians, so who were these people?

There are many different ideas about the **origins** (beginnings) of the Native American. Probably the best explanation is that at some time, on a date far back in the past, before written history, a group of hunting tribes crossed the Bering Strait from Asia to North America (at that time there may have been a land bridge). These nomad hunters moved southeastward. Their journeys, which took thousands of years to complete, did not stop until all of North and South America had been crossed and settled.

The various groups developed different physical characteristics, different languages and customs, and different handmade articles (artifacts). Thus, when the Europeans arrived, they were met by many different Native American peoples.

The Maya

The Maya built their civilization in present-day Guatemala and on the Yucatán Peninsula in Mexico. Their civilization was at its peak between the 4th and 10th centuries; after that time, the Maya civilization began to slowly fade away.

The Maya mainly lived in cities that were separate from one another; these are called city-states. The city-states were often at war with one another. Wars were fought to obtain tribute (payment for submission) and to acquire prisoners for religious sacrifice. Wars were considered the duty of the king and the ruling class of the military-priestly nobility.

Centers in Guatemala and the Yucatán

The Maya built an advanced culture in Guatemala. Then suddenly, late in the 10th century, they left all they had created and moved to the Yucatán Peninsula to begin all over again. Although no one knows why they moved, historians have suggested many theories (ideas). Some believe that the Maya lost a war and were forced to leave. However, there is no evidence now available that supports this theory. Others believe that the soil became so poor that the Maya could not produce enough food for their people. Another theory is that some disease swept through the area and forced the Maya to move. Finally, some think a great earthquake or volcanic eruption caused the movement. Whatever it was, the Maya moved in A.D. 987 to the Yucatán, where they remained until the Spanish arrived. Today, the remains of the Mayan cities and temples can be seen in the dense jungles and highlands of Guatemala, British Honduras, and the Yucatán Peninsula.

Achievements

The Maya were the only Native American people who successfully developed a writing system. It was, in some ways, similar to the hieroglyphic system of the Egyptians. Unfortunately, the Spaniards destroyed most of the Mayan carved or written records. Today, it is still difficult to translate completely the records that remain.

The Maya carved symbols on large stone shafts called **stelae**. A stela was often placed in front of a large building, and the exact date on which the building was completed was carved on it. Hundreds of stelae are left today, and archaeologists have found them to be important in their study of the Maya. (If you were an archaeologist, how would the stelae help you?) In addition, the Maya sculpted in cement, clay, and wood.

The Maya built temples on top of great terraced pyramids. The sculptured work that decorated the temples and cities is still looked at with wonder. They also made pottery and developed textile weaving, mat-making, basket-weaving, and jade carving.

The Maya were also fine mathematicians. They understood the idea of zero and developed a counting system using bars and dots. A bar stood for 5 and a dot for 1; thus .. was 2; ⋮ was 8; and ≅ was 16. The Maya used their ability in mathematics to study astronomy. They developed a 365-day year calendar, which was more accurate than the European calendars of the same time.

The largest group of Maya farmed their fields of maize. Corn was their main food, and its planting and harvesting were important parts of their economic and religious life.

The Aztecs

In the highlands of central Mexico, the Aztecs rose to power. They started out as nomads, who moved about northern Mexico looking for a place to settle. At the beginning they were not very good in war and lost almost every battle with their neighbors. As a result, they moved constantly. However, in the 13th century, they came into the central valley of Anahuac, and settled near a chain of lakes. Again they were involved in wars, which they lost, and then fled to the islands of Lake Texcoco. There, in 1325, they built the city of Tenochtitlán (where the modern Mexico City is now). At first the city was made up of huts, elevated on poles to keep them above the swampy earth. Later the Aztecs drained the area and filled it with dirt. They built a beautiful city with large public buildings. Since no

Mayan hieroglyphic writing and other symbols decorate this 30-foot-high stelae in Quirigua, Guatemala, a site of many Mayan ruins.

Closeup of Mayan hieroglyphics.

A Mayan temple.

one wanted this once-swampy area, the Aztecs were left in peace, but they were still among the weakest of the Native American tribes.

Slowly, through marriages and **alliances** (cooperative joining) with their neighbors, the Aztecs began to build their power. In time, they started to conquer their neighbors. Within 50 years they had defeated most of the other Native American nations and become the rulers of Mexico.

Military Interest

The Aztecs became a military people. Training for war took on importance, and rewards were great for military performances. All the leaders of the Aztecs were soldiers.

Aztec merchants traveled through Mexico, trading products and acting as spies and map makers for the army. The king was a soldier-priest.

Religion

As with the Maya, religion had a central place in Aztec life. The god of war—*Huitzilopochtli* (the "hummingbird")—was one of the most important of the Aztec **deities** (gods). The power of the gods was so great, the Aztecs believed, that all success and failure was due to their actions. A large group of priests was needed for religious ceremonies.

The Aztecs believed in human sacrifice. A victim (usually an enemy captured in battle) was killed, and the blood and heart were offered to the gods. The custom of human sacrifice came about because of an Aztec **legend**. The Aztecs believed that at one time in the past all Aztecs were killed in a great war. Quetzalcoatl, an important Aztec god, took his own blood and sprinkled it on the bones of the dead Aztecs to create a new Aztec nation. Therefore, the Aztecs believed, they had to give human blood to Quetzalcoatl in repayment. The Aztecs often waged war to get more victims for sacrifice to the gods.

Farming

The Aztecs were also farmers. Because the army was considered so important and the rulers wanted to be sure there was a food supply for it, farming was placed under the strict control of the government. The government owned all land and gave each family a number of acres to farm. The amount of land could be increased as the family grew, or reduced when family members married or died. The land stayed with the family as long as male heirs existed. If no sons survived, the land went back to the government to be given to others.

Part of the crops were given to the government as taxes and for support of the army. The main crops were corn, beans, squash, and peppers. The Aztecs also raised cotton, tobacco, and the maguey plant. (*Pulque*, a liquor used in religious ceremonies and for celebrations, was obtained from the maguey.) Turkeys captured for special celebrations were a favorite delicacy.

Language and Arts

The Aztecs spoke a language called *Náhuatl*. The same language is spoken today in the backcountry by Mexicans of Native American ancestry. The Aztecs had a large oral (spoken) literature and made picture books on parchment and on paper made from the leaves of the maguey plant.

Although war was the most important activity in the lives of the Aztecs, they were also creative in the arts. Artisans worked in gold. Unfortunately, very little of this work remains because the Spaniards melted the gold objects into bars, which could be shipped back to Spain more easily.

Aztec artists created beautiful feather mosaics that were worn as capes or used to decorate shields. They also made fine pottery and gold and silver jewelry.

Science and Engineering

The Aztecs must have been skilled engineers and architects. A complicated system of bridges, dikes, and canals was built to protect the city of Tenochititlán. Many houses several stories high were built of stone. The pyramids used for religious ceremonies remain as an example of Aztec abilities.

The Aztecs probably borrowed the idea of the calendar from the Maya. The calendar was carved on a large, round disk, the calendar stone. The Aztecs also had a rough method of counting and arithmetic, not as advanced as that of the Maya.

The Aztecs did not use wheels for transportation or for lifting weights. Having no work animals, they used human muscles for all labor and transportation.

The Incas

In the highlands of the Andes, the *Quechua*, or Incas, set up a large empire. From southern Colombia to northern Argentina (Tucumán) and Chile, the Inca Empire stretched nearly 3,000 miles along the high plateaus of the Andes.

The true history of the Incas is still not fully known, and we do not know their original name. We call them by the name they themselves gave only to their ruler, the Inca. Quechua is the name given to the language spoken by these plateau people. We are not sure who the Incas were or where they came from.

Tiahuanaco and Other Pre-Inca Remains

We do know that people lived on the plateau of Peru and Bolivia before the Incas. During the building of the Pan-American Highway, in the 1930s and 1940s, buried cities were discovered. They contained fine linens (cloth) and pottery. They seemed to prove that groups of creative and advanced Native Americans lived on the plateau 5,000 years ago. When the Incas conquered the plateau, they found the accomplishments of these peoples. The conquered people took on the traditions of the Incas and forgot their own history, languages, and customs.

Ruins of pre-Inca times are slowly being uncovered even today near the shores of Lake Titicaca. These ruins belong to the Tiahuanaco culture, which reached its peak between

Quechuans (Incas) wearing traditional and local dress.

A.D. 1000 and 1200. Tall stone pillars and beautifully carved stone doorways still stand on the Bolivian Altiplano. Although the Tiahuanacos were also conquered by the Incas, these people did not forget their language or their customs. The Aymara people of Bolivia are their descendants.

Building the Inca Empire

It is believed that the Incas came to the plateau near Cuzco, Peru, about A.D. 1200. Little by little, they conquered the peoples living near them and began to build their capital city, Cuzco, which is the oldest continuously lived-in city on the American continent. Cuzco was believed to be the center of the world. By 1500 the Incas had reached their Golden Age.

The Incas did not build their empire only by force or warfare. They were masters at getting other tribes to join with them. They built a society in which everyone was taken care of: the very young, the old, the sick, and the crippled. The Incas proved to many neighbors that they would be better off within the Inca Empire than outside it.

The government was headed by a powerful ruler called the Sapa Inca, or just the Inca. Thought of as a god, not just a man, he was assisted by his sons and other nobles. Each time a new tribe was conquered, its leaders were taken to Cuzco. They were treated like royalty and told of the greatness of the Incas. The conquered rulers soon became loyal to the Inca and then taught their people to show this same loyalty.

Machu Picchu was the last stronghold of the Incan people. It was built high in the mountains of Peru.

The descendants of Incans still live in areas of the original empire. The animal is a llama, a traditional beast of burden. The wall in the background is from an Incan temple.

The Incas worked out many ways to keep the peace. Conquered peoples were forced to move to lands near Cuzco, and loyal groups were moved to the conquered lands. Sometimes troublemakers were sent in small groups to distant parts of the empire, where they were surrounded by loyal Inca peoples.

To set up good communication and to be able to move soldiers quickly, the Incas built two parallel roads that ran the length of their empire, north to south. Several smaller roads, east to west, ran into the two main roads. Inca engineers built suspension bridges to span the rivers and canyons of the Andes. Some of those bridges still exist today.

Quipus—Records

Once a new area became part of the Inca Empire, a team of officials would go into the area and make a map of it in clay. They counted the people, buildings, equipment, and the amount of food stored. This information was all kept on a *quipu*.

The Incas never invented an alphabet. They had no books in which to keep records. Instead, they used the quipu, which was made with a long piece of wood or string. Smaller, colored strings were tied in knots at various points along the main string. Special people called *amantas* (wise men) were trained to read the meanings of the quipus.

Agriculture

Agriculture was very important to the Incas. Land was not owned by individuals, but was divided into four parts. One part was distributed to individual farmers, and another section was set aside for the sun. The crops grown here were given to the priests of the temples. The third part belonged to the emperor, who used the crops to feed himself, the royal family, the army, the engineers, nonfarming workers, and government workers. Some of those crops were set aside to help feed people in case of earthquakes, floods, or famine. The fourth section was farmed for the old and sick members of the village.

The Incas made many advancements in agriculture. They built an excellent irrigation system. Canals were built to carry water from streams and rivers to the farmers' fields, where corn, barley, and wheat were raised. Since the Incas lived in the Andes, they had to build terraces, and they enriched the soil by adding nitrates as fertilizers.

In addition, they developed a new crop, the potato. (Europeans did not raise potatoes until after the Spanish conquest of Peru.) The Incas also tamed three animals related to the camel—the guanaco, the alpaca, and the llama. All three are surefooted and are excellent for use in moving people and goods through the Andes. The Incas and the Andean people today use the furs and hides of these animals for trade as well as for clothing and shelter.

Architecture and Metalwork

The Incas were skilled architects. Evidence of their solid construction ability may be seen in the walls of the Inca temples and palaces that still stand today in Cuzco and at Machu Picchu, not far from Cuzco. The stones in these buildings, laid without cement, were fitted so closely that even today a knife blade cannot be run between them. Incan pottery, gold and silver work, and textiles were also of high quality. Of all the Native Americans, the Incas were the most advanced in the field of metalwork. They made beautiful jewelry and other ornaments from gold and silver, and axes, needles and pins, and weapons from copper and bronze.

Religion and Literature

The religion of the Incas had many ceremonies that were closely related to food, harvesting, and curing diseases. Viracocha, the Creator, was the most important god. All other gods and supernatural powers were created by Viracocha. The sun god was given the job of protecting the crops. Following the sun god, in order of importance, came the thunder god of weather; the moon goddess, wife of the sun; the various gods of the stars; and the goddesses of the earth and sea.

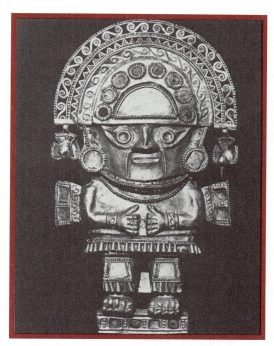

The Inca were advanced in metalwork. Here we see intricate designs in gold.

The Incan religion was headed by the Emperor, who was thought to be the son of the sun god. A large group of priests led the ceremonies and took care of the temples. The Incas hoped that through their worship they would have good crops, keep the evil spirits of sickness away, and receive aid in healing the injured or sick. The favorite way to win the help of the gods was through sacrifice, usually of grain, food, animals, or valuable objects. Sometimes, but far less often than the Maya and Aztecs, the Incas sacrificed human beings—usually young women.

The Aztec religion included a belief in a future life, with a comfortable heaven. There was also a hell, which was very cold. Those sent to hell got no food.

Like the Aztecs, the Incas developed poetry and a religious, dramatic, and historical literature. The literature was passed by word of mouth from storytellers in one generation to storytellers in the next, a process called **oral tradition**. Today some Incan stories are still repeated. The best known are the dramatic story of Ollantatay, the hymns to Viracocha, and the tales of the Chosen Women (*accla-cuna*).

Fall of the Empire

The fall of the Incas came suddenly. Huayna Capac, the twelfth Inca, died in about 1527. He made the mistake of dividing his kingdom between two of his sons, Huascar and Atahuallpa, with Huascar in Cuzco and Atahuallpa in Quito. The two half-brothers fought a civil war for five years. In 1532 Atahuallpa finally won and put Huascar in prison. Atahuallpa was ready to unite the empire when he was murdered by Spaniards in the same year. Without a central ruler the empire could not function.

Other Native Americans

Other Native Americans were also important in Latin America before the arrival of the Spanish.

In Mexico, the Toltecs, a Náhuatl-speaking tribe, began to move into Mayan lands in about A.D. 1000. The Toltecs reached their peak under their King Quetzalcoatl, who persuaded them to adopt Mayan culture. The Toltecs built roads and revived Mayan learning. The Mayan calendar was translated and later passed on to the Aztecs.

After King Quetzalcoatl died, he was made into the Feathered Serpent, god of the winds, peace, and industry. Today Quetzalcoatl's memory is kept alive in the temple next to the Pyramids of the Sun and Moon, at San Juan Teotihuacán near Mexico City, and in a long poem that was part of the Toltec-Aztec religious literature. Part of the legend says that Quetzalcoatl sailed off to the east, promising that someday he would return from the direction in which he sailed. This belief explains why, when Cortés landed, the Aztecs thought that he was the returning god (see page 647). As a result Cortés was not attacked by the Aztecs when he landed. He was accepted as the god in the legend.

Other Native Americans in Mexico and the Caribbean

Besides the Toltecs, there were Chichimecs, Mixtecs, Tlaxcalans, and Zapotecs living in Mexico. Almost all of these tribes were taken into the Aztec Empire, or else they paid the Aztecs for protection. On the islands of the Caribbean Sea lived a fierce, warlike group called the Caribs. Another group, the Arawaks, were peaceful farmers who were conquered by the Caribs.

Other Native Americans in South America

In South America, the Chibchas of Colombia had an organized government and were expert in their handicrafts. The Chibchas are often ranked next to the Aztecs, Maya, and Incas in terms of their cultural and political development. The Araucanians of Chile never developed a strong political or cultural life but survived the conquest by the Spanish; the Chibchas did not. The Guaraní in Argentina and Paraguay were another large Native American group.

Influence of Native Americans

The Native American groups of Latin America influenced the area greatly and left many traces of their cultures. Many of the foods still used in America came from these groups. Among the important plants of Native American origin are the following:

agave, or maguey (source of Mexican pulque and tequila)	maize (corn)	beans
	papaya	rubber
cacao (chocolate)	mushroom	elderberry
maté (Paraguayan tea)	yam	strawberry
avocado (aguacate)	blackberry	vanilla
wild grapes	squash	pumpkin
maple syrup	peanut	pineapple
sarsaparilla	white potato	sweet potato
guava	raspberry	blueberry
quinoa (a cereal)	tobacco	wild plums
sunflower seeds	nuts: acorn, black walnut,	cranberry
aji (chili pepper)	chestnut, cashew, pecan	tomato
manioc, or cassava (tapioca)	piñon (pine nut)	vanilla

Native American languages have added numerous words to all New World languages, especially in matters related to food, clothing, and other items of everyday life:

elote	corn (Ecuador)	*jitomate*	tomato
chicha	a liquor (Venezuela, Colombia, and Ecuador)	*cacique*	chief (all countries)
		canel	Indian (Guatemala)
pulque	a liquor (Mexico)	*machete*	cane cutter (all countries)
maiz	maize, or corn (all countries)	*cacahuate*	peanut butter (all countries)
quetzal	money of Guatemala	*cabaya*	sisal hemp (all countries)
chocolate	chocolate	*champu*	cereal grain (Ecuador)
aguacate	avocado		

Arrival of Europeans in Latin America

The conquest, exploration, and early colonization of Latin America were mainly the work of the Spanish and Portuguese. To understand why these Europeans acted as they did in Latin America, it is important to learn something about Spain and Portugal.

Spain and Portugal

Spain and Portugal are part of the Iberian Peninsula in southwestern Europe. (Iberia was the name the Romans gave the peninsula.) The Pyrenees Mountains separate Iberia from the rest of Europe. North Africa is just 12 miles across the Strait of Gibraltar from Spain and Portugal. Geography has therefore played a part in making Spain and Portugal culturally different from the rest of Europe. The mountains and the strait have acted as barriers.

Along with the original peoples, Carthaginians, Arab and Berber (Moroccan) Muslims, and Jews have made important contributions to a unique culture in Iberia.

Two events in the history of the peninsula strongly influenced the Iberian people of the 15th century. The first was the coming of Christianity to the peninsula about 1,800 years ago. The second was the Arab invasion from North Africa about A.D. 700, which brought the Muslim religion (Islam) and Muslim culture to Iberia. The history of Iberia from this event to about A.D. 1500 revolves around the efforts by the Spanish and Portuguese to drive the Arabs out of the peninsula.

The Muslim Arabs ruled Spain and Portugal as one country for a long time. By A.D. 1250, however, the Portuguese had driven out the Muslims, more than 200 years before the Spanish did. The Portuguese built their nation in the western part of Iberia facing the Atlantic Ocean. The Portuguese did not have to fight as long or as hard as the Spanish to free their land. (Can you give reasons for this?) As a result, the Portuguese developed their own culture and language. In addition, their religious feeling and warlike spirit were not as great as those of the Spanish.

The Spanish did not completely drive out the Arabs until 1492. Because of their long struggle, the Spanish developed a deep respect for religion and became adventuresome and warlike. Their nation faced the Mediterranean Sea.

Spain Gains Control of the Caribbean

In 1453, the Turks captured the city of Constantinople, at the eastern end of the Mediterranean Sea. The Turks now controlled the main trade routes to India and the East Indies.

Almost immediately the Portuguese began to look for a new route to India by sailing around Africa. In 1498, Vasco da Gama went around Africa to India. Pedro Cabral, on his way to India in 1500, was driven off course in a storm and found himself on the coast of Brazil.

In August 1492, Columbus set sail from Spain. By sailing west across the wide ocean, he hoped to reach India. In October 1492, his ships came to what is today called Watling Island. From there he sailed to Cuba, which Columbus called "Juana." Then he sailed to Haiti, which he named "Española" (Hispaniola), or "Little Spain." Even though he did not know it, Columbus had discovered a "new world," that is, a world new to Europeans.

The Spanish sent many expeditions into the Caribbean area after Columbus' discovery. They conquered the Native Americans first on Hispaniola and then on Cuba. Puerto Rico was conquered by Ponce de León in 1509. In the same year a settlement was made on Jamaica.

Spanish Conquest of the Mainland

While Columbus was making his four voyages of discovery, others were planning or making similar expeditions. Cabral reached the coast of Brazil in 1500. In 1503, Amerigo Vespucci also reached Brazil. Finding a wood similar to the brazilwood of Asia, he gave the name "Brazil" to the area. When he returned to Spain he wrote about his experiences. A mapmaker, Martin Waldseemüller, read Amerigo's story and published a map of the New World, using the name "America."

Having conquered the Caribbean area, the Spaniards turned their interest toward the mainland. It is important to note that the conquest of the mainland by the Spanish was carried out by private persons at their own expense. Three motives for conquest developed: "gold, glory, and gospel" (spreading Christianity).

Among the leaders of the conquest in America were four men who made possible the setting up of a permanent colonial empire for Spain.

Hernán Cortés and Mexico

The man picked to lead the expedition to conquer the Aztecs of Mexico was Hernán Cortés. He arrived in Mexico in 1519 with about 500 soldiers, 16 horses, and 10 cannons. When he landed, Cortés burned the ships that the expedition had come in to remove any idea of retreat. Victory or death was the only choice. Later, reinforcements arrived. Cortés set up the first Spanish settlement in North America at Veracruz.

Although greatly outnumbered, the Spanish conquered the great Aztec Empire. There were many reasons for their success. Cortés was a very fine leader, and his soldiers were disciplined and skilled. In addition, the cannon and muskets of the Spanish were far better weapons than the war clubs of the Aztecs. Horses were even more important. The Aztecs had never seen a horse with a rider on its back; they believed that rider and horse were one strange, powerful animal.

Another Spanish advantage was a religious legend of the Aztecs. This legend said that a white god, Quetzalcoatl, had left Mexico some time in the past and was supposed to return on the wings of a giant eagle. When the Aztecs first heard of the Spanish fleet with its white

EXPLORERS COME TO THE AMERICAS

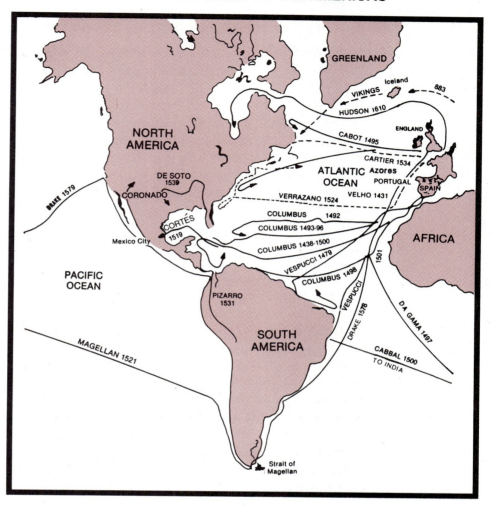

sails coming over the horizon, they believed that the ships were large birds and that the white-skinned Cortés was Quetzalcoatl. This belief at first kept the Aztecs from attacking the Spaniards. Cortés also made agreements with other Native Americans in the area, such as the Tlaxcala, who supplied troops and information. These tribes were willing to assist Cortés because they hated and feared Aztec power and domination.

Also important was a smallpox epidemic that broke out among the Aztecs. The Aztecs had never been exposed to this disease and as a result had no immunity (protection) from it. Consequently, many died. Within two and a half years, the Aztecs were conquered and Mexico became Spanish territory.

Francisco Pizarro and Peru

Soon after "New Spain" (Mexico) was won for Spain, the Inca area of Peru was added to Spain's New World Empire. Using Cortés' conquest as a guide, Francisco Pizarro led a small force (183 men and 37 horses) against the Inca Empire. In November of 1532, Pizarro met the Inca ruler, Atahuallpa, who was at war with his half-brother, Huascar, over control of the empire. With the Incas busy fighting among themselves, the Spanish were able to win control. In November 1533, Hernando de Soto took Cuzco, the Incan capital. In January 1535, Pizarro founded Lima, the "city of the kings," as his capital. As in New Spain, the surrounding territory was quickly explored and brought under Spanish rule.

After the conquest of Peru was completed, an expedition was sent into the south to conquer the rest of the Pacific coast area. Under Pedro de Valdivia, the leader, the Spanish made their way into central Chile and set up the settlement of Santiago. Although Valdivia won some victories over the Chilean Indians, the Araucanians, he was never able to conquer them. Even after he was killed in a battle, the Spanish managed to hold on, but Chile never became a very important colony of Spain.

Northern South America was conquered by Jimenez de Quesada. With an army of 600 men and 100 horses, he conquered the Chibchas. In 1538, he founded the town of Santa Fe de Bogotá, which he planned to be the capital. During the conquest Quesada heard stories of El Dorado ("the city of gold"), and he roamed Colombia in search of the city and the gold. He was not successful in finding either, but he did bring a large area under Spanish control.

Effect on the Pre-Columbian Civilizations

The Spanish conquests in the New World had a devastating effect on the Native Americans and their civilizations. Hundreds of thousands of them died during the fighting, especially in Mexico. After the conquest, the Spanish, according to plan, destroyed the Native American cultures. The conquerors destroyed temples, burned books, and killed the Native American kings, leaders, teachers, and priests. The Spanish forbade the Native Americans to practice their religion and other customs of their civilization and forcibly converted them to Catholicism. Their original Native American names were changed to Christian names.

In addition, the Spanish brought with them several diseases previously unknown in the New World; the worst were measles and smallpox. Native Americans did not have natural immunity or body resistance to these diseases, and several millions died. Also, thousands of Native Americans died throughout the Colonial period as a result of forced labor in the mines and on the plantations.

Colonial Period

Government

The king of Spain's chief representative in the conquered lands was the **viceroy**, who ruled what was called a viceroyalty. He had all the powers of the crown. To assist the viceroy, the **audiencia** was set up. The audiencia was a court; it carried out the laws; and it acted as an advisory group to the viceroy. The members of the audiencia usually had legal training, and were men of good name. There were paid high salaries so they would not be tempted by bribery. The audiencia was also a territorial division in the court that had jurisdiction to carry out the laws in various areas.

Each colonial town was ruled by a *regimiento*, or town council. *Regidores*, or councilmen, were elected by the landholding white citizens of the town. From this group, which wrote the laws, were selected *alcaldes* (justices) and an *alcalde mayor* (mayor).

Economic System

Spain developed the **mercantile system** in the 16th century. At the heart of this system was the idea that colonies were markets where the products of the mother country could be sold. In addition, the colonies were to produce cheap raw materials, which were needed by the mother country.

Taxes

The colonists were taxed to help support both the colonial government in America and the king in Spain. Many collectors were dishonest, and the methods of collecting taxes were often cruel. Many times property was taken by force. When a tax collector arrived in town, it was not unusual for the people to run away in fear of their lives.

Labor

The Spaniards were mostly fighting men or nobles who did not believe they should work in the fields or the mines. Under a system called **encomienda**, they forced the Native Americans to work the farms for them. The Spanish landlords treated the Native Americans as slaves and overworked them until they dropped. They paid little attention to Native American desires or needs, as for education. Native Americans also worked in the mines under the *mita* system. This too, was hard, and thousands died as a result.

The first black slaves were brought from Africa to the West Indies in about 1502. They were looked upon as animals and were treated cruelly. The Africans excelled in agriculture. They were strong and disciplined workers and were also craftspeople with a knowledge of smelting and iron working. Unlike the Native Americans, Africans were able to survive the white people's diseases. Therefore, many were highly desirable workers on the plantations.

Agriculture

As is the case today, the land was the most important part of the colonial economy. As early as 1532, the Spanish government ordered that all ships taking colonists to America should carry animals and plants there. Therefore, cattle, sheep, pigs, bananas, sugarcane, grapes, olives, coffee, rice, citrus fruits, and many cereals and vegetables were taken to America. Also, many American products, such as the potato, certain beans, and corn, were soon planted by the Spanish in America. Several regions were found to have good climate, good water, and good soil, especially Argentina, Uruguay, Paraguay, Chile, Colombia, Venezuela, and the West Indies.

The chief agricultural products of colonial Brazil were sugarcane, brazilwood (from which dyes were made), cacao, coffee, tea, vanilla, manioc (cassava or tapioca), tobacco, indigo (a dye), rice, cotton, citrus fruits, and tropical woods. The best agricultural lands in Brazil were found in the northern part of the country along the coast. Cattle and sheep raising were carried on in the highlands and interior of southern Brazil.

Other Industries

Besides mining and agriculture, pearl fishing was an important industry, especially along the Pearl Coast (Colombia and Venezuela). In addition, because of the demand for fish as food, offshore and deep-sea fishing were important. The manufacture of textiles, pottery, jewelry, and furniture, especially by Native Americans, also became important local industries. The dairy industry thrived in some areas, and families made wines, liquors, cigars, and cigarettes for home use and for sale.

Life

In the Spanish colonies there were great plantations or large ranches called **estancias**, haciendas, or *fincas*. (The Portuguese called them *fazendas*.) Each plantation or ranch was self-sufficient. Often the owner lived on his hacienda only part of the time. He spent most of his life in the nearby town or in the capital city, where life was much more comfortable. Life in the villages and on the hacienda was dreary, and hard work was all the people had to look forward to.

One of the leading colonial amusements was gambling. It became so widespread that both the Spanish and Portuguese governments tried to control it. Both mother countries stopped sending playing cards to the colonies. (Why do you think they did this?) In response, the colonists used free time to make their own cards.

Other amusements were bullfights, cockfights, jousting, horsemanship, dancing, and singing. All adults drank alcoholic beverages, and almost all smoked tobacco. Even children drank and smoked from early childhood.

Church holidays and public holidays were held often. A fiesta to celebrate a holiday sometimes lasted for days. At the fiesta there were fireworks, parades, and contests of physical skill.

Education, which was carried on by the church, was mainly for the rich. Only a very small minority of Native Americans went to school. Girls were given no formal education except in convents, and there were no schools that both sexes could attend. Marriages were arranged by the families of the young people.

Because of the warm climate, and because there was nothing else to do during the heat of the day, resting or sleeping or simply killing time was a regular part of life. In all of the Latin American colonies the midday *siesta* (nap or rest) became the law. All places of business were closed, and the streets were deserted.

Revolution and Independence

Conditions in 1800

The Spanish Empire in Latin America lasted approximately 300 years. However, throughout these years forces were working to bring about its end. Under the mercantile system much of the wealth of the colonies was exported to Spain. Taxes were many and high, and government officials appointed by the king were dishonest and cruel. The Native Americans and blacks were held in slavery. Many poor white farmers were barely able to make a living.

Factors Leading to the Desire for Independence

Discontent of the Criollos
    There was one group that had both wealth and education. Colonial landlords and traders had gained great wealth, and with this wealth they were able to educate their children, often in European schools. Many of the children were born in America. They were called criollos. Spaniards born in Spain but living in the colonies were called peninsulares. Only the peninsulares could hold high offices in the colonial government. The best the criollos could hope for was to win seats in the town councils. As the criollos became better educated, they also became more unhappy. They read about such ideas as all men having the right to life, liberty, and property. If the government tried to take away these rights, the people could then rise up and overthrow the existing system. This was known as the **social**

contract idea. In addition, the ideas of the Enlightenment, expressed in the works of Locke, Rousseau, Montesquieu, and others, led to the spread of revolutionary ideas in Latin America.

The American Revolution

The American Revolution was an important event for the criollos. They saw the North Americans rebel against a European king and win their independence. Such revolutionary North Americans as George Washington, Thomas Jefferson, Benjamin Franklin, and Thomas Paine were heroes to them, and many read translations of their writings. What the English colonists had been able to do, the Spanish and Portuguese colonists believed they could do also.

The French Revolution

The French Revolution, which broke out in 1789, also influenced the Latin Americans. The French overthrew their king. In the series of wars that followed, France fought against almost all of Europe. The French, led by Napoleon, came out of the early years of the wars victorious. Napoleon overthrew the Spanish king and put his own brother on the Spanish throne. The Latin American colonies refused to obey this foreign king. Also, the ideas of the French Revolution—"Liberty, Fraternity (brotherhood), and Equality"—made Latin Americans think of independence.

Economic Policies

Another important source of unhappiness was Spanish mercantile trade and economic policy. The criollos felt, with justification, that this policy and the laws that enforced the policy limited the economic development and prosperity of Latin America.

Rise of "American" Feeling

Finally, many of the colonists began to feel like Americans rather than Europeans. They began to develop patriotism and pride in the local areas in which they lived. These feelings led to even greater dislike for being ruled by "foreigners."

The Rise and Fall of the Portuguese Empire in Brazil

After the discovery of America, Spain and Portugal agreed to draw a line on the map to divide their colonies (Treaty of Tordesillas, 1494). Portugal was to have all the lands east of the line, and Spain the rest. The only part of Latin America that was east of the line was the "bulge" of land that is now the main part of Brazil.

Portugal claimed Brazil in April 1500 when Pedro Cabral landed on the coast. He called the land "Isla Vera Cruz" ("Island of the True Cross"). Later, the Portuguese called certain trees that they found "brazilwoods" because the wood was red, the color of a glowing ember (*brasa* in Portuguese). They changed the name of the country to Brazil, after the trees.

From 1501 to 1533, Portuguese trading expeditions came to Brazil almost yearly. However, an actual colony was not begun until 1533. The most successful early settlements were developed on the coast at Recife and Salvador in the northwest and São Vicente in the south. Large sugarcane plantations were set up in the northwest. Cattle hides, cotton, and tobacco, in addition to the sugar, were exported to Europe and brought great wealth to the planters.

The Portuguese colonists forced the local Native Americans to work on the plantations as slaves. Large numbers of Native Americans died of overwork and from European diseases. Many refused to become slaves and died fighting the Portuguese. To replace the Native Americans, Portugal began to bring thousands of black African slaves to Brazil.

When the Dutch started to settle in Brazil, fighting with the Portuguese broke out and the last Dutch settlement was destroyed by 1654. In the 1690s and early 1700s, adventurers from São Paulo discovered diamonds and gold in central Brazil. These discoveries brought thousands of Portuguese into Brazil's interior.

Much of this land was in territory that the Treaty of Tordesillas had given to Spain. In 1750, Spain and Portugal signed a new treaty in which Spain recognized Portugal's claim to almost all of what is now Brazil.

At the same time, Rio de Janeiro became a major seaport. Miners sent gold and diamonds to Rio, and ships took them to Portugal. In 1763, Rio became the capital of Brazil. By 1800, 3.5 million people, half of them slaves, were living in Brazil.

Portugal profited from the system of mercantilism it forced on the colony of Brazil. It limited the economic growth of the colony by not allowing the development of manufacturing. Portugal wished to sell its manufactured goods to the colonists in return for the gold, diamonds, and plantation crops imported from Brazil.

In 1807, when Napoleon of France invaded Portugal, Prince John, the ruler of Portugal, fled to Rio de Janeiro with his family. In 1808, Rio became the capital of the Portuguese Empire, and in 1815, the prince created the Kingdom of Brazil. When John returned to Portugal in 1821, he left his son Pedro to rule Brazil.

In September 1822, Pedro declared Brazil an independent kingdom and granted the people a constitution. A few months later he was crowned Emperor Dom Pedro I. Thus ended the Portuguese Empire in Brazil.

José Bonifaco Andrada was the architect of Brazilian independence and has been called the "Father of Modern Brazil." In 1822, he helped guide Brazil out of the Portuguese Empire. He persuaded Dom Pedro to remain in Brazil. He advised that Brazil become a limited constitutional monarchy with Dom Pedro as Emperor.

Andrada felt a constitutional (limited) monarchy was the best bridge from being a colony with little or no freedom to becoming a republic with complete freedom. Part of Andrada's program was put into affect in 1822 when Brazil became a free limited monarchy. Many of his ideas were included in the Brazilian Constitution of 1824.

The Independence Movement

The battle for independence in Latin America lasted about 35 years. It began in the early 1790s when the black slaves of Haiti threw out their French masters and set up a small island republic in the Caribbean. This small nation won its independence in 1803–1804, after more than ten years of fighting. For most of the region, the independence movement ended in 1824, when Simon Bolivar's army of South Americans defeated a Spanish royal army at Ayacucho, high in the Andes Mountains of Peru.

There were three kinds of independence movements in Latin America:
1. A true revolutionary uprising in which the ruling class was violently and totally overthrown and driven out by the people.
2. Civil war, with criollos fighting on both sides along with other South Americans. (This was much like the American Revolution.)
3. Easy achievement of independence, with little or no fighting. Few changes took place in these cases except that Spanish and Portuguese royal officials disappeared, and were replaced by local citizens (usually the criollo landowners and traders).

Below is a table that summarizes the independence movement in Latin America until 1828. For each country the type of movement that brought independence is indicated.

LATIN AMERICAN INDEPENDENCE MOVEMENT TO 1828

Country	Year of Independence	Leader in Independence Movement	Type of Movement
Haiti	1803–1804	Toussaint L'Ouverture	1
Mexico	1821	Father Miguel Hidalgo José Morelos Agustín de Iturbide	2
Colombia	1819	Simón Bolívar	2
Venezuela	1821	Francisco de Miranda Simón Bolívar	2
Ecuador	1822	José de Sucre Simón Bolívar	2
Argentina	1816	José de San Martín	
Chile	1818	José de San Martín Bernardo O'Higgins	2
Peru	1824	José de Sucre Simón Bolívar	2
Bolivia	1825	Antonio José de Sucre Andrada	2
Uruguay	1814, 1828	José Artigas	2
Brazil	1822	José Bonifácio Emperor Dom Pedro	3
Paraguay	1811	Fulgencio Yegros	3
Central American Republics	1812–1825	José Delgado José del Valle	3

After Independence: Latin America in the 19th Century

After winning their independence, Latin Americans were faced with many economic and political problems. With Spanish and Portuguese control at an end there was a time of confusion. During the colonial period, Spain had made all major decisions and policies through the viceroy and the audiencia. Now criollos took over the leadership. However, as we have seen, they had little leadership experience in government. Some men wanted to rule not as representatives of the people, but as dictators. The early governments of the new Latin American states had many political problems. Factions came into being, all trying to gain control of the government and ready to go to war with each other to gain that control.

The political problems came about in the following way. During the colonial period the foreign king had always been honored as the only person who had the right to rule and make laws. When the colonists did not like a law, they blamed the king's ministers. The king was above criticism. This attitude made for great stability in Latin American politics during the colonial period.

Changing Presidents and Constitutions

After independence had been won, the new nations elected presidents who went in and out of office every few years. Sometimes the people suffered under dictator-presidents, who seized power with the help of the army. The new Latin American presidents, whether elected by the people or put in power by the army, were not respected by the people as the king had been. No one knew for sure when the army or a part of the nation might start a rebellion.

Such rebellions often caused the overthrow of a president, as well as the constitution under which he ruled. During the first 100 years after independence there were few Latin American countries in which presidents or constitutions won the respect and loyalty of the people.

There was no country in Latin America in which a government was not overthrown or a constitution torn up. Since independence, the average life of a Latin American constitution has been about 20 years. (The U.S. Constitution, with only a few changes, has existed since 1789.)

Rise of Powerful Armies

Another important change was the position of the army in Latin America. The kings of the colonial period did not need armies to keep law and order; they had the fear and respect of the people. During the wars, however, armies of independence came into existence. They were not under good control and were neither well clothed nor well fed.

In many places, these armies took food from the peasants and the landowners. They forced towns to give them food, clothing, and money. If the money and goods were not given, the soldiers took hostages or killed the town leaders.

After the wars for independence, the new governments were too weak to control their armies. At the same time, the presidents needed the armies to remain in power and to keep law and order. In many cases, the leader of the army became the dictator of the country. **Golpe de estado** (coup d'état) has been a traditional method for army officers to gain control of Latin American governments.

Rise of the Caudillo ("Strong Man")

The lack of national unity, weak political leadership, and inexperience in government were great problems for Latin American rulers to overcome. As we have seen, politics was marked by violence. Democratic elections very seldom took place. A desire for peace and law and order at any cost soon developed among the peoples of Latin America.

As a result new forces were created that tried to bring about order and stability. Two of these were the **caudillo** or **cacique** ("strong man"), and the power of the army.

The caudillo ruled as a dictator with little opposition and with a strong, firm hand. Many a caudillo gained power with the help of the army and without being elected. Therefore, his power and continuing rule depended on protecting himself. Aware of the power of the army, the caudillo attempted to gain and keep its support by rewarding the officers with large salaries and other benefits. These rewards were paid at the expense of needed reforms to aid the less advantaged.

Persistence of Serious Inequalities

After the wars for independence, the social system in Latin America remained as unequal as it had been under foreign rule. A small group of large landowners, merchants, mine owners, lawyers, and foreigners continued to control wealth and power. The church also remained powerful. It struggled to keep the lands and privileges it had gotten during the colonial period.

This concentration of wealth and power led to the formation of two political groups and, in time, two main political parties. The Conservatives were the party of the rich and the church. This group was sometimes called the Clerical (Church) party. The Liberals, sometimes called the Anti-Clerical party, were also Catholics. However, they were against the church owning so much land; they wanted the land to be divided more fairly. The Liberals also wanted a better distribution of wealth and more control of the army.

There were several other results of the wars for independence. Many mestizos, mulattos, and black slaves had fought in the wars. About one-third of the army of José de San Martín, independence leader in Argentina and Chile, was made up of black soldiers. Therefore, the old colonial laws, which had strict rules classifying people according to birth (noble or peasant) and color, were swept away. So were the laws that gave legal privileges to whites while denying them to people of color. All the new constitutions contained written statements that all citizens were equal regardless of birth or color. (Haiti was the exception; whites were not given equal treatment in this black republic.) These constitutions no longer allowed the terms "criollo," "mestizo," "mulatto," and "indio" to be used in legal documents, or in setting taxes or owning land.

Independence probably hastened the end of slavery in Latin America. Haiti and Chile abolished (did away with) slavery during the wars of independence. Most other nations abolished slavery before 1850. It continued in Peru until 1851, and in Colombia and Venezuela to 1854. Brazil waited until 1888 and therefore was the last nation in the New World to end this terrible and brutal practice.

Economy

A visitor traveling through Latin America would notice many differences in the economies of the various countries of the region. Agriculture varies widely, according to the soil and climate. Mineral deposits are very plentiful and important in some countries but have little or no importance in others. In some areas there have been impressive advances in industry and manufacturing and industry has a firm base; in other areas it is still largely absent.

Agriculture

Partly because industrialization is only in its beginning stages in most of Latin America, agriculture is unusually important in the economies of most of the countries.

Agriculture is the way of life for most Latin American people. The main method of earning a living is farming. Agriculture has been the backbone of the economy of Latin America from the earliest days of human existence in the region.

The Pre-Columbian peoples developed a great variety of food plants that contributed to the creation of successful economies. The Maya, Aztecs, and Incas never invented the plow since much of the farm land was mountainous. In areas where fertile and plantable land is scarce, as in the Andes, digging the soil with a hoe resulted in the production of more food per acre than was possible with plow agriculture. (In Japan, where the land is similar, hoe agriculture also developed, while plow agriculture did not.)

Because of the rugged topography, the Incas of the Andes had to develop techniques that were remarkably "modern" and scientific. They terraced the mountainsides, irrigated the soil, and grew only the crops that would flourish best.

The Land

At the time of the Spanish conquest, Indian agriculture was concentrated in the fertile valleys of Mexico and in the carefully irrigated terraces of Peru. The Spaniards were more interested in raising livestock than in producing food crops. After the conquest, they seized the best lands and made them into pastures for animals. In Peru, the terraced fields were overrun by livestock and ruined.

The best lands eventually became part of large Spanish estates, while the majority of the Native Americans and immigrants had to farm on land that had limited agricultural value. This tragic situation has had much to do with Latin America's historic poverty. In all of Latin America only a very small part of the land can be used for farming. As we have seen, much of the land is covered by mountains, jungles, and desert. Large parts of the Andes Mountains are too high and cold for large-scale farming. The soils of the rain forest and dry grasslands are poor, and the deserts cannot support life.

Main Crops

Yet despite these difficulties, much is raised. The chief crops of the Amazon and Orinoco rain forests are bananas, yams, and manioc (tapioca). Every two or three years the Indians of this jungle area have to move from one clearing to another because the soil wears out quickly. Heavy rains leach the minerals from the soil. From the rain forest also come many products that are useful to people in other parts of the world. These products include mahogany and other hardwoods, chicle for chewing gum, and cinchona bark, from which is made quinine (a medicine used to treat malaria). Bananas are the main product of the rain forest and bring in the most money when they are exported.

As you remember, grasslands (savanna) are found north and south of the Amazon rain forest. The southern half of Brazil and the llanos of Venezuela in the north have a tropical savanna climate. This means there are two seasons, one rainy and one dry.

The savannas have poor soil for growing crops because of leaching. However, a number of cash crops for export are grown here. Sugarcane is the chief crop of these tropical grasslands; the hot weather, the rainy growing season, and the dry harvest time are good for growing sugar. Brazil, Puerto Rico, and Cuba are among the world's leading sugar producers. Another important export crop is *henequen* (sisal), from which rope is made. An important area for raising henequen is the Yucatán Peninsula of Mexico.

The vertical climate has a great effect on farming. (See page 626.) It should not surprise you that the farming can also be described as vertical. As the climate changes when you go higher, so does the farming. In the hot, dry lowlands (Tierra Caliente) there are plantations of bananas and cacao beans. Cacao beans grow inside large, green, cucumber-shaped pods on the trunk and larger branches of a tree called the *theobroma* ("food for the gods"). The beans are dried, ground, and roasted. From them chocolate, cocoa, and cocoa butter are made. Brazil, Ecuador, and Venezuela are large producers of cacao.

As you travel higher into a cooler climate (Tierra Templada), coffee becomes the main crop. In Brazil coffee is grown on large plantations called fazendas. In the Brazilian highlands the *terra roxa* (red soil) is rich in iron and potash. Coffee trees grow best in this soil. The trees are planted on the sloping hillsides, which allow the rainwater to run off easily. At first the coffee beans are green, but during the hot, rainy summer they turn red and open. During the dry, cooler winters the beans turn brown and are picked. Two-thirds of the world's coffee comes from Brazil. Other producers of coffee are Colombia, El Salvador, Guatemala, Mexico, Venezuela, and Cuba.

Many Native Americans live in the higher altitudes (Tierra Fría). On the steep mountainsides they raise subsistence crops (crops that meet their needs), such as wheat, barley, beans, potatoes, and maize (Indian corn). They graze herds of sheep, llamas, and burros.

Corn, a basic food in the diet of millions of Latin Americans, was raised by the Native Americans long before the Spanish came. Brazil, Argentina, and Mexico are leading producers of corn. In Brazil and Argentina, corn is grown chiefly as feed for livestock. In Mexico, it is an important food for people.

Three countries in Latin America have become leading producers of cotton. Mexico grows more cotton than any other Latin American country. The irrigated lands of north-central Mexico are the most important areas of cotton raising. The best-quality cotton in Latin America comes from the irrigated valleys in the deserts of Peru. Two areas, one near Natal and the other centering around São Paulo, have helped to make Brazil a leading producer. Cotton is also raised, although in lesser amounts, in the Gran Chaco of Argentina. It is interesting that the finest cotton can be grown in dry areas all over the world because of the miracle of irrigation.

Cattle Raising

The humid subtropical area along the southeast coast of South America has the best cattle-grazing land. The summer is long and hot; the winter, short and mild. The famous *pampas* (plains) of Argentina are in this area.

The deep, black soil of the pampas is so rich that fertilizers are hardly ever needed. The pampas are divided into estancias, where the cattle are taken care of by **gauchos**. The gauchos of the pampas of Argentina, Uruguay, and Paraguay are in some ways like the cowboys of the American West. Like the cowboys, the gauchos hold a place in the exciting and romantic legends of their countries. Also, the gauchos developed an independence and a free way of life on the vast open plains, as their North American counterparts did in the West.

In the 16th century, Spanish colonists brought cattle and horses to Argentina. Some of these animals escaped into the open grasslands of the pampas. Without natural enemies, the horses, sheep, and cattle began to multiply rapidly.

In the meantime, a mestizo population began to develop on the edges of the pampas. Some of these mestizos captured the wild horses, tamed them, and used them to hunt down the wild cattle. The cattle were killed for their meat and hides.

By the beginning of the 18th century a nomadic gaucho culture had grown. Living by their own laws and customs, the gauchos created a "Wild East" in the open lands of the pampas, east of the Andes. In the late 19th century, the equivalent of the "sodbusters" came to the pampas, just as they did to the Great Plains of the American West. These Spanish and Italian immigrant farmers began planting wheat and putting up fences, closing the open range and ending the gaucho's way of life as it had been created.

Today, gauchos continue to work on ranches in Argentina and Uruguay. But now they collect wages and live in houses with their families. Their nomadic, outdoor life and culture are a romantic part of their past history.

The cattle are raised chiefly for the meat. Large amounts of alfalfa are grown as food for the cattle. Wheat and corn are grains grown in this rich, black earth. Argentina is the world's leading exporter of beef and wheat. Unlike the rest of Latin America, most of Argentina's trade is with Europe, not the United States. (Can you discover the reasons for this?) Brazil has more cattle than any other country of Latin America, but Brazilian cattle are of poor quality and are used mainly to provide hides. Argentina and Uruguay are among the world's leading sheep-raising countries.

Cattle raising is also important in the **llanos** of Venezuela. The land is divided into haciendas, and is worked by *llaneros* (cowboys). Cattle graze near the rivers where there is grass. They are raised for their hides, and rarely for their meat.

Land Ownership Systems

After Mexico was conquered by Cortés, the king of Spain gave large sections of land to the Spanish soldiers and their officers as a reward for their services. As time passed, these land grants were turned into large farms and ranches called haciendas. Farmers (peons or campesinos) without land worked on the hacienda for little or no pay. In most cases the peon was given a small piece of land to farm for his own use. In other cases he received a part of the crop in return for his labor.

The hacienda system lasted through the entire 19th century and well into the 20th century. In the 1920s, after the Mexican Revolution, the largest haciendas were broken up. Smaller blocks of land were given to the landless peasants (peons). In addition, the government built houses for the peasants. The individual farmers worked as a group. The new system of land holding was called the **ejidos system**. In this system, farms are owned and operated by individuals, by several families, or by whole villages. In some cases the peons share in all of the work and all of the profits. On other ejidos the peons work only their own plots of land and keep all the produce and profits. Mexican farmers like this system because it allows them to own the land they work.

Ejidos are an important part of Mexico's agriculture. About half of all Mexico's farmland belongs to ejido peons. On most ejidos, each peasant owns 25 to 50 acres. These farms produce about half of Mexico's cotton, wheat, and rice. Harvests are low, however, because most farmers need better tools, machines, and fertilizer. They must be taught about the planting and care of other crops and new methods of farming. But most of all they need more land.

Problems of Agriculture

Latin America has sometimes been called a region of "one-crop countries." For example, Brazil and Colombia have at different times depended on one crop, coffee, for their incomes. The countries of Central America depend on the sale of bananas. Guatemala and El Salvador get more than half their export sales from coffee. Cuba and Puerto Rico depend on sugarcane; Argentina relies on beef. This kind of single-crop economy is called **monoculture**. If the crop is poor or its market price drops, the whole country suffers greatly.

Much of the fertile land in Latin America is occupied by large plantations, many of them owned by foreign businesses or by a few wealthy families. Because much of the land is in the hands of a few owners, and there are few factories, many Latin Americans have become agricultural workers. The plantations are in many ways like factories. Workers live and are fed in large buildings. They are paid low wages and have few luxuries and not very many of the necessities of life.

There are millions of campesinos whose farms are small and who have a low standard of living. Many of these campesinos are Native Americans whose land is poor in quality or is located where transportation is very poor. Because they have almost no education, their ways of farming are backward. They find it hard to grow enough to give their families more than a subsistence living.

The poverty of the people is the biggest problem of the area. They do not eat the right foods. They grow barely enough food for their families, and their health is poor. Because they have so little money, they cannot afford good school and health services. Many cannot read or write.

The number of people in Latin America is increasing so fast that the population will probably double in the next 20 years. Most of the growth is taking place among the poor families. This fact only makes the situation worse, since there is already a problem in raising enough food for the present population.

Despite the money that the plantation crops may bring into the countries of Latin America, economic growth in the region has not been great. Most of the people earning a living by agriculture remain subsistence farmers or poorly paid agricultural workers.

Better agricultural production is necessary to improve the economy of Latin America. The region's leaders agree that their nations must increase production from the land, and most important—give more of the profits to the people who do the farming.

It is estimated that between 10 and 15 percent of all Latin Americans own 90 percent of the agricultural lands. The big landowners organize political parties and, through them, control local government. They are unwilling to support land reform laws that would weaken their power and lessen their wealth.

In spite of the big landowners' opposition, several nations have started land reform programs. As we have seen, the ejido system in Mexico is an attempt at reform. Also in the 1950s and 1960s several nations acted to break up large estates. Venezuela began a planned program of land reform in 1957. Since then, millions of acres have been broken up into smaller farm units. Fidel Castro, following the Communist model, divided most of Cuba's large estates into collective and state farms. In addition, reform-minded military governments began farmland reform, but their work was interrupted by poor world economic conditions and revolution. In Chile, for example, land reform was begun in the 1960s and continued through 1973. When Salvatore Allende was overthrown by a repressive military junta in 1973, most land-reform plans ended.

Even if all land were divided equally, other reforms would be needed. Farmers must be given the opportunity to learn modern ways of farming and proper scientific care of the land. Also, loans must be made available at low interest rates to allow farmers to buy better tools, seeds, and fertilizer. Despite improvements in transportation, more improvements are needed to enable Latin American farmers to get their goods to market. Unless these improvements take place, division of the land into smaller plots would mean less production, not more.

Solution of the Debt Crisis in Brazil

Experts had feared that the 44 billion dollar debt that Brazil owes to private banks would crush the economy of the country. In 1991 and 1992, however, Brazil, the biggest Third World debtor, worked out an arrangement with 19 banks representing 300 private creditors. The banks agreed to extend the time for repayment of the debt. Brazil in return promised to repay the entire amount in smaller payments of principal and interest. In addition, Brazil agreed to enact economic reforms, mainly to control inflation and open up the country to foreign investment.

Natural Resources

Latin America has abundant natural resources. Within the vast area of Latin America there are rich mineral deposits, dense forests, and fast-flowing streams. The forests and the mineral deposits provide raw materials for modern industry in many parts of the world.

Forest Resources

About 40 percent of Latin America is covered with forests. Half of this area is in Brazil, from which mahogany, ebony, cedar, and pine are obtained. In Argentina, quebracho trees supply tannin, which is used to cure (tan) leather. The quebracho has a hard wood that decays (rots) very slowly. It is used for housing, railroad ties, and fence posts. Another forest product is **yerba maté**. The leaves of the yerba maté bush are used to make a drink called maté, something like our tea. The tropical forests of Latin America also produce rubber, carnauba wax (used as a polish and in phonograph records), Brazil nuts, and chicle.

Mineral Resources and Mining

Compared with the number of people who work on farms in Latin America, there are not many people working in the mines. Yet minerals are an important resource for the area. Much of this great mineral wealth is not used in Latin America but is exported to the industrial nations of the world.

MINERALS AND COUNTRIES WHERE THEY ARE PRODUCED

Mineral	Where Found
Silver	Mexico (first in the world), Argentina, Colombia, Peru, Bolivia, Costa Rica, Ecuador
Tin	Bolivia
Copper	Chile (Atacama Desert), Argentina, Bolivia, Colombia, Cuba
Nitrates (fertilizer)	Chile (Atacama Desert) (first in the world)
Oil	Venezuela, Mexico, Colombia, Argentina, Trinidad, Peru
Iron ore	Venezuela, Peru, Chile, Brazil, Argentina, Guatemala
Aluminum (bauxite)	Surinam (first in the world), Guyana (second), Jamaica
Iodine	Chile
Manganese	Brazil, Cuba
Antimony	Bolivia, Mexico, Peru
Platinum	Colombia (third in the world)
Diamonds	Brazil (second in the world)
Uranium	Brazil

Manufacturing and Industry

There are six main reasons for the growth of industry and manufacturing in a nation or a region: (1) available natural resources, (2) capital (money or property) available for development, (3) number of skilled workers, (4) transportation and communication, (5) home markets, and (6) government support and policy.

If you looked at a list of products exported from Latin America, you would see such items as bananas, coffee, sugar, oil, beef, copper, and bauxite. All of these are raw materials. Only in recent years have the nations of Latin America begun to manufacture goods.

Reasons for Slow Growth in South America

Industry and manufacturing have developed very slowly in South America. Let us use the six factors listed above to discover why the growth of industry has been slow.

1. Natural resources. Although Latin America is rich in many minerals, it has little of one of the most important, coal. Coal is important as a source of power for mills and factories, for running railroads, and for making steel. Some coal is found in Chile, Peru, Brazil, Argentina, and Colombia. Most of it, however, is either low grade or far from centers of population. A possible substitute for coal is water power; Latin America has the potential for over 75 million horsepower from water power. However, little of this resource has been developed because most of the water power is located far from centers of population.

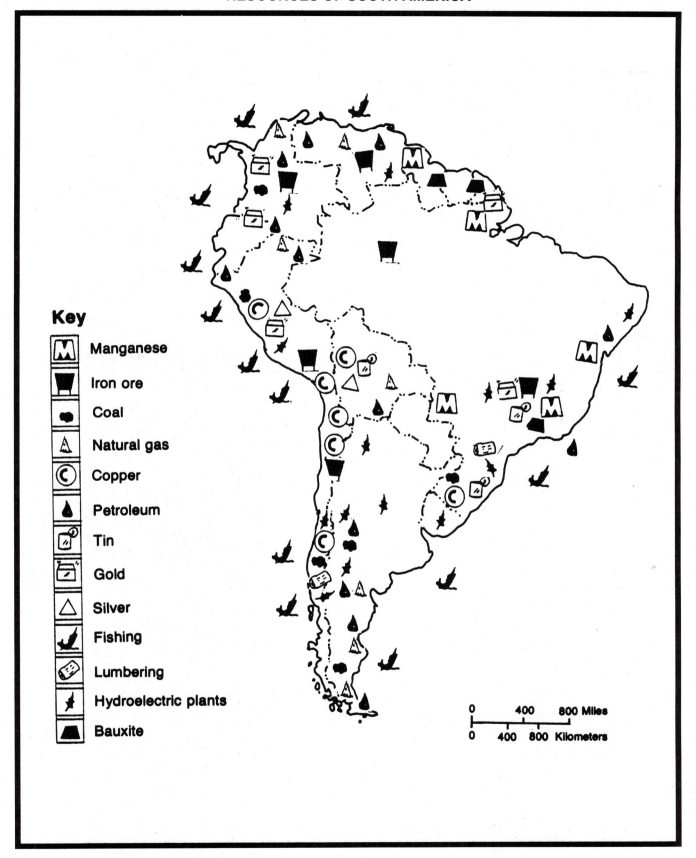

Key

M	Manganese
◢	Iron ore
•	Coal
◬	Natural gas
C	Copper
◗	Petroleum
⬡	Tin
▣	Gold
△	Silver
✦	Fishing
▱	Lumbering
✹	Hydroelectric plants
◣	Bauxite

0   400   800 Miles

0   400   800 Kilometers

2. <u>Capital</u>. Money is also needed. Money that is used to build factories and power plants is called capital. Latin America has lacked capital for several reasons.

First, the region has a history of rapid changes of government. Foreign businesses are not eager to invest money in countries that have revolutions all the time. They are afraid that their property will be damaged or taken away.

Second, foreign investors believe they can get greater profits from the mines and plantations than by investing capital in factories.

Third, the profits that do come from the mines or plantations go outside the country, since in many cases these sources of income are owned by people or businesses in other countries.

Fourth, wealthy Latin Americans, most of whom are large landowners, use their extra money to buy more land rather than to build factories.

3. <u>Labor</u>. Skilled workers are needed for factory work. You have already learned that a large number of Latin Americans cannot read or write. Literacy is necessary for the development of industrial skills.

4. <u>Transportation and Communication</u>. Mountainous topography, thick tropical forests, and centers of population that are far apart have hampered the development of transportation and communication in Latin America. Few paved highways have been built, and dirt roads often cannot be used by automobiles and trucks. Latin America has few railroads to cover its large area. Good transportation infrastructure (basic framework) is necessary to bring raw materials to factories and to take goods to markets for sale.

5. <u>Home markets</u>. Latin Americans buy imported manufactured goods rather than products made in their own countries. Why? In Latin America most people have so little money that they cannot buy manufactured products. For this reason, few large factories are needed.

6. <u>Government policy</u>. Latin American leaders have tried to reduce the influence of foreigners in raw materials production. They followed a policy known as economic nationalism, in which the amount of taxes paid by foreign-owned companies were increased. In some cases, the government took over the foreign-owned companies, an action that does not encourage others to invest in Latin American industry.

Another fact related to this situation is that most wealthy Latin Americans do not pay taxes. To make up for this nonpayment, Latin American governments put high taxes on the profits of foreign-owned companies. As a result, profits are too low to make foreign investment worthwhile.

Despite the situation described above, progress has been made in industrialization.

Situation in Central America

For the most part Central American countries lack mineral wealth. Only Nicaragua has significant mineral deposits. In the late 1960s, gold, silver, lead, and zinc were discovered in northern Nicaragua. Mining is slowly becoming an important part of Nicaragua's economy.

In Honduras, silver was discovered in the 19th century. By now the silver deposits have been almost used up. Honduras is turning to smaller industries, such as sugar refineries and factories that produce cement, beer, and soft drinks.

El Salvador and Costa Rica are the two most industrialized countries of Central America. Water power is the key to both countries' success. A power station on the Lempa River fuels El Salvador's large textile and food-processing plants. Costa Rica also has plentiful supplies of water power. Costa Rica's main industrial products are textiles, chemicals, and leather goods.

Situation in Mexico

Mexico is far ahead of its Central American neighbors in industrial development. It is the world's largest producer of fluorite (used in glass making) and graphite. Mexico is also well supplied with other minerals, including silver, zinc, lead, and copper.

The most important boost to industry has been the discovery of many oil deposits on Mexico's Gulf coast. Mexico may have the world's largest supply of oil. Known deposits already exceed (are greater than) those of the United States.

Oil money has been used to build dams in the northern mountains to develop power for use in the steel and textile mills of Monterey. In addition, these dams supply water to irrigate the cotton and winter vegetables grown on the dry lands of northern Mexico.

Oil money has also been used to start up new industries and expand existing ones. But when the price of oil dropped in the mid-1980s, Mexico developed a serious debt problem that threatens to halt progress.

Mexico City, with a population of over 17 million, which makes it the largest **urban** (city) area in the world, is the leading industrial city of Mexico. Textiles, food processing, and chemical, paper, and fertilizer production employ thousands of workers.

North American Free Trade Agreement

If the North American Free Trade Agreement (NAFTA) among the United States, Canada, and Mexico, goes into effect, it will join 363 million consumers into the world's largest trading zone with a combined gross domestic product of more than 6 trillion dollars.

The pact's big winner at the outset will probably be Mexico, which lags behind the United States and Canada in industrial development. It is estimated that Mexico could gain 600,000 industrial jobs by 1995 as a result of the rollback of tariffs and reduction of quotas that now limit Mexico's exports. In time, the United States and Canada would benefit greatly from an expected explosion of sales from a growing Mexican market.

	U.S.	Canada	Mexico
GDP (Gross Domestic Product) in billions of dollars (1991)	$5,673	$501	$283
Population in millions (1991)	253	27	83
Per capita income (1991)	$22,400	$21,980	$3,400
Hourly compensation in manufacturing	$14.77	$16.02	$1.80
Literacy rate	99%	99%	87%
Median age	33	33.5	19
Infant mortality per 1,000	10	7	29

Source: U.S. Bureau of the Census, U.S. Dept. of Commerce, CTA; Data Resources, Inc.

Situation in the West Indies

As we have learned, the West Indies do not have enough mineral resources and water power to support industry. As a result, the industries that do exist revolve around agricultural products grown on the islands. Sugarcane is sent to industrial plants in the Dominican Republic and Cuba. Tobacco is processed into cigars and cigarettes in Cuba and Puerto Rico. Other industrial plants in the islands prepare coffee, cacao, and tropical fruits for export. Textiles are produced in Haiti, the Dominican Republic, and Cuba. The Dominican Republic supplies most of its neighbors in the Caribbean with dairy products, such as cheese, butter, and whole milk.

Industry plays an especially strong role in the economy of Puerto Rico. More than half of all Puerto Rican workers are involved in industry, and most of Puerto Rico's wealth comes from industry rather than from farming. The main reason for this is the Puerto Rican self-help program, "Operation Bootstrap," which encouraged investment from the United States and put money into the education of Puerto Ricans.

Recent Progress in South America

Most South American countries still depend on the export of raw materials, such as food products and metals, for most of their income. In some countries, however, manufacturing industries are growing quickly.

Steel mills, chemical and cement factories, and wood-processing plants are increasing in Argentina, Brazil, and Chile. Transportation facilities and roads are being improved and expanded. The area around São Paulo and Rio de Janeiro in Brazil has become a huge manufacturing district. Brazilian petroleum products, machinery, automobiles, tires, furniture, radios, television sets, and clothing are exported throughout the world.

Food processing and canning are important industries. Argentina is the leader, with a large meat-packing and meat-processing industry. Colombia and Brazil process sugar and coffee. Chile converts grapes into wine that is sold at home and abroad.

The wood products industry is growing in Latin America, particularly in Colombia. Wood is made into pulp, paper, and building materials, and plywood for the building industry is produced in Colombian factories. The manufacture of furniture, exported to the United States for the first time in 1969, is a promising industry.

The textile industry is spreading widely throughout Latin America. Ecuadorian and Peruvian mills usually make products from natural materials—wool, cotton, or silk—rather than synthetic materials such as Orlon, nylon, and Dacron. The major reasons for this growth have been:

1. Loans from the World Bank and the International Monetary Fund were used to improve roads and build factories.

2. Under a plan called "Alliance for Progress," the United States lent money to Latin American countries for agricultural and industrial projects.
3. Most important were the loans and private investments made by Americans, Europeans, and the Japanese that enabled the Latin Americans to continue their industrialization progress.

The Arts in Latin America

Three groups of people have influenced the arts in Latin America—the Native Americans, the Europeans, and the Africans.

The oldest buildings in Latin America were built by Native Americans. Machu Picchu, in the Andes of Peru, stands as a monument to the genius of the Incas. The pyramids of the Maya and the Aztecs still stand in Mexico.

Even today the Native Americans of Latin America are skilled makers of handicrafts, many of which are considered of good quality. The patterns used for decoration often are symbols of nature or the gods. These designs show a connection with the past and provide much information about past Native American life. Among the many Native American tribes certain dances, ceramics, and rituals (practices) still survive and also inform us about the past.

The African style of dance and music, which reflects these people's tribal background, has greatly influenced the folk dances and music of Brazil. In the West Indies the intricate drum rhythms of Africa have become an important part of the music. Jazz is basically African in style. Dances showing African influence have been popular in various sections of Latin America and the United States.

Painting

For a long time after the Spanish and Portuguese came to Latin America the artists of Latin America copied the styles of Europe. The Mexican Revolution of 1910 (see page 675) had an important impact on art. Diego Rivera was the leader in "revolutionary art," which might also be called "the art of the people" because it showed how the people struggled and how they lived. Rivera also painted scenes of Mexico's history, which were a major contribution to the growing Mexican interest in the country's Native American past. José Orozco and David Siqueiros were other Mexican artists who painted the people as they were. These artists made the Native Americans and other poor people the subjects of their paintings. The people were shown as the victims of the Spanish, the landowners, and the foreign capitalists. For these painters the purpose of art was to educate. Although each took different subjects, their paintings all told the story of the Native Americans and their enslavement by the Spanish and the struggle of the modern working class.

In Peru, Ecuador, and Bolivia, artists have created strong, colorful paintings of the Incas. Brazilian artists, such as Candido Portinari, have shown the joys, the sorrows, and the problems of black Latin Americans.

Some Latin American artists, Roberto Matta of Chile and Wilfredo Lam of Cuba, were surrealists. They sought to portray life as if it were a dream. Haiti is noted for painters who show African and voodoo influences.

Other artists of importance include Pedro Figari and Joaquin Torres Garciá (Uruguay), Frida Kahlo (Mexico), and Antonio Sequí, Julio le Parc, and Luis Felipe Noé (Argentina).

Literature

Ever since the conquest by Spain, Latin America has had many writers. The early explorers wrote about their adventures. One of the earliest writers born in Latin America was Garcilaso de la Vega, the son of an Inca princess and a Spanish captain. He wrote about Inca legends and stories. From him we have learned much about Inca festivals and ceremonies and about the suffering of the Incas under the Spanish.

One of the great poems in the Spanish language is "La Aracaña," which praises the bravery and courage of the Native Americans of Chile in their wars with the Spanish. It was written by Alonso de Ercilla y Zuniga, a captain in the Spanish army.

Domingo Sormiento, in his book *Civilization and Barbarism*, followed the Spanish style. One who did not was Andrés Bello. Writing in the 1820s and 1830s, Bello believed that Latin Americans should build their own literary style. Another who did not was José Hernandez in *Martin Fierro*. The hero of this epic work is the Argentina gaucho, symbol of the bold reality of life on the pampas.

Romanticism

Nevertheless, most writers followed the style of the Europeans. The **romanticism** of European writing in the 1850s greatly influenced Latin Americans. Romanticism emphasized human emotions (love, hate, fear, and so on) rather than human reason (thinking and looking for facts). Romantic writers believed human feelings were more important than the power to think and reason.

New Movements

In the late 19th century, a new movement in literature, called **modernism**, developed in Latin America. The Modernists were led by Rubén Dario of Nicaragua. Dario, both a poet and a diplomat, led the movement to help awaken an awareness among Latin Americans of the ties that bound them together. Dario also objected to the use of European Spanish themes and to the Romantic movement in Latin America.

José Martí, a Cuban, was another Modernist. He objected to the ideas of Domingo Sarmiento of Argentina. In his book *Our America*, Martí argued against Sarmiento's idea of dividing Latin Americans into "the civilized and the barbarians." Martí believed that the "barbarians" had qualities that would prove to be more valuable than those copied from Spain.

Along with Dario and Martí, writers like José Asunción Silva of Colombia, José Enrique Rodó of Uruguay, and Manuel Gutierrez Najera of Mexico wrote of the similar cultural ties among all Latin Americans. They emphasized that this unity of culture reached beyond political boundary lines and political ideas.

By the end of the nineteenth century, **realism** became important; authors and poets began to describe life as it really was. Alberto Blest Gana in Chile, and Joaquim Machado de Assis in Brazil, were leading realist writers. The Revolution of 1910 in Mexico led more people to write about things realistically.

Today many Latin American authors write about the poor and the unhappy. Some of their novels and short stories are about people who lie in crowded city slums. Some write about people who struggle in tiny mountain villages or in the jungles of northern Brazil. The Nobel Prize for Literature was won by Miguel Angel Asturias of Guatemala in 1968, and by Gabriel Garciá Márquez of Colombia in 1982.

Poetry has always been an important part of the culture of Latin Americans. Two important Latin American poets are Gabriela Mistral, a Chilean who won a Nobel Prize, and Pablo Neruda, also a Chilean, who has won many honors around the world.

Music

The Incas, Maya, and Aztecs played musical instruments, sang, and danced. The *quena* (reed flute) of the Incas is still played in the Andes of Peru today.

Spain also influenced the area's appreciation of music. The guitar and piano are two of Spain's contributions. As we have already read, the music and dance of Brazil are based on African rhythms and melodies.

Many modern Latin American composers have used the rhythms and melodies of folk songs in their music. Hector Villa-Lobos of Brazil was probably the most famous Latin American composer. In his composition *Amazonas* he combined many of the folk tunes he heard as a boy to produce a concert masterpiece. Villa-Lobos wrote about 700 pieces of music, all seeking to bring out the life and culture of the Brazilian people.

In Mexico, Carlos Chavez was a well-known composer. Because Chavez had fought in the Mexican Revolution, he knew how the common people felt. One of his compositions, *Llamadas,* is sometimes called the "Workers Symphony." As the name shows, this piece was written for all Mexican city workers.

Another Latin American in the field of music who became known throughout the world was Pablo Casals, who was born in Puerto Rico. He played his cello for the enjoyment of all, not only the rich.

The Fiesta

Music and dancing come together in the fiesta, a community, village, or town celebration. Usually, the fiesta is partly religious and partly social. It is a happy time, with music, dancing, and eating. Fiestas come at planting or harvest times or on special religious days. The whole fiesta is a group activity and everyone has a part to perform.

Summary of the Situation

The history of most of the Latin American countries in the 19th century was almost a continuous parade of revolutions, dictators (caudillos and caciques), and constitutions. Many have said that these numerous changes show a lack of ability for self-government, but there is a far more realistic way to see the problem. The revolutions, dictators, and constitutions were only symptoms of a serious problem. They were evidence of the struggle of the people to overcome the handicaps of a difficult physical environment and an unfair economic system. In addition, the people had to struggle against the twin curses inherited from Spain—an aristocratic refusal to do physical labor and a lack of training in the democratic idea of government.

It is with these ideas in mind that we should view Latin America in the 19th century and into the 20th century. Whatever progress was made should not be measured by comparison with the advances made by the United States. Rather, it should be measured by the number and difficulty of the obstacles overcome in each of the Latin American countries.

The Caribbean Islands (West Indies)

Geography and Climate

The West Indies are a chain of islands that separate the Caribbean Sea from the Atlantic Ocean. The islands form a curve about 2,000 miles long that stretches from Florida in the United States to Venezuela in northeastern South America.

Three main island groups make up the West Indies:

1. *The Bahamas*, in the north, consist of about 3,000 small islands and reefs.
2. *The Greater Antilles* lie in the center to the south and east of mainland North America. This group includes the large islands of Jamaica, Cuba, Hispaniola (Haiti and the Dominican Republic), and Puerto Rico, as well as the U.S. Virgin Islands.
3. *The Lesser Antilles* are a long chain of islands beginning to the east of Puerto Rico and continuing south to almost the mainland of South America.

Most of the islands of the West Indies were formed by volcanic eruptions (a few are made of coral and limestone). The climate is mainly hot and wet in the summer (tropical) and warm and drier in the winter.

The People

The West Indies has about 34 million people; about one-third of them live in Cuba. More than half inhabit rural areas and earn a subsistence living by farming.

A majority of the people of the West Indies are descendants of black Africans brought to the islands as slaves to work the sugar and tobacco plantations. Most of the rest have British, Dutch, French, Portuguese, or Spanish ancestors. Some people are the descendants of Chinese or East Indian farm workers who arrived in the 19th century after slavery was abolished. Others are the offspring of mixed marriages between blacks and Europeans. The area's original Native American peoples have died out, except for a small group of Caribs who live in the mountainous regions of the island of Dominica.

The Languages and Literature

The many languages and dialects spoken in the West Indies show the mixed cultural traditions and backgrounds of the many African and European groups that settled the regions. Below are listed the most important languages and the islands where each is spoken.

Spanish: Cuba, Dominican Republic, Puerto Rico
Dutch: Aruba, Netherland Antilles
French: Haiti (Creole), Guadalupe, Martinique
English: Jamaica, Barbados, Monserrat, Grenada, Trinidad and Tobago, St. Vincent, Antigua, Dominica, Bahamas

Many West Indians use a dialect called patois (in Haiti, Creole), which is a mixture of African words and English or French. Another dialect, *Papiamento*, which is a combination of Dutch, English, Portuguese, and Spanish, is widely used in Aruba and the Netherlands Antilles. In short, the language situation in the West Indies is a fine example of cultural diffusion and adaptation.

Derek Walcott—Nobel Prize Winner

Derek Walcott, a West Indian poet, won the Nobel Prize in Literature in 1992. His writings clearly show the cultural diversity and richness of the Caribbean experience. The Swedish Academy of Letters, which offers the prize, honored Mr. Walcott for his "historical vision and sensitivity, the outcome of a multicultural commitment."

The New York Times, in the issue of October 9, 1992, described the poet's achievements as follows: "In his literary works Walcott has laid a course for his own cultural environment, but through them he speaks to each and every one of us. In him, West Indian culture has found its greatest poet."

Mr. Walcott is noted for his ability to use the classics, folklore, history, and the **vernacular** (native language) to bring life to his efforts. His latest poetic work, "Omeros" (1990), is a perfect example. Although the principal characters have names taken from the *Iliad* and *Odyssey* of Homer, the work is meant to capture, in the words of *The New York Times*, "the whole experience of the people of the Caribbean."

The Economy

The Greater Antilles (Cuba, Hispaniola, Puerto Rico, Jamaica, and the Virgin Islands) account for more than 90 percent of the Caribbean region's total land area. On the Greater Antilles, mountain highlands slope from the center of each island to the sea. Frequent earthquakes rock the islands.

The Bahamas consist of a chain (archipelago) of about 3,000 small islands and reefs lying off the southeast coast of Florida. These are low-lying coral and limestone islands with few rivers.

The Lesser Antilles include an arc of mountainous islands with active volcanoes and five islands off the coast of South America. Volcanic crater lakes and bubbling hot springs attract tourists to many of the islands.

The small total land area and the mountainous topography of the area limit its resources. Volcanic deposits help to make the soil fertile, but there is little level land for farming. The sides of hills and mountains provide arable sites for raising coffee. In valley regions, with their mild climate and fertile soil, citrus fruits, tobacco, and bananas are grown.

More than half the people of the West Indies earn their living by farming. Many work on large sugar, coffee, or banana plantations owned by rich landowners. Some own or rent small plots of land on which they raise crops and livestock, but only enough to live on at a subsistence level. The crops that make up the diet of most West Indians are rice, beans, sweet potatoes, and such tropical fruits as bananas, mangoes, and oranges. This is supplemented by fish and crabs.

Most of the cities and towns of the Islands are located in coastal areas. Most city people earn their living by working in hotels or service businesses connected with the tourist industry. The few that make up the middle class own small shops or work for the government.

Sport fishing attracts tourists to the Caribbean throughout the year. Local fishermen catch shrimp, lobsters, and a variety of fish for local markets. However, there is little commercial fishing for export because the waters of the area are too shallow for large schools of fish.

The region's mineral resources include small deposits of bauxite, oil, iron, and chromium. These are exported to the United States and Western Europe to be refined.

Early History

Cibony tribespeople were the first group to settle in the West Indies, over 3,000 years ago. Members of the Arawaks, a South American tribe, began moving to the West Indies during the 11th century. They settled on the islands of the Greater Antilles (Cuba, Jamaica, Hispaniola, and Puerto Rico). The Arawaks were a peaceful people who farmed near their permanent villages.

They were followed by the Caribs, who settled in the many islands of the Lesser Antilles to the south of the larger islands. The Caribs were more warlike than the Arawaks. Their economic life was based on hunting and fishing.

Colonial Period

Christopher Columbus landed on the island of San Salvador in the Bahamas in 1492. During the next 10 years, he reached and claimed almost all the West Indian islands for

Spain. The Spanish set up the first permanent European settlement in the West Indies in 1496 at Santo Domingo on Hispaniola.

The lure of gold and other riches brought thousands of Europeans to the West Indies. In the early 16th century, Spaniards set up colonies in Cuba, Jamaica, and Puerto Rico. They made slaves of the Native Americans and forced them to work in the gold mines and on the plantations. Disease and overwork killed almost all of these Native Americans.

The wealth of the West Indies brought pirates from England, France, and the Netherlands to the area. These pirates attacked Spanish ships and ports and stole valuable cargoes.

In the 17th century, the Danes, Dutch, English, and French set up colonies on the smaller islands of the Lesser Antilles. In 1655, the English conquered Jamaica, and in 1697 the French took the western part of Hispaniola (Haiti).

During the 17th and 18th centuries, the colonial powers gained great wealth from sugar grown in the West Indies. The Europeans brought millions of black Africans to the islands to work as slaves on the sugar plantations.

Independence Comes

During the 18th century, the revolutions in the United States and in Europe brought new ideas of freedom to the islands. The revolutions also weakened the power of the Europeans.

Haiti

In 1804, a slave revolt led by Toussaint L'Ouverture broke out in Haiti against the French. Although L'Ouverture died during the revolt, Haiti became the first independent nation in the West Indies. (The Dominican Republic, in the eastern half of Hispaniola, broke away from Haiti and declared its independence in 1844.)

Cuba, Puerto Rico, and the U.S. Virgin Islands

In 1898, the people of Cuba revolted against Spain and the United States became involved in a war with Spain. After the United Sates won the war, Cuba became independent, and Puerto Rico became a U.S. colony and, later, a **commonwealth** of the United States.

In 1917, the United States bought the U.S. Virgin Islands from Denmark. Today the Virgin Islands is a self-governing **possession** (territory) of the United States. The governor and legislature are elected by the people of the Virgin Islands.

The British West Indies

The British had ruled Jamaica and many small islands of the so-called West Indian Federation (Antigua, Barbados, Dominica, Grenada, Jamaica, Monserrat, St. Kitts-Nevis-Anguilla, St. Lucia, St. Vincent, and Trinidad and Tobago). In 1962, Jamaica and Trinidad-Tobago became independent, and in the next 20 years the other members of the federation also gained independence.

The End of Slavery

Before the end of the 19th century, slavery was abolished in all of the West Indies. The plantation system then became less profitable because plantation owners lost most of their cheap labor. As a result, Europeans began to lose interest in the West Indies.

The Situation Today

The nations of the West Indies face a number of economic and social problems, including overcrowding, poverty, and unemployment. Large numbers of West Indians cannot find jobs or must work for low wages. Consequently, many of the best educated and most skilled West Indians have left the islands and moved to Canada, Great Britain, and the United States. The basic cause of these economic problems is that the islands lack natural resources and capital for development.

In an attempt to remedy the situation, regional organizations such as CARIFTA, CARICOM (Caribbean Community and Common Market), and the Caribbean Development Bank have been set up to stimulate industrial and economic growth.

Puerto Rico

In considering the West Indies today, it will be helpful to look at the present situation in each of four large countries—Puerto Rico, the Dominican Republic, Haiti, and Jamaica—and in the smaller French possessions, Dutch territories, Trinidad and Tobago, and Barbados. Puerto Rico is located on the eastern end of the Greater Antilles. In the center, mountains extend east and west toward the coast. A narrow coastal plain surrounds the island.

Puerto Rico is a self-governing commonwealth of the United States. Puerto Ricans are U.S. citizens, although they do not pay federal income taxes while living on the island. They elect their own governors and legislature, as well as a nonvoting representative to the U.S. Congress. However, they cannot vote in presidential elections. As a result, some Puerto Ricans want their island to become the 51st state of the United States. Others like things as they are. A small but very active group is in favor of complete Puerto Rican independence.

Sugarcane is the most important crop of Puerto Rico. Coffee, tropical fruits, and tobacco are also grown. Unlike most of Latin America, less than one-half the population works in farming.

In fact, the most important economic activity of Puerto Rico is manufacturing. As recently as 1940, Puerto Rico had little industry, but in that year "Operation Bootstrap" was introduced. Under this program, many incentives (advantages) were given to businesses that came to Puerto Rico. These incentives included lower or no taxes for industry and special training programs for workers.

Because of Puerto Rico's special relationship with the United States and its easy access to the American marketplace, many businesses moved to Puerto Rico. Wages are lower there than in the United States, and products can be manufactured more cheaply. Today, petrochemicals, medicines, and electrical equipment are produced in Puerto Rican plants.

The Dominican Republic

The Dominican Republic is located on the eastern two-thirds of Hispaniola (the western third is Haiti). The people of the Dominican Republic are Spanish speaking and Roman Catholic in religion. Seventy-five percent of the 7.1 million inhabitants are mulattos of mixed Spanish and African descent. The Dominican Republic was one of Spain's earliest colonies in the New World. As a result, Spanish culture and influences remain strong.

The topography of the Dominican Republic is made up of steep mountains, fertile valleys, and coastal plains in the north and south. Its forests contain valuable tropical woods for export. Large deposits of ferro-nickel and gold ores also provide valuable exports. Sugarcane, plantains, rice, bananas, coffee, mangoes, and cacao are raised. These products serve as staples for export and also make up most of the Dominican people's diet.

In the last 20 years, tourism has become the most important industry of the Dominican Republic.

Haiti

Haiti, located at the western end of the island of Hispaniola, lies directly east of Cuba. Its population is about 6 million.

Most of Haiti's people are black. Although French serves as the official language, only a small, highly educated minority speak it. Most people speak Haitian Creole, a language of African and French origins.

Voodoo, a type of religion based on West African beliefs and ceremonies, is practiced by many Haitians. Voodoo exists alongside Roman Catholicism, which was introduced into the island by the French.

Haiti ranks as one of the world's poorest and least developed nations. Most Haitians earn less than $200 a year. There is a very high infant mortality rate, and life expectancy is only 45 years.

Seventy-five percent of all Haitians make a living as subsistence farmers. They raise cassava (tapioca—an edible, starchy root), plantains (like bananas), and yams (sweet potatoes). On larger farms, coffee, sugarcane, and cotton are raised for export.

The capital city of Haiti, Port-au-Prince, is the island's sole manufacturing center. In a country with low literacy, industry often depends on hand labor and simple machines. Among the country's exports to the United States are clothing and baseballs.

Haiti faces many problems. It has a dense population that cannot be supported by the island's few resources. Overuse of the land has caused severe erosion and ruined the soil for farming.

Also, democracy has never really been part of the Haitian tradition. Unstable governments, civil unrest, and rebellions form a large part of Haiti's history. Into the late 1980s, attempts to end dictatorial government had not been successful. Because of these problems, many Haitians continue to migrate to the United States.

In 1986, Jean-Claude Duvalier, Haiti's most recent dictator, was overthrown by the army. For the next four years the army ruled Haiti. Army leaders regularly promised free elections, but at the same time they feared the results of any elections. They did not wish to give up power.

In late 1990, General Herard Abraham, leader of the military junta, finally agreed to allow a free election. Father Jean-Bertrand Aristide, a Roman Catholic priest, won a landslide victory. He took office in February 1991 and became Haiti's first democratically elected president.

Aristide won because he pledged to work to improve the lives of the Haitian people. After becoming president, he met with leaders from the international community. The United States, France, and Venezuela and the International Development Bank pledged 511 million dollars in aid to the Aristide government.

In early October 1991, however, the military, led by General Raoul Cedras, drove Aristide from office and out of the country. Cedras claimed that the coup d'état was caused by the arbitrary, violent, and undemocratic actions of the president, who seemed to condone violence to achieve his ends.

Aristide asked the United Nations for assistance in restoring democratic rule to Haiti and also requested help from the Organization of American States (OAS). The OAS voted to reject the coup and also to apply diplomatic and economic pressure on Haiti, including trade embargoes and sanctions. It was hoped that these actions would isolate the army leaders and force them to accept the return of Aristide.

Jamaica

Jamaica lies directly west of Haiti and just south of eastern Cuba. It is a mountainous island with only about one-fifth of the land available for farming. Nevertheless, Jamaica was Great Britain's major sugar supplier for nearly 300 years. Other important crops include bananas, coffee, tobacco, and citrus fruits. The Blue Mountains of eastern Jamaica are noted for the high quality of the coffee grown on their slopes. Jamaica produces nearly all the world's supply of a seasoning called allspice.

The discovery of bauxite in the 1950s gave Jamaica a valuable mineral export, mainly to the United States. Bauxite is used in the making of aluminum.

Jamaica's economy is based on a mixture of small plantations, small farms, food processing, and tourism. The policy of the government has been to encourage foreign investment by reducing taxes and offering other incentives.

Jamaica was an important British colony until 1962, when it was granted independence. Jamaica follows the British parliamentary system. Two parties have shared political power. One follows capitalist economic policies; the other, socialist economic policies.

French Possessions

Martinique and Guadalupe are French possessions located in the Lesser Antilles. Both are volcanic islands with active volcanoes. Sugar and bananas are raised and exported to France. Tourism is the major industry of the islands.

Dutch Territories

The Netherlands has ruled an area that includes three small islands—Aruba, Bonaire, and Curaçao—in the northeast Caribbean off the coast of South America. Aruba and Curaçao have major oil refineries that process oil from Mexico and Venezuela. Tourism has become a major industry on the three islands.

Trinidad and Tobago

The two-island country of Trinidad and Tobago is located off the coast of South America just north of Venezuela. The country's economic activity revolves around its oil deposits. Petroleum products make up about 80 percent of its exports. Although oil refining and oil services provide many of the jobs available on the islands, most people are employed in agriculture and the tourist industry.

Barbados

With over 250,000 people, Barbados is one of the world's most densely populated countries (1,548 people per square mile). It lies farther east than any other island in the West Indies. Historically Barbados was a major British sugar colony. Today about 60 percent of the land is still used for sugar plantations and sugar is the most important export. It is sent to other Caribbean islands, the United States, the United Kingdom, and Canada. Other industrial exports are electrical components, chemicals, clothing (textiles), and rum. Tourism is an important industry and supplies many jobs. Barbados has an excellent educational system and a relatively high per capita income.

Latin America in the 20th Century

In the 20th century, after almost 100 years of disturbance and weak government, the Latin American states began to gain stability and make political and economic progress.

As we have seen, Latin America has had many uprisings; however, it has had only a few real **revolutions**. A revolution is a complete overturning or change of a political system or social structure. The many uprisings, on the other hand, kept the same political and social systems. Changes were made in leaders and on paper (new constitutions). It might be said that the many uprisings took the place of free elections, which were not allowed by those in power.

The "real" revolutions took place in Mexico (1911), Bolivia (1952), Cuba (1958), and Nicaragua (1979). A possible fifth in Chile was not allowed to finish its course.

Mexican Revolution

The Mexican Revolution began in 1911 against the dictatorship of Porfirio Díaz, who had been in power since 1876. He was overthrown and replaced by Francisco Madero, an idealist (someone who dreams of a better world) devoted to the interests of the Mexican people. However, Madero was not a good leader. As president he tried to make changes, but he simply could not solve the problems that existed after 35 years of the Díaz dictatorship.

In 1912, Madero was forced out of power and was assassinated. For the next eight years violence and civil war ruled Mexico. Men like Victoriano Huerta, Pancho Villa, and Emiliano Zapata led troops that fought each other and the government.

Finally, in 1920 peace came to Mexico, and reform could take place. The large estancias and haciendas were broken up, and the land was divided among the peons, who were offered credit (loans). The system of land division, copied from the Aztecs, was called the ejido system.

The Mexican government encouraged the building of industry and labor unions. In 1938 oil wells and oil lands were taken away from foreign owners, including Americans. Mexico from that time on has been a producer of oil. Recently, new oil wells have been developed in northern Mexico.

Today, the ideals and the hopes of the Mexican Revolution continue to guide Mexico. As a result, the country has developed a stable government. In addition, Mexico has become one of the most prosperous nations of Latin America.

Mexico City is a modern city with wide boulevards and plazas.

Bolivian National Revolution

Bolivia also had a national revolution. Most of the people of Bolivia were mestizos or Spaniards. A large minority of Native Americans lived in lonely, isolated villages in the mountains. The Native Americans were always poor, had few rights, and never thought of themselves as Bolivians.

In the 1930s, Bolivia lost a war with Paraguay. The main outcome of the war was unrest. Returning soldiers were not happy with their treatment. Wages in the tin mines were low, and conditions became dangerous. At the same time, Native American war veterans now felt that they were Bolivians, and demanded greater rights and better living conditions. Many small revolts broke out and governments changed every few months.

In 1952, the small revolts turned into a great national revolution. The miners, who began this uprising with a strike for higher pay and better working conditions, were joined by students and the unhappy Native Americans. All of these groups fought the army and won. The tin miners set up their own government.

For the next 12 years the leaders of the miners tried to correct the evils of the past. Most people were given the right to vote, and the army was made much smaller. Land was taken from the large landholders and was divided among the peasants. The government ran the tin mines. There was much confusion, and the economy of Bolivia was upset.

In 1964, the army revolted against the government of the workers and took control of the country. Little progress had been made in the 12 years to improve the lives of the people. Today Bolivia still suffers from many of the same problems that it had in the past. Unlike Mexico, Bolivia did not benefit much from its social revolution.

The Cuban Revolution

The second revolution that brought complete and lasting, as well as far-reaching, changes in Latin America took place in Cuba.

Cuba has an important location near the United States. It lies at the mouth of the Gulf of Mexico, a short distance from both the United States and the Panama Canal.

The Situation from 1898 to 1956

Until 1898, Cuba was a colony of Spain. When the U.S. Congress declared war on Spain, it stated that the United States would "leave the government and control of Cuba to its people" (Teller Amendment). However, after Spain was defeated in the Spanish-American War, the United States army stayed in Cuba while Congress debated what to do about the island nation. Many members of Congress believed that the Cuban people were not ready to run their own government. Also, American business leaders wanted to protect their investments in Cuba and therefore opposed complete independence for that nation.

Finally, in 1901, Cubans were allowed to write a constitution for an independent Cuba. The United States then forced the Cubans to agree to the Platt Amendment.

The Platt Amendment limited Cuban independence. It gave the United States the right to intervene in Cuba "to protect American life and property." The United States took the power to veto Cuban decisions in foreign policy and money matters. The amendment also gave the United States the right to intervene "to preserve Cuban independence." Under the Platt Amendment the United States leased (rented) an area of Cuba on a permanent basis and built the Guantánamo Naval Base [The Platt Amendment was **abrogated** (done away with) in 1934 but the United States still in 1992 controls the base at Guantánamo.] In fact, the Platt Amendment meant that Cuba was not really independent.

Between 1902 and 1933, Cuba was ruled by shaky or do-nothing dictatorships. Civil violence was frequent, and three times U.S. troops were sent to Cuba to maintain law and order.

Most Cubans were poor. They were unhappy about the fact that few Cubans gained from their country's riches. Cubans objected to U.S. businesses that were making large profits from Cuban resources without sharing the wealth with Cuban workers.

President Fidel Castro of Cuba.

In 1933, an army sergeant, Fulgencio Batista, led a gulpe de estado. Although others appeared to rule Cuba, in fact Batista ruled for the next 25 years. He restored order but ended all political opposition and severely limited civil liberties. The economy improved, but the old social problems of poverty and inequality remained and grew.

The Castro Regime

Revolutionaries tried several times to remove Batista from power, but failed. Then in December 1956, Fidel Castro, his brother Raul, and Ernesto (Che) Guevara began a rebellion. After two years of guerrilla warfare, Batista was overthrown. By January 1959, Fidel Castro was in complete control.

Castro immediately started land reforms. Sugar and tobacco (Cuba's main products), lands, and cattle production were placed directly under the control of the government. Soon after, Castro nationalized all banks, industries, and foreign-owned companies. Much of this nationalized property was owned by Americans. In response, the United States embargoed all trade with Cuba.

Castro was left without a source of foreign aid and without Cuba's largest market for sugar. Castro turned to the Soviet Union for help and in 1960 announced publicly that he was a Communist.

As a result of the revolution the living standards of most Cubans improved. Education is free and available to everyone. In 1958, almost one-third of Cuban workers were unemployed. Today, full employment is provided by the Cuban government. Public health care has been greatly improved. Every Cuban has the right to a proper diet and decent housing. Corruption and violent crime have been brought under control.

The price paid for this improvement, however, has been high. In government, Castro and a small group of supporters have determined policy and rule the nation without calling for elections. Civil rights accepted in democratic countries, such as freedom of the press and free dissent (right to disagree), are not permitted. Many Cubans have chosen to leave Cuba rather than live under a dictatorship. Those who remained and showed opposition to Castro often were sent to jail.

The Cuban government did not enjoy the bad publicity it got because of its poor record on human rights. Since the middle of 1988, many hundreds of political prisoners have been released. As a reward, Cuba was elected to the United Nations Human Rights Commission, despite the opposition of the United States.

Throughout the 1980s and into the 1990s Cuba was forced to rely heavily on Russian economic and financial aid. In April 1989, President Gorbachev of the former Soviet Union promised to continue economic and financial aid but did not try to persuade Castro to follow Russia's policies of *perestroika* (reconstruction) and *glasnost* (openness).

At present Cuba is a nation of young people. Nearly 60 percent of the almost 11 million Cubans were born after Castro came to power in 1959. These youths, the healthiest and best educated younger group in Latin America, have created the greatest pressure for change in Cuba. They do not know or care what Cuba was like before Castro. They want jobs, dollars, and consumer goods.

Despite the grave problems that exist in Cuba, there has been progress. Since early 1990 Castro has encouraged criticism from "within the revolution." He has promised to debate the idea of change in future party congresses. However, any discussion of a multiparty system or a free-market economy will not be tolerated.

While many millions live in poverty in much of Latin America, there are no beggars on the streets of Havana or other Cuban cities. The infant mortality rate is now about 11 per 1,000 births, compared to about 60 per 1,000 when Castro came to power. Although Cubans may view their society as not fulfilling all of their needs, the majority feel that it is humane and just, treating all with equality—a situation not known in Cuba before Castro.

Cuba and Reformed Communism

The wave of economic and social reforms that swept Eastern Europe recently reached Cuba in 1990 or 1991. However, the Cuban government continued to follow the Marxist-Leninist ideas of government central planning and the control of the government through the Communist party.

When hard-line Communists in the Soviet Union tried to take over the government in August 1991, the Castro government seemed to be neutral. But when the coup failed the Cubans were not happy. The Cuban Communist party said it would continue with its Socialist policies.

However, these Socialist policies have not been working too well. Although production of export goods has remained at satisfactory levels, not enough consumer goods are produced. In addition, military aid has been discontinued, and Russian economic and financial help has been greatly reduced. In August 1990, the Cuban government was forced to tighten rationing because of these Russian cutbacks and the U.S. trade embargo. Every Cuban citizen was limited to two rolls a day and less than a pound of meat every nine days.

To add to the problems, President Gorbachev of the Soviet Union announced in September, 1991 that the Soviet Union would be stopping all military assistance to the Cubans and would further decrease all economic and financial aid in the coming years.

Pan American Games

In August 1991, the Pan American Games were held in Cuba. These games gave Cubans a tremendous lift in terms of self-image and pride. The favorable publicity and television coverage throughout Latin America and the United States could not but improve the image of Cuba in the eyes of the peoples of the region.

However, in December 1992, the United Nations voted to ask the United States to remove its blockade of Cuba. The United States voted against the request and has not, as of this time, removed the blockade.

The Sandinista Revolution in Nicaragua

Like other countries in Latin America, Nicaragua had been ruled by weak and unstable governments since it gained independence from Spain in 1821. These governments favored the rich and powerful at the expense of the majority, who were poor and weak. They did little to develop Nicaraguan resources for the good of the Nicaraguan people.

In the late 1920s and early 1930s, a leader, Augusto César Sandino, emerged to challenge the existing situation. Sandino captured the imagination and sympathy of Latin Americans everywhere as he led the guerrilla movement against the corrupt government of Nicaragua. A peace was arranged in 1933 and Sandino was given **amnesty** (freedom from arrest and forgiveness of past crimes). In exchange for the amnesty Sandino promised to lay down his arms and cooperate with the new government to set up a democratic Nicaragua.

Rule by the Somozas

A year later Sandino was arrested and put in prison, although no charges were ever made against him. While in prison Sandino was murdered by officers of the Nicaraguan National Guard, the Guardia. The Guardia commander was Anastasio Somoza, who became president of Nicaragua in 1936.

Between 1936 and 1979, members of the Somoza family ruled Nicaragua. The Somozas tolerated no opposition and granted no civil rights to the people. In 1977, a rebellion broke out, led by a guerrilla group called the "Sandinista National Liberation Front." The group took its name to pay tribute to Augusto Sandino.

The Sandinista Government

In 18 months, in 1979, the Sandinistas were able to overthrow the Somoza government and take control of Nicaragua. The Sandinistas had wide support from the majority of the Nicaraguan people. The actions taken to overthrow the Somoza government were true to the people's wishes.

Once in power, the Sandinistas received aid from Western Europe, the United States, and Cuba. The Sandinistas established close ties with the Soviet Union and other Communist nations.

When they first came to power, the Sandinistas promised to bring democracy and prosperity to Nicaragua, but these promises proved difficult to keep. Some land was redistributed to landless farm families. However, most of the land was put into **collectives** (ownership of land and farm machinery is shared). In addition, much of the land was taken over by the government for state-owned and -operated farms. The United States stopped its aid to the new government when the Sandanistas put political opponents in jail and welcomed Cuban military and political advisers as well as Russian military aid.

In a further attempt to reform the economy the Sandinista government nationalized the banks, mines, and coffee and cotton plantations. In addition, the army was built up and the government requested aid and advice in this matter from the Russians and the Cubans.

Social programs brought improved health care and nutrition. Education was made available to all, and illiteracy greatly reduced.

When Ronald Reagan became president of the United States, relations between the two countries became strained. The United States feared the close relationship between the Sandinistas and the Russians. Reagan also was unhappy about the Sandinista attempt to turn Nicaragua into a Socialist country. (Nationalization of banks, mines, and the land are steps to socialism.) In addition, the United States accused the Sandinistas of helping Communist guerrillas in nearby El Salvador.

Opposition from the Contras

Many Nicaraguans also disliked the new government. Calling themselves "Contras," a shortened term for antirevolutionaries in Spanish, they were former Somoza supporters and onetime Sandinistas who no longer could support the government. Their forces numbered between 8,000 and 10,000 men.

The Contras began a guerrilla war against the Sandinistas in 1982. President Reagan approved giving aid to the Contras, both by official and by secret means. In 1984, the Central Intelligence Agency helped the Contras to plant mines (explosives) in the harbors of Nicaragua. The International Court of Justice ruled that the United States should stop any blockading or mining of Nicaraguan ports because under international law, mining harbors is an act of war.

Faced with increasing guerrilla attacks and fearing an invasion by the United States, the Sandinistas asked for and received tanks, helicopter gunships, small arms, and ammunition from the Soviet Union. All males were required to register for military service. Fifteen-year-old boys could be drafted.

To further protect itself, the Sandinistas severely limited civil rights. The press was closely censored, and public, outdoor political meetings were forbidden. Citizens had to have travel passes to move from place to place. Political party opposition was limited, and some opposition leaders were thrown in jail. Speaking out against the Sandinistas was regarded as a crime, thus limiting freedom of speech.

Events from 1984 through 1989

In 1984, Daniel Ortega, who headed the revolutionary government, was elected president. By mid-1986, the economy of Nicaragua was in trouble. Because of guerrilla raids, the coffee crops had been cut by 25 percent. More and more money had to be spent on the military; about 50 percent of Nicaragua's budget was used to fight the Contras.

To improve the situation the government took control of large parts of Nicaragua's industry (by 1986 about one-half of it was under government control) and about one-quarter of agricultural land and production. Severe shortages continued to exist throughout the country, and unemployment kept increasing. Nicaragua's foreign debt climbed to about 5 billion dollars.

In the Nicaraguan situation, the U.S. Congress, which reflected the differences of opinion regarding U.S. involvement in other countries that existed since the Vietnam War, did not always follow a consistent policy. In 1984, Congress voted nonmilitary aid—food, clothing, and medicines for the Contras. At the same time, Congress prohibited the Central Intelligence Agency and other government agencies from helping the Contras in any way. Two years later, in 1986, Congress voted to give the Contras 100 million dollars in military aid.

In February 1987, President Oscar Arias of Costa Rica proposed a Central American peace plan. In January 1988, President Daniel Ortega of Nicaragua agreed to a cease-fire and peace talks with the Contras. However, the peace talks failed and fighting continued.

The End of the Struggle

In February 1990, President Ortega was defeated in an election by Violeta Barrios de Chamorro, who was supported by the United States. Ortega, who had said the election was held to end the civil war, pledged to comply with the results.

When Chamorro became president of Nicaragua in April 1990, she appointed Humberto Ortega, the brother of Daniel Ortega, as head of the armed forces. She took this action to try to gain the loyalty of the Sandinistas.

Since taking office, President Chamorro has succeeded in ending the nine-year civil war between the Sandinista army and the Contras, backed by the United States. She has also eliminated the military draft. Economic conditions in Nicaragua are slowly improving since the United States lifted its economic and trade embargo.

The Long Conflict in El Salvador

From 1931 through the late 1970s, El Salvador was ruled by harsh military dictatorships. Nevertheless, with assistance from the United States, a great deal of economic progress was made, especially between 1951 and 1965. The military junta began to allow opposition groups to form. Labor unions were made legal, and women were granted the right to vote for the first time. As a result the Salvadoran people began to protest the long years of corrupt military rule, the cheating in elections, and the lack of protection for civil liberties. The greatest protests came over the unfair distribution of land and wealth.

The Beginning of Civil War

The protests led to several unsuccessful attempts to reform the economic and political situation. In 1979, however, in a U.S.-backed program, almost 500 privately owned plantations were turned into cooperatives where the farmers shared the ownership of the land, the crops, the cattle, the equipment, and the profits. This attempt at land reform divided the nation. Most landowners and high army officers opposed any reform. The poor farmers in the cooperatives and other landless farmers joined with the urban poor to support the reform. Rival armed groups were formed, and El Salvador was soon involved in a civil war.

By late 1980 armed conflict, murder, illegal arrests, and torture occurred daily. Right-wing anti-Communist "death squads" killed those who favored social change, whether they were Communists or not. Left-wing guerrillas supported by Communists waged war on the government. Between 1980 and 1986, about 60,000 people were killed in the civil war, and about half a million were forced to leave their homes.

The United States charged that the Cubans and the Sandinistas of Nicaragua were actively helping the guerrillas. President Reagan sent arms and military advisers to El Salvador. He also put pressure on the Salvador government to hold democratic elections.

Election of Duarte

In 1984, elections were held in order to set up a new civilian government. José Napoleon Duarte, a moderate, was elected president. The leftist opposition did not take part in the election, by its own choice. After the election Duarte promised to bring the bloodshed to an end. However, efforts by the Duarte government to negotiate peace with the guerrillas were unsuccessful.

The economy of El Salvador remained in deep trouble. By mid-1986, El Salvador had become almost totally dependent on economic aid from the United States. The cooperatives had fallen deeply in debt. A second land-reform program, "land for the tiller" (plower or farmer), was started. Poor farmers working as tenants on rented lands were given loans at low interest to buy the lands they rented. These farmers have made much progress but still find it difficult to repay the loans.

Cristiani and the Peace Agreement

In 1988, Duarte, seriously ill with cancer, decided not to run for re-election. In July 1989, Alfredo Cristiani of the right-wing Arena party became president of El Salvador. Throughout the rest of 1989 and into 1990 Cristiani made a number of moves to achieve a peaceful settlement of the civil war. At the same time, however, he intensified government military crackdowns on opposition groups, especially religious groups who had been the most outspoken opponents of him and his government.

In September 1991, the government of El Salvador and the leftist rebels of the Farabundo Marti National Liberation Front (FMLN) signed an agreement, reached after 10 days of negotiation under the guidance of the United Nations. Included in the agreement were these provisions:

1. The guerrillas would lay down their arms and act out their opposition within the existing political process. Elections would be held in the near future.
2. The Salvadoran military would be prevented from using its "death squads" to prevent free exercise of political rights.
3. Civil rights abuses would be investigated, and the abusers would be removed from the army and punished.
4. Economic and land reforms would be instituted as soon as possible.
5. Members of the guerrilla forces would be taken into the new national civilian police force, which might eventually replace the army.
6. The size of the armed forces would be immediately reduced.
7. Families and supporters of the guerrillas would not be forced to leave the lands they had lived on for years in guerrilla-controlled areas of El Salvador.
8. A commission made up of members of the government and the guerrillas would carry out the agreement.

In January 1992, in Mexico City's Chapultepec Castle, the government of President Alfredo Cristiani and the rebel FMLN formally signed a comprehensive peace treaty, putting an end to 12 years of conflict. The war in El Salvador was over.

In advance of an expected "purge" of human rights violations, the Salvadoran armed forces reassigned two dozen ranking officers, including several linked to the November 1989 murders of six Jesuit priests. The National Assembly passed an amnesty paving the way for the return of thousands of FMLN guerrillas, but leaving the door open to try human rights violators on both sides. Rival troops have been confined to areas under United Nations supervision. The army is being trimmed, and the Cristiani government has announced a large-scale plan for reconstruction.

Despite the difficulties lying ahead, the Salvadoran accord is a watershed. It represents a genuine compromise: the left gave up its hopes to seize the state by force and impose radical economic reforms, the right giving up its historical control and violent opposition to change. Such compromise was made possible by a combination of several factors: (1) a military stalemate; (2) increased flexibility on both sides, brought about by momentous events in El Salvador and the world; and (3) the pressure of a respected neutral arbitrator in the United Nations.

Lessons the United States Can Learn from the El Salvador Experience

El Salvador's success demonstrates how the end of the cold war has created new opportunities for the United States to set up a different approach to policy in Latin America. By disconnecting worldwide strategic concerns from local political consequences, the United States changed its traditional opposition to leftist (radical) movements and distanced itself from past efforts to seek a military victory over the FMLN. This shift created more space for Salvadorans to negotiate what may be the foundations of a long-term social peace.

Future policy for dealing with regional conflicts can benefit from the experience of El Salvador. First, U.S. policy assumed that low-intensity warfare plus reform would overcome armed resistance. This assumption led the United States into an alliance with right-wing reactionaries who were opposed to the very reforms necessary to defeat the rebels. Policymakers believed that U.S. aid created leverage (influence) to force through these reforms. However, leverage, as Salvadoran military officers well understood, works only when the United States is willing to use it. Only after the end of the Cold War and the murder of the Jesuits was Congress ready to cut aid.

Second, regular elections alone will not guarantee democracy. Especially in the early years of the war, U.S. policymakers showed an appalling disregard for the violation of human rights and the exclusion of democratic left parties from the Salvadoran government. The United States failed to understand that regularly scheduled elections cannot channel conflicts in a democratic manner unless they are joined with effective civilian control over the military and respect for the civil and human rights of all citizens, regardless of their political opinions.

Finally, cooperative efforts, especially under the auspices of an international organization, is more likely to lead to settlements than one-on-one negotiations with the United States as a party. In the 1980s, overtures from Mexican and French authorities, the Contadora group, and Costa Rica's President Arias were distinctly unwelcome to the United States. The Bush administration's decision to support U.N.-sponsored talks and the involvement of the third countries was essential for bringing a conclusion to the civil war.

In short, the experience in El Salvador suggests that the United States should learn what Salvadorans are already learning: in regional conflicts the deliberate effort not to use all of ones power can be most conducive to a successful outcome.

Central America Today

Today, Central America is an area undergoing serious and important changes. The economic and political problems are difficult to solve, and therefore the future of the area is difficult to foretell.

American involvement in Central America has stirred heated debate in the United States. Many Americans and refugees from Central America felt that the United States was supporting undemocratic governments. The United States feels its policy will eventually lead to greater stability and more personal freedom for the people.

Latin America and the United States

The long history of relations between Latin America and the United States has been marked by extremes. Intense friendship and great ill-will, understanding and misunderstanding, total cooperation and unbending opposition, progress and retreat have been the keys to this relationship. Interdependence and common desires tie the two areas together. More often than not, self-interest has torn them apart.

When the Latin American nations gained their independence from Spain, the U.S. government quickly recognized the government of each Latin American state. In other words, the United States said to the world that it welcomed the Latin American states as equal and independent nations. The United States and Latin America began to trade on a large scale.

Monroe Doctrine

Spain wanted to regain her colonies, and the United States wished to protect the independence of Latin America. President James Monroe started what is called the Monroe Doctrine. Monroe said that the United States would go to war if necessary to stop European nations from setting up new colonies or trying to gain control of the free nations of the New World. However, the United States was not powerful enough in 1823 to back up this idea with force.

Great Britain was also interested in the freedom of the Latin American countries because it had set up a great deal of trade with them. England told the world that it supported the Monroe Doctrine. In case of war, England's large navy would be used to support the United States. No European nation would challenge this power.

Mexico-United States Disputes

Twice between 1835 and 1850 Mexico and the United States became involved in disputes (disagreements). First the Mexicans, led by Santa Anna, tried to prevent a group of Americans living in the Mexican state of Texas from setting up an independent nation. In 1835, Texas defeated Santa Anna at the battle of San Jacinto. With the blessings of the United States, Texas set up an independent nation.

Later, in 1847, Mexico and the United States went to war when the United States annexed Texas as a state. As a result of the Mexican defeat in the war, Mexico was forced to cede the territories we know today as California, New Mexico, Utah, and Colorado. This was called the Mexican Cession. In all, during this 15-year period, Mexico lost one-third of its territory.

Other Disputes

In 1864, Napoleon III tried to set up a French colony in Mexico. He sent French troops to Mexico to support an Austrian archduke named Maximilian as emperor of Mexico. When the Civil War ended in the United States in 1865, the United States sent 50,000 troops to the Mexican border. The French were told to get out or there would be war. Faced with this threat, the French began to leave. By 1867 the Mexicans had regained control of their government.

Toward the end of the 19th century a boundary dispute developed between Great Britain and Venezuela. Gold was discovered near the border of British Guiana and Venezuela, and both nations claimed the gold field. In 1894, the United States asked that the issue be sent to arbitration. Arbitration is the settling of a dispute between two sides by a person, a group, or a nation agreed upon by both sides. After much discussion the

British finally agreed to arbitration because they wished to avoid a war with the United States.

The court of arbitration included two U.S. Supreme Court judges, two British judges, and a Russian judge. In 1899, the court reached a decision. It gave most of the disputed territory to Great Britain.

Spanish-American War

War between Spain and the United States broke out in 1898. One cause was the way Americans felt about the treatment of Cubans by Spain. In 1895, the Cubans had revolted against Spanish rule. To crush the rebellion the Spanish government forced hundreds of thousands of Cubans into concentration camps, where many died of disease, starvation, and cruel treatment. American newspapers spoke out strongly against Spanish brutality. Also, in 1898 the United States battleship *Maine* was blown up in Havana harbor. Spain was blamed, and the United States declared war. The United States won the war in three months. Under the peace treaty, Cuba was given its independence and Puerto Rico became a territory of the United States.

United States-Latin American Friendship Strained

After 1900, the friendship between the United States and Latin America, which had begun to grow, started changing. Because the United States wanted an apology for the arrest of American sailors by Mexican troops, U.S. troops occupied Veracruz in Mexico in 1914. In addition, American troops invaded Mexican territory in 1916 to capture the Mexican patriot Pancho Villa. Villa had attacked Americans in Columbus, New Mexico, because he was angered by American policy toward Mexico.

The American role in building the Panama Canal did not help matters. The United States had assisted Panama to become independent from Colombia in 1903. Panama then gave the United States permission to build the canal (Colombia had refused).

Several Caribbean and Central American nations had not paid the money they owed to European nations. To prevent the collection of the debt by force, the United States took control of Nicaragua (1909–1933), Haiti (1915–1934), and the Dominican Republic (1916–1924). The United States collected taxes and paid the debts. The United States also sent troops into Honduras in 1924 and Panama in 1925 to keep order. This policy of **intervention** (getting involved) was resented by the nations of Latin America.

Trade relations between the United States and Latin America were also a cause of trouble. The Latin Americans sold raw materials to the United States. The money was needed to buy manufactured goods from the United States. In the 1920s, the United States raised tariffs on raw materials, decreasing sales and causing hardships in Latin America.

In addition, a quota system was set up. Exporters of certain products, such as sugar, were allowed to send only certain amounts to the United States so as not to flood the U.S. market. This caused problems especially for nations that depended on the sale of one crop for economic survival.

Good Neighbor Policy

In the 1930s, President Franklin Roosevelt tried to bring about better relations. Under his Good Neighbor Policy, the United States stopped sending soldiers into Latin America. Also, the United States began to discuss situations with Latin Americans and to treat them as equals.

Latin Americans began to look with friendship toward the United States. During World War II the nations of Latin America, with a few exceptions (Argentina, for one), united behind the Allies in their efforts to defeat Germany and Japan. The rest were either neutral or supported the Axis.

Although the old resentment had lessened, it was still there. In 1948, after the war, a meeting in Bogota, Colombia, of the Organization of American States was scheduled to take place. The meeting had to be postponed for several days when a riot broke out. A mob ran wild through the city, carrying anti-American signs and burning American flags. This event was called a *bogotazo*. Today this word is still used in Latin America to describe any violent public demonstration.

In the 1950s, relations worsened again. Latin Americans felt they were being ignored by the United States. Armed mobs attacked the automobile of Vice-President Nixon in Venezuela in 1958. The United States supported dictators who were disliked by the people, such as Marcos Perez Jimenez in Venezuela.

When John Kennedy became president in 1960, he announced a new policy, called the "Alliance for Progress." However, any good the announcement of the policy caused was destroyed by the Bay of Pigs invasion.

Cuban Missile Crisis

As we have learned, American relations with Cuba had become worse after Fidel Castro became leader of Cuba in 1958 (see pages 677–679). On April 17, 1961, Cuban exiles trained by the Central Intelligence Agency landed at the Bay of Pigs on Cuba's southern coast. The invasion failed. As a result of the attempt Cuba moved closer to the Soviet Union for protection. The invasion also weakened U.S.-Latin American ties because the United States was once again intervening in another country's affairs.

In October 1962, the United States had proof, through aerial photographs, that the Soviet Union was setting up missile bases in Cuba. The United States acted quickly. President Kennedy ordered a **quarantine** (blockade) to prevent the shipment of missiles to Cuba. Kennedy stated that a missile attack from Cuba against any country in the Western Hemisphere would be regarded as a Soviet attack against the United States. United States forces were readied for war with the Soviet Union. An emergency meeting of the Organization of American States was called to discuss "the threat to the security of the area." The United States also asked for an emergency meeting of the Security Council of the United Nations.

The Russians saw that the Latin American nations would back the United States and therefore gave in. The missile sites were taken down, and 42 missiles were shipped out of Cuba. The Cuban missile crisis did much to bring the countries of the New World together in the face of a common threat to all.

Dominican Republic Crisis

In 1961, Rafael Trujillo Molina, the dictator of the Dominican Republic, was assassinated. After several weak governments, power came into the hands of a committee of generals. In April 1965, a reform party, made up of civilians and young military officers seized power. They wished to make Juan Bosch president.

President Lyndon Johnson of the United States worried that the reformers might include Communists, and that Bosch would set up a Communist-type government. Johnson was also afraid the Dominican Republic might become another Cuba.

In 1965, a group of Dominican army officers forcibly overthrew a newly formed government led by Juan Bosch. Bosch wished to have a democratic government with guaranteed civil liberties for all. He had the support of a majority of the people, including many Communists.

As a result of the gulpe d'estado, fighting broke out between the army and Bosch supporters. President Johnson sent in the U.S. Marines because, he said, they were needed to protect Americans living in the Dominican Republic. His major reason, however, was that he was afraid Bosch might let the Communists take over. The marines, with the help of an additional 20,000 soldiers, remained in the Dominican Republic until August 1965. The American forces helped the military rulers remain in power.

Bosch said that "this was a democratic revolution smashed by the leading democracy in the world." To Latin American leaders in other countries it led to a belief that, if the United States did not like their policies or politics, it would support revolutions to overthrow them.

Most of the suspected "Communists" turned out to be anti-American, Dominican nationalists with no known Communist connections. Johnson made an error in reasoning that had been made before him and would, at times, be made after him: that anyone who is anti-United States must be a Communist. The American intervention in the Dominican Republic increased distrust of the United States and increased anti-American feeling.

In the United States opinion is divided. Many think that the United States should not help dictators and military rulers gain power. Others believe that revolutions in Latin America are often supported by anti-American Communists or by Communist-backed groups. Therefore, the United States should support certain governments even if they are ruled by the army or dictators to preserve order.

Unsettled 1970s and 1980s

In the 1970s, under President Richard Nixon, the United States decided to drop the social and economic aims of the Alliance for Progress. Instead, Nixon called for a partnership between the United States and Latin America. Nixon also made it "perfectly clear" that the United States would not accept the seizure of property belonging to American businesses in Latin America.

During the Nixon years the Central Intelligence Agency was very active in Latin America. Its activities included supplying money and training groups in Chile who wished to overthrow the government of President Salvador Allende.

In the administration of President Jimmy Carter, the United States tried to reassure Latin Americans that our policy was to work for reform and progress. The centerpiece of the Carter policy was his program on human rights and a concern for individual civil and political freedom in the hemisphere. This new policy was aimed at governments in Latin America that had taken repressive measures against people who disagreed with government actions. In particular, Carter threatened to cut off aid to Argentina and Chile unless the governments of those two countries protected the rights of their people.

Grenada

In October 1983, U.S. military forces landed on the island of Grenada in the Caribbean Sea. Grenada had been ruled by a government friendly to Cuba since 1979. In early 1983, Cuba began assisting in the construction of a large and modern airport in Grenada by workers heavily armed with modern weapons. President Ronald Reagan feared that the airport would be used by the Cubans and the Russians as a military base. He was also concerned about the safety of Americans, such as medical students, on the island if there should be trouble.

More than 6,000 U.S. troops were sent to Grenada. U.S. citizens were evacuated (taken away to safety). Several hundred armed Cubans on the island were captured and ordered to leave. U.S. troops remained on the island until a democratically elected government was set up a few months later.

Governments in Latin America

The United States is a **republic**, and so are the nations of Latin America. This means that each of the 22 independent nations of Latin America has its own written constitution. Each of these constitutions describes the way the government is supposed to work.

In a republic the people are supposed to elect their president and other government officials. Republics also have branches (arms) of the government that make the laws.

Most nations of Latin America have been free for more than 160 years. Some of the nations have a **tradition** (history) of honest and fair election of their leaders. Venezuela, Uruguay, Colombia, Costa Rica, and Chile (until 1974) offer good examples of peaceful and constitutional change of leaders. However, many Latin American nations have not been able to set up good, strong governments to serve the people. In these countries the governments change often. Bolivia has had more than 60 revolutions since 1820. Ecuador has had 11 different constitutions. Colombia has had 27 civil wars. These are only a few examples of unstable governments in Latin America.

You might think that, because the United States is also a republic, its politics and government are very similar to those of Latin American nations. There are, however, important differences.

In the United States we, the citizens, play an important role in governing ourselves. By voting, we elect the president (our executive branch) and the members of Congress (our law-making, or legislative, branch). For this reason we feel that the United States is a government "of the people and by the people." The leaders of our government are changed by peaceful election.

In Latin American countries only certain people may vote. Many people do not have the right to vote and do not take part in the government. Leaders in Latin America are often changed by military takeovers.

Many Dictatorships

During most of their history, many Latin American nations have been ruled by dictators. In a dictatorship, one person (the dictator) or a small group of persons rule the country. They make the laws and do whatever they want, without regard to the wishes of the people.

In Latin America, a dictator is called a *caudillo*. Many caudillos have been generals or powerful military leaders. Latin Americans like their leaders to be bold, brave, and powerful and to be *macho* (very masculine). The people have confidence in this type of man. They believe he will serve them better than other types of leaders.

The caudillos force their way into power with the help of a small group of supporters. They hold power because they control the army and navy. This type of government is not stable because the leaders remain in power only until the next revolution.

Political Parties

Political parties are important if governments of the people are to work. Latin American parties can be divided into three groups: Conservative, Liberal, and Workers. During most of the history of Latin America the Conservatives and Liberals fought over the power of the church and control of power in the government.

The workers and the poorest people had no party to speak for them. Therefore, the government paid little attention to labor reforms and the improvement of social conditions.

Workers' parties came into existence in the 20th century. Members were usually Socialists or Communists. The Socialist Worker parties and Communist Worker parties have not been able to cooperate (except in Chile in 1938 and again in 1970). As a result, few reforms for the people have been put into action.

The Future and Possible Change

One event has greatly influenced the situation in Latin America. That event is the Cuban Revolution. As you have already read, Fidel Castro led a people's revolution in Cuba. Because this was a revolution in which most of the people took part, many changes have occurred in Cuba.

What lessons were learned by other Latin American countries? They saw poor people who were no longer satisfied with their living conditions. They learned that when such conditions are not improved there can be revolution.

Many governments are now showing interest in the welfare of the people. Education laws are being more strictly enforced. Colombia has set up a system of radio schools to reach the poor mountain and country people. Chile uses television for group teaching. The governments now realize that, in order to bring about improvements in people's lives, the people must be educated. If more people learn to read and write, more people will be able to understand how their governments work. By using their votes more wisely, they will elect leaders who will bring about reform.

Latin American leaders have made it possible for more people to vote. Only with time, education, and the widening right to vote will Latin American countries encourage the setting up of governments "of the people, by the people, and for the people."

Chile: The Failure of a Peaceful Revolution

Chile was one of the few countries of Latin America to have a stable government and economy in the 19th and early 20th century. However, problems did exist. The majority of the Chilean people were farmers. Few of them owned the land on which they worked in poverty. Most of the land and wealth was held by a few hundred families. There was, however, a small but growing middle class living in the cities of Chile.

The unequal distribution of wealth and power led to protest from the middle class and peasants (poor farmers). Also, economic problems began to arise. Chile's economic well-being was based on the sale of nitrates and copper. When sales of these two resources began to fall, great unemployment resulted.

In 1970, Dr. Salvador Allende won a narrow victory in a democratically held election. Allende was the head of a coalition of Communists and Socialists. He gained the support of the defeated party by promising to follow democratic and constitutional procedures while in office.

Allende wished to help the poor. His program called for equal distribution of income and land. He began a process of nationalizing Chile's natural resources (copper, nitrates, and iron ore). Allende scolded the owners of the copper and nitrate mines for not using the profits from the mines to help the Chilean people. He hinted that the owners, many of whom were from the United States, would not be paid for their property because of the excessive (very large) profits they had taken out of the country in the past. Actually, much of the property that was nationalized was paid for. However, the owners felt they had not received the true value.

Allende then ordered a 35 percent wage increase for the miners and at the same time set up a system of price controls. These price controls prevented the raising of prices on food and other products sold in Chile. In addition, 1,300 farms were taken away from their owners without payment. The government also took control of the banks.

Salvador Allende became President of Chile in 1970. His "peaceful revolution" and attempts to change the economic situation in Chile failed. In 1973 he was killed and a military junta took control of Chile.

The poor peasants, the miners, and the urban poor benefited from these changes. But the middle class in the cities and the urban (city) middle-class workers did not. They became very unhappy and dissatisfied with Allende and his government. Strikes took place in the cities, and members of groups opposed to Allende carried out a series of terrorist acts. To make matters worse, food shortages developed and the market for copper and nitrates shrank.

President Richard Nixon had made it part of his policy that the United States would not accept the seizure of property belonging to U.S. businesses in Latin America. Nixon considered Allende's nationalization of natural resources a direct threat to U.S. interests. To help bring down the Allende government, the United States and American banks and businesses withheld loans and further investments in Chile.

By late 1972, Chile's economy was in deep trouble. Strikes continued. Allende accused the United States of "strangling" Chile's economy and asked for assistance from the Soviet Union. Even with the aid of technicians and experts from the Soviet Union, Cuba, and other Communist nations the economy continued to worsen.

Strikes and street rioting in the cities increased. In September 1973, the army attacked the presidential palace, killing Allende. A military junta under the leadership of General Augusto Pinochet took control. Pinochet immediately suspended all civil liberties, disbanded all political parties, and prohibited strikes. Pinchot ruled Chile as an absolute dictator until March 1990.

The failure of this "peaceful revolution" has been blamed on middle-class greed and upper-class terror. Additional blame is placed on the antidemocratic military and U.S. interference in the form of Central Intelligence Agency aid to the army and the opposition to Allende. Allende's opponents believe that the ideas and actions that he promoted would have destroyed Chilean democracy.

Argentina: From Democracy to Dictatorship to Democracy

Argentina in many ways was the most advantaged of the Latin American nations. The fertile soil and the wealth of natural resources made Argentina's future look bright. However, Argentina had to attract Europeans who know how to raise the crops that European customers would buy. In addition, railways were needed to haul the new crops to the seaports of Argentina.

To achieve these ends Argentina encouraged European immigration and investment. By 1900, Argentina had more foreign-born people in its population than native-born. The English invested in and constructed the best rail system in Latin America for the Argentines.

The immigrants (mainly Italians and Germans) made a great industry of agriculture. In the early years of independence many farms had surrounded the towns and cities in order to feed the local population. After the Europeans came, thousands of acres were planted in wheat. Grain now went to the city people of Europe as well as to the people of Argentina.

On the pampas, the grazing of cattle was transformed into a stock-raising industry. Cattle was raised for export. The development of the meat-packing industry brought great profits. Along with grain exports, meat product exports brought great prosperity and wealth to Argentina.

After Argentina became independent, the country, as was the case in all of Latin America, went through a period of local wars, weak leaders, and unstable government. Then, from 1835 to 1852, Argentina was ruled by Juan Manuel de Rosas, a caudillo considered to be one of the most brutal ever to appear in Latin America. However, he did establish order, and he taught the Argentines the value of the civil liberties and freedom he had taken away from them. In 1852, Rosas was overthrown, and from then until 1930 Argentina had a constitution, regular elections, and movement toward more democratic government.

In 1930, however, Argentina fell victim to the worldwide depression. Exports of beef and wheat fell sharply, and unemployment grew. The government did little to improve the situation. At this point the military took control. One president, picked by the army or navy, followed another. None stayed in power long. Then, in 1943, Colonel Juan Perón took over and ruled through people he controlled. In 1946, he became president and ruled for 9 years.

Perón established order and reformed the economy. He began by encouraging outside investment in Argentine industry. He aided the growth of labor unions and used them as a base for increasing his power. Perón increased wages and benefits for the workers and their families. He nationalized the railroads and used government money for public works. Although he protected and widened workers' rights on the job, he outlawed freedom of speech and limited freedom of the press. He abolished the clause (part) of the constitution that would have prevented him from succeeding himself as president of Argentina.

Eva Perón, his wife, helped him to win the support of the people. She had the title "Minister of Health and Labor." Women's rights and welfare programs were her special interests. She helped women gain the right to vote and had hospitals and schools built. When she died in 1952, the Argentine workers wept for her.

Perón lost the support of the army when he threatened to arm the workers. He also lost the support of the Roman Catholic Church when he tried to weaken its power with the people.

In 1955, Perón was driven from power by a group of army officers. During the next 18 years the people of Argentina faced a worsening political and economic situation. When elections did take place, the army removed from office people whom it did not like. Civil liberties disappeared entirely, and the days of the brutal Rosas returned to Argentina.

By the 1970s, unemployment and inflation were high. In 1972, Perón was re-elected president, but he died in 1974 before he could do anything to improve the situation. The army continued to rule, and conditions kept getting worse.

In 1982, Argentina invaded the Falkland Islands, a British colony in the South Atlantic. Argentina had long claimed ownerships of the Falklands. The military government hoped to unite the country by this popular action and to draw the people's attention from the troubled economy and the loss of freedom. After a two month war, however, Argentina was defeated and the British regained control of the islands.

In 1983, in a democratic election, Raul Alfonsín was elected president. He was faced with the worst inflation in Argentina's history. In addition, high employment and a huge foreign debt existed. Since Alfonsín took office, he has restored civil liberties, ended human rights violations, and attempted to solve Argentina's economic problems.

The recent past haunts the government of Raul Alfonsín. During the "dirty war" against "Marxists" between 1976 and 1983, the army resorted to illegal methods. At least 9,000 Argentines were arrested, never charged, and disappeared without trace. Torture and murder were the usual methods used by many army officers to gain their objectives.

When Alfonsín became president, he promised to investigate and punish the officers involved. Five former military junta leaders and five other generals were sent to prison. Another 360 officers were to face trial on human rights violation.

In April 1987, however, an army mutiny broke out, led by a junior army officer, Lt. Col. Aldo Rico. Rico said he was not leading a mutiny against the government but protesting the continuing military trials. In May 1987, a law was proposed that would exonerate all lower-ranking officers of atrocities on the ground they were following orders.

The army felt that it fought a successful war against a Marxist attempt to overthrow the legitimate government between 1976 and 1983 and that it should be honored, not put on trial. The opposition is convinced that the army acted illegally and that thousands of innocent people were tortured and murdered, and that the "assassins" must be brought to justice.

In the middle, the majority of Argentines are uncertain. They are anxious for reconciliation and peace but are not sure how to achieve them. They are committed to democracy, but because of lack of experience are unsure of how to make it work successfully.

The army was not satisfied to allow a civilian government to put army officers on trial. As a result, army rebellions took place in April 1987, January 1988, and November 1988. The reason for the rebellions in each case was the same—a demand for amnesty for those officers accused of human rights violations during the 1976–1983 period of military rule. In each case, Alfonsín put down the rebellion and refused to give amnesty.

In May 1989, elections for the presidency were held. A rule in the constitution prevented President Alfonsín from seeking a second consecutive term of office.

In the election, the Peronista's Partido Justicialista candidate Carlos Saúl Menem won with 47 percent of the vote and became president on July 8, 1989.

Inflation continued to be the major economic problem that faced Argentina. Rates of inflation reached a monthly figure of almost 200 percent in July 1989.

When Menem became president he put in motion an economic program which included: (1) devaluation of the Argentine currency; (2) new taxes; (3) reduction of tariffs to encourage exports and imports; (4) declaration of a state of emergency to allow for large public spending cuts and privatization of state-owned industries; (5) price controls on basic goods; and (6) an increase in utility rates by 200 to 900 percent.

This program seemed to be succeeding and the inflation rate fell. However, when price controls were lifted and raises were given to workers in December 1989, inflation again began to rise. Inflation continued to be a problem in 1991 and 1992 but has been more controlled than it was in the 1980s.

Early in December 1990, a new army rebellion broke out which was quickly put down. However, on December 30, 1990 President Menem pardoned many of the officers who had been involved in the human rights violations during the 1976–1983 period. After the pardons were granted, the army was satisfied and seemed to become a loyal supporter of the Menem presidency. Most Argentineans (70%), however, objected to the pardons.

The Road Ahead: A Swing to Democracy?

Between 1980 and 1990 military governments were forced to give up power in Latin American nations. The list of countries that moved toward civilian and democratic rule included Argentina, Bolivia, Chile, Uruguay, Brazil, Peru, Panama, Paraguay, and Honduras. In Ecuador an elected civilian president replaced a military junta in 1979.

In March 1990, 71-year-old Patricio Aylwin Azocar took office as the democratically elected president of Chile, ending 17 years of harsh military rule. Aylwin was elected at the head of a 17-party coalition. General Pinochet, the last of the military dictators, was named commander of the army.

Democratic elections took place in Peru in 1985, when Alan Garcia Perez was elected, and in 1990, when Alberto Fujimori, the son of Japanese immigrants, was elected president. The events that followed in Peru are described in the following section.

In Bolivia elections took place in 1985 and in 1989. The current president of Bolivia is Jaime Paz Zamora.

Guatemala held elections in November 1985 and in November 1990. In the most recent election neither of the two major candidates won a majority of the votes, and as a result a run-off election was held in 1991.

In Honduras, a presidential election took place in 1985 and again in 1989. In January 1990, Rafael Callejas took office. This event marked the first time since 1932 that a change to a president from the opposition party was achieved peacefully through a democratic election.

Recent Crises in Three Latin American Countries

Shining Path (Sendero Luminoso), led by Abimael Guzman, has carried on a 12-year campaign to destroy all of Peru's "capitalist and imperialist" institutions through violence and to set up a peasant-worker state on the Maoist-Chinese model. The Shining Path movement is perhaps the most radical leftist rebellion still in operation in the world. It has waged a war of terror throughout Peru that has taken 25,000 lives and damaged 22 billion dollars worth of property.

To put down the rebellion, Alberto Fujimori has turned his presidency into a virtual dictatorship. In April 1992, he unilaterally dissolved Peru's congress, shut down the courts, and suspended the constitution, largely on the grounds that these measures were necessary to destroy Shining Path. The United States and most European and Latin American countries disapproved, and the United States went so far as to suspend aid to Peru.

As the rebels were closing in on Lima, Fujimori set up a *dictablana* (soft dictatorship). He has suspended civil liberties, loosened controls on the police, and changed the judicial system so that convictions are easier to obtain.

Abimael Guzman, the leader of Shining Path, was born in Arequipa. As a university student he was influenced by Communist ideas. He was also influenced by Mao Zedong's Cultural Revolution in China. In 1962, he became a teacher of philosophy at Huamanga University, where his students called him "Shampoo": he could wash one's brains, making everything crystal clear.

As he built a guerrilla organization, he ruthlessly stamped out opposing ideas and opinions. His followers were compelled to memorize his "Gonzalo Thoughts" (named after his alias) and to learn Maoist hymns in Chinese, syllable by syllable. In a way Guzman was trying to create a collective brain: the individual was to become an instrument for the greater good.

In September 1992 Guzman was captured by government forces. The capture of its leader was a blow to the bloodiest and most self-sufficient revolutionary movement in Latin America. Money to support Shining Path flowed, not from foreign sponsors, but from the Haullaga Valley in central Peru, a prime cocoa-producing area.

Even with the capture of Guzman, however, Shining Path will continue to exist and spread terror. The conditions that gave rise to the rebellion back in the late 1970s—poverty, injustice, and deep resentment over racial and class distinctions—still prevail. Until Fujimori finds a more stable, equitable, and democratic course, thousands of impoverished Peruvians will be willing to support an alternative vision, no matter how ruthless or violent. To explain the appeal of Shining Path for many Peruvians, a review of the **dichotomy** (division into two parts) that exists in the country will be helpful.

In the Andes, near the town of Cuzco, sculptors are raising what will be the largest statue in Peru. It is a 114-foot-high bronze sculpture of Inca Pacha Kuteq, a 15th-century ruler of the Inca empire.

Far away, near the coast in the capital city, Lima, is a statue of the Spaniard Francisco Pizarro, conqueror of the Inca Empire.

The two statues symbolize the regional and racial divisions of modern Peru. It is impossible to understand the violence of the Shining Path rebel movement by looking only at poverty and political oppression. Racial and ethnic discrimination is also a very important factor.

Of Peru's 22 million people, about 60 percent are mestizos, that is, people of mixed Spanish and Native American (Quechuan) heritage, 30 percent are Andean Native Americans, and 10 percent are whites. A Quechuan who moves into the city, cuts his braids, puts on Western clothes, and learns to speak Spanish then considers himself a mestizo, or "cholo." Most Shining Path supporters come from Peru's Andean heartland—Cuzco, Ayachucho, Huancavelica, and Huancayo—all centers of Peru's Quechuan population.

On the 500th anniversary of Columbus' arrival in the Americas (1492), Peru's Association of Economists delivered a bill for 647 billion dollars in colonial reparations to Spain's ambassador to Peru. In addition the association requested an apology for the **genocide** (mass killing) perpetrated by the Spanish conquerors and colonists. The largest item on the bill was for a ransom of seven tons of gold and 13 tons of silver that a captive Inca, Atahuallpa, paid Pizarro for his release. After the ransom was paid, Pizarro had Atahuallpa killed.

After Pizarro founded Lima, the Spanish adopted racial controls to maintain their power. Indians were not permitted to own horses, to wear Spanish dress, to enter the churches of Lima, or to own or carry weapons.

Thousands of the Quechua people worked and died as slaves in Spanish mines. Also, when British companies hired contract laborers from India, China, and Polynesia to mine nitrates (guano), they allowed hundreds to be blinded by the ammonia fumes in the mines. In the 1920s, uncounted workers died from an unregulated copper smelter run by an American company.

This history of mistreatment of course contributes to the extreme xenophobic (hatred of things foreign, or "white" in this case) ideas of Shining Path and to the feelings of the poor of Andean Peru. They see whites as foreigners, and they have strong feelings of vengeance. It is also interesting that Quechua and Aymara peoples feel like foreigners in their own country, since Peru is ruled by descendants of the Spanish conquerors or later immigrants who gained success in their new homeland.

In November 1992, the Peruvian people elected members of a new Congress to replace the one President Fujimori had dissolved earlier in the same year. The results were a vote of confidence for Fujimori, as the people chose members of his party to represent them.

Brazil—Democracy in Turmoil

Fernando Collor de Mello won the Brazilian presidency in 1989 by promising reforms that would help the *descamisado* (shirtless ones), the Brazilian poor. By the summer of 1991, Brazilians by the thousand had put on shirts—black ones—to show their disgust with the Collor government.

In September 1992, a congressional commission concluded after a three month investigation that President Collor and members of his family had received 6.5 million dollars from his campaign fund raiser. The fund raiser extorted large sums from businessmen who hoped to get government contracts or favors. Also, an inflation rate of 20 percent a month and record unemployment helped to destroy support for the once-popular Collor.

In September 1992, the Brazilian Congress voted to accuse Collor formally. Officially Collor has been "suspended" from office for up to 180 days while the Brazilian Senate tries him on the charge of receiving bribes and kickbacks. They will hear the evidence and then vote on whether to remove him from office.

If Collor is removed, Vice President Itamar France would then be sworn in as president with the right to rule for up to six months. It would be his job to run the government and try to revive the very sick Brazilian economy.

However, Latin America's largest nation has shown one very impressive sign of democracy. For the first time it has settled a government crisis by strict constitutional methods without out military intervention.

Nevertheless, Brazil's democracy is still weak. A long and painful impeachment process could do great harm. Many Brazilians are convinced that the best solution is for Collor to resign, but he has said several times that he never will.

In February 1991, a small group of soldiers led by an army colonel attempted unsuccessfully to overthrow the Venezuelan government. For 34 years, Venezuela has been a stable democracy, and the failed coup sent shock waves throughout Latin America. Like President Carlos Andres Perez of Venezuela, most Latin American leaders have begun painful free-market reforms and have asked their people to cooperate.

Perez's own policies were a factor in the coup attempt. He has often been charged with tolerating corruption. Also, in a recent year Venezuela's economy grew by 9 percent and earned 15 billion dollars from oil exports. Yet Perez kept social spending in check and allowed real wages of Venezuelan workers to drop. In addition, the army killed 300 people to put down food riots in 1989, yet the poor still resent cuts in food and gasoline subsidies.

As a result of the coup attempt, a new 4-billion-dollar economic-development program has been introduced in Venezuela.

However, in late November 1992, the second unsuccessful coup of the year was attempted by the same army group. In the coup attempt, 230 people died and rebel planes bombed the presidential palace.

In a December 1992 poll, just after the coup attempt, Perez has a disapproval rate of 92 percent. To underline this disapproval and unhappiness, Venezuelan voters in several sections of the country did not vote for candidates from Perez's party in the elections held 10 days after the coup attempt. With this unrest, it is difficult to believe that there will not be other attempted coups in the near future.

Problems That Latin American Democracies Face

Although civilian rule is still weak in most countries in Latin America, the trend toward democratic elections and popular rule is clear.

The movement toward democracy is taking place at a time of many problems. The major factors that brought the military to power in the past were high inflation, local high unemployment and recession, and severe foreign debt problems.

The military was not able to solve these problems. In fact, the situation became worse. The new democratically elected governments now have to deal with high inflation, high unemployment, and a large foreign debt. The success of the democratic movement may depend on how quickly these problems can be solved.

Summary
of
Key Ideas

Latin America

A. **Latin America is considered a region of diversity.**

1. Latin America is divided into three major regions: Central America and Mexico, the islands of the Caribbean (West Indies), and the continent of South America.

2. Most of the people of the region have a heritage from the Iberian Peninsula in Europe.

3. The Native American and African heritages are also prevalent throughout the area.

4. "Latin America" is not a geographic term but is used to describe an area that has similar historical roots.

B. **The geography and climate of Latin America have greatly influenced the culture and history of the area.**

1. Latin America covers a wide geographic area, about 7,000 miles north to south and about 3,200 miles at its widest point.

2. Latin America is an area of great physical diversity; it has high mountains, plains, tropical rain forests, deserts, semiarid areas, and large bodies of water, all of which influence the region and its peoples.

3. Latitude, altitude, nearness to large bodies of water, ocean currents, and the direction of winds greatly influence the climate of the region.

4. Geography has affected the lives of the people of Latin America.

   a. Most of the region is remote from the large land areas of the world, its population centers, and major east-west trade routes.

   b. Ocean currents played an important role in the early Spanish and Portuguese conquest and exploration.

   c. Geographic factors have encouraged South America to traditionally "face" toward Europe.

   d. Geographic factors have served to divide and isolate parts of the area.

   e. Geography has created obstacles to transportation, trade, inter-American cooperation, and even, in some cases, national unity.

   f. Large areas have not been productively utilized because they are too arid, too mountainous, too cold, or too infertile for agriculture.

5. In the seven countries of Central America, similar natural environments have influenced similar cultural and economic development.

C. **The first Americans made great contributions to civilization.**

1. It is important to look at the culture and civilization of pre-Columbian Latin America through the eyes of its people.

2. Many local civilizations were at different levels of development during the same time period.

3. The Maya

   a. The Maya built a significant culture and civilization in present-day Guatemala and the Yucatán Peninsula in Mexico.

   b. The Maya were the only Native Americans to develop a writing system.

4. The Aztecs

   a. The Aztecs were late arrivals to central Mexico.

   b. Aztec uniqueness is related to the high degree of the organization of their society and to a highly developed culture based on complex rituals.

   c. Aztec culture and religious practices were based on the Aztec cosmography (how the earth was created and sustained).

5. Incas

   a. The early history of the Incas is not fully known because they lacked a written language.

   b. The Incas spread their empire by war and by a form of social welfare that persuaded their neighbors that they would be better off within the Inca Empire than outside it.

   c. The Incas developed stable government and an excellent system of communications.

   d. The Incas' system of land ownership and distribution was an important feature of their society.

   e. Agriculture was the mainstay of the Incan economy (irrigation system, canals, a new crop—potatoes—and the use of nitrates).

   f. Oral tradition was the means of transmitting poetry, religion, drama, history, and legend.

D. **The Latin American past provides us with a key to understanding Latin America today.**

1. The coming of the Spanish changed pre-Columbian society.

   a. Geography played an important part in making Spain and Portugal culturally different from the rest of Europe.

   b. The discovery and early settlements in Spanish and Portuguese America were incidental in the search for a passage to China and the East Indies.

c. As the size and wealth of the area became known, the Spanish Crown set up greater imperial control and imposed restrictions on the economic and social life of the people of the region.

d. The introduction of the Roman Catholic religion and its impact greatly affected the culture and civilization of the region.

2. Spanish colonial policy led to discontent in the colonies.

a. There are many parallels between the U.S. war for independence and the Latin American wars for independence.

b. Forces were at work throughout the 300 years of Spanish rule that would lead to the doom of the Spanish Empire.

c. The impetus for revolt came largely from *criollos,* who often were jealous and resentful of special treatment given to *peninsulares.*

d. Blacks and Native Americans were active in the fight for independence, but the movement was not designed for their benefit.

3. Latin Americans achieved independence in a 20-year struggle.

a. There were three types of independence movements in Latin America:

(1) true revolutionary uprisings in which the ruling group was violently overthrown and driven out by a united people;

(2) movements, almost civil wars, with criollos fighting on both sides;

(3) the achievement of independence with little or no fighting.

b. The major movements for independence were as follows:

(1) Simón Bolívar led a long and difficult struggle in northern South America (type 2) (1812–1824).

(2) José de San Martín and Bernardo O'Higgins were the leaders in the southern cone of the continent (type 2) (1816–1818).

(3) Fathers Miguel Hidalgo and José Morelos and Agustín de Iturbide led Mexico to independence (type 2) (1810–1821).

(4) Toussaint L'Ouverture led the Haitian movement against France and Napoleon (type 1) (1803–1804).

4. In Latin America the 19th century was a time of struggle, revolution, and dictatorship.

a. After gaining independence the new nations of the region faced many problems.

b. In colonial times the idea that the king was above criticism had established stability and inspired a respect for law and order.

c. For a long period after independence was achieved, frequent revolts against elected presidents and established constitutions undermined stable government.

d. Economic and political inequality remained and led to the formation of the two main political parties.

e. Conservatives generally supported strengthening the central government; Liberals wanted more power in local units of the government.

f. Liberal criticism of centralized government, the role and power of the church, and established privilege for the few led to challenges to oligarchic (a type of government or rule by a few people, often for their own interests) and authoritarian rule.

g. In much of Latin America, personalities emerged as more important than ideas as the "era of the *caudillo* and *cacique*" began.

h. *Gulpe de estado* (coup d'état) has been a traditional means to power, prestige, and wealth for the Latin American military.

5. The twentieth century has marked a period of revolutionary change in Latin America.

a. The Mexican Revolution opened an era of democratic and social change.

b. The Bolivian Revolution attempted to bring about democratic and social changes, but failed.

c. The Cuban Revolution was a successful attempt to bring social and economic change by implementing Communist ideas and methods.

d. The Sandinista Revolution in Nicaragua, which seeks social, economic, and democratic change, is still in motion.

e. The Chilean Revolution, an attempt to bring democratic change, was defeated by antidemocratic military leaders.

E. The economic situation in Latin America is the key to Latin America's future.

1. Latin America's riches are both a blessing and a curse.

a. Important mineral resources, with the notable exception of coal, can be found throughout Latin America.

b. Latin America is rich in its variety of foods and its potential for growing them because of its extensive area and its various climatic regions.

c. The development of one-crop or one-product economies (monocultures) is an example of the paradox "Latin American economic problems are those of a starving man with a gold mine under his feet."

2. Agriculture has been the economic base of Latin America.

a. The greatest natural resource of Latin America is its land.

b. The origins of the large landholding systems (latifundia) can be found in the 16th-century Spanish conquest.

c. Modern agricultural techniques were not used extensively because an abundance of low-paid farm workers was available.

d. A variety of problems have beset agricultural development. These problems include monoculture, poor land use, the landholding system, lack of modern equipment, and the lack of modern scientific methods.

3. Obstacles have delayed Latin America's industrial development.

    a. Latin America's slow development is marked by low per capita incomes, uneven distribution of wealth, export dependence, inadequate housing and educational facilities, illiteracy, and rapid population growth (about 3 percent annually).

    b. Lack of coal has hampered the development of a steel industry.

    c. Capital for industrial development has not been adequate.

    d. Geographic factors have hampered the development of an infrastructure necessary to support industrialization.

    e. The lack of a strong educational system has limited the development of a skilled labor pool.

    f. Industrial development has not proceeded at an even pace throughout the region. Mexico, Argentina, Brazil, and Venezuela are at a more advanced stage.

    g. Urban industrial workers have been exploited as a labor force.

4. Latin Americans have tried to solve their problems in many ways.

    a. Agrarian reform is viewed as one method of correcting social inequalities, but large landowners fear it will destroy the foundations of their political power.

    b. Organizing rural and urban workers into unions has been a key factor in the process of agricultural and industrial reform.

    c. In urban centers, industrialization created conditions and opportunities that stimulated the growth of organized labor and a middle class.

    d. Scientific methods have compensated for the lack of coal and energy resources, such as obtaining coke from petroleum, the use of gasohol in Brazil, and the exploitation of hydroelectric power.

    e. Agrarian reform policies include taxing programs, credit extension, development of education, and development of transportation.

5. Regional economic interdependence is important to Latin American development.

    a. It is an important first step toward the concept of a "united" Latin America.

    b. It will encourage the formation and investment of capital within the region.

    c. It will lessen dependence on and control by foreign investors and will lead to strengthening of the economic autonomy of the nations of the region.

    d. The creation of regional rather than national markets will give Latin Americans a united voice in commercial negotiations with countries outside of the region.

F.   **Cultural factors have played an important role in the development of Latin America**

1. Each nation of Latin America has developed in its own distinctive manner, although there are many similarities in culture, history, society, and political and economic development.

2. "The Latin American" is a mixture of many groups

    a. The origins of pre-Columbian Native Americans probably can be found in Asia.

    b. Many of the cultural traits of Latin Americans can be traced to Iberian sources.

    c. Immigrants from many parts of Europe have influenced Latin America.

    d. An important result of the Spanish colonization was the forced immigration of Africans as slaves into Latin America.

3. Religion has played an important role in Latin American culture.

    a. The Catholic religion touches every aspect of life in Latin America.

    b. Over the past 50 years the Catholic church in Latin America has moved from support of the status quo (existing situation) to a force for economic, political, and social change.

4. Latin Amercians have developed their own cultural traits.

    a. Latin American culture can be seen as a combination or mixture of Native American, European, and African cultures.

    b. The extended family system has created great stability in a difficult political, economic, and social situation.

5. Latin America has developed distinct traditions in art, music, and literature.

    a. Widespread illiteracy and a lack of national feeling caused early writers and artists to look to Europe for subjects and styles.

    b. By the beginning of the 20th century, Latin American authors and painters began to find their subjects in local rural areas and pre-Columbian Latin America.

    c. In Latin America, art, music, and literature have played a significant social role, with the artist, musician, and author acting as a guide, teacher, and conscience of the country.

    d. The themes, melodies, and rhythms of Latin American music reflect the mixing of Iberian, Native American, and African influence.

    e. Latin American authors and poets have achieved worldwide fame and have won Nobel Prizes in Literature.

G. **The islands of the Caribbean Sea (the West Indies) are an important part of Latin America.**

1. The West Indies are a chain of islands that separate the Caribbean Sea from the Atlantic Ocean. The major islands are Cuba, Haiti, the Dominican Republic, Puerto Rico, and Jamaica.

2. A majority of the people of the West Indies are descendants of black Africans brought to the area as slaves.

3. The culture and the society of the West Indies have been greatly affected by African, European, Asian, and North American influences.

4. The economy of the area is based mainly on agriculture and a one-crop economy.

5. The history of the region has been dominated by European and American interests.

6. The revolution led by Fidel Castro in Cuba and political and social instability in Haiti and the Dominican Republic are important elements in the modern history of the West Indies.

7. Puerto Rico has enjoyed some prosperity as a Commonwealth of the United States.

UNIT VIII

Exercises and Questions

Vocabulary

Directions: Match the words in Column A with the correct meaning in Column B.

Column A

1. tropical
2. reforms
3. artifacts
4. origins
5. peon
6. revolution
7. agriculture
8. bauxite
9. capital
10. leaching
11. social contract
12. delta
13. fiesta
14. pampas
15. regionalism

Column B

(a) a field worker or poor farmer in Latin America
(b) strong interest in local economic and social affairs, customs, and traditions
(c) having to do with the hot areas near the Equator
(d) a large, grassy plain in Argentina
(e) sources; beginnings
(f) the mineral from which aluminum comes
(g) objects made by either hand or machine
(h) using the land to produce crops; farming
(i) money used to develop a country's economy
(j) family, community, village, or town celebration
(k) making basic changes in government, economics, or culture
(l) the washing away of nutrients from the soil
(m) the land that is formed at the mouth of a river
(n) changes intended to improve the situation
(o) the right of the people to overthrow an existing government if their rights are not protected

Directions: Match each word in Column A with the correct meaning in Column B.

Column A

1. barrios
2. favela
3. maize
4. Contras
5. gulpe de estado
6. caudillo
7. mita
8. criollo
9. encomienda

Column B

(a) corn raised by the Native Americans of Latin America
(b) a large farm or ranch in Latin America
(c) the system of landholding of Mexico in which individual farmers work in groups and share all profits
(d) a cowboy of Argentina
(e) a large plantation in Portuguese Brazil
(f) the system by which Spanish landholders forced the Native Americans to work for them
(g) a dropout from school

10. quipu
11. fazenda
12. deserción
13. ejidos
14. hacienda
15. gaucho

(h) the method of forcing Native Americans to work in the mines of the colonial period

(i) a long piece of wood or string used by the Incas as a method of communication

(j) the slum area of a Latin American country other than Brazil

(k) a guerrilla group that opposed the Sandinista government in Nicaragua

(l) the forcible overthrowing of a government in Latin America

(m) the slum area of a Brazilian city

(n) a dictator or "strong man" in Latin America

(o) a person born in America of Spanish parents

Who Am I?

Directions: From the names listed below, select the person described in each of the sentences.

Francisco Pizarro   Father Hidalgo   Gabriela Mistral
Hernán Cortés   José Martí   Pablo Neruda
Toussaint L'Ouverture   Rubén Dario   José Orozco
Simón Bolívar   Martin Fierro   Diego Rivera
José de San Martín   Cândido Portinari   Juan Perón

1. I was a Chilean poet who won a Nobel Prize. _____

2. I was an Argentinian dictator in the 1940s and 1950s. _____

3. I was the Spanish conqueror of Mexico. _____

4. I was the leader of Mexican "revolutionary art." _____

5. I am the Argentine gaucho hero in a novel by José Hernandez. _____

6. I was the leader of the 19th-century Mexican Revolution. _____

7. I was a Mexican artist who made the Mexican Indians the heroes of my paintings.

   _____

8. I was the spanish conqueror of the Incas in Peru. _____

9. I was the leader of the Haitian rebellion against the French. _____

10. I was a famous Chilean poet. _____

11. I was the leader of South America's fight for indepedence in the North.

   _____

12. I was the leader of Argentina's fight for independence. _____

13. I was a Brazilian artist who painted scenes relating to the lives of black Latin Americans.

   _____

14. I was a Nicaraguan poet. _____

15. I was a Cuban writer. _____

Multiple Choice

Directions: Select the letter of the correct answer.

1. Which of the following statements best describes the use of the term "Latin America"?
    (a) It is accurate and is accepted by all Latin Americans.
    (b) It is the best name available, although inaccurate in some ways.
    (c) Hispanic people accept the term because it shows Spanish contributions.
    (d) Since the area was discovered by Spain, the term is accurate.

2. All of the following statements are true about Latin America *except*
    (a) parts of Brazil are closer to Africa than to the United States
    (b) Latin America has many volcanoes but all are extinct
    (c) the pampas are the most important plains of Latin America
    (d) the islands of the Caribbean are really the tops of underwater mountain peaks

3. Which river is correctly paired with the country in which it is located?
    (a) Amazon River (Brazil)
    (b) Orinoco River (Colombia)
    (c) Magdalena River (Venezuela)
    (d) Rio de la Plata (Chile)

4. The main mountain range of Latin America is found
    (a) along the north coast.
    (b) along the west coast.
    (c) along the east coast.
    (d) on the plateau of Brazil.

5. The geography of Latin America has served to
    (a) unify Latin America.
    (b) force Latin America to "face west."
    (c) limit regional differences.
    (d) divide and isolate parts of Latin America.

6. Cuba is to Jamaica as Costa Rica is to
    (a) Mexico.
    (b) Haiti.
    (c) Argentina.
    (d) Venezuela.

7. The mountains and rivers have affected life in Latin America because they have
    (a) always been used as travel and trade routes.
    (b) protected the people from invaders.
    (c) been barriers to transportation and communication.
    (d) aided the development of agriculture.

8. Geography played an important role in the history of Latin America in all of the following ways *except*
   (a) ocean currents helped Spain set up trade routes between Latin America and Spain
   (b) the horse latitude winds carried Columbus' ships into the Caribbean Sea
   (c) from the West Indies Spanish explorers moved to the mainland
   (d) from Panama winds and currents carried Spanish ships across the Pacific Ocean

9. Most people of Latin America live
   (a) near the west coast.
   (b) near the rivers not far from the coast.
   (c) on the pampas and llanos.
   (d) in the Atacama and Chaco areas.

10. Regionalism exists in Latin America today for all of the following reasons *except*
    (a) Latin America was divided by Spain in colonial times
    (b) communication is poor because of geographic barriers
    (c) groups of people are isolated because of Latin American topography
    (d) a long, irregular coastline prevents the growth of harbors and cities

11. The factor of geography that explains the differences in climate between Quito, Ecuador, and Belém, Brazil is
    (a) latitude.   (b) wind direction.   (c) altitude.   (d) vertical climate.

12. The factor of geography that best explains the difference in climate between Lima, Peru, and Salvador, Brazil, is
    (a) latitude.   (b) ocean current.   (c) altitude.   (d) nearness to water.

13. Which of the following statements is *true* about Latin American climate?
    (a) The climate is hot and rainy.
    (b) Ocean currents have little or no effect on the climate.
    (c) Because of many factors Latin America has a wide variety of climates.
    (d) The seasons in all of Latin America are the same as in North America.

14. Which of the following ocean currents is *correctly* paired with the country it affects?
    (a) Humboldt Current (Peru)
    (b) Falkland Current (Chile)
    (c) Gulf Stream (Argentina)
    (d) Westwind Drift (Brazil)

15. Which of the following statements about the geography/climate of Latin America is accurate?
    (a) Geographic features prevented European imperialism.
    (b) Harsh climatic conditions prevented the development of large-scale agriculture.
    (c) Geographic barriers made the development of transportation and communication systems easier.
    (d) Great differences in landforms and latitude resulted in many different climatic areas.

16. Which statement about the West Indies is accurate?
    (a) It is a country 100 miles west of India.
    (b) It is a collection of islands in the Caribbean Sea.
    (c) It is the second largest river in Central America.
    (d) It is the largest mountain range of Latin America.

17. The children of a European-Native American marriage are called
    (a) mestizos.   (b) Spaniards.   (c) mulattos.   (d) zambos.

18. Which is a valid generalization about the nations of Latin America?
    (a) Mestizos are the main ethnic group.
    (b) Most people live in the countryside or small villages.
    (c) The political systems of these nations are copied from those of the United States.
    (d) The most widely practiced religion is Roman Catholicism.

19. The language that is *correctly* matched with the country in which it is the *main* language spoken is
    (a) Spanish (Haiti).
    (b) French (Guyana).
    (c) Quechua (Argentina).
    (d) Portuguese (Brazil).

20. Control of education in Latin America is given to the
    (a) local boards of education.
    (b) mayor of each town.
    (c) national ministry of education.
    (d) state board of regents.

21. A recent change in the attitude of the Catholic Church in Latin America is
    (a) growing favoritism toward the wealthy.
    (b) greater support for military dictatorships.
    (c) frequent support for social and political reform.
    (d) lessening desire toward reducing illiteracy.

22. The term *quechua* is related to a
    (a) language of the Aztecs and present-day Mexican Native Americans.
    (b) language of the Incas and present-day Peruvian Native Americans.
    (c) prehistoric language of the pre-Columbian Native Americans of Central America.
    (d) patois language spoken in Haiti.

23. Which of the following *correctly* pairs the Native American group and its location?
    (a) Incas (Colombia)
    (b) Maya (Guatemala)
    (c) Aztecs (Peru)
    (d) Chibchas (Argentina)

24. An example of cultural diffusion in Central America was
    (a) the use of the quipu by the Incas.
    (b) the Toltec translation of the Mayan calendar.
    (c) the Aztec development of an oral literature.
    (d) the Mayan development of a written language.

25. Which of the following statements is *true* about the Maya, Aztecs, and Incas?
    (a) All three developed written languages.
    (b) All three depended on agriculture to survive.
    (c) All three were conquered by the Spanish.
    (d) All three were warlike and had large armies.

26. Quetzalcoatl, which means "feathered serpent," was
    (a) the name of an Incan god.
    (b) the Aztec name for Cortés.
    (c) the Incan name for Pizarro.
    (d) the name of an Aztec god.

27. The Maya had knowledge of all of the following *except*
    (a) the idea of zero
    (b) a 365-day calendar
    (c) a decimal system of numbers
    (d) a written language

28. Which of the following words is *not* from a Native American language of Latin America?
    (a) maize   (b) machete   (c) manioc   (d) hacienda

29. Human sacrifice was a part of the religious practice of the
    (a) Toltecs.   (b) Aztecs.   (c) Incas.   (d) Caribs.

30. The Toltecs made an important contribution to civilization by
    (a) developing a 365-day calendar.
    (b) passing on the learning of the Maya to the Aztecs.
    (c) keeping written records that were useful to historians.
    (d) making important discoveries in mathematics and astronomy.

31. The city of Cuzco was the capital of the
    (a) Maya.   (b) Aztecs.   (c) Incas.   (d) Toltecs.

32. Which of the following is the result of the other three?
    (a) dissatisfaction of many native peoples with Aztec rule
    (b) legend of Quetzalcoatl believed by the Aztecs
    (c) conquest of the Aztec Empire by the Spaniards
    (d) superiority of Spanish war technology

33. Which statement about ancient American civilizations expresses an historical theory rather than an historical fact?
    (a) The Incas did not have a written language.
    (b) The spread of disease caused the downfall of the Mayan Empire.
    (c) Human sacrifice was an element of the Aztec religion.
    (d) The Pyramid of the Sun was located at Teotihuacán.

34. An important result of the Spanish conquest of Mexico and Peru was
    (a) an increase in the Native American population because of improved health conditions.
    (b) the end of all forms of local slavery and forced labor.
    (c) the education of Native American leaders in the ways of Spanish government.
    (d) the near destruction of the local Native American cultures.

35. The Iberian Peninsula is located in
    (a) Central America.
    (b) South America.
    (c) southwest Asia.
    (d) southwest Europe.

36. The countries of the Iberian Peninsula are
    (a) Nicaragua and El Salvador.
    (b) Argentina and Brazil.
    (c) Haiti and the Dominican Republic.
    (d) Spain and Portugal.

37. During most of the 15th century the Spanish were involved in
    (a) driving the Muslims from Spain.
    (b) exploring the New World.
    (c) fighting against the English in America.
    (d) conquering the Portuguese part of the Iberian Peninsula.

38. A reason that may explain the differences in Spanish and Portuguese culture is
    (a) the two countries are separated by the Pyrenees Mountains
    (b) the Portuguese drove the Muslims out of their country two centuries before the Spanish did
    (c) the Muslims were never able to conquer all of Portugal but did conquer all of Spain
    (d) the Portuguese were more quickly converted to Islam that the Spanish

39. Ponce de León was the first European to discover
    (a) Puerto Rico.
    (b) Hispaniola.
    (c) Cuba.
    (d) Panama.

40. The island of Hispaniola is made up of the two countries of
    (a) Spain and Portugal.
    (b) Puerto Rico and Cuba.
    (c) Nicaragua and El Salvador.
    (d) Haiti and the Dominican Republic.

41. Which statement is *true* of Catholic Church leaders, the military, and the landowners in Latin America during colonial times?
    (a) They often opposed each other on major economic issues.
    (b) They formed an elite class and held political power.
    (c) They challenged the political power of Spain and therefore lost their own political power.
    (d) They made up the majority of the population.

42. Under the economic idea of *mercantilism* the Spanish colonies existed for the benefit of
    (a) all European nations.
    (b) the people of the colony itself.
    (c) the Spanish mother country.
    (d) the people of all the Spanish colonies.

43. The economic policies of Spain in the 17th century gave rise to a spirit of
    (a) contentment.
    (b) apathy.
    (c) friendship.
    (d) enlightenment.

44. Among the causes of the independence movement in Latin America were all of the following *except*
    (a) unequal sharing of power between criollos and Spanish-born colonists
    (b) the increase in the number of Native Americans and non-Spanish people in Latin America
    (c) the dishonest and cruel behavior of Spanish government officials
    (d) the ideas of the American and French revolutions

45. The Latin American leaders Símon Bolívar, Miguel Hidalgo, and Toussaint L'Ouverture are most closely associated with
    (a) independence movements.
    (b) Communist revolutions.
    (c) economic reforms.
    (d) education and social reform.

46. Which of the following events occurred *first?*
    (a) Peru won its independence.
    (b) Brazil won its independence.
    (c) Haiti won its independence.
    (d) Mexico won its independence.

47. The major events of the Latin American struggle for independence took place in
    (a) the beginning of the 18th century.
    (b) the first three decades of the 19th century.
    (c) the last quarter of the 19th century.
    (d) the last two decades of the 18th century.

48. An important result of independence for Latin America was that
    (a) democratic rule was brought to the area.
    (b) slavery and racial discrimination were done away with.
    (c) stable governments were set up under dictators.
    (d) great progress was made in eliminating poverty.

49. In Latin America the emphasis on the role of the military and the strength of the Roman Catholic religion have their origins in
    (a) ancient Native American village organizations.
    (b) cultural exchanges with the United States.
    (c) English practices in the New World.
    (d) Spanish colonial rule.

50. If the headlines "Juarez Defeats French Troops in Mexico," "Bolívar Leads Revolutions in South America," and "Haiti Becomes Independent from France" appeared in newspapers, they refer to the emergence of
    (a) colonialism.   (b) nationalism.   (c) Marxism.   (d) mercantilism.

51. Which of the following events occured *last?*
    (a) Porfiro Diaz set up a dictatorship in Mexico.
    (b) Pancho Villa and Emiliano Zapata fought against the Mexican government.
    (c) The Mexican Revolution was successfully completed.
    (d) Francisco Madero was assassinated.

52. A major reason for the Mexican Revolution was
    (a) unequal distribution of land.
    (b) lack of freedom of religion.
    (c) limited freedom of speech.
    (d) the assassination of Francisco Madero.

53. Which of the following men is *correctly* paired with the revolution he was involved in?
    (a) Fidel Castro (Mexico)
    (b) Augusto Sandino (Nicaragua)
    (c) Pancho Villa (Cuba)
    (d) Simón Bolívar (El Salvador)

54. Among the causes of the Cuban revolution were
    (a) lack of stable government in Cuba under Fulgencio Batista.
    (b) a *gulpe d'estado* led by Fulgencio Batista.
    (c) unequal land distribution with foreigners holding most of the land.
    (d) failure of the Cuban banking system to pay for a land reform program.

55. Which of the following is *true* about American relations with Central America and th Caribbean at present?
    (a) The United States supports the Sandinistas against the Communists.
    (b) The United States supports the present government of Haiti.
    (c) The United States supports the Contras who oppose the government of El S: vador.
    (d) The United States supports the elected government of El Salvador.

56. Which headline best reflects events in Central America during the 1980s?
    (a) "Prosperity Comes to Central America."
    (b) "European Powers Set Up New Colonies."
    (c) "The Fighting Never Stops."
    (d) "Economic Gains Are Impressive."

57. Which of the following statements accurately describes the present political status Puerto Rico?
    (a) It is a colony of the United States.
    (b) It is one of the states within the United States.
    (c) It is an independent nation.
    (d) It is a self-governing commonwealth.

58. In 1972 a democratically elected government was replaced by a military junta in
    (a) Argentina.
    (b) Chile.
    (c) Cuba.
    (d) Nicaragua.

59. A fact that is common to most countries of Latin America is that
    (a) stable governments have been set up since independence.
    (b) single parties dominated their politics in the 19th century.
    (c) during most of their history dictators have ruled.
    (d) few civil wars and revolutions have occurred.

60. Which of the following men is *incorrectly* paired with the nation he ruled?
  (a) Alberto Fujimori (Peru)
  (b) Juan Perón (Brazil)
  (c) Raul Alfonsín (Argentina)
  (d) Augusto Pinochet (Chile)

61. The basic food of most Latin Americans is
  (a) wheat.   (b) corn.   (c) beef.   (d) beans.

62. All of the following are problems of agriculture in Latin America *except*
  (a) monoculture
  (b) poor transportation
  (c) small farms
  (d) overuse of scientific methods

63. The ejido system is found in
  (a) Brazil.
  (b) Chile.
  (c) Mexico.
  (d) Dominican Republic.

64. An attempt by the United States to aid the improvement of Latin American economies was the
  (a) Common Market.
  (b) Good Neighbor Policy.
  (c) Alliance for Progress.
  (d) Organization of American States.

65. In recent years human rights violations have been reported in
  (a) Cuba and Costa Rica.
  (b) Argentina and Chile.
  (c) Puerto Rico and Colombia.
  (d) Jamaica and Virgin Islands.

66. One of the most important barriers to economic progress in developing Latin American nations has been a shortage of
  (a) raw materials.
  (b) unskilled workers.
  (c) land.
  (d) capital.

67. A major problem for many Latin American countries has been the
  (a) payment of their debts to foreign countries.
  (b) shortage of water.
  (c) rapidly declining population.
  (d) shortage of labor in agricultural areas.

68. A major purpose of the Organization of American States (OAS) is to
  (a) prevent Communist expansion in Latin America.
  (b) control the sale and production of minerals in Latin America.
  (c) provide a means for settling disputes in Latin America.
  (d) promote a unified trading zone in Latin America.

Thought Questions

1. "Geography helps determine how people live." What is the meaning of the statement? Explain why you agree or disagree with the statement.

2. If you were going to move to a nation in Latin America, what factors of geography would you have to know?

3. How has its geography helped in the development of Latin America?

4. Why is the term "Latin America" inaccurate in many ways?

5. How would living in a region such as the Andean altiplano be different from living on the Argentine pampas?

6. In what ways has the climate of Latin America influenced the development of cities, industries, and agriculture?

7. What factors made possible the Spanish conquest of Mexico? Peru?

8. How did the Incas build and maintain their empire?

9. Why would it have been important for the Maya to have a calendar? What information was available to the Maya that allowed them to develop a calendar?

10. Describe the culture developed by the Maya.

11. Compare (state the similarities and differences) in the cultures and histories of the Aztecs and Incas.

12. What were the reasons that led Spanish Americans to revolt against Spanish rule?

13. If you were living in Latin America in the early 19th century, why might you feel you had the right to revolt against the rule of the king of Spain?

14. Why did Latin American nations suffer from so many civil wars and revolutions after they gained their independence from Spain?

15. How did the United States and Europe contribute to the independence and progress of Latin America in the 19th century?

16. "The roots of Latin America can be found in Europe and Africa." What evidence exists to support this statement? What evidence exists to show that this statement may not be entirely true?

17. What forces have moved nations to revolts and revolutions in 20th-century Latin America?

18. What role did each of the following men and women play in the history of Latin America?
    (a) Simón Bolívar
    (b) Domingo Sarmiento
    (c) Fidel Castro
    (d) Eva Perón
    (e) Gabriela Mistral
    (f) Diego Rivera

19. Pretend you are a newspaper reporter. Write an editorial relating to American policy in Nicaragua and El Salvador.

Developing Answers to Regents-Type Essay Questions

Helpful Hints

In developing your answers to the essays be sure to:

1. Include specific factual information and evidence whenever possible.

2. Answer the question being asked; do not go off on tangents.

3. Keep these general definitions in mind:
    (a) *discuss* means "to make observations about something using facts, reasoning, and argument; to present in some detail."
    (b) *describe* means "to illustrate something in words or to tell about."
    (c) *show* means "to point out, to set forth clearly an idea or position by stating it and giving data that support it."
    (d) *explain* means "to make plain or understandable; to give reasons for or causes of; to show the logical development or relationship."

Sample Essay Questions

1. Issues or problems in one part of the world often have an impact on other areas of the world.

    Problems

    Destruction of the rain forest in Latin America
    Castro's establishment of communism in Cuba
    Human rights violations in Latin America
    Nonpayment of debts by Latin American nations

    A Choose *two* problems listed above.
       (1) Define each problem.
       (2) Explain how each problem affects other parts of the world.

    B Base your answer to Part B on your answer to Part A. Write an essay explaining how a problem in one part of the world can have an impact on other areas of the world.

2. Geographic factors have influenced the development of many nations. The pairs of nations in Latin America listed below have been influenced by geographic factors.

Pairs of Nations

Dominican Republic—Nicaragua   Mexico—Haiti
Argentina—Brazil   Bolivia—Venezuela
Peru—Chile

For *each* pair, use specific examples to show how geographic factors have had similar or different effects on the economies or the political or cultural developments of the two nations.

3. Revolutions can be political, social, or economic. Whatever their nature, they produce long-term effects on regions or countries.

In Latin America the following revolutions have been significant:

Latin American Revolutions

Mexican Revolution   Nicaraguan Revolution
Bolivian Revolution   Chilean Revolution

For *each* revolution:
a. Describe one major cause.
b. Explain one effect on the country in which it occurred.

4. Certain civilizations have achieved success in the following areas:

Areas of Success

Centralized government   Art and architecture
Technological improvement   Communication

For *each* of the following people—Incas, Aztecs, and Maya—discuss the extent of success achieved by their civilization in two of the areas listed above.

5. Many changes have taken place in the nations of Latin America in the past 90 years. These changes have affected many aspects of life in these nations.

Changes

Women's roles and status   Rise of democratic movements
Role of the church   Industrial development
     Growth of nationalist movements

For *each* of the above changes, describe one example of this change in a specific nation of Latin America, and discuss *either* a positive or a negative effect of the change on the nation.

6. Throughout history, nations have been organized under authoritarian or dictatorial leadership. Political figures and military leaders have assumed power and have tried to shape their nation's development.

Authoritarian Leaders

Fidel Castro (Cuba)   Duvalier (Haiti)
Juan Perón (Argentina)   Trujillo (Dominican Republic)
Augusto Pinochet (Chile)

For *each* of the leaders listed above:
a. Discuss the reasons why he was able to come to power.
b. Describe the influence he had on his nation's development.

Puzzle

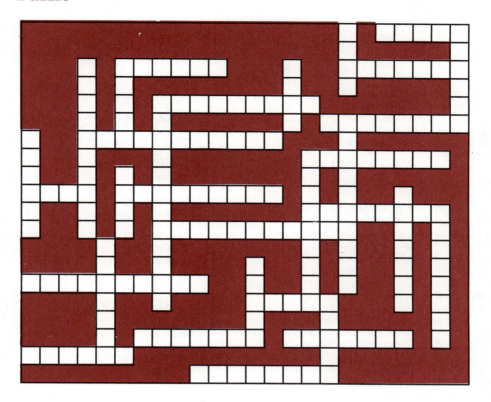

Directions: Place the words below in their proper place in the puzzle.

4 LETTERS	**5 LETTERS**	**6 LETTERS**	**7 LETTERS**	**8 LETTERS**
INCA	AZTEC	LLANOS	LA PLATA	CAUDILLO
MAYA	ANDES	PAMPAS	ISTHMUS	REPUBLIC
GULF	LATIN	AMAZON	PLATEAU	HACIENDA
PEON	CANAL	STAPLE	MESTIZO	HERITAGE
	CHACO		MULATTO	VERTICAL
			FINANCE	

9 LETTERS	**10 LETTERS**	**11 LETTERS**	**12 LETTERS**
ALTIPLANO	REVOLUTION	MONOCULTURE	DICTATORSHIP
DEMOCRACY	ENCOMIENDA	REGIONALISM	
HURRICANE	ESCARPMENT		

Glossary

abrogate   do away with

acculturation   process by which two cultural groups have contact over a long period of time and influence each other

acupuncture   an ancient Chinese practice of sticking needles into certain parts of the body to treat disease and to relieve pain

adaptation   adjustment to the conditions of the environment or culture

agriculture   using the land to produce crops and raise livestock; farming

agronomist   a person who studies soil management and field crop production

ahimsa   Indian idea of nonviolent action as suggested by Mohandas K. Gandhi

ainu   among the earliest known people to live in Japan

Allah   the one God of Islam

alliance   joining together of groups by formal agreement

altitude   height of the land above sea level

amnesty   granting of pardon

animism   the worship of spirits that are part of the natural environment

annex   to join or add to a larger or more important thing

anthropologist   social scientist who studies people, their culture, and their different ways of living and behavior

anti-Semitism   hostility and prejudice against Jews

apartheid   a policy of segregation and political and economic discrimination against non-European groups in South Africa

aquaculture   cultivation of the natural products of water such as fish

arable   fertile; suitable for growing crops

arbitrator   a person chosen to settle a dispute between two groups

archaeologist   scientist who studies the cultures of prehistoric and historic peoples through their artifacts, such as tools, pottery, building, and writing

archipelago   a group of islands

artifacts   objects made by either hand or machine representing a particular culture

artisan   trained or skilled worker; craftsman

audiencia   the highest court of Spanish colonial America

autonomous   self-governing; independent

balance of payments   a summary of international trade (exports and imports) of a country or region over a period of time

Bantu   a large group of Africans who speak a common language

barrio   a neighborhood or district of a town

bauxite   an ore used in making aluminum

bazaar   marketplace in many Middle Eastern and Oriental countries

bedouins   nomadic Arabic livestock-raisers and -herders

bicameral   a two-house legislature

bilateral   affecting two sides or parties in any negotiation

Boers   South Africans of Dutch or Huguenot descent; from the Dutch word for farmers

boycott   to refuse to buy and use certain goods

bride price   payment made by a man to a woman's father to be allowed to marry her; bride wealth

Bunraku   Japanese puppet play

Bushido   Japanese Samurai Code of Behavior; similar to the feudal code of behavior of the European knights, called chivalry

cacao   the seeds of a tree from which cocoa and chocolate are made

caliph   a successor of Muhammad as spiritual and temporal head of Islam

calligraphy   artistic writing, especially common in China and Japan

canyon   a deep valley with steep sides, usually with a river flowing through it

capital   the things used to produce goods and services; money used to develop a country's economy

capitalism   an economic system based on private rather than government ownership

cash crop   crop that is raised for sale rather than for personal use

caste   social system in which people are grouped according to occupation, wealth, inherited position, or religion

caudillo or **cacique**   powerful South American leader or dictator

cede   to give up or give over; to yield by treaty

civilization   level of development of a group; includes food-producing ability, government, and methods of communication

clan   people within an ethnic group who are descended from a common ancestor

class   people grouped according to similar social and economic levels

climate   the general existing weather conditions over an area for a long period of time

coalition   voluntary union of interest groups, political parties, or nations

collectives   a system in which a farming community shares ownership of land and farm machinery

colonialism   a situation in which one group, often a nation, has control over and is depended upon by another area or people

colony   a body of people living in a separate territory but retaining ties with the parent state

commonwealth   a nation or state

commune   often rural community characterized by collective ownership and use of property

communication   the ability to send or receive information and ideas

communism   economic system in which a single party controls the means of production with the aim of establishing a classless society

community   a group living together, having the same laws, and sharing common interests

confederation   alliance or league

conservation   protection of natural resources; conserve, to save for the future

continent   a large landmass; one of the seven great divisions of land on the globe

contractual   a binding agreement between two or more parties or groups

cooperative   a community system operated by and benefiting all members who contribute to it

coup d'etat   sudden and violent overthrow of a government by a small group

Creole (criollo)   a white person descended from French or Spanish settlers of the U.S. Gulf states

crusades   military campaigns and pilgrimages by European Christians to win the Holy Land from the Muslims (1096–1204)

cultivated   prepared land for the raising of crops

cultural diffusion   spread of cultural traits from one group to another

culture   the customary beliefs, social forms, and material traits of an ethnic, religious, or social group

cuneiform   writing in wedge-shaped characters

customs   usual ways of acting in a particular situation

cyrillic   the alphabet used for Russian and other Slavic languages

deficit   lacking in amount or quantity

deforestation   the action of clearing forests of their trees

deity   a god or godess

delta   the land that is formed by mud and sand at the mouth of a river

democracy   a political system in which the people participate in the making of their own laws or elect representatives to make the laws

density   the quantity of anything per unit of area

desert   a barren, extremely dry area

devaluation   an official reduction of the value of a currency of a nation

dharma   the law in the Buddhist religion; correct behavior, virtue in Hinduism

dialects   a regional or local variety of languages

dichotomy   a division into two individual groups

dictator   someone who has taken complete control of a country's government and the lives of the people

dissident   one who disagrees with the general opinion or actions of a group

diversity   not alike; variety

doctrine   a position or principle taught and believed in by a church or government

domesticate   tame; the adaptation of plants and animals for human use

drought   a long period of dry weather over an area

dynasty   a powerful group or family that rules for many years

economic   relating to the production, distribution, and consumption of goods and services

ecosystem   an ecological unit consisting of a community and its environment

ejidos system   a type of communal farm found in Mexico

elevation   the height of land above sea level; altitude

embargo   complete restriction or restraint of trade; refusal to buy a product

encomiendo   a grant of land given by the King of Spain for loyal services

environment   all of the natural, physical, and cultural conditions that surround and affect people

equator   an imaginary line circling the earth and equally distant from the North Pole and the South Pole

erosion   the process by which soil is worn away from the earth's surface; caused by running water, wind, waves, and ice

escarpment   sharp, steep cliffs

estancia   a large sheep or cattle ranch in South America

ethnic group   a group of people who have common physical traits, history, and culture

ethnocentrism   belief that one's own group or culture is superior to others

exploit   to make unfair or selfish use of something or someone

extended family   a family that includes other members besides mother, father, sons, and daughters; for example, grandparents

extinct   no longer existing

extraterritoriality   existing or taking place outside of the territory of a nation

extremists   people who go to the greatest extent, including violence, to achieve their goals

faction   clique; a party or a group

fallow   plowed land that is not planted for one or more seasons

favela   a part of a Brazilian town or city where the poor and landless live

federation   a union of equal organizations that give power to a central group

fellahin   the farmers of Egypt

feminism   the theory of the political, economic, and social equality of the sexes

fetish   any real object worshipped by people for its supposed magical powers

feudalism   the political and economic system in which the vassal pledges loyalty and service to a lord in return for land and protection

fragmentation   to break up or into parts

gaucho   an Argentine cowboy

genocide   the destruction of a particular group of people

gentry   people belonging to the upper or ruling class of society

ghats   low mountains on the east and west side of the Deccan in South India

"global village"   describes the current state of our world, in which events or actions in one part of the world affect other parts of the world

golpe de estado   coup d'etat in Latin America; the military overthrow of a Latin American government

greenhouse effect   harmful warming of the earth's surface and lower layers of the atmosphere, caused by an increase in carbon dioxide in the atmosphere

gross domestic product (GDP)   the total value of all goods and services provided in a country during a year

guano   manure from seabirds; used as fertilizer and   a source of nitrates

guerilla   member of a group that carries on raids and fights an established government

guru   a personal religious teacher and guide to Hinduism; one who is a recognized leader or authority

habitat   the natural environment in which people, animals, and plants live or grow

hacienda   a large land estate or ranch in Spanish America, mainly in Mexico

haiku   a Japanese form of poetry

hegira   Mohammed's journey from Mecca to Medina in 622 A.D.

heritage   that which is passed from one generation to the next

hieroglyphics   a writing system using mainly pictorial characters

Hindi   the major language of India

Hinduism   the major religion of India

hydroelectric   relating to the production of electricity through the use of water power

ideology   the ideas, concepts, and thinking of an individual, group, or culture

Ife   a town in Nigeria in sub-Saharan Africa, where sculpted heads made of bronze were found

illiterate   not able to read or write

imam   leader of the Shi'ite Muslims; prayer leader of a mosque

imperialism   a nation's policy of extending its power and dominion over other nations by using force or indirect economic and political control

indemnity   security against hurt, loss, or damage

indigo   a plant that produces a dark blue dye

indoctrination   to instruct and impose ideas, opinions, points of view, or principles on a group of people

inflation   the great increase in the amount of paper money in relation to the available goods for sale; this situation leads to rising prices

infrastructure   the basic transportation and communication system of a nation

interdependence   people's dependence on one another

intervention   the policy of interfering in the affairs of another nation

irrigation   the watering of crops or other plants by pipes, canals, and ditches

Islam   a major world religion that recognizes Allah as the only God and Mohammed as his Prophet

island   a land mass completely surrounded by water

isolation   separation from others

isthmus   a narrow strip of land connecting two large land masses and separating two large bodies of water

jihad   Islamic holy war

Judaism   the oldest of the Middle East religions; the main idea of Judaism is the belief in one God (monotheism)

junta   a board or ruling body

jute   a plant raised mainly in India from which burlap and twine are made

Kabuki   a form of Japanese drama with song and dance

kami   good spirits of nature to the Japanese

kaoliang   a cereal grain grown in China

Karma   Hindu idea that every human action brings about certain reactions

kibbutz   an Israeli community of farmers who work together and share all the property and income

kiln   pottery oven

Koran   the holy book of the Muslims

landlocked   describes an area or region completely surrounded by land without access to a sea or ocean

language   a systematic verbal method of communication among a group of people

latifundia   large farms, ranches, or plantations in Spanish America

leaching   the washing away of nutrients from the soil

leftist   a person who favors change or reforms, usually in the name of greater freedom

lines of latitude   imaginary parallel lines running east and west around the globe; these lines measure distance north and south of the equator

livelihood   how people earn a living

llanos   plains in Colombia and Venezuela; from the Spanish word for "plains"

loess   a thin layer of rich soil left behind by glaciers and carried by the wind

mandate   an order or command; a commission set up to rule an area

marxist   one who believes in socialism as a method of government

matriarchal   a family group led by the mother

mediation   the process of settling disputes by compromise and discussion. A third party is usually present to act as mediator

mercantile system   a system in which a colony's only purpose is to provide raw materials for the mother country and act as a market in which products from the mother country can be sold; the colony exists solely for the support of the mother country

mestizo   a person of mixed European and Native American ancestry

migration   the movement of people from one area or country to another

militarism   policy in which the armed forces are made powerful and military interests are most important

militia   citizens who can be called to help defend a nation; this generally does not include the regular armed forces

minerals   nonliving materials found on or near the earth's surface, such as gold, silver, and lead

missionary   person who brings his religion to people who are not members of that religion

moderate   not extreme

modernism   a late 19th-century writing style that stressed unity among Latin American cultures

moksha   the final resting place for all deserving Hindus

monarchy   government headed by a king or queen

monoculture   cultivation of a single product,   the land is used for nothing else

monotheism   the belief in one god or supreme being

monsoon   a wind in Asia that brings a wet season when it blows from the sea and a dry season when it blows from the land

mosque   a building used for public worship by Muslims

most-favored nation   a part of most trade agreements that gives each nation the same rights as all other trading partners

mouth   the place where a river empties into a sea, lake, or ocean

mulatto   a person having one European and one African parent, or a person of mixed European and African ancestry

multilateral   involving more than two nations or parties

Muslim   someone who practices the religion of Islam

myth   a traditional story of supposedly real events that explains a world view of a people or a practice, belief, or natural phenomenon

nationalism   loyalty and devotion to one's own country, especially placing it above all others

nationality   a group of people who feel they belong together because of common cultural characteristics like language, religion, history, and traditions

nationalization   the government take-over of industry and property

natural resources   industrial materials and capacities provided by nature

navigable   deep enough and wide enough for ships to sail on

negotiate   to confer or bargain in order to arrive at a settlement or solution to a problem

neutralism   a policy of not taking sides in relation to the great world powers

nirvana   the stopping of the wheel of rebirth (reincarnation); the goal of all Buddhists

Nō (Noh)   a Japanese form of drama developed in the 14th century

Nok   a town in Northern Nigeria where terra-cotta pottery and figurines were found

nomad   a member of a group that moves from place to place to secure its food supply

nonalignment   a policy of not being allied with the great world powers

nuclear proliferation   the possession of nuclear weapons by more and more countries

oasis   a place in the desert where there is a natural spring or surface water

ocean   a great body of water that covers 3/4 of the surface of the earth

ocean current   a regular movement of the surface water of an ocean caused mainly by winds and by differences of water temperature

opium   an addictive narcotic drug

oral tradition   the practice of passing down stories and information from generation to generation by word of mouth

origin   thing from which anything comes; source; starting point

overpopulation   a situation in which an area contains more people than available resources can support

pact   an agreement between two or more nations

paddies   rice fields in Asia

pagoda   temple or sacred building with many stories (levels) found in India, Southeast Asia, and Japan

pampas   the large grassy plains of southern Latin America, especially in Argentina

panchayat   a local council in India

parliament   a supreme legislative body

partitioned   divided into parts

patois   a local dialect

patriarchal   a family group in which the father is the head of the family

patriotism   love and devotion to one's own country

peasant   a small landowner or laborer

peninsula   land mass surrounded on three sides by water

peon   in Latin America, a field worker who owns no land

per capita GDP   the average value per person of the goods and services a country produces in a year

permanent   lasting; remaining for a long time

petrodollars   money paid to oil-producing countries

petroleum   an oily, inflammable liquid used in making gasoline and chemicals

pharaoh   a ruler of ancient Egypt

pictograph   an ancient or prehistoric drawing or painting on a rock wall

plain   an extensive area of flat or rolling treeless country

plateau   a broad land area with a usually level surface raised sharply above the land next to it on at least one side

population density   the average number of persons per unit of area

possession   an area under the control of another government

prairie   a large area of flat land with tall grass and few trees; steppe; from the Latin word meaning "meadow"

prehistoric   refers to a period of time prior to written history

primitive   very simple; of early times in a civilization

propaganda   the spreading of ideas, information, or rumor for the purpose of furthering one's position or cause to injure another

provincial   local;   relating to a province or district

quarantine   to blockade in order to prevent the transfer of goods

Quechua   the language of the Incas, still spoken by the Indians of Peru, Bolivia, Ecuador, Chile, and Argentina

quota   the limit placed by one nation on the amount of goods that may be imported from other nations

rabbi   a Jewish religious leader

race   a division of people having certain similar physical characteristics

radical   one who favors extreme changes in government or society

rain forest   a forest of hardwood evergreen trees that requires very heavy rainfall

rajah   Indian ruler

realism   a writing style which attempts to portray life as it really happens

rebellion   armed resistance or fighting against one's government, political system, or culture

referendum   a practice of submitting by popular vote a measure passed or proposed by a legislative body or by popular demands

reforestation   the act of repopulating forests by planting seeds or young trees

region   an area of land whose parts have one or more similar characteristics

regionalism   loyalty to local economic and social affairs, customs, and traditions

reincarnation   the act of returning to some form of life after death

remote   distant; far from settled areas

republic   a nation in which the leaders are elected by the people

revolution   basic change in or complete overthrow of an existing government, political system, or culture

rift valley   a split or separation in the earth's crust; the Great Rift Valley extends from southwest Asia (Jordan) to Mozambique in East Africa

rightist   one who supports conservativism and resists change

romanticism   a writing style that emphasizes human emotions rather than human reasoning

rural   having to do with farming and the countryside

samuri   the military class of feudal Japan

sanskrit   an ancient Indian language; the classical language of Hinduism

sari   garment worn by Hindu women

savanna   a grassland in subtropical areas with drought-resistant undergrowth and few trees

secede   to withdraw from a group or organization

sect   a group believing in a particular idea or leader

sectarian   a member of a sect; or a narrow or bigoted person

self-sufficient   able to meet one's own needs without help

sepoy   a native of India employed as a soldier by the English

serf   a member of a subservient feudal class bound to the soil and subject to the will of a lord; serfs had few rights or privileges

sheik   an Arab or bedouin chief

Shi'ite   Muslims who believe Ali and the imams to be the only rightful successors of Muhammad

Shinto   the original religion of Japan, having gods (Kami) of nature (sea, river, winds, forests, and sun)

shogun   a military leader of Japan before 1867

silt   a deposit of sand and mud along a river

slash-and-burn   a method of clearing land so that it is temporarily usable for farming; used in tropical areas

social contract   the idea that all people have a right to life, liberty, and property, and that, if a government tries to remove these rights, people also have the right to revolt

socialist economy   a system in which the government owns the means for production and distribution of goods

source   origin; place where something begins

species   a category of related organisms (plants or animals) or populations that are potentially capable of interbreeding

sphere of influence an area or region within which the influence or the interest of one nation is more important than any other nation

stable steady; firm; not likely to fall

standard of living the level of comfort enjoyed by an individual or a group

stelae large stone columns

steppe flat, treeless plain with short grass found in southeastern Europe or Asia

strait a narrow channel of water connecting two larger bodies of water

subcontinent a landmass of great size but smaller than a continent; for example, India

subsidy a grant or gift of money to assist an enterprise, business, or individual

subsistence farming the production of all or almost all the goods required by a farm family, usually without any significant surplus for sale

sultan ruler of a Muslim country

Sunni the Muslims of the part of Islam that follow the orthodox tradition

suttee the act or custom of a Hindu widow being cremated on the funeral pyre of her husband

Swahili a Bantu language of East Africa used for trade and government; has many Arabic, Persian, and Indian words

swaraj Indian term for self-rule

taiga a forested area in the Soviet Union and other places near the Arctic

Talmud books containing Jewish civil and religious law and tradition

tariff a tax on goods brought into a country from another country

terraced farmland flat shelves of land, arranged like wide steps on a mountainside

terra-cotta baked clay used to make pottery

terrorism the idea of using violence and fear of violence to gain an objective

textiles fibers and yarns made into cloth and then into clothing

Third World refers to the developing nations of Asia, Africa, and Latin America

topography the surface features of a place or area

totalitarianism all parts of life —economic, social, political, religious, and educational—are controlled by the state

trade surplus exports of a nation are greater than the imports of that nation

tradition the handing down of information, beliefs, and customs from one generation to another

tribalism tribal relationships, feelings, and loyalties

tribe a group of people who share a common language and religion and are united under one leader

tributary the arms of a large river

tropical having to do with the hot areas near the equator

typhoon a tropical storm or cyclone found in the China Sea and Indian Ocean

underdeveloped an area with little industry that is in an early stage of economic development

unilateral an action taken by one party or person

uninhabitable an area where, due to the environment, people are not able to survive

unique one of a kind

untouchable a person belonging to the lowest caste of the Hindu social order

uprising revolt; rebellion; an act of popular violence in defiance of an established government

urban relating to a city

values attitudes or beliefs considered to be important by a group

vassal a person under the protection of a feudal lord to whom he has vowed his loyalty and service; a subordinate or follower

veld South African steppe or prairie

vernacular the style of language used in a certain area

viceroy the governor of a country or a province who rules as the king's representative

wadi gully; the bed of a stream which is usually dry except during the rainy season

xenophobia the fear and dislike of anything unfamiliar

yerba maté popular tea beverage in Argentina, Paraguay, and Uruguay

Yoruba an African tribe living in present-day Nigeria

zambo a person of mixed Native American and African parentage in Latin America

Zionism a theory for setting up a Jewish national community in the Middle East and supporting the modern state of Israel

PICTURE CREDITS:

Index

(Page numbers in *italics* refer to captions.)

Abadan, 123
Abdullah, King (Jordan), 73
Abraham, Herald, 673
Abu Nidal terrorists (Damascus), 96
Achebe, Chinua, 176
Acholi tribe, 214, 215
acid rain
  and pollution, 19
Aconcagua Mountain, 619
acupuncture
  in China, 274–275
Addis Ababa, 217
Advani, Lal Krishna, 415–417
Aesop, 174
Affonso I, King (Congo), 198
Africa
  and agriculture, 27, 176–184, 188
  Arab role in, 197–198
  arrival of Europeans in, 198
  arts of, 170–176
  climate of, 159–160, 177–184, 186
  continent of, 5
  as cradle of civilization, 187
  crops of, 176–180, 188
  deserts of, 159
  diamonds in, 184
  disease in, 178
  early history of, 187–191
  European control of, 204–205, 205
  European explorers of, 202–204
  fables in, 173–175
  families in, 163–166
  famine in, 180–184
  farmers in, 176–177, 186
  geography of, 153–155
  gold in, 184, 199
  and independence, 209–223
  and independence, chart, 210
  industrial development in, 184–187
  Islam in, 197–198
  isolation of, 153–154
  languages of, 163, 173, 189, 225
  masks of, 172
  medicine men in, 169–170
  missionaries in, 204
  mountain of, 155
  and oil imports, 181
  ores of, 184, 219, 232
  people of, 160–163
  political map of, 152
  politics in, 213
  population of, 6, 180, 187
  rain forests of, 21, 159–160
  rainfall in, 160
  religions in, 168–170, 207
  resources of, 184–187, 185
  rift valley of, 156
  rivers of, 155
  savannahs of, 159–160
  size of, 155
  Soviet-Cuban influence in, 217
  topography of, 155–159
  trade in, 189
  transportation in, 181, 186, 207
  tribes of, 166–168, 191
  urbanization of, 181
  See also individual countries
African National Council (ANC), 220,
  225, 227–228, 233–235, 242
Africanus, Leo, 198
Afrikaans language, 225
Agrarian Reform Laws, 75
agriculture
  and civilization, 10
  and crops, 45, 176–177
  and development, 74
  and global warming, 21
  and irrigation, 60, 62, 74, 477, 656
  and population growth, 25–27, 58
  slash-and-burn, 178
Aguinaldo, Emilio, 485
Ahimsa (non-violence), in India, 395,
  403
Ahu De (Chu Teh), General, 314
Akali Dal Party
  of Sikh people, 412, 415
Akbar the Great, 397–399

al-Fatah of Palestine Liberation
  Organization, 89
Albert Lake, 203
Alexander the Great, 393, 405
Alfonsín, Raul, 692–693
Algeria, 41, 44
  under French rule, 69, 204
  and nuclear energy, 28–29
Alhambra palace, 66
Ali, Rashid, 71
Ali, Sunni, 193
Allah
  and Muslims, 53–54
Allende, Salvatore, 659, 687, 689–691,
  690
alphabet
  defined, 12
  origin of, 63
altiplano
  of South America, 620, 628
altitude, defined, 159
Amazon River, 620, 622
Amin, Adi, 213–215
Amritsar, 406, 412
An-Yang, 264
ANC, See African National Council
Anderson, Terry, 116
Andes Mountains, 619, 656
Andrada, José Bonifaco, 652
Angola
  civil war in, 182
  independence of, 210, 217–218
  under Portuguese rule, 205, 217
  treaty with Zaire, 219
animism, defined, 473
Antarctica
  continent of, 5
anthropologist, defined, 9
anti-Semitism
  in Europe, 82
Antigua, 619, 668
Antilles, Greater, 668, 670
Antilles, Lesser, 668, 670
Aoun, Michel, 114
apartheid
  in Africa, 176, 220, 223–242, 230
  defined, 223
  movement away from, 232–242
  struggle against, 225–227
Aqaba, Gulf of, 85
aquaculture, defined, 574
Aquino, Benigno, 489
Aquino, Corazon, 489–490
Arab Common Market, 73
Arab Fund for Economic and Social
  Development, 73
Arab-Israeli conflict, 82–88, 99–101,
  108–110, 127, 131
  Arab side on, 86–88
  Israeli side on, 82–86
Arab League
  and Arab-Israeli conflict, 108
  formation of, 73
  and Lebanese civil war, 114
Arabian American Oil Company
  (ARAMCO), 76, 77, 78
Arabian Nights, 66
Arabic numerals
  origin of, 66, 396
Arabs, 64–66
  and Israel, 82–84
Arafat, Yasir, 89, 91–93, 108–109
ARAMCO, See Arabian American Oil
  Company
Araucanians, 644, 648
Arawaks, 644, 670
archaeologist, defined, 11
archipelagos, defined, 477
architects, 60
architecture, 61, 66, 396, 552–553
Arctic Ocean, 5
Arctic survival, 2
Arena party (El Salvador), 682
Arequipa, 694
Argentina, 655, 657, 660, 691–693
Arias, Oscar (Costa Rica), 681, 683
Aristide, Jean-Bertrand, 673

artifacts, defined, 189
Aruba, 668, 674
Aryans
  conquerers of India, 385, 391–392,
  405
ASEAN, See Association of Southeast
  Asian Nations
Ashanti tribe, 166
Ashikaga period (Japan), 547–548,
  565–566
Asia
  continent of, 5
  population of, 6
Askia Mohammed, 194
Asmara (Asnera), 217
Assad, President of Syria, 126, 133
Assam, 415, 420
Assis, Joaquim Machado de, 666
Association of Southeast Asian Nations
  (ASEAN), 503–504, 511
astronomy, 63
Asturias, Miguel Angel, 666
Aswan High Dam, 74, 189
Atacama Desert, 627
Atahuallpa, 643, 647, 695
Atlantic Ocean, 5
Atlas Mountains, 44
attack, preemptive, defined, 85
Aurangzeb, 398–399
Australia
  continent of, 5
Austria, 68
Awami League Party (Bangladesh), 428
Ayacucho, 652
ayatollahs
  of Iran, 118, 120
Aymara, 640, 695
Ayodhya, 416, 420
Aziz, Tariq, 127
Aztecs, 636–639, 646

Babangida, Ibrahim B., 212
Babur, 397, 405, 415
Babylonians, 63
Baganda tribe, 213, 214
Baghdad, 67, 123
  and Gulf War, 127
Bahadur, Jung, 431
Bahamas, 668, 670
Bahrain, 41
Bahujan Samaj
  in India, 417
Baker, James, 109, 127
Baker, Sir Samuel, 203
Bakongo tribe, 168, 219
balance of payments, defined, 418
Balfour, Lord, 83
Balfour Declaration, 83, 87
Bali, 504
Balkok, 465, 474, 481, 494
Bangladesh, 371, 405, 424–430
  famine in, 427
    map, 370
  origin of, 422, 425
Bangladesh Nationalist Party (BNP),
  426
Bangwa figure, 173
Bantu
  language of Africa, 163
Bantu tribes, 196, 224
Barbados, 668, 674
Basra, 123
Batavia, See Djarkata
Batista, Fulgencio, 677
Bay of Pigs invasion, 686
bazaar, 66, 118, 373
  defined, 48
Bedouins, 46
  See also nomads of desert
Begin, Menachem, 17, 104–107
Beijing (Peking), 296, 307, 310, 327
Beirut
  after civil war, 114–115
  and Palestine Liberation
    Organization, 90
  terrorism in, 96
Belem, 625
Belgian Congo, See Zaire
Belgium
  and Congo (Zaire), 204
Bello, Andrés, 666
Bengal, 424–425

Bengali language, 422
Benghazi
  United States bombing of, 95
Benguela (cold ocean current), 160
Benin
  art of, 171
Bey, General, 424
Bhagavad-Gita, 388
Bharatiya Janata Party (BJP) of India,
  414–418, 420
Bhumibol Adulyadej, King of Thailand,
  493
Bhutto, Benazir, 423–424
Bhutto, Zulfikar Ali, 422–423, 425
Biafra, 212
  See also Nigeria
Bible
  and Talmud, 53
Biharas (non-Bengali Moslems), 426
Biko, Steven, 227
biologic weapons, 127, 130
biotechnology
  and rain forests, 20
bipedalism, defined, 188
Birendra, King of Nepal, 431
Biswas, Abdur Rahman, 428
BJP, See Bharatiya Janata Party
Black September
  events of, 89–90
Blue Nile River, 202
BNP, See Bangladesh Nationalist Party
Bodos tribe
  of India, 415
Bolivar, Simon, 652
Bolivia, 640, 688
Bonaire, 674
Bonsai (Japan), 548
Bophuthatswana Republic, 225
Bosch, Juan, 686
Bosnia
  and United Nations intervention, 18
  and World War I, 17
Botha, President P.W., 227–228, 231
Botswana, 202
Boxer Rebellion, 309
Brahmaputra River, 372
Brahmins, 385, 392–394
Brazil, 651–652, 656, 657, 659, 660,
  695–696
  and oil, 82
  and rain forests, 20–21, 620, 622
Brazilian Highlands, 620
Brezhnev, Leonid, 434
British East India Company, 400, 406
British Honduras, 636
British Petroleum, 80
British South Africa Company, 220
Bruce, James, 202
Brunei, 503
Buckley, William (hostage)
  of Beruit embassy, 115
Buddha, Gautama, 405, 475
Buddhism
  in China, 273, 278, 295
  in India, 393–395
  in Japan, 538, 540, 553–555, 558
  in Korea, 591–592
  origin of, 394, 406, 475
  in Southeast Asia, 473–476
  terms used in, 476
Buenos Aires, 620
Bunraku theater (Japan), 549
Burma, See Myanmar
Burma Road, 486–487
Burton, Richard, 203
Burundi, 212
Bush, George, 109, 119, 125,
  127–133, 424, 683
  and China, 346–347
Bushido, Code of, 559, 563
Bushmen
  of Africa, 163, 170, 188
Buthelezi, Gatsha, 234–235, 238
Byelorussia
  and nuclear energy, 27

Cabral, Pedro, 646, 651
Cai Lun
  inventor of paper, 299
Cairo
  and Middle East Peace Conference,
    109
  summit in, 126
Calcutta, 372, 374, 377, 410

calendars
  origin of, 60, 636
caliph, defined, 56
Caliphs, 66
Callejas, Rafael, 693
Callié, René, 202
calligraphy, 554
  defined, 281, 553
Cambodia (Kampuchea), 479, 481,
  483–485, 493, 511–513
  economy of, 501–502
  and Vietnam, 512–513
camels
  in Africa, 189
Cameroon
  under German rule, 205
Camp David Accords
  between Israel and Egypt, 106–107,
    133
Canaan, See Israel
Canton, See Guangzhou
canyon, defined, 156
capital (money)
  and development, 15–16, 74, 186,
    662
caravans
  in deserts, 159
Caribbean Sea, 623
Caribs, 644, 670
Carnatic (eastern) coast of India, 372
carpenters, 60
Carribean Islands, See individual
  countries; West Indies
Carter, Jimmy, 79, 106–108, 687
  and China, 345
  in Egypt, 107
Casals, Pablo, 667
Caspian Sea
  and oil, 82
caste, defined, 384–385
Castro, Fidel, 219, 659, 677–678, 686,
  689
Castro, Raul, 677
Catholicism, See Christianity
CCP, See Chinese Communist Party
Cedras, Raoul, 673
Central America, 683
  geography of, 623–625
  and rain forests, 20
  See also individual countries
Central Intelligence Agency (CIA), 506,
  681, 686, 687, 691
Ceylon, See Sri Lanka
CFC, See chlorofluorocarbons
Chad
  famine in, 180
Chaldeans, 63
Chamorro, Violeta Barrios de, 681
Chams
  people of Southeast Asia, 466
Chang River, See Yangtze River
Changamire Empire, 196
Chao Phraya (Menam) River, 463, 464
Chapala Lake, 623
Chapultepec Castle, 682
Chavez, Carlos, 667
chemical weapons, 127, 128, 130
chemicals
  and greenhouse effect, 21–22
Cheney, Dick, 127
Chernobyl
  nuclear accident at, 22–24
Chiang Kai-shek, 310–311, 322
Chibchas, 644, 648
Chichimecs, 644
Chickamatsu, 549
Chidambaram, P., 419
Chile, 627, 648, 660, 689–691, 690
  independence of, 655
China, 263–347, 308
  acupuncture in, 274–275
  and agriculture, 26, 267–269, 270,
    317–319
  civil war in, 279, 311
  climate of, 265–267
  as cradle of civilization, 58
  crops of, 267
  and cultural diffusion, 14
  education in, 291–292
  families in, 274, 279, 282, 284–286
  and foreign policy, 342–347
  history of, 292–298
  industry of, 272
  isolation of, 263

and language, 12, 289–290
map of, *265*
mountains of, 264–265
Nixon's visit to, *327*
and nuclear energy, 29, 586
people of, 272–275
philosophy of, 277–279
population of, 24, *266*, 275, *276*
resources of, 269–272, *271*
rivers of, 263–264
role of women in, 286–287, *288*
science and technology in, 299–303
Second Republic of, 310
social classes in, 281–283
social revolution in, 315–316
Special Economic Zones of, 333
topography of, 263–265
writing system of, 290–291
China, People's Republic of, 312–326
agriculture in, 330–331
cultural revolution in, 292, 322
Five-Year Plan of, 317, 318, 333
Gang of Four in, 322, 328–329
Great Leap Forward of, 318–319
Great Proletarian Cultural
Revolution of, 319–321, *321*
and India, 434–436
industry in, 331–333
and Japan, 310–311, 586–588
and Third World, 347
China, Republic of, 309–312
Chinese Communist Party (CCP), 310,
315
Chinese Nationalist Revolution, 310
Chinese Revolution
beginning of, 309
Chittagong, 428
chlorofluorocarbons (CFC)
and ozone layer, 21, 23
Chongqing (Chungking), 311
Chou En-lai, *See* Zhou Enlai
Christianity, 42, 110, 207
in Japan, 540–541
in Korea, 591
in Latin America, 633–634, 648, 672
in Southeast Asia, 475
Christopher, Robert, 589
Chulalongkorn (King Rama V)
of Thailand, 483
Chung Ju Young, 595
church
and state, separation of, 117–118
Churchill, Winston, 70
CIA, *See* Central Intelligence Agency
Cibony tribe, 670
city
and civilization, 9
Civil war
in United States, 202
civilization, 9–13
characteristics of, *table*, 9
defined, 9
early Middle East, 58–63
Cixi, Dowager Empress, 308
clan, defined, 46
Cleopatra, 191
Click
languages of Africa, 163
climate
and agriculture, 45
defined, 3
and deserts, 44, 186
and land, 44–45
and rainfall, 44
and rivers, 45
of world, *table*, 8–9
Clive, Robert, 400, 406
coastline, defined, 5
Collor de Mello, Fernando, 695
Colombia, 660, 688
Colorado River, 623
Columbus, Christopher, 624, 646, 670
commerce
and trade, 60
communes, defined, 318
communique, defined, 326
Communism, 131–132, 435, 687, 689
in China, 273, 291, 311–319, 323,
338
in Cuba, 659, 678
in El Salvador, 681
in India, 414, 417
in Korea, 596
in Vietnam, 493

Communist National Revolution, 310
compasses, *301*
Conference of Islamic Nations, 123
Confucianism, 277–279, 540, 591
Confucius (Kung Fu-tzu), 277–279
Congo River, *See* Zaire River
Congo (Zaire)
under Belgian rule, 204, 206
Congress Party (India), 402–403, 406,
416, 418
conservation
and energy, 22
Constantinople, 646
Contadora group, 683
continents, *4*
defined, 5
Cornwallis, Lord, 400
Cortés, Hernán, 644, 646, 658
Costa Rica, 662
Council of Arab Economic Unity, 73
crafts
of Egypt, 60
of Sumerians, 62
Cristiani, Alfredo, 682
crops
distribution of, in Africa, 179
effect of altitude on, *626*
of Latin America, 656–657
rice, *268*, *471*
rubber, 206
sugar, 74
Crusades, 67
Cuba, 95, 623, 656, 657, 664, 668
and Africa, 217
revolution in, 676–679
Cuban missile crisis, 686
culture, 5
and art, 5
defined, 2, 5
and diffusion, 13–14
and education, 5–6, 15
and government, 5–6
and habitat, 2–6
and language, 5, 10–13
and occupations, 5
and religion, 5–6
and survival, 1–2
Curaçao, 674
currents, ocean, 160, 536, *626*
Cuzco, 640, 642, 647

Dahomey
under French rule, 204
Dalai Lama, 273
damage, environmental, 19
Damascus, 96
Daoism (Taoism), 280–281, 590–591
Dario, Rubén, 666
Dark Ages
of Europe, 192
David, King, 85
"Day of Five Billion"
and United Nations, 24
de Cuellar, Javier Perez, 125, 127
de Gaulle, Charles, 72, 209, 492
de Klerk, Frederick W., 232
Deccan (south) Plateau of India, 372,
392, 395
Declaration of Independence
(American), quoted, 402
decolonization
British, 71–72
French, 72
reasons for, 71
deficit, defined, 419
deforestation
and reforestation, 22
Delhi, *See* New Delhi
Delhi Sultanate, 397, 405
deltas, defined, 464
democracy
defined, 309
parliamentary, 84
Democratic Republic of the Congo, *See*
Zaire
Deng Xiaoping (China), 275, 319–320,
322, 328–336, *329*, 342
foreign policy under, 342–347
opposition to policies, 335
Denham, Dixon, 202
Desai, Morarji, 406, 411–412
desert
caravans in, 159
and Middle East, 74

oil in, 77
survival in, 2
devaluation, defined, 419
development
and aid, 16, 26
economic, of Middle East, 74–75
dhow, *65*
Diaz, Bartholomew, 198
Díaz, Porfirio, 675
dictatorship, defined, 688
divorce
and Islam, 58
Djarkata (Batavia), 468, 481, *505*
Djibouti, 216
DNA, human, 188
Dominica, 668
Dominican Republic, 664, 668, 672,
686–687
independence of, 671
Dravidians (original people of India),
391–392, 395
drought
defined, 179
in India, 407, 412
Druzes
religion of, 110
Duarte, José Napoleon (El Salvador),
682
Duong Van Minh, 511
Duvalier, Jean-Claude, 673

Earth Day, 19
earthquakes
and Japan, 534
East Africa, *158*, 194–196
kingdoms of, *192*
lakes of, 156
See also Africa
Eastern (Great) Rift Valley
of East Africa, 156
economy, free-market
in India, 420
economy, Socialist
defined, 497
ecosystems, defined, 20
Ecuador, 627, 656, 688
Edo (Tokyo) painters, 556
education
and culture, 5
EEC, *See* European Economic
Community
Egypt, 41, 45, 99, 102, 133
and agriculture, 60
ancient, *map*, *61*
and Arab League, 73, 108
architecture in, 61
and art of writing, 60
under British rule, 204
as cradle of civilization, 58
exports from, 75
farmers in, 188
government of, 60
history of, 60–62
and language, 12
religion of, 60
science in, 62
and United Arab Republic, 73
El Alamein
British victory at, 71
El Chicó Mountain, 619
El Dorado, 648
El Salvador, 662, 681–683
elephants
in Nubia, 191
embargo, oil, 79
"Empty Quarter," *See* Rub ál Khali
energy, nuclear, 22, 27–29
energy, solar, 22
Enfield rifle, 401
England
and slavery, 201
Entebbe Airport
in Uganda, 215
environment
and culture, 2–5
environment, defined, 2
EPLF, *See* Eritrean People's Liberation
Front
Ercilla y Zuniga, Alonso de, 666
Eritrea, 216
under Italian rule, 205
Eritrean People's Liberation Front
(EPLF), 216

Ershad, Hussain Muhammad, 426
escarpment, defined, 154
Ethiopia, 216–217
civil war in, 181
famine in, 180, 182, *183*, 216
under Italian rule, 205
refugees in, 182
ethnocentricity, defined, 273
Euphrates River, 45, 58, 62
Eurasian land mass, 5
Europe
continent of, 5
population of, 6
European Economic Community (EEC),
18
Everest, Mount, 371, 430
exports
of Africa, *table*, 177
extraterritoriality, defined, 306

Fahd, King of Saudi Arabia, 108
Faisal, King of Iraq, 73
Faisal, King of Saudi Arabia, 103
Falkland Islands, 692
famine
in Africa, 180–184
Fanti tribe, 166
Farabundo Marti National Liberation
Front (FMLN) (El Salvador),
682–683
farmers, 47, 60, 188, 376, 681
and herders, 3, 10, 45–47, 188
Farouk, King, 71
Fascists, 88
FBI, *See* Federal Bureau of
Investigation
Federal Bureau of Investigation (FBI),
99
Feisal, Amir, 87
Ferdinand, Archduke, 17
Fertile Crescent, *See* Mesopotamia
fetish, defined, 171
feudalism
defined, 564
in Japan, 563–564
Fez, Morocco, 108
Figari, Pedro, 666
Filipino, *See* Phillipines
fishers
in Africa, 188
in early China, 292
in Japan, 535
FLN, *See* Front de Libération Nationale
floods
and agriculture, 74
FMLN, *See* Farabundo Marti National
Liberation Front
FNLA, *See* National Front for the
Liberation of Angola
food
and development, 74
importation of, 74
foreign aid
in Africa, 186–187
Formosa, *See* Taiwan
fossil fuels, 22
FPR, *See* Rwandese Patriotic Front
France, 71–72
and African colonies, 209
and nuclear energy, 29
France, Itamar, 695
Front de Libération Nationale (FLN), 17
Fuji (Fujiyama), Mount, 533
Fujimori, Alberto, 694–695
Fujiwara period (Japan), 550, 552,
561–562
Fulani tribe, 211
Funan Empire
of Southeast Asia, 479

Gama, Vasco da, 198, 199, 298, 375,
399, 405, 480, 646
Gambia
under British rule, 204
Gana, Alberto Blest, 666
Gandhi, Indira, 406, 410–413, *413*,
415–416, 432, 434, 438
Gandhi, Mohandas K., 209, 395, *403*,
403–404, 416
Gandhi, Rajiv, 406, *413*, 413–414,
416–417, 432, 434, 436, 438
Ganges River, 372, 393, 426
canals of, *373*, 377

Gao
mosque at, 193
Muslims in, 197
Garciá, Joaquin Torres, 666
Garratt, G. T. (quoted), 404
Gatun Lake, 623
gauchos, 657
Gautama, Siddhartha, 393–394
Gaza Strip
population of, 101
and Six-Day War, 84–85, 99–100, 103
Gemayel, Bashir, 91, 112
Geneva
Baker and Aziz meeting (1991), 127
Germany
and nuclear energy, 28
Ghana
empire of, 191–193
famine in, 180
independence of, 209
Ghats (India), 374, 399
defined, 372
Ghazni, Mahmud of, 397, 405
ghettos, defined, 82
Ghori, Muhammed, 397, 405
Giles, H. A., 290
Giza, Pyramids of, *43*
global warming
and greenhouse effect, 21–23
Gobi Desert, 264
God
and Africans, 169
and Hebrews, 50, 52
Golan Heights
and Six-Day War, 85, 99–100, 103
gold
in Africa, 184, 199
Gold Coast
under British rule, 204
Gorbachov, President, 343, 414,
678–679
Gordimer, Nadine, 176
Gorkha
kingdom in Nepal, 431
government
of Ottoman Empire, 68
Gowon, General
of Ibo tribe (Nigeria), 211
Grande, Rio, 623
Great Britain
and China, 306–309
and Egypt, 69
and global warming, 21
and India, 399–402
mandates of, 70, 83
and Middle East, 71–72
Great Lake, *See* Tonle Sap
Great Wall of China, 293, *294*
Greece
and India, 393
and language, 12
green revolution
in India, 379
greenhouse effect, 19, 21–22
Greenland
and global warming, 21
Grenada, 668, 687
Gromyko, Andrei, 585
Guadalupe, 668, 674
Guangzhou (Canton), 304–306
Guaraní, 644
Guatemala, 635–636, 657, 693
guerrillas
in Africa, 218
defined, 94
in El Salvador, 682
in Ethiopia, 217
in Latin America, 682
in Lebanon, 110, 113
in Pakistan, 425
in Rhodesia, 220
in Southeast Asia, 486, 487
and war in Palestine, 87–88
Guevara, Ernesto (Che), 677
Guiana Highlands, 620
Guinea
independence of, 209
Gulf War, 42, 56, 81, 93–94, 109,
125–128, 424
and nuclear energy, 28–29, 127,
130
in retrospect, 131
Gupta Empire, 396–397, 406
Gurkha soldiers, 430–431

gurus, defined, 399
Guzman, Abimael, 694

habitat
  defined, 3
  and environment, 2–5
Haddad, Saad, 113
haiku poetry (Japan), 552
Haiti, 664, 668, 672–673
  independence of, 652, 671
Halabjah
  bombing of, 129
Hamas (Islamic Resistance
  Movement), 93
Hammer, Armand, 333
Hammurabi, 63
Han Dynasty, 272, 295, 479, 510,
  591
Han Sen, 513
Hanabusa Itcho, 555
Hangzhou (Hankow), 310
Hanj Sen, 501
Hannibal, 191
Hanoi, 465, 492, 510, 588
Harappa, city of, 390–391
Hausa
  conversion to Islam, 197
  language of Nigeria, 163
Hausa tribe, 166, 211
Hayat, Sandar Shaukat, 424
He Di, Emperor, 299
Hebrews, 63
  history of, in Middle East, 82
  religion of, 42, 50–53
Heian period (Japan), 550, 553,
  561–563
Heilbroner, Robert
  quoted, 14–15
heiroglyphics, 637
herders
  and farmers, 3, 10, 45–47, 188
  nomadic, 78, 167, 391
Hernandez, José, 666
Herzl, Theodore
  The Jewish State, 82
Hezbollah organization, 115
hijacking, See terrorism
Hillary, Sir Edmund, 431
Himachal Pradesh (India), 389
Himalaya Mountains, 371, 374
Hindi language, 380
Hindu Kush Mountains, 371
Hinduism
  in Bangladesh, 425
  defined, 384–386
  and Dharma, 385–386, 397
  in India, 376, 378, 384, 384–385,
    395, 397, 399
  and Karma, 385
  and mathematics, 66
  and reincarnation, 385
  in Southeast Asia, 473
Hirohito, Emperor, 572
Hiroshige, 556
Hiroshima, 572
Hispañiola, 623, 646, 672
Hitler, Adolph, 83
Hittites, 63
Ho Chi Min (Nguyen Ai Quoc), 483,
  492–493, 510
Ho Chi Minh City (Saigon), 465, 481,
  508
Hoabinhians
  of ancient Vietnam, 476
Hokkaido Island, 531, 579, 581, 585
Hokusai, 556
Honduras, 693
Hong Kong, 306, 343–344, 344
Honshu Island, 531
Horn of Africa, See Djibouti; Ethiopia;
  Somalia
hostages
  in Middle East, 115–116, 120, 131
Hottentots
  of Africa, 160
Hu Yaobang (China), 330, 338–339
Hua Guofeng (China), 330, 343
Huascar, 643, 647
Huayna Capac, 643
Huerta, Victoriano, 675
Huks
  of Phillipines, 488–489
human resources
  and development, 15

humanitarian intervention
  principle of, 18
hunters, 3, 11
  in early China, 292
  and gatherers, 3, 10, 188
Hussein, King of Jordan, 73, 85, 90,
  108–109, 126
Hussein, Saddam, 18, 28, 56, 93,
  120–123, 125–131
Hussein, Sharif, 70, 87
Hutu tribe, 212

Iberia, 645
Ibo tribe, 166–168, 211
Ieyasu, 566
Ife
  city of, 171
Ihara Saikaku, 552
Ikabana (flower arrangement; Japan),
  547–548
imperialism
  in Africa, 204–207
  defined, 308
  European in Middle East, 69–71
Incas, 639–643, 694
indemnity, defined, 306
independence
  and nationalism, 70, 74, 87, 101
India, 371–439
  agricultural production in, table,
    379
  agriculture in, 372, 372–374,
    376–379
  art and architecture in, 396
  under British rule, 399–402
  British trade in, 69
  Buddhism in, 393–395
  caste system in, 385–386
  and China, 434–436
  climate of, 374–377
  coasts of, 372
  as cradle of civilization, 58
  crops of, 377–379
  diet in, 382–383
  economy of, 407, 418
  elections in, 417–418
  exports from, 408
  farmers in, 376, 378, 383, 390
  Five-Year Plans of, 407, 413
  geography of, 371–372
  and Great Britain, 399–402
  Hinduism in, 384–385
  history of, 390–397, 405–406
  history of, table, 405–406
  housing in, 382–383
  independence of, from Great Britain,
    402–407
  industry of, 408
  and Kashmir, 437–438
  languages of, 380–381
  languages of, table, 380
  literature of, 386–388, 396
  literature of ancient, 386–389
  map, 370
  medicine in, 396
  and Middle East, 439
  modernization of, 407–421
  Muslims in, 397–399
  and nuclear energy, 408
  ores in, 407–408
  and Pakistan, 436–437
  partition of, 403–405
  people of, 380–383
  political parties in, 416–417
  population of, 24, 371, 380, 407
  population of, table, 383
  rainfall in, 377–378, 382
  reforms in, 418–419
  resources of, 407–408, 409
  and role among nations, 438–439
  and Russia, 433–434
  in the 1990's, 414–421
  science in, 408
  sea route to, 67
  social problems of, 408–410
  and Soviet Union, 408, 433–434
  and Sri Lanka, 438
  topography of, 376
  transportation in, 401
  and United States, 402–403,
    432–433
  and Vietnam, 439
  village life in, 381–383
  and world politics, 432–439

India and Pakistan
  partition of, 404, 406, 436
India National Congress, 402, 406
Indian Ocean, 5, 42, 375
  and Portuguese traders, 194
Indochina, See Cambodia; Laos;
  Vietnam
Indonesia, 462, 467, 479–480,
  482–483, 491–492, 504
  economy of, 499–501
  houses of, 469
Indus River, 372, 390–391, 405, 421,
  424
Industrial Revolution, 3, 19
industrialization
  and slavery, 200
industry
  and development in Africa, 184–187
  and development in Middle East,
    74–75, 118
  in India after independence, 408
  reforms in China, 331–333
industry, cottage
  in India, 408
infanticide, defined, 275
Inkatha Freedom Party
  in South Africa, 234–235
Inland Sea (Japan), 535
interdependence
  cultural, 18
International Atomic Energy Agency,
  130
International Court of Justice, 120
International Monetary Fund, 215, 419,
  433, 664
intifada
  causes of, 92
  defined, 92
  effects of, 93
  Israel's response to, 92
IRA, See Irish Republican Army
Iran, 41, 44, 116–117
  and discovery of oil, 76
  and nuclear energy, 28, 127, 130
  oil wells in, 76
  population of, 118
  revolution in, 118–120
  and terrorism, 95–96
  and trade embargo, 125, 130
  War with Iraq, 42, 120–125, 129
Iraq, 41, 45, 93–94, 102
  and Arab League, 73
  independence of, 70–71
  and India, 439
  invasion of Kuwait, 125–128
  and nuclear energy, 28
  oil wells in, 76
  and terrorism, 95–96
  and United Nations intervention, 18
  War with Iran, 42, 120–125, 129
Irazú Mountain, 619
Irish Republican Army (IRA), 17
iron
  and development, 189, 191, 346
Ironsi, General
  of Ibo tribe (Nigeria), 211
Irrawaddy River, 463, 464, 473
Islam, 41, 42, 53–58, 64–66, 101
  in Africa, 197–198
  and Arab unity, 72
  defined, 53
  Five Pillars of, 54
  and freedom of expression, 119
  and Muslim civilization, 64–66
  origin of, 197
  and politics, 117–118
  religious revival of, 116–118
  resurgence of, 116–118
  in Southeast Asia, 475, 480
  spread of, 64–65, 375, 480
  and Westernization, 116
  See also Muslims
Islamabad (Pakistan), 422
Islamic Council
  in Cairo, 101
Islamic Jihād, 115
Islamic Republic of Iran
  establishment of, 116
Islamic Resistance Movement, See
  Hamas
Island
  Australia as, 5
Ismailia, Egypt
  meeting of Sadat and Begin, 106

Israel, 41, 52, 100
  air force of, 102, 128
  and Egypt, 104–108
  exports from, 84
  formation of, 83–84, 88
  and Hebrews, 50
  and Lebanese civil war, 113
Israel Security Zone, 115
Israeli-Egyptian Agreements, 103–104
Israeli Parliament (Knesset), 106
Itsukushima Shrine, 539
ivory
  in Africa, 199
Ivory Coast
  under French rule, 204
Izalco Mountain, 619

Jaffa
  riots in, 87
Jahan, Emperor Shah, 398, 405
Jainism, 395
Jamaat-i-Islam Party
  in Bangladesh, 428
Jamaica, 668, 673–674
Jammu, 415
Jammu and Kashmir Liberation Front,
  415
Janata Dal Party
  in India, 416–418
Janata Party
  in India, 411–412
Japan, 531–589
  agriculture in, 558, 579–580
  architecture in, 552–555
  art in, 552–556, 563
  arts in, 547–556, 562
  and China, 310–311, 586–588
  climate of, 535–536
  culture of, 546–547
  diet of, 546
  early history of, 556–567, 556–573
  economy of, 573–583, 586, 587
  education in, 543–545, 544
  exports from, 576–577
  feudalism in, 563–564
  gods and goddesses of, 567
  government of, 573
  history of, table, 557
  imports of, table, 576
  industrialization of, 569–570
  influence of China on, 541–542, 553
  language of, 537–538, 562
  life in, 541–556
  literature in, 549–550
  and Nippon (Nihon), 531
  occupation by United States,
    572–573
  opening to the West, 567–568
  people of, 536–537, 545
  rainfall in, 536
  religion of, 538–541
  role of women in modern, 542–543
  in the 1990's, 589
  and Southeast Asia, 485–486,
    588–589
  and Soviet Union, 585–586
  topography of, 531–536
  and trade relations, 582–583
  village life in, 575
  war with United States, 571–573
  young people of, 545
Japanese Red Army, 18
Java, 472, 482, 491, 499–500
Jerusalem, 50, 55, 85–86, 86, 101
  East (Old City), 85, 89
  riots in, 87
  West (New City), 85
Jesuits, 682
Jewish National Home, 87
Jewish State, See Israel
Jews, 49–53
  Orthodox, 51
  See also Hebrews
Jiang Qing, 320–322, 328–329
Jihad (holy war), 54–56, 96, 101
Jimenez, Marcos Perez, 686
Jimmu Tenno, legend of, 557
Johanson, Donald, 187
John, King of Portugal, 198
John, Prince of Portugal, 652
Johnson, Lyndon, 506–507, 686
Jomon period (Japan), 557–558
Jordan, 41, 94, 100, 102
  and Arab League, 73

and Palestine Liberation
  Organization, 89–90
  population of, 89, 101
Jubail
  city of, 78
Judaism, 49–53
Jumklatt, Kemal, 112
jungle survival, 1
junta, military
  defined, 487
justice
  and righteousness, 52
jute, defined, 377, 408
Jutiya Party (Bangladesh), 428

Kabuki drama (Japan), 549, 567
Kahlo, Frida, 666
Kahn, Genghis, 397, 405
Kaifu, Prime Minister of Japan, 582
Kakuei Tanaka, 580
Kalahari Desert, 159
Kamakura period (Japan), 539, 540,
  555, 563, 565
Kampala
  capital of Uganda, 214, 215
Kampuchea, See Cambodia
Kana syllables, 538
Kan'ami, 548
Kanchenjunga Mountain, 430
Kanji syllables, 538
Kanto plain
  of Honshu, 533
Karachi (Pakistan), 421
Karakorum Mountains, 371, 421
Karami, Roshid, 112
Karen National Union (KNU)
  (Myanmar), 487
Kashatriya, 385, 392, 399, 401, 475
Kashmir, 406, 415, 421, 435, 437–438
Katanga Province of Zaire, See Shaba
Kathmandu, 431
Kaysone Phomvhan
  Prime Minister of Laos, 506
Kazakhstan
  and nuclear energy, 27
Kendo, 544
Kennedy, John, 686
Kennedy, Malcolm, 542
Kenya, 167
  under British rule, 204, 206
  independence of, 210, 214
Kenya Mountain, 155
Kenyatta, Jomo, 17, 207, 208, 213
Khalafahs, See Caliphs
Khalistan, 412, 415
Khalsa (military brotherhood of India),
  399
Khan, General Ayub (Pakistan), 422
Khan, Ishaq (Pakistan), 423–424
Khan, Sayyid Ahmad (India), 402
Kharg Island, 123
Khayyám, Omar, 66
Khmer Empire (Southeast Asia), 479
Khmer Rouge, 512–513
Khmers (people of Cambodia), 466,
  479
Khomeini, Ayatollah Ruhollah, 92, 96,
  117–123, 121
Khrushchev, Nikita, 324
Khyber Pass, 371
kibbutzim, defined, 47
Kikuyu tribe, 166, 210
Kilimanjaro, Mount, 154, 155, 202
Kilwa, East Africa, 194
Kim Dae Jung, 595
Kim Il Sung, 596
Kim Young Sam, 595
Kinai plain
  of Honshu, 533
Kirkuk, 123, 129
Kissinger, Henry, 103–104, 221,
  326–327, 510, 511
KMT, See Kuomintang
Knesset, See Israeli Parliament
KNU, See Karen National Union
Kobe, 535
Koran (Muslim holy book), 53–54,
  56–58, 165, 401
Korea, 589–596
  agriculture of, 594
  climate of, 590
  divided, 593–594
  economy of, 594–596
  history of, 591–593

industry of, 594–595
people of, 590
religions of, 590–591
in the 1990's, 596
topography of, 589–590
Korean War, 322, 325, 572–573, 576, 593–594
Koreans
  in Japan, 537
Koryŏ Dynasty
  of Korea, 592
Kosygin, Alexei, 102
Kuala Lumpur, 468
Kublai Khan, 296, 300
Kuomintang (KMT)
  (Nationalist Party in China), 310
Kurdish rebellion, 129–130
Kurdistan, 128
Kurds, 128–130
Kurile Islands, 585–586
Kush, Kingdom of (Nubia), 191
Kuwait, 41, 102, 124
  economic development and, 78
  Iraq's invasion of, 93–94, 125–128
  oil wells in, 76
  See also Gulf War
Kuwait National Museum
  looting of, 126
KwaZulu, 238
Kyoto, 539, 551, 555
  See also Heian period
Kyushu Island, 531, 532

Lahore (Pakistan), 422
Lam, Wilfredo, 665
Landers, John, 202
Landers, Richard, 202
landlocked, defined, 501
Langi tribe, 214, 215
language
  of Africa, 163, 173, 189, 225
  Akrikaans, 225
  alphabets and, 12, 63
  Arabic, 41, 66, 72, 197–198
  Bantu, 163
  Bengali, 422
  Click, 163
  and culture, 5, 10–13
  cuneiform, 62
  and Cyrillic alphabet, 12
  defined, 10
  English, 11
  Greek, 12
  Hausa, 163
  and hieroglyphics, 60
  Hindi, 380, 399
  of India, 380–381, 405
  Indo–European, 11
  of Israel, 84
  of Japan, 537–538, 562
  of Latin America, 630–631, 668
  Native American, 12
  "Newspeak," 11–12
  of Nigeria, 163
  of Persia, 399, 422
  of Phillipines, 488, 491
  Phoenician, 12
  and pictography, 12, 60, 289
  Roman, 12
  Romance, 617
  of South East Asia, 466, 468
  Spanish, 630
  Sudani, 160
  Swahili, 163, 197
  Urdu, 399, 422
  and writing, 12–13, 60
Lao Tzu
  founder of Daoism, 280
Laos, 481, 483, 493, 506
  economy of, 501
Latin America, 617–696
  agriculture in, 649, 655–659
  arrival of Europeans in, 645–648
  arts in, 665–667, 668
  climate of, 625–628, 668
  colonial period of, 648–650
  economy of, 649, 655–665, 670
  education in, 634–635
  farmers in, 639, 642, 655, 658, 670, 673, 682
  geography of, 618–624
  governments in, 688–696
  history of, 667
  independence in, 650–653

independence in, table, 653
industry of, 660–665
languages of, 630–631, 630–632, 668
literature in, 666
map, 616
minerals in, table, 660
mountains in, 619–620
music in, 667
people of, 629–630, 629–635, 650, 668
Pre-Columbian, 635–645
religions of, 633–634, 642
resources of, 659–665, 670
rivers of, 622–623
social classes of, 632–633
Spanish empire in, 650
in the 19th century, 653–655
in the 20th century, 674–683
and United States, 684–687
viceroys of, 648
  See also individual countries
latitude, defined, 159
Le Duc Tho, 510
League of Nations, 70
Leakey, Dr. Louis, 187
Leakey, Mary, 187
Leakey, Richard, 187
Lebanon, 41, 63, 102
  and Arab League, 73
  Christian domination of, 110, 114
  civil war in, 42, 90, 110–116, 112
  foreign involvement in, 112–113
  independence of, 110
  Israeli invasion of, 90–91
  and Palestine Liberation Organization, 90–91, 95
  religions of, 111
  terrorism in, 96
Legalism (China), 279–280
legends and epic tales
  of Africa, 173
Lempa River, 662
León, Ponce de, 646
Lesseps, Ferdinand de, 69
Li Peng, Premier, 339, 436
Liberia
  civil war in, 182
Libya, 41, 117
  and Italian takeover, 69
  and Ronald Reagan, 95
  and terrorism, 95
  See also Eritrea
Lima, 647, 694, 695
Limpopo River, 155, 196
Lin Biao (Lin Piao), 320–322
Lin Zexu (Lin Tse-hsu), 305
Lincoln, Abraham, 16
Linton, Ralph
  quoted, 13
Lisbon
  and slavery, 200
literacy
  and Middle East, 74
literature
  of ancient India, 386–389
  in Japan, 549–550
  of modern Africa, 175–176
  of Muslims, 66
  oral, in Africa, 172–173
Liu Shaoqi (Liu Shao-ch'i), 314, 319–320, 330
livelihood (in China)
  defined, 309
Livingston, David, 202, 203
Lockerbie, Scotland, 99
Lod Airport, 18
lodestone, 301
Lon Nol, 485, 511–512
L'Ouverture, Toussaint, 671
Lucy
  discovery of skeletal remains, 187–188
Lunda tribe, 219
Lydians, 63

MacArthur, Douglas, 572
Machu Picchu, 642, 665
MacPherson, Hugh (quoted), 404
Madagascar
  settlement of, 188
Madero, Francisco, 675
Madras (India), 374, 384

Madrid
  and Middle East Peace Conference, 109
Magdalena River, 622
Magellan, Ferdinand, 481
Magsaysay, Ramon
  President of Phillipines, 489
Mahabharata (India), 388
Mahavira
  founder of Jainism, 395
Mahendra, King of Nepal, 431
Malabar (western) coast of India, 372
Malawi
  refugees in, 182
Malay Peninsula, 465, 480, 498
  houses of, 469
Malaysia, 493
  economy of, 498
  and rain forests, 20
Mali
  conversion to Islam, 197
  empire of, 191, 193
  famine in, 180
  under French rule, 204
Man, dignity of, 52
Managua Lake, 623
Manchu Dynasty, 296, 303–309
Manchuria, 265, 272
  Japanese invasion of, 310, 571
Mandal, B. P., 414
Mandela, Nelson, 233, 235–236, 237, 242
Mandela, Winnie, 236
Mangope, Lucas, 225
Manila, 468, 481
Mao Zedong (Mao Tse-tung), 275, 290, 292, 310, 312–322, 313, 325–326, 327, 694
Marathis (people in India), 399
Marayama Okyo, 555
Marco Polo, 296, 302, 303
Marcos, Ferdinand, 489
Marcos, Imelda, 489
Mariam, Mengistu Haile, 216–217
Maronite Christians, 110, 113
Márquez, Gabriel García, 666
Marshall, General George, 311
Martí, José, 666
Martinique, 668, 674
Masai tribe, 166, 167
masks
  uses for, in Africa, 172
Mass Democratic Movement (MDM) (South Africa), 233
mathematics
  and ancient Egypt, 61–62
  and ancient India, 396
  and Sumerians, 62
Matope, King of Rozwi (East Africa), 196
Matsuhito Meiji, 568
Matsuo Basho, 552
Matta, Roberto, 665
Mau Mau, 210
Mauritania
  famine in, 180
Maurya, Asoka, King (India), 393–395, 405
Maurya, Chandragupta (India), 393, 405
Maya, 635–636, 638
MDM, See Mass Democratic Movement
Mecca, 54
  and Muslims, 53, 101
  pilgrimages to, 193, 194
Medina, city of
  and Muslims, 53, 101
Mediterranean Sea, 42, 62
Meiji Restoration
  in Japan, 534, 543, 559, 568–571
Mekong River, 464, 473, 501
Memphis, ancient capital of Egypt, 191
Menam, See Chao Phraya River
Menem, Carlos Saúl, 693
Mengistu, Lieutenant Colonel, 181
Meo tribes (Southeast Asia), 468
Meroë, capital of Nubia, 191
Mesopotamia
  as cradle of civilization, 58, 62–63
  See also Iraq
mestizo, defined, 488, 629
Mexico, 657, 663, 684
Mexico City, 620, 663, 675
MFN, See most favored nation

Middle East
  after Gulf War, 128–130
  and agriculture, 74–75
  cities of, 48–49
  cities of, table, 48, 49
  climate of, 41, 44
  conflict in, 42
  decline of, 66–67
  decline of kingdoms of, 63
  defined, 41
  early history of, 58–63
  economic development in, 74–99
  European imperialism in, 69–72
  importance of, 42
  industry in, 75
  and international terrorism, 42
  language of, 41
  people of, 45–49
  population of, 49
  religion of, 41–42, 53–58
  trade in, 42
  in world affairs, 131–133
  World War I, 70
  World War II, 70–73
Middle East Peace Conference
  in Madrid (1991), 109–110, 131
migrations, defined, 371
militia, defined, 111
millet, 165
Minamoto family (Japan), 562–564
Minamoto Yoritomo, 563–564
Mindanao Island, 491
mines
  and economic development, 75
Ming Dynasty, 296
missionaries
  in Africa, 198, 201, 204
Mistral, Gabriela, 667
Mixtecs, 644
Modigliani, Amedeo, 172
Mogadishu (East Africa), 194
Mogul Empire (India), 397–399
Mohammed
  biography of, 66
  heirs of, 56
  and Islam, 53–54, 64–65
  and Muslims, 117–118
  teachings of, 53–54
Mohenjo-Daro, city of, 390–391
Moi tribes (Southeast Asia), 468
Molina, Rafael Trujillo, 686
monarchy, defined, 483
Mongkut (King Rama IV)
  of Thailand, 483
Mongol Dynasty, 296
Mongolia, 264
Mongols
  invasion by, 67, 296, 397, 405, 564–565
Monomotapa (East Africa)
  empire of, 196
monotheism, 53, 399
  defined, 50
Monroe, James, 684
Monroe Doctrine, 684
Mons
  people of Myanmar, 466, 480
Monserrat, 668
monsoons, 465–466
  in Bangladesh, 426, 429
  defined, 267
  in India, 374–375, 375–376
  and Japan, 536
Montreal Protocol, 23
Morocco, 41, 44, 69, 102
  exports from, 75
  under French rule, 204
  independence of, 72
  and invasion of Ghana, 192
  and invasion of Songhai, 194
Moronobu, 556
Morwat, Irfanullah, 424
Moses, 82
mosque, defined, 48
Mossawa (Mitsiwa), 217
most favored nation
  China, 347
  defined, 306, 345
mountains, 45, 155, 263–264
Mozambique (East Africa), 194, 196
  famine in, 180
  independence of, 210, 218
  under Portuguese rule, 205
  war in, 182

Mozambique National Resistance, 182
MPLA, See Popular Movement for the Liberation of Angola
Mubarek, Hosni (Egypt), 105, 126
Mugabe, Robert, 220–223
Muhammad, See Mohammed
Mujib, See Rahman, Mujibur
mulatto, defined, 629
Murasaki Shikibu, 550
Musa, Mansa, of Mali, 193
Museveni, General Yoweri, 215
Muslim Brotherhood, 117
Muslim League, 402–403, 406, 423
Muslims, 41, 64–66
  in Africa, 194
  and architecture, 66
  and art, 66
  and astronomy, 66
  in Bangladesh, 424–425
  and chemistry, 66
  in China, 273
  contribution of, 65–66
  and culture, 66
  in India, 397–399
  and mathematics, 66
  and medicine, 66
  in Pakistan, 421
  religion of, 110
  Shi'ite, 56, 96, 110, 115, 120, 122–124, 128–129
  Sunni, 56, 110, 120, 124, 128–129
  See also Islam
Mussolini, Benito, 70
Mutota, King of Rozwi (East Africa), 196
Muzorewa, Bishop Abel, 220
Mwene Mtapa, 196
Myanmar (Burma), 465–466, 474, 480, 481, 483, 486–488, 504, 529
  economy of, 495
  education in, 496
  ethnic groups of, table, 487

NAFTA, See North America Free Trade Agreement
Nagasaki, 572
Nagoya, 535
Najera, Manuel Gutierrez, 666
Namib Desert, 159
Namibia (South-West Africa)
  independence of, 218
Nanak, Guru, 399
Nanjing (Nanking), 309–310
  Treaty of, 305–307, 343
Nanking, See Nanjing
Napoleon
  and Egypt, 69
Napoleon III, 684
Nara period (Japan), 550, 553, 561
Narayan, Java Prakash, 411
NASA, See National Aeronautics and Space Administration
Nasser, Gamel Abdel, 71, 72, 73, 75, 84, 105
Nasser Lake, 74
nation, defined, 17
National Aeronautics and Space Administration (NASA), 23
National Front for the Liberation of Angola (FNLA), 218
National League for Democracy (NLD) (Myanmar), 487
National Liberation Front (NLF) (North Vietnam), 506–507, 510
National Reconciliation Pact
  in Lebanon, 114
National Union for the Total Independence of Angola (UNITA), 218
nationalism
  and Africa, 17, 207–211
  and Arab unity, 72–73, 87
  and Canada, 17
  defined, 16–17, 207
  defined (in China), 309
  growth of, in Middle East, 70, 118
  in India, 402–403
  and Middle East, 17, 70
  and terrorism, 17–18
Nationalist Party in China, See Kuomintang (KMT)
Nationalists (NP) (party in South Africa), 223–224, 227, 232, 234

nations
    development of, 14–15
Native Americans
    influence of, 644–645
    and language, 12
    in Latin America, 629, 644–645
NATO, See North Atlantic Treaty
    Organization
Nazi
    concentration camps, 83
Nazis, 88
NCP, See New Congress Party
Ndebele tribe, 220
negritude
    defined, 175
Negroid race, 160
Nehru, Jawaharlal, 403, 403, 406, 410,
    416, 435
Nehru, Jawaharlal (quoted), 404, 438
Nepal, 430–431
Neruda, Pablo, 667
Netherland Antilles, 668
Neto, Agostinho, 219
Nevada del Ruiz Mountain, 619
New Congress Party (NCP) (India), 411
New Delhi, 372, 374, 398
New Democratic Youth League
    (China), 316
New Peoples' Army (NPA)
    (Phillipines), 489
Ngami Lake, 202
Ngo Quyen, 510
Nicaragua, 662, 679–681
Niger
    famine in, 180
Niger River, 155, 202
Nigeria, 165, 168
    under British rule, 204
    civil war in, 211–212
    culture of, 170
    languages of, 163
Nile River, 45, 62, 74
    and artifacts, 189
    exploration of, 202
    sources of, 155, 203
    See also Blue Nile River; Victoria
        Nile River; White Nile River
Nile Valley
    as cradle of civilization, 58–60
Nippon, See Japan
nirvana, defined, 475
Nixon, Richard, 326, 343, 432, 507,
    511, 686, 687, 690
Nkomo, Joshua, 220–223
Nkrumah, Kwame (Ghana), 207
NLD, See National League for
    Democracy
NLF, See National Liberation Front
Nō theater (Japan), 548–549
Nobi plain
    of Honshu, 533
Noé, Luis Felipe, 666
Nok (Nigeria)
    culture of, 170
nomads
    of Africa (Sahel), 179
    of desert, 45–47, 64
non-violence, See Ahimsa
nonalignment, policy of, 432
Norgay, Tenzing, 431
North Africa, 41
    and agriculture, 45
    climate of, 45
    religion of, 53–58
    rivers of, 45
    See also Middle East
North America
    continent of, 5
North America Free Trade Agreement
    (NAFTA), 663
North Atlantic Treaty Organization
    (NATO), 18, 132
North Indian Plain, 372, 377
North Korea, 102
    and nuclear energy, 28–29
    and terrorism, 95
North Sea
    and oil, 80, 82
NPA, See New Peoples' Army
Nubia, 189–191, 190
nuclear proliferation
    defined, 27
Nyerere, President of Tanzania, 213
Nzinga, King of Congo, 198

OAS, See Organization of American
    States
oasis, 43
    defined, 45
Obote, Milton, 213–215
Occupied Territories
    of Israel, 101
oceans, 4
    defined, 5
Ogata Kōrin, 555
Ogoni mask, 173
oil
    in China, 269
    control of, 76–77
    crisis of 1973, 79–80
    crisis of 1979, 80
    discovery of, 76
    exporting, 75–76
    income from, 78
    in India, 408
    and international politics, 79
    in Latin America, 675
    in Middle East, 42, 47, 75–81
    and modernization, 78
    new sources of, 82
    Nigerian export of, 212
    oversupply of, 81
    pipelines for, 76, 78
    price of, 79–80
    production quota of, 81
    reserves of, 76
    reserves of, chart, 80
    as weapon, 79, 82, 103
    See also petroleum
Old Silk Road, 302
OLF, See Oromo Liberation Front
Oman, 41
OPEC, See Organization of Petroleum
    Exporting Countries
Open Door Policy
    in China, 333, 335
Operation Desert Storm, 125
    See also Gulf War
opium
    in China, 304–307
Opium War, 305, 306, 343
Organization of American States (OAS),
    673, 686
Organization of Petroleum Exporting
    Countries (OPEC), 79–82, 103
Orinoco River, 620, 622
Orissa (India), 387
Oromo Liberation Front (OLF), 216
Oromos, people of, 216–217
Orozco, José, 665
Ortega, Daniel, 681
Ortega, Humberto, 681
Orwell, George, 11
    See also language, "Newspeak"
Osaka, 535
Osaka Castle, 562
Ottoman Empire, 67–68, 82
    decline of, 68–70, 83
    government in, 68
    rise of, 66–68
ozone layer
    defined, 22
    depletion of, 22–23

Pacific Ocean, 5
    Fire Rim of, 531, 533, 534
Pahlavi, Mohammed Riza, 118–120
Pahlevi, Riza, 118
painting, 61
Pakistan, 371, 403–407, 415,
    421–424
    East vs. West, 422
    geography of, 421–422
    and India, 436–437
    map, 370
    origin of name, 421
    population of, 423
Pakistan, East, See Bangladesh; Bengal
Pakistan Peoples Party (PPP), 423
Palestine, 71, 82, 87–94, 101
    and Gulf War, 93–94, 126
    partition of, 88, 108–109
    population of, chart, 89
    See also Israel
Palestine Liberation Organization
    (PLO), 17–18, 73, 95, 108
    formation of, 89
    international recognition of, 91–92
    and Jordan, 89–90

in Lebanon, 90–91
    and United Nations, 91
    and United States, 91
Palestinian refugees, 88, 110
pampas, 620
Pan-African Congress, 225
Pan Am
    flight 103, 99
Pan-American Highway, 639
Pan Arabism, defined, 72–73
Pan Islamism, defined, 72
Panama, 624
    Isthmus of, 5
Panama Canal, 619, 685
panchayat (council of five)
    in villages of India, 382, 397, 401,
        431
paper
    origin of manufacture, 298, 299
Parc, Julio le, 666
Paris Peace Conference (1919), 87
Park, Mungo, 202, 204
Parliament
    in India (Lok Sabha), 405, 411, 414
Parliament (British), 400
pass laws
    in South Africa, 225, 231
Pathet Lao, 506
patois, defined, 630
Patriot missiles, 128
Patriotic Front (PF), 221
Peacock Throne, 399
Pearl Harbor, 486, 571
peasants
    in Middle East, 74–75
Pedro, Dom I, 652
Peking, See Beijing
Pemba
    in East Africa, 194
Pentagon Papers, 507
People's Republic of China, See
    China, People's Republic of
Perez, Alan Garcia, 693
Perez, Carlos Andres, 696
Perón, Eva, 692
Perón, Juan, 691–692
Perry, Matthew C., 567
Persia, 63
    and India, 392
    See also Iran
Persian Gulf
    and oil reserves, 72, 118
    war in, See Gulf War; war between
        Iran and Iraq
Persian language, 399
Peru, 647–648, 657, 660, 694
petrodollars
    defined, 79
petroleum
    See also oil
Petroleum College, 78
petroleum (oil), 75
    by-products of, 75
Phalangist Party, 91, 110–111
Pharaoh
    of Egypt, 60
Phillipines, 462, 466, 481, 485,
    488–491
    independence of, 486, 488–491
    languages of, 488, 491
    origin of name, 488
Phnom Penh, 511–512
Phoenicians, 63
    and language, 12
physics
    and Muslims, 66
Picasso, Pablo, 172
pilgrimage, defined, 54
Pinatubo Mountain, 491
Pinchincha Mountain, 619
Pinochet, Augusto, 691, 693
Pinyin, defined, 290
Pipeline
    Alaskan, 79
Pizarro, Francisco, 647, 694–695
plains
    of Latin America, 620
Plassey, Battle of (1757), 400
Plata, Rio de la, 622
plateaus
    of South America, 620
Platt Amendment, 676
PLO, See Palestine Liberation
    Organization

pogroms, 82
Pol Pot, 512
politics
    and instability, 74
    international and oil, 79
pollution
    effects of, 19
polygyny, defined, 164
Popocatepetle Mountain, 619
Popular Democratic Front for the
    Liberation of Palestine
    of Palestine Liberation Organization,
        89, 96
Popular Front for the Liberation of
    Palestine
    of Palestine Liberation Organization,
        89, 96
Popular Movement for the Liberation of
    Angola (MPLA), 218, 219
population
    density, 6–7
    and desirable location, 7, 10
    distribution, 6–7
    explosion, 6
    growth of, 24–27, 75
    of South Africa, table, 223
    tables, 6, 7, 587
    of World, 6–9
population, urban
    of Middle East graph, 50
Port-au-Prince, 673
Portinari, Candido, 665
Portugal
    African colonies of, See Angola;
        Mozambique
    and Brazil, 651–652
    conquest in Latin America, 645–648
    and India, 399–400
    invasion of East Africa, 196,
        198–199
    and Southeast Asia, 480
    and trade with China, 298
Potsdam Declaration, 571
Powell, Colin, 127
PPP, See Pakistan Peoples Party
Prester John (Kingdom of Africa), 198
progress
    in Middle East, 78
prophets
    of Hebrews, 52
    of Muslims, 53–54
Puerto Rico, 623, 646, 656, 664, 668,
    671–672
pundits, defined, 380
Punjab (North India), 372, 412–413,
    415, 421
Pygmies
    of Africa, 161
pyramids
    of Egypt, 61–62

Qaddafi, Colonel Muammar, 95, 117
Qatar, 41
    oil wells in, 76
Qin (Ch'in) Dynasty, 263, 279–280,
    280, 293, 295, 369
Qin Ling (Tsinling) Mountains,
    266–267
Qin Shi Huang Di, 369
Qing (Ch'ing) Dynasty, See Manchu
    Dynasty
Qom, 124
Quechua
    See also Incas
Quechuas, 630, 640, 694–695
Quesada, Jimenez de, 648
Quetzalcoatl, 638, 644, 646–647
Quito, 619, 625
Qureshi, I. H. (quoted), 404
Qustul, capital of Nubia, 190, 191

Rabat, Morocco
    Arab summit at, 91
Rabbis, defined, 53
racism
    in Africa, 208
Rafsanjani, President of Iran, 125
Rahman, Mujibur, 422, 425
railroads
    in Africa, 186, 204
    in Argentina, 691
    in India, 401

in Japan, 534, 588
    in South America, 628
rain forests
    destruction of, 20–21
rajah, defined, 391
Rajasthan Desert, 408
Rajputs, of India, 399
Ram, Kanshi, 417
Ram Das, 399
Ramayana
    of India, 388
Ramos, Fidel V., 491
Rana
    family of rulers in Nepal, 431
Rangoon, See Yangon
Rao, P. V. Nershimhe, 405–406,
    418–421, 433
Reagan, Ronald
    and apartheid, 231
    and China, 345
    and India, 414, 432
    and Latin America, 681, 687
    and Libya, 95
    peace plan of, 108
Rebmann, Johann, 202
Red Guards
    of China, 320, 321
Red River, See Songkoi
Red Sea, 42
Reform, Land, See Agrarian Reform
    Laws
refugees
    in Africa, 182
regionalism, defined, 625
Reischaur, Edwin O., 542
religion
    of Africa, 168–170, 207
    and culture, 5–6
    of Druzes, 110
    of Egypt, 60
    of Hebrews, 50–52
    Hinduism, 384–385
    of Korea, 590–591
    of Latin America, 633–634, 642
    of Lebanon, 111
    of Middle East, 41–42, 53–58
    Muslim, 110
    of Southeast Asia, 473–476
repatriation, defined, 103
republic, defined, 688
Resolution 242, 100
Revolution, American, 651
Revolution, Bolivian, 676
Revolution, Cuban, 676–679
revolution, defined, 309
Revolution, French, 651
Revolution, Mexican, 665, 666,
    675–676
Revolution, Sandinista (Nicaragua),
    679–681
Rhodes, Cecil, 204, 220
Rhodesia, 206
    under British rule, 204, 220–223
    See also Zimbabwe
Rico, Aldo, 692
Rio de Janeiro, 652, 664
Rivera, Diego, 665
rivers, 45, 263–264
    and civilization, 58
Rodó, José Enrique, 666
Roh Tae Woo, 595
Romans
    and language, 12
Rommel, Erwin, 70
Ronin, Tale of, 560
Roosevelt, Franklin D., 571, 685
Rosas, Juan Manuel de, 691
Rosetta Stone, 59
Rub ál Khali, 44
Rushdie, Salman, 119
Russia, 68
    and nuclear energy, 27
Ruwenzori Mountain, 204
Ruwenzori (Runsoro or Kokora)
    Mountains, 155
Rwanda, 212
Rwandese Patriotic Front (FPR), 212

Sabra
    and Shatila, camps of, in West
        Beruit, 91
Sadat, Anwar, 73, 91, 104–107, 105,
    107

Sahara Desert, 44, 153–154, 159
  changes in, 188
Sahel drought
  in West Africa (1970–1974),
    179–180
Saigon, *See* Ho Chi Minh City
Saladin, *See* Sala-al-Din
Salah-al-Din (Saladin), 67
Salween River, 464
samurai, 543, 559, 568, 569
San Martín, José de, 655
Sandinista National Liberation Front,
  679
Sandino, Augusto César, 679
Sanskrit language, 380, 391–392, 396,
  478
Santa Anna, 684
Santa Fe de Bogatá, 648
Santiago, 648
Santiago, Miriam Defensor, 491
Santos, 628
São Paulo, 628, 664
Sapporo, *581*
Sarmiento, Domingo, 666
Sass, Florence Von, 203
Sato, Prime Minister
  of Japan, 589
Saudi Arabia, 41, 117, 133
  and Arab League, 73
  and economic development, 75–76,
    78
  and Gulf War, 125
  independence of, 70
  and oil production, 81
  and slavery, 202
Schwarzkopf, Norman, 127
science
  and Egypt, 62, 66
Scotland Yard, 99
SCUD missiles, 29, 128
sculpture, 61, 393, 396
  African, 171–172
Seami, 548
secession, defined, 212
sectarian violence
  defined, 111
Security Council
  of United Nations, 100, 125, 130,
    513
segregation, *See* apartheid
Sei-Shonagon, 550
Sejong, King
  of Korea, 590
Selassie, Haile, 180, 216
Sendero Luminoso, *See* Shining Path
Senegal, 175
  famine in, 180
Senghor, Léopold Sédar, 175–176
Seoul, 592
Sepoy Rebellion, 399–402, 406
sepoys, defined, 401
Sequi, Antonio, 666
Sese Seko, Mobuto (Zaire), 219
Sesshu, 553, 555
settlement
  and civilization, 9
SGPC, *See* Shiromani Gurdwara
  Prodandhak Committee
Shaanxi (Shensi) Province, 310
Shaba (Katanga Province of Zaire), 219
Shah, King Tribhuwan, 431
Shah, Prithwi Narayan, 431
Shah of Iran, *See* Pahlevi
Shan, *See* Thai
Shang Dynasty, 292, 591
Shanghai, 272, 310
Sharif, Mian Nawaz, 423, 424
Sharpeville massacre (South Africa),
  225–226
Shatt al-Arab waterway, 122, 124
Shen-nung, 267
Sherpas, 431
Shi Huangdi (Shih Huang-ti), 280, 293
Shiba Kōkan, 555
Shi'ite rebellion, 129–130
Shikoku Island, 531
Shin Kanemura, 583
Shinaino River, 533
Shining Path (Sendero Luminoso)
  movement, 694
Shintoism, 538–540, *539*, 569
Shiromani Gurdwara Prodandhak
  Committee (SGPC), 412
Shogun, 564

Shona tribe, 220
Shōtoku, Prince, 558–559
Shuban, 555
shuttle diplomacy, defined, 103
Siam, *See* Thailand
Sichuan (Szechuan) Province, *268*
Sierra do Mar, 628
Sierra Leone
  under British rule, 204
Sierra Madre Occidental Mountains,
  619
Sihanouk, Norodom, 483, 485,
  511–512
Sikhs, 399, 401, 412–413, 415
silk, 301, *302*, 303
Silla monarchs
  of Korea, 592
Silva, José Asunción, 666
Sinai Peninsula, 72, 99–100, 106–107
  and Six-Day War, 84–85
Sind, state of, 391, 397, 405
Singapore, *463*, 468, 481
  economy of, 502
Singh, Manmohan, 419
Singh, V. P., 406, 414–417
Siqueiros, David, 665
Sisulu, Walter, 233
Sithole, Ndabaningi, 220–221
Sivaji, 399
slavery
  in Africa, *199*, 200–202
  origins of, in Africa, 198
  ships used for, *201*
Smith, Ian, 220, 221
Socialist Janata Party
  in India, 417
society, prehistoric, *table*, 11
Sofala
  in East Africa, 194
Solanski, Madhav Singh, 434
Solomon, Temple of, *55*
Somalia, 216
  famine in, 180
  people of, 159
  and United Nations intervention, 18
Somaliland, 203
  See also Eritrea
Somoza, Anastasio, 679
Son Sann, 513
Song (Sung) Dynasty, 296
Songhai
  conversion to Islam, 197
  empire of, 191, 193–194
Songkoi (Red River), 464, 473, 501
Soto, Hernando de, 647
South Africa, Republic of, *162*, 218,
  223–242
  apartheid in, 223–242
  under British rule, 204
  constitution of, 234
  homelands of, 224–226
  since 1984, 227–232
  violence in, *229*–230
South America, *See individual*
  countries
  continent of, 5, *621*
  geography of, 624
  resources of, *661*
South India, 374, 395
Southeast Asia, *460*, 461–513
  agriculture in, 472–473, 477, *500*
  arrival of Westerners in, 480–482
  climate of, 465–466
  early history of, 476–478
  economy of, 495–504
  empires of, *478*, 479–480
  European trade and, 480–482
  farmers in, 470–473, 476, 482
  foreign relations of, 504–508
  geography of, 461–462
  and independence, 486–495
  and Japan, 485–486, 588–589
  languages of, 466, 468
  mountains of, 462
  nationalism in, 482–485
  origin of term, 461
  people of, 466–472
  population of, 468
  rainfall in, 465–466
  religions of, 473–476
  resources of, *497*
  rivers of, 464–465
  topography of, 462–465
  trade and commerce in, *table*, 502

village life in, 470, 472
  and World War II, 485–486
  See also individual countries
Southeast Asia Treaty Organization, 432
Southern Rift Valley
  of East Africa, 156
Southwest Africa
  under German rule, 205
Southwest Africa People's Organization
  (SWAPO), 218
Southwest Asia, *See* Middle East
sovereignty, defined, 307
Soviet Union
  and Africa, 217–218
  and Arab-Israeli conflict, 102, 132
  and Chernobyl, 23
  and China, 317, 323–325, 342–343
  and India, 408, 433–434
  and Middle East, 42, 71, 132
  and nuclear energy, 27–28
  and terrorism, 95
  and war between Iran and Iraq, 124
Soweto (South Africa)
  riots in, 226
Spain
  conquest in Latin America, 645–648
Spanish language, 630
Speal, Percival (quoted), 404
Speke, John, 203, 204
Sri Lanka (Ceylon), 371, 417, 438
Srivijaya Empire
  of Southeast Asia, 479
Ssu-ma Ch'ien, 295
St. Vincent, 668
Stalin, Joseph, 17, 323
Stanley, Henry M., *203*, 203–204
state
  and church, separation of, 117–118
steppe (veld)
  of Africa, 160
stipend, defined, 78
stonemasons, 60
Strait of Hormuz, 123
straits, defined, 556
subcontinent, defined, 371
subsidies, defined, 418
Suchinda Kraprayoon, 493–494
Sudan, 102
  under British rule, 204
  civil war in, 181
Sudanic
  languages of Africa, 160
Sudras, 385, 392, 393
Suez Canal, 42, 69, 72, 78
  Company of, 71
  and Six-Day War, 84–85
Suharto, General, 492, 499, 505
Sui Dynasty, 295
suicide squads
  and terrorism, 96
Sukarno, Ahmed, 482, 491–492,
  499–500, 504
Suleiman the Magnificent, 68
sultan, defined, 68
Sumatra, 499
Sumerians, 62
Sumi-e art, 555
Sumo wrestling, *551*
Sun Yat-sen, Dr., 309
Sundiata, of Mali, 193
suttee, defined, 400
Swahili
  language of East Africa, 163, 197
  origin of, 197
SWAPO, *See* Southwest Africa
  People's Organization
Swift, Jonathan
  quoted, 153
Syria, 41, 95, 99–100, 102–103,
  112–113, 131
  and Arab League, 73
  and Lebanese civil war, 112–113,
    115
  and terrorism, 96, 115
  and United Arab Republic, 73

Taiho Code
  of Japan, 561–562
Taiki program
  of Japan, 559, 562
Tainjin (Tientsin), 306–307
Taiping Rebellion, 308
Taiwan (Formosa), 311–312,
  322–323, 345

Taj Mahal, 398, 405
Takeshita, Prime Minister
  of Japan, 583
Tambo, Oliver, 242
Tamerlane (Timur Leng), 67, 397, 405
Tamil, 395, 438
Tamil Nadu, 417
Tana Lake, 202
Tanaka, Prime Minister
  of Japan, 585, 587
Tang (T'ang) Dynasty, 295–296, 542
Tanganyika
  under German rule, 205
Tanganyika Lake, 203
Tanzania, *154*, *162*, *167*
  human remains in, 187
  independence of, 214
Taoism, *See* Daoism
tariff, defined, 306
Tea ceremony (Japan), 547
Teheran, 120, *122*, 123, 124
Tel Aviv, *50*
Tenochtitlán, 636
terrorism
  1968–1991, 96–99
  defined, 94
  growth of, 81, 95
  international, 17, 42
  in Israel, 96
  as nationalist weapon, 94–99
  state-supported, 95–96
  in Uganda, 215
terrorism *chart*, 97–99
Texcoco Lake, 636
Thai (Shan)
  people of Southeast Asia, 466, 468,
    479
Thailand (Siam), 468, *471*, 481, 483,
  493–495, 505
  dancers, *484*
  economy of, 498–499
Thar Desert, 372
theocracy, defined, 117
Thieu, President
  of South Vietnam, 508, 511
Third World
  and China, 347
  defined, 16
  and green revolution, 26
  and oil, 79–80
  population growth of, 24
Thor Desert, 421
Three Mile Island, 22
Tiahuanaca culture, 639–640
Tiananmen Square (Beijing)
  massacre at, 338–342, *340*, 346,
    587
Tibet (Xizang), 264, 273, 435
Tierra Caliente, 626
Tierra del Fuego, 620, 628
Tierra Fría, 626
Tierra Puna, 626
Tierra Templada, 626
Tigre People's Liberation Front, 216
Tigris River, 45, 58, 62
Tilak, Bal, 402
Timbuctu, 193, 194
  exploration of, 202
  Muslims in, 197
Timur Leng, *See* Tamerlane
Tiran, Strait of, 85
Titicaca Lake, 623, 639
Tlaxcalans, 644
Togoland
  under German rule, 205
Tokugawa Shogunate, 543, 555,
  566–567
Tokyo, 535, *575*, 576
Toltecs, 644
Tomahawk missiles, 127
Tonkin Gulf, 506, 510
Tonle Sap (Great Lake)
  of Southeast Asia, 465, 501
topography, defined, 3
Tordesillas, Treaty of, 651–652
Touré, Sekou, 209, 213
Tours, battle of (732), 64
trade
  in ancient India, 395
  and commerce, 60, 189
  and development of Africa, 189, 206
  exchange of, 18
  in India, 400
trade embargo, defined, 125

trade winds, 624, *627*
trains, *See* railroads
Transjordan, *See* Jordan
Transkei Territory, 224–225
Treaty of Brotherhood, Cooperation,
  and Coordination, 115
Treaty of Nanjing (Nanking), 305–306
Treaty of Sevres (1920), 128
tribes, 211–213
  defined, 45, 166
  and tribalism in Africa, 211–213
Trinidad and Tobago, 668, 674
Tripoli
  United States bombing of, 95
Truman, Harry S, 311, 322, 571
Truman Doctrine (1947), 132
Tshisekedi, Etienne, 219
Tshombe, Moïse, 218–219
Tunisia, 41, 92, 102
  under French rule, 204
  and French takeover, 69
  independence of, 72
Turkey, 41, 44–45, 68
  exports from, 75
Turks, 67–68
Tutsi tribe, 212
Tutu, Bishop Desmond, 228, 231, 240,
  241

UAR, *See* United Arab Republic
UDPS, *See* Union pour la Democratie
  et le Progress Social
Uganda, 213
  under British rule, 204
  independence of, 214
Ukiyo-e period (Japan), 553
  art of, 555–556, 567
Ukraine
  and nuclear energy, 27
ULFA, *See* United Liberation Front of
  Assam
Ulmann, Liv, 183
U.N., *See* United Nations
UNEF, *See* United Nations Emergency
  Force
UNICEF (United Nations Children's
  Fund), 183
Union of Soviet Socialist Republics
  (USSR), *See* Soviet Union
Union pour la Democratie et le
  Progress Social (UDPS) (Zaire),
  219
UNITA, *See* National Union for the
  Total Independence of Angola
United Arab Emirates, 41
  oil wells in, 76
United Arab Republic (UAR), 73
United Liberation Front of Assam
  (ULFA), 415
United Nations Emergency Force
  (UNEF), 84
United Nations (U.N.), 17, 18, 24, 28,
  83, 84, 130, *237*, 679
  Charter of, 209
  in El Salvador, 682–683
  and famine in Africa, 180, 182
  General Assembly of, 91–92, 104,
    490
  and Gulf War, 125
  and hostages, 120
  and Palestine Liberation
    Organization, 91–92
  peace keeping forces of, 103, 114
  and refugees, 88
  and two Chinas, 322
United States (U.S.)
  and apartheid, 231–232
  and China, 311, 322, 325–326, *337*,
    344–346
  and El Salvador, 683
  and Gulf War, 125–131
  and India, 402–403, 432–433
  and Israel, 103, 106, 128
  and Japan, 571–573
  and Latin America, 684–687
  and Middle East, 42, 71, 132–133
  and nuclear energy, 28
  and oil imports, 82
  and Palestine Liberation
    Organization, 92
  and slavery, 201
  and South Africa, 232
  and war between Iran and Iraq,
    124–126

—410, 412

(India), 387
language (Persia), 422
in of, 399
., See United States
USSR (Union of Soviet Socialist
Republics), See Soviet Union

Vaishya, 385, 392
Valdivia, Pedro de, 648
Varnas (social groups) in caste system,
385
Vedas (India), 386, 391
Vega, Garcilaso de la, 666
Venezuela, 656, 657, 696
Vespucci, Amerigo, 646
Victoria, Queen, 401, 406
Victoria Falls, 202
Victoria Lake, 156, 203
Victoria Nile River, 203
Vietnam, 102, 479, 481, 483,
492–493, 506–512
and Cambodia, 512–513
children in, 509
and China, 343, 511
economy of, 501
history of, table, 510
and India, 439
Viking Press, 119
Villa, Pancho, 675, 685
Villa-Lobos, Hector, 667
village
global, 18–19
of Japan, 575
life in India, 381–383, 397
life in Southeast Asia, 470
Virgin Islands, 671

volcanoes
in Latin America, 619–620
voodoo, 673

Wade, Thomas F., 290
Wade-Giles
defined, 290
wadis
defined, 44
Wahan (China), 332
Wailing Wall, See Western Wall
Waite, Terry, 116
Wajid, Husina, 426
Walcott, Derek, 669
Waldseemüller, Martin, 646
War
of 1948, 85
Arab-Israeli, 79
between China and Britain (Opium
War), 305, 306, 343
between China and France, 306
between Ethiopia and Somalia
(Ogaden War), 181
holy, See Jihad
between Iran and Iraq (1980–1988),
42, 120–125, 129
between Iraq and Kuwait, See Gulf
War
Israeli, 42
Six-Day (1967), 79, 84–85, 96, 103,
132
Spanish-American, 676, 685
See also individual Wars
Washington, DC
and Middle East Peace Conference,
109
Water Buffalo, 268, 471
Watusi tribe, 161, 166
weavers, 60, 467, 630

Weizman, Dr. Chaim, 87
West Africa
kingdoms of, 191–194
West Bank
Jordanian ownership of, 89, 108–109
population of, 101
and Six-Day War, 85, 100
West Indies, 664, 668–674
British, 671
climate of, 668
colonial period of, 670–671
early history of, 670
economy of, 670
geography of, 668
independence of, 671
languages of, 668
literature of, 668
people of, 668
slavery in, 671
West (Xi) River, 264
Western Rift Valley
of East Africa, 156
Western Wall, 51
of Jerusalem, 85
Westernization
and Muslims, 116–117
White Nile River, 203
White Paper
British (1939), 88
Women
in Africa, 172
in China, 286–287, 288
in India, 382, 392, 400
in Iran, 118, 120
and Islam, 56–58
in Japan, 542–543, 550, 563
in Southeast Asia, 477, 482
World Bank
and Africa, 187, 215

and China, 341
and India, 433
and Latin America, 664
World War I, 17, 70
World War II, 117
and African nationalism, 207, 209
Axis of, 70
and growth of nationalism, 209
and Japan, 485–486
and Middle East, 70–82, 74, 118
and Southeast Asia, 485–486
World Zionist Organization, 87
writing, See language
Wuchang, 309

Xia (Hsia) Dynasty, 292
Xinjiang, 273
Xizang, See Tibet

Yahya, Mohammed Khan, 425
Yamoto kingdom
of Japan, 541–542
Yangon (Rangoon), 465, 481, 487,
529
Yangtze (Chang) River, 264, 268, 307
Yayoi perod
of Japan, 558
Yedo (Tokyo) Bay, 567
Yellow River (Huang He), 263–264
Yeltsin, Boris, 27, 434, 586
Yemen, 41, 95
and Arab League, 73
Yenan, 310
Yi Dynasty (Korea), 592
Yokohama, 576
Yom Kippur War, 101–103
Yoruba tribe, 166, 168, 211
Young Pioneers (China), 316
Yuan Dynasty (Mongol Dynasty), 296

Yuan Shih-kai, 309
Yucatán Peninsula, 620, 635–636, 656
Yugoslavia
and United Nations intervention, 18

Zaire (Congo), 168, 218–219
treaty with Angola, 219
Zaire (Congo) River, 155, 168
exploration of, 204
Zambezi River, 155, 196, 202
zambo, defined, 629
Zanj (East Africa), 194
ZANU, See Zimbabwe African National
Union
Zapata, Emilio, 675
Zapotecs, 644
ZAPU, See Zimbabwe African People's
Union
Zen Buddhism
in Japan, 540, 553–555, 559
Zhao Ziyang, 330, 339
Zheng He (Cheng Ho), Admiral,
296–297
Zhou (Chou) Dynasty, 278, 293
Zhou Enlai (Chou En-lai), 313, 314,
321–322, 326, 435, 587
Zia, Begum Khalida, 426, 428
Zia ul-Haq, General, 423, 436
Zimbabwe
in East Africa, 195–196, 220–223
ruins at, 195
See also Rhodesia
Zimbabwe African National Union
(ZANU), 220–223
Zimbabwe African People's Union
(ZAPU), 220–222
Zionists, 82–84, 87, 104
Zoroastrianism, 63
Zulu tribe, 166, 234–235, 238